Other books by Herbert M. Shelton

The Science and Fine Art of Fasting

The Science and Fine Art of Natural Hygiene

Fasting Can Save Your Life

Natural Hygiene: The Pristine Way of Life

Fasting For Renewal of Life

HERBERT M. SHELTON

The SCIENCE and FINE ART of FOOD and NUTRITION

The Hygienic System: Volume II

American Natural Hygiene Society, Inc.

The Science and Fine Art of Food and Nutrition
First Edition 1935
Second Revised Edition 1947
Third Edition 1951
Fourth Edition 1956
Fourth Edition (2nd Printing) 1962
Fifth Edition 1969
Sixth Revised Edition 1984
Seventh Edition 1996

Mailing Address:
American Natural Hygiene Society, Inc.
P.O. Box 30630
Tampa, FL 33630

ISBN 0-914532-39-1
Library of Congress Catalog Number: 96-085470

PRINTED IN THE UNITED STATES OF AMERICA

Printed on Recycled Paper

HERBERT M. SHELTON

The SCIENCE and FINE ART of FOOD and NUTRITION

The Hygienic System: Volume II

This book describes an approach to diet and nutrition that has had beneficial effects for thousands of people who sought Dr. Shelton's advice for a variety of health problems.

Nothing in this book is intended to constitute medical treatment or advice of any nature. Moreover, as every person responds differently to diet and lifestyle changes, it is strongly emphasized that any person desiring to implement the recommendations in this book should consult his or her doctor.

In publishing and reprinting *The Science and Fine Art of Food and Nutrition,* it is the intention of the American Natural Hygiene Society to keep information about the work of Herbert M. Shelton available to the reading public. Dr. Shelton's theories and teachings are his own and are not necessarily consistent with those of the American Natural Hygiene Society.

The American Natural Hygiene Society is dedicated to teaching people how to live the healthiest, happiest lives possible. For membership information about the Society and its award-winning *Health Science* magazine, write: American Natural Hygiene Society, P.O. Box 30630, Tampa, FL 33630, Phone (813) 855-6607.

Contents

	From the Publisher	5
	Preface	6
	Introduction	7
1	Philosophy of Nutrition	21
2	Food Elements	27
3	The Minerals of Life	52
4	Vitamins	61
5	Calories	90
6	Law of the Minimum	98
7	Organic Foods	109
8	Organic Acids	123
9	Fruits	127
10	Nuts	144
11	Vegetables	153
12	Cereals	159
13	Animal Foods	168
14	Drink	181
15	Condiments and Dressings	191
16	Salt Eating	200
17	Fruitarianism and Vegetarianism	223
18	Nature's Food Refinery	230
19	The Digestibility of Foods	246
20	Mental Influences in Nutrition	252
21	Enjoying our Food	259
22	Absorption of Food	263
23	Uses of Food	266
24	How Much Shall We Eat	274
25	How to Eat	289
26	Correct Food Combining	299
	Food Combining Charts	321
27	Effects of Cooking	327
28	Uncooked Foods	344
29	Salads	356

Contents

30	Conservative Cooking	369
31	Effects of Denatured Foods	376
32	Under Nutrition	392
33	Hypo-Alkalinity	400
34	Diet Reform Vs. Supplemental Feeding	405
35	Beginning the Reform Diet	411
36	Feeding Mothers	438
37	Building the Teeth	455
38	The Eliminating Diet	470
39	Feeding in Disease	478
40	The Three Year Nursing Period	496
41	Cow's Milk	501
42	Pasteurization	508
43	Mother's Milk	521
44	Should Baby Be Weaned	534
45	No Starch for Infants	539
46	Three Feedings a Day	542
47	Feeding of Infants	549
48	Feeding Children From Two to Six Years	565
49	Man Shall Not Die With Food Alone	577
50	Our Denatured Soil	584

From the Publisher

Every philosophic movement has its literary cornerstones, and the modern day Natural Hygiene movement is no exception.

Dr. Shelton's seven-volume *Hygienic System,* which he began crafting in 1934, indisputably serves as the literary foundation upon which the modern day Natural Hygiene movement is based.

In reprinting *The Science and Fine Art of Food and Nutrition* , the American Natural Hygiene Society is fulfilling an important part of its fundamental commitment to keeping the most valuable historical texts of Natural Hygiene in print.

The three volumes of the *Hygienic System* which the American Natural Hygiene Society has brought back into print: Vol. I *The Science and Fine Art of Natural Hygiene,* Vol. II *The Science and Fine Art of Food and Nutrition,* and Vol. III *The Science and Fine Art of Fasting,* are the most important works in the series. They describe the basic foundation upon which this profound health system is built. Subsequent volumes were more narrowly focused and are of a limited interest.

Dedication

To my three children: Bernarr Herbert, Walden Ellwood and Willowdeen La Verne, whose rugged health, sunny dispositions, mental alertness and unusual strength are due to Natural Hygienic Principles and Practices, this book is lovingly dedicated by

The Author

PREFACE TO SIXTH REVISED EDITION
by Vivian Virginia Vetrano, B.S., D.C., H.M.D.

Ever since the days of Sylvester Graham in the 1830's, Natural Hygienists have been stressing proper nutrition, the science of nourishing the body. However, many people mistake the term nutrition for diet, and believe that a person is well nourished so long as all the nutrients are present in every meal regardless of how the various foods are combined. According to modern nutritionists, a person is well nourished so long as there are a sufficient number of calories, vitamins, minerals, carbohydrates, fats and proteins in the diet. They are completely unmindful as to whether a person has the digestive or assimilative capacity to handle all that food.

Here is where Natural Hygiene differs. It takes into account the state of health of the individual and the activities, and nourishes the individual according to the ability to digest, assimilate and utilize the food at the time. Instead of haphazardly stuffing all the known nutrients into an individual at one time, Natural Hygiene insists that the laws of physiology be obeyed, that foods be combined for the most efficient digestion. It gives more food, less food, or no food according to the state of the individual.

Natural Hygiene adapts the diet to the current needs and capacities of the individual and does not expect every individual's digestive capacities to be the same. Nor does it expect the same individual to have the same digestive abilities under the varying circumstances of life, health, ill health, or emotional stress. This is the beauty of Natural Hygiene: it is instinctive living. When an individual has learned to live instinctively in every particular and eats only when genuinely hungry instead of for pleasure or out of fear of offending a host or hostess, then he or she is on the road to a state of superior health unmatched in modern times.

THE SCIENCE AND FINE ART OF FOOD AND NUTRITION

Living instinctively means more than just eating the right foods. One must supply all the requisites of physiology, such as fresh air, rest, sleep, sunshine, exercise, emotional poise, etc., when needed and in proper proportions one to the other. For example, when one is tired rest is needed, not more food or stimulants as is the custom.

Because many Natural Hygienists have recovered from formidable diseases solely by Natural Hygienic means and they feel so good most of the time, they become zealots for the new way of life, and undauntedly preach it to the world. They actually make some converts, especially since so many people are disappointed in their medical doctors who have done nothing for their health. This disenchantment with the medical profession has led many people to seek a knowledge of nutrition. More and more people are becoming aware of the important relationship of a wholesome diet to health.

Dr. Shelton has taught diet and nutrition to thousands of people since he first started writing articles and publishing books many years ago. What he said then is just as true today, for the broad principles of Nutrition do not change. A principle is a truth that is everlasting, invariable, inviolable, immutable and irrevocable; and since Natural Hygiene is based upon physiological truths it is everlasting, changing only in minute details according to the pathological changes in human beings because of environmental pollution.

There are present day critics who state that Natural Hygiene does not work. "Not all people can eat the *Paradise Diet,*" they reprove. They do not understand that our digestive system is the most abused organ system in the body, and as our general health deteriorates every organ in the body suffers, especially the most abused ones, the stomach and intestines. As a consequence, the digestive capacity weakens, and people become unable to digest fresh fruits and vegetables without some pain, flatulence, diarrhea or some other unwanted symptoms. They must first fast or remain on a restricted Hygienic diet until the digestive capacity improves. Regardless of the erroneous ideas of those with little knowledge of Natural Hygiene, this way of living and eating is efficacious in producing superior health in people of normal structure and function. Those who have had parts of their stomachs or intestines removed cannot be expected to have the hearty digestion of the robust individual with all digestive organs intact. Likewise, an individual who has gastric, or intestinal irritation, inflammation, or ulcers may be just as crippled in digestive capacity as the individual without a stomach. However, the one who still has all digestive organs intact can recover health if he or she persists in right living. The one without a stomach

PREFACE

may make a little progress, but will always have to be extra cautious regarding eating habits.

The varying stages between irritation, inflammation, ulceration, and cancer, and the various areas affected along the gastrointestinal tract, cause the numerous different reactions of individuals to the same foods. For instance, one person may be able to digest only bananas and carrots, whereas another one with inflammation or irritation in a different area may be able to digest only vegetables. The pathological condition causes the digestive capacity to vary. Once I had a patient who had ulcers, diagnosed by specialists in radiology and medicine, and the only thing her body would tolerate was oranges. This is extremely unusual. Most others with the same problem usually cannot handle any fruit, much less citrus.

The fact that many people in their present pathological conditions cannot eat the strictly uncooked diet does not mean that Natural Hygienic principles are unfounded and that the Natural Hygienic diet is in error as a means of nourishing the body. It means only that in a state of impaired health and impaired digestion the diet must be modified to meet the individual's lowered capacity to handle any and all foods.

Unfortunately, some people who criticize Natural Hygiene do not live according to the laws of physiology for a sufficiently long period of time to recover their health. They do not improve because of their failure to carry out a perfect Natural Hygienic way of life. These would declare Natural Hygiene "no good" for them, yet they did not give it a fair chance. They lack the necessary discipline to stay with it. They denounce Natural Hygiene instead of admitting their own weaknesses and lack of discipline.

Today we must take into account that we are a degenerate people. We are no longer the prototype of pristine man, but weaklings, lacking in vitality and normal healthy structures. The pollution of our environment with radioactivity, scattered electrons from power lines, which are radiomimetic, auto fumes, toxic fungicides, insecticides, herbicides, toxic household cleansers, plus recreational and medical drugs and x-rays, are causing our babies to be born lacking essential enzymes that are crucial to their existence. The number of enzymatic deficiencies, or losses due to mutations or simple damage during intra-uterine life, make diabetes fade into comparative insignificance. Environmental pollution is rapidly destroying our genetic pool, and far too many babies are being born defective. Some of the more vigorous ones will live to reproduce. The inheritable damage will be transmitted to future generations many times more frequently than presently, simply because those with mutations will mate with those who also have mutated genes. The deterioration of the race will increase so rapidly that, before we know it, we will be so far down the road to extinction, there will be no coming back.

Commonly children are born today lacking in enzymes necessary for normal metabolism and utilization of nutrients. They are sick their entire short lives and no one knows why. By switching to the Natural Hygienic life-style and diet these children are enabled to live more comfortably, but they will never be well, for they were born deficient in the ability to metabolize certain amino acids or other nutrients. It is not the fault of the Natural Hygienic diet, as some people contend, that these young people do not get well. The inability to attain superior health, when one supplies all the conditions of life and avoids all poisons, cannot be attributed to a failure of Natural Hygiene, for Natural Hygiene is basic to life. Without Natural Hygiene there can be no life. If recovery of health does not occur in a reasonable amount of time, it is due to a failure to find the true cause of the trouble, barring some irreversible pathology. Once it is discovered that one, or two, or more enzymes necessary to normal function and metabolism are missing, then the ill health can be properly ascribed to the missing enzyme, hormone, or other factor needed for normal metabolism. These problems are similar to diabetes in which an ingredient necessary to proper bodily function is missing. Eventually physicians, biologists, pathologists and people in general will learn wherein lies the fault when one fails to recover after applying Natural Hygiene when pathological degeneration has been ruled out. Then they will realize that Natural Hygiene is a valid and correct Science of life.

Presently many people complain that they cannot digest nuts. This has been a complaint for many years. However when these same people are taught to eat nuts in proper combinations, and not immediately after a seven course meal, they can digest them perfectly well. The more current objection to nuts is that they contain enzyme inhibitors and their digestion is very difficult because of their enzyme inhibitors. Animals and people ate and enjoyed nuts and seeds before anything was known about enzyme inhibitors. I am skeptical about this contention. The inability of certain people to digest nuts and seeds may well be because of impaired digestion of the individual, and not inherent in the nut or seed.

Returning to the present book, I assure you its principles are valid and anyone who is guided by these cannot keep from feeling younger, more vigorous, more alive, happier and at times euphoric. Don't let

PREFACE

those undisciplined people who know so little about the Natural Hygienic diet discourage you from eating properly. Dr. Shelton writes in generalities in some sections because many details were not known at the time he wrote the book, but details are known now, and they have proved his generalities true.

Synergistic action was understood many years ago, and experimenters wrote extensively about it, but for years those whose job it was to sell vitamins ignored the facts. Not so Shelton and the early Natural Hygienists. Their cry was loud and clear against the sale of vitamin and mineral pills and tablets because of their knowledge of the cooperative *action* of nutrients. Calcium tablets were sold under the pretext that more calcium was needed for the formation of good teeth. No mention was made by the purveyors of these pills that more nutrients than just calcium are needed for tooth formation. Indeed, for the proper formation of bone and teeth, calcium, phosphorus, vitamins A, C, and D, iron, and protein are needed. Shelton says, "It is folly to feed much calcium in an effort to produce good teeth and to ignore the other essential elements of the teeth."

Shelton emphasizes, "that it is not the sum total of nutrients consumed but their relative proportions which determines the nutritive value of any given dietary." He strongly insists that dosing oneself with a lot of mineral and vitamin preparations is not only useless but pernicious to health. It creates disproportions, excesses and deficiencies. For instance, according to the law of the minimum, "If one essential food element, which normally should compose one per cent of the food eaten, is present in only half this amount, then the body will only be able to utilize the other elements, in tissue building, in the same reduced quantity."

When reading the various health magazines, almost every article in most of the magazines stresses the value of a particular vitamin or mineral and urges you to take the vitamin or mineral in tablet or pill form. Rarely are the synergistic actions discussed. Rarely is the reader made aware of the fact that when one takes calcium, phosphorus is also needed, or of the calcium/phosphorus ratio and how much calcium is needed in proportion to phosphorus. Nor are we taught calcium is necessary for the absorption of vitamin B 12. Vitamin B 12 is sold with no thought as to how it will be absorbed.

Only by feeding natural foods, will we secure the various vitamins and minerals in their proper proportions relative to one another. Only by eating natural foods in proper combinations in their uncooked state will we be assured of securing all the vitamins and minerals in their

THE SCIENCE AND FINE ART OF FOOD AND NUTRITION

proper proportions relative to the others. Only by eating natural foods will we be assured of not creating imbalances, excesses, or deficiencies of the various minerals and vitamins and other known and unknown nutrients.

At the time of the first writing of this book, Shelton contended that, when carrying out their experiments, the biochemists neglected to study the trace minerals. It is true, the trace minerals were very much neglected until it was observed that cattle became sick when fed on food which was grown on soil deficient in certain trace minerals. More is known about the trace minerals today.

In fact, for a long time only vitamins were stressed in health circles. Years before others began talking about minerals, Natural Hygienists were proclaiming the importance of minerals to our health. Shelton says, "If we are to have normal development, the mineral elements in our diet must also be present in minimum quantities, but they must also represent proper ratios one to another. The mineral salts are most sensitive to any deficiency of any of them in the diet. Many common foodstuffs are deficient in iron and calcium, and these deficiencies reduce the ability of the body to assimilate the other elements. On the other hand, in experimental diets, any increase of one element raises the mineral requirements of all the others."

This is precisely why one should not take vitamin or mineral supplements, but rely solely on natural foods in their uncooked state. It is too easy to create deficiencies by taking too much of one vitamin or mineral. Mother Nature knows what she is doing. The best of all scientists can muss up things that Mother Nature does with ease. Many of the vitamin and mineral correlations are brought out in this volume by Shelton. Many of these same correlations are ignored in other textbooks on health.

It is significant that when animals are fed on refined and denatured food, they sicken and die. Much to the chagrin of those who advocate fruit and vegetable juices (and who think they can eat all the refined foods they desire so long as they take plenty of fresh vegetable juices), it was shown that when the fresh juices of vegetables were added to the refined foods, the animals recovered partially and survived but did "not regain their normal weight and strength, nor their resistance to disease. These vegetable juices contain no fuel value. The animals are restored to normal vigor and health only after they are fed unrefined foods such as cabbage, spinach, celery, lettuce, whole grains, whole milk, etc." Shelton brings out facts that are seldom mentioned by other nutritionists. He contends that we must understand that we cannot eat

PREFACE

a refined diet and take a few vitamin pills or a few juices and expect superior health. It is impossible.

There are so many wonderful principles (which others ignore) that Dr. Shelton teaches in the present volume, that it is a shame this book cannot be used as a textbook in colleges for advanced courses in nutrition.

Shelton stresses the effects of indigestion on the body. I've never read of anyone else doing this except those who have followed Shelton. He shows how acid fermentation robs us of calcium and other organic minerals. When food is not digested, but undergoes fermentation, much calcium is used in neutralizing the acids which are formed as a result of the decomposition of carbohydrates. As a consequence there may be a calcium deficiency as a result of indigestion from improperly combining our foods. Most other books on nutrition simply have you shovel in the food, in any haphazard combination. In fact you are encouraged to have a food from each basic category at each meal without any respect to our enzymic limitations and without any thought at all as to whether or not the meal will be digested, absorbed or assimilated. Poor combinations rob us of many minerals and vitamins and most assuredly cause the absorption of poisonous fermentation and putrefactive products such as the various toxic alcohols, acetic acid and indole, skatole and other highly toxic and carcinogenic products of rotting proteins. The chapter on Food Combining brings out the many other reasons why it is important to respect our digestive limitations for better nutrition.

Other wonderful facts that are not found in the average book on nutrition are found in this illuminating *Volume II of the Hygienic System*. Since it is based upon physiology, the facts in it are immutable and will be just as valid a thousand years from now as they are today. Although this book was written many years ago, it is still the paramount book about food and feeding extant. Though other books may have more details and specifics about each vitamin and mineral, calories, "RDA's", etc., this book still reigns supreme, because it coordinates this information into a system that works, whereas other books, lacking this cohesiveness, give you myriads of facts, but no fundamental principles upon which to base your diet or your life. A knowledge of Natural Hygiene and the principles of nutrition as taught in this volume will prevent ricocheting from one cure-all to the next, one vitamin to another, one mineral to another, and one diet to the next. If read with understanding, this book sets the course straight ahead and guides you to the most ideal diet for man, *The Frugivore*. If you adhere to its principles, it leads to superlative health and an unbelievable happiness. Some days you will feel so good and cheerful you'll wonder if something is wrong with you. It's so pleasant. You'll say, "I haven't felt like this since I was a kid!" So read on and soak up all that good knowledge and then put it into practice!

INTRODUCTION TO SECOND EDITION

Among the civilized as among savages, social activities center about sex and food. Civilization grew up in fertile sections, where food was abundant — where food was scarce nomadic tribes roamed in savagery or semi-savagery. Man's food and his ways of procuring his food have largely shaped his whole social, political and religious history.

The study of food and its relations to the structures and functions of the body constitutes one of the most important subjects that can occupy our minds. It is unfortunate that the knowledge of diet possessed by the ancients was permitted to perish during the Christian era and people were taught to "take no thought of what ye shall eat or drink," for "it is not what goeth into a man's body, but that which cometh out that defileth him."

It is now over a hundred years since the study of food was revived and, while much valuable knowledge has been accumulated during that time, it has been slow in reaching the minds of the people. The spread of such knowledge has met with organized opposition from the medical profession, which has been able to keep many people in almost complete ignorance of how to feed their bodies.

Modern dietary science (trophology) may be said to have had its beginning with Sylvester Graham, and his *Lectures on the Science of Human Life* is still abreast of our time in most particulars. If you want "the newer knowledge of nutrition," you'll find most of it in this book.

It will be recalled that in Vol. I of this series we recounted Graham's experiences in preventing cholera by dietetic and general hygienic means and how the movement initiated by him grew and spread. Despite its overwhelming success, the medical profession, as stubborn then as now, in its opposition to dietary advancement, heaped ridicule and slander upon Graham and the Grahamites.

In his efforts at diet reform, as in all of his other efforts at living reform, Graham ran up against the stone wall of established prejudices and practices and the active opposition of vested interests who saw in his efforts a serious threat to their incomes and investments. Not the least of these interests was the medical profession.

From Europe the early American settlers had brought the idea that fruits and vegetables and, especially uncooked fruits and vegetables, were to be avoided. The *New York Mirror* warned, Aug. 28, 1830, that fresh fruits should be religiously forbidden to all classes and especially to children. Two years later the same paper carried the information that all fruit is dangerous and, because of the cholera epidemic city councils prohibited their sale in the cities. "Salads were to be particularly feared." Robley Dunglison, the famous physiologist of the period, appears also to have shared this view.

In August 1832 the Board of Health of Washington, D. C. prohibited, for the space of ninety days, the importation into the city of "cabbage, green corn, cucumbers, peas, beans, parsnips, carrots, egg plants, cimblings or squashes, pumpkins, turnips, water melons, cantaloupes, muskmelons, apples, pears, peaches, plums, damsons, cherries, apricots, pineapples, oranges, lemons, limes, coconuts, ice cream, fish, crabs, oysters, clams, lobsters and craw fish.

"The following articles the Board have not considered it necessary to prohibit the sale of, but even these they would admonish the community to be moderate in using: potatoes, beets, tomatoes and onions."

Beef, bacon and bread, with beer and wine were about all they left for the people of Washington to eat. The Board said that the prohibited articles, "are, in their opinion highly prejudicial to health at the present season." The Board were probably afraid that these wholesome foods would cause ague, chills, fever and even cholera.

In that very year (1832) Dr. Martyn Paine, of the New York University Medical School was arguing that garden vegetables and almost every variety of fruit had been known to develop the deadly cholera and that to avoid it the people should restrict themselves to lean meat, potatoes, milk, tea and coffee.

It was in New York City in 1832, the very year that the cities were prohibiting the sale of fruits and vegetables because they cause cholera, that Graham launched his attack upon the false beliefs concerning fruits and vegetables and endeavored to induce Americans and, indeed, the world, to eat more fruits and vegetables and cease eating animal foods.

Graham not only challenged the view that fruits and vegetables cause cholera and that plenty of meat and wine will prevent it; but he declared that a diet of fruits and vegetables with entire abstinence from all alcoholics, tobacco, condiments, etc., and from all animal foods, was the best preventive of cholera.

It is interesting to note, in this connection, that Graham's first observations of the effects of diet upon health were made in Philadelphia and related to the part a vegetable diet apparently played in

INTRODUCTION

preventing Cholera. A small sect of *Bible Christians* had migrated from England to Philadelphia. These people abstained from all animal foods — flesh, eggs, milk, cheese, etc. — and from all condiments and stimulants. They used no tea, coffee, alcohol or tobacco. It was their view that flesh eating violated the first command given by God to man—the instruction to Adam that he should eat the fruit of the trees of the Garden.

Ten years before Graham lectured in Philadelphia for the Pennsylvania Temperance Society, this city had experienced a severe epidemic of cholera. There were many cases with a high death rate. Contrary to what was expected from the medical teachings of the time, not a single member of the *Bible Christian Church* had cholera. This fact made a deep and lasting impression upon Graham and caused him to turn his attention to the study of diet. No longer was he a mere temperance lecturer. His first series of lectures given the following year in New York were upon the causes and prevention of cholera. So radical and revolutionary did his lectures seem to the medical profession and most of the educated people of the time that it required nearly another quarter of a century for them to discard their false notions about vegetables and fruits causing cholera and concede that Graham may have been right. Fallacy dies slowly. Deep-rooted prejudices are not easily uprooted. Old habits are not quickly abandoned. The world's leaders do not like to admit that they have been wrong and have been misleading the people. They did not give up without a struggle — indeed, it may be truthfully said that they have not given up entirely to this day.

Many who heard Graham's lecture followed his advice and, thereupon, the physicians, butchers and others of New York reported that the Grahamites were dying like flies of the cholera. Graham returned to New York and being unable to find a single instance of death from cholera, and only one or two instances of cholera (these in people who had not carried out his advice) among those who had adopted the plan of eating and living he offered, challenged, through the public press of the city, his traducers to bring forth a case of death among his followers. This they did not and could not do, but they did not cease to peddle the lie.

Graham pointed out in reply that in America, where animal food is almost universally consumed in excess, and where children are trained to the use of it, even before they are weaned, scrofulous affections are exceedingly common, and lead to that fearful prevalence of pulmonary consumption, which has rendered that complaint emphatically the *American Disease.*" In addition to this, Graham pointed to "well-fed vegetable-eating children of other countries in all periods of time" and to examples of "feeble and cachectic children, and even those who are born with a scrofulous diathesis," who had been "brought into vigorous health on a well ordered vegetable diet, under a correct general regimen" as proof that the "very best health can be preserved in childhood without the use of flesh-meat."

Graham was an educated man and the same can not be said of most physicians of the period. It were folly to say to a man who knew the history of Sparta, that health and strength cannot be built and maintained on a vegetable diet.

The people were not all fools and the colleges and universities were not then, as now, dominated by big business interests. The teaching profession gave strong suport to the movement for diet reform. Professor Reubin Mussey of Dartmouth College openly advocated vegetarianism and invited Graham to address the students of Bowdoin College and also to speak in Hanover. Professor Edward Hitchcock delivered a series of lectures on diet and regimen in Amherst College and these were enthusiastically received by the students. Even the unexpected happened: The *Boston Medical and Surgical Journal*, a conservative and established periodical, endorsed his cause in its issue of Oct. 21, 1835 and declared that Graham's introductory lecture in Boston would have reflected honor upon the first medical men in America. No doubt the *Journal* later repented of this serious breach of medical ethics, for its editors missed few opportunities to lampoon Graham, although accepting an occasional article from his pen.

The fear of the produce of garden and orchard lingered on for many years after Graham's work began. Indeed, the author recalls many stories of how water melons, cantaloupes, cucumbers and a few other fruits and vegetables cause malaria, which he heard when a boy.

During the cholera year of 1849 the *Chicago Journal* strongly condemned the city council of that city, for not prohibiting the sale of fruits and vegetables as had been done in other cities, since, as the *Journal* said, the "sad effects," of using such foods were "so apparent." The *Democrat* carried the story of two boys who ate freely of oranges and cocoanuts and then went to the circus. "In a short time one was a corpse and the other reduced to the last stage of cholera." Even as late as 1867 it was reported by the press that someone by merely passing a fruit stand laden with spoiled peaches had suffered an "attack" of the *gripes,* a not impossible psychic reaction. But they reached the conclusion that "if bare proximity to those peaches caused him so much pain, the eating of them would have been certain death." Today we witness a similarly asinine procedure in the prohibition of the sale of raw milk in the cities.

Certain of the old physio-medical physicians condemned the eating of tomatoes because these contained calomel; lettuce was long said to contain opium; acid fruits were held responsible for rheumatism, arthritis and other "acid diseases." Apples were condemned by many physicians because they "derange digestion." I recall hearing one aged physician (this was over thirty years ago) telling of the evils of apples and say: "I would rather give my patients a dose of poison than to give them apples." He was daily dosing them with poisons, though withholding apples.

"Medicine" does not easily give up; it does not readily admit its mistakes. If Graham and his co-workers and successors had demonstrated that fruits and vegetables were not dangerous and they did not produce cholera and other "diseases," the profession of medicine would find other reasons for rejecting these foods and sticking to their meats and meat soups. They invented the idea that while these things may be pleasing to the sense of taste they have no food value.

As late as 1916 we find Dr. Richard C. Cabot of Harvard writing: "Lettuce for instance, is a food practically without value — nice and pleasant to look at, and valuable so far as it has dressing (made with oil). But the dressing is the only thing that has any food value." Also: "Tomatoes are ninety-four percent water; there is hardly any nutrition in them." These statements are typical of the medical view of fruits and vegetables in general.

In their efforts to discourage the eating of uncooked fruits and vegetables the regular profession pictured these as reeking with typhoid germs and the germs of other diseases. Cooking was necessary in order to destroy these germs. Lettuce, now shipped all over the country and eaten raw by everybody, was especially covered with hidden dangers in the form of disease germs. Not until the discovery of vitamins did the medical profession lose its fear of germs on vegetables and fruits sufficiently to enable it to sanction the use of uncooked foods. Even so, they never mention Graham, except to ridicule him.

But it was too late to stop the civilized world from eating fruits and vegetables. Graham and the other food reformers had done their work too well. The annual per capita consumption of plant foods was then, and still is, increasing. The medical profession still opposes vegetarianism and continues to insist upon the use of meat and meat soups, but they have lost on all fronts and have been forced to acknowledge the value of the fruits and vegetables, even if they do continue to ignore Graham.

INTRODUCTION

When the discovery of vitamins was first anonunced, the physiologist, Professor Percy G. Styles, stated that the theory is a restatement of Graham's views. Professor Styles was probably duly penalized for this breach of scientific ethics; for, apparently, neither he nor anyone else has dared reaffirm such a scientific heresy. The medical and so-called scientific crowd have long since decreed that "nothing good can come out of Nazareth" and with derisive scorn they point to Graham, when they condescend to notice him at all, and ask: "is not this the carpenter's son?" It is agreed that no discovery is a discovery unless it is made by one of the boys in the inner circle of "science." If they have not educated him; if he teaches not their doctrines; he is unworthy of a place in the Hall of Fame; or, is it the Hall of Infamy in which the "scientists" sit?

Graham made the "mistake" of offending the bakers, millers, brewers, distillers, saloon keepers, tobacco growers and sellers, butchers, packers, etc. There was no dairy industry then, but had there been one the members of this would have joined in the effort to mob him as they now join in the conspiracy of silence against him. Despite professional opposition and the opposition of the vested interests who saw their interests threatened, Graham's work prospered and grew. Soon he had many helpers, among them, Dr. Trall.

In his *Hydropathic Encyclopedia*, 1851, Dr. Trall declared to the world that all fresh fruits and green vegetables are antiscorbutic (opposed to the development of scurvy). Trall soon joined Graham in his crusade for vegetables and fruits and whole grain bread and against meat, eggs, milk, white bread, wines, narcotics, etc. Graham died in 1851. Trall carried on until his death in 1879. By this time the workers were many. Dr. Jennings joined them early in Graham's crusade. After Dr. Trall's death, Drs. Page and Densmore added to our fund of knowledge about trophology.

The next great advance in our trophologic knowledge came in 1891 when Dr. H. Lahmann, of Germany published his *Dietetsche Blutentmischung*, in which he presented the results of his investigations of the "ash" (minerals) of food. Lahmann was a German "regular" practitioner who had forsaken the pill bags and poison bottles and joined Louis Kuhne in his establishment. Lahmann gave us our first real knowledge of the value of food minerals. His work was rejected by the medical profession, though eagerly accepted by Hygienists and "faddists," with whom he had associated himself. Forty years ago Dr. H. Lindlahr brought Lahmann's discoveries back to America with him. Otto Carque and Alfred W. McCann quickly seized upon this new advance and began the work of acquainting the American public with it.

Ragnar Berg, a Swedish chemist, associated himself with Lahmann and began the development of the world's greatest food scientist. Lahmann died, but Berg still carries on. Lahmann's sanitarium fell into the hands of others. Lahmann's work was declared obsolete, the institution was given over to "experiments a la Steinach" and Berg was discharged.

It should be borne in mind that "with the exception of certain investigations made by Ragnar Berg, absolutely no research of any kind has been undertaken on the complete metabolism of the mineral salts, either in man or animal." — *The Physiology of Nutrition*, London, 1927.

Within recent years laboratory workers have attacked the subject of diet and these have added to our detailed knowledge of foods if not to our practical knowledge. These experiments have now been carried on long enough that we feel safe in asserting, on the strength of their results, that foods are really good to eat and that they do actually nourish the body. We feel safe in going even further and asserting that we must have foods to grow.

These "biochemists" discovered that cabbage, lettuce, celery, tomatoes, apples, oranges, etc., are really valuable foods. Their discovery so shocked and surprised the medical world that it completely forgot that the "faddists" had been eating these foods for a long time and had declared them to be superior to white flour, salt bacon, pigs knuckles, sausage, lard pies and coffee. It was really a remarkable discovery — all they now need to do is to become "faddists" with the rest of us and make use of the things Graham, Trall, Alcott, Densmore, Page, Oswald, Kuhne, Lahmann, Berg, etc., had long taught.

Much of the experimental "findings" is sheer nonsense. Many of the experimenters are subsidized by interested commercial firms. There are many green vegetables that are as valuable as spinach, but none that have "growers" organizations back of them to subsidize research. The manufacturers of yeast, of cod-liver oil and halibut-liver oil have subsidized research workers. So have the big milk producing companies. The same is true of the citrus industry. The gatherers and sellers of sea weeds have their scientific prostitutes also. When we see some special food heralded as an apple from

INTRODUCTION

the "Tree of Life" and see its value over-emphasized in books, magazines, newspapers and in physicians and "research" workers' reports we may be sure that there is money behind it.

The work of the biochemist tends to center around the vitamins and is confined largely to animal experimentation. It lacks the importance possessed by the work of those who feed human beings and who do not confine their attention to one food factor, but attend to the whole diet and to the whole program of eating.

I do not desire to minimize the serious work of the laboratory experimenters, but I would call attention to the fact that the "faddists" have preceded them with a whole series of much more important experiments. The "faddists" are of all varieties and kinds and they have many different notions and practices. They have, in other words, carried out, in human beings, many dietetic experiments. Some of these experiments have involved thousands of individuals and three or four generations. These experiments and their results are not to be lightly cast aside because those who make them lack training in the diploma mills of medicine, or because they were not "controlled." Hail to the faddists! They have performed a necessary work.

In this work we do not intend to ignore the work of the "fadists" but shall make use of it just as we shall draw upon the work of the laboratory men to confirm the findings of the "faddists." For it was the "faddists" and not the "bio-chemists" who initiated the movement for dietary study and reform and, who, by their results, compelled the medical world to take notice. Except for the "faddists" the "biochemists" may not have been born.

The medical profession showed no interest in dietetics until an awakened public demanded to know how to feed itself. Trophologists were ridiculed as faddists, fanatics, extremists and unqualified practitioners, or quacks by the medical fraternity.

Dr. Trall's words in his *Hydropathic Cook-Book* (1853) are still true: "However strange may seem the assertion, it is nevertheless true, that the philosophy of diet has never been taught in medical schools! Physicians generally are as profoundly ignorant of the whole subject as are the great masses of people."

Back in 1916 Dr. Richard C. Cabot, one of the outstanding physicians of the world, wrote: "Almost nothing is known about diet. There are numerous books on the subject which are useful for pressing leaves, but not for much that they contain." I believe that Dr. Cabot's evaluation of medical literature on diet was correct at the time he first published his statement and that the condition has not greatly improved since.

In Nov. 1926, R. G. Jackson, M.D., Toronto, Canada, declared that although diet had "long been ignored and its few advocates been relegated to the category of 'cranks,' proper feeding is beginning to be recognized by the medical profession as a most important adjunct to our therapeutic armamentarium." He adds: "Diet was not 'scientific medicine,' therefore it was not anything. And besides, diet was a measure advocated by 'cults' outside the profession; therefore it ought to be frowned upon."

Note that Dr. Jackson recognizes that his profession are accepting diet merely as an adjunct to their "therapeutic armamentarium," and not as a very foundation stone of life and health. He adds: "Moreover, modern dietetics is not the creation of our profession. It has been developed in its scientific aspects largely by our friends, the biochemists, and through them almost forced upon us. But now our authorities are beginning to put their O.K. upon it and marking it as their own; so it becomes respectable and will soon belong to 'scientific medicine'."

The "bio-chemists" entered the field of dietetics at a rather late stage and have succeeded, by laboratory experiments, in confirming practically the whole of the trophologic philosophy and practice of the *Hygienic* school. They, like Dr. Jackson, omit to mention this fact, however, in their public writings.

There is not a medical college in the United States that has a course in dietetics and the number of physicians who make an effort to acquire a knowledge of dietetics after graduation is exceedingly small. They usually plead lack of time and opportunity, but they find time and opportunity to play golf, take post-graduate courses in other and much less important subjects and even to go abroad. Dr. Phillip Norman ascribes their persistence in ignorance of how to feed the body to a lack of interest in the subject.

Dieting has never been an essential part of a physician's prescription and physicians have never known and do not know anything about diet, as they so freely admit. Eighteen years ago doctors were still ridiculing those who advocated dietary measures. Thirteen years ago it was still not a factor in the treatment of the sick and oc-

INTRODUCTION

cupied no place in the discussions in medical journals. Much fun was poked at "diets," "dieting," and "diet systems" by the regular medical profession until it suddenly dawned on them one fine day that the people were asking for diet. Today it is a factor in the care of patients in the practice of only a few physicians, has just reached the point of discussion by the profession and is still subject to ridicule by many of the dignitaries in the profession.

Despite their confessed ignorance of diet, despite their lack of training in dietary science and their lack of experience in dietary practice, they are ever ready to assume an air of pontifical infallibility in their criticisms of those of us who do employ a knowledge of food science in our care and feeding of the well and the sick. Some of our medical critics, some of the leaders in the ranks of materia medica, accuse "diet fads" of causing "nutritional diseases," "metabolic disorders" and cancer. Diet "fads" cause fewer evils than poisonous drugs, putrid serums, rot vaccines, dirty soups, and unnecessary surgical operations. Although freely admitting that they know nothing of diet and of trophology, they declare "it's all wrong anyway."

Another objection frequently met with is that "only a fool will bother about his diet when he is the right weight, sleeps well, enjoys life and is happy." This objection assumes either that correct eating is only for the invalid, or, else, that one should not make an effort to preserve his health, but should eat haphazzardly until he becomes ill and then should try to restore his health. The intelligent person will seek to prevent rather than remedy ill health.

It too often happens that when a medical man does become interested in dietetics he absorbs as much of the work of the *Hygienic* school as he can and passes it out to the public as his own. For example, some of them tell us that they "have found" that raw starch is digestible and that it is not well to eat proteins and starches at the same meal, but they forget that those they decry as "faddists" preceded them with these discoveries.

I do not want to be understood as saying that there are no medical men who possess a knowledge of diet. The leaven is at work in the profession and its more progressive and honest members have seen the light and have shown the rare courage that is required to break with professional precedent and follow that light. I am happy to have a number of such men, in various parts of the country, among my friends. To these men, I look with confidence, to lead their profession out of its self-imposed darkness. But for the great mass of physicians there is no newer knowledge of nutrition. They make no advance in dietary science. Indeed, some of their leaders labor to prove that the discoveries in the field of diet only reveal that they were feeding correctly all the time. It is lamentable, but true.

A tubercular specialist wrote a booklet a few years ago on feeding in tuberculosis. He briefly reviews the high-lights of dietary research and says that these findings only prove that they have been feeding tubercular cases correctly all the time. Physicians really seem to be unable to grasp the truths that have been uncovered about diet and seem incapable of comprehending their significance. They have never fed their tubercular patients correctly and are not doing so now.

Logan Clendening asserts that "Researchers on diet have not created a new dietary: they have simply proved why the old one so long in use was effective.° ° ° °It is really safer to stick to the long-established diets we have been all using and liking than to the pronouncements of the food dogmatists."

He here expresses the old "conservative" resistance to change and progress, the inertia of the "long-established." In the same article he asserts that the present eating habits of "the average human being" were formed "since he became a prosperous animal" and this is tantamount to the admission that our eating habits are not "long-established" ones. If he will look a little deeper he may discover that the food manufacturers are responsible for many of our recent eating habits and that processed foods are of recent modern origin.

I agree with Clendening that dietary research has not caused the medical profession to change its feeding plans and programs. They are still feeding their families and their patients as they were forty years ago. They are still defending white flour and coffee. They are still counting calories and lauding meat and a high protein diet.

Go into the hospitals and there you will find white flour, white sugar, denatured cereals, coffee, tea and the like served to patients. You discover that these same foods are eaten by the nurses. The hospital diet is notoriously unsatisfactory, as is testified to by physicians, internes, nurses and patients. It is miserably prepared and served with no consideration for its dietary value and with no regard for combinations. Meat, potatoes, white bread, corn starch pudding and tea are likely to form the bulk of the hospital diet. The dis-

INTRODUCTION

coveries of dieticians and scientists in the realm of food science are utterly disregarded in these medical institutions.

Dr. Victor Lindlahr admirably expresses the *Hygienic* view of this matter when he says: "Certainly marble halls, X-ray apparatus, microscopes, rounded corners, patented beds and all the frills and doo-dads that the hospital heads so delight in, do not contribute to the building of a patient's body cells. The human tissues that heal a wound do not sprout from equipment, architecture, or spaciousness. Wouldn't it be better to have less pretentious hospitals, less equipment, less staff but more vitamins, mineral salts and better cooks and care of the preparation of food."

Visit the homes of their patients and see these eat; or, better still, consult the written or printed diet prescriptions the physician gives to his patients, where he gives any thought to diet at all, and note the whole long list of denatured foods prescribed. They are still advising "standardized" and antiquated diets and pleading as an excuse that they "are too busy to keep up with the news of progress or are too far away from the places in which that information is readily obtainable."

This is the poorest kind of an excuse for ignorance of a subject so vital, all the more so when we consider that these same physicians manage to keep up with the "advances" in drugs, serums, operations, etc., Dietary knowledge is too easily obtained for us to accept this as an excuse for their failure to acquire and make use of it. Medical colleges certainly cannot offer this as an excuse for not establishing a Chair in dietetics.

Go into the homes of physicians and you soon discover that they and the members of their families are eating denatured foods of all kinds. There is white bread on the table. There is also white sugar, commercial syrups and sulphured and canned fruits. Denatured cereals are there, as are also coffee and tea. Their food is prepared according to conventional methods and is eaten in the customary, haphazzard manner, with no regard for combinations or other essential orthotrophic factors.

Dr. N. Phillip Norman, Instructor in Gastro-enterology, New York Polyclinic Medical School and Hospital, says, in an article in the *Journal of Clinical Medicine*, July, 1925: "The average medical man seems to have so little interest in dietary matters that I feel I should like to say or write something, at every possible opportunity, to stimulate his interest to a more definite understanding of the

THE SCIENCE AND FINE ART OF FOOD AND NUTRITION

nutritional principles that should be applied to every person, regardless of whether he is sick or well."

Progress in dietary science (trophology) makes it essential that intelligent men and women reform their eating habits, even if physicians will not. I always suspect commercial motives in the physician, however high his standing, who disparages dietary reform and who sings that "the old time religion (diet) is good enough for me."

Orthotrophy, from the Greek *Orthos* — straight, erect, true — and *Trepho* — nourish, was coined by the author to designate correct nutrition and separate it from the great mass of fallacies that make up what now passes under the term dietetics. Orthotrophy — correct nutrition — is broad in its meaning and covers more than is implied under the term, food. We, therefore, employ the term *trophology* the science of food, in the narrow sense of food and food chemistry. Trophology will be used to supplant the term dietetics.

Orthotrophy means correct nutrition. There are times when to abstain from food is not only right but imperative; when to eat is not to nourish the body, but to poison it. Therefore fasting, or negative nutrition, comes, properly, under the heading of orthotrophy. Although frequent references to fasting will be made in this volume, the subject will be fully covered in Vol. III of this series.

Sunshine is also a nutritive "substance" of great importance. It will likewise be covered in Vol. III.

Philosophy of Nutrition
CHAPTER I.

Several generations of study of cell development and heredity have ignored almost completely the more important study of nutritional habits as these determine and predetermine cell developments and affect reproduction and survival. The role of nutrition in integration, reintegration, and disintegration has been shamefully neglected.

For the most part, it has been taken for granted that it matters not what kind of food an organism consumes, so long as it consumes "enough" and more than "enough." Plenty of food and lack of food are chiefly considered as of importance. This places most importance upon quantity rather than quality and kind.

Only recently have we begun to seriously investigate the physiological basis of life and the incidences of nutrition as they affect growth and reproduction, both in a physiological and pathological sense. It is true that hints of the role of nutrition in *health* and *disease* have come to thinking members of our race during the past several thousand years; but scientists have considered such things unworthy of their notice.

Nutrition is the sum total of all the processes and functions by which growth and development, maintenance and repair of the body, and, by which reproduction are accomplished. It is the replenishment of tissues and not the accumulation of fat and not the "stimulation" (excitation) of the vital powers. Due to the great misunderstanding and confusion that exists about "stimulation," we are inclined to associate it with nutrition.

"Pure and perfect nutrition," says Dr. Trall, "implies the assimilation of nutriment material to the structure of the body, without the least excitement, disturbance, or impression of any kind that can properly be called stimulating." "All stimulus, therefore, is directly opposed to healthful nutrition, and a source of useless expenditure or waste of vital power."

Food, we define as any substance the elements of which are convertible into, and do form, the constituent matters of the tissues and fluids of the body and are employed by the organism in the performance of any of its functions. Life depends on food. All growth, repair and maintenance of tissues and all development of vital power are the results of nutrition. All parts and products of the body are elaborated from the blood, and all the functions of the body depend upon the blood for material supplies. The blood is elaborated from air, water, food and sunshine. These are essential and all. that are essential, so far as materials are concerned, for the production of good blood and sound tissues and organs and functional results.

During life two simultaneous processes are in continual progress —a building up and a breaking down process. The two processes taken together are called metabolism. The contructive process is known as anabolism; the breaking down process as katabolism. In the healthy organism, during childhood and youth and well into maturity, the constructive process exceeds the destructive process. During sickness and in old age the destructive process exceeds the building up process.

During complete rest and sleep all the general life functions are carried on as during waking hours, only less actively. The heart continues to pulsate, the chest to rise and fall in breathing, the liver and digestive organs and other internal organs all go on working. All of the body cells work.

The metabolism carried on at complete rest is called basic metabolism. The metabolic rate is determined by measuring the amount of oxygen used. This varies with age, sex, climate, race, habits, diet, mental state, etc. It is lower in women than in men, higher (nearly double) in infants than in adults, lowest in advanced age. It is lower in Orientals (Japansese and Chinese); higher in athletes than in sedentary men. Americans living in Brazil show a lower basal metabolism than in this country. It is greater after effort (but during sleep) due to muscular tension. It rises during the day, being higher in the afternoon than in the morning. It is lower in vegetarians than in meat eaters.

Orthodox science cannot tell what is a standard metabolism and a standard of biological relation. As in everything else, the standards for "normal basic metabolism" are mere statistical averages made, for the most part, on over-stimulated, over-fed and particularly over-protein-stuffed subjects. The ideal or biological norm can be determined only from healthy individuals living a truly bionomic life.

PHILOSOPHY OF NUTRITION

It is the *Hygienic* view that normal metabolism must be based on a normal mode of nutrition which involves not only the kind, quality and amount of food eaten, but also, and very importantly, the kind and amount of work — "sweat of the brow" — expended in earning this food. No mode of nutrition can be considered normal that does not involve work—counter-service—in procuring it. Predacity, parasitism, saprophytism, and similar modes of stealing supplies or of living without work involve, not only a disturbance of the normal work-food ratio, but also feeding upon inferior foods. Metabolic abnormalities growing out of such modes of nutrition result in losses and exaggerations of structure and in disease in general.

7,000,000 of the 25,000,000,000,000 red blood cells in the body of an average man die every second, so that 7,000,000 new ones must be produced every second of our lives—a wonderful example of the creative operations always at work in our bodies. The materials out of which these new cells are built are supplied by food. This represents only a small part of the creative work that goes on. Similar destruction and reconstruction occur in other tissues of the body.

The human body is made up of twenty-two chemical elements, as follow:

		Zinc
Oxygen	Manganese	Chlorine
Hydrogen	Sodium	Flourine
Carbon	Silicon	Bromine
Nitrogen	Iron	Nickel
Calcium	Lithium	Copper
Phosphorous	Iodin	Arsenic
Potassium	Sulphur	Magnesium

The nutritional roles of about a dozen elements, such as aluminum, arsenic, boron, bromide, nickle, silicon, vanadium and tin, which appear in human and animal bodies in minute amounts, are still unknown. They are all supposed to be concerned with *catalysis*, or the instigation and speeding up of chemical reactions in the body. It is not certain that they belong in the body. They may be found there only as foreign elements. The evidence offered of the need for boron is very circumstantial and far from conclusive.

These elements do not exist in the body in their "free" state, but in organic combinations with each other, and are variously distributed in the various tissues and fluids of the body. Roughly, they are grouped in our foods as proteins, carbohydrates, hydrocarbons, water, mineral salts, vitamins, and indigestible portions — bulk or roughage. Each element serves a definite and indispensible function which no other element can serve for it. All of them are essential to wholeness of life, to health, growth and to continued existence.

It is to supply material with which to carry on the building up of tissue and replace that which is broken down; in other words, to supply material for growth and repair, that we eat. At least this is one of the purposes served by food.

Other processes besides those of growth and repair are continually going on in the body. For example, there is the work of preparing food for use by the body. This work is known as digestion and is accomplished largely by the action of certain juices or secretions which act upon the food chemically. These juices have to be manufactured by the body for its own use. Food furnishes the materials necessary for the production of these and the many other secretions of the body.

The broken down products of the cells are acid in character and are highly irritating and poisonous. If permitted to remain in the body unchanged they would soon destroy life. Therefore, they are not only eliminated, but are changed chemically by being combined with certain alkaline mineral elements, thus rendering them less irritating and harmful and also preparing them for elimination. The mineral elements with which this detoxifying change is made are supplied by our food.

Foods are burned in the body to supply heat and energy. At least this is the present theory of scientists. There are those who deny this and who insist that both the heat and energy of the body are independent of its food supply, that food serves solely as replacement material in building up new and repairing old tissues and in forming the body's secretions. The claim has been made that heat is derived from the assimilation of food rather than from its oxidation. It is also claimed that the body's heat is due to friction.

We eat carbon, take in oxygen and give off carbon dioxide. It is quite evident that the carbon is oxidized in the body. It would certainly give off heat in this process. The body may have other sources of heat, but this seems to be certainly one of them. The amount of heat produced by the body seems to parallel the amount of carbon dioxide it gives off.

PHILOSOPHY OF NUTRITION

The chemical energies of the body are directed by something which is not itself a chemical energy, but which is intimately associated with the organic synthesis which the chemical energy serves to maintain. At least, I cannot see how we can escape this position. I have no doubt that chemical as well as mechanical energies are utilized in the body, although, they are subordinate to a controlling and unifying non-chemical force. However, this is still a much mooted question and will be solved only in the future. I do not think that all the energies of the living body are derived from foods.

The normal specific gravity and normal alkalinity of the blood are maintained by food. As will be shown later, these two functions are performed chiefly by the minerals of the diet.

These uses of food may be summed up in a few words by saying: food is any substance which, when taken into the body, can be used by it for the replenishment of tissue (growth and repair) and for the performance of organic function. This definition can be made to include water and the oxygen of the air; however, water and oxygen are not usually classed as foods. Such substances, if they are to be classed as true foods, must be with deleterious effects. Many things that are eaten by man have deleterious effects, although, they do possess food value. Obviously, such foods should be abstained from so long as other foods are to be had.

The human body is a wonderfully complex and ingenuous mechanism made up of thousands of different parts and containing hundreds of different chemical compositions. Yet all of these must be nourished by a single blood stream, a stream which itself is of remarkably uniform composition so far as any chemical analysis can determine.

If the blood derived its substance from a single source of supply, as does the blood of a nursing baby, for example, life would seem marvelous enough. But, when one considers that the blood is often nourished by hundreds of different food substances, particularly in the case of modern civilized man, it seems almost inconceivably complex. We find it difficult to comprehend how life can exist at all.

The body must secure all the necessary food elements from all the great mass of diverse foods, in order to avoid the deficiencies or "starvations" and, at the same time, it must avoid all excess of certain materials which we almost always consume in excess. Food substances which are not needed and cannot be used, injure and do not help the body.

THE SCIENCE AND FINE ART OF FOOD AND NUTRITION

As the study of nutrition continues, the essentials of man's diet multiply. The older books gave man's nutritive requirements as proteins, carbohydrates and fats. Today we say he needs proteins, fats, carbohydrates, minerals, vitamins and cellulose, or roughage. The normal dietary should include all of these factors.

Since food serves so many and such vital functions in the body, it is highly important that we supply our bodies with all of the needed food elements. It is essential that the diet adequately nourish the whole body and not merely some part or parts of it. The dietary ensemble must meet all of the needs of the ensemble of nutrition. The whole of the diet and not one article of food or one element of nutrition, determines the nutritive result. The adequacy of a given dietary to feed the whole body and not its theoretical adequacy to meet the needs of one organ, will determine its fitness in any given case.

The human body has never been fully analyzed nor has there ever been made a full and complete analysis of all foodstuffs. This, however, is not a matter of great importance. Neither man nor foods can be analyzed without thoroughly destroying him or them. The products of the destructive processes are not the same as those that exist in the cells and tissues of the body or of the food. It is only possible to analyze a dead body and this throws but little light on the chemistry of a live one. An analysis of a dead body and an analysis of a handful of soil will show them to both be composed of the same elements, but no one can mistake the flesh of a man for a handful of soil. An apple, too, is made up of the same elements as the soil, but we easily recognize the vast difference between this product of vital synthesis and the soil in our garden. Fortunately it is not necessary to know the exact chemistry of the body nor the exact chemistry of foods in order to properly feed ourselves, our families and our patients. If we feed our bodies natural foods, so that we may be sure they contain all the nutritive essentials, we can trust the orderly and very ancient processes of life to take care of the rest of the matter for us.

Food Elements
CHAPTER II

By food elements the reader is not to understand, chemical elements. The chemical elements—nitrogen, carbon, iron, calcium, etc.—in foods were named in the preceding chapter. By food elements is meant the various distinct compounds that exist in foods and that are useful, after digestion, as nourishment for the body. The chemical elements of the body do not exist in the body in their "free" (uncombined) or pure state. They are always present in various complex combinations, both in the human body and in the simplest forms of food-stuffs. The animal body does not make use of the "free" elements, with the exception of oxygen, but employs only certain acceptable compounds prepared by the synthetic processes of the plant. The plant is the ultimate source of all animal food.

Foods are materials which supply the "elements" necessary for promoting growth of the body and repairing its waste, yield energy for msucular work, yield heat, regulate the body processes, and make reproduction possible. According to their chemical composition, foods are classified as:

    Proteins.
    Carbohydrates (starches and sugars).
    Hydrocarbons (fats and oils).
    Salts (organic).
    Vitamins.

According to their functions, foods are divided into:
    1. Fuel and energy foods—carbohydrates, fats, proteins.
    2. Building foods—proteins, salts, water.
    3. Regulators of body processes—minerals, vitamins, water.

According to their sources, foods are classified as:
    1. Vegetable foods.
    2. Animal foods.

Food substances as they come from the plant and animal contain: (1) Nutritive matter; (2) Water; (3) Refuse—or waste. The different articles of food are placed into different classes according to the food elements that predominate. Thus, there are protein foods, carbohydrate foods, hydrocarbon foods and foods rich in organic salts, vitamins and water. Let us briefly discuss each of these classes of food substances and notice the chief sources of each.

PROTEIN FOODS

These are rich in protein which contains nitrogen as a distinguishing element. Proteins also contain carbon, hydrogen and oxygen. Most proteins contain sulphur and some other elements. Chief among the protein foods are:

Fruits—olives, avocados.
Nuts—all kinds except chestnuts, cocoanuts and acorns.
Grains—all kinds.
Legumes—beans, peas, lentils, peanuts.
Eggs—all varieties.
Lean meats of all kinds—including fish, poultry, etc.

CLASSIFICATION OF PROTEINS

The plant and animal proteins most commonly met with in physiology are collectively designated "native proteins." This is a more or less arbitrary classification for which there seems to be little need. Formerly there existed considerable confusion in naming and classifying proteins and we still meet some differences of usage in the literature of the subject, but the tendency is more and more to follow the recommendations of the joint committee of the American Physiological Society and the American Society of Biological Chemists made in 1907. The following classification follows this recommendation in general:

1. *Simple Proteins:* These are defined as proteins that yield only amino acids or their derivatives on digestion or hydrolysis. This definition, however, is faulty as many of these proteins have been shown to have some carbohydrate material in their composition. Among these are:

A. *Albumens:* egg albumen, lactalbumen, serum albumen are of animal origin. Albumens of plant origin are legumelin of peas and leucosin of wheat.

B. *Globulins:* egg globulin, lactoglobulin, serum globulin, fibrinogen of the blood, myosin (muscle globulin) are of animal origin. Of plant origin are legumin of peas, tuberin of potatoes, edestin of wheat and seeds, and excelsin of the Brazil nut.

D. *Albuminoids, or Scleroproteins:* These are found in the connective tissues of the body. Among these are collagen which forms the ground substance of bone and cartilage and in the white fibrous or inelastic conective tissue (tendons, aponeuroses, ligaments, dura mater, pericardium, fascia); elastin found in the yellow (elastic) connective tissues in the walls of the blood vessels (especially arteries), and of the air tubes of the lungs; keratin, found in the outer layer of the skin and in nails, hair, feathers, hooves, etc.

E. *Glutelins:* Glutenin of wheat is an example of the glutelins.

F. *Prolamines*: Gliadin of wheat, zein of corn, and hordein of barley are examples.

2. *Compound (complex or conjugated) Proteins*: These are composed of a simple protein united with some other substance and are named according to the character of the other substance, as:

A. *Chromoproteins:* a simple protein united with a pigment—hemoglobin is an example.

B. *Nucleoproteins:* One or more simple proteins united with nucleic acid found chiefly in the nuclei of the cells, but also in the germ of wheat and in the thymus gland.

C. *Phosphoproteins:* Proteins containing phosphorus, as ovovitelin (vitelin of egg yolk), casein or caseinogen of milk.

D. *Glycoproteins:* A protein united with carbohydrate as mucin in saliva and mucus.

E. *Lecithoproteins, or Lecithans:* a protein united with lecithin, a compound of fat containing phosphorus and nitrogen and found in the brain, seminal fluid, and in many plants.

3. *Derived Proteins:* Proteins produced from the previously named proteins in various ways, but chiefly by means of digestion or hydrolysis, that is, by the action of digestive enzymes and by acids and alkalies. These are:

A. *Coagulated protein,* formed by heat.
B. *Acid Metaproteins* formed by the action of acids.
C. *Alkali Metaproteins* formed by the action of alkalis.
D. *Casein, Fibrin.*
E. *Secondary Derivatives* formed in the process of digestion—peptoses or albumoses, peptones and peptoids or peptids.

AMINO ACIDS

Every species of plant and animal has its own characteristic proteins. The proteins of closely related species are different. Indeed the proteins of different structures of the same organism are different. It has been estimated that there are 1600 different proteins in the human body. Similar complexity of protein constitution exists in the tissues of practically all animals. Each plant, also, possesses several different proteins in its makeup, each different tissue possessing its own characteristic protein. The proteins of the food supply are very different to those of the animal taking that food. These have to be broken down and reconverted into proteins peculiar to the eater.

When protein digestion is completed the protein has been broken down into simpler compounds known as amino acids. These are organic acids containing nitrogen. It does not seem necessary that I here enter into any detailed and technical discussion of the complexities of their chemical constitution. This can be of no value to my lay readers and my professional readers may consult their text books and reference books to refresh their memories upon this subject.

Amino acids, called also, the "building stones of the body," are much talked about today. Indeed, it begins to look as though they are now to go through the same over-emphasis, high pressure consideration and commercial exploitation that the vitamins are just now beginning to emerge from. Already synthetic amino acids and amino acids extracted from food sources are offered for sale to the food-conscious public. These offers are accompanied with the usual misleading and unfounded claims for their superior virtues.

The body cannot absorb any protein as such. If protein is absorbed directly into the blood stream, without first undergoing the processes of digestion, it is poisonous. Proteins must be broken down into simpler compounds known as amino acids before they can be absorbed and assimilated. Introduce the amino acids out of which proteins are made and all is well.

Proteins are colloids—amino acids are crystalloids. Plant and animal material should or must be in the colloidal state. Each plant and animal, however, must build its own colloids and in order that the animal body may utilize the substances in plant colloids in building its own colloids, it must first break them down into crystalloids.

While it is not entirely correct to speak of protein as containing such and such amino acids, for these are known to us only after the protein has been decomposed; still, for convenience we say proteins are made up of chemical units called amino acids, just as words are made up of letters. Just as the twenty-six letter of the alphabet

FOOD ELEMENTS

are sufficient to form millions of words; so, the twenty-two or more amino acids are sufficient to form the many different proteins known and unknown. It is generally believed that there are amino acids that have not been isolated and identified.

Proteins are numerous, each one being different from every other. The protein molecule is exceedingly complex, containing from twelve to twenty different amino acids. Amino acids, themselves, are complex nitrogenous bodies, synthesized by plants in the process of growth. Animals are able only to analyze proteins in the process of digestion, and resynthesize the resulting amino acids into new and different proteins.

There exists a certain amount of confusion in naming and classifying the amino acids. Berg names the following twenty-one: glycocoll, alanin, serin, valin, leucin, isoleucin, asparaginic acid, asparagin, glutamin, arginin, ornithin, lysin, cystin, cystein, B-phenylalanin, tyrosin, trytophan, histidin, prolin, and oxyprolin.

Sherman lists the following twenty-two: glycine, alanine, valine, leucine, isoleucine, norleucine, phenylalanine, tyrosine, serine, theonine, cystine, methionine, aspartic acid, glutamic acid, hydroxyglutamic acid, argenine, lysine, histidine, proline, hydroxyproline, tryptophan and serine.

Amino acids serve the following five general functions in the animal body:

1. They serve as building stones out of which the proteins characteristic of the various cells of the body are synthesized. Thus, they serve as the materials of growth and repair.

2. The cells use them in manufacturing the many and various enzymes of the body, in producing the various hormones and in producing other nitrogenous products. They are supposed to be employed in the production of genes and antibodies; but as these two "substances" are merely hypothetical entities, who knows.

3. The blood proteins are made from the amino acids. These proteins, because of their colloidal osmotic pressure, are indispensable.

4. They are said to be used as a source of energy. In this the nitrogen of the amino acid is regarded as being of little value. But when the amine has been split off from the amino acid the remainder of the molecule, which constitutes the larger part of it, contains no nitrogen, but much carbon. Thus, if they are not immediately needed, certain of the amino acids, such as glycine, alanine, cystine and arginine are transformed into glucose and glycogen.

—31—

5. Some of the amino acids are supposed to serve certain specific functions. A deficiency of trytophan in young rats leads to cataract and blindness and to poor development of tooth enamel. In old as well as in young rats a lack of tryptophan causes blindness and impairs the generation of spermatozoa. Tryphtophan is essential to generation in rats. Tyrosine is thought to be essential to the production of the hormones adrenalin and thyroxin. A reduction of the number of spermatozoa is said to result from a deficiency of arganine.

ESSENTIAL AMINO ACIDS

The various amino acids are specific in their functions. They are not interchangeable. Of the twenty-two known amino acids only ten or twelve are regarded as essential or indispensable. Tryptophan, tyrosin, lysin, cystin, glutamic acid, histidin and ornathin are among the essential amino acids. If the diet supplies the essential amino acids in adequate quantities, growth, maintenance and reproduction are normal. If one or more of these is lacking or deficient this is not true. Examples: A deficiency of valine in the diet of young animals stunts growth and development to a remarkable degree. If lysin is lacking in the diet there is more or less maintenance but no growth. No matter how much protein and other elements supplied in the diet, if lysin and tryphtophan are lacking, life soon comes to an end.

It is held that the amino acids other than the ten or twelve indispensable ones can be made by the tissues from the essential amino acids, apparently by oxydizing them. Glycine apparently can be manufactured in the animal body from the other amino acids if it is lacking in the diet. Prolin, which may be readily produced in the body by oxidation of histidin is, therefore, not considered an essential amino acid. Its production from histidin depends, however, upon an over supply of this latter acid. Glycocoll is also of such constitution that it may be produced in the body by the oxidation of several different amino acids. Casein of milk is devoid of glycocoll, but rats fed upon casein thrive.

By an essential amino acid, then, is meant, one that the body cannot produce by oxidation (reduction) of another amino acid. The animal body cannot synthesize amino acids out of the elements of earth, air and water, but must receive these from the plant, which, alone, has the power to synthesize these substances. The animal body is capable only of producing some of the less complex amino acids out of the more complex ones by a reduction process.

Since the lower grade amino acids are formed within the body out of the higher compounds, they are regarded as of no vital importance. This, in my opinion, is a mistake. The body does seem to require them so that they are actually essential, even if it is not essential that they be taken in as such, but can be produced from other amino acids. On the other hand they can be produced from the higher amino acids only if these latter are present in excess of need. It may also be true that a saving of energy is secured if the lower grade amino acids are taken in with the food stuffs and the body is not compelled to reduce the higher compounds to lower grade. There is another theoretical possibility. The older theories of nutrition overlooked the universal validity of the *Law of the Minimum* to be explained in a later chapter. Investigators ignored the extent to which every tissue builder is dependent upon all the others. As Berg puts it: "They failed to realize that what is decisive for development, is not so much the absolute quantity of the various nutritive elements, as their relative proportions. They did not understand that the bodily need in respect of any one constituent of a diet can be determined only when we simultaneously take into account all the other factors of nutrition." There is the possibility that when one of the "non-essential" amino acids is lacking in the diet and the body is forced to make it from one of the essential amino acids, an actual reduction, below normal requirements, of the essential amino acid takes place with a corresponding lag in development.

PROTEIN EVALUATION

Proteins are made up of amino acids. Some of these amino acids are indispensable, others may be made from the essential amino acids. No two proteins have the same amino acid content. Some of them are very deficient in one or more of the essential amino acids. Either the amino acid is entirely absent or it is present in such minute quantity that one would be forced to consume enormous quantities of the protein to secure an adequate supply of the deficient amino acid. Proteins lacking in an essential amino acid are inadequate proteins. According to their adequacy, individual proteins are grouped as:

1. *Complete*: Those maintaining life and providing for normal growth of the young and reproduction in the adult when fed as the sole protein food. Examples of complete proteins are *excelsin* of the Brazil nut, *glycinin*, of the soy-bean, *casein* and *lactalbumen* of milk, *ovalbumen* and *ovovitallin* of eggs, *edestin*, *glutenin* and maize *glutel-*

lin of cereals. Rose showed that the proteins most suitable for maintaining growth in dogs are lactalbumen (milk), ovalbumen and ovavitellin (eggs); that next in order of suitableness are glutenin (wheat), casein (milk), glutelin (corn) and glycinin (soy bean). Gliadin (wheat and rye) and legumin (peas) are capable of maintaining nitrogen balance, but not growth. Zein and gelatin can do neither.

2. *Partially Complete*: Those maintaining life but not supporting normal growth. Examples of these are *gliadin*, of wheat, *hordein* of barley and *prolamin* of rye, *legumin* of peas, *legumenin* in the soy bean, *conglutin*, in blue and yellow lupin, *phaseolin* in the white kidney bean, *legumin* and *vignin* in vetch.

3. *Incomplete*: Those incapable either of maintaining life or of supporting growth. *Gelatin* from horn and other hard parts of the animal is the most conspicuous example of an incomplete protein, *Zein* of corn (maize) is another example of this class.

Let us take a look at an incomplete protein. With zein as the sole source of amino acids, growth is impossible. In fact, experimental animals fed zein as their sole protein, lose weight. If tryptophan is added to the zein, weight is maintained but growth does not occur. Only after both lysine and tryptophan are added can normal growth take place. Zein is deficient in tryptophan, glycine, lysine and glycocoll.

Gliadin, found abundantly in wheat and rye, lacks sufficient lusine to maintain growth. Gelatin lacks tyrosin and tryptophan. Unless these are supplied to the animal fed on gelatin as its sole source of protein, it soon dies.

Thus it may be seen that since the nutritive value of proteins is determined by the kinds and quantities of amino acids they contain, all proteins are not of equal value to the body and cannot be used interchangeably. The nutritive value of foods cannot be determined by reference to a table of food composition. This fallacy was exposed by Prof. Huxley many years ago. Sophie Leppel followed him in protesting against the belief that tables of food analysis give reliable indexes to food values. All the fuss made about the need for 118 grams of protein daily, without specifying the kinds of proteins, does not amount to much.

While I have emphasized the fact that the various proteins are not interchangeable, it is necessary to distinguish between the various isolated proteins and the common protein foods. All protein foods contain two or more proteins. The deficiencies of one protein of a food are often made up by the other protein of the same food. For example, tryptophan may be lacking in one protein and one of the other proteins in the same food may be rich in this amino acid. Returning to zein of corn, which, as we have seen, will not maintain life; it is supplemented by glutelin, of which the corn possesses almost an equal amount, and these two proteins are capable of supporting a normal rate of growth. Gliadin of wheat and rye lack sufficient lysine to maintain growth. But wheat contains other proteins which supply liberal portions of this amino acid.

We do not eat isolated individual proteins and do not depend upon but one such protein as our source of amino acids. On the contrary, we eat whole foods which contain two or several proteins. We also eat several foods, all of which contain proteins. Just as one protein in a food may supplement another protein in the same food, so the protein of one food may supplement the protein of another food. Two inadequate proteins may prove adequate when supplied to the same individual. This can be so, of course, only when they are not both inadequate in the same amino acids. If each is abundant in what is lacking in the other, the combined proteins will prove adequate. The sum total of the various proteins in the diet, if the diet is varied, will prove fully adequate.

It is customary to use young rats in testing the value of the various proteins. It is obvious to everyone that young rats never attempt to live on isolated and single proteins. They eat the whole food and eat different kinds of protein foods so that they receive all of the needed amino acids. Most of the experiments with the different vegetable and grain proteins have been made with denatured proteins and may not prove all that they are supposed to prove. They have been performed with isolated, individual proteins and Hindhede aptly says of these substances that, far from being remarkable that these isolated proteins have so little value, "it is remarkable that such substances, isolated by complicated chemical processes, have any value at all."

It may be ideal for experimental purposes, in testing the value of the different proteins, to use only single isolated proteins, but it is a far cry from this experimental condition to the eating practices of man and animals. It is not only true that the diets of both man and animals commonly contain more than one kind of protein food, but it is also true that all protein foods contain two or more proteins. If only a single protein food were consumed, the diet would contain more than one protein. Note the different proteins in corn, wheat, milk and eggs. It frequently happens that the protein in one food is abundant in the amino acids in which the protein in another food is deficient. Thus the two proteins supplement each other so that, together, they constitute a complete protein. Often the deficiency in a protein is so small that a very slight addition of the deficient amino acids from another source suffices to support normal growth and maintenance. All proteins are, therefore, capable of supplying the body with important nutritive substances. The mere fact that a protein is inadequate is not sufficient reason for rejecting it completely.

It is true that some mixtures of protein foods have been shown to be inferior, even, to certain single articles of protein. This is especially true of the grains as compared to milk. Some of the cereal proteins are adequate, but only so when fed in large amounts. Glutenin from wheat may be made to supply a sufficiency of amino acids in which it is deficient only by separating this protein from the wheat and feeding it in concentrated form and in amounts one could not secure by eating wheat. Edistin of hemp is another example of this kind. In small quantities it does not supply sufficient lusine. The same thing is true of the casein of milk. It is low in cystine, hence in small quantities, does not supply sufficient of this amino acid. Thus it becomes apparent that some complete proteins may prove to be partially incomplete when fed in reduced amounts.

A mixture of grains will not suffice to maintain growth and repair. Rye and barley are about the only grains that are adequate for the adult body. Even a mixture of as many as ten varieties of grains does not provide adequate protein for growth due to the fact that all of them are poor in lysin and cystin and most of them contain too little tryptophan.

In regular practice we do not consume casein as our sole source of protein, nor do we live upon an exclusive grain diet. We regularly consume many other protein-containing foods. *Hygienists,* on the other hand, have long contended that grains form no normal part of man's diet and have long considered them to be inferior foods. Dr. Densmore was the first to point out the inferiority of grains as an article of human consumption. We are not surprised that the experimenters have fully verified most of his contentions. More of this in a later chapter.

VEGETABLE VERSUS ANIMAL PROTEINS

Animal experimenters are prone to overemphasize the importance of the food substances that they regularly use with which to supplement inadequate diets and to ignore, almost wholly, the natural order of feeding. For example, milk is a very handy item of food and is used very much as a dietary supplement in these experiments. It usually suffices to render adequate an otherwise inadequate experimental diet, hence the experimenters are prone to emphasize the "value" of milk and to completely ignore the obvious fact that in nature, animals secure an adequate diet without resort to milk after they are weaned. Their experimental diets are almost never the diets of the people; nor are they the diets of animals in nature. There is a tendency of this class of experiments to mislead both the experimenter and the people as a whole, inasmuch as they ignore the many other food supplements that are equally capable of suplementing the inadequacies of a monodiet or of a deficient but somewhat varied diet.

In experiments on dogs deficient diets were fed to a group of dogs. To this diet was added, for some of the dogs, a given quantity of milk. The dogs that got the milk grew and developed normally. The dogs not receiving the milk were stunted and poorly developed. It would be folly to reason from this that dogs require milk for normal development, for we know that dogs can and do develop normally without getting milk after they are weaned. All that such an experiment proves is that milk added to an otherwise deficient diet will render the diet adequate. But there are hundreds of other ways of rendering the diet adequate as all animals in the wild state are well aware. Indeed, it is probable that many of the other ways of rendering the diet adequate are superior to the milk. Milk after the normal suckling period has ended is far from being an unmixed blessing.

Experiments with the different proteins would easily lead the unwary to believe that the elephant, cow, horse, buffalo, deer, rabbit and other strictly vegetable eating animals cannot live and grow on their vegetable diets, but, actually, we know that they do very well on such diets. This is because they never eat but one kind of protein (never eat individual isolated proteins). Their diet is varied One protein corrects the defects of another.

Another fact strikes the serious student of dietetics: namely, the experimenters never seem to consider nuts, which are certainly important constituents of man's normal diet, as worthy of their attention; yet most nuts contain complete and high grade proteins. Green vegetables also contain high grade proteins, although in very small amounts. But when these are added to the diet in large quantities, as in consuming large daily salads, they are capable of supplementing the deficiencies in an all-cereal diet and rendering this adequate. The experimenters are fond of comparing legumes and cereals with flesh foods, and neither of these classes of foods form parts of man's normal diet.

The biological value of the different proteins is tested on animals, commonly on rats. These are rapidly growing animals. A protein may prove to be incomplete or partially complete when fed to animals of rapid growth and may prove to be complete when fed to animals of slow growth. No doubt, too, different species require the differnt amino acids in varying amounts, even for maintenance. We know that the protein in human milk is especially rich in tryptophan, more so than the protein of cow's milk, an amino acid vitally important in the growth of the infant and young child. No broad generalizations about the value of the different proteins are, therefore, possible. When a protein has been shown to be complete, partially complete or incomplete for a particular species it can be said to be so only for this species. It may prove to be otherwise when fed to another species with different requirements. The underworld notwithstanding, man is not yet a rat, and "rat-pen" results are not fully applicable to his nutrition. The final test must be upon man.

We are frequently told that meat protein is more easily assimilated than vegetable proteins. There is no evidence for this statement, but it may be argued on the other side that the frequency with which allergic manifestations follow the use of animal foods indicates that these are less easily assimilated than vegetable proteins. The assertion is based upon a failure to take into consideration, not the difficulties, but the differences (largely of timing) in the digestion of the various foods: not of various proteins, but of various foods.

Muscle meat, the kind most commonly consumed, is a very poor food. Its inadequacy is made manifest by the failure of captive lions to reproduce themselves on a diet preponderantly of this food. Berg says that the protein of potatoes is more efficiently utilized by the body than that of flesh. Hindhede has also shown the protein of potatoes to be adequate.

On the other hand, we are not concerned so much with the relative values of specific proteins, or even of the proteins of one protein-carrying food, but with the total value of all the proteins contained in our customary diet: and not with the proteins alone, but with the total diet. The whole question involved is best expressed thus: *Is meat, as a whole, superior to vegetables as food?* When we consume flesh or vegetables, we do not confine ourselves to their protein constituents, but eat the whole of them and they must be considered in their entirety.

There is nothing in the protein of the flesh that the animal did not derive from the plant. Not being able to synthesize amino acids, the animal merely appropriates these, ready-made, from the plant, in the form of plant proteins. Man can do this as efficiently and as easily as the lower animals. Plants yield up their amino acids to man as readily as to the cow.

Green vegetables contain proteins of a very high· quality, though in small quantities. Nuts, on the other hand, rank with or even surpass, flesh foods in the quantity of their proteins, while their proteins are of equal rank with those of flesh. At the same time, nut proteins are "free from pathogenic bacterial or parasitical contamination," to use Clendening's words.

It is argued that plant proteins are "poor" because "they contain unnecessarily large amounts of some amino acids and little or none of others." It should not be overlooked, however, that we consume several vegetable protein foods and the deficiencies of one are made up by the richness of another. The excess of amino acids in vegetable proteins is never great.

That the individual proteins in grains and some other plant foods are physiologically inadequate is sufficiently demonstrated, but the sum-total of the various proteins in those foods, or shall we better say, in the diet as a whole, is usually fully adequate.

A protein is said to have higher physiologic or biologic value the smaller the amount of it required to supply the needs of the animal. Based upon this standard, the whole egg is ranked at 94; milk, 85; liver and kidney, 77; heart, 74; muscles meat, 69; whole wheat, 64; potato, 67; rolled oats, 65; whole corn, 60; white flour, 52; navy beans, 38. By this standard, vegetable proteins in general are said to be nearly always inferior to those of animal origin. The proteins of peanuts and soybeans are listed as exceptions, their proteins being compelte. There is no appreciable difference between the muscle meat of cow, hog or sheep. These relative values were determined by tests made on rats, dogs, etc., and are not necessarily valid for human nutrition. It will be noted that nuts are again ignored in this classification of biologic values.

The fact that proteins are completely digested, that is broken up into their constituent amino acids before absorption proves, we believe, that highly complex proteins are not really wanted as foods. While it is true that it is part of the function of the digestive tract to extract impurities and non-congenial substances from the food and avoid these, it is not well to abuse the digestive system by foods that are too rich, that is, too complex. This will be made more clear in the chapter on food allergies.

The plant is the best and original source of building materials that our diet can supply. The really "vital and abiding union sought after in animal nutrition, is between the amino acids of the plant and the blood of the animal." In conformity with the principle of reciprocity and reciprocal differentiation operating in the organic world, we want in our diet proteins quite different from our own.

There is a tendency in many quarters to exalt meat proteins as superior to all other forms of protein. The adequacy of flesh proteins as growth factors is especially stressed. That flesh proteins contain all of the essential amino acids is frequently asserted. Meat (flesh) protein is the most valuable of all forms of protein, is a frequent assertion. Berg points out that "this cannot be accepted as a positive fact as regards the protein of individual muscles, only as regards the aggregate proteins of an animal body used as food." Abderhalden also points out this fact. This is especially true if the meat is not accompanied with a large supply of base-forming foods. Berg points out that carnivorous animals, living in a state of nature, "ensure a supply of bases by drinking the blood of their victims and devouring the bones and the cartilages as well as the flesh." It is also true that wild carnivores consume considerable quantities of fruits, berries and buds. Cats are often observed to eat vegetable foods. Wild carnivora especially eat such foods in the Autumn, although in the Spring they are likely to subsist exclusively upon the fruits of the kill.

It has long been known that if a dog is fed on flesh from which the juice has been extracted, he becomes ematiated after a time, toxic symptoms devlop, and death rapidly follows. Skeletal changes characteristic of osteoporosis and oteomalacia are found upon postmortem examination. The extraction of the salts of the flesh causes death.

It is well to keep in mind that the different organs of the animal body differ in their amino acid content. As has been pointed out before, not merely every species of animal, but also, within each animal, every organ, has its own peculiar kind of protein. For this reason the different organs of the animal body are not equally complete or "valuable" as sources of amino acids. One advocate of flesh eating deplores the fact that "some patients are unfortunately averse to eating entrals. Entrals, like liver," he says, "kidneys, heart, spleen, etc., are extremely rich in certain vitamins and other valuable constituents and their regular use in this diet is to be greatly encouraged." To receive all the value of a flesh diet, it is necessary to eat the whole animal—not, however, as is the case in eating whole oysters, the feces, also.

We want, not merely amino acids, but amino acids in ideal combination with other indispensable substances—minerals, vitamins, carbohydrates—such as only plants can furnish. These other substances are essential to the full utilization of proteins. Meat protein, when deprived of its minerals, destroys life. Animal proteins are not ideally combined with these other substances. The most ideal substances for animal and human nutrition and the most ideal blends of these substances are to be found in the spare products of plants.

There is also a tendency of the experimenters to place too much importance on gains in weight. They find more rapid growth, or a greater gain in weight, or even greater ultimate growth, on some diets than on others. Too much reliance should not be placed in reported gains unless the kind of weight gained is specified. We are not interested in fattening beef cattle nor in mere bigness. Accelerated growth and precocious development are far from desirable accomplishments. Nor are results in one generation nor in a short time sufficient to establish the ultimate effects of a particular diet.

It is now asserted by all experimenters that the duration of the earlier dietetic experiments was usually too short. Berg says that his own first experiments lasted for a week. Later he extended them to two weeks, then to several months. It is now known that an experiment must often run through several generations to yield dependable results. Unfortunately the importance of the time factor is not yet fully appreciated. Nature has carried on countless dietetic experiments, lasting not just a few weeks, or a few generations, but for ages. Our experimenters have failed to notice the results of long-time experiments of this nature. Their belief in "struggle" and "survival" has prevented them from recognizing the role of nutrition in integration, disintegration and re-integration—in two words, *evolution* and *degeneration*.

The advocates of flesh eating are particularly prone to close their eyes to the results of ages of flesh eating. With no valid standard of normal growth, they fix their attention upon the growth promoting effects of flesh. They ignore the evils of precocious development and an accelerated growth. Their standard of mere bigness is the same as that of the stock raisers. One could easily think that they are growing children for the market; that the children, after they reach the "fryer" or "broiler" stages are to be sold by the pound. The larger they grow, the more money they will bring. Accelerated growth tends to be unbalanced growth. There is likely to be overgrowths and undergrowths that render the finished organism inferior. But, I must again emphasize, one generation or even three generations of such feeding is not sufficient to unfold its ultimate results.

CARBOHYDRATES

This is the name given to certain organic compounds of carbon that are produced by plants in the process of growth from carbon, hydrogen and oxygen, with the oxygen and hydrogen in proportions to form water. In everyday language we know the most important of these carbohydrates as starches and sugars. As will be seen later, carbohydrates are complex substances composed, in most instances, of simpler substances, or building blocks, called sugars. Chief among the carbohydrates are:

Fruits—Bananas, all sweet fruits, hubbard squash, etc.
Nuts—A few varieties—acorns, chestnuts and cocoanuts.
Tubers—potatoes, sweet potatoes, carrots, artichokes, parsnips, etc.
Legumes—Most beans, except some varieties of soybeans, all peas, peanuts.
Cereals—All grains and practically all cereal products. (Gluten bread is not a carbohydrate.)

FOOD ELEMENTS

The reader will notice that grains and legumes are classed both as proteins and carbohydrates. This is due to the fact that they contain enough of each of these food elements to be placed in both classes. Nuts, for the same reason, are classed both as proteins and as fats. Milk, commonly classed as a protein is really low in protein. It may with equal jusification be classed as a sugar or carbohydrate. All foods contain more or less carbohydrates, as they all contain more or less protein. Most foods contain some fats, but there is none in most fruits nor in the green leaves of vegetables.

Carbohydrates, like proteins, are composed of simpler compounds known as simple sugars or *monosaccharides*. According to their composition, these are classed as follows:

1. *Monosaccharides:* Sugars containing only one sugar group or radical. Among the monosaccharides are grape sugar (glucose or destrose), fruit sugar (fructose or levulose), and galactose of honey. These are the assimilable forms of carbohydrate. Dextrose is the principle member of the glucose group and much less sweet than cane sugar. It is known as grape sugar and is found in fruits, some vegetables and honey. Glucose occurs in both plants and animals and is formed by the action of heat and the ultraviolet rays upon starch in the presence of an acid. Corn syrup is commercially known as glucose. Glucose may also be made by treating starch with sulphuric acid in the presence of heat. Fructose and levulose are derived from fruits and honey. Galactose is a crystaline glucose obtained by treating milk sugar with dilute acids.

2. *Disaccharides:* Sugars containing two simple sugars, or that can be broken into two monosaccharides. The ordinary cane sugar or sucrose of commerce is a disaccharide composed of glucose and galactose. Invert sugar found in honey is a mixture of glucose and fructose. Maltose or malt sugar is composed of galactose and glucose. Maple sugar (sucrose) and milk sugar (lactose) are also disaccharides.

3. *Trisaccharides:* Sugars containing three sugar groups or radicals. Beet sugar is the best known example of this sugar.

4. *Polysaccharides:* Colloids or non-crystalizable organic substances known as starches. There are three main groups of polysaccharides: 1. Starches; 2. glycogen (animal starch), and 3. pentosans. Pentosans are numerous and include the cellulose or woody fibre of cotton, linen, walls of plant cells, etc. They are usually indigestible, although, in tender cabbage and other very tender veg-

etables, they are digestible. Galactose found in sugar, seeds, and algae; pectans found in unripe fruit and the gummy exudate on trees and plants are also pentosans.

Starches and sugars are well known to everyone as they are found in all fruits and vegetables. Sugars are soluble carbohydrates with a more or less sweet taste. When heated to a high temperature they form caramel. Sugars are crystalloids, starches are insoluble and are colloids. Glycogen and milk sugar are the only carbohydrates of animal origin and even these are derived originally from the plant. Animals are incapable of extracting carbon from the air and synthesizing carbohydrates.

While the sugars are all soluble, raw starch is insoluble. Boiling will render part of it soluble. This, however, as will be shown in a later chapter, hinders its digestion. Starch is converted into a disaccharide in the mouth and this is, then, converted into a monosaccharide in the intestine.

The body cannot use starch. It must first be converted into sugar before it can be utilized by the cells. This is done in the process of digestion and begins in the mouth. Disaccharides and polsaccharides are converted into monosaccharides in the process of digestion, as carbohydrates can be absorbed and assimilated only as monosaccharides. Starch must first be converted into sugar and the complex sugars must be converted into simple sugars before they are absorbed. The body's need for sugar may easily be supplied without eating commercial sugars and syrups, or any form of denatured carbohydrate. Child and adult, alike, should eat only natural sweets and starches.

Sugar is the most important building material in the plant world. A characteristic difference between plants and animals is that, whereas, the animal is built up largely out of proteins, the plant is built up largely out of carbohydrates. Plants may be truly said to be made of sugar. They contain various minerals and some nitrogen, but practically the whole fabric of the plant or tree is composed of sugar in some form. Sugars are essential constituents of all plants without which they cannot exist. Indeed, sugars are the most important and most abundant building materials in plants. Out of the *immature* or *sap sugars* plants build their roots, stems, flowers, fruits and seeds. The finished plant is almost literally made of sugar.

Nature produces sugars out of three gases—carbon, oxygen and hydrogen. Oxygen and hydrogen in proportions to form water are

FOOD ELEMENTS

taken from the water in the soil. Carbon is taken from the carbon dioxide of the air. Out of these gases, or out of this fluid and gas, the plant synthesizes sugar, a thing the animal cannot do. The green coloring of plants is due to the presence of a pigment known as chlorophyll. This pigment takes part in a chemical process known as photosynthesis, by which, carbon-dioxide (or, at least the carbon in the carbon-dioxide), with the aid of sunlight, is united with water to form sugar. Recent experiments have shown that enzymes contained in the leaves of the plants are the chief agents in the production of this sugar. Some plants can produce sugar in the absence of light.

Not only the starches of plants, but also the pentosans, the woody fibers, cellulose and gums are made of sugar and may be reconverted into sugar. When carbohydrates are stored for long periods they are stored as starches. When they are used, they are reconverted into sugars. Corn, peas, etc., are sweet (full of sugar) before they mature. The sap of the corn is also sweet. The sap of the cane plant is very sweet. In the matured state, corn, cane seed and peas are hard starch grains. In the germinating process the starch is reconverted into sugar. As starches, these seeds will keep for long periods of time; as sugars they would not keep until the following spring. It will be noticed that the enzymes in seed do not require ultra violet rays and acid to bring about this reconversion, any more than do the enzymes in digestive juices.

Fruits are ready for immediate use and if not used soon after ripening, tend to decompose rapidly. Grains are intended for storage. It is significant that fruits are composed of insoluble starches and are usually rich in acids before they ripen. In this state they are usually avoided by animals. The starch is reconverted into sugar in the ripening process. This arrangement protects the seed of the fruit until it is matured and ready for dispersal. Then the fruit is ripened and made ready for food.

The animal, like the plant, builds its carbohydrates out of sugar. All starch foods must be converted into sugar (in the process of digestion) before they can be taken into the body and used. Animal starch (glycogen) is made from sugar. It, like the starch of grains, is a storage product. Like the starch of grains, it must be reconverted into sugar before using. The sugar in milk may be made from starches.

THE SCIENCE AND FINE ART OF FOOD AND NUTRITION

The *matured* or *fruit sugars* of plants, especially those of fruits, are particularly appropriate for food. They are never concentrated and are always well balanced with other ingredients. They are built up out of the immature sugar and impart to both fresh and dried fruits their delicious flavors. Matured sugars in flowers are collected by bees and made into honey. Fruit sugars are, in truth, export products produced by plants.

All the sugar the body requires may be obtained from fresh ripe fruits. This is especially so during the summer months. During the winter months when fresh fruits are not so abundant, dried (but unsulphured) fruits are excellent sources of sugar. These should not be cooked. Owing to the absence of water, dried fruits are more concentrated foods then fresh fruits and should not be eaten in the same bulk.

Just as fruits are savoured with their matured sugars, so vegetable foods are savoured with the imature juices (saps) of the plants. In the plants, as in the fruits, the sugars are combined with vitamins, mineral salts, fibre and other elements of foods .

It is essential to emphasize that sugars constitute but one of the ingredients of plant life and are never put up in their pure state. In fruits and plants they are always combined with and balanced by other ingredients, particularly with salts, vitamins and water. Man, not nature, produces concentrated sugars. Man, not nature, separates the minerals from sugar. Sugars should be eaten as nature provides them.

Commercial syrups and molasses are concentrated saps. Besides being concentrated, usually by the use of heat in evaporating the water, they are commonly deprived of their minerals and vitamins, often have preservatives, artificial colors and flavors added and are often bleached with sulphur dioxide, with which they become saturated. Comercial sugars—maple, cane, beet, milk—are crystalized saps. They too, are unbalanced, commonly bleached, and thoroughly unfitted for use. So concentrated are these syrups and sugars, so denatured and so prone to speedy fermentation in the digestive tract, that it is best not to employ them at all. If they are used they should be used very sparingly. The same rule should apply to honey. This food of the bee contains all the other nutritive elements in very minute quantities, being largely water and sugar with flavors from the flowers. If it is eaten, it should be taken sparingly.

What a difference between eating sugar cane and eating the extracted, concentrated and refined sugar of the cane! It is said that it takes a West Indian native an hour to chew eighteen inches of cane from which he derives the equivalent of one large lump of sugar—less than the average coffee-drinker puts into a single cup of his favorite poison. (The boys and girls of Texas and Louisiana can chew sugar cane faster than the West Indian native, it seems.) In thus securing his sugar, the cane-eater secures the minerals and vitamins that are normally associated with sugars—he does not eat a "purified" product.

Sugar is regarded as an energy food, but it is a remarkable fact that the heavy sugar-eater prefers to watch athletic games to taking part in them. We, of course, have reference to the heavy-eater of commercial sugars. They seem to stimulate and then depress the muscular powers.

It has long been the *Hygienic* theory that the catarrhal diseases are based on carbohydrate excess—sugar excess, as all starches are converted into sugar in digestion. It is interesting to note, in this connection, that the *British Medical Journal* for June 1933 carried an article discussing "the relation of excessive carbohydrate ingestion to catarrh and other diseases," in which it was pointed out that during World War I, the incidence of catarrhal illnesses was reduced seemingly corresponding with the great reduction of sugar consumption. The writer of the article concludes that "restriction in the use of sugar would result in improvement in the national health as regards catarrhal illness, as well as in other directions."

HYDROCARBONS

Hydrocarbon foods are those rich in hydrocarbon—fats and oils. Hydrocarbons are composed of carbon, hydrogen and oxygen. In the animal body, fats may be manufactured out of sugars and proteins. Fats are produced in the plant out of sugar. Chief among the hydrocarbon foods are:

Fruits—olives, avocados.
Nuts—almost all varieties.
Legumes—peanuts, soy beans.
Dairy products—cream, butter and some cheese.
Flesh of dead animals, especially pork and mutton and beef that has been fattened. Fat fish—herring, shad, salmon, trout.

There are many kinds of fats—solid and liquid. Fats and oils are formed in plants, and fruits when ripening. A decrease in sugars accompanies the increase in fats. It is but another evidence of the importance of sugar in the life of the plant and, thereafter, in the life of the animal. While the animal is capable of synthesizing fats out of starches and sugars, it is not capable of taking hydrogen, oxygen and carbon and synthesizing fats out of these.

The fat of the animal differs from the oil of the plant, just as do the proteins of the animal differ from those of its food supply. Each animal builds its own characteristic fats out of its foods. Fats and oils are complex substances that are made up of simpler substances which we may call the "building stones" of fat. True fats are composed of fatty acids and glycerol—or glycerides. Fats differ according to the fatty acids and glycerides which they contain.

Stearic, palmitic butyric and oleac acids are the most common glycerides found in edible fats. The stearates are combinaitons of stearic acid with glycerol—stearin. Several fatty acids are present in all fats. In butter there are palmitic, oleic, myristic and butyric acids. Stearic acid is present in suet (hog fat), palmitic acid is abundant in vegetable and animal fats. Oleic acid is found in most fats and oils. Such vegetable oils as olive, cottonseed, peanut, almond and cocoanut oils contain large amounts of olein.

Fats are split up during the process of digestion into fatty acids and glycerol. Fats and oils, like proteins and carbohydrates, are not usable as such, but must be broken down into their constituent "buliding stones" and these "building stones"—fatty acids and glycerol—are used with which to build human fats.

Mendel asks "are there essential fatty acids that must be supplied in the diet because they cannot be produced *de novo* by the animal organism?" Although both he and Hindhede have shown that green stuff can take the place of fat in the diet, there are facts that lead us to believe that it is, at least, a great saving to the body if some fat is supplied.

Although the body can synthesize fats out of carbohydrates and proteins, there are certain fatty acids that it is incapable of synthesizing and these are essential to animal life. Three *unsaturated fatty acids*—linoleic, linolenic and arachaidonic—cannot be synthesized by the animal organism. Only one of these is considered essential, for, as in the case of certain amino acids, they can replace one another in animal nutrition. Rats fed on diets lacking in the essential fatty acids cease to grow, develop scaliness of the skin, caudal necrosis, emaciation, kidney lesions and early death. Certain blood deficiencies are also seen when these fatty acids are lacking in the diet of animals.

Besides the fatty acids supplied by the fats in our diet, fats also contain fat soluble vitamins and minerals. Large quantities of fat are not required, but a small quantity daily is essential to normal development and maintenance and to good health.

Fat serves as a protection and as a packing and support for organs, forms emulsions and lubricants, serves as storage for reserve "fuel," enters into the constituents of the walls of the body's cells, and is an essential element of the nervous system. Lecithin, a widely distributed fat is very important in human nutrition, being an essential ingredient of the brain and nerves and also of the semen. Lecithin contains, besides the fatty acids, phosphorus. Insufficient fat tends to lessen nervous efficiency.

On the whole, vegetable oils are superior to animal fats as human foods. Cream and butter (unpasteurized) are the best of the animal fats employed as foods. Fats, like sugars, are best taken as nature prepares them; that is in the foods in which they exist. Most nuts are rich in oil and form the best sources of fat for human consumption. Fats, when extracted from their sources, concentrated, purified, and preserved, form poor foods. Many of them have all their vitamins destroyed and are devoid of all minerals. For example, in the process of rendering hog fat into lard, the fat is boiled for a long period and everything skimmed from the top until nothing remains but "pure" fat. All the minerals and vitamins are destroyed and removed. Long cooked in this way, the lard is practically indigestible. Olive oil, peanut oil, soybean oil and other vegetable oils are best eaten in the fruits, legumes and other plant substances in which nature prepares them.

Fats must be digested before they can be used. The cells of the body cannot use complex fats. The fats must first be reduced to a few simple acceptable substances in the process of digestion. The skin is not a digestive organ. It is not able to take complex fats and break them down into their simpler constituents and then make use of the fatty acids and glycerol thus formed. For these reasons "skin foods," composed of some cream or oil, to be rubbed on or into the skin, cannot nourish the skin. They only grease it—that is, make it dirty. The skin must be fed from within. It contains very little fat and this must come from the blood. Blood is the only food of the tissues of the body. It is folly to try to feed our tissues with any other substances.

THE SCIENCE AND FINE ART OF FOOD AND NUTRITION

ORGANIC SALTS AND VITAMINS

As separate chapters will be devoted to these two classes of substances, little more will be done here than to classify the chief sources of them. The mineral salts enter into the composition of every fluid and structure of the body. Inorganic salts cannot be substituted for them as will be shown in a subsequent chapter. The animal lacks the ability to take the crude elements of the earth and synthesize these into acceptable organic compounds.

Vitamins, of which there are a number, are also produced only by the plant. The animal body is capable of taking certain pro-vitamins and completing their synthesis. But it is not capable of producing vitamins *de novo*. They serve as enzymes.

Vtiamins and organic salts are distributed throughout nature and are present in varying quantities in all food substances. Fruits and fresh vegetables are especially high in them. Fruits and vegetables will be treated in separate chapters. Here we are intersted in them, largely as sources of these food substances. Chief among these rich sources of vitamins and salts are:

(1) *Succulent (watery, juicy) Vegetables:*

Leafy Vegetables—celery, lettuce, kohlrabi, cabbage, spinach, dandelion, endive, turnip tops, mustard, parsley, cauliflower, brussels sprouts, kale, chard, lotus, cress, field lettuce, romaine, chicory, rhubarb, beet tops, radish tops, etc.

Fruiting Plants—okra (gumbo), cucumbers, squash summer squash, pumpkin, string beans, green peas, corn "in milk" (fresh), etc.

Tubers—Asparagus, beet, carrot, turnip, radish, onion, cone artichoke, rutabaga, garlic, oyster plant (salsify).

(2) *Juicy Fruits:*

Acid: Orange (sour), lemon, lime, sour apple, grapefruti, pineapple, peach, sour plum, apricot, cranberry, loganberry, pomegranate, strawberry, tomato.

Sub-Acid: Melons—watermelons, musk-melon, cantaloupe, casaba, honey dew, etc.,—sweet grapes, huckleberry, fresh figs, pears, etc.

Many other foods are used, both in America and other parts of the world, but all may be placed in some one or the other of the above classes. Some foods such as nuts, grains and legumes, may be placed in two classes.

The bountiful hand of mother nature has supplied us with an abundant and pleasing variety of foods. This wonderful variety of

FOOD ELEMENTS

foods which are designed to please the senses of sight, taste and smell, as well as supply the needs of the body, are all made of but a few simple elemnts of the soil—"the dust of the earth."

Together with water, oxygen and vitamins, proteins, carbohydrates, fats and minerals form the constituents of the body. These must be taken into the digestive tract and there prepared for the use of the body, before they are allowed to enter the body and before they become part of the body.

The material composing a leaf of lettuce cannot be anything but a leaf of lettuce, until it has died from that state and then, after it has been disintegrated, its elements may be built up into the tissues of man. Digesion is the disintegrating process.

Our present knowledge of the role of digestion in nutrition shows positively that the parental administration of food is without value. The process of digestion disintegrates food into fragments which represent the true nutrients—proteins are reduced to amino acids, carbohydrates to simple sugars, fats to fatty acids and glycerol and it is claimed that ions may be liberated from the organic salts during the process of digestion. These things serve as the structural or metabolic units and nothing else will or can.

The Minerals of Life
CHAPTER III

It seems quite clear that the vital importance of the organic salts of foods was established by men who were outside the regular folds. The older physiologists and physiological chemists gave no attention to them. In the tables of food analysis they were relegated to the "ash" column and ignored.

The great German Physiologist and Chemist, Bunge, said in 1889, "As to the developed organism, we do not, a priori, understand why it should need the constant ingestion of salts. The purpose served by the inorganic salts (minerals) is totally different from that served by the organic substances (carbon, nitrogen, fat). °°° The organic food substances are, therefore, of use to us through their very decomposition.°°° The case is quite different when we turn to the inorganic salts. These are fully saturated oxides, or chlorides which cannot combine with oxygen. As they are not subject to decomposition or oxidation, they can develop no work power in the body, they cannot possibly be used up so as to become unserviceable. What is therefore the good of renewing them?"

In 1904 Dr. Harvey W. Wiley wrote to Otto Carque: "I regret to say that no one in this country has undertaken a complete analysis of all the mineral constituents of foods. An analysis usually relates to the nutritive value and general composition, but does not give, as a rule, the composition of the ash." His words plainly imply that the salts have no nutritive value.

Perhaps H. Lahman, a German physician who had forsaken the regular methods of care and had allied himself with Louis Kuhne, was the first to make a study of the roles of the minerals in nutrition. Ragnar Berg, a Swedish biochemist, who associated himself with Lahmann, soon became one of the world's foremost biochemists. In this country, Otto Carque, Henry Lindlahr and Alfred W. McCann emphasized the importance of these minerals. At the present day their importance is everywhere recognized. It is no longer thought that only the "nutritive values"—proteins, carbohydrates, fats—are important.

THE MINERALS OF LIFE

Animals fed on foods deprived of their salts soon die. In the same manenr, they die if, to these demineralized foods, are added inorganic salts in the same quantities and proportions as are found in the ashes of milk. The salts must come to the body in the organic form. These inorganic salts are not used except in the presence of vitamins.

Berg has pointed out that there does not exist one single complete analysis, either of the human organism or its excretions or of our foodstuffs. Not everything is known about the function of minerals in the body and of some of them almost nothing is known. Some of them, such as zinc and nickel, apparently perform functions similar to those of vitamins. Prof. E. V. McCollum showed that animals deprived of manganese lose the maternal instinct, refuse to suckle their young, do not build a nest for them, and even eat their young. Their mammary glands do not develop properly and they are unable to secrete proper milk for their young. Here are effects commonly attributed to vitamin deficiency.

This "ash" enters into the composition of every fluid and tissue in the plant and animal body and without even one of these minerals, life could not go on. They are of the utmost importance. They serve a number of purposes. They form an essential part of every tissue in the body, and predominate in the harder structures, such as bones, teeth, hair, nails, etc. The bones consist largely of calcium phosphate. They are the chief factors in maintaining the normal alkalinity of the blood as well as its normal specific gravity. They are also abundant in all the body's secretions and a lack of them in the diet produces a lack of secretions. They are also used as detoxifying agents, by being combined with the acid waste from the cells. The wastes are thus neutralized and prepared for elimination. Their presence in the food eaten also aids in preventing it from decomposing. Acidosis produced by the fermentation of proteins and carbohydrates often comes because the mineral salts have been taken from the food thus favoring fermentation.

In a simplified sense we may consider the blood and lymph as liquids in which solids are held in solution—much as salt is dissolved in water. The cells, which are bathed at all times in lymph, are also semi-fluid with dissolved matter in them. If the lymph outside the cells contains much dissolved solid, as compared to that within the cells, the cells shrink in size. If there is more dissolved solid within the cell than without, the cell expands and sometimes bursts. In either case the result is pathological.

If the amount of dissolved solids within and without the cell is equal, so that internal and external pressure are equalized, the cell remains normal. It falls very largely to the minerals of the food to maintain this state of osmotic equilibrium.

The waste formed in the body, due to its normal activities, is acid in reaction. The greater part of the work of neutralizing these acids is done by the mineral elements—the "ash."

These minerals enter into the composition of the secretions of the body. The hydrochloric acid in the gastric juice, for example, contains chlorine. Clotting of the blood does not take place without the aid of calcium or lime.

The mineral matters in food undergo no change in the process of digestion, prior to absorption, as do proteins, fats and carbohydrates. They are separated from these other elements in the process of digestion and pass directly into the blood.

If our foods do not contain enough of the right kinds of mineral salts we simply starve to death. It does not matter how much "good nourishing food," as this is commonly understood, that we consume, if these salts are not present in sufficient quantities we suffer from slow starvation, with glandular imbalance or disfunction, lowered resistance to "disease" and other evidences of decay. McCarrison showed, definitely, that foods and combinations of foods, which are inadequate and unsatisfactory in feeding animals, are equally as inadequate and unsatisfactory in feeding man.

Life and health are so directly related to these salts, of which little enough is known, that we can never have satisfactory health without an adequate supply of them. We may be sure that each salt has its own separate function to serve, while certain combinations of them have long been known to perform vital services in the body.

No drug salts can be made to take the place of those found in food. As Dr. William H. Hay, says: "Nature provides all her chemicals for restoration of the body in the form of colloids, organic forms, and man has for a long time sought to imitate her in this, but he has not been so very successful that we are now able to insure the recouping of the mineral losses of the body by any artificial means, and must still depend on Nature's colloids as found in plant and fruit." Well or sick, no compound of the chemist, druggist or "bio-chemist" can recoup your mineral losses.

THE MINERALS OF LIFE

Let us here notice, in alphabetical order, the minerals of the body, and their most abundant plant sources.

Arsenic: Arsenic, it is claimed, is a normal constituent of the body existing in minute quantities in the skin, hair, nails, brain, thyroid gland and other glands. Arsenic in organic combination with phosphorus and iodine, as found in vegetables, is not, however, to be confused with drug arsenic. A human body weighing 150 lbs. contains a mere trace of arsenic. It is found in most fruits and vegetables and in egg yolk.

Bromine: This element, found in sea plants, has been found in the liver, thyroid gland, adrenal glands, and in the nails. It is not known definitely whether or not it serves any physiological function, or is a foreign element.

Calcium: Calcium (lime) constitutes more than 50% of the mineral elements of man's body. Much of this is contained in the bones and teeth. It is also an essential of the blood and muscles. There are about 3 lbs. of this mineral in a body of 150 lbs. It hardens the bones and teeth, strengthens the muscles, coagulates the blood, causes the heart to beat, and counteracts acids. The richest sources of calcium are, in the order named, *Vegetables:* savoy cabbage, kale, lettuce, dandelion (if young and sweet), cabbage, okra, celery and tomatoes; *Fruits:* strawberries, blackberries, oranges; *Nuts:* beechnuts, brazil nuts, filberts, almonds, pinions and pecans.

Chlorine: Chlorine helps to form the gastric juice and is found abundantly in the blood where it assists in the elimination of the nitrogenous end-products of metabolism. About 1 lb. is found in a body of 150 lbs. The richest sources of chlorine are in the order named, *Vegetables:* tomatoes, celery, lettuce, cabbage, parsnips; *Fruits:* avocados, dates, black raspberries, cherimoyas, bananas, pineapple, raisins and mangos; *Nuts:* cocoanut and beechnut.

Copper: Copper is found in the liver, bile and blood and seems to be essential to the assimilation of iron and the manufacture of hemoglobin. There are about 15 grains of copper in a human body weighing 150 lbs.

Copper is present in the leaves of celery, lettuce, in the roots of salsify, carrot, turnip, beet and in the stalks of the latter, potatoes, in green beans, in the pumpkin, cucumber, tomato, pear, apple, grape, olive, banana, date, orange, chestnut and in such seeds as peas, beans, soy beans, lentils, wheat, barley, oats, maize, rice and in various nuts, sweet and bitter almonds, hazelnuts, walnuts.

Fluorine: Fluorine is found in the blood, teeth and bones and in the iris of the eye. There are about 3 oz. in a body weighing 150 lbs. It is essential to the formation of enamel and to hardness of the bones. The richest sources in the order named are, *Vegetables:* watercress, cauliflower, swiss chard, red cabbage, cabbage, garlic; *Fruits:* olives. Other fruits and nuts as well, contain this element, but analyses are lacking.

Iodine: Iodine is found in the thyroid gland in a very minute quantity. It is thought to be essential to the elaboration of thyrosin —an internal secretion of the thyroid. There is about $\frac{1}{4}$ gr. in a body weighing 150 lbs.

The richest sources of supply are in the order named: *Vegetables:* green kidney beans, asparagus, cabbage, garlic, tomatoes, lettuce, potatoes, *Fruits:* pineapple, strawberries, grapes, and pears. The reader should know that both as regards iodine and other minerals, analyses of nuts have not been as complete as those of fruits and vegetables.

Dr. Barwise, an English Medical officer, in an official report made by him in 1924, gave the following summary of the part iodine plays in our life: "1.—It is necessary for effective metabolism and especially promotes respiratory exchanges and physical growth. 2.—It promotes efficient mental development. A severe shortage before birth results in cretinism. An inadequate supply may produce anything from imbecility to mere mental dullness. 3.—It is especially required in the pregnant condition, and antenatal clinics bear this point in mind. 4.—It is needed at the age of adolescence for the development of the reproductive organs, particularly in the female, in whom the change-over takes place more rapidly than in the male. 5.—It is needed to keep the skin and its appendages in a healthy condition. A dry skin and falling hair frequently mean thyroid deficiency. 6.—It is required for the digestion, assimilation and combustion of fats. When a shortage occurs the fats cannot be satisfactorily dealt with, and it is stored in the subcutaneous tissue. Many cases of obesity may be occasioned in this way. 7.—It is required for the metabolism of calcium. 8.—It is needed to enable us to resist the invasion of microbes, and to render harmless the toxins (poisons) they produce."

THE MINERALS OF LIFE

Iron: Iron is the chief constituent of the red cells and enables man and animals to take in oxygen. It gives color to the blood and complexion. The presence of copper seems to be essential to the assimilation of iron. Nature stores up iron in the liver to guard against deficiency.

There is about 0.1 oz. in a body weighing 150 lbs. The richest sources of supply are, in the order named: *Vegetables:* sorrel, leek bulbs, spinach, small radish, asparagus, kohlrabi, romaine, lettuce; *Fruits:* strawberries, watermelons, gooseberries; *Nuts:* most nuts contain iron, but none of them contain much.

Lithium: Lithium has been found in minute quantities in almost all parts of the human body, but chiefly in the lungs. It is thought to influence the metabolism of albumenous food substances.

Magnesium: Magnesium (chiefly in the form of phosphate of magnesium) adds firmness to the bones and hardness to the teeth. The teeth contain more magnesium than the bones. Magnesium takes part in the formation of the albumen of the blood. The muscles contain much of this element. It also aids in reducing waste and foreign matter. Magnesium is valuable only in the presence of lime; in its absence magnesium is injurious. There are about 1.2 oz. in a body weighing 150 lbs.

The richest sources of supply are in the order named: *Vegetables:* tomatoes, dill, spinach, lettuce, dandelion, sorrel, water cress, swiss chard, romaine lettuce, sugar beet leaves, rutabagas, cabbage and cucumbers; *Fruits:* blackberries, black dried figs, apples, huckleberries, bananas, avocados, raisins, pineapples, watermelons and gooseberries; *Nuts:* beechnuts, pinions, almonds, brazil nuts, English walnuts and pecans.

Manganese: Manganese is also contained in the red cells and is an oxygen carrier. It seems to exert a beneficial influence on the vegetative functions and on the glands in general. There is about ½ oz. in the body of a man weighing 150 lbs.

The chief sources of supply are, in the order named: *Vegetables:* water cress, parsley, nasturtium leaves; *Nuts:* walnuts, almonds, pignolias, chestnuts.

Nickle: Nickle is found in exceedingly small quantities in different organs of the body, but more especially in the insulin of the pancreas, of which it may be an active ingredient, just as iodine is the active agent in thyrosin of the thyroid gland. Nickle may be essential for the proper oxidation of sugar.

THE SCIENCE AND FINE ART OF FOOD AND NUTRITION

Phosphorus: Phosphorus, chiefly in the form of lecithin, appears to be an essential of oxidation and to take part in many of the body's chemical processes. The brain and nervous system contain considerable lecithin. There is much phosphorus in the bones and teeth. There are about 1.5 lbs. in a 150 lb. body.

The chief sources of supply are, in the order named, *Vegetables*: kale, large radish, pumpkins, watercress, sorrel, dill, brussel sprouts, cucumbers, swiss chard, romaine lettuce, savoy cabbage, cauliflower, turnips, rutabagas, spinach, leek bulbs, lettuce, asparagus; *Fruits*: currants, huckleberries, peaches, gooseberries, limes, cherries, watermelons, lemons, breadfruit, mirabellas, oranges, apples, red raspberries, plums, grapes; *Nuts:* brazil nuts, pinions, beechnuts, peanuts (a legume), almonds, English walnuts, filberts, pecans, chestnuts, (dried), water chestnuts, cocoanut.

Potassium: Phosphate of potassium is the mineral basis of all muscular tissue. Potassium is a predominant element in the red-blood cells and brain and is essential to the formation of glycogen from sugar, of proteins from peptones and proteoses, and of fats from glycogen. The spleen and liver are both abundantly supplied with potassium. There are about 8.4 oz. in a 150 lb. body.

The chief sources of supply are, in the order named; *Vegetables*: tomatoes, kale, lettuce, turnips, sorrel, celery, rutabagas, cabbage, romaine lettuce, swiss chard, cauliflower, cucumbers, eggplant, beets, parsnips, brussel sprouts, savoy cabbage, small radish; *Fruits:* currants (dried), limes, olives (dried), huckleberries, lemons, cherimoyas, prunes (fresh), peaches, apricots, mangos, oranges, grapes, watermelons, cherries, blackberries, breadfruit, figs (dried smyrna), white currants, bananas, plums, avocados; *Nuts*: acorns (dried), water chestnuts, beechnuts (dried), cocoanut, filberts, brazil nuts, pecans, pinions.

Silicon: Silicon is present in the muscles, hair, nails, pancreas, connective tissue, teeth, skin and the walls of all cells. It combines with flourine in forming the enamel of the teeth. There is only a trace in a body weighing 150 lbs.

The chief sources of supply are, in the order named; *Vegetables*: lambs lettuce, lettuce, parsnips, asparagus, dandelion, spinach, onions, beets; *Fruits*: strawberries, cherries, apricots, watermelons, apples, prunes (fresh); *Nuts*: beechnuts.

In vegetables silica is found chiefly combined with cellulose, and in the skin of fruits and vegetables and the coats of cereals.

It is essential to the formation of certain tissues and is also a protective agent in that it tends to prevent chemical disintegration and putrefaction.

Those who eat white flour, polished rice, corn meal, etc., from which the outer coats of the cereal have been removed; who peel their apples, pears, peaches, etc., and who reject the skins of grapes are most likely to suffer from a deficiency of this mineral.

Sodium: Sodium, in combination with chlorine, is a principal constituent of the blood and lymph. It renders the lime and magnesia salts of the blood more soluble and prevents their deposit in the body. It prevents a too ready coagulation of the blood, being able to re-dissolve coagulated fibrin and return it to the liquid state. It is an essential ingredient of the saliva, pancreatic juice and bile. Sodium phosphate and sodium carbonate in the blood enable the body to excrete carbon-dioxide. There are about 3-oz. of sodium in a body weighing 150 lbs.

The chief sources of supply are, in the order named; *Vegetables*: celery, spinach, swiss chard, romaine lettuce, tomatoes, small radish, red beets, water cress, pumpkins, carrots, leek bulbs, dandelion, rutabagas, lettuce, okra, cabbage, lambs lettuce; *Fruits*: strawberries, pomegrante, black figs (dried), apples, avocados and bananas.

Sulphur: Sulphur is a constituent of practically all proteins. It is found in all tissues of the body. In the red blood cells it serves as an oxidizing agent. There are about 6 oz. in a 150 lb. body.

The chief sources of supply are, in the order named; *Vegetables*: kale, water cress, brussel sprouts, dill, cabbage, sorrel, spinach, turnips, cauliflower, *Fruits*: cranberries, red raspberries, currants (red), avocadoes, currants (black), pineapples; *Nuts*: filberts, brazil nuts and chestnuts (dried).

Zinc: Zinc is found in connection with phosphorus in the brain. It exists in very minute quantities. It is thought to be connected with the action of the "vitamins," which it seems to be able to replace to some extent, at least, in the animal organism. It seems to be essential to the nutrition and growth of certain plants and has been found in milk.

These mineral elements are divided into base-forming (acid-binding) or alkaline elments, and acid-forming elements. The bases are potassium, sodium, calcium, magnesium, iron, manganese, copper, lithium, zinc and nickel and the acid-formers are phosphorus, sulphur, silicon, chlorine, flourine, iodine, arsenic and bromine.

Aluminum: Aluminum is often found in both fruits and vegetables in the form of aluminum oxide, or alumina. It is sometimes found in the body, but does not seem constant. If it has any function in the body this is unknown and McCollum says: "Recently I have proved that aluminum is not essential."

Vitamins
CHAPTER IV

Although much uncertainty and obscurity still surround the subject of vitamins, the condition is somewhat clearer than when the first edition of this volume was published. Much speculation and nonsense still exist in the literature of the subject. It is still not possible to satisfactorily define them and they are frequently referred to as "vital chemicals." It is still said: "we do not know exactly how the vitamins act in the body," although it is now generally agreed, as I suggested in the first edition of this work, that they are enzymes.

Although certain of the vitamins are of a protein nature, some of them being somewhat like the amino acids, vitamins do not constitute a group of chemically related compounds, as do the proteins or carbohydrates. Chemically, about the only thing they have in common is that they are organic compounds. Functionally, rather than structurally, they are of a group. It is said to be merely accidental that they are classed together as "vitamins" (Berg preferred the term "complettins" which, perhaps, more correctly expresses their roles in nutrition.).

Vitamins are regulating substances. They are appropriately described as part of the chemical regulators of the activities of living organisms. They share this work with the hormones of the internal secretions and the various enzymes of the body. I have thought that they may be essential to the formation of hormones and the various enzymes. They are very complex substances and are derived from a wide variety of sources. Not all vitamins are known and of those now known only certain ones are thought to be essential to human life. They are not foods in the regular sense of the term, but they enable the body to untilize and assimilate the proteins, carbohydrates, fats and minerals. As enzymes they lose much of their mysteriousness.

Some vitamins are found in almost every living cell indicating that their role in nutrition is a very fundamental one. Indeed, it is probable that they constitute an integral part of the grand admixture of many ingredients that we know as protoplasm. They are required in very small amounts; certain of them being required in unbelievably small amounts, yet they are indispensable to the life and well-being of the higher animals. Not all the known vitamins are required by all animals. Although about twenty-two vitamins have been announced (only about twelve of these have been isolated in pure form), only about seven or eight have been definitely shown to be needed by man. It is thought that there may be many vitamins that have not yet been discovered. Perhaps not more than one to three of the unknown vitamins will prove, when discovered, to be essential to human nutrition. I know of no reason to doubt that the lower forms of animal life also require vitamins for their life and well-being.

Vitamins are one link in a chain of essential nutritive substances requisite for the harmonious regulation of the chemical and organic processes of the body. Although the several vitamins are closely related and inter-related, at least, functionally, it is believed that each one plays a specific role in nutrition. Summarizing from McCarrison's *Studies in Deficiency Diseases*, vitamins are constant constituents of living tissues, being present in small amounts and, although, they do not contribute to the energy-supply of the body, they do make it possible for the body to untilize proteins, carbohydrates, fats and salts and are essential to growth, regeneration and to maintenance of health. There exists a distinct relation between the amount of vitamins required and the other food elements, so that efficiency of the vitamins is dependent upon the composition of the food mixture. There is also a distinct relation between the amount of vitamins required and the rate of metabolism.

The capacity of any given cell for work is impaired in proportion to the degree of vitamin starvation. The result of vitamin deficiency is destruction — the greater the deprivation, the more rapid the development of deficiency states; the lesser the deprivation, the slower their development.

NOMENCLATURE

In the first edition of this book I stated that both systems of naming vitamins (that of naming them A, B, C, D, X, Y, Z, etc., and anti-scurvy, anti-rachitic, etc.) are wrong. I said: "they should be named according to their positive qualities and not according to their negative virtues." This would mean designating them physiologically or functionally and not "therapeutically" or "prophylactically." They play certain roles in the production and maintenance of certain body structures and functions and are not mere "antis." Today, while the tendency is to name each vitamin according to its chemical nature (at least, as rapidly as their chemical natures are discovered), we retain the older designations. Vitamin A, for example, is called the "antikeratinizing" vitamin; yet its true role is not that of preventing keratosis (keras, horn), but that of promoting normal development of the epithelial tissues. The same thing may be said for vitamin B_1 the "antineuritic" vitamin, and D, the "antirachitic" vitamin. The true role of the first of these is not to prevent neuritis, but to promote normal nervous structure, that of the latter not to prevent rickets but to promote normal bone formation. Because they function physiologically, they should be designated physiologically. The present perverted terminology results from permitting medical men to name things according to their perverted views of life. Why not designate them *epetheliogenic, neurogenic* and *osteogenic*, etc. These or some similar designations would be more in keeping with their true and positive roles.

The following rather condensed summary of the results of vitamin investigation is not guaranteed to be up to date, for every few weeks a new vitamin is announced. Before this book comes from the press several new vitamins may be discovered or hinted at.

VITAMIN A, or: ANTIKERATINIZING VITAMIN

This is a fat soluble vitamin and is found chiefly in the green leaves of plants, tomatoes, butter, sweet potatoes, yellow corn, green peas, cream, egg yolk, palm oil, broccoli, kale, dandelion, parsley, lettuce (there is thirty times as much vitamin A in the outer as in the inner leaves of lettuce), spinach, apricots, yellow peaches, etc.

All yellow vegetables and fruits are sources of this vitamin, or rather carotene, which is pro-vitamin A. Provitamin A is converted into active vitamin in the liver. Carotene is also found in green plants where it is masked by the chlorophyll. "The solids of tomatoes," says Carque, "contain more of vitamin A than butter fat." The cream and butter of the Jersey cow is especially rich in carotene when there is an abundance of green pasturage. This is not so of the butter and cream of the Holstein. It is claimed that the Holstein converts the carotene into vitamin A with greater efficiency than does the Jersey. This may and may not be true.

White varieties of corn, potatoes, asparagus, celery, lettuce and turnips are deficient or devoid of vitamin A. Bleached vegetables are lacking in this substance. Vitamin A may be stored in the liver, in fat and in milk.

Lack of A checks growth, hence it was formerly called the growth-promoting vitamin (in keeping with the rest of their nomenclature, it should have been called the anti-dwarfing vitamin) but since it is now realized that there are several dietary deficiencies that stunt growth, vitamin A has been renamed the *antikeratinizing vitamin*.

Keratinization is the acquisition of a horn-like character by the epithelial tissue in many parts of the body. This is to say, the epithelial tissue becomes like the outermost layer of the skin. It then loses function. The epithelium atrophies. Such conditions as dry skin, night blindness, zerophthalmia, defective enamel formation in the teeth, changes in the tissues and glands of the mouth, digestive tract, respiratory organs, urinary and genital tract, and keratinization of other structures are attributed to vitamin A avitaminosis.

Vitamin A deficiency is credited with the following abnormal developments:

1. Failure of the processes of growth.
2. A greatly reduced resistance to infectious agencies.
3. Failure in the development of bone, cartilage, and teeth and in calcium metabolism.
4. Tendency to edema.
5. Failure of the nutrition of the cornea.

Deficiency of vitamin A is supposed to be concerned in the development of rickets, keratomalacia, deficient calcification of the teeth, nutritional edema and phosphatic urinary calculi (stones).

Vitamin A is destroyed by oxidation, so that when foods are chopped or ground this vitamin is lost. Grated carrots have far less vitamin A than whole carrots. Long cooking in an open kettle also results in loss. It is not affected by heat, but is injured by being exposed to light and especially by being exposed to ultraviolet rays. Freezing does not affect it.

The estimated average daily requirement of this vitamin is 5,000 units. More is required by infants and children and by pregnant and nursing mothers. Children and mothers need an abundance of fruits and vegetables.

VITAMIN B COMPLEX

What was formerly thought to be a single vitamin and called Water Soluble B is now called the "vitamin B complex." It is not one vitamin but many that occur together and are so complementary in their physiological effects that they are classed together. The

VITAMINS

more the substance is investigated the more complex it becomes. There are now at least thirteen B vitamins with other possible ones to be discovered. The thirteen B vitamins at the last authentic count do not include all of the suspected B factors. Biotin, inosital, P-aminobenzoic acid, thiamin, riboflavin, niacin, pantohhentic acid, pyroxine, choline, folic acid the "extrinsic factor" and two other chemically unknown factors said to be needed by the chick for growth and feather production and one or more factors of significance in guinea-pig nutrition complete the tally of known B vitamins.

If this vitamin business becomes any more complex the minds of our researchers and nutritionists are going to crack. It is lucky for them that the other vitamins — A, C, D, K, etc. — are not as complex as the B vitamin. No human mind could ever hope to unravel such complexity.

The vitamins of the B complex are fundamental to life, being found in all living things. It is difficult to differentiate between the disturbances caused by a deficiency of the individual members of the complex and it has more than once been the case that a deficiency attributed to a lack of one of the group was later found to be due to multiple lack. Beriberi is the most outstanding example of this; (A few years ago vitamin B was thought to be made up of only two factors. One of these was called vitamin F and the other vitamin G.) Only three of the B complex group have been shown to be of importance to man. We will here consider more than these three.

B_1, or *Thiamin*: the antineuritic vitamin: This vitamin is said to prevent and cure beriberi. It is an organic compound of two parts, one of which contains sulphur and the other nitrogen. It is not destroyed by absorbing oxygen, but is destroyed by heating, especially above the boiling point, if the heating is continued for some time, as in roasting, baking and frying. Thiamine is not destroyed by cooking at 100° for an hour, but it is soluble in water so that much of it is found in the water in which the food is cooked. Soda added to the food in cooking adds to the destruction of B_1.

As an enzyme it instigates the transformation of glucose into carbon-dioxide and water. If there is a deficiency of this vitamin this change is incomplete and an accumulation of *pyruvic acid* results. It promotes and is essential to growth, is essential to normal nerve function, is essential to the utilization of carbohydrates, is said to "stimulate" the appetite and normal intestinal functions and is essential to reproduction and lactation. It is said to prevent and "cure" beriberi and certain other forms of neuritis and the "diseases" of the heart and circulation associated with this.

Beriberi, or multiple neuritis, characterized by inflammation and degeneration of the peripheral nerves, intense pain, resulting, finally, in paralysis and wasting of the muscles, is said to result from B_1 deficiency. It should be noted, however, that the diets that result in beriberi are deficient in more than B_1.

One of the first symptoms of B_1 deficiency is loss of appetite, but the reader should not think that this is the sole cause of loss of appetite. The amount of B_1 needed varies with activities. Any increase of the metabolic rate increases the need for this vitamin. Muscular work as well as growth increase the need for it. No doubt cold, also, does the same. More is required during pregnancy and lactation than at other times. The liver can store this vitamin to some extent. A few other organs do the same. We require a daily supply because of this limited storage.

B_1 is said not to be widely distributed and green vegetables and fruits are said to be poor sources. Emphasis is placed upon yeast, soybeans and wholewheat as sources of this vitamin. This will be found to be a mistake as there are many vegetarian animals that never eat neither of these products. Milk is said to be a poor source, yet the amount necessary for normal growth is from three to five times as much as required by the adult to prevent beriberi. This milk is the sole diet of the calf during its period of most rapid growth. Yeast and wheat germ are emphasized as sources. Always the "authorities" place the emphasis on some commercial product of the food factories.

Synthetic B_1 or thiamine chlorine is not to be used, nor does one have to eat liver or liver extract to obtain this vitamin. Yeast preparations should be avoided. All of the B_1 required for all of the purposes of life is obtainable from green vegetables, fresh fruits and nuts. Wheat germ and rice polishings are also rich in it as are most beans and peas.

B_2 or *riboflavin* (also flavin and vitamin G) is composed of a single type of sugar (*ribose*) and a yellow pigment (*flavin*), hence the name. It is slightly soluble in water, does not withstand exposure to direct light, but is largely unaffected by heat. It is made up of carbon, hydrogen, nitrogen and oxygen. It is decomposed by both visible and ultraviolet light. It was first discovered in milk in 1879 before anything was known about vitamins and has also been called *lactoflavin*.

In conjunction with thiamin and niacin, riboflavin plays an important role in the oxidation of carbohydrates. It promotes and is essential to health. Its lack in the diet of rats is said to result in the loss of hair and atrophy of the oil-secreting glands. A deficiency of riboflavin is said to result in skin lesions, especially cheliosis, or fissures in the corners of the mouth, and cheilitis. Bloodshot eyes and increased susceptibility to infections, especially to pneumonia, are also said to result from its deficiency. In adequate quantity it is claimed to prevent abnormal changes in the eyes, thus preventing cataract and failing vision. In lower animals severe disturbances, including great loss of weight and blindness, are said to result from a deficiency of B_2.

The "authorities" emphasize milk, eggs, kidneys and soybeans as sources of riboflavin. Milk is said to be the best source of all. It is said also to be formed in the intestines by bacterial action. Fresh fruits, fresh vegetables, nuts and seeds of all kinds will supply all the riboflavin neded. There is no need to purchase commercial products or laboratory products to secure this vitamin.

Vitamin B^3 has not been isolated and its nature is not known. It is thought to be identical with pentothentic acid.

Pantothenic acid is said to be distributed in all living cells, hence its name, which is derived from a Greek word meaning "from everywhere." It is an organic compound containing calcium, carbon, hydrogen, nitrogen and oxygen. Its office in human nutrition is not established, but it is thought to be necessary to nutrition in all the higher animals, man included, and is "probably associated with the distribution of riboflavin." It is also said to one of the two factors that prevent graying of the hair. Nothing has yet prevented graying of the hair.

Pantothenic acid is so widely distributed in foods that no person who eats plenty of natural, unprocessed foods, need ever worry about not securing enough.

Vitamin B^4 is a heat-destructible, water soluble factor different from B_1, B_2 and B^3, which is said to prevent a type of paralysis in rats. Human need for it has not been demonstrated.

Vitamin B⁵ is a heat-stable factor that prevents loss of weight in pigeons. This is about all that is known about it.

Vitamin B⁶ or pyridoxine is an organic compound composed of hydrogen, oxygen, and nitrogen. In the tissues it is thought to exist in combination with a protein. It is claimed to enable the animal to utilize the amino acid tryphtophan. In its absence tryphtophan is said not to be utilized. Little is known about its office in nutrition and it has been used chiefly along with riboflavin and niacin in the treatment of pellagra. It is also supposed to "correct" muscular fatigue, in which case it is a substitute for rest. It melts at 205° C and is not decomposed by acids, alkalies or heat. Fresh fruits, green vegetables, nuts and seeds contain ample supplies of this vitamin.

Vitamin B⁷ (I) is a factor Centanni claimed in 1935 to have isolated from alcohol extract of rice polishings and which prevents digestive disturbances in birds. It has no effect on beriberi.

Vitamin P-P or *Niacin* (*nicotinic acid*) was discovered about the time of the Civil War, but nothing was known of its function. The term *niacin* was adopted to avoid confusing it with nicotine. It is an organic acid composed of carbon, hydrogen, oxygen and nitrogen and is also called *carboxylic acid*. It is soluble in water, but does not oxydize and is not affected by heat.

A deficiency of niacin is credited with causing pellagra, but it will be noted that the diets of pellagra sufferers are deficient in many other food factors. We see in the diets of these people multiple deficiencies. Its use is credited with curing the sores of pellagra in man and the analogous disease of dogs called black-tongue.

The "authorities" emphasize yeast, liver, veal, pork, peanuts, milk, eggs and wholewheat as sources of this vitamin. A diet of fresh fruits, green vegetables, nuts and seeds supplies all the niacin required. Yeast, capsules, tablets and concentrates are not needed.

Folic Acid, the newest member of the B-complex is thought to be important in the production and maintenance of normal blood. Sulfa drugs administered to rats, also to man, cause granulocytosis, or a destruction of the granulocytes of the blood. They also cause a depletion of the bone marrow cells which leads to the production of anemia. It is asserted that the administration of folic acid prevents and cures this condition. This assertion must be received with the proverbial, "grain of salt." Medical claims of "cures" are never trustworthy.

The "authorities" emphasize liver, kidneys, yeast and immature grass as sources of folic acid. Folic is from *folium* meaning leaf and should indicate the proper sources of this vitamin.

Cholin, another member of the B-complex, is thought to be necessary to the storage and mobilization of fats. It is said that in its absence the liver becomes loaded with fat.

Vitamin H or *Biotin* is described as the most powerful of all the vitamins. Discovered by three different investigators, one of whom called it vitamin H, a second called it biotin and a third called it "coenzyme R," this vitamin is regarded as essential to the respiration of certain lower organisms. It is said to "cure" a type of skin inflammation produced in rats by eating raw egg whites.

Only about three or four of the B vitamins have been shown to be essential to human nutrition. Others are said to be necessary to some of the lower animals. An assumed anti-alopecia factor is supposed to be essential to the growth of hair in animals. Why call it anti-alopcia; why not call is pro-hair? An assumed anti-graying vitamin (why not call it pigment-promoting) is supposed to maintain the color of animals' hair.

VITAMIN C, ASCORBIC ACID; ANTISCORBUTIC ACID

This is a water-soluble vitamin that is called antiscorbutic because it is supposed to prevent and remedy scurvy or scrobutus. Water Soluble C, (anti-scorbutic) is found chiefly in fresh fruits and in lesser degree in raw vegetables. Lack of it produces:

1. Swelling and tenderness of joints.
2. Spongy, hemorrhagic and painful condition of gums.
3. The teeth become loose.
4. Swelling of the ribs and fracture at junctions of bones and cartilages.

Unlike most vitamins, more of this vitamin is required by adults than by children. More is also required during pregnancy and lactation. For a change, the "authorities" discover this vitamin in plant foods—the sole source of all vitamins. Citrus fruits are emphasized as sources although all leafy plants, all growing leaves, green and red peppers, etc., are well-supplied with C. Apples and potatoes have a fair share of them also.

Ascorbic acid is destroyed by heating, drying, salting, contact with air and is deteriorated by prolonged storage, due to oxidation.

Raw cabbage contains about twenty times as much of C as when it has been boiled in water in the usual manner. Baking soda or other alkalies used in cooking hastens the destruction of the vitamin. Since C is soluble in water it is leached out when vegetables are cooked in water.

VITAMIN D; ANTI-RACHITIC VITAMIN

This is a fat-soluble vitamin which is essential to the assimilation of calcium and phosphorus. It is of vital importance in the formation of good bones and teeth. By some magic of numbers the "authorities" have decided that there are vitamins D_2 and D^3 but no vitamin D_1. Vitamin D_2, or *calciferol,* is produced by irradiation with ultra-violet light of the sterol, *ergosterol.* "It is not the vitamin found in cod liver oil," although it serves the same purpose. Identical with vitamin D of cod liver oil is vitamin D^3 produced by irradiation of the sterol, 7-*dehydrocholesterol,* stored abundantly in the skin. It may be stored in the liver. The production of this vitamin by irradiation of the provitamin stored in the skin accounts for part of the value of sun bathing.

The "authorities" emphasize cod liver oil and other fish liver oils, butter and cream as sources of this vitamin. Green vegetables, peas, peanuts, almonds and other nuts, wheat bran and many other vegetable foods are abundant in vitamin D.

Due to greater calcium and phosphorus metabolism in early life, vitamin D is most needed in the first year of life. Mothers need it during the last two months of pregnancy and during lactation. Sunbathing by mothers will also be of great value.

VITAMIN E: ANTI-STERILITY VITAMIN

Fat-soluble E, found in green leaves, the germs of seeds, in olives and olive oil. and in other foods (lettuce is rich in it), is supposed to energize and potentize the reproductive glands. Many forms of E are said to exist in foods. It seems to be essential to reproduction in rats in which its absence causes the germ cells to perish and the seminiferous tubules, in which the germ cells are produced, to atrophy. The ovaries of the female remain normal but the fetus dies a few days after fertilization. No evidence of the need of this vitamin by man has been produced.

The alphabet has not been exhausted. There are a few other vitamins about which little or nothing is known. No doubt others will be discovered as the search continues. But brief space will be devoted to these other vitamins.

Vitamin J has not been shown to have any value to man. Von Euler reported in 1935 that he had succeeded in extracting from fruit juices a factor that has no effect in preventing scurvy, but that protects guinea pigs from pneumonia.

Vitamin K or the anti-hemorrhage vitamin (why not call it the blood coagulating vitamin?) is a fat-soluble vitamin that we are said not to require in our food as it is produced for us by the action of bacteria in the intestines. It is supposed to be essential to the coagulation of the blood.

Factors L_1 and L_2 are substances said to be essential to milk productoin. L_1 is obtained from beef liver and L_2 from baker's yeast, neither of which is ever eaten by most milk-producing animals. These two vitamins are thought to aid in maturing the milk-producing tissuse. If they are really essential vitamins, they are produced by plants and not by the liver of the cow. The cow only stores them in her liver.

Factor M: When it was found that niacin and combinations of this vitamin with B_1 and B_2 will not correct pellagra symptoms in Rhesus monkeys another vitamin was assumed. Dried brewer's yeast and liver extract are said to clear up these symptoms. Factor M is, therfore, assumed to exist. As dried brewer's yeast and liver extract are never eaten by monkeys in nature, Factor M must be present in the fruits and vegetables eaten by these animals, else Factor M is a fiction.

Factor U: This is a vitamin apparently essential to the growth of chicks. Its significance, if it has any, in human nutrition is unknown.

Factor W: Thought possibly to be related to Pyridine, is an additional growth-promoting factor needed by rats. Its relation to human nutrition, if it has any, is unknown.

Grass Juice Factor: In addition to the usual vitamins found in grass, the existence of a vitamin, or of other vitamins, in the juice of the grass is assumed, but its nature has not yet been established.

SOURCES

Ultimately, the animal is dependent upon the vegetable kingdom for vitamins. Plants, alone, can synthesize these substances.

It is asserted that, while man cannot synthesize any of the vitamins, a few animals are able to make one vitamin. In a few cases the animal is able to transform the immediate precusor of the vitamin (the provitamin) into the vitamin. It can complete but connot initiate the synthesis. Examples of this are the transformation of provitamin A (*carotene*) into A and the transformation of provitamin D (*ergosterol*) into D. In this respect, vitamins do not differ from the essential amino acids, the highly unsaturated fatty acids and the minerals. The plant kingdom is the true source of animal nutrition. Green plants on land and algae and other small plant organisms in the sea produce the world's vitamin supply. Man, like the cod and other animals, is capable of storing up vitamins in the liver and elsewhere.

Berg says: "The germs of seeds are especially rich in vitamins. In like manner the vitamin content of eggs, which are animal counterparts of seeds, is concentrated in the yolk." In potatoes the vitamins are in the eyes.

Foods that are richest in minerals are also richest in vitamins. Those portions of foods that are richest in minerals are also richest in vitamin. Processes that favor the assimilation and fixation of minerals, the production of fats, starches, sugars, etc., also increase the vitamin content of foods. Those "refining" processes that remove the salts from foods or that impair the nutritive value of the salts also remove and impair the vitamins. These facts may simply mean that anything that influences food influences vitamin production as much as sugar production or salt formation,

Vitamin B, in cereals, "seems to be closely associated with phosphorus. The determination of the total phosphorus content of cereal products seems to give a fairly accurate index to the relative amounts of vitamin B present. While phosphorus does not enter into the vitamin molecule, the dsitribution of phosphorus and vitamins within the grain runs practically parallel."

Darker colored vegetables have more vitamins. They are known to have more minerals. Sunshine favors vitamin storage. The green outer stalks and leaves of lettuce, cabbage, celery, etc., are –more abundant in vitamins than the pale inner leaves and stalks. The green leaves of tubers possess more vitamins than the tubers.

The more sunlight fruits receive, the more vitamin C they "possess." Oranges, lemons, grapefruit, pineapples and other tropical fruits, requiring nearly a year of tropical sunshine to perfect their chemistry, are the best known "sources" of vitamin C. Fruits and vegetables grown under glass are poor "sources" of vitamin C. Among vegetables, tomatoes, lettuce, cabbage and carrots are excellent "sources" of vitamin C.

Vitamins exist in connection with the processes of life in plants and animals and are more or less completely destroyed by whatever destroys the life processes. They are present only in very small quantities in those foods that are richest in them. Only two of them are considered to be likely to be deficient in the average dietary.

Dr. Percy Howe says: "Every refining process of which I can think at the moment is more or less destructive to at least some of the vitamins which were in the organized food materials. There are important vitamins in animal fats, such as butter, but rendering those fats into lard so completely destroys the vitamins that very serious consequenses result if an animal is fed for a long time upon a diet which contains no animal fat except lard."

Since butter is never rendered into lard, Dr. Howe must have reference to those fats which are so altered and refined. These fats also contain mineral salts and these are all taken out in the process of rendering the fats into lard.

Dr. A. Adams Dutcher, of the Department of Agricultural Chemistry, Pennsylvania State College, says: "Drummond and his coworkers, Golding, Zilca and Coward, have shown that lard does not usually contain the fat soluble vitamine, due to the fact that the ration of the hog is invariably deficient in this particular food factor." Lard is simply fat — refined fat. Lard couldn't possibly contain vitamins for the reason that it is such a highly processed fat when it leaves the rendering tank, following its treatment by heat, fuller's earth, clarifiers, bleachers, etc., it pours from the spout a so-called purified hydrocarbon, deficient in every food factor but the one factor found in all oils.

Dr. Dutcher says: "That the vital organs of the type represented by the liver and kidneys are rich in vitamins scarcely needs comment."

Dutcher further says: "It is possible to produce milk which is almost devoid of vitamins, depending upon the vitamin content of the cow's ration." Feed a cow upon beet pulp, which represents the exhausted residue of the beet sugar mill, after the makers have extracted the vitamins and salts of the tuber, and a deficient milk is the result.

One of the most popular dairy rations of the recent past was a mixture of beet pulp, brewer's waste and distiller's grain. These exhausted byproducts of brewery and distillery have been robbed of their vitamins. There is overwhelming evidence that malnutrition and anemia, leading to tuberculosis, have been the most common sequels of feeding cows on vitamin and mineral exhausted commercial foodstuffs.

When the tissues of the animal are robbed of the nutritional factors upon which they depend for tissue-tone, the milk of such animals is grossly deficient in the substances not present in the cow's food. Her milk is not normal. "Disease" is inevitable.

"Silage does not appear to enrich milk as far as the anti-scorbutic vitamin is concerned," says Dr. Dutcher. Silage is a fermented product and because it has undergone fermentation, it falls into the class of oxidized foods. Its whole chemistry is changed.

Dr. Dutcher also declares: "We have observed that green alfalfa seems to influence the nutritive value of the milk, increasing its nutritive properties, but in just what way we are not prepared to say." Good green alfalfa is one of the richest of plants in minerals and vitamins.

VITAMINS PERISHABLE

Vitamins are perishable substances. They are destroyed in a variety of ways. Some of them are destroyed by oxidation, some are destroyed by high temperatures, as in cooking, apparently some are destroyed by freezing, some are destroyed by light, some are affected by the presence of minerals, such as copper or iron. Some are thought not to be affected by any of the conditions to which food stuffs are subjected. The vitamin content of foods is often reduced by methods of storage, marketing and cooking. The full value of foods is obtained only by eating them in the fresh, raw state.

White flour, polished rice, degerminated corn meal, all denatured cereals, white sugar, jellies, jams, pasteurized milk and cream, refined syrups, sulphured fruits, and a whole long list of processed, refined and over-cooked foods that constitute a major part of present-day diet are devoid of vitamins as they are deficient in minerals.

What is the answer? This should be obvious enough. Eat more fresh, whole, raw fruits and vegetables and cease consuming the refined and denatured products. "Return to Nature" in your eating habits. Forsake the commercialized and spoiled foods that are fostered by the manufacturers of foodless foods.

VITAMIN EXTRACT

The observing reader cannot miss the fact that in all books and articles dealing with vitamins, commercial products are emphasized and foods as sources of vitamins are slighted. Yeast, cod-liver oil, halibut-liver oil, shark-liver oil, Black Strap Molasses, and other food extracts, even synthetic "vitamins" are recommended, even insisted upon, instead of natural foods. Indeed natural foods are often pictured as indigestible, even dangerous. Our efforts to get vitamins and organic salts the "easy way" has led to many foolish practices.

Prof. E. V. McCullum says: "An examination of the labels on the containers of the vitamin preparations which we have studied suggests at once their promotion for therapeutic purposes represents a repetition of the 'patent medicine' propaganda which has for so long been inflicted on the American public. Thus the same general symptoms that have been used in labels of sarsparillas, blood-purifiers, kidney remedise, remedies for female weakness, etc., reappear as conditions for which the vitamin preparations are said to be specific remedies.

"The claims set forth on the labels, of the medicinal value of these preparations are extravangant and misleading. They do not contain the vitamin 'B' in concentrated form, as they are represented to do. The marketing of the preparations represents an attempt and unfortunately, a successful one, to substitute a commercial vitamin propaganda for the nefarious patent medicine business."

Prof. Casimir Funk says: "Science is very much in the dark yet as to the composition and function of vitamins. The combined research has taught us that all we do know about the subject is of tremendous importance. But it is not detracting from the valuable place that vitamins hold in the list of food elements to say that we are just beginning to understand them a little.

"Reputable scientists do not countenance the efforts that are being made to deceive the public into believing that the time has come when it can be said satisfactorily that such and such a result will follow the practice of taking certain proprietary vitamin preparations.

"To put it briefly, the people who are promoting such preparations do not know what they are talking about. And they certainly are leading the public into deception. If their claims for these products could be substantiated, science would greet them with open arms. There are several hundred scientists experimenting, but, as yet, vitamins have not been isolated, much less concentrated.

"Besides, vitamins so far have proved of value only where there have been cases of very distinct vitamin deficiency. When the diet is complete, we do not yet know whether an additional supply of vitamins is needed or even advisable. No one has established the quantity of vitamins necessary for the maintenance of the average healthy person. (Since Prof. Funk made these statements, some experimenters claim to have demonstrated that an excess of vitamins is harmful.)

"There is nothing mysterious about vitamins. They are just food constituents that should be in our diet, just as other food properties should be found there.

"I do not know what use, particular or otherwise, will be made of isolating vitamins when we have succeeded in separating them. I could not even venture a guess — no one can know. I confidently predict that the time will come eventually when we shall succeed in such isolation. But no one has succeeded in doing it yet.

"What would be the use in preparing all our foods artificially, so long as nature is producing her own foods with sufficient abundance to supply an increasing population? It would be folly even to think of turning ourselves into domestic manufacturers and consumers of self-made food so long as nature gives us enough."

McCullum reported tests made with six widely advertised nostrums supposed to carry large percentages of vitamins, the test showing them to be not only worthless, but injurious. "Fed to test groups of rats and other animals," he says, "not only was growth most positively not promoted, but was checked, halted and inhibited. Continuous feeding resulted in the death of the animals subjected to the test." Other investigators making similar tests with widely advertised vitamin carrying patent foods, etc., agree with McCullum's finding. Our safest and most dependable source of vitamins, as of salts and other food elements, is the plant kingdom — fresh fruits, green vegetables and nuts.

It is true that the above quoted statements were made a few years ago, but the essential facts have not changed. Vitamins work best in cooperation; cooperation, not alone with each other, but also with the other nutrients in the diet.

Nature puts up her foods in complete *ensembles* and our efforts to separate the various food elements and put them up in bottles and boxes have not been very successful. Science is better at building bridges or tunnels than at building men. In this latter we must still follow the ancient, the primitive, pattern.

IRRADIATION-VITAMINS

The announcement that ultra-violet irradiation of foods produces "vitamin D" in them caused irradiation of all manners of foods. "Sunshine pills" were marketed in England; irradiation of cows with ultra-violet lamps in winter was advocated; quartz tubes for use in the ears, nose, throat, rectum, vagina and to introduce into the stomach, in cases of indigestion, were used. It was proposed to fit up restaurants with ultra-violet lamps. Irradiated cigars, cigarettes, laxatives, and toilet paper were placed on the market. Vitaminized face powder and vitaminized cleansing creams are advertised.

The whole lesson is learned from the wrong end. *Hygienists* have long advised: "Eat the sunshine," that is sunkissed foods. Nature irradiates her foods during growth, as the sun's rays stream down upon orchard and garden. The essential work in food production she does well. To irradiate white flour or other denatured foods and expect this to render them wholesome is absurd. Irradiated white flour is still lacking in calcium, iron, sodium, etc.

Drummond showed that ultra-violet irradiation of milk has its drawbacks in that "milk which has been exposed to the radiations of a mercury-vapor lamp for as short a time as five minutes, not only becomes unpalatable in that it acquires an unpleasant tallowy odor, but actually suffers chemical changes which are highly undesirable from the standpoint of nutrition. One of these is the destruction of vitamin A by oxidation." He says children fed on such milk are likely to show retarded growth and diminished resistance, which appears to be due to a deficiency of vitamin A.

Nature irradiates her products of garden and orchard. Throughout the Spring, Summer and Fall the rays of the sun beat down upon the growing plant giving it the needed assistance in producing vitamins. Why accept substitutes?

DAILY VITAMIN NEEDS

The daily minimum requirements of the various vitamins have been worked out in both growing child, adult and pregnant and nursing mother. These statements of our vitamin needs are no more valid than statements of our daily calorie needs; they are no more reliable than the statements of our daily protein needs.

Recent experiments by workers in the Department of Home Economics of the University of Chicago showed that the accepted standards of riboflavin requirements for young women are too high. The fact is that no reliable standards of requirements for any of the vitamins have been worked out and it is more than probable that all the, at present, accepted standards are too high, as they are for other nutrient factors. Vitamin requirements are correlated with the intake and utilization of other nutrients. They do not work in a vacuum.

To secure an adequate supply of all needed vitamins it is not necessary to know the amount of each vitamin contained in each food consumed; it is needful only that we have a broad understanding of what constitutes the so-called "protective" foods. To put this more simply, it is necessary that you understand that you should have a daily supply of fresh, uncooked fruits and vegetables. Other so-called protective foods, such as milk and eggs, are not essential if the fresh fruits and vegetables are taken in abundance.

UTILIZATION OF VITAMINS

It has been found that the ability of the body to utilize vitamins from different sources varies considerably. Spinach is rich in carotene or pro-vitamin A. Fish liver oils are rich in vitamin A. But it has been found that, in terms of international units, a baby can derive from spinach ten times that which it can get from a similar dosage of various fish liver oils. To be of equal value to spinach, fish liver oil would have to supply 10,000 units of vitamin A to equal 1,000 units of vitamin A in spinach. The difference in these two substances is the difference in the availability of their vitamin A. The vitamins and minerals contained in fruits, vegetables and nuts are much more available than those derived from other sources. The results of the use of synthetic vitamins indicate that these substances are not available at all.

Besides the many abnormal conditions that prevent the absorption and untilization of vitamins, it is said that there is faulty util-

VITAMINS

ization of vitamins in the absence of disease. It is said that there is a congenital inability to utilize vitamins well. Indeed, it is claimed that faulty utilization of this character is very common. The condition is said to be seen in both the young and the aged.

It is my opinion that congenital inability to utilize vitamins, if it exists at all, is extremely rare. The "absence of disease" from the standpoint of orthodox scientists means merely the absence of physical signs. Individuals that pass as healthy are often on the verge of complete collapse. A "biochemist" will talk learnedly about congenital inability to utilize vitamins and have a cigar in his mouth all the time he is talking. He does not recognize the inhibiting effects of tobacco upon digestion. He will prepare menus containing coffee, tea and other such substances. He will not exclude vinegar and condiments, that inhibit digestion, from the diets of his patients. He will talk learnedly of the "dramatic" way in which patients who have been for years on a "very good diet," respond to vitamin concentrates, all the while wholly unaware that he is witnessing, not improved nutrition, but mere temporary stimulation.

The utilization of vitamin C is improved by iron and the B complex. The B complex is helped in its work by A and D. Such minerals as zinc, manganese, magnesium, help in the utilization of vitamin C and the B complex.

"Biochemists," watching the assistance given the vitamins by the minerals, do not see in this the need for mineral-rich foods, but the need for mineral concentrates from their own laboratories. Unfortunately, these chemists know little of *bios*, hence mislead all with whom they come in contact. They seem never to think of foods as sources of vitamins and minerals.

Physicians, biochemists and dietitians employ a number of tricks in an endeavor to force the utilization of vitamins in those cases where there is failure of utilization. Such tricks as adding wheat germ oil to the vitamin A ration, or if this fails, using bile salts with the vitamin A. Bile salts are also used in connection with vitamins D, E and K. Lecithin is also employed to help the utilization of vitamin A.

In catarrhal conditions in which vitamin C is not well utilized they give additional carbohydrates, which tends to increase the catarrhal condition. Honey in addition to vitamin C is a favorite carbohydrate among the vitamin cure mongers. It is recommended that ascorbic acid tablets always be taken with honey, or other "easily digested" carbohydrate. This is because there is bacterial destruction of vitamin C in the colon. It does not seem to matter what happens to vitamin C or any other vitamin after it reaches the colon, for it has already gone beyond the point where it can be absorbed. Vitamins are also given by injection and then there is the method of giving such large amounts of the vitamin concentrates that "limited utilization will still mean adequate stores." In some quarters it is recommended that natural vitamins (extracts) be used along with the synthetic vitamins to assure the use of the latter. All of this nonsense belongs to the drug superstition and will not be engaged in by any rational man or woman. Every hospital, clinic and every physician's office is full of the failure of this program.

When we are not physical and mental drunkards, when we have not surfeited ourselves—our metabolism—we can find all the elements we need in the everyday natural foods found in our markets, or grown in our gardens and orchards, but when surfeited, we can starve to death with our system loaded with "good nourishing food" — the very elements for the lack of which we are dying. No more obvious example of this fact can be given than that of the great and rapid increase in the number of red blood cells in anemic patients when placed upon a fast, or the improvement of the bones of rachitic children and animals when fasted.

It is asserted that allergies to fruits rich in C are common and those so afflicted must turn to other sources for their supply of C. Fruit "allergies" are largely or wholly fictions and grow out of improper use of fruits. I take people who are "allergic" to the citrus fruits and put them on a citrus fruit diet and their supposed allergy does not show up. Fruit "allergies" are largely the outgrowth of wrong combinations.

There are other sources of C besides fruits. Cabbage, green and red peppers, practically all fresh green leaves, etc., possess this vitamin in adequate amounts. One does not have to rely on extracts and synthetic concoctions. It is characteristic of dietitians, "biochemists," physicians, etc., that they turn to artificial sources of 'vitamins" instead of resorting to natural foods.

Vitamins tend to crowd out all other important nutrients and to cause dietitians, physicians and others to neglect other important food elements. This is a very unfortunate fact, for even the vitamins are valueless in the absence of these other nutrients. "Investigators have conclusively shown," says Dr. Philip Norman, "that there are other principles as important as the vitamins and that their absence negatives the value of the vitamins just as much as the absence of the vitamins negatives the food value of the others. *Paradoxical as it may sound, it is the very element of the population which could afford a good food balance among which a devitalized diet is observed most frequently.* The poorer classes, eating coarser bread and utilizing all the vegetable parings and fats, subsist on a diet much richer in vitamins and minerals."

We must also avoid over-emphasizing the importance of vitamins in nutrition. They are but one of many factors, all of which are of equal importance and none of which is of value in the absence of the others. Health, growth and strength cannot be maintained in an ideal manner without any of the essential nutritive elements. A lack of any of the nutritive elements constitutes a deficiency and the resulting effects of this lack may rightly be termed a "deficiency disease."

Dr. Casimir Funk has said: "We are handicapped by imperfect knowledge. Views are often expressed as to the exaggerated importance assigned to the vitmains. There is no doubt vitamins do not mean everything in nutrition."

Above all we must not permit ourselves to be mislead by the present commercial exploitation of vitamins. "Concentrated" vitamin-carrying substances are offered us as supplements to our diets. Great claims are made for the value of these things. Man's nutritive needs are coordinated with the supplies of Nature, we may be sure that their concentration (assuming that they are really concentrated in the advertised preparations) can be of no special value to us.

As will be shown in another chapter, our ability to utilize vitamins depends upon the presence of other elements in our diet. To eat concentrated vitamins and not consume these other elements in equal proportions would simply waste much of the vitamins. We need not only vitamins, but vitamins in ideal combinations with other elements and only the plant kingdom knows how to put up these vitamins. The plant kingdom is our ideal source of vitamins.

SYNTHETIC VITAMINS

Nature puts up her vitamins in ideal combinations with the other essential elements of our foods. She gives us lettuce, apples and grapes; the demi-goda of "science" give us the quintessences of these and other natural products and tell us that these are better than Nature's own creations. They give us devitalized foods and synthetic "foods" — substances with nutrition rejects, preferring to starve.

At first, after the discovery of vitamins, they gave us vitamin extracts. The chemist extracted the vitamin but the vital element was lost, and we were forced to eat uncooked fruits and vegetables to get it. Later, after some of the vitamins were isolated and analyzed (more or less accurately), he gave us synthetic vitamins, which, he assured us, are chemically identical with the natural vitamin. He is unable to manufacture acceptable fats, sugars, amino acids, salts, but he can manufacture "acceptable" vitamins. He can't produce a viable egg, but he insists that his dummy eggs are just as good as the real article.

The chemist is not only an egomaniac, but he is the faithful handmaiden of the commercial firm that employs him. He is engaged in the production of "just as good" substitutes for nature's products, because there "are millions in it." There was never any reason, except commercial reasons, for the attempt to manufacture synthetic vitamins. The plant kingdom, the sole source of supply, manufactures these in super-abundance. Old mother nature puts them in all foods. No prudent eater need ever suffer from a lack of any of them.

Chemists can play with the elements — analyze, synthesize, combine and take apart again — but they cannot produce living substance. Their syntheses lack many important refinings which only the metabolic processes of the plant and animal kingdom can accomplish. They say their synthetic vitamins are chemically identical with those produced by plants, but the results of their use prove unmistakeably that they are not functionally identical. The garden and orchard turn out products far superior to those of the laboratory.

It is folly to think you can mix together a lot of synthetic and extracted vitamins and produce a salad that is equal to a salad of uncooked vegetables or fruits. It is equally as foolish to think you can mix together a dozen or more different salts supplied you by the druggist and produce a salad that will equal a salad of fresh, uncooked vegetables or fruits. Nor can you do so by mixing a dozen synthetic vitamins with a dozen salts from the druggist.

Synthetic vitamins, that is, "vitamins" made in the chemical laboratory, although having practically the same chemical composition as those of nature's products, are not vitamins and do not have the effects of vitamins. Despite the claims made for them by the commercial firms and by the drugging fraternity, who know no difference between nature and their laboratories, except that their laboratories are "superior," made vitamins are no more valuable than the mineral salts sold at the drug stores and prescribed by physicians. Certain synthetic vitamins, such as K, are water soluble, whereas the same vitamins from natural sources are not. This difference in solubility rests upon fundamental differences in their structure. Synthetic "vitamins" are "paste," not true diamonds.

Manufacturers and their subsidized scientists with commercial motives assert that their synthetic vitamins are as good as those the cow gets from grass and alfalfa and passes on to your child in her milk — providing the milk is not pasteurized. This is a gross misrepresentation.

They also emphasize the fact that synthesis brought the price down much below the cost of extraction. The fact that extracting the vitamins is neither necessary nor helpful is ignored.

Ansel Keys and Austin F. Herschel of the University of Minnesota tested vitamin tablets and concentrates to determine their values. The whole alphabet from A to Z was tested. Twenty-six soldiers were used as subjects for these tests. A total of 256 experiments were made. During the whole of the period of observation every effort was made to assure standardized conditions. The men were fed the usual army post rations, wore regulation army clothing and packs at all times and marched on motor-driven treadmills for definite periods.

Both vitamins and placeboes were used in these tests. The placebos were made up in pill form to resemble in every way the "vitamins," so that the men could not know when they were getting vitamins and when they were getting placebos. The two forms of pills looked alike and tasted alike. The synthetic "vitamins" and the placebos were given both before and after each meal. The soldiers were divided into two groups. During the first part of the test one group would have his meals supplemented with "vitamins," the other group would get the placebos. During the second part the first group would receive the placebos and the second group would receive the "vitamins."

Careful tests of circulatory, metabolic and blood-chemistry responses were made after each period on the tread-mill. These two men report as a result of these tests that:

"In neither brief extreme exercise nor in prolonged severe exercise and semi-starvation were there any indications of any effect, favorable, or otherwise, of the vitamin supplementation on muscular ability, endurance, resistance to fatigue, or recovery from exertion.

"It is concluded that no useful purpose would be served by enrichment of the present U.S. Army rations with the vitamins studied."

Among the vitamins studied were the much advertised thiamin chloride (B_1), riboflavin (B_2), nicotinic acid (a B factor), pyridoxine (B_6), pantothentic acid (a B factor), and ascorbic acid (C).

Similar negative results were obtained in experiments conducted in England during the late war. Both school children and working men were given synthetic "vitamins" for several months and the results carefully checked. School children who took multiple vitamin pills for a period lasting from seven to nine months failed to register a superior record in relation to weight, height or sickness in comparison with the children who went without the synthetic "vitamins." The tests showed that, despite the war, the home and school diets of the children contained sufficient real vitamins so that the synthetic "vitamins" contributed nothing. Similar experiments conducted in war workers failed to result in any health gains among those workers who received the synthetic "vitamins" as compared to those who did not.

Baffin and Caper of Duke University give some details in an issue of the *Journal of the American Medical Association* of the results of an investigation made at the request of the Office of the Quartermaster General of the U.S. Army to determine the value of adding vitamins to the Usual American diet. I think it significant that the "usual American diet" which is by no means an ideal diet, was used in this series of tests. It carries me back to Chittenden's experiments made years before vitamins were heard of. For some time now, I have been convinced that: either Chittenden did not obtain the results he claimed, or else, the vitamin researchers are kidding themselves and the public about their findings.

Two hundred volunteer medical students and technicians were used in these tests. The volunteers were divided into five groups. They were all "in apparent good health" and were consuming the "usual American diet," whatever this may be in any given instance.

VITAMINS

The tests were run for thirty days, "because that period is found sufficient for recovery under vitamin treatment," of patients actually ill from vitamin deficiency.

One group was given vitamins tablets and liver extract tablets.

A second group was given yeast extract tablets and vitamin pills.

A third group was given vitamin pills and sugar pills made to resemble the others.

A fourth group was given vitamin pills only.

The fifth group was given sugar pills only.

None of the volunteers were permitted to know what was in the pills they were taking. Each man kept a daily record of his weight and of such symptoms as "gas" or indigestion, nausea, vomiting, abdominal pain, diarrhea. Also he kept a daily record of his impressions of any effect on his appetite and on his "pep" or energy.

Baffin and Caper report that "a significant increase in diarrhea and a highly significant increase in abdominal pain and nausea and vomiting occurred in those receiving liver extract and yeast." They found no evidence to substantiate the view that the use of vitamins will increase one's efficiency and sense of well-being in cases where no real deficiency exists.

But are we to believe that the "usual American diet" of white bread, denatured cereals, white sugar, refined syrups, canned goods, pasteurized milk, embalmed and cooked muscle meats, cakes, pies, preserves, candies, coffee, etc., is not deficient in vitamins? No one claims that present methods of determining vitamin deficiencies are sufficiently delicate to reveal the earliest stages of deficiency.

It is not to be supposed that the diet fed to soldiers in the army or the war-time diets of the British people were so good that they could not be improved upon. At best, the British war-time diet was a subsistence diet. Good nutrition is necessarily based on a good diet of natural foodstuffs and health cannot be assured anybody by taking a certain number of vitamin capsules or vitamin pills regularly A good diet will supply all the vitamins needed, while taking "vitamin" pills to supplement a poor diet is ridiculous. Synthetic "vitamins" are doing incalculable harm in inducing people to depend upon these to the neglect of real vitamins.

What, then is the trouble? First, the vitamins are only imitations. Second, they are not properly used. They are useful only in the presense of elements of food stuffs that are almost invariably deficient in the "usual American diet." Better nutrition may be had by better diet, not by eating vitamin pills.

The fact that vitamins are employed best in combination should show the reader that taking large amounts of vitamin C and not securing sufficient amounts of vitamin B will result in failure of nutrition. This has led to the preparation of pluri-vitamin pills and extracts. But these fail, not alone because the vitamins are not real, but also, because the vitamins are not useful in the absence of the minerals that "act" synergistically with them. Even mixtures of vitamins and minerals fail, for the reason that the minerals are not available and the vitamins are only imitation.

I would emphasize two other important facts: namely, with all the work that has been done, we do not yet know all the chemistry involved in a single one of our common foods, nor in the human body. There may be other vitamins or other food factors of which we know nothing at present. Certainly we do not know all that we need to know about the mineral composition of foods or of the body. There is every reason to think that there are amino acids that are as yet unknown. Mineral concentrates contain only the known minerals of the body. Vitamin concentrates contain only the known vitamins. Amino acids now sold on the market contain only the known amino acids. The unknown factors of foods are lacking in all of these substances. Foods contain all food factors now known as well as those now unknown. Manufacturing chemists, druggists, food manufacturers, etc., cannot compete with nature in preparing food for man.

VITAMIN PROMOTION

The manufacture of artificial vitamins is an industry organized along the lines of the famous international cartels and at least one of the corporations of this country was party to an agreement with the I. G. Farbenindustrie. Millions are spent in advertising and in subsidizing research. Vitamins are sold over the counters in America today in excess of a quarter of a billion dollars a year.

During the early part of the last War much publicity was given to the fact that industrial workers were given daily quotas of vitamins to increase their productiveness. This was accomplished by the vitamin makers or their advertising men going to the heads of these industrial plants and persuading these men to permit the manufacturers to supply the vitamins to the men as a "scientific" test. It was done as an advertising program and the cost was charged off to advertising. It resulted in no good. No doubt many thought they were benefitted, just as many think they are benefitted by taking drugs in other forms. One of the soldiers used in the tests at the University of Minnesota reported that he felt much better after taking the tablets given him in the tests. A careful check disclosed that he had been taking the placebos and not "vitamins" at all.

The German experience with a vitamin pill called piroxin is instructive. The German government requested the workers to take these pills. At first they thought they were getting wonderful results, because the pills seemed to lessen the fatigue of the workers. For a few weeks there was a step-up in production but after a few months industrial accidents had increased thirty per cent. Investigations showed that the piroxin had undermined the workers' nervous systems and had made many thousands of drug addicts. Synthetic vitamins are drugs.

TOXICITY

The literature of the subject contains frequent references to the toxicity of vitamins. Numerous tests have been made in an effort to determine their toxicity. In some of these tests death has resulted from the use of large doses of these substances. Other vitamins slackened the growth rate. Niacin has been shown to be somewhat toxic. Thiamine is less toxic than niacin. Pyridoxine is about as toxic as niacin. Other vitamins have shown varying degrees of toxicity.

Three important facts stand out in these tests, namely:

1. The tests are made with synthetic vitamins, which are drugs, not vitamins,

2. Large doses are employed, such as one would never consume in eating.

3. The so-called vitamins are frequently administered by injection into the skin, a method of vitamin intake that we never employ in eating.

There is a complete lack of evidence that an excess of natural vitamins, such as an animal might receive by consuming an enormous quantity of green grass, or a man might receive by eating a large quantity of oranges while on an orange diet, is harmful. The toxicity of natural vitamins in quantities that may consumed in eating is not demonstrated. What is demonstrated is that artificial or imitation "vitamins" are toxic. This is another good reason why we should rely upon nature's own products and avoid the laboratory concoctions of the manufacturing chemists.

Records of cases of hypervitaminosis (excess of vitamin) A, D and K exist in vitamin literature and we are told that "certain of the vitamins may possess pharmacologic actions which are not apparent when administered in the small quantities usually provided in nutritional experiments." These cases of hypervitaminosis are seen in those dosed with drug "vitamins." There is no such thing as pharmalogic action.

Dr. Casimir Funk, who coined the term "vitamin," says: "Synthetic vitamins are less effective and more toxic." The sober fact is that the evidence for the "toxicity" of natural vitamins is almost nil, while the evidence for the toxicity of the synthetic vitamins is great. It is essential that we understand the differences between the two kinds of vitamins. Dr. Royal Lee very appropriately says of the synthetic vitamins: "Unnatural vitamins like unnatural foods, are dangerous." The "synthetic vitamins" are really drugs. They behave as irritants rather than as enzymes. A *Textbook of Physiology* by Wm. D. Zoethout, Ph.D., and W. W. Tuttle, Ph.D., says of the synthetically produced vitamins: "their consumption in this form is less desirable than eating natural foods in which they are found." These physiologists think there are advantages to be gained by "re-enforcing" white flour with vitamin B_1 so long as "people insist on eatnig fine white bread."

VITAMIN CURES

The use of certain vitamins is said to "cure" certain "diseases." We must not permit ourselves to be misled by these claims. They have no more value than the claims that drugs, or other such substances, "cure" disease. There is no so-called disease that is due to a unitary cause — every disease is the complex effects of a number of correlated antecedents — and no disease is *curable* by a unitary *cure*. On the other hand, practically all of the so-called deficiency states that are said to require vitamins for their *cure*, will and do get well while the patient is fasting and drinking only distilled water. The wild enthusiasm caused by the discovery of vitamins will sooner or later, give way to sober reflection and it will then be recognized that the research workers and others have permitted their enthusiasm to run away with their judgement.

Thousands of people are taking vitamin pills, pellets, powders, vitamin extracts, etc., and taking mineral concentrates in powder and pill form, they are supplementing their diets with these minerals.

VITAMINS

Both vitamins and minerals are being taken in specified doses for supposed specific conditions. The drugstores and health food stores, along with the manufacturers of these products, are growing rich off their sale. But no lasting good is coming out of the practice.

The vitamin devotees tell us that vitamin A dissolves kidney stones, vitamin B aids the deaf, vitamin C softens cataracts, vitamin C helps hayfever, vitamin C relieves arthritis. These things are not true, of course. The thousands of sufferers who have been dosed with the vitamins for these conditions and have grown worse instead of better are sufficient proof of this statement. The statement that vitamins can "help, perhaps cure magically," is an exaggeration by an over-enthusiast or a commercial-exploiter of vitamins.

Vitamins do not prevent colds; they do not give energy nor prevent fatigue; they do not prevent nor cure arthritis; they do not prevent graying of the hair nor do they restore the hair to its normal color.

The drug-store pill eater is led to believe that he can have health by taking these synthetic "vitamins" without the necessity of removing the many causes of his disease. Taking vitamins to "cure" disease and neglecting to correct the habits of life that have produced and are maintaining that disease, is the same in principle and is equally as ridiculous as taking drugs for the same purpose while ignoring the habits of life. Vitamins cannot erase the effects of tobacco, alcohol, coffee, worry, fear, anxiety, domestic irritations, overwork, lack of exercise, overeating, insufficient rest and sleep, foul air in workshop, office, bed room and elsewhere.

Calories
CHAPTER V

Food values continue to be measured in calories. The calorie is a unit of measurement, just as the inch or yard is a unit of measurement. The small calorie is the amount of heat required to raise the temperature of one gram (about 20 drops) of water one degree. The large calorie is the amount of heat required to raise one kilogram (equal to about two and a quarter pounds) of water one degree centigrade.

Heat and energy are considered equivalent and transformable. Thus, the orthodox scientist considers that those foods that give off most heat per pound are the best foods for human consumption. It was decided that the average individual requires about 2,500 calories a day and diets were figured out on this basis. This was worked out simply by finding out how much people do eat and using this as a right or average standard. In fact, the matter was worked out by Voit, of Germany, on the basis of an enormous compilation of what German laborers, students, etc., actually do eat. It was presumed that people eat what they ought to eat in amount and kind, an assumption that is now known to be wholly false.

This method of determining food needs resulted in the absurd proposition that *everybody ought to overeat because the average person does overeat.* It led also to the ruinous notion that white flour, white sugar, denatured cereals, lard, etc., being high in caloric value, are man's best foods, while, fruits and green vegetables are almost foodless. It taught people to look upon vegetarians, fruitarians, and raw food advocates as cranks and fanatics.

This system of fire-box dietetics led to such ridiculous statements as the following from Dr. Richard C. Cabot's *Handbook of Medicine*: "Tomatoes are ninety-four per cent water; there is hardly any nutrition in them." "Lettuce for instance, is a food practically without value—nice and pleasant to look at, and valuable so far as it has dressing (made with oil). But the dressing is the only thing that has any food value." "If we take a teaspoonful of olive oil we are getting more food than if we took a large potato, for instance, because oil is a food which produces so much heat." "A workingman who buys a can of beans ought to know that he is getting many times the food for the same money as when he buys a can of tomatoes."

A few teaspoonfuls of olive oil a day should suffice to supply a man with all the food (heat units) he requires, but everyone nowadays knows that man cannot live on such a diet. The great value of lettuce is now everywhere recognized. Fruits and vegetables, formerly almost valueless, except in the estimation of a few cranks like Graham, Trall, Densmore, Page and Tilden, are coming to be more and more recognized for what they are — man's best food. It is even asserted on experimental evidence that green foods are absolutely necessary.

The estimated calorie requirements of a resting man weighing 160 lbs., is 2200 calories. Sleeping twenty-four hours, this man would expend only 1680 calories. The calorie requirements of woman are estimated to be much lower — a seamstress requiring 1800 calories a servant 2800 calories and a wash-woman 3200 calories. The seamstress requires fewer calories than the resting man, a thing I seriously doubt. Her requirements are but 120 calories more than that of the sleeping man.

Harrow says: "The calorie is a true guide to muscular activity; it seems to be no guide to the activity of the brain." Where, then, does "mental energy" come from?

The human body is more than a mere furnace or fire box into which we must continue to shovel fuel. The fuel value of food is the least valuable thing about it. White sugar is a very high grade fuel having a fuel value of 1750 calories a pound as compared to 165 calories for buttermilk, 100 calories for tomatoes and 95 calories for spinach. Yet animals fed on white sugar and water soon die. The nutritional value of food can no more be measured in calories than the value of water in the system can be stated in pounds or quarts, or in units of steam pressure.

A man may starve to death on a high calorie diet of white bread, white sugar, white rice and refined fat. He will starve on such a diet while consuming more calories each day than the standards call for. Indeed he will die quicker on a diet of this kind than he will if he takes nothing but water.

In measuring the caloric value of foods, only the combustible portions are considered. That portion of the food that does not burn, commonly referred to by the orthodox food scientist as "ash" (meaning ashes), and which is made up of the mineral content of the food, is not even considered. By such a standard oleomargarine with 3410 calories a pound is one of the greatest of food, while lemons with 155 calories, oranges with 150 calories and strawberries with 150 calories are practically worthless. Salt pork with 3555 calories a pound is a food for the gods by this standard, while celery and lettuce with only 65 calories each a pound and skim milk with but 165 calories consume more energy in digestion than they produce when oxidized. Yet neither oleomargarine nor salt pork will sustain life, health and growth. Animals fed on such a diet soon perish.

Let us bear in mind that the caloric value of food is no index to its surplus in acid or alkali elements, although most foods that rank highest in caloric value are decidedly acid-forming and rapidly break down the body.

Osborn and Mendell fed animals on a diet of denatured starches and fats, refined sugar and refined proteins and found that when so fed they rapidly declined in health. The addition of inorganic salts to the food was found to be absolutely valueless.

When the whey of milk was added to the diet their decline in health ceased. The refined sugars, starches, fats and proteins have a very high caloric value while they possess almost no food value. The whey contains none of the fats or proteins of milk but does contain iron, phosphorus, calcium, potassium and other organic salts. These tests prove that organic mineral salts are of more importance than heat units. Indeed, it may easily be shown that those foods that are the most deficient and worthless of all are the very foods which rank highest in fuel value.

Foods that are so high in caloric value that they are estimated by thousands, when fed to animals result in early death. Add to these foods the juices of foods of low caloric value and they live and grow.

Consider white bread with 1200 calories a pound and refined corn meal with 1625 calories a pound, and then think over the fact that high as these foods are in caloric value, they not only will not sustain life but actually produce death in animals fed upon these, exclusively, quicker than starvation itself. White sugar, oleomargarine, polished rice, salt pork, etc., do the same. Animals fed on these foods, or on tapioca, corn syrup, corn grits, cream of wheat, macaroni, puffed rice, corn starch, corn flakes, and other such foods possessing a high fuel value, sicken and die.

CALORIES

If the fresh juices of vegetables are added to the refined foods the animals survive but do not regain their normal weight and strength nor their resistance to disease. These vegetable juices contain no fuel value. The animals are restored to normal vigor and health only after they are fed unrefined foods such as cabbage, spinach, celery, lettuce, whole grains, whole milk, etc. These foods are so low in caloric value as compared with the refined starches, sugars, proteins, etc., that orthodox scientists formerly regarded them as being practically valueless.

A pound of apples gives but 190 calories while a pound of watermelon only yields 50 calories, but either of these foods is superior to the refined high caloric foods.

McCullum's experiments have shown that some foods will sutain growth while others will not. It is assumed that those foods that sustain growth and development contain substances to which the term vitamin has been applied. These substances are found abundantly in spinach, lettuce, cauliflower, cabbage, celery and milk. All of the refined foods already mentioned are absolutely lacking in this respect. They will neither sustain nor promote growth. Grass and grass seeds, oranges, lemons, grapefruits, tomatoes, in fact all fresh fruits and green vegetables, all of which are very low in caloric value, are rich in growth promoting elements.

Cereals and pastries are high in caloric value, but eating these in excess makes one not only look tired by actually be tired. An excess of sugar makes one lazy.

As many of the important elements of food are not oxidized in the body, a diet that is based on the assumed calorie requirements of the patient or of the non-patient, is likely to have these other elements ignored. The minerals and vitamins of foods are not employed in the production of heat and energy. Proteins, though oxidizable, therefore possessing calorie value, do not serve primarily as fuels in the body, but as building materials. Knowing the caloric value of a protein will give you no index to its amino acid content. Its building value is not measured by the amount of heat it produces when burned in the laboratory.

The assimilation and final oxidation of carbohydrates, for example, depends upon the presence of adequate amounts of other food factors that are associated with the metabolism of carbohydrates. If these are lacking in your diet, as they commonly are in conventional diets, carbohydrate metabolism will be crippled. The presence of certain vitamins is essential to proper utilization of carbohydrates.

A given amount of fat will produce a given amount of heat when burned in the laboratory. In the body, fat burns best and most efficiently in the presence of sugar. Uder many conditions of the body, fat is poorly oxidized so that it does not yield the amount of heat listed in the calorie tables. In diabetes, for example, fat metabolism is very much crippled.

Measuring food value by calories ignores the body's mineral and vitamin needs. It gives no attention to the relative values of the various proteins, and overlooks the acid-alkali ratio of the diet. It wholly forgets the *Law of the Minimum*.

In determining the fuel value of foods, not only are the growth promoting substances wholly ignored but also those elements which, though absolutely worthless from the calorific standpoint, are absolutely essential to the regulation of the specific gravity of the blood, the functioning of the blood corpuscles, the contractility of the muscles, the preservation of tissue from decomposition, the chemical reaction of the secretions, for maintaining normal alkalinity of the blood and for use in preparing the cell wastes for elimination.

Iron and manganese, which are the oxidizing agents of the blood, have no caloric value. Flourine, which forms a hard protective shell around the teeth, and calcium, which forms a large percentage of the normal composition of bone, are wholly lacking in heat producing properties. Sodium, magnesium, sulphur, potassium and other elements that are used in the processes of assimilation and elimination cannot be substituted by calories.

Calories do not build bones and teeth nor do they neutralize the acidity of the end-products of metabolism, or preserve the alkalinity of the blood and lymph. It is precisely those foods that are least fitted to perform these functions that are richest in calories.

Prof. Sherman says of the calorie: "In connection with such comparisons of food value, while of primary importance, is not alone a complete measure of its nutritive value, which will depend in part upon the amounts and forms of nitrogen, phosphorus, iron and various other essential elements furnished by food." We may add that the value of any food to the individual is partly determined by its digestibility and by the individual's present nutritive needs and powers of digestion and assimilation. It is obvious that no part of food that is not digested can be of use, however high its caloric or other value. Again food eaten, when not required or when the digestive apparatus is not prepared for the work of digestion can only produce harm.

A table giving the caloric values of different foods tells us merely how much heat can be produced in the laboratory by burning these foods. Such tables are fairly accurate indexes to the fuel values of the foods listed, but they are not an index to the nutritive values these foods have for you. You must digest them, absorb them, assimilate them and then metabolize them. If you fail to digest and absorb them, you certainly cannot assimilate and metabolize them. You can produce no heat by the oxidation of foods that pass out in the stools.

The amount of heat and energy required by various individuals varies so greatly with the conditions of sex, climate, occupation, age, size, temperament, etc., that food values based on the calorie standard are of no pracfical value. Aside from this, most of the heat produced in the body is used in maintaining normal body temperature and not for the production of energy. If health is destroyed, if the nutritive functions are impaired, to stoke up on fuel foods is not only valueless but is positively harmful. This is easily proven when we compare the results of such treatment with those obtained by the fast or by a low calorie diet which is rich in the organic mineral elements.

The burning of food in the body is a vital or physiological process and does not take place in a dead body. Food, to be burned in the body for the production of calories, is dependent upon the condition of the tissues that do the burning, a fact that is completely overlooked in feeding the sick. If the functions of the body are impaired this process is also impaired and foods that are high in fuel value cannot be properly cared for. The digestive and assimilative powers of the individual are ignored in fire-box dietetics. If energy is low, feed up the fires by shoveling in more coal.

To declare that man requires a given number of calories a day and to feed these, all the while ignoring the individual's condition, is the height of folly. In a state of nature, demand reaches forth to supply and satisfies itself. The calorie feeders force the supply even when there is no demand or when there is lack of ability to properly care for the supply. Along with this, their standard of measuring food values wholly ignores the most important elements of the food and the further fact that not all the food elements of the food that are combustible are burned in the body. Those proteins that are used in building new tissue are not used for the production of heat and energy, even if we assume that man derives his energy from food.

It should be easily seen that a system of feeding based on the caloric or fuel value of foods must inevitably lead to mischief. And this is exactly what it has done for it invariably causes patients to be stuffed with fuel foods that are deficient in the other and more vital elements. These patients are forced to eat beyond their digestive capacity in the effort to feed them the standard amount of calories. A standardized treatment without a standardized patient is a farce and a stadarized patient is an impossibility.

Hospital diets, because they are based on calorie computations, are likely to be very inadequate diets, besides being poorly prepared. Hospital diets and many other prescribed diets are still based on the supposed calorie needs of the patients. The inactive person "needs" 2000 calories a day; a moderately active person "requires" 3000 to 4000 calories a day and the vigorously active person requires 6000 calories a day. Not only is this standard based on faulty experiments, but it fails to take into account differences in individual efficiency in utilizing the food eaten.

This rule-of-thumb method of prescribing diets does not take into account individual needs and capabilities. It is as ridiculous as to say that every man at the age of twenty should be able to run a hudred yards in ten seconds. Without a standardized humanity, and we certainly do not have one, there can be no standardized diets.

It is necessary that we lose our test-tube conception of dietetics and learn to feed human beings. Man is no chemical apparatus that can be manipulated as can such a device in the laboratory. Theoretically he may need a certain amount of protein or a given number of calories, or a certain minimum of vitamins: actually, he may not be able to digest and absorb anything. Feeding must be a personal, not a rule-of-thumb affair. Formula feeding is a fallacy.

Consider for a minute the lesson of the German Raider, The Crown Prince Wilhelm. The crew was fed on a large variety of high caloric foods such as:

Breakfast: Oatmeal with condensed milk, fried potatoes, white bread, oleomargarine, coffee, white sugar and cookies.

CALORIES

Dinner: Beef soup, pea soup, lentil soup, potato soup, pot roast, fried steak, roast beef, salt fish, canned vegetables, potatoes, white bread, cookies, soda crackers, white sugar, oleomargarine, coffee, and condensed milk.

Supper: Fried steak, corned beef hash, cold roast beef, beef stew, white bread, potatoes, white sugar, cookies, oleomargarine, coffee and condensed milk.

Nearly every one of these foods possess a high calorie value, but every one of them is lacking in the organic minerals and growth promoting factors. After two hundred and fifty-five days on a diet like this, the ship steamed into Norfolk with many of her crew dead, 110 ill on their bunks and many others about ready to break down. Their ailment, which was similar to beriberi or pellagra, was "cured" by a diet that possessed almost no fuel value whatsoever, but was rich in organic salts and vitamins.

The Law of the Minimum
CHAPTER VI

The metabolic process by which an apple, a tomato or a portion of cabbage is made into hair, or muscle or nerve, or some of the cells of the eyes, or into a hormone of some of the ductless glands is beyond our present comprehension, although a few steps in this process are supposed to be known. What we do know is that if the foods we eat are to be made into tissues and secretions, they must contain adequate amounts and due proportions of all the elements needed in the production of these things. Just as we cannot make concrete with cement alone or with sand alone, but must, if our concrete is to be good, have due proportions of both, so, if we are to have good structures in our bodies, we must have adequate amounts and proper proportions of all the food elements that go into the construction of these structures.

To make the best use of any food element, such, for example, as the proteins, certain other food substances and possibly a variety of them must be available in the diet in definite proportions. No food element is of itself of more importance in the body than another. It is only by the combination of all the necessary ones that the whole may be obtained.

Liebig laid down a *"law of the minimum"* in these words: *"The development of living beings is regulated by the supply of whichever element is least bountifully provided."*

The law of the minimum implies that the nutritive value of any food-mixture, however abundant most of the food elements therein may be, is limited by the minimum quantity of any essential element it may contain; unless, as it happens in certain food constituents, the lacking factor may be synthesized from some of the more abundant food elements, fat from sugar, for example.

Calcium cannot be utilized in producing enamel in the absence of phosphorus. If phosphorus is present in inadequate amounts, the enamel will be of poor quality. If iron is lacking, there will also be poor enamel. If any one of the vitamins is lacking poor enamel is the result.

THE LAW OF THE MINIMUM

The united "action" of minerals, proteins, vitamins, etc., in the production of tissues and fluids in the body is called "synergistic action." Since they do not act, but are used, it may be more correct to say that the body makes correlated use of them. At any rate, a knowledge of the "synergistic action" of the food elements and vitamins is of vast importance and helps to make clear to us the *Law of the Minimum*.

Tooth enamel is made up largely of calcium and phosphorus with small quantities of iron. But the fusion of these substances into enamel requires the presence of vitamines A, C and D. At least half a dozen elements and factors are essential to the production of this tissue. In the absence of either of these factors the enamel of the teeth cannot be made. It is folly to feed much calcium in an effort to produce good teeth and to ignore the other essential elements of the teeth.

Many different tissues are being built and repaired in the body at all times. These tissues are constantly engaged in a wide variety of activities. This means that there is a continuous use of vitamins, minerals, amino acids, sugars and fatty acids in the body. Consuming an abundance of a single vitamin or of a single mineral is not sufficient to meet the needs of the many "synergistic actions" that are in constant process in the body. All of the vitamins and all of the minerals are required. If all the nutritive elements are present in adequate quantities and in due proportions, all the synergisms of all the minerals, vitamins, amino acids, sugars, etc., are at work piling up their benefits.

It is well to keep in mind that these "synergistic actions" are far more complex and broader than our description of them would indicate. The many functions of the body are also *synergistic*. The function of one part of the body is dependent upon the functions of all other parts. Feeding vitamin B in certain forms of nervous trouble with the aim of remedying the nervous impairment, and ignoring the correlated functions of the body that support nerve function, is doomed to failure. All of the "synergistic chemical actions" in all parts of the body must be adequately provided for before the actions of any part can be ideal. This is the thing that makes specific diets so unsatisfactory.

The work of potassium in promoting the formation of proteins, fats and glycogen, is not essentially unlike the work ascribed to vitamins. Zinc is thought to be connected with the action of the vitamins, which it seems to be able to replace to some extent, at least in the animal organism. Lithium is also thought to influence metabolism in a way not unlike that of the vitamins. The same is true of copper, nickel and of arsenic. It should be borne in mind that little is known about the offices of zinc, lithium, copper, nickel and arsenic in the body and that experimenters, carrying out their experiments, have wholly neglected these elements.

In plant life and growth the *Law of the Minimum* has long been known. If perfect growth is to be procured in plants, these must find a certain minimum of each of several elements in the soil in which they are grown. If only half the needed amount of potassium, for example, is present, then, regardless of how abundant all the other soil elements may be, their normal utilization is reduced one-half. The rate of growth of the plant and its ultimate development are correspondingly depressed.

Prof. Osterhout showed that seeds placed in distilled water grow better than when placed in water containing but one salt, and that each salt exerts a specific toxic effect according to its chemical nature. He found that one salt "counteracts" the effects of another.

An excess of nitrogen in the soil retards the formation of grain, roots and tubers and gives rise to sickly plants. Nitrogen excess in the soil of rose beds leads to the production of soft, sappy tissues, a luxuriant growth of leaves, and roses with little or no perfume.

Plant processes, from germination to ripening of their seed, are a drama of physiological minerals and gases. Without a sufficiency of lime or potash in the soil, acids, sugars and starches cannot be formed; without iron no chlorophyll and no albumen can be formed. Without silica no fibre or plant skeleton, etc. Each mineral plays a definite role in the growth of healthy plants.

The actual amount of potassium requisite for plant growth is very small compared with the needed amount of carbon or nitrogen. But if this relatively small quantity is not available the utilization of other constituents in tissue growth or repair is always deficient.

If one essential food element, which normally should compose one per cent of the food eaten, is present in only half this amount, then, the body will only be able to utilize the other elements, in tissue building, in the same reduced quantity.

The organic whole — the unit — is official to animal nutrition. Not the sum total of the minerals consumed, but their relative proportions, determines the nutritive value of any given dietary.

THE LAW OF THE MINIMUM

A certain minimum amount of organic salts is essential to optimal growth. A further increase in these, even a great increase, does not further influence growth. Not only the total quantity of these salts, but also the quantities of the individual minerals and their mutual quantitive relationships are of decisive importance in regulating the assimilation of proteins.

If we are to have normal development the mineral elements in our diet must also be present in minimum quantities, but they must also represent proper ratios one to another. The mineral salts are most sensitive to any deficiency of any of them in the diet. Many common foodstuffs are deficient in iron and calcium, and these deficiencies reduce the ability of the body to assimilate the other elements. On the other hand, in experimental diets, any increase of one element raises the mineral requirements of all the others.

If health and development are to follow, certain relationships must prevail between the various salts. Berg, McCarrison, McCollum and others have amply demonstrated this. Rose found that a certain relationship must prevail between calcium and magnesium if the maximum development of the body is to be attained. Between lime and potassium, lime and sodium, potassium and magnesium and between the metals on the one hand and sulphur and phosphorus on the other, an optimum ratio exists.

The proper exploitation of both proteins and carbohydrates is determined by mineral metabolism, since they can be more readily oxidized in an alkaline medium than when an excess of acids is present. It has been repeatedly shown that an excess of bases over acid-forming foodstuffs ingested promotes the utilization of proteins. Zunts, of Berlin, showed that diabetics can more easily oxidize sugar if the body has an abundance of bases at its disposal. Abderhalden performed investigations which showed that a diet rich in bases is essential for the proper functioning of the hormones of the ductless glands.

Without iron there can be no oxygen supply for the cells. Without copper there can be no assimilation of iron. Without sodium there is no elimination of carbon-dioxide from the tissues of the body. Every physico-chemical process of the body is correlated with others and any failure in one spells a corresponding failure in the correlated processes.

May Mellanby says that the evidence shows that the calcium in the diet does not in itself directly control the calcification of the teeth, but that it is subservient to other dietetic factors. One of these is vitamin A. She thinks that she has demonstrated the existence of factors in some foods, particularly in cereals, and more especially in oats, that inhibit calcification. Phosphorus is as essential to the formation of good bones and teeth as is lime.

The present furore over vitamins has caused many ex-spurts to concentrate their whole attention upon these substances and almost forget the other elements of nutrition. We pick up a book or a magazine article or a report dealing with nutritional problems and we learn that a diet rich in vitamin A does thus and so, or a diet poor in vitamin B results in such and such effects. The minerals in the diets are particularly overlooked. Interest in vitamins is causing us to forget the importance of other food elements.

The present over-emphasis on vitamins is as absurd as if we were similarly to over-emphasize sodium, or magnesium. To ignore the organic salts, as is so often done in our mad rush for vitamins, is as foolish as would be the ignoring of the vitamins.

It has been demonstrated that regardless of the amount of vitamin A supplied in the diet, if some other constituent of the diet is wholly lacking, vitamin A can have no effect. Berg shows that on a cereal diet complettin A is without effect unless sodium and calcium are added to the diet in sufficient quantities to produce an excess of bases. McCollum and his co-workers have shown that when there is an abundance of vitamin A in the diet, the mother cannot secrete sufficient milk for her progeny, unless her food contains an adequate amount of organic salts in proper proportions.

The absence of anyone of the essential vitamins prevents the rest of them from functioning at all. If any one of them is present in but one-half or in but one-fourth the required amount, then the others, though abundantly present, will function only up to one-half or one-fourth of their full effectiveness.

Lack of vitamins disturbs calcium metabolism. A lack of calcium or an excess of calcium in the diet renders vitamin A of no effect. Vitamins are valuable only in the presence of each other. Calcium seems to be usable only in the presence of vitamin A.

McCarrison says that "in the absence of vitamins or in their inadequate supply, neither proteins, fats nor carbohydrates nor salts are properly utilized; some are largely wasted, while others yield products harmful to the organism. In such circumstances life may be sustained for a longer or shorter period, during which the body utilizes its stores of vitamins and sacrifices its less important tissues to this end. But there is a limit beyond which such stores cannot be drawn upon, and once this is reached the cells of higher function — secretory, endocrine and nerve cells — begin to lack vigor, and to depreciate in functional capacity, although the tissues may continue to hold considerable stores of vitamins. The disintegration process is delayed or hastened, lessened in severity in one direction or increased in severity in another, according to the character of their lack of balance."

There are many kinds of proteins and where one is securing his protein from one source only he is likely to suffer from protein inadequacy even though he is consuming an excessive amount of protein. The biological value of the various proteins varies considerably.

Proteins are broken down into their constituent amino-acids in the process of digestion and these amino-acids are employed in constructing new and different proteins in the body, but amino-acids may be utilized by the body only to the extent that the diet supplies other protein constituents which enable the body to synthesize them into proteins proper to man. If more amino-acids are introduced into the blood than the presence of other elements will enable the body to utilize, the amino-acid content of the blood rises and there is an increased excretion of amino-acids in the urine.

It is at once apparent from this, that growth can proceed at an ideal rate only as rapidly as all of the essentials of growth become available to the growing organism.

It is found, in harmony with this law, that in the case of proteins, the value of a protein or mixture of proteins for structural purposes in the body, is limited if one of the indispensable amino-acids is deficient or wholly lacking. If and when this deficiency is remedied, a deficient supply of some other indispensable amino-acid constitutes a further limitation.

Attempts are often made to determine the value of an article of food by using as an index to its fitness, the amount of some element contained in it; let us say phosphorus. This effort is based on a misconception of the office of these elements in nutrition. To over-emphasize the importance of any of the salts — iron, calcium, potassium — or of any of the vitamins or complettins, or of protein or carbohydrate is to overlook the essential fact that these things function in nutrition only in union with the other elements.

This law of the minimum applies even to water. It has been shown repeatedly that if water is limited to a certain extent in the diet of infants, and all the other growth essentials are adequate, growth will not take place. Children placed on dehydrated diets can be taught within a very short time to take and be content with a small amount of water. The body establishes a water balance on a very low level but does not grow.

Many scientists have concentrated on single issues, seeking in these the secrets of life. But this concentration on one detail caused them to overlook the importance of the *tout ensemble*. Schaumann, for example, attempted to show that beriberi (polyneuritis) is due to the loss of a phosphorus compound in the milling of whole grains. Chamberlain checked up on his assumption and found it to be wrong. Several elements are lost in the milling of grains and the troubles resulting from consuming denatured grains grow out of the total deficiency.

The effort to supply us with isolated vitamins and minerals is essentially a medical rather than a tropholgic procedure and harks back to the antiquated notions that there are "specific diseases," having specific causes and requiring specific remedies.

Every tissue builder is dependent upon all the others. The decisive factor in development is not so much the absolute quantity of the various food elements in the diet, but their relative proportions. The organism's need for one element of food may be supplied only when all other elements are supplied in relative proportions. The diet must contain a sufficiency of all essential food elements, but there must be no great excess of any of these.

The amount of any given element available for utilization by the body depends, not alone upon the proportions of other elements present in the diet, but also upon other factors. The organic salts enter into important reciprocal relationships, especially in the work of secretion, but also in the process of synthesizing new organic compounds, so that we are concerned with both a qualitative and a quantitive minimum. If an element is being fed in quantities that are adequate *per se*, but some other and antagonistic substance is also being given, the quantity of the first is thereby rendered inadequate. An adequate amount of calcium, for example, would be ren-

THE LAW OF THE MINIMUM

dered inadequate by the medical administration of acids, or by acid fermentation in the digestive tract. The calcium would be exhausted in neutralizing the acids and little or none would be left for the body. An abundance of calcium coupled with a lack of sodium means trouble, for the sodium is essential to keep the calcium in solution.

The availability of a food element depends, not alone upon the amount and form of this element present in the food, but also upon the quantities of other elements present. The quantity of available calcium, for example, does not depend wholly upon the absolute quantity of calcium in the diet, but upon the quantity of mineral bases generally present in one's food. A shortage of these bases involves a drain on the calcium for purposes of acid-neutralization, and cosumes an amount of calcium which would otherwise be available for assimilation.

After the alkaline salts have been consumed in neutralizing the acids in the foods thmselves, the residue of these are available for storage in the body as a reinforcement of its alkaline reserve. The availability of the alkaline elements is proportioned to their excess over the food acids. This is the reason that our diet should at all times be preponderantly alkaline. McCarrison showed that an excess of fat or of unsaturated oleic acid in the food may cause a relative deficiency of iodine and enlargement of the thyroid.

MacCollum, of Johns Hopkins, states in his *Pathology* that there seems to be some relation between the deposition of calcium and the available supply of iron. Iron is not assimilated in the absence of copper.

An excellent example of this matter, on the positive side, is the increased protein-calcium-phosphorous retention produced by the use of oranges. The regular use of oranges results in an increased retention of these elements out of all proportion to the amounts of these actually present in the fruit itself.

It has been found that a diet with an acid-ash residue results in a greater excretion of minerals than one with an alkaline ash. Oranges give an alkaline ash. Indeed, the addition of oranges to a decidedly acid-ash diet of much cereal, meat, and few vegetables, gives such a marked alkaline result that it shifts the reaction of the urine from a decidedly acid reaction to a decidedly alkaline one. This means increased mineral retention and also increased nitrogen assimilation.

Drs. Miller and Newell, of Iowa State College, added an ounce and a half of orange juice daily for three months to the otherwise unchanged diet of fourteen underweight children and tabulated the results. The weight of these children increased 146 per cent of the expected gain, in contrast with only 46 per cent observed during the preceding three months.

Dr. Cheney, of California, fed a group of undernourished children an orange a day. To another group he gave no oranges. During two different periods of two months each, the children who received the oranges gained an average of 141 and 118 per cent above the expected increases. The other group, without oranges, gained only 28 and 18 per cent above the expected gain. During the non-orange juice periods, including the preliminary days, the children gained an average of .08 pounds a day; with the oranges they gained an average of .3 pounds a day — approximately four times as much as without the fruit.

Failure of growth may rightly be considered a deficiency disease although, on certain types of diets, both animals and man maintain good health and proportionate development, failing only to attain their normal sizes. Except for size they seem to be normal animals. This is explained by the law of the minimum given at the beginning of this chapter. Such diets contain all the needed food elements and growth is determined by the elements least bountifully supplied.

Unfortuate experiences such as famine, war, poverty, and the ignorance that causes many people to feed upon denatured diets, prove that the laws of nutrition and growth are the same in man as in the lower animals and plants. The wise will understand.

To secure the highest possible development from food, it must be adequate in every respect. All of the food nutrients must be present in sufficient quantities and in due proportions and in digestible and assimilable, that is, available, form. This adaptation in the food is relatively more important while the child is growing most rapidly, and less important as the birth period, is receded from. Suitable variety and proper blending of foods, therefore, cannot be ignored, if we desire the highest vigor and greatest development in our children. Happily, except in isolated places and among the most poverty-stricken classes, the diet of the child may be easily controled. Knowledge of correct feeding is needed by mothers.

McCarrison noted that under about the same conditions of filth and squalor, the Sihks and Pathans were much larger than the Madrassis and other peoples of India. He found the Sihks and Pathans eating leafy vegetables, curds and cheese, and these are lacking in the general Indian diet.

He fed a group of rats on the Sihk and Pathan diet and another group on the general Indian diet. The first group grew to great size; the second group remained small. He fed other groups on the customary Japanese diet, Philipino diet, Javanese diet and the characteristic diet of the ill-nourished English working man. The results of these diets he checked with the results of the Sihk-Pathan diet. The results were the same. All groups, except those fed on the English diet, were small in size; while the latter group attained nearly the size of the group fed on the Sihk diet but had rough coats and a combative disposition.

Experiments with Japanese school children, covering several years, show that similar additions to the regular diet of Japanese children cause them to grow to be several inches taller and several pounds heavier than the average Japanese child.

A few years ago the New York Times carried the picture of three boys of the same age (eight years); one an average American boy, of average size for his age; the other two, European boys, whose growth had been stunted by inadequate food. Neither of the European boys reached to the horizontally outstreched arms of the American boy. The European boys were victims of the war that had deprived them of food. In accordance with the law of the minimum, the growth of these two boys was relative to the element least abundant in their diet.

McCollum has repeatedly demonstrated that if a litter of rats is divided into two groups of four each, and one group is fed distilled water and whole wheat only, and the other group exactly the same quantities of distilled water and whole wheat, plus the addition of turnip or beet leaves, each rat in the first group will only attain the size of a large mouse; whereas, those in the second group will attain nearly double the size of those in the first group. Except as to size both groups of rats are "normal" in all respects.

We cannot better sum up what has gone before than in the following words of McCarrison: "It is unwise to consider any of the essential ingredients of food, whether proteins, carbohydrates, fats, salts, water, or vitamins, as independent of the assistance derivable from their associates in the maintenance of digestive and nutritional harmony. No doubt some of these have special relations to others, as for instance that of iodine to fats, that of vitamin B to carbohydrates, that of vitamin A to lipoids, calcium and phosphorus holding substances, and that of vitamin C to inorganic salts. But whatever be their special relations to one another they are all links in the chain of essential substances requisite for the harmonious regulation of life's processes; if one link be broken, the harmony ceases or becomes discord."

Organic Foods
CHAPTER VII

The words *organic* and *inorganic* have undergone considerable change of meaning within recent years and these changes have led to much confusion in thought and practice. *Organic* means pertaining to an organ; connected with or pertaining to the bodily or vital organs of plant or animal — *organic structure, organic disease, organic chemistry, organic function;* combined with function; having a definite, systematic structural arrangement; organized; an organic whole; a complete unity. Originally, *organic chemistry* was that dealing with the products of animal and vegetable organisms. At present, it is largely restricted to the study of carbon and hydrogen compounds.

Not long since, *anatomy* was defined as "the science of organization." The anatomist differentiated between the words *organized* and *organic.* The term *organized* was used to refer to things which have organs — parts which are differentiated from each other. *Organic* was applied to things which result from the vital (synthetic) activities of organized bodies. Substances which did not result from vital synthesis were referred to as *inorganic.*

Today this is all changed. The term *organic* is used to designate all carbon compounds, whether formed in the body or not. The term *inorganic* is now regularly applied to food substances that result from the synthetic activities of the living organism which were formerly called *organic.* The best examples of this are the food salts contained in all plant and animal foods. There is a tendency to make no distinction between the salts in foods and those in the chemist's laboratory. Indeed, it is commonly thought that the salts of the laboratory may be readily used by the body as substitutes for the salts that should exist in our foods.

All of this confusion has come about by defining *organic* to mean carbon and hydrogen compounds, whereas, it really means products of the synthetic activities of the organs of an *organized* being — an *organism.* Bear in mind that the basic meaning of *organic* is pertaining to an organ. Chemists should stick to their own terminology and cease trying to pervert the terms of biology.

The chemist observes that silt may eventually become flesh, but he overlooks the many refining metabolisms through which it must be carried by both plant and animal before it can be "made flesh." He can only feebly imitate, he cannot duplicate, Nature's creations.

The chemist manipulates the elements that filled the great void before the spirit of the Supreme Synthesizer acted upon it. He can produce a dummy egg, but he cannot make a viable one. A viable egg contains all the potentialities of a new animal. The chemist's egg seems to have everything — that is, everything except the power to evolve into a new animal. Man's creations turn out to be clay, slag, delusion. The chemist cannot make an egg that will hatch. His science is no match for the rooster. The compounds of evolution are vastly different from the synthetic compounds of the chemist. Only his egomania causes the chemist to think he can create a viable egg out of lifeless elements.

The natural order of nutrition is for the plant to "eat" the soil and the animal to eat the spare products of the plant. This order was established many long ages ago and has been in operation as long as plant and animal life have existed side by side on our globe. It has worked very successfully throughout all this time and our present efforts to skip the refining work of the plant and go directly to the soil for our sustenance makes us appear ridiculous. The common use of table salt (sodium chloride), the employment by physicians of calcium salts, iron salts, and other such preparations and the employment of so-called "tissue salts" by certain types of physicians amount to an effort to skip the plant and eat the soil. Sprinkling various salts of this nature on foods is a similar effort. These practices are direct outgrowths of our science mania.

The body does not employ nitrogen as such — it uses proteins, or, more specifically, amino acids. Acceptable amino acids are manufactured by the plant kingdom only. The animal cannot manufacture them out of the elements. The body does not use carbon as such— it uses carbohydrates, or, more specifically, simple sugar: *monosaccharide*. Acceptable sugars are prepared by the plant kingdom only. The animal can convert some of the protein compounds into sugar, but it cannot manufacture sugar out of the elements. The body does not use carbon in making fats. It uses chiefly fatty acids. It can manufacture fat out of sugar and protein, but it cannot manufacture it out of the elements. It is dependent upon plants to take the "dust of the earth" and make this into acceptable compounds — *organic substances*. The animal body cannot manufacture *organic salts* out of the elemnts of the soil. It must receive these ready prepared from the plant. The animal is incapable of manufacturing vitamins out of the elements. From the plant it must receive either the vitamin or the pro-vitamin. The synthetic activities of plants manufacture the food supplies of the whole animal world.

Can the chemist supplant the work of the plant? This has long been his dream. He has sought to duplicate the products of the plant world and make these serve as foods for man and animals. He claims a certain measure of success. But, since the body draws a sharp line of distinction between laboratory compounds of all kinds and those resulting from the synthetic activities of plant life, we prefer to apply the term *organic* to these latter and inorganic to the crude substances of the earth and to the products of the laboratory.

We have not learned to make, nor even to imitate living substances. We know that animals are dependent upon plants for their food and cannot go directly to the soil for it. We can neither synthesize these substances in the laboratory, nor can we tear them down in the kitchen or in the laboratory in "purifying" them (extracting their salts from them) without greatly impairing their food values. It is a mistake to assume, as these experimenters do, that chemical substances constitute nourishment irrespective of their form or condition.

Chlorophyll is the great organic laboratory. By its aid and the aid of sunlight plants take up the crude elements of the soil and carbon and nitrogen from the air and synthesize these into organic combinations. Plants alone can do this. Animals cannot do it. Man cannot do it in the laboratory.

Plants, at least working plants as distinguished from parasitic and saprophytic plants, manufacture proteins, carbohydrates, hydrocarbons, organic salts and vitamins. We say that soil is the food of plants; we could, with equal propriety say that plant substances are the soil of animals.

"All nutrient material is formed in the vegetable kingdom, in the growing process — the green state," says Trall. "No animal organization can create or form any food of any kind. All that the animal can do is to use or appropriate what nutrient material the vegetable kingdom has provided. The vegetable kingdom is intermediate between the mineral and animal kingdom."

Animals cannot use soil materials, nor can they synthesize carbohydrates out of carbon and water. For the same reason that they cannot utilize the minerals of the soil, but must receive them in the form of organic salts resulting from plant processes, they cannot utilize drug minerals or the inorganic salts produced in the chemical or pharmaceutical laboratory.

The animal cannot synthesize amino-acids, the constituent "building stones" of proteins; nor sugars, the constituent "building sctones" of fats; nor vitamins. He must receive these from the plant kingdom. Synthetic vitamins, now so much advertised, are no more useful than the inorganic salts offered by the chemists. Animals are dependent upon plants for organic foods — for proteins, sugars, starches, fats, organic salts and vitamins. All foods come, either directly or indirectly from the plant kingdom.

We have it contended by the proponents of the use of various inorganic salts, called by them, "tissue salts," "bio-chemical remedies," "vito-chemical remedies," etc., that there is no difference between crude minerals and organic salts except in the fineness of the particles. They contend that if these inorganic substances are ground finely enough, the body can make use of them. So, they grind these in a suitable medium and prescribe and administer them.

Physical chemistry reveals that a mineral may be divided into the smallest possible particle — individual ions — by simply dissolving it in water. Eperience with these salts proves that they are not remedial. Dr. Tilden's testimony is to the point. He says he gave them a thorough trial at one time in his career and found them to be worthless.

No animal — there are a few lowly forms that are said to be exceptions to this, but these exceptions are very doubtful — can make constructive use of any mineral unless he gets it through the plant kingdom. The mineral salts must be synthesized into living tissue before the digestive and metabolic systems of man, or animal, can use them in body building, body cleansing or for any other constructive purposes.

The inability of the animal organism to take the elements of earth, air and water and synthesize amino-acids, carbon chains, organic salts, vitamins, etc., from these renders the animal absolutely dependent upon the plant kingdom for its food supply. As these food constituents cannot be synthesized by the animal body its needs for these substances can be satisfied in no other way than by their provision, ready made, in plant foods. The ultimate source of all food needs of the animal body, except water and oxygen, is, therefore, the vegetable kingdom. The main supply would appear to be derived from the green and growing parts of plants.

The animal body is capable of building up the most complex forms of protein providing the necessary carbon chains and amines are supplied in the diet. The cow, the sheep, the pig, the chicken, or other animal that you may eat, is compelled to secure the absolutely indispensable amino acids from external (that is, plant) sources. There is nothing in the animal body that was not derived from the plant kingdom — nothing, that is, except water and oxygen.

The proven fact that the organism of higher animals. is incompetent to synthesize carbon chains, or to effect ring closure and that only in rarest cases can they achieve amination and then only by making use of ready prepared and more complex amino acids, that it cannot synthesize vitamins and organic salts — this lack of ability to make the fundamental syntheses compels the animal to rely exclusively upon organic substances for its food supply. I repeat: the normal order of feeding is, *plants feed upon soil and animals feed upon the spare products of plants.* The dream of the chemist to be able to reverse this order is an expression of his egomania.

Organic salts are in the colloidal form. Colloidal iron or calcium or phosphorus are usable. Inorganic salts are crystaloids and are not usable. Crude minerals, after they have been organized by the plant kingdom into highly complex compounds, are assimilated and used by the body, but taken in their elementary state, are injurious, some of them even deadly poison, to the body. The plant takes the elements of the soil and synthesizes these into acceptable compounds. The animal is limited to these compounds.

Carque very appropriately says: "Even the embryonic plant must feed on the organic compounds of the seed until its roots and leaves are grown. The elevation and characteristic change of inorganic matter, which takes place principally in the green leaves of the plant, by means of the chlorophyll, is the starting point of all organic combinations. Chlorophyll is, therefore, a substance of great physiological importance."

Only along special lines have chemists been able to repeat or feebly imitate the productions of nature. The essentially living products not only carnot be produced in the laboratory, they are, as yet, but little known. So-called bio-chemistry is not what its name implies. Life can exist only in a complex mixture; the chemist studies merely isolated fragments. The physiological and biological chemists all seem to have missed the conception of the individuality of the living mass, as a complex of elements and compounds, each of which bears a special and vital relationship to each other. Each element is vitally essential to the welfare of the whole mass.

Biochemistry is largely guess work. The chemists do not know exactly what processes take place in the living organism. They write learned treatses on bio-chemistry, but it is 98% guess work.

Just as the animal body is unable to synthesize amino acids, but is confined for its supply of these, to the plant kingdom; so, it cannot synthesize "organic" salts from the crude or "inorganic" salts supplied by doctors and druggists. The plant kingdom is the great laboratory in which animal food is synthesized and our chemists have not learned to duplicate vegetable processes. Imitate some of them, yes, but there is a vast difference betwen the ability to produce urea and the ability to synthesize proteins.

We must secure our mineral salts from food. We cannot get them from any other source. The power to assimilate crude matter, as it exists in the soil, and convert it into structures of living bodies is a monopoly of the vegetable kingdom. It is the office of plant life or vegetation to take the primary elements in their crude form and convert them into the organic state. No synthetic process known to the laboratory can do this.

After the plant has raised the crude earth-elements to the plane of plant substance, the animal may then take them and raise them still higher, that is, convert them into animal matter. The animal is forced to secure food either directly or indirectly from the plant kingdom. He either eats the plant, or else he eats the animal that has eaten the plant. Air and water form the only exceptions to this rule.

We know that the same elements, with practically the same chemical compositions may be wholesome food in one case and virulent poison in another. The protein of nuts and nitric acid both owe their distinctive characteristics to the nitrogen they contain. Sugar and alcohol not only contain the same elements, but represent very nearly the same chemical combinations. One is a good food, the other a strong poison. They taste and smell unlike and when consumed do not produce the same effects.

ORGANIC FOODS

The air is rich in nitrogen. Plants are able to absorb it and assimilate it — to make proteins out of it. But animals cannot. We must get our nitrogen from foods.

It was pointed out in a previous chapter that the body it unable to manufacture vitamins and the essential amino-acids. It is capable of manufacturing sugars out of more than one kind of organic substance, but cannot produce this from crude carbon. Only in organic combinations are minerals usable. Only plants — vegetables and fruits — with the aid of sunshine, are capable of taking the crude mineral elements of the soil and organizing them.

Salts built up by plants, we shall call organic salts and those built up by other processes we shall call inorganic. The chemist may continue to declare that he can find no difference in the two groups of materials, but the animal body continues to make a distinction and to draw a sharp line of demarkation between the salts the chemist turns out and those turned out by the plant.

Iron is an essential element of the body. It is especially found in the red blood cells. We get it from fruits and vegetables. As we there find it, it is usable. But we cannot supply our bodies with iron by eating saw fillings or pig-iron. Its frequent use in drug form upsets digestion, producing headache, gastric distress and constipation.

Elements are *available* only in certain forms. We must draw our minerals from foods. In like manner must we draw our vitamins from foods. Synthetic vitamins are as useless as earth salts before these have been organized by the plant.

McCann truly says: "We must not assume because the chemist has calculated the iron of the red blood corpuscles as 'iron oxide' that it would be a good thing, therefore, to go to a drug store and purchase a dose of iron oxide. The iron in the blood does not exist in such form. The chemist has to reduce it to such form before he can recover it from the organic compounds in which it is found in life.

"Herein lies the great error made by the patent medicine manufacturer (also by the ethical practitioner. Author), who tries to make the people believe that because certain salts are found in the human body therefore medicines containing them are good for the human body.

'To assume that because 'calcium oxide' appears in an analysis of the blood serum it must therefore appear in the blood serum itself as calcium oxide is a childish error.

"The calcium, iron and other mineral salts as they appear in the blood and internal secretions are present in such wonderfully complex forms that they cannot be reproduced in the drug store or laboratory."

Otto Carque says: "In natural foods iron is found solely in the form of complicated iron compounds which have been built up by the life processes of plants. From these compounds hemoglobin is produced in the animal organism, which is not able to construct the highly complex organic molecule from inorganic substances." He points out that foods are organic wholes, "in which the tissue salts are chemically associated with the organic substances, and only in this form are they able to sustain vital force."

Experiments on anemic rats with diets containing drug iron, food ash containing iron, flour to which copper was added, etc., showed that by no kind of trick or makeshift diet could the anemia be overcome. The rats had to have real foods from nature's own food laboratory — the plant kingdom — in order to recover.

Thousands of invalids, feeble children, chlorotic girls and anemic patients are taking iron daily, often by injections, in drug preparations, and upon the prescription of a doctor. This is supposed to supply any deficiency in this element and give them health and strength. The practice is a snare and a delusion. It sometimes induces a facetious simulation of health, and deceives both the physician and his patient. But it has long been known that such iron is not assimilated by the body, while, when given to chlorotic individuals of the tubercular diathesis, it hastens the development of tuberculosis.

Phosphorus is a necessary constituent of the bones and nerves. But we must supply it to the body as we find it in plants. Crude rock phosphorus as it comes from the earth, is a powerful poison. Laws now prohibit its use in the manufacture of matches, because of its poisonous character. It particularly affects the jaw bone producing a condition known as "Fossy jaw." Its continued use, as a medicine, even in small doses, produces anemia and emaciation. Although so vitally essential to bone and nerve, phosphorus, when not "organized," as we find it in plants, is the most virulent poison of any of the normal elements of the human body. A man of average size contains, normally, about two pounds of phosphorus, but two grains of this "disorganized" (this may be done by calcination of a bone), given to a healthy man, produces great excitement, particularly of the brain. Delirium, inflammation and death may be the result in a single hour. Ten times this amount, taken as nature gives it to us in food, produces no such trouble.

Phosphorus poisoning is characterized by nervous and mental symptoms, jaundice, vomtiting, general fatty degeneration, the presence of bile pigments, albumen and other abnormal constituents in the urine, followed by death.

Chronic phosphorus poisoning was quite common among workers in match-factories. Necrosis of the jaw bone was one of its frequent results. It ranks with mercury in its power to wreck the bones.

It is claimed that animals and children are able to utilize inorganic phosphorus in building up their bones. Hens seem able to use inorganic phosphorus in making egg shells. But when we come to the question: Is the animal organism capable of building up organic phosphorus compounds out of inorganic phosphorus? — we are face to face with a different and vital problem.

Berg says "here most physiologists make the mistake of failing to distinguish between salt-like or ester-like compounds (the so-called mixed-organic compounds) and compounds into which the phosphorus has entered as a constituent part of an organic complex. Yet the chemical distinction is vital." "So far as the more highly organized animals, at any rate, are concerned, we do not know a single instance of such genuine reduction of phosphorus and the incompetence of the animal organism to achieve this reduction is the probable explanation of the inability of the higher animals to synthesize carbon chains." "Innumerable investigators have studied the problem, and almost all of them have come to the conclusion that no such synthesis can be effected within the animal body."

Sulphur is poisonous. Yet sulphur is a necessary constituent of the body, and when supplied as nature prepares it in food, is wholesome. But as a medicine it is unwholesome.

Berg reviews all of the experiments made, which are claimed to show that the animal body can make use of inorganic salts, and shows that faulty experimental methods have been present in every case. Taking the case of sulphur he says, "We know this element in the organism only in the form of cystein or its 'anhydrite' cystin, although there can be do doubt that quite a number of sulphur compounds are represented in the 'neutral sulphur' of the urine. *** Cystin is a vitally essential substance which cannot be synthesized within the animal body." Osborn and Mendel have repeatedly noted that growth, and even the mere maintenance of weight, are impossible unless ready-made cystin is supplied. Sulphur compounds are available for assimilation only in the forms in which they exist in organic matter.

Lime, or calcium, cannot be supplied to the body by feeding it crude rock lime or chalk. In such a form, lime is an irritant and a corrosive. In the "unslacked" form, it is highly destructive of the tissues of the body. Lime water, so often given to infants, is of no value to them and produces much injury. We must take this as it is supplied by plants.

Inappropriate food may actually "drive out" appropriate food. "Large doses of calcium chloride," says Berg, "induce severe losses of calcium, which may culminate in osteoporosis and osteomalacia in the experimental animals." The calcium chloride actually induces a hyperacidity within the body and so great an impoverishment of the alkali reserves of the body that those of the bones are called upon to neutralize the acids.

A "biological antagonism" between soluble alkalies and the alkaline earths is known to exist in animal physiology. "If the bicarbonates, or indeed, any salt of sodium or potassium, be administered to a human being in fair quantity for any brief but appreciable period, the following extraordinary phenomenon is manifest: large quantities of calcium and magnesium salts immediately make their appearance in the urine, thus showing that sodium or potassium when administered to an animal in excess at once exhibits so strong a contrast in the economy of that animal that immediately a large output of calcium and magnesium occurs."—Reinheimer.

Berg says, "With the exception of calcium carbonate and tricalcium phosphate all the inorganic calcium salts induce acidity in the organism. Rose has repeatedly noted the production of acidity in adult human beings by calcium chloride and calcium sulphate; and Fuhge, Erich Muller's assistant, noted the same thing in testing my statements by giving lime salts to children."

Berg has pointed out that the acid radical (carbon) in calcium carbonate can be freely discharged in the gaseous form through the lungs, so that no bases are requisite to assist in its excretion."

ORGANIC FOODS

Copp and others, investigating the nutritional factors in arthritis, found that it is essential to restore the calcium balance before recovery can take place. They found that when inorganic calcium salts or other basic salts in the inorganic form are given these are rapidly eliminated and are not assimilated by the tissues. The bodies of animals can make use of salts only as these are prepared for them by the plant kingdom, a symbiotic dependence of great significance.

There is no doubt that the inorganic salts of the drug store may be absorbed into the body more or less and, perhaps, some of them may be employed to a limited extent in such purely chemical processes as the neutralization of acids. But they cannot become parts of the teeth, muscles, nerves, blood or glands of the body.

Experiments seem to show that where there is a deficiency of salts in the diet, the use of inorganic salts—wood ashes, for example—will enable the animal body to use all or nearly all of the available organic salts in building tissue. There is no evidence, however, that such additions to the diet can make the diet equal to one adequate in organic salts. In most cases, however, these things seem to merely induce fatty degeneration.

Iodine is supplied in a usable form in foods. Drug iodine is a rank poison. The prolonged use of iodine and its compounds produces a condition known as iodism; characterized by violent colds, headaches, increased salivary secretion (insalivation), a metallic taste, gastric irritation and an acne rash. It has accounted for many deaths, while its use in goitre has proven not only a failure but disastrous. Food iodine never does this.

The following quotation from *American Medicine*, May, 1926, gives a partial picture of the effects of inorganic iodine compounds:

"In view of the wide publicity that has been given to the value of iodine as an absolute preventive of goitre, and the commendation that has been given to the communal use of iodized salt, it is important that the hazards attendant upon such wholesale employment of iodine should be given equal publicity. Iodine is a drug, although the bodily need for it suggests that it may be employed as a food. Its use has to be safe-guarded because of its pharmacologic properties and, indeed, as a result of its peculiar effects when ingested in too large quantities by those having a susceptibility to its effect or by those who have physical conditions likely to become pathologically activated through its administration. There is ample evidence that iodine rashes are appearing more frequently than heretofore and that acne vulgaris is more difficult to cure among those making use of iodized salt. Further, the appearance or recurrence of hyperthyroidism amply demonstrates that the technique generally employed for administering iodine to adults is attended with serious disadvantages and dangers."

It is now claimed that a small amount of arsenic forms a normal part of the human body. I need not dwell on arsenical poisoning. The doctor's arsenic is not mistaken for food arsenic, or "organic" arsenic.

Common salt (sodium chloride) is not an exception to the rule that inorganic salts are not acceptable to the animal body, as will be fully shown in a succeeding chapter.

Berg has shown that when mixtures of "artificial nutritive salts" (drugs) are given they play the part of foreign bodies in the organism, "for they increase the osmotic pressure to an intolerable degree," and "hence they are eliminated as rapidly as possible."

"When an acid-rich diet is being taken," he says, "and we aim at neutralizing the excess of acid by administering inorganic bases in the form of salts, the use of litmus paper will show that the urine speedily acquires an alkaline reaction. During the night, however, the period when the great cleaning up of the organism after the day's exertions takes place, the amount of available bases is greatly reduced owing to the rapid excretion of the ionized salts, the result being that the morning urine (which contains the products of tissue change during the night) has again become acid, and is rich in uric acid although its power of holding uric acid in solution is small. In other words, when the requisite bases are supplied in the form of inorganic salts they are excreted so rapidly that the organism suffers from alkaline impoverishment at the time when its need for alkalies is greatest.

"Conditions are very different in the case of natural nutrients. Here the inorganic bases are, to some extent at least, present in masked forms, in stable organic combination, and their presence can in many instances not be detected until after the destruction of the organic combination. To some extent, compounds of this character are even able to resist the disintegrating effects of digestion, as I have myself proved in the case of milk. In this form, the bases do not irritate the animal organism in any way, and they can be retained by the body for a considerable period, until the bases are restored to an ionisable condition by the breakup of the organic combinations. If, therefore, the organism be provided with an abundance of bases by supplying it with a food naturally rich in bases, ere long morning urine will be found to have an alkaline reaction. In such cases the uric-acid content of the urine will tend towards a minimum characteristic of the particular diet; and at the same time the capacity for excreting uric acid, that is to say the competence of the urine to dissolve uric acid, will rise to a maximum. Thus whereas the effect in artificial mixtures of inorganic salts is restricted to an hour or two after their ingestion, the bases in the natural nutritive salts remain effective over long periods, and are always on hand when the organism needs them. I have found that the water in which potatoes, greens, etc., have been boiled, or protein-free milk (whey), is speedy and effective."

Berg says: "Calcium carbonate, therefore, acts in the animal body as a free base in this respect, that it is competent to neutralize acids, and thus reduce acidosis. Obviously, all inorganic bases in the free state can act in the same way, provided that they can be absorbed by the organism in a soluble form. The free bases, however, have, like the free acids, and even more than these, the disagreeable quality of being corrosive. They dissolve organic matter, and can therefore not be tolerated by the organism except in extreme dilution."

Indeed, the use of inorganic lime-salts, with the exception of calcium carbnoate and tri-calcium phosphate, produces acidosis. Large doses of calcium chloride induce severe losses of calcium from the body and may even result in osteoporosis or osteomalacia. Chloride of lime, if given for a long time, results in severe losses of calcium and even in bone deformity. Calcium chloride induces hyperacidity within the body and the alkalies of the bones and other tissues are used up in neutralizing the acids. There is only one source from which to secure your calcium—namely, natural foods.

In plants the minerals are combined in some peculiar way in the living system of the cell which makes them acceptable to the animal body, which is unable to take chemically pure substances and synthesize these into animal tissues. Schussler's salts and Carey's salts, even though administered in the sixth decimal trituration of homeopathic therapeutics, as is the common way of giving them, are not used by the body. Homeopathic trituration is not identical with the synthetic processes of plant life and does not produce the peculiar plant substances that are alone acceptable to the animal.

These same facts apply to the many "cell salts," "vegetable salts," "essential foods," etc., now exploited in this country.

Members of the Biochemic school of medicine, followers of Schuessler, homeopaths and others, who declare that these crude substances may be used in and by the body as "tissue salts," if only they are finely enough ground and sufficiently triturated are greatly in error.

Strictly speaking there is no science of biochemistry. All so-called biochemistry is the chemistry of the dead. Those who have cell-salts, tissue salts, biochemic salts, etc., to sell are merely exploiting popular ignorance. Their "remedies" are worthless.

The body possesses the power to manufacture the chemical substances it requires and this it is continuously doing, the exercise of this power depending upon the supply of acceptable raw materials. Thyroxin, for example, manufactured by the thyroid gland, is tri-iodo-trypophane. The production of this hormone is dependent, not alone upon the supply of the amino-acid, tryptophane, but upon the supply of acceptable iodin. Drug iodine, in whatever form, does not enable the body to synthesize thyroxin, and its use is a frequent cause of the very condition it is given to prevent or *cure*.

Physicians have long prescribed iron in various forms in anemia, chlorosis, and other conditions. Abderhalden, a German scientist, performed an extended series of experiments upon several species of animals, to determine to what extent they were able to absorb and utilize different forms of iron. He discovered that animals fed upon iron-poor diets, to which were added inorganic iron substances, were unable, in the long run, to produce as much hemoglobin as those given normal food. He came to the conclusion that inorganic iron salts act chiefly, if not wholly, as "stimulants," and that hemoglobin is derived essentially from the organic iron compounds of food. Hemoglobin is a protein compound into which the iron salts enter and the iron salts of the drug store do not enter into this compound.

Organic Acids
CHAPTER VIII

Organic acids, as we employ the term here, are those acids that result from the synthetic activities of plants and animals, as distinct from decomposition acids, like uric acid, etc. For the purposes of this chapter, organic acids are those acids found naturally in fruits and vegetables, such as acetic, citric, malic, oxalic, etc., acids.

Carque says: "Organic acids are used by the living plants in their synthetic processes. In the ripening of some fruits some of the acids are progressively utilized in the formation of ethers and carbohydrates. Others are combined to form salts of potassium, sodium, calcium, magnesium, etc."

Organic acids in varying percentages exist in all fruits and vegetables. In many foods the acid exists in minute percentages, in none of them is the percentage of acid very great. They have a very pleasing flavor and are relished by everyone. A few of these, the most common ones, are as follow:

Citric acid, is found in oranges, lemons, limes, grapefruit, tangerines, qumquats, pineapples, pomegranets, tomatoes, citrons, quinces, goosberries, raspberries, strawberries, currants, cranberries, and many others, either as an acid or else combined with alkaline salts forming citrates. Citric acid is absorbed from the digestive tract and, after being decomposed in the body, is eliminated by the kidneys as sodium carbonate.

Oxalic acid is perhaps the most widely distributed of all the organic acids, occurring in both fruits and vegetables. Cocoa, chocolate, coffee, and tea are particularly rich in it. So also are cranberries and rhubarb. The leaves of the rhubarb contain more than the stems. Tomatoes really have very little oxalic acid. Spinach contains many times as much oxalic acid as tomatoes. White bread, and even potatoes, contain much more of this acid than tomatoes. Sorrel is rich in oxalic acid.

Oxalic acid is most difficult for the animal body to oxidize and use. Opinions differ about its availability to the body. In excess it is probably productive of harm and is held responsible for some kidney stones. The percentage of this acid in most vegetables and fruits is so small that there is little danger of excess. A diet of spinach, tea, coffee and cocoa will easily introduce an excess into the body. In the normal person oxalic acid, whether entering the body as a free acid or as a salt, usually a calcium salt, undergoes oxidation into carbon dioxide and water, leaving its bases at the free disposal of the body.

Acetic acid is found in many plants. It combines readily with sodium, potassium, ammonium and other alkalies, forming salts or acetates, these acetates existing naturally in the juices of many vegetables. The acid and its salts are converted into alkaline carbonates in the body.

Malic acid is found in apples, apricots, cherries, cherimoyas, currants, loquats, mangos, papayas, pears, peaches, pineapples, plums, prunes, quinces, tomatoes, blackberries, cranberries, raspberries, strawberries, either in the free state, or in combination with alkaline bases, as malates, such as malate of calcium, malate of potash, malate of magnesium; and is found also in parsley, carrots and potatoes.

Tartaric acid is one of the most common organic acids. Grapes, mangos and tamarinds and other fruits contain this acid. As grapes ripen their tartaric acid disappears and sugar and other carbohydrates increase. The acids are apparently converted into sugars and starches.

Lactic acid is produced in the fementation of milk sugar (lactose), when the milk sours. It exists in cheese and also in ripened cream. The fermentation of various sugars and starches and other substances, in the precense of protein, also gives rise to lactic acid as a by-product.

Nelson, of the Bureau of Chemistry found the acids of the strawberry are citric acid, 90%, malic acid 10%; pineapple acids, citric acid 87%; malic acid 13%; red raspberries acids, citric acid 97% and malic acid 3%; black raspberry acids, citric acid; concord grape acids, malic acid 60%, tartaric acid 40%.

Fruit acids and vegetable acids are beneficial only in their organic forms or as acid salts. The artificially prepared acids, sold in soft drinks and in other forms, never produce the beneficial effects that one obtains from the organic acids. Extracted acids are also not beneficial. Fruit and vegetable acids should be taken only in the fruit or vegetable in which they were formed or in the form of fruit juices and vegetable juices.

The older view that fruit acids produce acidosis, or that they increase blood acidity, still prevails in many quarters. This view is erroneous. Fruit acids actually do just the opposite of this — they increase blood alkalinity. Prunes, plums and cranberries are perhaps the only exceptions to the rule that acid fruits are all alkaline-ash foods.

Most of the various organic acids, such as citric and malic acids, are completely oxidized within the body. Benzoic acid contained in prunes, plums and cranberries is an exception. This is detoxicated by being converted into innocuous hippuric acid and eliminated in the urine. It has been found that more hippuric acid is eliminated than the limited amount of benzoic acid will account for. It is thought that the excess is derived from the quinic acid in these fruits.

Carque says: "The combined organic acids or salts consumed in food are generally changed in the body into alkaline carbonates, thereby increasing the alkalinity of the blood and secretions. The uncombined acids either form alkaline carbonates, or are oxidized into carbon dioxide and water."

The terminal product of the combustion, the acid radical of calcium salts of combustible organic acids, is carbonic acid and is excreted through the lungs and requires no bases to assist in its excretion. The entire calcium content of the salt remains at the free disposal of the body as a base. The same is true of the potassium, sodium and magnesium contained in the salts.

Blatherwick and Long found that drinking even large quantities of orange juice always results in producing an alkaline urine. They say: "It was impossible to over-reach the organism's ability to oxidize the contained citric acid," even though the amount drunk was the equivalent of twenty-four large oranges eaten daily.

It is, nevertheless, true that in certain patients, after a considerable period on an acid-fruit diet, symptoms are produced that necessitate a change of diet. These patients become tense, restless, irritable, nervous and do not sleep well. The acid fruits begin to irritate them and they are uncomfortable after eating them. Such cases are relatively rare and are found almost wholly among thin, nervous patients. This would indicate that at least in some conditions of the body there is a limit to its power to oxidize organic acids. Like all other good things their use may be over done.

When organic acids are taken in excess of the body's abilities to effect their complete combustion into carbonic acid and water, they have the same effect as inorganic acids, as they have to be neutralized by being combined with bases before they can be eliminated.

The entrance of organic acids into the blood through other than the regular channels of digsetion and absorption has proven fatal in experimental animals. In entering the body by the digestive tract, they enter the blood by first passing through the devious route of the lymphatic system, where they are at least partially changed and neutralized.

Berg mentions symptoms of acid poisoning arising out of the immoderate use of lemons (citric acid) in those undergoing the "lemon cure," popular in parts of Germany. Obviously, therefore, the body's power to utilize organic acids is limited and this power must vary with individuals and in the same individual, with the varying conditions of the body. The same fact must be true of these as inorganic acids — namely, that not until large doses of acids have been given for a considerable length of time, does the real "acidosis" result. A temporary excess, therefore, will result in no particular harm.

Most, if not all, of those cases where digestive troubles are occasioned by the use of acid fruits are due, not to the fruit or the acid *per se*, but to the combinations. Hundreds of patients have told me that they cannot eat fruits, that they cause indigestion, gas and discomfort. Almost invariably I have found that they were having oranges or grapefruit with a breakfast about as follows: Cereal with sugar and cream, egg on toast, coffee. Usually sugar was used on the grapefruit. When these patients are given an abundance of acid fruits, uncombined with other foods, they experience no discomfort or trouble.

Acid fruits are usually tabooed in gastric hyperacidity. As most cases of hyperacidity are not this at all, but are cases of acid fermentation in the excess of carbohydrates consumed, acid fruits taken with the meals, make the condition worse by their interference with salivary digestion. Taken when there is no other food in the stomach, they cause no trouble. A few cases of "sour stomach" (these may be cases of real hyperacidity) have their distress increased by the use of acid fruits, whether taken alone or in combination with other foods. A short fast usually enables these few to take the acid fruits. Acid fruits do not always aggravate gastric ulcer but should not be employed until the ulcer is healed. A fast best accomplishes this result.

Fruits
CHAPTER IX

"Figs or Pigs, Fruit or Brute?" is the title of a little book on fruitarianism which I have in my possession. The question is a pertinent one and its correct answer is freighted with increased health and happiness for everyone. Dr. Alcott declared, and this at a time when the regular profession declared fruit to be practically without food value, that; "The purest food is fruit. Fruit bears the closest relation to light. The sun pours a continuous flood of light into the fruits, and they furnish the best portion of food a human being requires for sustenance of mind and body."

Botanically, fruits are the edible parts of plants that result from the development of pollinated flowers, such as peaches, oranges, cucumbers, tomatoes, peppers, nuts, beans, peas, etc. Although, scientifically, beans, peas, nuts and other such articles of food, are classed as fruits, popularly such seed, because they do not possess an edible capsule (we do eat the green pods of the bean), are not considered as fruits. Botanically, the wheat grain or other cereal is a fruit. We shall here consider under the term of fruit, however, only those foods that possess the edible capsule surrounding the seed and shall consider nuts and cereals in separate chapters.

The soft, delicious pulp of the peach, pear, plum, apple, orange, etc., constitute fine food and is prepared by the plant especially for export purposes. Primarily, seeds are produced for reproduction. Secondarily, they are produced in great over abundance, that some of these may be used as export products. Some fruits, such as the banana, pineapple and the seedless orange, do not surround a seed. Other fruits, like the pomegranate, are largely seed, with but little edible pulp.

Edible fruits exist in greater variety than any other form of foodstuffs; over 300 different edible varieties are known. The tropics are especially abundant in them. Long before Bichat proved, by comparative anatmy, that man is naturally frugivorous, the race had recorded this fact in a thousand ways. The very word frugal refers to fruit. Dr. Oswald tells us of the Romans of the Republican age that, "in their application of the word, a frugal diet meant quite literally a diet of tree-fruits."

Ancient peoples realized the great importance of fruits. The Bible is full of references to fruits and vineyards. The same is true of other ancient literature. Moses exempted the man, who had planted a vineyard, from military service. The pagans consigned the olive tree to Minerva, the date to the Muses and the fig and grape to Bacchus for protection.

"And the Lord God planted a paradise eastward in Eden and there He put the man whom He had formed. And out of the ground made the Lord to grow every tree that is pleasant to the sight and good for food; And God took the man and put him into the Garden of Delight to dress it and keep it. And the Lord God commanded the man, saying, 'of every tree of the garden thou mayest freely eat'."

In these few words the writer of Genesis explains to us that man was originally a gardener or rather a horticulturist and lived upon the fruits of the trees. In this, many of the ancient myths, legnds and tradition agree perfectly with Moses. These also picture man as living in a state of perpetual bliss with health, strength and a very long life, so long as he remained on his fruit and nut diet and as becoming depraved, weak, short-lived and diseased when he forsook this and took to a diet of meat. This early age of man was called the "Golden Age."

The tradition of the deluge has it that the first thing Noah did after the waters of the flood had subsided was to plant a vineyard. The account of the spies sent by Joshua to investigate the land of Cannan tells us that they brought back "unto all the congregation, and showed them the fruit of the land."

The Latin poet, Ovid, pictures for us, a Golden Age when "Western winds immortal spring maintained," and when man lived on fruits, berries, and nuts. He says: "The teeming earth, yet guiltless of the plough, and unprovoked, did fruitful stores allow." During this age there was no vice and crime. Then, after describing the horrible cruelties inflicted upon animals, in order to appropriate their flesh as food, he says:

"Not so the Golden Age, who fed on fruit,
Nor durst with bloody meals their mouths pollute."

FRUITS

Referring to a subsequent "Silver Age," Ovid says:
"Then summer, autumn, winter did appear,
And spring was but a season of the year;
The sun his annual course obliquely made,
Good days contracted, and enlarged the bad.
The air with sultry heat began to glow;
The wings of winds were clogged with ice and snow;
And shivering mortals, into houses driven,
Sought shelter from the inclemency of heaven.
Those houses, then, were caves, or homely sheds;
With twining osiers fenced, and moss their beds,
Then ploughs, for seed, the fruitful furrows broke,
And oxen labored first beneath the yoke."

Geology proper knows only one climate — a universal spring-like climate which reigned from pole to pole. Then, there came a great change in earth's climate. Ovid describes man before and after this change. He pictures agriculture and dwelling in caves and houses, as succeeding the Golden Age. Almost without exception, the poets, philosophers and historians of antiquity picture the diet of primitive man as being very simple and consisting largely of fruits and nuts. Porphyry, a Platonic Philosopher of the third century, after carefully investigating the subject of diet, tells us that "the Ancient Greeks lived entirely on the fruits of the earth."

Making all allowances for the accretions of time and the loss of accuracy which time brings to traditions, these ancient myths embody important truths. They were not manufactured "out of whole cloth." They are not only important as blurred pictures of a more remote antiquity, but are also important as indications of the importance the peoples of less remote times attached to fruits and nuts. The myth of Promethus, who first stole fire from heaven, points back to a time when man did not cook his food; when he was not a deformed, sickly, suffering creature as we see him today, but a long-lived, healthy, happy being.

The Greeks always served two courses of fruits, while the Romans, if they ate breakfast at all, had a fruit breakfast. The third course of the principal daily meal of the Romans consisted of a super-abundance of fruits from their own orchards. Rich Romans planted fruit trees on the tops of high towers, and on the tops of their houses. The ancient Gymnosophists, of India, lived entirely upon fruits and green vegetables. It was a part of their religion to eat nothing which had not been ripened by the sun, and made fit for food without any further preparation.

Fruits are rich in alkaline minerals and in those qualities or characteristics which are called vitamins and complettins and also in organic acids. Sweet fruits are especially valuable for their delightful sugars, so easily digested (sometimes almost pre-digested), which sustain the body with so little energy expenditure in digestion.

Fruit sugars are better than starch. Even bananas, commonly condemned as indigestible, are a superior food and easily digested if fully ripened. Fruit sugars require very little work in digestion and consume far less energy than starch. "The ordinary dried figs of commerce," says Dr. Densmore, "are said to contain about 68 per cent of glucose, which when eaten, is in the identical condition that the starch of cereal food is converted into after a protracted and nerve-forcing-wasting digestion." The same is true of grapes, dates, raisins, bananas, etc.

Starch is an almost insoluble carbohydrate and is converted into sugar in the process of digestion in rendering it soluble. The following brief description by Milo Hastings, of the storing of starch by plants and its later conversion into sugar is both interesting and instructive: "Many plants store future food material in this form of starch and later, when nature requires this material in soluble form so it can move and flow through the cells, the starch is changed into sugar.

"This is the change that occurs in the sprouting or malting of all grains, and malt syrup is sugar made in this fashion from the starch of the barley grain. Even the starch of the potato turns to sugar when the potato is planted, and sometimes after long storage we get a little of this sugary taste in our potatoes and wonder what is the matter with them.

"When we get starch in any form it is changed into sugar before absorption from our digestive organs and yet after absorption some of this sugar is changed back into gycogen or 'animal starch,' which is stored in the liver, or to a lesser extent in the muscles, until it is needed as fuel for our muscles. Then before it is actually oxidized or burned in the muscles this product must again be changed back to sugar."

Fruits are rich in *levulose* (fruit sugar), which is the choicest of all sugars. It represents starch in a state of complete digestion and is ready for instant absorption and assimilation. It is the ready absorption of this sugar that renders fruit juices so refreshing to the fatigued person.

The best source of sugar for the body is sweet fruits—grapes, dates, bananas, figs, raisins, etc. These sugars come to us almost pre-digested and well-balanced with minerals and vitamins. These fruits are wholesome, natural, delicious and are full of life-sustaining qualities. No cook, confectioner or manufacturer can even remotely imitate these delicious products of nature's solar-vital laboratory.

Sweet fruits are superior to starches as a source of carbohydrates. Man is a sub-tropical animal and his craving for sweets is, undoubtedly, a survival of his habit of subsisting largely on the sweet fruits which grow so abundantly in the sub-tropics and tropics. Sweet fruits serve the same heat and energy purposes that starch does and need almost no digestion. The digestion of starch foods consumes much more energy than does the digestion of sweet fruits. Dr. Densmore, indeed, strenuously advocated a non-starch dietary and insisted upon the substitution of sweet fruits for starch foods. For he claimed, and rightly, that sweet fruits give the greatest amount of nourishment for the least amount of digestive strain.

Herbert Spencer, who stigmatized bread and milk and butter, as insipid, and who praised fruits because they were savoury and wholesome, declared that "the more the labor of digestion is economized, the more energy is left for the purposes of growth and atcion." He perceived, also, that considerable energy is consumed in converting starch into sugar, in making it available for use in the body.

Starch digestion takes place largely in the duodenum. Indeed, combined, as it usually is, with proteins and acids, starch is almost wholly digested in the duodenum, and has usually undergone considerable fermentation before it reaches there.

Starch must first be converted into sugar before the body can use it — fruit sugars have been converted from starch to sugar while ripening under the influence of the sun. The sun and the life force of tree having done this part of the work, man may save his energy by eating the fruit instead of cereals or potatoes, which certainly do not form any part of man's naural diet.

Fruits produce more food per acre than any other food, except pecans. Humboldt calculated that the ground required to produce thirty-three pounds of wheat or ninety-nine pounds of potatoes, will produce four thousand pounds of bananas — a delightful fruit that is more valuable than both of these foods. Grapes and other fruits will all produce comparatively large yields.

A grapevine planted in 1775, at San Gabriel, Calif., now has a base eight feet and nine inches in circumference; its branches spread over an area of twelve thousand square feet — a space the size of a city lot 100 ft. by 120 ft. It produces a ton of grapes a year. No tilled crop can equal fruits and nuts in the amount yielded. Fruit culture will simplify agriculture and lessen the farmer's burdens.

Fruits are commonly divided into three classes according to the amount of sugar and fruit acid they contain, viz., acid fruits, subacid fruits and sweet fruits. The most common fruit acids are malic, tartaric, citric and oxalic. These occur usually in acid salts of potassium, sodium or calcium.

Malic acid is found chiefly in apples, pears, currants, berries, pineapples, grapes and cherries. Tartaric acid is found in grapes. Citric acid is found in oranges, lemons, limes, grapefruit, tangerines, tangeloes, tomatoes, gooseberries and currants. Oxalic acid is found in small amounts in raspberries, tomatoes, grapes and currants, with but a trace of it found in apples, plums, oranges and lemons. Cranberries are rich in it. During the ripening process, fruit acids are slowly transformed into sugar. As the orange, for example, ripens, its acid content decreases and its sugar content rises.

The principal sweet fruits are dates, figs, sweet grapes, raisins, bananas, prunes and the pawpaw.

The chief subacid fruits are apples, pears, apricots, blackberries, blueberries, raspberries, cherries, grapes, peaches, persimmons, plums and practically all deciduous friuts.

The acid fruits are oranges, lemons, limes, pineapples, grapefruit, tangerinse, tangeloes, strawberries, loganberries, cranberries, loquats and tamerinds.

The world teems with a profusion of kinds and varieties of edible fruits and no effort will be made here to consider all of them individually. A few of the more commonly known fruits will be briefly noticed. They will be considered alphabetically, rather than under their classifications.

Apples: These fruits are poor in vitamin C and are not especially rich in B, but added to a scurvy-producing diet, they prevent scurvy. They are also described as curative in scurvy.

Apples contain calcium, phosphorus, sulphur, iron and magnesia. Their phosphoric acid is in the most soluble form, while the iron in the apple is more easily taken into the blood than iron from any other source. Dr. Tilden especially recommends apples for rachitic children, and for building good bones and teeth. Dr. Claunch stated that cavities in his teeth healed while he was on an apple diet. There are many varieties of apples, all of them a delight to the sense of taste, and they are obtainable throughout the year.

Avocado: The avocado is coming more and more into popularity and as its cultivation increases, is destined to become one of the finest articles of diet on the American bill-of-fare. At present the best avocados we get in this country are raised in California. Florida and West Indian avocados are not as tasty as California avocados and do not possess the food value of the latter. A good California avocado contains about 3.39% protein. This is about the protein content of milk and that of the avocado is equal to the protein of milk in its content of amino acids essential to growth and repair. It is low in carbohydrates, containing but 2.9% of these of which 1% is invert sugar. They are rich in a very tasty emulsified oil which has a high degree (about 93.8%) of digestibility. The total minerals of a good California avocado amount to 1.18% of the total edible portion. This includes an ample proportion of the bases: calcium, potassium, magnesium and sodium. It contains considerable iron while phosphorus is found in generous combination with its protein. Copper, essential to the assimilation of iron, and manganese are present in smaller quantities. The avocado contains liberal supplies of several of the vitamins. It is a good source of thiamin (B_1) and riboflavin (B_2 or G) and is a fair source of A and C (ascorbic acid). The avocado requires no preparation, but is ready to eat when it reaches the mellow stage. Due to its high fat content it is not wise to eat it with other protein foods.

Bananas: The banana is a tropical plant and together with figs, dates and a host of other such fruits, are demonstrations that nature has not designed sweet fruits for cold regions and juicy and subacid fruits for the tropics. People who live on banana plantations consume them in large quantities and withstand the heat well. Figs and dates are favorite foods of the desert peoples.

Chemical analysis shows the banana to contain: water 73.3 per cent; protein 1.3 per cent; fat .06 per cent; total carbohydrates 22 per cent; mineral element .8 per cent. The mineral content of the banana is largely potash, sodium and chlorine. Lime and iron exist in but small amounts.

Prof. Jaffa says that green bananas contain: sugar .94, starch 22.26. Ripe bananas contain sugar 18.87, starch, .82. When bananas are thoroughly ripened the almost indigestible starch of the green banana has been converted into an almost pre-digested sugar ready for immediate absorption. A well-ripened banana is almost predigested. It is then good for food, not before.

Bananas are rich in vitamins A and B, which promote growth. The antiscorbutic vitamin C is abundant in bananas. Vitamin D, which is supposed to prevent rickets, is said by some investigators to be deficient, although Berg declares it is present in sufficient quantity. Vitamin E, which is supposed to promote fertility, is present although its quantity is supposed to be small.

Tested on rats, banana protein proves to be inadequate; yet there is a So. American parrot that lives exclusively on bananas and attains an age that makes the oldest rat look like a day-old infant. The fecal discharges of this parrot have the fragrance of bananas and are as inoffensive as bananas themselves.

Banana protein has been proven to be of about equal value to those of grains and potatoes. "An abundant supply of bananas," says Berg, "is a guarantee that the food will contain an excess of bases," although there may be a partial lack of calcium salts. They are too poor in calcium to be adequate growth promoters. Bananas plus nuts, plus green vegetables would make an adequate diet for child or adult and for a pregnant or a lactating mother.

Berg says: "Bailey Ashford relates that indigenes convalescing from yellow fever, eat nothing but bananas, consuming from thirty to forty of these fruits daily without any supplement whatever, health and strength returning in a marvelously short time. I have myself proved that, after habituation to the strange diet, it is possible to live very well on bananas and butter, with a much lower consumption of protein than is requisite, for instance, upon a wheaten diet."

Thousands of rubber gatherers perform prodigious feats of muscular strength and endurance on almost no other food than bananas. The banana is higher in nutritive value than any other fresh -fruit. Mr. Mcfadden, who once declared the banana to be a complete food, thought one could live a life-time on it and be thoroughly nourished, providing only, that the bananas were eaten when thoroughly ripened. He stated that he had known many athletes of more than ordinary ability to live almost entirely on bananas for an extended period and maintain their strength to a high degree on this food.

There is little doubt that a mature individual could live for some time on bananas alone, without any appreciable decrease in strength or health, and this is especially true if the bananas eaten had fully ripened on the tree. But bananas do not form a complete food and one could not live a life-time on these alone. Mr. Mcfadden made the above statement at a time when we knew less about the life-sustaining and growth promoting value of foods than now. He was not for from right, at that.

Bananas that are shipped are pulled green and are ripened after reaching the dealer. They are usually sold to the consumer and eaten by him in only a partially ripened state. Often they are sold with green tips. More often, however, the banana is all yellow. A yellow banana is still an unripe banana. A fully ripened banana is flecked with little brown spots. It resembles the complexion of a much freckled boy, except the banana freckles are darker and become black. Fully ripened bananas are usually sold much cheaper than the unripe ones because they do not keep long after ripening. It is just then, however, that they should be eaten.

No fruit that is pulled green and ripened afterwards, is as good as are those that are permitted to ripen on the tree. The ripening process is less complete, their food value is not so great, their flavor is not so delightful. These things are due to two chief causes: (1) they are deprived of the sap from the tree, and (2) they are deprived of the influence of the sun's rays.

I have been informed that if a stalk of bananas is placed in the sunshine, with the end of the stalk in water, the bananas will ripen almost as well as if they had been permitted to ripen on the tree and will have almost as delicious a flavor.

Bananas are excellent food for children and should be given them instead of candy, cakes, pies, sugar, etc. They will supply the child with the needed sugar in an easily assimilated form. All children relish them and will prefer them to the above abdominations. Give them well-ripened bananas and let them chew them well.

A lady once saw the writer give his little two year old son a banana to eat, and thought it a crime that I did not mash the banana up well before giving it to the boy. She had a girl only a few months older and fed her bananas this way. It is the writer's conviction that the wrong was on her side. Mashed bananas can be swallowed without chewing, but the whole banana requires some chewing before swallowing. The mother chewed the food of her daughter with a masher, but this did not insalivate it. The daughter then swallowed it without insalivating it.

It is true that a well-ripened banana does not require much insalivation but it should be given all that naturally comes to it in the necessary chewing. Other than this, children should not be fed in a manner that encourages them to swallow their food without chewing it.

Popular and quasi-scientific opinion has it that the banana is difficult to digest. So it is if eaten green,' as is usually the case, while they are still starch, the green starch being almost insoluble. In this state they are much like green apples, green peaches, etc., and may result in trouble when eaten. There are few foods that are more easily digested than a fully ripened banana, and surely none with a stronger appeal to the unperverted taste. The use of tobacco seems to deprive the user more or less of his natural relish of fruit.

Berries: The acid of berries is chiefly citric, with small amounts of malic acid. All berries, except cranberries, are excellent foods. The strawberry possesses a delicate, sweet-acid flavor and a delightful aroma. It is rich in iron and lime, containing about a fourth of a grain of lime to the ounce. It excels all other fresh fruit, except figs and raspberries, in richness in iron. Strawberries are richer in iron than most vegetables, being excelled only by green peas and fresh lima beans.

Cranberries, unlike other fruits, contain an excess of acid minerals.

Cherries: Over two hundred varieties of this excellent fruit are grown in the United States, and their composition varies with the variety. They are rich in sugar, minerals and vitamins.

Dates: A sweet fruit of the palm, the date is an excellent source of simple sugar. It is richer than most fruits in protein, being richer, even, than mother's milk, and is relatively high in minerals.

Figs: A prince among the sweet fruits are the many varieties of this anciently cultivated fruit (or flower). Native figs were found growing in Mexico, Central and So. America when the New World was discovered. Many varieties are grown in this country, although few varieties are known to the general public. The mineral content of figs closely resembles that of human milk. They are rich in sugar and are excellent sources of vitamins.

Grapes: Grapes merit their title, "King of Fruits." They are rich in iron and fruit sugar and vitamins. Their use in the famous "grape cures," of France and Southern Germany, has demonstrated their wonderful nutritive and "cleansing" value.

They contain from fifteen to thirty per cent sugar and, like most fruits, are low in protein. They are also rich in vitamin C.

Raisins: or dried grapes, are very rich in a readily assimilable sugar.

Haws: A delicious fruit growing wild in Southern United States and known as red haws and black haws, according to their color, these fruits are deserving of cultivation and wider use.

Mangoes: The mango is a tropical fruit and has long been cultivated by man. It does well in Florida, Southern Texas and in a few sheltered spots in California, although the best magoes our market affords come from Central America. It is one of the most delicious of fruits and is destined to grow in popularity.

Melons: All melons are excellent foods. There was an old notion, fostered by the medical profession, that melons cause "chills" and "feners," remnants of which still exist and cause many people to reject these foods. Three general types of melons are produced in America. These are:

Casaba: Also known as the winter melon, is represented by several varieties, such as the casaba, honey dew, golden beauty, Christmas melon and other types.

Musk-melon: Most musk-melons are commonly known as Canteloupes. There are many varieties called canteloupes. In the South the term musk-melon is reserved for one variety which is much larger than the others and is ridged or sectional. The persian melon and the banana melon belong to this group. The banana melon gets its name from its shape, similar to that of the banana, although it grows to great length and is large in diameter.

Watermelons: These are among the largest of our fruits, often weighing more than a hundred pounds. There are many varieties of water melon. It is common to describe the outer skin of the water melon as green; some of them are golden yellow. It is also common to refer to the inner part or meat as red; there are water melons with yellow meat.

All kinds and varieties of melons are valuable for their minerals, vitamins, sugars and pure water.

Contrary to popular and professional belief, probably nobody is ever allergic to melons. My experience has been that so-called allergic individuals can take all the melons they desire without distress, if the melons are eaten alone. Melons do not combine well with other foods, except perhaps, other fruits.

Nectarines: are closely related to the peach and are sometimes classed as a variety of the peach. In appearance they seem to be a cross between a peach and a plum, as they have a smooth skin. The composition of the nectarine is similar to that of the peach, although its flavor is distinctive.

Oranges are rich in lime and other alkaline salts. They have a delightful flavor and may be relished by everyone. Their use combats "acidosis" and prolongs youth. These, with grapefruit, are our best agents in feeding the sick. As a cleansing diet, I prefer the grapefruit.

The experiments of B. Leichtentritt (on guinea pigs) in an effort to determine the relations between the presence of "accessory food factors" in the diet and the course of tuberculosis provide wonderful testimony in favor of acid fruits. When he added lemon juice to a "basal diet" this made a very great difference. The lemon juice improved the general nutrition of the pig — especially the fat storing power—and "raised its resistance to the tubercle bacillus." The bacillus was forced to live on the dead tissue and excreta (were restored to their normal saprophytic work) and forced to abandon their parasitic activities. The different diet compelled the bacillus to change its tactics and, if it continued to grow freely, did so without producing any definite toxic effect.

I have not discussed grapefruit (pomelo), lemons, tangerines, tangeloes, etc., under separate heads, because, in general, what is said of the orange applies also to these fruits. Even the pineapple is not greatly different from these foods. The orange is richer in sugar than most other citrus fruits. The Texas grapefruit is richly supplied with sugar and is not bitter. The pinks and ruby reds are very popular, though not superior in flavor or food value to the white grapefruit.

Papayas: Called also a "tree melon" because of its resemblance to a melon, this fruit grows on a giant herbaceous plant and not on a tree. It is a valuable and delicious fruit, but lacks all the magic and *medicinal* virtues with which the salesmen of papaya juice and papaya extracts invest it. It is a tropical fruit but does well in Florida and the Lower Rio Grande Valley section of Texas. It does not stand shipping and must be eaten "on the ground" to be really appreciated.

The vitamin content of the papaya is a feature that has attracted considerable attention. *Bulletin* No. 77 of the Department of Agriculture tells us that the papaya contains four vitamins. The vitamin content occording to international units per 100 gms., is about 2,500 units of vitamin A, 33 units of vitamin B and 70 units of vitamin C. Vitamin D is present but the amount is as yet, undetermined. This is a relatively high vitamin content.

Prescribing papaya with protein meals because of the presence in it of the enzyme, *papain*, or vegetable pepsin, as an aid to digestion is wrong. Because of the presence of this enzyme in the fruit, it should never be eaten with protein foods. Teaching the stomach to rely upon outside sources of digestive enzymes, instead of removing the cause of digestive impairment, is a ruinous practice.

Pawpaws: The American Pawpaw must be distinguished from the papaya, which is also sometimes spelled "papaw" and "pawpaw." Our pawpaw, a native of the United States, grows best in the Mississippi Valley where it was highly valued by the Indians. Someday it will be more widely cultivated in America. Unfortunately, it does not ship well and is but little known outside its native haunts. Carque says it is fully equal, if not superior, to the banana in nutritive value. It surpasses all other varieties of fresh fruit in protein content, its edible portion possessing 5.2 per cent protein. It is also rich in sugar.

Peaches: Flavored by the presence of a very small quantity of hydro-cyanic acid and fruit ethers, the peach is one of the most delicious of fruits. Low in protein and fat, comparatively rich in sugar, the many varieties of peaches are chiefly valuable for their vitamins and the sodium, potassium and calcium that make up most of their mineral content.

Pears: Botanically related to the apple, pears are similar to apples in composition, but contain more sugar and less malic acid. Pears are not especially rich in vitamin A.

Persimmons: Carque says the persimmon comes to us from Japan. This is true only of certain varieties. We have many varieties of persimmons that are native to the Southern part of the United States, and they are more tasty than the Japanese persimmon, though smaller. He says that in color, the persimmon resembles the tomato. This is also true only of certain varieties. There are black persimmons. The persimmon is among the most delicious of fruits.

Plums and *Prunes*: The many delightful varieties of plums are rich in sugar, minerals and vitamins. The dried prune may contain seventy per cent sugar, hence deserves to be classed as a sweet fruit. Plums are not especially rich in vitamin A.

Tomatoes: are commonly classed as vegetables but we shall consider them as fruits. They are the equal of oranges, both in vitamins and in alkaline elements and are the finest of foods. For a long time tomatoes or "love apples" were regarded as poisonous and were grown in flower beds as ornaments. People would not eat them, although the Indians had eaten them for ages. The old physio-medicalists claimed that they contained mercury and would rot the liver. Regular medical men eschewed them because they "make the blood acid." There are still people who believe that tomatoes are poisonous and that they build acidosis. There are still physicians who proscribe the tomato in rheumatic cases.

The tomato contains 1.40 per cent alkaline salts as against .34 per cent acid salts. It is so predominantly alkaline that its use cannot be too strongly urged. The juice of the tomato ranks next to orange juice in its beneficial effects. We can recommend it to babies and adults in large quantities. Tomatoes should be eaten uncooked and properly combined.

Tomatoes are also rich in vitamin A.

THE FRUIT DIET

The great nutritional value of fruits is unquestioned by the well-informed. Supplemented with nuts, they form the ideal diet of man. All fruits are rich in vitamins and mineral salts and are especially valuable in preventing or remedying deficiency "diseases." Dr. Oswald says: "From May to September fresh fruit ought to form the staple of our diet."

A few years ago, in one of his articles in *The New York Evening Graphic*, Milo Hastings wrote: "'A daily reader' without name, sex or address, notes that fruit is always recommended to purify the blood, drive diseases from the body, etc. He, or she, wants to know why we should not live all the time on this superior type of food and so maintain perfect health.

"The idea, with slight modification, has been tried. A generation ago, Prof. Jaffa, of the University of California, made a scientific study of a group of fruitarians, only these persons included nuts in their fruit diet. The professor found them underweight and undersized folks, but all in fine health. He also calculated the total amount of food they ate and found, as measured in caloric units, that they were living on much less total food than the teachings of those times held to be possible.

"At the time this report was issued food authorities taught us that we all ought to overeat because the average man did overeat, and that we all ought to be somewhat fat because the average man was overfat. Looking over that report today, we realize that these minimum eaters were really in first class physical condition and were living the way of long life and freedom from the ills of fleshpots. They were able to live on fruits by including nuts, which are very rich in protein and fat, neither of which elements exist in fruit proper to a sufficient degree to maintain normal life.

"The chief reason we cannot live on fruits is that they contain practically no protein. This is also one reason why adding them to the average diet is beneficial, for the average diet is too rich in protein. Going on a fruit diet is 'cleansing' chiefly because it is a protein fast, and most of the accumulated wastes and poisons of the body are of a protein nature."

Dr. Gibson says of the nut and fruit diet: "In the light of the latest notations in the science of human nutrition, there is no activity in the human system, no process of digestion, assimilation, and nutrition, no nervous expenditure or structural strain, that cannot be sustained and maintained to its highest constitutional potency by a judicious dietetic balance of fruit and nuts. The former gives it sugar for the maintenance of fats and heat of the system; its organic salts to sustain the chemical composition and metabolic balance of the blood; its acids for breaking up tissue congestions, due to accumulation of waste matter; while the nut, with its storage of nitrogen and fat, furnishes material for anatomic repairs, and lubrication of the various joint movements. Finally the carbons contained in both the fruit and nut unite to generate the cerebro-vital explosions which set free the energies of high tensioned nervous life."

Dr. John Round (England) reports that, "In 1854 cholera attacked the Midland counties; there were many deaths in Staffordshire and elsewhere, but the fruit-growing and cider-making villages of Herfordshire escaped. The physicians of that time attributed this to the custom of eating fresh fruit; it is certain that the villagers did not peal their apples, and so consumed vitamins freely, it being a fact that the vitamins exist near the peel in all such fruits."

Dr. Gibson says: "The gains accruing to an individual from a well-established nut-and-fruit-diet would be far reaching. His domestic economy, by virtue of the time-and-labor-saving simplicity of a mostly fireless housekeeping would give rise to surprising assets. Furthermore, the relation between man and his associates in the animal kingdom would find a perfect moral and ethical adjustment. There would be no justification for killing or taking of life, for the sake of life; no dependence on animal sacrifice for our existence. Released from this awful task of compulsory 'slaughter of the innocents,' man would rise into a living protective power of peace and good will to every creature within his zone of influence, aiming at a consecration in place of a desecration of expressions and opportunities of life. His attitude towards his dumb and helpless neighbors would be serene, sweet and peaceful, with no grim implement of murder, concealed in the caressing hand."

Because of the rapidity with which fruits leave the stomach, and the readiness with which they decompose after they have been broken up, fruit is best eaten alone and not in combination with other foods. A fruit meal is the ideal.

Under all conditions and circumstances fruits should be taken alone and not eaten at the same meal with other foods. Fruits digest in the intestine, not in the mouth and stomach, and should not be held up in the stomach to await the digestion of other foods before being passed on to their own digestive fields.

Sugar on fruit means fermentation. Two sugars do not go well together. Cane sugar and beet sugar must be converted into simpler sugar before they can be utilized. Fruit sugars do not. Cane and beet sugar tend to prevent the absorption of fruit sugars until they both ferment.

Preserved fruits are confections, not fruit. We do not advise them. Canned fruits have little to recommend them.

The use of fruit juices as desserts and as appetizers, so strongly advocated in some quarters, is pernicious. The practice is based on the belief that we must secure all of the needed food elements at each meal. It is advocated in total disregard of the limitations of the digestive enzymes. Such eating guarantees indigestion to evryone who practices it.

Drinking fruit juices at all hours of the day, instead of water, is a sure road to indigestion. Fruit juices are foods, not drink, and should be taken as foods. Troubles arising from the misuse of fruits should not be blamed on the fruits.

Dried fruits are superior to bread in nutritive value, besides which they supply the bases so commonly lacking in cereals and cereal products. Sulphured fruits should never be employed. Sun dried fruits are best. Eat them dry or soak them but do not cook them. Fruits should never be cooked. Nor should they be frozen. They should be eaten ripe, fresh and uncooked. Their taste is not always as agreeable in this stage, but they are richer in vitamins before fully ripened. They lose vitamins in ripening. Fruits, like vegetables have more vitamin C in proportion as they are green. Fruits in general, like many nuts, are poor in vitamin A.

Allergies to fruits are commonly not that at all. The troubles attributed to allergy are, in almost every instance due to misuse of the fruit. Eaten in proper combinations, people who imagine they are allergic to fruit, find they have no difficulty with them. Placing these "fruit allergic" people on a diet of fruits, using the very fruits to which they are supposed to be allergic, proves them not to be allergic.

Nuts
CHAPTER X

Nuts are seeds of certain trees. Unlike the seed of the peach and plum, they possess no edible capsule. The peach, once a bitter almond, has developed, under cultivation, a delicious edible capsule. The peach seed, has a taste like that of the almond. The capsules of the pecan, walnut, chestnut, cocoanut, almond, hazelnut, hickory nut, etc., are not edible. They are tough, fibrous materials containing tannic acid and other foul tasting substances that protect the seed from being eaten until it is matured. Botanically, nuts are classed as fruits, as they develop from pollenated flowers. Because the nut is the seed of the tree and is not the edible pulp that surrounds the seed, as is the edible portion of the peach or plum, nuts are discussed in a separate chapter and are not considered in the chapter on fruits.

Paleontologists tell us that primitive man was a nut eater. All over the face of the earth man has used nuts as food from time immemorial. There are many kinds of nuts and these have all proven excellent sources of food, not alone for man, but for the lower primates and many other animals, including many birds. They are rich in food values, delightfully flavored and keep for extended periods so that man, as well as the squirrel, may store them for future use. Many animals besides squirrels eat large quantities of nuts. Many of the birds make use of the nut as an article of food. Horses will consume great quantities of acorns. While they will eat fruit from the trees, they eat acorns off the ground after they have fallen. Hogs eat so many hickory nuts that in certain parts of the country they are called pig-nuts. Horses are also fond of pecans.

The nut tree, like the fruit tree, strikes its roots deep into the earth, where they take up the precious minerals, and sends its limbs high into the space above, where, from air and sun, they take in the carbon, that enable the majestic tree to produce its wonderfully nutritious seed.

Day after day, through spring, summer and autumn, the great sun drives the river mists before it and sends down through the softly whispering foliage a thousand shafts of burnished gold that

NUTS

drain the nectarous dew-drop from its chalice and kiss the nut until its youthful, mineral-laden sap changes to delightful food beneath their passionate caresses.

It takes months of sunshine to perrect the nut and when it is completed it is a veritable store house of mineral sand high-grade protein, emulsified oil and health-imparting vitamins. Packed in a nature-made, water-proof and air-tight shell, the nut-meat comes to us clean and wholesome. Hermetically sealed the nut does not become contaminated and spoiled as does meat, for example. Nuts are free from waste products, are aseptic and do not readily decay, either in the body or outside of it. They are not infested with parasites (trachinae, tape-worm, etc.), as are meats.

Nuts, particularly the pecan, produce more food per acre than any other product and no one need eat animal products so long as these delightful foods are to be had. They are not to be considered as a "meat substitute." The meat is the "substitute," as Prof. Sherman, of Columbia University, says.

Kellogg says that "nuts are the choisest of all substances capable of sustaining life," and that in "nutritive value the nut far exceeds all other food substances." Also, "The nut is the choisest aggregation of the materials essential for the buildnig of sound human tissues, done up in a hermetically sealed package, ready to be delivered by the gracious hand of Nature to those who are fortunate enough to appreciate the value of this finest of earth's bounties."

Nuts are rich in minerals, particularly iron and lime. Pecans are rich in potassium, magnesium and phosphorus. Almonds, pecans, walnuts, chestnuts and hazelnuts contain an average percentage of iron of about two and a half times that of fruit, three times that of vegetables, greater than that of cereals and more than average meats. The almond is rich in iron and lime. One pound of almonds contains as much calcium as twenty-five pounds of beef, or eleven pounds of bread and potatoes. The almond is twice as rich in blood-building elements as meat and is very rich in bone-building elements, in which meat is sadly lacking.

Most nuts are abundant in vitamins A and B. The researches of Cajori demonstrated the abundant presence of growth-promoting vitamins in pecans, English walnuts, chestnuts, almonds, pine nuts, filberts, and hickory nuts.

Most nuts are rich in oils. The fats (oils) of nuts are the most easily digested and assimilated of all forms of fat. Kellogg says: "The fat of nuts exists in a finely divided state and in the chewing of nuts a fine emulsion is produced so that the nuts enter the stomach in a form adapted for prompt digestion."

Nuts are fairly rich in starch and sugar, and are three to four times richer in vitally important salts than animal flesh, even richer than milk in these vital substances. Not albumen is easily assimilated and does not form uric acid. Nuts are rich in fat, which, like that of milk, is in a state of emulsion — that is, ready-made, prepared, or pre-digested, as it were — for circulation through the lymphatic system.

Measured in calories, most nuts rank high. One example must suffice. Measured in calories, two ounces of shelled pecans contain as much food as a pound of lean beef.

Everything that can be had from flesh foods can be gotten in better condition and more usable form from other sources, and especially from nuts. Nuts are not only cleaner than meat, they come in hermetically sealed shells that prevent contamination.

Nut proteins are of the highest order, most nut proteins being complete. Kellogg maintains that nut proteins are the best of all sources upon which the body may draw for its supplies of tissue building substances and that the proteins of nuts are superior to those of ordinary vegetables or meat. "Nuts furnish perfect proteins." Nut proteins are superior to those of cereals and are claimed to be more complete than those of eggs. Indeed, Kellogg says: "The special method of research adopted by Dr. Hoobler of the Detroit Women's Hospital and Infant's Home, provides a most delicate biological test for the nutriment value of food. The test shows the nut to be superior to meat, milk or eggs or all these foods together in producing the highest degree of nutritive efficiency. Nut protein is the best of all sources upon which the body may draw for its supplies of tissue-building material."

Carque says: "Investigations made at Yale University have proven that all nuts furnish a relatively high amount of basic aminoacids, and that the nut proteins are of high biological value, fully adequate to maintain life and growth and for the elaboration of mother's milk. Professor Cajori found in his experiments, conducted at the Sheffield laboratory, that the protein and fat of nuts were generally absorbed to a large extent."

Studies of the proteins of nuts by Osborn and Harris, Van Slyke, Johns and Cajori demonstrated that the proteins of nuts are at least equal to those of meat. This was shown to be true ot the almond, black and English walnuts, butternut, pecan, filbert, Brazil nut, pine nut, chsetnut, hickory nut and cocoanut. Observations have shown that, in general, the proteins of oily seeds are complete proteins. Johns, Finks and Paul found that the globulin of the cocoanut is an adequate growth-factor in rats and that cocoanuts are almost completely sufficient as the sole source of protein in human beings. Para nuts have also been shown to be rich in superior protein. Not all workers are agreed about hickory nuts, many maintaining that these possess a low-grade protein. The others named are rich in high-grade proteins, promoting growth, development, reproduction, lactation, and the rearing of the young, not alone in animals, but also in man.

Nuts are acid-ash foods, as are all proteins, but they are not so much so as are animal proteins. The comparative degrees of acidity of the proteins run walnuts, 8; oysters, 15.3; veal 13.5; eggs, 12; chicken, 11.2; beef, 9.8; etc. Nuts contain less acid minerals than meat.

A brief consideration of a few of the nuts best known in this country will help us to appreciate their great value and, perhaps, cause us to encourage the production of more nuts. It would be difficult to overestimate the tremendous gain that would accrue to the people of our country if the millions of acres now devoted to grain-raising were devoted to nut and fruit culture. Let us look at the nuts in alphabetical order:

Acorn: A farinaceous nut produced by the oak tree. It was used to a great extent by the ancient Greeks and by the early inhabitants of the British Isles. It is still used extensively as food in certain parts of Turkey. When the white man first visited California he found 300,000 Indians thriving on a diet in which acorns were staple. They had thrived for hundreds of years on the acorn diet.

Almond: This is one of the finest of nuts, being higher in its phosphorus content than any other product of the vegetable kingdom. It also possesses considerable calcium. It is low in potassium. Contrary to popular teaching, the almond is not a base-forming food. It is definitely acid-forming, as are practically all nuts, Its skin should be removed before eating the almond as it contains a strong astringent. Avoid the sulphur-treated almonds sold in the market. An average analysis presents: water, 6.0; protein, 24.00; fats, 54.33; carbohydrates (no starch), 10; cellulose, 3; organic salts, 3.3.

Brazil nut: In our younger days we knew this nut as the "nigger-toe." It is one of the most important of the nuts. It is high in fat and rich in calcium and magnesium. Like the almond, its skin should be removed before eating it. An average analysis reveals: Water, 4.8; protein, 17.2; fat 66; carbohydrates (mostly sugar), 5.7; cellulose, or fibre, 3; organic salts, 3.3.

Cashew: Technically, this is not a nut, but the seed of the cashew apple. Unlike other seeds of fruit, it grows on the outside of the apple, at its lower end. It cannot be eaten in its natural raw state and the "raw" cashews sold in the market have been treated with low heat to dissipate the cardol and anacardic acids in them which acids burn the mouth and throat. The skins have also been removed.

Chestnut: Though having all the appearance of a nut, its shell is thinner than that of most nuts, the chestnut, in composition, is more closely related to the starchy grains. Almost as many people the world over live on bread made from chestnut-flour as upon that made from any kind of grain. It is superior to cereal flour as a food. An average analysis of the chestnut shows the following: Water, 6; protein, 10; fats, 8; carbohydrates (mostly starch), 70; cellulose, 3; minerals, 2.4.

Cocoanut: This is a very popular nut which, unfortunately, is usually consumed in horribly incompatible mixtures. Both its meat and its milk are fine foods and in some tropical places it makes up almost the whole bill-of-fare. An average analysis of the cocoanut gives the following figures: water, 3.5; protein, 6.3; fat, 57.4; carbohydrate, sugar and fiber, 31.5; organic salts, 1.3. Its minerals are chiefly phosphorus and potassium with small amounts of iron, sodium and manganese. It should be eaten with green vegetables or, like melons, taken alone.

The cocoanut is a remarkable sugar food. Its meat is an excellent and tasty food; its juice is a delicious and nutritious "drink." In its unripe or custard-like state it forms an almost perfect food for those who live in the tropics. When sprouted the "milk" of the cocoanut is transformed into a snow-white, sponge-like ball that is very sweet and very much in demand in countries where the nut is grown. Its oil, an emulsified fat, is employed as butter, and not used solely for soap-making.

Hickory-nut: Like the pecan, the hickory is strictly an American nut and many of us can recall the days we spent gathering them and eating them before the fire in the winter. The Indians stored these nuts in great abundance for winter use. Unfortunately, like the black walnut, it has a thick hard shell that prevents it from becoming popular with our effete people of today. An average analysis of the seventeen varieties of this nut that grow in America shows: water, 3.7; protein, 15.15; carbohydrates (almost all sugar), 12; organic salts, 2. The protein of this nut is of a high order, but it is claimed to be inadequate as a sole source of protein.

Pecan: This is the king of nuts and is a native of America. It was first used by the Indians who planted it all over large sections of our country. Dr. G. E. Harter of the Defensive Diet League of America, says that "one can live a full life, amply nourished, upon an exclusive diet of pecans and fruits." Members of the League demonstrated this fact. He says: "The fatty elements of this nut are more easily assimilated by the human body than any other obtainable." Here is an average analysis: water, 3.5; protein, 13; fat, 70.8; carbohydrates (mostly sugar), 8.5; cellulose (fiber), 3.7; organic salts, 1.5. The pecan is lower than most nuts in protein, but contains an ample quantity; it is highest of all nuts in a delicious and easily digested oil.

The pecan is not only rich in food value but possesses great appeal to the sense of taste. The pecan is a low protein food. Its fat is the easiest to digest of the nut oils. Pecans are easily digested. If well-chewed and properly combined they may be digested by all save the weakest digestions. Many chronically underweight persons pick up weight at once, when, in the pecan season, they consume pecans in great quantities. Pecans are not constipating, as is asserted in some quarters. On the contrary, due no doubt to the large quantity of oil they contain, they tend to be mildly laxative.

Pignolia or *Pine nut*: This is not really a member of the true nut family. There are many varieties of pignolias and they are highly esteemed. This nut possesses the highset percentage of protein of any natural food, a small portion of them supplying all the protein needs of the body. They are also rich in an easily digested oil. Well-chewed, as all nuts should be, they are easily digested. An average of a number of analyses shows the following composition: water, 6.4; protein, 33.9; fat, 49.4; carbohydrates (simple sugar),

6.9; organic salts, 3.4. Its mineral content is made up largely of calcium, magnesium and iron.

Pistachio: These nuts are greenish in color and the greener they are the better nuts they are. Although high in protein, this nut has been found to be non-acid, inclining to be alkaline-forming when digested. Its oil is very easily digested. It contains no indigestible cellulose, but is all food. Broadly the pistachio contains: water, 4.2; protein, 22.5; fat, 54.5; carbohydrates (largely simple sugar), 16; organic salts, 3.

Walnuts: Under this head it is customary to include, along with the English walnut, which came originally from France and Italy, and the black walnut, which is a native American nut, the Butternut. Each of these three nuts are excellent and tasty foods. For taste, the author's preference is the black walnut, but it has a thick, hard shell that renders it difficult to get at. Unfortunately, most present-day Americans know the black walnut only as a source of fine and beautiful wood out of which some of our most beautiful furniture is made. Compared with the black walnut, the English walnut is flat and stale. The following table of comparative analyses of these three nuts will tell you nothing of the flavors of each of them:

	Black	English	Butternut
Water	2.5	2.5	4.5
Protein	27.5	18.5	27.9
Fats	56.3	64.5	61.2
Carbohydrates	11.7	12.5	3.4
Cellulose	1.7	1.4	none
Minerals	1.9	1.7	3.0

In addition to the above listed nuts with which we are acquainted in this country, there are many other varieties of nuts. Some of these are very good nuts, others are not so good. The *Castanopis* or California chestnut is considered a link between the oak and the chestnut. It is eaten chiefly by birds and squirrels. The *Chufa*, known also as the earth-chestnut, is not really a nut. It grows underground like the peanut and when slightly parched has a flavor resembling the nut. The *Queensland nut*, grown only in Eastern Australia, resembles the Brazil nut, but has a superior flavor. The *Pilinut* or Javanese almond grown in the Philippines, East Indies and Asia, is seen in the U. S. only when brought here by immigrants. The *Sapucaia* or Paradise nut, is little known in this country outside our seabord cities. The *Suari* or tropical butternut is a native of British Guiana and is seldom seen in this country.

Peanuts are not nuts, but legumes. They are also known as ground-peas, ground-nut, goober, etc. In England they are called monkey nuts. The peanut grows underground, but does not grow on the roots of the pea vine. Ranked high in biological value because of its high protein content, its protein being of high quality, the peanut is a very much overrated food. Harter declares it to be the most dangerous of the bean family. It is high in protein; its mineral content is made up largely of phosphoric acid and it contains a high percentage of starch. The combination of these three substances makes it highly acid-forming and, when eaten with anything but green vegetables, very difficult to digest, if, indeed, it is digestible at all in other combinations. It is a great favorite of the candy-makers and this is certainly a vicious use of the peanut. The composition of the many varieties of the peanut depends upon soil, climate, etc. Its protein composition ranges from 25 to 35 percent, its fat content from 40 to 55 percent. The average of over two thousand analyses shows the following: water, 7.9; protein, 30; fat, 50; starch and cellulose taken together because inseparable by present methods, about 12; minerals, 2.9. I do not share Harter's view that eating peanuts is "literally playing with fire," but I know from experience how much trouble they can cause when not eaten correctly. Roasted peanuts are almost indigestible. Peanut butters are commonly roasted, salted and have hog lard added. At its best, raw peanut butter is oxidized to some extent and not equal to the peanut.

Nuts are commonly thought to be difficult of digestion. This thought seems to have its basis in the common habit of eating nuts as a last course in a several course dinner. The nuts are blamed for the discomfort that results from such eating. Biochemists assert that they have shown that nut proteins are not as digestible as flesh proteins. Even if this were true, it would not place flesh proteins above nut proteins. But this is not true. Their tests are not worth anything inasmuch as they were not properly carried out. The ability to digest nuts may be very low in one who is not accustomed to eating nuts; whereas, the same person, perhops habitually eating flesh, will have marked ability to digest flesh. If he begins the daily use of nuts his ability to digest these foods will increase day by day until maximum ability is reached, after which it levels off and remains at this maximum level, providing, of course, that he continues to eat nuts. To ignore this fact in determining the digestibility of any food, is to make tests that are of no practical value.

Finely ground and emulsified nuts have proven to be the very best substitutes for milk, when the mother's milk fails and the child is sensitive to cow's milk. There are many children who are sensitive to cow's milk and to the prepared milk foods on the market. Many children have been killed by milk whose lives might have been saved by nuts. Nut-butters are not to be recommended for this purpose. These are cooked, contain considerable "free" fatty acids, are usually salted, and often have other denatured oils added to them. Only the raw or unfired nuts are to be used.

Being concentrated foods, nuts must be eaten moderately and require to be thoroughly masticated. Combined with green vegetables, eaten as a regular part of the meal, and not at the end of a hearty meal, as is the usual practice, and thoroughly and slowly chewed, they are not difficult to digest and may be eaten by everyone. Their delightful flavours make them palatable to all save the most depraved appetites.

Vegetables
CHAPTER XI

We think of vegetables as plants cultivated for their edible portions. This loose definition includes leaves, stems, roots and tubers, pods, buds, flowers, seeds and fruits.

Leaves: spinach, chard, beet greens, turnip greens, chinese cabbage, mustard greens, kale, cabbage, etc.

Stems: rhubarb stalks, celery, cardoon, fennel, etc.

Roots and tubers: potatoes, sweet potatoes, turnips, radishes, carrots, salsify, parsnips, Jerusalem arthichoke, onions, etc.

Buds and flowers: French artichoke, broccoli, cauliflower, etc.

Seeds: beans, peas, peanuts, okra (of okra and green beans we also eat the pods), etc.

Fruits: Tomatoes, peppers, cucumbers, melons, squash, pumpkins, egg plant, etc.

The plant is the basis of all animal life; all animals deriving their food either directly or indirectly from plants. Plant eating animals always consume vegetables when they can get these and, while we speak of certain forms of animal life as graminivorous, it is a well-known fact that these animals, pigeons, for example, become ill, breed badly and rear fewer young, if they are unable to procure green food as well as grains.

The most marvelous chemical laboratory known resides in the green leaf. Here are formed all the marvelous products of the vegetable world — delightful colors, delicious aromas, foods, poisons, vitamins. But this is not all. Here in this scene of marvelous activity and growth are produced substances that impart the power to grow to young animals, which are unable to synthesize the highly complex organic materials essential to cell functioning out of crude inorganic matter.

Vegetables are one of our most important sources of food; the green leafy ones being, usually, more abundant in alkaline minerals than fruits. They are also rich in vitamins and carry small amounts of proteins of the highest quality. Experience and experiment have shown that the addition of green vegetables to a fruit and nut diet improves the diet and it is a fact that practically all frugivora include green vegetables in their diet.

Many valuable plant foods, weeds we call them now, have been used by peoples at various times, which are no longer in use. The American Indian used many plants, "wild," which we do not use. The Chinese make use of many greens unknown to us. So do the New Zealanders and Abyssinians. Archeologists find evidence that our progenitors made use of a vast number of plants which we ignore. During the Middle Ages salads were in high repute.

The North American Indians cultivated extensive gardens and cultivated many plants, some of which we have dropped from our gardens, perhaps to our detriment. They employed various kinds of greens, many fruits and a number of varieties of nuts and berries. Corn was practically their only cereal.

As shown in the introduction, the medical profession once taught that practically all the fresh fruits and vegtables which we eat, especially in the summer when they are most abundant, are causes of disease. It has required years of constant effort on the part of vegetarians and fruitarians to overcome this fallacy.

It will not be necessary to do more than briefly refer to a few of the more common vegetables. Let us being with the lowly lettuce which is one of the finset vegetables. It is safely alkaline and does not contain the opium that popular superstition says it does. Old fashioned leaf lettuce is superior to head lettuce in food value. Young lettuce is better than old lettuce. Hot house lettuce is of little worth, because it lacks sunshine.

Mr. Harter says: "Now that we in the North are getting Texas-grown lettuce, full of sunshine and good cheer, we feel that the winter lettuce problem is approaching solution." "Eat some lettuce every day. Eat garden-grown lettuce when you can get it — grown right where you live. The next lettuce is that 'shipped in from' Texas. Then comes Florida lettuce, not so good, not probably because of lack of sunshine, but because Florida soils are said to lack something that plant life needs. Texas soil needs no fertilizers while they must be used heavily in Florida. All fertilizers are questionable. Some are very bad; some destroy the value of foods; some make them injurious."

Bulletins Nos. 94-95 of the Defensive Diet League of America say: "We know definitely that lettuce, spinach and other products grown on the comparatively exhaustless soil of Texas and the far

VEGETABLES

West are so much more valuable as foods that it seems almost unbelievable, as for example, such a comparison of vitality as one to ten thousand. Of course loss in shipping long distances must be taken into account."

Spinach, a native of Persia, grows wild in Asia minor. It was cultivated in ancient Babylon and Nineveh. It is a fine food, but it has been much overrated, particularly as a food for children. Beet tops, turnip tops, kale, mustard, dandelion, leeks and other green leafy vegetables may be used instead of spinach.

Cabbage, which grew wild on the shores of the Mediterranean, was gathered for the tables of Rome. It is one of our most valuable vegetables and should not be spoiled by converting it into sourkraut. A head of cabbage, weighing two pounds, contains more organic salts of iodin than the thyroid gland can use in a week.

The cucumber was among the first cultivated plants and has been known for 2000 years. Fresh, green or ripe, they make excellent foods. Our parents thought they were poisonous. The poison resided chiefly in the skin, which nobody dared to eat, but some of it existed in the body of the cucumber. These excellent foods were first carefully pared and then soaked in salt water to "take the poison out of them." They were accused of causing "fevers." These prejudices, although they persist in the public mind, are unfounded. Cucumbers are not poisonous and do not cause fevers. Their skins are rich in minerals which are valuable to the body.

Cucumbers are especially rich in iron, potash, magnesium and calcium. They rank high among the alkalinizing vegetables. Containing about ninety percent pure water, they form excellent summer foods. They should never be pickled (pickled they are indigestible) nor soaked in salt water. They are best eaten unpeeled, whole, seeds, skins and all. Everyone may relish them whole—unpeeled, unsalted and fresh.

In the eighteenth century, New Englanders burned large stocks of potatoes because they were thought to be harmful and it was believed that if the cattle ate them they would be poisoned.

Okra is a food that comes to us from Africa, where the negroes call it *gumbo*. It is a tasty and valuable food, though not widely known outside the Southland. In its young, raw state it is very sweet. It is excellent for thickening soups instead of using the usual starches.

Mushrooms, falsely reported to rank high in food value, are as indigestible as boot straps. Simple observations show that they pass through the digestive tract unchanged. Untoward results have been reported as coming from their use.

Many superstitions cluster about the onion family — onions, scallions or shallots, garlic, leeks, chives — are numerous and some of them are very old. They possess none of the curative and prophylactic virtues attributed to them. Garlic will not reduce blood pressure, it is not an intestinal antiseptic, onions will not "cure" gall stones. None of the *curative* powers attributed to these foods are real.

These bulbs and their blades are rich in mustard oil that imparts to them their irritating quality and renders them unfit for regular articles of diet. The oil is eliminated through the kidneys and must, if used regularly, ultimately impair the kidneys. Their irritating effects upon the digestive system cannot but enervate these. For all their richness in certain valuable food factors, they should be eaten only rarely — and then, only when you are going to be alone.

All foods that grow above ground in the sun are superior to foods that grow under the ground, a fact known to the ancients. Roots and tubers are usually deficient in calcium and sometimes in sodium. This is especially true of potatoes and carrots. Beet tops, radish tops and turnip tops are more important foods than the beets, radishes and turnips.

There is a seasonal rise and fall in the nutritive value of vegetables caused by the varying amounts of sunshine in the different seasons. Spinach, for example, grown in summer is richer in vitamins and basic minerals, such as iron, calcium and manganese, than spinach grown in winter. This is also true of other green vegetables and of fruits and berries. Winter vegetables grown in the far south, Florida, Southwest Texas, etc., are far superior in these respects to winter vegetables grown farther north.

There is a marked difference between the green parts of plants and the seed from the nutritional standpoint. The seeds contain an excess of acids, while the leaves contain an excess of bases. Leaves are richly supplied with sodium and calcium, whereas, all seeds are deficient in these bases. Animals fed on grain, must also be given plenty of green fodder, if they are to rear their young. Even birds must have greens along with their grains. Green leaves contain considerable quantities of vitamin A — more, usually, than most fats contain.

Due to the greater abundance of salts and vitamins in young, rapidly growing plants and also to the fact that most of them are

VEGETABLES

alkaline in reaction, they are better than the matured ones for food. It will be noticed by all who observe them that animals and birds prefer young tender grasses, herbs and seeds to the older forms of plant life. Migratory birds follow the vegetation northward in the Spring and southward in the late Fall.

Young onions, young cabbage, etc.,, are better than old onions or old cabbage. The same is undoubtedly true of potatoes, popular opinion to the contrary notwithstanding. Young lettuce is better than old lettuce. Young peas, young beans, etc., are basic foods, but matured pulses of all kinds are acid formers. Those of us who are located in the winter-garden and valley regions of Texas, where we have fresh fruits and vegetables all year are to be envied by our less fortunate kinsmen of the North and East.

The outer, greener leaves and stalks of lettuce, celery, cabbage, etc., are superior to their white, inner leaves and stalks. Lazy people, who do not like to chew, dislike the tough outer stalks of celery, or the outer leaves of lettuce. They prefer the "hearts" of these and other such foods. But these outer leavs contain more minerals and are possessed of more of those food qualities to which the name *vitamin* (or complettin) has been attached. In well-to-do families these better parts of such foods are thrown away; in the poorer families they are not discarded.

In general, green vegetables are the richest sources of minerals and vitamins. Practically all green leaves are rich in vitamin C. Cabbage is also rich in B. Cucumbers are rich in C, as is also the bell pepper. Leaves contain an excess of bases (alkaline salts) while seeds contain an excess of acids. Even nuts, with perhaps one or two exceptions, contain an excess of acids. Green leaves also contain small quantities of very high grade proteins.

The following paragraphs are from the third edition of *Chemistry of Food and Nutrition*, by Prof. Sherman, of Columbia University: "They (vegetables and fruits) tend to correct both the mineral and the vitamin deficiencies of the grain products, and in a sense they supplement the milk also, in that many of the vegetables and fruits are rich in iron or vitamin C, or both *** This increasing use of vegetables and fruits improves the food value of the diet at every point at which the American dietary is likely to need improvement.

"The benefit to health which so generally results from a free use of milk, vegetables and fruits in the diet may be attributed in part to the fact that these foods yield alkaline residues when oxidized in the body; but this point should not be too greatly emphasized, for there are several other respects in which the eating of liberal amounts of milk, vegetables, and fruits is certainly beneficial, notably in supplying calcium (lime), iron and vitamins, and in improving the intestinal condition.

"It becomes apparent that a dietary made up, as so many dietaries are, too largely of breadstuffs, meats, sweets, and fats, may be satisfying to the palate and to the traditional demand for variety, may furnish ample quota of protein, calories, with fats and carbohydrates in any desired proportion, and yet may be inadequate because of faults in its mineral and vitamin content. We now understand how it is that fruits, vegetables and milk in its various forms serve (in ways which until recently could not be fully appreciated) to make good the deficiencies of breadstuffs, meat, sweets, and most fats."

Cereals
CHAPTER XII

Cereals, after Ceres, goddess of the harvest, are grains. Oats, wheat, rye, rice, barley, millet, and similar grass seed, used as foods, are denominated cereals. They grow and mature in short seasons, can be grown in parts of the world that have short growing seasons, will grow almost everywhere, may be produced with a minimum of effort and will keep almost indefinitely. For these reasons they have been the mainstay of whole populations, despite the many objections that may be offered to their use. Until recent modern times, they were used almost wholly as whole grain and not as refined products.

I should not have to remind my readers that the only grain products that are permissible in the diet of an intelligent and informed individual are whole grains in the dry state. But after this has been said, it is necessary to sound a warning against the use of grains in the *Hygienic* diet. At their best, grains are inferior articles of food and they certainly form no part of the normal diet of man. Every man, woman and child in the land will be better off by leaving them out of their diet.

Dr. Emmet Densmore was the first to raise a voice against the use of cereal products. He pointed out that man is a frutarian animal, not adapted to the use of cereals, and traced many evils to the employment of grains, even whole grains, as food. He declared bread to be the "staff of death" instead of the "staff of life" as it is usually referred to.

Considering man a frutarian and finding that fruits (ripe) contain plenty of sugar, but little or no starch, whereas the cereal and vegetable diet of civilization is largely starch, he began to investigate the subject still more. He soon found that starch requires much more time and energy to digest than fruit and that cereals are the most difficult of all to digest. "Fruits are best, cereals are worst" he declared. He quotes, approvingly, Dr. Evans as saying: " 'Cereal and farinaceous foods form the basis of the diet of so-called 'vegetarians,' who are not guided by any direct principle, except that they believe it is wrong to eat animal food. For this reason

THE SCIENCE AND FINE ART OF FOOD AND NUTRITION

vegetarians enjoy no better health, and live no longer than those around them'."

Declaring man not to be naturally a grain-eating animal, Densmore says: "The only animals that may be truly said to be grain-eating are birds. Many species of birds eat a considerable portion of grass seeds (and all cereals are developed from grass)°°° birds are the animals for which starchy seeds are the natural food, and birds have altogether a different digestive apparatus from other animals." Even birds do not feed their young on grains—"They generally feed their young on insects and ollusces, while feeding themselves on fruits and seeds," declares Densmore.

Squirrels often are forced, from scarcity of food, to eat cereals. They bite off the end containing the germ and eat this, leaving the rest of the grain. Berg says "the proteins of most seeds, and especially those of cereals, are especially characterized by inadequacy due to a lack of cystin and lysin. In like manner, it is a common characteristic of seeds, not only to contain an excess of acid, but also to exhibit a deficiency of calcium. For lime is almost always present in the soil, so that seeds need not contain any more calcium than is requisite to provide for the growth of the first rootlet. In animal organisms, on the other hand, the need for calcium is very great. Cereals, consequently, quite apart from the fact that they contain an excess of acid, are about the most unsuitable food we can force upon the growing animal organism. The best proof of this is that even graminivorous birds collect insects to nourish their young. The fledglings of the most strictly vegetarian birds are carnivora."

All experimenters seem to agree that the much vaunted cereal diet is inadequate. Funk, Simmons, Pitz, Hess, Unger, Hart, Halpin, Steenbock, Davis, Hogan, Mendel, Wakeman, Parsons and others of equal standing agree with Berg who agrees with Densmore. Oats are deficient in basic salts. Wheat is deficient in sodium and calcium, while the germ of the wheat is inadequate as a growth-factor. Rice is deficient in salts, and especially in calcium. It does not contain enough calcium to support an adult hog. It is also deficient in sodium and chlorine. They are all lacking in iodine.

Mineral deficiency is a common fault in the diet of young animals fed largely on cereals and it has long been known to farmers and stockmen that their animals must have grass and other green foods—that they will not thrive well on an all-cereal diet. In his laboratory experiments with whole wheat bread, Milo

Hastings found that the animals used thrived better and grew more rapidly as the percentage of green foods was increased and the percentage of whole wheat bread was decreased in their diet. If the green foods constituted well over half their diet, they thrived best.

"We have learned," says Berg, "that all cereals have certain defects which may be looked upon as characteristic of these nutriments. As regards inorganic salts, they are deficient in sodium and calcium; they are also poorly supplied with organically combined sulphur and with bases generally; but they contain a superabundance of inorganic acid-formers and of potassium. The cereals are also poor in A, B and C, the poverty being more marked in proportion to the fineness of the flour. Finally, the proteins of the cereals are always inadequate; they are lacking to some extent in the ringed amino-acids, and are especially poor in lysin and cystin."

The contention, so frequently heard, that whole wheat is a perfect food, is a foolish statement of over-enthusiastic salesmen. A few years ago an acquaintance of the writer's made an effort to walk from New York to San Francisco on a diet of whole raw wheat alone. Before starting, however, he consulted me and I advised him not to try it, but to have an abundance of lettuce and celery and some fruit in addition to his wheat. He would not hear of such a plan. Whole wheat is a perfect food and he was going to prove that one could accomplish such a walk on a whole wheat diet. He didn't get as far on his wheat as George Hassler Johnston got on his water diet (fasting) before he discovered that whole grain wheat is not the perfect diet that the "health" food exploiters and amateur dietitians say it is.

"It has long been known," says Berg, "that when herbivora, and still more when rodents, are fed exclusively on grain, acidosis rapidly ensues. In rabbits on a maize diet, for example, the acid urine contains far more phosphorus than is being introduced in the food. (Showing that phosphorus is being lost from the animal's tissues.— Author). °°° Rats, again, can only endure an exclusive grain diet for a short period, speedily succumbing to such a regime. An abundant addition of protein to the grain does not help. Hogan, however, tells us that that an addition of alkalies preserves life and has a marvelous effect in furthering growth."

McCollum fed rats on a diet restricted to grains — only one kind of grain being used at a time — and found that they became restless, irritable and apprehensive. They were "on edge," rather than "full of pep." He inclines to the belief that the "obstreperousness" of the horse that "feels his oats" is due to the fact that he is suffering from an "attack" of nerves; that he is displaying pathological irritability and apprehensiveness, rather than healthy activitiy.

There are vegetarians who might more properly be called *cerealists;* that is, they drop flesh from their diet and substitute large quantities of cereals therefor. Usually they do this because they are told that whole wheat, for example, is an almost perfect food—"has all the elements the body needs in about the right proportion." These people not only consume too much cereal for which they suffer, but they eat their cereal in forms that tend to ferment before it digests.

Take, for example, the mush dish of boiled oat-meal, to which has been added milk and sugar, so commonly eaten. It is one of the worst abominations that ever slipped down the human throat. It is practically indigestible. No saliva and no ptyalin are poured out upon such a dish and it may remain in the stomach for hours, undergoing little or no digestion, before it is permitted to pass into the intestine. Fermentation is inevitable. Cracked wheat, soaked and boiled, and then served with milk and sugar, milk and honey, milk and sweet fruits, is equally indigestible.

The oatmeal, or cracked wheat or other soaked or boiled cereal does not undergo salivary digestion, even when, and if, eaten without milk and sugar. When eaten in the usual combination, digestion is doubly impossible.

Flaked cereal foods (various types of corn flakes and other such foods) are much in use. Chemical analysis shows them to be possessed of abundant food value, though, actually, they are largely charcoal. They are said to be ready-cooked and predigested. This is a fallacy that the public must outgrow. They are pressed between rollers at intense heat and are rendered practically valueless as foods.

Whole wheat alone will not sustain life, health and growth in an ideal manner. After a shorter or longer period on such a diet, the rate of growth slackens unless, in addition to the whole wheat, the animal is also fed some green foods. Furthermore, if growth is to continue in an ideal manner, the amount of green foods must be greater than the amount of whole wheat. Hasting's experiments only serve to corroborate the correctness of the long-

CEREALS

time observations of farmers that their horses, mules, etc., must be given grass or other green foods and cannot be fed exclusively upon grains or other dry foods for any considerable time without harm.

Wheat is the most acid-forming of the cereals. Oats seem to have the worst effect on the teeth. Rice which is probably the best of the cereals, is the staple article of food in the diet of more than half the world's human inhabitants. Cases of beri-beri in human beings have been reported in which whole and not polished rice constituted the bulk of the diet.

I have repeatedly referred to the dangers of attempting to feed man after the results of experiments on animals. For, as Berg says, "The same nutriment has very different effects on different species of animals." Maize proves harmless to fowls and pigeons. Rats maintain health on it. It produces marked polyneuritis in rabbits and scurvy in guinea pigs. Pigs fed on maize die from general malnutrition. Fowls fed on wheat maintain health while pigs and rats develop polyneuritis on this diet, and guinea pigs develop scurvy thereon.

Says Berg: "The varying reactions of different species of animals to an identical diet is still a complete enigma, and in my opinion insufficient attention has been paid to the matter. Speaking generally it would seem that graminivorous birds thrive on whole grains, but suffer from polyneuritis when the grain is hulled. In mammals, on the other hand, grain feeding may cause polyneuritis in certain circumstances, especially in rodents (except for the omnivorous rat), which are highly susceptible to acidosis. In many mammals, however, a grain diet induces scurvy instead of polyneuritis; while some animals perish from general malnutrition owing to the inadequate supply of inorganic nutriments in the grain. When grain has been thoroughly hulled, almost all animals, human beings included, become affected with polyneuritis. Are these variations due to varying requirements in respect to vitamins; or are the polyneuritic disorders due to the absence of various vitamins which act differently in different species of animals, or are essential to different species in varying degree?"

This last question of Berg's completely ignores the mineral deficiencies of grain and the varying requirements of various animals for these minerals. It completely ignores the individuality of the organization and functions of the various species. It is enough for us, at this point, that we note the evils of the largely grain diet and the confirmation of Densmore's earlier claims. While fowls thrive on a grain diet (this is only true of adult fowls), we must not overlook the fact that in a state of nature the graminivorous birds all consume large quantities of green grasses, and even consume most of the seeds or grains in their green or "milk" state, when they are alkaline and not acid.

Corn, while green and still growing, contains almost no starch, but considerable sugar. During the last two or three weeks of its maturing period, this sugar is converted into starch which, unlike sugar, is insoluble in water and therefore not readily fermentable. What is true of corn is true of other grains.

Green corn is not classed as a starch. It ranks relatively high as a base-forming food. Some of our State Agricultural Experiment stations have shown that, when green corn is detached from the stalk, it immediately begins to ripen and will accomplish as much of the ripening process in twenty-four hours, as it would have done in several weeks, had it been left on the stalk. So rapid is the transformation of the sugar into starch that in twenty-four hours, it is changed from an alkaline-ash to an acid-ash food.

Germinated grains make better food than dry grains. Grains "in milk," this is, before they have been matured, are alkaline foods, but the matured grains are acid. Fresh corn on the cob, not off the stalk for twenty-four hours or longer, is an alkaline food.

Never before in history have as much cereals and refined flours been consumed, as in America and parts of Europe, since the perfection of the rolling mill process in 1879. Bread is consumed in enormous quantities. Breakfast foods (denatured cereals) are eaten in considerable quantities in almost every household. "Health" food stores and "health" food factories turn out more cereal products than all other products combined. The advocates of whole cereals, in preference to the denatured kinds, did their work too well. Vegetarians are usually great eaters of cereals. They would receive less harm from moderate amounts of meat.

Cereal (denatured) with cream (pasteurized) and sugar (white) is a staple breakfast in most households. A predominantly acid forming breakfast, a horrible combination — and plenty of sickness as a result. The physicians continue to tell us that germs cause our diseases!

CEREALS

Bread eating is one of the great curses of modern life. Made of cereals, largely of denatured cereals, mixed with salt, soda, yeast, lard and often other ingredients and subjected to a high degree of temperature, in cooking, and then eaten three and four times a day, in considerable quantities, mixed indiscriminately with all classes of foods and taken in addition to much other starch food, bread is one of our chief sources of woe.

The so-called enrichment of white flour has given people a false sense of security. Various states have passed laws requiring the "enrichment" of all flour manufactured in or shipped into them. The people are lead, by this requirement, to believe that the "enriched" flour is good food. Never was a greater fallacy entertained. These laws were lobbied through the state legislatures by the milling companies, in an effort to head off the rising demand for whole-wheat flour. They seem to have temporarily succeeded.

This "enriching" process adds a small quantity of "synthetic vitamins" but does not return to the flour the minerals that have been extracted. Seventy-five percent of the minerals of the wheat are extracted in the process of making white flour. All of the vitamins, and not just one, are removed. The present process of "enrichment" is similar to the process of sixty and seventy years ago of adding phosphorus to the flour to replace the phosphorus extracted in milling.

In the milling process organic salts are extracted. These are not returned by the "enriching" process. In the milling process real vitamins are removed. Part of these are replaced, by the "enriching" process, with fraudulent or imitation vitamins. What folly to remove the vitamins in the first place! Why not leave them in the flour and why remove them at all?

Dr. Anton J. Carlson, noted physiologist of the Department of Physiology of the University of Chicago, recently uttered a warning about this very matter in which he said that the term "enriched" applied to white flour to which a little vitamin B is added is misleading. "Such flour is still impoverished," he said. Referring to the fact that the idea is "put across" that "enriched" flour is better than whole grain flour he pointed out that refining actually takes out salts, vitamins and proteins, only a small part of which are replaced by the "enrichment" process. The learned physiologist added that the theory that some races cannot physiologically tolerate whole grain is without foundation. He declared it to be not a matter of toleration but of acceptance, adding that food acceptance is a question of what a person is used to from childhood. "You cannot overnight change the diet of a healthy people," he declared, although, since he never saw a healthy people, it would be interesting to know how he came to this conclusion.

Grain alone was shown, by experiments conducted by the Defensive Diet League, to be a much safer food than grain and meat — the combination of these at the same meal being the chief trouble-maker. We know that too much bread, if taken alone, will break down one's health. But the combination of bread and meat causes even more trouble. Such a diet, when fed to experimental animals (young ones), resulted in high blood pressure, Bright's disease and troubles which usually accompany these conditions in man. Neither do the animals grow as they should.

Cereals are about the most difficult to digest of any habitual sources of starch except beans and peas. They are difficult for the infant and growing child. They ferment easily and cause much gas and intoxication.

Cereal starches require from eight to twelve times as long to digest as does potato starch. Grierson found that two full hours are required to digest the starch of wheat, corn and rice, and eighty minutes to digest the starch of oats, whereas the same amount of potato starch digests in ten minutes.

Doctors frequently recommend the feeding of cereals to infants and children. Densmore declared: "Cereal or grain and all starch foods are unwholesome for all human beings; but this diet is especially unfavorable for children, and more especially for babies. The intestinal ferments which are required for the digestion of starch are not secreted until the babe is about a year old; and these ferments are not as vigorous for some years as in adults. All starch foods depend upon these intestinal ferments for digestion, whereas dates, figs, prunes, etc., are equally as nourishing as bread and cereals, and are easily digested — the larger proportion of the nourishment from such fruits being ready for absorption and assimilation as soon as eaten." No starch and, more particularly, cereals, should be given any child before it is two years old.

Dr. Percy Howe, of Harvard University, says: "Mrs. Mellanby and Dr. Pattison, in England, have just concluded a very interesting experiment on 71 children in a bone-tuberculosis hospital, for a period of 28 weeks, which may help to establish the fact that

CEREALS

cereals, especially oatmeal, exert an anti-calcifying influence." Calcification is the deposit of lime salts in the tissues. Cereals would prove a distinct evil in rickets, tuberculosis and in growing children, if this is proven to be true. Of course, these people had no right to experiment on these children, but since human vivisection goes on in every hospital and sanitorium in the world, they probably thought they had as much right to flirt with human health and life and produce suffering, as do the other physicians, surgeons and "research" workers.

We may state a few conclusions about cereals from the above facts:

(1) Cereals do not form any part of the natural diet of man and are not necssary to health and life. (I believe geologists and anthropologists are agreed that man did not become a cereal eater until late in his history).

(2) They are best omitted from the diet entirely and especially from the diet of infants and children.

(3) Where they are eaten, only the whole, undenatured, unprocessed cereal should be taken.

(4) They should form but a small amount of the diet and shoud be offset with an abundance of fresh fruits and green vegetables — properly combined.

(5) To insure the conversion of their starches into sugar they must always be eaten dry and not as porridges and mushes.

Animal Foods
CHAPTER XIII

The unfitness of certain substances for assimilative purposes is manifest by the anaphylactic symptoms that so frequently follow their use. Alimentary anaphylactic phenomena are confined almost exclusively to substances of animal origin. The more closely these animal substances resemble the human body in composition, the more frequently do they give rise to these phenomena. Thus flesh is the worst offender, eggs come second and milk is last.

Little can be said in defense of the use of animal foods except in instances of dire necessity. Let us consider them briefly.

HONEY

Honey is popularly considered a legitimate sweet for promiscuous and perfectly safe use, where other sweets are considered to be dangerous. This is a delusion. Its sugar does not combine with other foods any better than do other sugars, while the manite acid it contains renders its combination with other foods undesirable.

The presence of manite acid in honey renders its combination with other foodstuffs more injurious than ordinary cane sugar. Its combination with starchy or protein foods is sure to produce indigestion. Those with impaired digestions will be sure to hvae gas following its use.

Honey made from certain flowers is positively poisonous. In many parts of the world poisonous honeys are produced. I have eaten honey that was as bitter as quinine. Its color, its flavor and its poisonous or non-poisonous quanlities depend on the flowers from which the bees extract the pollen.

From time immemorial honey has been used as a stimulant. It has played a prominent role in the materia medicas of a number of different peoples. Herodotus tells that the Egyptians employed it in mummyfying the dead, because of its preservative qualities.

In spite of my warning against the use of honey many are going to continue to use it, declaring it to be a "natural sweet." Most honeys are delicious and the appeal to the gustatory sense is often irresistible. Those who cannot resist its lure and those who refuse to listen to any advise must find out the hard way as many others have had to do.

I cannot and do not recommend its use. But I know that there are those who are going to continue to use it. These should know that people who are engaged in active outdoor work, using their muscles rather than their brains, can use honey to best advantage. It should not be mixed with fruit, milk, cereals, mushes, meat or bread. Thoroughly charcoalized (toasted) bread may be used with honey.

No person with gastric or intestinal ulcer, or any marked catarrhal condition should ever use honey. Highly organized, nervous and sensitive people should also avoid this food.

EGGS

Eggs at best are poor foods while modern methods of egg production, involving great overstimulation of laying strains, produces eggs of a very poor quality. Egg eating usually involves over consumption of protein.

Raw egg white, so often urged as food for invalids, is poorly digested and assimilated. From thirty to fifty per cent of the amount consumed passes through the digestive canal without being digested and absorbed. Raw egg white may produce diarrhea and sometimes vomiting.

Egg whites are acid forming, and produce in some stomachs almost deadly acids. It is asserted that "practically all constipated people are sensitive to white of egg poisoning."

Invalids, inactive people and those inclined to constipation should especially avoid egg whites. They are bad food for children. Eggs should certainly never be eaten by one whose liver or kidneys are not in perfect condition.

Because Beaumont, in his experiment upon Alexis St. Martin, noticed that raw egg whites left the stomach very quickly, in less time in fact than the other foodstuffs he investigated, the idea grew that raw egg white is the most easily digested of all food substances.

Pavlov showed that egg white, unlike other proteins, does not stimulate the flow of gastric juice. Abderhalden discovered that pepsin does not act readily upon egg white. Okada showed that pancreatic juice and bile are both indifferent to egg white. Very little bile is poured out and trypsin has no effect whatever upon raw egg white. Other investigators have confirmed these findings.

Vernon, Hetin and others have shown that raw egg white hinders the digestion of other substances. Bayliss, Prof. of Physiology, University of London, (*The Physiology of Food and Economy in Diet*), says that raw egg white contains some substance which even in small amounts, hinders the action of the digestive fluids. Lemoine, a French authority, after careful study, says raw egg white contains a poison which damages the kidneys.

The yolk of the egg seems to be less objectionable and is an alkaline-ash food, whereas the white is an acid-ash food. Egg yolks are easily digested and, if taken raw are not the source of any trouble. I can, however, see no reason for using egg yolks, a practice that is rather expensive.

MILK

Milk is nature's food for the new-born mammal. It is highly diluted and well adapted to the delicate and undeveloped stomach of the young for which it is prepared. Cow's milk is prepared to meet the nutritive needs of the calf; goat's milk is prepared to meet the nutritive needs of the kid; the milk of the bitch is designed to meet the nutritive needs of her puppies. The same with the milk of other animals. Each animal produces milk for its own young.

The young of all mammallian species naturally subsist for a certain period exclusively on milk — the milk of their own mothers which is especially prepared for them. But there comes a time when they begin instinctively to add other foods to their diets. Finally, they abandon milk completely and the fountains of supply dry up.

The lactating period of all mammals is brief. The same is true in human mothers. From this fact, it is evident that nature has not designed us for a milk diet. She has made no provision to supply us with milk beyond a certain stage of our development. The nursing period of various mammallian young varies according to the rapidity of their growth, those animals that grow slowest having the longest nursing periods. The length of the nursing period is in direct ratio to the time required to reach maturity. It is but natural that in man whose growth is slowest and who requires longest to reach maturity, the nursing period should be longest.

The digestive organs of babies are in a condition requiring liquid food and milk, particularly their mother's milk, is peculiarly adapted to their physiological needs and powers. As they grow, new organs and new powers are developed. The new functions adapt the child

ANIMAL FOODS

to new kinds of food. Simultaneously with the development of the teeth, corresponding developments in the physiological powers of the digestive system take place so that they are fitted to digest solid foods and are ready to discontinue the use of milk. As in the case of the lower animals, there is a transition period, during which the child eats both milk and other articles of diet, but there should also come a time when milk is no longer needed and should no longer be taken. Man should be weaned.

Milk has grown to be the basis of one of the country's staple businesses. New York city alone pays more than half a million dollars a day for milk. The profits of milk distributing are very high, consequently, the business has attracted some of the nation's wealthiest and most influential citizens. The result has been the creation of a milk trust that is ever expanding and more and more monopolizing the milk industry. Laws requiring pasteurization of all milk sold in commerce is one of their weapons against the small dairymen and the individual farmers who seek to sell their milk.

This milk trust, assisted by certain members of the medical profession, medical organizations and even by Boards of Health, has fostered the idea that man should remain a suckling all his life. He should never be weaned. By this they do not mean that he should continue to nurse at his mother's breasts all of his life (this would net them no profits) but that he should suck the teats of the cow throughout life, even if he lives to be ninety or a hundred years old. This fallacy is promoted for purely commercial reasons.

In Japan male children are nursed at the breast durnig childhood and sometimes to the age of nine years. Viewing the physique and the mentality of the Japanese one can see no evidence of any advantage to be gained from such prolonged use of milk.

There can be no doubt that the present practice of forcing children to consume a quart of milk (sometimes more) a day is a vicious practice. The children are certainly getting too much milk. There are better foods that the children should be given and the forced feeding program should be abandoned.

For adults milk is both an inefficient and uneconomical food. It is certainly not an essential element of the adult diet. No mammal in a state of nature ever receives milk after it is weaned. This is also true of those peoples who have no herds or flocks that produce milk. Before man domesticated the cow, goat, camel, ass, horse, reindeer, etc., he received no milk after weaning. In various

—171—

parts of the earth today, he consumes the milk of a variety of different animals, but there are still large portions of the human race that do not drink milk.

It is important to note that milk is totally absent from the diet of adults in many virile peoples and certainly cannot be regarded as an indispensable item of adult diet. Indeed, there are important reasons to think that it is not a good article of diet for children after they have passed the normal nursing period. It is not employed by any other mammal after the period of infancy has passed and, with a few exceptions, has not been an article of diet in the human family after weaning, until compartively modern times. The dairy industry is very new.

When the Americas were discovered they were inhabited by millions of "red" men who possessed no milk animals. After an *Indian* child was weaned, usually at the age of four years, he never again had milk to drink. In 1624 the first cattle were introduced into New England and by 1632 no farmer was satisfied without a cow. The cow was raised for both domestic and export purposes. But, "the market was soon over-stocked, and the price of cattle went down from fifteen and twenty pounds to five pounds; and milk was a penny a quart." "This latter statement about the price of milk means very little, as cows were seldom milked at this time, being raised principally for their hides, and secondarily for meat, and only incidentally for milk."—*Social Forces in American History*, A. M. Simons.

In the earlier editions of his *The Newer Knowledge of Nutrition*, before he became a highly paid consultant on nutrition to the National Dairy Products Co., Prof. E. V. McCollum stressed the fact that milk is not an essential in the diet of man. He pointed out that the inhabitants of southern Asia have no herds and do not drink milk. Their diet is made up of rice, soy beans, sweet potatoes, bamboo sprouts, and other vegetables. According to Prof. McCollum these people are exceptional for the development of their physique and endurance, while their capacity for work is exceptional. They escape skeletal defects in childhood and have the finest teeth of any people in the world. This is a sharp and favorable contrast with milk-drinking peoples. The professor found it expedient to delete these facts from all editions of his work published subsequent to his becoming Consultant to National Dairy. Truth must be suppressed when and if it threatens profits and salaries.

ANIMAL FOODS

For a time Graham favored the use of milk by adults, but he tells us: "eight years of very extensive experiment and careful observation, have shaken many of my preconceived opinions concerning milk as an article of human food." Hundreds of Graham's followers who tried the experiment of using milk and of doing without it all stated that they did better with milk and vegetables than with flesh and vegetables, but that they did better when they confined themselves to a purely vegetable regimen and drank only water. Physical workers of various kinds — farmers, mechanics, etc., — found they were more vigorous and active and had more endurance when they left milk out of their diets. They stated that they experienced less exhaustion and fatigue at the end of the day if they ate only vegetable fare and no milk. "I have found," says Graham, "that dyspeptics and invalids of every description, do better when they abstain from the use of milk than when they use it, and in many cases it is indispensably necessary to prohibit milk." He adds: "Dyspeptics almost invariably find it oppresive to their stomachs, causing a sense of distention and heaviness."

Graham conceded that there may be conditions of life, outside of infancy, when milk may be used to advantage, but gave it as a general rule for adults, that they should abstain from milk entirely.

It is now quite generally admitted that milk is not as valuble as a "proctective" food as it was thought to be a few years ago. That the free use of milk will prevent tooth decay is a fallacy that can be seen on every hand. There is no evidence of its superiority in providing for bone development.

Dr. Victor Lindlahr says "close to one-half of the daily protective food intake should be composed of fresh raw foods. This will include milk." Yet all over the country, almost all the milk the people can get is pasteurized milk and this is no longer a "protective food." Too many dietitians, doctors and physicians are feeding pasteurized milk under the delusion that it possesses all the virtues of raw milk.

Milk is held to be the "carrier" of a number of serious diseases such as tuberculosis, colds, septic sore throat, rheumatic fever, heart disease, undulant fever, typhoid fever, scarlet fever, measles, dysentery, and other infections which are said to be frequently "traceable to contaminated milk." Epidemics of ulcers of the stomach and intestinal tracts of children have also been said to have been traced to drinking milk from cows with inflamed udders. *Hygienists* consider all this to be sheer nonsense that will be outgrown in time. Robert

Koch first "discovered" that tuberculosis may be transmitted from cow to man by drinking milk from tubercular cows. The so-called scientific world accepted his alleged discovery. Koch continued his investigations of the matter and came to the conclusion that he had been wrong. He repudiated his "discovery" and said that tuberculosis is not transmitted in this manner. The so-called "scientific" world refused to accept his repudiation. They had found the "discovery" profitable and useful — they refused to give it up.

Intensive and high-priced propaganda has been employed to make the people believe that pasteurizing makes milk "safe," and that no milk save pasteurized milk is "safe." Millions of people are literally afraid of unpasteurized milk. They are convinced that they take their lives in their hands when they drink a glass of unpasteurized milk. The big dairies and certain medical organizations, helped in some states, by the Boards of Health, have fostered this deliberate fraud upon the people for commercial reasons. The first and, so far as is conceivable, the only reason for the existence of laws and regulations requiring the pasteurization of milk is the protection of the interests of the big milk distributors.

The milk trust has also fostered the belief that bottled milk is "safer" than loose milk. There is not a shred of evidence for the truth of this idea, but its acceptance by the public has led to the outlawing of the sale of loose milk, hence has helped the milk trust in securing its monopoly of the industry.

Despite the law, milk is regularly adulterated and the adulteration is never put on the label. Although this is a violation of the Pure Food and Drug Act, the dairying industry has never been prosecuted for its adulteration of milk. One of the most common adulterations put into milk is the so-called "alkalinizers." These are used most during the summer months to mask the taste of milk produced by the growth of bacilli in it. This enables the milk industry to sell old milk as "fresh milk."

Modern methods of milk production — overfeeding of cows on rich fare and forced long periods of milking, everproduction of milk with its inevitable drain on the organism of the cow, tuberculin testing and vaccination of cows, etc. — are not designed to produce the best quality of milk. Certified milk, produced by cows kept in sunless barns and fed on dry foods, is an especially inadequate food.

ANIMAL FOODS

FISH LIVER OILS

Although the majority of vegetarians and drugless practitioners recommend and prescribe cod-liver oil to children and adults, I have consistently rejected this grease. About twelve years ago there came out of England, from thoroughly orthodox medical sources, evidences that I am no longer to stand alone in this matter. The *British Medical Journal* (Aug. 1929) declares that "there is some difference of opinion as to the effects of cod-liver oil in ordinary doses, and the present evidence is suggsetive enough to warrant a definite answer to the question: "Can cod-liver oil do harm?"

Agduhr testing the oil on rabbits and Malmberg using children for his tests, both came to the conclusion that oil is harmful to the heart, and is often responsible for cases of death in children. Agduhr working with Dr. N. Stenstron, proved definitely, by animal experimentation, that cod-liver oil produces pathological changes in the heart muscle. P. Hendricksen concludes, from his tests, that large doses may produce general cell degeneration throughout the body. C. W. Herlitz, I. Jundell and F. Wahlgre, after conducting an extensive and elaborate series of experiments, showed that doses quite comparable with those given to children in ordinary practice can produce considerable degeneration in the heart muscle. These men feel that the public should be warned of these dangers as well as of the dangers from radiated milk.

In an article in the *British Medical Journal,* Dr. A. A. Osman shows that many of the cases of marked debility of children are cases of ketosis —a form of disturbed sugar metabolism. He says that the treatment of such conditions with cod-liver oil increases the ketosis, yet many hundreds of children so suffering have been treated with this oil. Cod-liver oil increases rather than relieves the symptoms of ketosis.

FLESH

The use of meat, particularly its use in the usual quantities, is detrimental to man's health and strength of mind and body; due chiefly to four factors:

First: Meat is very rich in protein and its use in the usual quantities means the intake of considerably more protein than is required, with harmful consequences. The average digestion can care for not more than four ounces of meat at a time without some putrefaction.

Second: Meat contains considerable quantities of the end-products of metabolism which are held up in the tissues at the time of death. These wastes are poisonous and irritating and lend to meat a stimulating property that is usually mistaken for added strength.

Third: No matter how carefully handled, meat very readily undergoes putrefaction and it is impossible to get it so fresh that more or less putrefaction has not already taken place. It also putrefies as readily in the digestive tract and the putrefactive poisons it forms in the stomach and intestine are the same as those it forms when allowed to putrify in the ice box.

Fourth: The conditions under which animals that are intended for use as food are kept, and the manner in which they are fed to fatten them, are not conducive to health. It is very seldom, if ever, that a fattened animal is killed that is free of disease and the eating of diseased meat is not a healthful practice.

Discussing carnivorous animals, Berg says: "a diet of meat (flesh) exclusively is *per se* an unsuitable diet for a growing animal." They require the blood, internal organs, bones, bone marrow, etc., of the animal (or of different animals) and frequently supplement this diet with fruits, berries and vegetables. Muscle meat, so popular among human carnivores, is poor food.

THE ECONOMIC SIDE

Meat, egg and milk production is a great economic loss. It is one of our most wasteful follies. As the earth's population continues to increase man will be forced to be contented with a proportionately smaller area in which to produce his food. The land now used for hunting purposes and cattle-raising purposes can be (and will be) more economically utilized in raising fruits, nuts and vegetables.

Scientists estimate that about 40 square miles of land are required to maintain one man in a primitive hunting community. It requires ten times as much acreage to grow cattle as it does to grow corresponding food values of wheat. Many more acres are required to grow game than to grow cattle. A tract of well-cultivated land will sustain at least twenty times more people by its crops than can be nourished on the meat of cattle supported by the same tract. Reinheimer says: "A pair of ravens or peregrines require a square mile of territory for a hunting ground, but twenty linnets will nest in one hedge.

It is roughly estimated that "about 24 per cent of the energy of grain is recovered for consumption in pork, about 18 per cent in milk, and only about 3.5 per cent in beef and mutton." The farmer who feeds wheat, oats or corn to pigs and cows "is burning up 75 to 97 per cent of them in order to provide us a small residue of roast pork or beefsteak."

The American farmer, in what Milo Hastings calls, "The Official Method of Making Human Food Abundant by Feeding It to a Pig," gives "to his 100,000,000 fellow human consumers only one-twelfth as much of the vegetable food he produces as he does to the country's 529,000,000 cattle, hogs, sheep and poultry." Our livestock consume sufficient food to support a population of 500,000,000 men, women and children.

Mr. Hastings says that "for each unit of human food produced in the beef industry there is consumed about sixteen units of vegetable food substances. In the production of milk the ratio is about one to twelve; in pork production the ratio is about one to eight.

"Refiguring these proportions on the basis of our present livestock industries, we find that enough food is derived from the animal products to food units required to support forty million humans.

"Meat food sufficient to support but two-fifths of the human population is the return we get for the loss of vegetable food supply sufficient for five times our population."

Hindhede calculated that if people lived on vegetable foods Europe could sustain a population 5.4 times and the United States 15.1 times their present populations and "everybody be well-fed." He pointed out that the starving Central Powers, during World War I, "in converting grains and vegetables into pork and milk," lost "a food value of 80 per cent and into beef of 95 per cent."

In a paper read before the Association of American Geographers, April, 1922, Prof. O. E. Baker, of the U. S. Dept. of Agriculture, said: "Fully three-fifths of the crop acreage in the United States is used to provide feed for farm animals; and in addition our livestock consume the product of about seventy-five million acres of unimproved grass land and pasture in farms and national forests, besides that of perhaps five hundred million acres of arid and semi-open range land in the west. It seems safe to say that the livestock consume two-thirds of the product of unimproved pasture, or fully eight per cent of the total food and feed produced by tame and wild vegetation in the United States."

The folly of this immense economic waste should be immediately apparent to every intelligent person. And yet, in the greater part of the North American continent the chief work of agriculture is the raising of cereals, grasses and vegetables as food for animals for meat production. Instead of raising wholesome vegetables, fruits and nuts for man, agriculture gives most of its attention to first feeding the animal and then we prey upon the animal.

For each 100 pounds of digestive organic matter eaten, the cow gives back 18 pounds of digestible milk solids. The cow must be fed 100 pounds of nutritious matter in order to produce 18 pounds of nutriment. It would seem that it is a great economic waste to first feed the cow and then let her feed us.

Egg production is as much of a waste and expense as milk production. It involves feeding enormous quantities of food to poultry and receiving back from them, in the form of eggs, a small percentage of the food material fed to the poultry.

A thousand acres of wheat will feed ten times as many people as a thousand acres of cattle. A thousand acres in many other foods will feed more people, and feed them better, than a thousand acres in wheat. Minerals are drawn from greater depths by fruit and nut trees than by cereals, as the strong roots of the trees are capable of reaching the deeper and richer strata of soil, permitting, therefore, a more intensive utilization of an area of land. Fruit and nuts are not only man's best food, but his most fruitful and least wasteful crop. Besides this, the trees themselves serve many other very useful offices, such as the purification of the air, protection against sudden changes in atmosphere, etc. The garden and the orchard should soon supplant the ranch, the dairy and the grain fields.

Agriculture has always been the backbone of civilization. The more advanced civilizations have depended more on the farmer and less on the herdsman and the hunstman. Hunting is a sport, not a livelihood among the civilized — a cruel sport, but a sport and nothing more. The herdsman is passing. There is no longer room for his great herds. Economic necessity will force vegetarianism and fruitarianism upon our grandchildren. The tremendous waste of feeding grain to cows and getting back just one-tenth its food value in meat will not be tolerated.

THE ETHICS OF FLESH EATING

Meat eating, or, perhaps, more properly, meat getting, involves a certain moral impairment of man. Butchering animals is a brutalizing and demoralizing occupation; because brutality *brutalizes*.

ANIMAL FOODS

The taking of life is highly revolting to the higher nature of man and, as our feelings are as much a part of our better natures as our teeth are parts of our bodies, this intinctive revolt against butchery and preying must always bear great weight in any decision respecting the dietetic character of man.

George Bernard Shaw, writing on the wastefulness and stupidity of those who find pleasure in destroying animal life, says: "Wanton slaughter of birds is caused by indifference to the beauty and interest of bird and song, and callouness to glazed eyes and blood-bedabbled corpses, combined with a boyish love of shooting." Who can say that this indifference and callousness and love of shooting never results in the killing of men? Or, even if it never goes this far is it not probable that it results in much other of "man's inhumanity to man?" Who can confine the callousness of a man to one channel? Who can prevent the hunter or the butcher, or the fisherman from being cruel to his children or to his wife?

While comparatively few meat eaters today kill their own flesh-food, and are therefore saved from the brutalizing influence of this brutality, they are not absolved from the brutalization of those proxies who kill for them. I have seen many women who delighted in eating chicken but who could not be induced to kill a chicken under any circumstances. Which is the ideal: the tenderness of such women or the callousness of the butcher or the hunter or the fisherman.

Tenderness and mercy and gentility, and all the spiritual qualities that set man off so greatly from beasts of prey, are lacking in the lion, tiger, wolf and other carnivora.

The claim that man has evolved to such a high mental and spiritual plane that he must have meat is exactly the opposite of the facts. He must crush and harden his higher nature in order to hunt and fish and prey. If he relishes the carion feast, or the jackal's or the vulture's meal, it is either because he is debased, or because someone else is debased. If we eat meat miles from the shambles, after the butcher has done the bloody work, we must not think that we are not responsible for the debasement of the butcher.

The hunter and the butcher are not symbols of spirituality. They are not embodiments of the higher mental, moral and social powers of man's nature.

Meat, egg and milk production involves man's slavery to animals. G. B. Shaw truly says: "My own objection to being carnivorous, in so far as it is not instinctive, is that it involves an enormous slavery of men to beasts as their valets, nurses, mid-wives, and slaughterers."

Man's slavery to meat-animals is appalling. He li·es with them in the most unhygienic conditions, in order that he may eat dead carcasses. He little dreams of the gigantic waste of human energy and of food that this practice involves.

Drink

CHAPTER XIV

Drink we define as pure water only. No other fluid except water deserves the name of drink. Other fluids commonly referred to as drinks are either foods or poisons and should be classed under these heads. Thirst is a demand for water — not for food or for a so-called beverage. Fruit juices, milk, etc., are foods, and should be taken as such.

The body is largely water and its water content is greater during its period of most rapid growth than at other periods. Water supports all of the nutritive processes, from digestion on through absorption and circulation through the body, assimilation and disassimilation, to excretion. It is the chief agent in regulating body temperature, serving much as does water in the radiator of an automobile.

Some of the most important offices of water in the body are:

1. It is an essential constituent of all tissues and cells and of all body fluids — blood, lymph, glandular secretions, etc.

2. It holds the nutritive materials in solution and serves as a medium for the transportation of food to the various parts of the body.

3. It holds waste and toxins in solution and serves as a medium for the transportation of these from the body.

4. It keeps the various mucous membranes of the body soft and prevents friction of their surfaces.

5. It is used in regulating body temperature.

The body is constantly throwing off water and this must be replenished. It gets much of its water in foods in the form of juices. Other water is taken as drink. A good part of the water taken in becomes an integral part of the tissues, that is it becomes "living water."

Fresh rain water and distilled water are best. Distilled water is not dead, as some foolishly say it is. Pure water from a rock spring is excellent drink.

Drinking water should be as pure as possible. Hard waters, mineral waters, etc., contain considerable mineral matter, and are injurious in proportion to the amount of mineral they contain. The delusion that mineral water is curative is an old one and has resulted in incalculable harm to countless thousands.

One of the dogmas of modern so-called science is that man should drink so much water a day. People are advised to drink at least a given amount daily regardless of the quality and quantity of their diet, the nature of the environments (climate, season, occupation, etc.) and without consideration for the instinctive demands of their bodies. If they are not thirsty they are advised to drink anyway; to cultivate the habit of drinking a glass of water at regular intervals. The advise usually given is to drink at least six glasses of water between meals each day.

I do not believe in routine drinking anymore than I believe in routine eating. There is not and never was any necessity to drink any specific number of glasses of water a day. Indeed, many have gone for years without drinking water as such.

A peculiar feature about this drink-lots-of-water dogma is that it is held by those who advise one never to eat unless truly hungry as much as by those who preach the belly's gospel of three squares plus and go by your appetite. Why should one drink without thirst? Is this more appropriate than eating without hunger? Does not the body know when water is needed?

The great importance of pure water should be recognized, but all of the facts about water given in this chapter do not teach us that we should be constantly taking water into our stomachs.

Water needs vary with season and activity and other factors. The man who is engaged in active physical labor in the summer's sun requires more water than the office worker who is in the shade, perhaps near an electric fan, and pushes a pencil or operates an adding machine. We require more water in summer than in winter, more during the day's activities than during the night's slumbers. The more food one eats the more water will his system demand. The fasting individual has little thirst. The person whose diet is chiefly fresh fruits and green vegetables gets large quantities of water in its purest form from these. He needs to drink less water than the man whose diet is largely dry. If milk is taken with meals this supplies considerable water.

The body's water requirements depend upon age, sex, activities, season, climate, etc. It needs a certain amount of water under given conditions, but it makes no difference to the body from whence it obtains this supply. It is perfectly satisfied with the juices of fruits and vegetables or the water in milk and, accordingly, we find that infants on a milk diet and adults who consume an abundance of juicy fruits and succulent vegetables have little or no desire for water.

The amount of solid matter in milk is small. It is nearly all water. The percentage of water in milk is greater than the percentage of water in the infant. There is, therefore, no reason to give much water to the milk-fed infant. If fruit juices (also nearly all water) are fed to the infant, in addition to the milk, there is absolutely no reason to give additional water to infants. This I have proved on several infants. They need no water save that contained in their milk and fruit juices, during their first year of life, and their growth will be above the average.

How about adults? Most green vegetables and fresh fruits contain a higher percentage of water than the adult body. If the diet contains an abundance of these foods little or no additional water will be required.

Dr. Lamb, of England, took the position that man is not by nature a drinking animal. Dr. Alcott and others of the vegetarian school proved by direct experiments that those who adopt an exclusively vegetable regimen and make a large proportion of their diet consist of juicy fruits and succulent vegetables can be healthfully sustained and nourished without water-drinking. Sophie Lepel, of England, also condemned the use of water.

If the fertilized ovum of some sea animal is placed in tap water and watched, its weight will increase to as much as a thousand times the original. The ovum develops despite the entire absence of all other nutrients except water. Obviously such growth is not normal and the cells formed under such conditions are deficient and weak. Growth of this kind can occur only within narrow limits and the water-logged cells are far from ideal.

Super-saturation of the protoplasm of plants submerged in water weakens and even kills them. Excesses of water produce rank, watery vegetation, while prolonged standing in water will kill most vegetation more surely than a drought.

If a sufficient amount of water is forced into man or animal it will produce all the symptoms of alcoholic intoxication. Nothing is to be gained by excessive water drinking at any time. Excessive water drinking tends to water-log man's tissues and fluids and to lessen the vitality of his cells. The power of the blood to absorb and carry oxygen is lowered and the body is weakened. One sweats more when he drinks more, but excessive transpiration is weakening. Observation will readily show that those who suffer most from the summer's heat are the ones who drink the most water. We naturally conclude that they drink more because the heat causes great thirst. If these individuals can be induced to drink less, their sweating will decrease, thus showing that the excessive drinking was largely responsible for the sweating.

I do not believe that a small excess of water is particularly harmful, but I believe that the safest rule about drinking is: *drink as little as thirst demands.* A false thirst induced by salt or some other irritant, is not to be "satisfied."

I have never been able to find any sound reason why we should deliberately drink a certain number of glasses of water a day just because somebody has arbitrarily decided that we require that much water. I know of no sound reason why we should take water in the absence of real physiological need for water, as expressed in genuine thirst. I am fully convinced from my own observations and experiments that there are many people who are injuring themselves by drinking too much water.

Dr. Trall severely condemned the "indiscriminate practice of large water-drinking" and said, "I have seen not a little mischief result from it." Drs. Shew, Cully, Johnson, Wilson and Rausse, of the hydropathic school, severely and justly repudiated the extravagant recommendation of large water-drinking contained in many works on water-cure. Dr. Tilden, though, like the author, once an advocate of much water-drinking, has for several years past condemned the practice. The late Dr. Lindhar did not favor the practice.

Shall we, then, affirm that all the water should be taken that instinct calls for? If so, how much does instinct call for? What is an instinctive call for water? How much of our present thirst is due to habit? How much to irritation? What part is normal? Is an abnormal thirst any better guide than an abnormal appetite?

Water drinking can become a habit like any other thing we do. Those who cultivate drinking large quantities of water will feel a "need" for much water. On the other hand, eating salt, spices, condiments, greasy dishes, concentrated foods, meats, eggs, cheese, sugar, starches, etc., creates an irritation that is usually mistaken for thirst. But water will not ally such a "thirst." One may inundate his stomach with water every five minutes and still be "thirsty." If he will refrain from drinking he will find that his supposed thirst will be satisfied much sooner. It is argued that people turn to strong drink because water will not allay such "thirst." Perhaps it is often true. If the supposed thirst is endured it will be satisfied with the normal secretions and this almost irresistable desire for water will pass away. On the other hand, if water is taken, these secretions are not used to allay the "thirst," while the water, upon leaving the stomach, carries the secretions that are there along with it.

Those who seek to do the body's work for it and are afraid of letting it do its own work in its own way will object to permitting these secretions to be used for this purpose and will maintain that it robs the system of that much water. The objection is unsound from first to last. The secretions can satisfy the "thirst" while water will not. Besides this the secretions will prevent putrefaction and fermentation in the digestive tract while water will favor these very processes. Lastly, the secretions are not lost to the body, but are reabsorbed.

Would we say to the glutton: Eat all your appetite calls for; or to the satyr and nymphomaniac; Indulge as much as your desires command? If not, then, why shall we say to the man of perverted thirst: Drink all your thirst calls for? Such advise could be beneficial only where thirst is normal.

How much should one drink? I don't know. How much should one eat, or breathe, or sleep? You answer — "All that nature calls for." Suppose we say the same in regard to water drinking — how much does nature call for? This will depend on a number of circumstances and conditions, such as; the amount and character of food eaten, amount and character of work performed, climate, age, sex, etc.

No hard and fast rules can be set down in this matter. The intelligent person will not attempt it. It is often stated that our bodies require a certain minimum of water daily. This is doubtless true, but it by no means follows that we should always drink this amount. We may get two-thirds or all of this amount in our diet.

Drinking with meals: There are many who advocate drinking with meals although animals and savages abstain from water at this time. Drinking with meals or soon thereafter is not compatible with good digestion.

While eating, large quantities of digestive juices are being poured into the stomach. If drink — water or beverages — is taken these are diluted. The water passes out of the stomach in ten to fifteen minutes and carries the digestive juices along with it. The food is deprived of these juices and digestion is greatly retarded. Fermentation and putrefaction follow.

Drinking water and beverages leads to bolting of food. The food is washed down instead of being properly masticated and insalivated. Many foods are dry and require much insalivation before they can be swallowed. Washing them down with drink prevents the completion of this first and necessary step in digestion. Forego the drink and the glands of the mouth will meet the demand for fluid by a copious supply of digestive fluids.

Drinking water with meals and directly after meals, leads to dilatation of the stomach. Chronic indigestion, gastritis, ulcers, and even cancer follow in their logical order.

A fictitious thirst often follows a meal. This is especially so if the food has been salty, greasy or full of spices and condiments. This "thirst" should be ignored. If thirst following a meal is not satisfied with water, it will be satisfied with digestive secretions and these will bring along enough enzymes to prevent fermentation and accomplish digestion in good order. The intake of fluids with meals and immediately after meals interferes with all the digestive secretions and results in indigestion. One may safely drink fifteen to twenty minutes before meals.

The person who eats fruit, green and succulent vegetables, and avoids condiments and has overcome his drinking habit, will have little cause for drinking at any time and no cause for drinking at meal time or immediately thereafter. Let him not fear that his health will suffer therefrom. I can assure him that it will improve and quickly at that.

Drinking with meals is a frequent cause of overeating. It stimulates the appetite, sometimes even creating an enormous one. Trall says: "Some persons have boasted of the 'ravenous appetite' produced by drinking twenty or thirty tumblers of water a day; but I cannot understand the advantages of 'ravenous appetites'; they are generally indicative of excessive morbid irritation of the stomach."

Distilled water: This is water that has been vaporized by heat and re-condensed by being cooled. In this process the mineral matters that are suspended or dissolved in the water and the vegetable and other organic matters that are suspended therein, are left behind, so that the water is rendered practically pure. The hardest and foulest of waters may be rendered practically pure by distillation. Certain noxious gases contained in water falling in the cities are not lost upon distillation. For this reason, it is best to use other water for distillation.

Nature is ceaselessly engaged in distilling water. Were this process not in ceaseless and eternal operation, the water of the earth would become so contaminated and foul as to be unfit for use. In spite of this, all *natural* water is more or less impure. Some of it is very impure. Hard waters are full of dissolved and suspended mineral matters. Surface waters are full of earthy matters and organic matters. Even fresh rain water contains gases and dust picked up in falling. Distillation provides us with the purest water obtainable.

Distilled and areated, distilled water has the taste of freshly fallen rain water. It is soft water, for it has lost its minerals. It contains so few impurities that it constitutes the best drinking water obtainable.

Objections are frequently offered to the use of distilled water. Distilled water is said to be "unnatural." It is as unnatural as the purest rain water. It is said to be *dead*. There is no such thing as live water. All water is lifeless. It is said that the body needs the minerals dissolved in the water. That the body needs minerals is certain, but it needs them, as previously shown, in the form of organic salts and derives these from foods. It is objected that the use of distilled water causes decay of the teeth and softening of the bones. This objection has no foundation. Observations will quickly reveal that decay of the teeth is very common in people who are habitually using hard waters. It is objected that the affinity of distilled water for minerals causes it to take up the minerals from foods so that the body derives no benefit from these. This objection is a peculiar perversion of physiology. One of the functions of water in the body is to take up these very minerals and take them to the cells and tissues. How absurd, to object to the use of distilled water because it serves this very function better than does contaminated water!

THE SCIENCE AND FINE ART OF FOOD AND NUTRITION

Mineral Waters: "According to the theory of the anti-Naturalists," says Dr. Oswald, "a man's instincts conspire for his ruin; whatever is pleasant to our senses must be injurious; repulsiveness and healthfulness are synonymous terms. To every poison known to chemistry or botany they attribute remedial virtues; to sweet-meats, fruits, fresh air, and cold spring-water all possible morbific qualities. But for consistency's sake, they make an exception in favor of mineral springs. Spas impregnated with a sufficient quantity of iron or sulphur to be shockingly nauseous, must therefore be highly salubrious. Solitary mountain regions afflicted with such spas become the favorite resort of invalids; dyspeptics travel thousands of miles to reach a spring that tastes like a mixture of rotten eggs and turpentine."

Saline and sulphur spring waters are purgative, since the alvine canal hastens to rid itself of these injurious waters. A stay at the watering place teaches the colon to rely upon the mineral excitant, hence the chronic constipation that so often follows upon the return from the spa; the excitant being withdrawn, the tired organs lie down for a rest. "From a hygienic standpoint," says Dr. Oswald, "a sanitorium without a spa is therefore by no means a Hamlet-drama minus the Prince."

In 1930 the town boosters of Seaton Delaval, England, desiring to advertise the curative properties of their water supply, hired a chemist to analyze it. The chemist found that its peculiar flavor was due to near-by miners washing their pedigreed dogs in the reservoir with kitchen soap. Some years ago a wonderful healthspring in one of Gotham's many suburbs was curing its patrons daily. It achieved a great reputation as a cure-all. So great was its reputation, a movement was started to improve the property. While improving the grounds a break in the sewer was found. This was quickly repaired and, to the sorrow of the exploiters and disgust of the drinkers, the spring promptly dried up.

So come and go the cures and neither the curing professions nor the people ever forsake their superstitious belief in cure. Those who were drinking the leaking sewerage and those who took Fido's bath water, like those who pin their faith in poisonous drugs, filthy pus, diseased animal serums, marvelous machines and apparatuses, colored lights, electrical currents, metaphysical formulas, and punches in the back, simply went elsewhere for a cure.

The poodle soup of Seaton Delaval and the Gotham sewerage effected their cures in the same way that the famous mineral waters from the mineral wells and springs effect theirs. All methods of cure, however absurd or fantastic, however impotent for good or potent for harm, could point to apparent cures. But sooner or later in the march of experience all cures are exploded.

Drugged Waters: Health (?) Boards no longer permit the drinking of pure water. They drug the drinking water of cities with iodine, chlorine, lime, alum, etc. This compulsory wholesale and indiscrimiate drugging of the people is made possible by reason of the fact that we have state medicine in America.

Just as examples of the wholesale drugging of our water supply the small city of Fort Lauderdale, Fla., uses 40,000 pounds of alum in three months in its city water supply, or a little over a pound per capita per month; while Columbus, Ohio, purchased for use in its water in 1933, 8000 tons of lime, 3000 tons of soda ash, 1200 tons of sulfuric acid, 500 tons of bauxite (an aluminum ore compound), 500 tons of coke and 8 tons of liquid chlorine. I shall not discuss each of these poisons separately. Iodine will be discussed elswhere. At this point I shall confine my remarks to chlorine.

Chlorinated water is water that has had chlorine, an "inorganic" acid-forming mineral, added to it, to destroy "typhoid germs." Chlorine is a poison and if enough of it is put into the water to destroy germ life, it will also destroy animal and human life. Chlorinated water is more to be feared than the "typhoid germs."

All poisons are cumulative in their effects, if they are habitually used. If there is not enough chlorine placed in city water to kill outright, it will produce its effects in time. Sprinkling the lawn with chlorinated water kills the grass and flowers and impairs the soil.

In Toronto, Canada, where chlorinated water has been used for a period of years, there has been no reduction of typhoid. During the five-year period from 1921 to 1925 there were more deaths from typhoid in Toronto than in the combined cities of Kingston, Cobourg, Cornwall, Brookville, Belleville and Hamilton. These later cities all used the same water and it was not chlorinated.

So much for its failure; now for its damages. Some authorities state that even the steam escaping from radiators supplied with chlorinated water has been known to cause death. The victims were gassed with the same gas that the soldiers were killed and injured with in World War I. Boiling this water may fill the room, day after day, with this gas. There is also a greater concentration of the mineral left in the water, which goes into the foods cooked in it. Mr. Harter, president of the Defensive Diet Legue, says: "The worst feature of all is the slowness with which the darned thing works and the absence of symptoms until the trouble has reached an incurable stage."

Clarke, of London, author of a medical dictionary, and a good authority, presents a long list of diseases which have resulted, in human beings, from repeated and long-continued dosess of water containing the approved percentage of chlorine. Among these diseases are colds, catarrh, acute rheumatism, inflamed and ulcerated mouth, malignant pustules, acne, carbuncles, nettle rash with fever and dry, yellow, shrivelled skin. Dr. Clarke seems to have proven his case. Even if the chlorine does not produce these troubles outright, it does not kill the germs that are held responsible for them.

Condiments and Dressings
CHAPTER XV

A condiment is defined as an appetizing ingredient added to food; a substance which seasons and gives relish to food. It is a sauce, a relish or a spice. The fallacy contained in this definition will be made fully apparent as we proceed.

In one form or another condiments are in almost universal use. In more advanced portions of the globe many condiments are employed and are regarded as quite a natural and necessary part of the diet. They are not foods and are not considered as foods, although they are frequently referred to as accessory foods, and almost everybody thinks he cannot live without them.

Common salt, (sodium chloride) is the most widely used condiment. Arsenic is also used in some parts of the world as a condiment. There is no more excuse for the use of salt than there is for the use of arsenic. As a separate chapter will be devoted to salt using, it will not be necessary to say more about it at this time.

Before considering the usual defenses of condiment using let us get an idea of what condiments are and what they do. Condiments are of two classes:

(1) Those containing irritating, but non-volatile oils, such as mustard, pepper, cayenne, capsicum, horse-radish, ginger, spices.

(2) Those containing irritating but volatile oils, such as mint and thyme.

Both classes are irritating to the delicate lining of the digestive tract and those that find their way into the body carry their irritating effects along with them to prick and goad the liver and other organs of the body. This should cause us to be suspicious of the truth of the claims made for them.

The use of condiments is usually defended on the following grounds:

(1) They make the food more palatable.
(2) They increase the appetite.
(3) They stimulate the flow of the digestive juices.

Spices were first used as *medicines;* this is to say, their use grew out of voodooism. From the black magic art of *curing* "disease" they were carried over into the black magic art of adding tastiness to foods that have been robbed of the natural flavors contained in their juices and salts by the black magic art of cooking. Dr. Moras says: "The sickly prevailing way of boiling vegetables in a lot of water, thereby extracting their curative and nourishing juices and salts, and then pouring these essentials away, is equal to feeding people the straw and residue, and pigs the nourishing and curative parts. Not only that, but in order to make the residue or straw eatable it is then fixed up with some flour paste or milk gravy or vinegar or other palate-tickling condiments or seasonings — thereby heaping insult upon injury to the poor stomach."

Condiments can improve the palatability of foods only for those who are accustomed to their use. No condiment is palatable when it is first tasted. Everyone is forced to learn to use them over the protests of the organic instincts. Condiment using is really a deliberately cultivated perversion of the sense of taste.

Condiments not only irritate the digestive organs and thus impair their functioning powers; they also blunt the sensibilities of the gustatory nerves and thereby diminish our enjoyment of simple foods. In thus trying to increase his enjoyment in eating, the surfeited gastronome defeats his own purpose; "the most appetizing dishes he values only as foil to his caustic condiments, like the Austrian peddler who trudges through the flower-leas of the Alpenland in a cloud of nicotine, and to whom the divine afflautus of the morning wind is only so much draught for his tobacco-pipe."

There are no flavors that appeal more to the normal sense of taste than the flavors that exist in natural foods. I always feel sorry for people who know nothing of the flavors that no condiment can ever equal or even imitate. When I see people adding salt to an apple, or a watermelon, pepper to a cantaloupe or dressing to lettuce I think of the real gustatory delights of which they are robbing themselves.

To the unperverted taste the attractiveness of alimentary substances is proportioned to the degree of their healthfulness and their nutritive value. No one is ever mislead by an innate craving for unwholseome food, nor by an instinctive aversion to wholesome foods. By beginning a carefully graduated plan of miseducation,

CONDIMENTS AND DRESSINGS

the sense of taste may be so depraved that it will reject wholesome foods and will demand the most unwholesome and innutritious substances.

There is nothing that entices us with greater appeal, nothing that awakens the desire to eat, nothing that arouses every organ of digestion and pleases the sense of taste more than Nature's richly colored, delicately flavored, highly scented — luscious and odorous — edibles.

He who is accustomed to eat unseasoned, unspiced foods, knows that condiment users are missing many fine, delicate flavors that are far more pleasing to the sense of taste than any sauce, relish or spice can ever be. Real pleasure in eating comes from tasting the natural flavors in foods.

Condiments cover up or camouflage the fine, delicate flavors that nature puts into her food products and prevent the user from enjoying these finer flavors. Millions of people live comparatively long lives without ever once experiencing the real taste of even the most common articles of food. The employment of sauces, condiments, salt, etc., on foods, in eating them, in the foolish belief that this makes them better, prevents them from once enjoying the real taste of foods themselves.

Condiment users protest that foods have no taste unless they are spiced or covered with relish or sauce. They are unable to enjoy an unspiced, unseasoned meal. This is true because their sense of taste has been perverted by the very practice. Condiments so deaden the sense of taste that it is not able to appreciate the finer flavors of foods. The natural flavors of foods are neither detected, nor appreciated, nor relished.

Dr. Edmond R. Moras well says: "Most people eat because eatables are salty or peppery or vinegary or sweetish, and not because they relish the taste of the eatables themselves. When you educate your taste back to enjoying the taste of articles of food because the foods themselves taste good, and educate your brain back to its autologic instinct, you are on the way to health."

Nature has seasoned all of her foods perfectly. If these are eaten in their natural state there will be no desire for harmful condiments, seasonings nad flavors.

While I was sitting at my desk writing this chapter the following words came in over the bunk box (radio) in advertising a fiery relish manufactured here in Texas: "here is something to arouse a jaded appetite and make foods a joy again." But should a jaded appetite be aroused?

Nature has arranged that Natural, unseasoned foods, eaten when required by the body and under proper mental or emotional and physical condition, will occasion the secretion of the digestive fluids in a perfectly natural way and the stimulation they afford is never sufficient to impair the functional vigor of the digestive glands. Artificial "stimulation" is not necessary, but is harmful.

One who discontinues the use of condiments soon discovers a returning appreciation for the more delicate flavors of foods, and develops a keen relish for foods for their own sake rather than for the seasonings. In time he finds that foods really taste better than seasonings and cannot be hired to return to the use of condiments.

Do condiments increase appetite? They do, and for this very reason their use should be condemned. The desire for food should arise out of actual physiological needs and when these needs are not present no food should be consumed. Appetite should not be stimulated by the use of condiments. This leads to overeating. Condiments do not produce hunger — we should eat only when hungry.

So great is the power of condiments to stimulate appetite that it is seriously contended that it is almost impossible to overeat if they are not employed. They induce eating when there is no natural need and desire for food, when no food should be taken. They induce eating long after the physiological needs of the body have been fully satisfied.

If there is a real need for food no condiments are essential to the production of desire for food. The artificially produced simulation of desire for food serves no useful purpose. If there is a natural desire for food condiments are not needed to enable us to enjoy eating.

While I have said condiments do increase appetite, it is perhaps best to say that this occurs only in the habitual condiment user and that the increased demand is less for food, than for the accustomed excitant, itself. Upon this very point Dr. Oswald says, in *Physical Education*, p. 58:

"By avoiding pungent condiments we also obviate the principal cause of gluttony. It is well-known that the admirers of lager-beer do not drink it for the sake of its nutritive properties, but as a medium of stimulation, and I hold that nine out of ten gluttons swallow their

CONDIMENTS AND DRESSINGS

peppered ragouts for the same purpose. Only natural appetites have natural limits. Two quarts of water will satisfy the normal thirst of a giant, two pounds of dates, his hunger after a two day's fast. But the beer-drinker swills till he runs over, and the glutton stuffs himself till the oppression of his chest threatens him with suffocation. Their unnatural appetite has no limits but those of their abdominal capacity. Poison-hunger would be a better word than appetite. What they really want is alcohol and hot spices, and, being unable to swallow them 'straight," the one takes a bucketful of swill, the other a potful of grease into the bargain."

Do condiments stimulate the flow of the digestive juices? Perhaps some of them do produce a temporary increase in the flow of such juices. Much juice may be poured out to counteract their irritation and wash them away. It is doubtful, however, that they increase the secretion of enzymes and it is certain that any juice poured out in response to these substances would not be adapted to the digestion or ordinary foods. The juice would be more likely to be mucous than a digestive secretion. In the mouth the increased outpouring of saliva mixed with mucus would not contain more pytalin; in the stomach more diluting fluid and mucus, not more pepsin and hydrochloric acid would be poured out.

The three defenses of condiment using add up to the contentions that their use increases the joys of eating and improves digestion, thus improving nutrition. I have previously showed that contrary to increasing the joys of eating, condiments rob us of these very joys. It is here necessary to consider only the contention that their use improves digestion.

"It is a fallacy," says Dr. Oswald, "to suppose that hot spices aid the process of digestion; they irritate the stomach and cause it to discharge the ingesta as rapidly as possible, as it would hasten to rid itself of tartarized antimony or any other poison; but this very precipitation of the gastric functions prevents the formation of healthy chyle. There is an important difference between rapid and thorough digestion." It is evident he is here contrasting rapid (and premature) emptying of the stomach with thorough digestion.

In the renowned experiments made by Beaumont on Alexis St. Martin (1825 to 1833), he found by repeated and careful tests that when precisely the same kinds of foods were taken at the same hour on successive days, and in exactly similar conditions of the stomach, food that had been dressed with liberal quantities of

—195—

strong mustard and vinegar was three-quarters of an hour longer in digesting than that which was taken without such condiments. All of this difference was noticed in a stomach accustomed by long use to such condiments and was unable, therefore, due to loss of tone and vigor as a result of their use, to properly perform its function.

Condiments interfere with digestion in still another way. We have learned of the part played by the taste of food in determining the character of juice poured out upon the food. Condiments disguise the taste of food and prevent the precise adaptation of juice to food. This factor is more important than it may seem to those unaccustomed to think in physiological terms. To discontinue the use of condiments means better digestion.

In the undepraved condition of mouth and stomach, their sensibilities enable them, with the nicest discriminating accuracy, to perceive and appreciate both the quality of the stimulus and the degree of stimulation. The habitual use of unnatural "stimulants" so blunts and depraves the sense of taste and the sensibilities of the stomach, that these often lose their powers of discrimination to such an extent that they are no longer able to perceive the quality of the stimulus and retain only their ability to appreciate the degree of stimulation. By such means their delicate susceptibility to the action of their natural stimuli (food) is impaired.

It was also found in Beaumont's experiments that when mustard and pepper were consumed with the food these remained in the stomach until digestion was complete and continued to emit a strong aromatic odor to the last; and that the mucous surface of the stomach presented a slightly morbid turgid appearance towards the close of the digestive process.

CONDIMENTS HARMFUL

All condiments act as irritants and, as a consequence, induce inflammation in the digestive tract. Their continued use results in hardening (toughening) of the mucous lining of the alvine canal. This hardening renders the delicate membranes less sensitive to their irritating qualities, but cripples the efficiency of the membranes. Cayenne or red pepper is about the most fiery of all condiments. It burns and "stimulates" these organs and is followed inevitably by a reaction with a corresponding lowering of the vital tone of these same organs.

The effect of condiments is the opposite of what it is popularly supposed to be. They depress and hinder rather than aid digestion.

CONDIMENTS AND DRESSINGS

The taste of condiments is repulsive to infants and those unaccustomed to their use.

The irritation caused by mustard, pepper, pepper-sauce, horseradish, cayenne, capsicum, and other hot and exciting substances, due to highly poisonous essential oils, which, in the pure state, quickly produce blisters upon the skin, and which in condiments when taken internally, exert their irritating effect upon the more delicate membranes of the digestive tract, excite the stomach to increased action in certain respects, but lessen the secretion of gastric juice and, later, decrease activity of the stomach. Mint and thyme lessen the activity of the stomach and diminish secretion. These substances "act" upon the digestive organs as a lash but the spasms they induce do not accelerate digestion. Their irritation, though temporarily increasing the tone of the mouth and throat "burn" like a coal of fire. If pepper is taken by the non-user its burning may be felt in the stomach. It may even result in diarrhea. When it passes out with the stools on the same or the following day the non-user experiences the same irritation and burning in the rectum that he experienced in the mouth and throat when he ate the pepper. If it is habitually employed nature is compelled to thicken and harden the membranes of mouth, throat, stomach, intestine and colon to protect these against its influence.

Black pepper and white pepper have the same effects differing only in the degree of their irritating qualities. Spices, nutmeg, cloves, ginger, mustard, casicum and all irritating sauces and condiments exert the same kind of influence and impair digestion rather than improve digestion. Repeated irritation from these things produces irreparable injury to the stomach, liver, intestine, kidneys, blood vessels, heart and other vital organs. Catarrh, chronic inflammation, hardening, glandular destruction, permanently impaired digestion, gastric ulcer, cancer of the alimentary canal and colitis are among the results of using condiments.

Boix, of Paris, showed that pepper will produce hardening of the arteries and "gin liver." He showed pepper to be six times as active as gin in producing cirrhosis of the liver. He also showed that the acetic acid in vinegar is twice as active as gin in producing cirrhosis of the liver.

Condiments, sauces (worcestershire sauce among them), dressings, vinegar mustard, alcohol, etc., possess absolutely no constructive properties, but all of them are, to a marked degree, destructive.

The only safe and proper stimuli for the digestive processes are the odors and flavors of foods, hunger and the digestive products themselves.

By repeated use we learn to tolerate the presence in the body of poisons and irritants. Toleration is gained at the expense of changes in the organism that are away from the ideal. That the body can tolerate the presence of any poisonous or irritating substance and does not react against it promptly and vigorously, is certain evidence of its far-advanced degeneration and depravity.

Contrary to popular opinion, wines, as well as strong drinks, are decidedly detrimental to digestion. Prof. Chittenden, in his classical resarches for the Committee of Fifty, clearly demonstrated this fact. He showed that alcohol increases the flow of gastric juice, but found that an equal amount of water would increase gastric secretion equally as much. Upon further investigation it was found that the secretion induced by water possessed much more powerful digestive properties than that induced by alcohol.

The secretion of hydrochloric acid is only temporarily increased by alcohol after which its secretion is diminished, while the alcohol hinders the formation of pepsin. It also causes the mucous glands to pour such quantities of alkaline fluid (mucous) into the stomach that it upsets gastric digestion.

Vinegar, with its alcohol and ascetic acid, certainly should be avoided by all who desire good digestion and good health. Its acid interferes with the digestion of both proteins and starches.

"HEALTH" CONDIMENTS

Man is the only condiment and dressing user and it is claimed with much justification, that it is impossible to keep alive an appetite for condiments, seasonings, alcohol, tobacco, tea, coffee and other "stimulants" when the body is properly nourished.

Few dietitians are ready to completely abandon the old diets and hashes. They give much attention to the effort to prepare their "healthful diets" in such a manner that they resemble as far as possible the customary diet. They not only have meat substitutes and coffee substitutes and health candies, but use condiments, as well.

Anise seed, celery and caraway seed, sage, paprika, nutmeg, etc., are used to take the place of pepper, spices and other condiments. Celery salt and various other "vegetable salts," made up large-

CONDIMENTS AND DRESSINGS

ly of common salt, are employed. Mayonnaise dressing is made with lemon juice instead of vinegar, lemon juice is put on salads in place of vinegar.

Granting that some of these things are not as bad as some of the things they displace, they still disguse the natural flavors of food, act as irritants and induce overeating.

There is no sound reason why we should imitate the customary dietary habits around us. Our efforts at dietary reform and revolution should not lead to the susbtitution of one form of food exploitation for another, but to a return to the simplicity of a natural diet.

Dr. Oswald says, in *Physical Education*, p. 53: "The carnivora digest their meat without salt; our next relatives, the frugivorous four-handers, detest it. Not one of the countless tonics, cordials, stimulants, pickles and spices, which have become household necessities of modern civilization, is ever touched by animals in a state of nature. A famished wolf would shrink away from a 'deviled gizzard.' To children and frugivorous animals our pickles and pepper sauces are, on the whole, more offensive than meat, and therefore, probably more injurious."

Salt Eating
CHAPTER XVI

Of all the substances added to our foods, salt (chloride of sodium) is the only one that is said to be indispensable. Many reasons are given for the use of salt and I shall discuss the most important of these in this chapter; but the two basic reasons for its use are commonly stated about as follows: 1. Salt is highly essential to animal life; and 2. Animals recognize its necessity by going to "salt-licks" for their periodic supply. I shall discuss these two basic assumptions first, after which, I shall consider some of the minor *reasons* for its use.

SALT

A salt is the result of the combination of a metal with an acid. There are many of these known to the chemist, as for example, sodium carbonate, sodium phosphate, etc. Only a few salts are known to the layman as such. Epsom salts, Glauber salts, Rochelle salts, smelling salts and bath salts, etc., are well-known salts. No one thinks it necessary to eat these salts daily. Although sodium, carbon and phosphorus are all essential ingredients of the living body, nobody thinks it essential to eat sodium carbonate or sodium phosphate daily. Only sodium chloride (a combination of sodium and chlorine) is thought to be essential as a daily addition to our diet.

DISTRIBUTION

Sodium chloride (common salt) exists in the soil and exists in all parts of the world. The waters of the ocean and salt lakes of the world are abundantly supplied with it as it is washed out of the soil by the rains and carried down the streams to the lakes and oceans. The drying up of salt lakes, of ocean arms and marshes, etc., has left large deposits of salt in many parts of the earth. Other parts are not supplied with the salt deposits. Few of these deposits are above ground. Almost all of them are covered over with and intermixed with soil. Outcroppings of salt are so rare that salt is not available to animal life in most parts of the globe.

Salt is plentiful in Northern Europe, scarce in China, Korea and India, scarce in the Malayan Peninsula , unknown in Western

Africa, plentiful in North America, but scarcely known to the pre-Columbian Indians of this continent.

By and large the white man gets much salt, the yellow man some, the brown man little and the black man none at all. These facts are generally known to scientists, yet they continue to ignore the fact that whole tribes and races have maintained health and strength for many centuries without the use of salt.

SALT INNUTRITIOUS

Is salt a necessity of life? There are a number of salts that are essential to animal (and plant) life. These are the various organic salts synthesized by plants in their processes of growth. Iron salts, copper salts, calcium salts, magnesium salts, etc., are needed, but these are not the salts referred to when salt is declared a necessity of life.

Eating salt is a violation of the provisions of nature that plants shall subsist upon the soil and animals shall subsist upon the spare products of the plant. We try to skip the vegetable and go directly to the mineral kingdom for our food when we eat salt. We contend not only that the only salts that are useful to the body are those contained in foods, but also that if salts are taken in any other form they are positively injurious.

Salt is wholly innutritious and affords no nourishment to the body. It is both indigestible and unassimilable. It enters the body as a crude inorganic salt which the body cannot utilize, it is absorbed unchanged, goes the rounds of the general circulation as an unassimilated salt, and is finally eliminated as such.

WILD ANIMALS DO NOT NEED SALT

Concerning the popular superstition that animals crave and seek salt Sylvester Graham says, "As to the instinct of the lower animals, it is not true that there is any animal in Nature, whose natural history is known to man, which instinctively makes a dietetic use of salt."

It is such an obvious fact that in a state of nature few, if any, animals ever receive salt from any source, save from their foods, that it should not require statement. The enormous herds of bison that once roamed the plains of America did not get salt. The numerous herds of wild horses that are now all but extinct did not receive salt. There are still large numbers of deer in America and these do not receive salt. Birds, rabbits, wolves, and other wild animals that still exist in abundance are not salt eaters. The vigor and fine condition maintained by the bison, horse and deer reveal how false is the contention that salt is essential to animal life. In those parts of the world where salt deposits are scarce or non-existent, so that man is without salt, the animal life of the regions is also without salt.

"SALT LICKS"

Popular superstition has it that animals frequent "salt licks" to procure their regular supply of salt. This superstition is held by scientific men who should know better.

Where are these much-talked of "salt-licks?" I have been unable to find one or to find anybody who has ever known where there is one. I have talked to large numbers of men who have roamed all over the whole of the western part of the U. S., from Kentucky to the Pacific and none of them have ever seen a salt lick. Some of them have never even so much as heard of such things. If they exist, they must be very rare and but a few animals ever have access to them.

A salt lick, if such a thing exists at all, would be an outcropping of a salt deposit. Salt deposits are not laid down in great numbers all over the world, but are commonly far apart. Rarely, if ever, are there outcroppings of them. This means that salt licks, if they ever exist, are so rare that few animals ever have acess to them. Brine springs do exist, but they are not common. Comparatively few animals have access to these.

Mr. Colburn says: "I have diligently inquired of old hunters and pioneers for confirmation of the story that deer and buffalo are in the habit of visiting regularly the salt springs or 'licks,' in order to eat salt. I have not been able to find one who has seen the licking process himself. There is reason to believe that hunters do take their positions at certain brine springs to find their game, and that the deer at certain seasons of the year resort to them — precisely why, is not determined. Nothing of the kind is claimed of the buffalo; that is a tradition."

I myself have been over considerable stretches of this fair land and have never seen a "salt lick." What is more, I have inquired of many old hunters, and have been surprised to find that most of these did not even know what I was talking about. One of these, of whom I inquired, had hunted deer over Texas, New Mexico, Colorado and Arizona and said he had never heard of a "salt lick."

If it is true, as Mr. Colburn seems to think, that deer do frequent brine springs at certain seasons of the year, it is not possible that all deer do so, for there are vast stretches of land in this country that are or were, at one time, inhabited by deer, where no such springs exist. This is especially true of the plains country of our great southwest, where a spring of any kind is a novelty.

DOMESTIC ANIMALS DO NOT NEED SALT

Whatever may be true of wild animals, it is generally agreed, in this country at least, that domestic animals, at least some domestic animals, require salt. Salt for these animals is taken for granted.

Man lived on the earth for ages before he acquired the salt-eating habit. Livestock were introduced to salt eating by man and did not bring the practice with them from their wild state. It is probable, in view of the comparative scarcity of salt until recent times and in view of its high cost, that is was long after man developed the salt eating habit before he introduced the practice to his livestock. Untold billions of men and animals have been born on this earth, lived their regular life cycles, and passed away without ever having tasted salt once in their life times.

It is not probable that when the first tribe began the use of salt, the people at the same time began to feed salt to their stock, if, indeed, at that time, they had domesticated any animals. Its use as a "food" for stock probably began much later and, no doubt, spread even slower than its use by man. We know that, even now, not all animals on the farm and ranch are given salt. We know, moreover, that there is a common superstition among farmers that salt is fatal to certain animals — hogs and chicken, for example.

Speaking of domestic animals Mr. Colburn wrote: "It is a common notion that salt is necessary to the well-being, if not the preservation, of horses and horned cattle. It is, I am persuaded, a great mistake. In the first place, although it is undoubtedly true that some domestic cattle will eat salt, and follow impatiently to get it, it is not true of wild cattle. I am assured by many of the great herders in Texas, Colorado and California, that the native cattle are not fed salt, never see it, and will not eat it if offered. Of course it is a transparent absurdity that salt could be hauled hundreds of miles to feed these great inland herds; and it is not done as is supposed."

In the early days of the cattle industry, which had its beginning in Texas, and spread from there throughout the west, it is true that salt was not hauled to the cattle and horses. With the coming of the railroads, many ranchmen do supply salt for their cattle and stock, not trom any need for it on the part of the cattle, but simply because popular superstition holds that they require it. No evil effects have been observed to result in cattle deprived of its use.

In a letter dated March 28, 1864, Mr. G. H. Ambrose, of Lexington, Mo., wrote to the *Herald of Health* as follows: "I have raised stock for fourteen years past without salt, and with satisfactory results. I know of several tribes of Indians in Oregon who occupy the country between the Rocky Mountains and the Coast Range, who have raised extensive herds of fine fat cattle as one would wish to look at, without the use of salt. Reared in that manner, stock will not use it, which proves conclusively that it is an artificial and morbid appetite. Anyone who has lived in Oregon in its early settlement, can bear testimony to the fact that stock was almost universally raised without salt. I regard the experiment of stock raising in Oregon as conclusive and satisfactory. I have seen thousands of head of stock raised in that country without salt, and when grown up they would not use it, and were as large, thrifty, fat and sleek as any like number of stock to be found anywhere. I have not written this for publication, but to call your attention to the fact that stock do quite as well if not better without the use of salt, at least my experience so teaches me; and I have tested it in Oregon for seven years and in this state the same length of time, and all the time owning several hundred head of cattle."

At my father's dairy, although the milk cows were given salt regularly in their diet, the calves were never given salt, nor were the dry cows in the pasture. The horses and mules were given salt but no salt was fed to the chickens and hogs. Our ducks and guineas were never given salt. As a boy I had a flock of pigeons which were never fed salt. We had a large pasture over which our animals grazed at will, but there were no "salt licks" thereon. The wild life on the pasture and on the wooded section did not get salt. There were no "salt licks" known to farmers and hunters in that whole region of the state. This was in North Texas. My *Health School* is in South Texas. I am unable to learn of a salt-lick anywhere in this region. The squirrels and rabbits here on the *Health School*

SALT EATING

grounds do not get salt. Neither do the quail, doves, cardinals, mocking birds, sparrows, etc., that abound here.

About 1914 I made my first experiment of withholding salt from a cow. I placed her with my father's dairy herd, every member of which was given salt regularly in her food. Every cow received salt except mine. Otherwise her feeding and care was the same as that received by the other cows. She did not lose health, there was no falling off in milk production and she developed none of the symptoms of "salt hunger" popularly supposed to result from lack of salt.

At the *Health School* a stallion and a mare were kept for more than three years without salt with no evidences of "salt hunger" or failing health. Indeed,, they both maintained splendid health and great vigor. The little stallion, the first offspring of the mare, was reared from before birth until nearly three years old without salt. Beautifully developed, a fine glossy coat of hair, as full of life as colts proverbially are, and in as fine condition as any animal can possibly be, the playful little fellow never knew what it was to be even slightly ill.

The finest oxen raised in Great Britain are not given salt. The enormous herds of cattle of the West are not given salt. Many have raised animals without salt as an experiment. Dr. Kellogg raised deer without salt and they refused to eat it.

On the other hand, cattle have to be taught to eat salt. It is put in their food, sprinkled on hay, after being dissolved in water, etc., until they acquire the salt eating habit. Often, when a man possesses but one or a few cows, he sprinkles the salt on their backs, where it works down through the hair and causes the cows to lick it off. In this way they acquire the habit. Cattle with the salt eating habit are like humans with the same habit — they like salt and will eat it if offered. The writer knows, however, from extended experience and observation, that cattle do not instinctively turn to salt under any condition, but must be taught its use.

Otto Carque says: "Extensive experiments made in Germany with the horses of ten squadrons of cavalry and two batteries of artillery, during two years, showed that the animals, if they had their choice, preferred the unsalted fodder. If half an ounce of salt was added to their daily rations, they ate them without difficulty, but if an ounce was given they showed apparent disgust. In every instance the use of salt was injurious rather than beneficial and did not increase the strength of the animals. With cows, a very small amount of salt increases the quantity of milk, but deteriorates the quality."

And thus the supposed instinctive use of salt is effectually disposed of. The supopsed need for salt is seen to be not real. Salt is not the one exception to the rule, that we cannot take mineral elements into our body in their crude state and make use of them.

Farmers and dairymen think that feeding salt to cows causes them to drink more water and, as a consequence, produce more milk. If this were true, the milk would be watery. But careful experiments by one of the largest dairying industries in the country have shown this to be false. They thus confirmed by large scale experiment, what I found in a limited test.

Although salt is thought to be necessary to some domestic animals, it is not thought to be essential to all. It is commonly considered to be fatal to hogs, pigeons, chickens, birds and dogs. We are told of these animals that excrete considerable nitrogen, that, if they are fed salt in small quantities they soon die and that autopsies of these animals reveal the liver and kidneys to be studded with uric acid concretions. (Milo Hastings found, by experiments on chickens, that salt does not kill them).

Only within recent years have the manufacturers of prepared foods for poultry begun to add salt to their abominable concoctions. Dogs were formerly not given salt, it not being supposed that meat-eating animals require salt, but salt is now added to the prepared dog food with which dog fanciers are killing their dogs.

It is asserted that salt-fed cattle will fatten faster than those not so fed. This may be true, at least the experiments of Boussingault point to the fact that this is true for a time. His trial showed that ten cattle, salted and fed alike in other respects, gained in weight, some forty pounds in about · one-hundred days, over ten unsalted cattle, and that, otherwise, both classes were equally good in health at the end of this period. The experiment made to determine the relation of salt eating to milk production did not reveal any tendency of the salt-fed cows to take on fat faster than the cows that did not get salt. In the case of healthy human beings, although, as far as we know, no such experiment has ever been conducted, one thing is certajn, everyone who indulges in salt does not gain weight. Many of them lose weight.

SALT EATING

Again, it should be borne in mind, that, if it were an actual gain in healthy flesh, due to temporary stimulation of the digestive organs of the cattle, one hundred days would hardly be a sufficient length of time in which to show the real and lasting effects of salt eating. But it was no gain in healthy tissue — in muscles, in health, in power. Rather it was a gain in fat. And it is a well-known fact that fat is a disease and not a desirable acquisition. We do not want to produce fatty degeneration.

MAN DOES NOT NEED SALT

If it were true that salt is indispensable we should find its use universal among mankind and nearly so among the lower animals. This is not the case. There are numerous peoples who do not use salt. Indeed, the greater part of the human race have lived and died without ever knowing of its existence.

Salt seems first to have been used as a preservative, although, it is more than likely that its use dates from the time the first voodoo priest used it in some fantastic and wierd ceremonial to drive away a ghost. It may have first been used by the shaman as a *medicine*.

Trall says, *Hydropathic Encyclopedia*, Vol. I, Page 336; "Millions of the human race have lived healthfully, and died of a good ripe old age, without employing it at all; . . . . furthermore, hundreds of thousands of human beings now live in the enjoyment of good health, who have never used salt either as a food or a condiment."

Richard T. Colburn, in *The Salt Eating Habit*, says: "I think it would not be difficult to show that there are whole nations and tribes of people who do not eat salt. I am told by an Italian, who has lived among them, that the Algerines do not. I was myself informed while in the region that the Indian tribes inhabiting the banks of the Columbia and Puget Sound do not. It is noteworthy also that those tribes are among the most graceful, intelligent and industrious tribes in North America, and are fine in personal appearance. I think that there is little doubt that the inhabitants of the islands of the Pacific Ocean lived from a period of vast antiquity, explorers have been left for weeks, months and years without a supply of salt by accident or otherwise, and have survived without apparent injury. Finally, there are many persons in the United States who have voluntarily abandoned the use of salt for periods ranging from one to twenty years (and for aught I know longer), not only without injury but with increased health, strength and activity. So far from being natural to man, the instincts of children, especially when born free from an inherited bias in its favor, go to show by their rejection of it that it is unnatural. Like the taste for coffee, tea and various seasonings, it is an acquired one; few, if any children but will prefer unsalted food."

Bartholomew found the Chinese of the interior to be healthy and that they do not use salt.

The Bedouins consider the use of salt ridiculous. The highlanders of Nepaul refuse salt, as do the Kamschatdales. Millions of natives of Central Africa have never tasted salt. The Darmas of Southwest Africa "never take salt by any chance."

The author of *The History of Robinson Crusoe* gives a somewhat amusing account of how Friday was taught to eat salt. His picture of Friday's antipathy to salt is instructive. In Thoreau's account of his life in the woods, he refers to salt as "that grossest of groceries," and tells us that he discontinued its use and found that he was less thirsty thereafter while suffering no ill effects. He also says that he found that the Indians whom he encountered in his wandering did not use it.

Dr. Benjamin Rush, who made a careful study of the habits of the American Indians a hundred years ago and found them to be very healthy, says: "Although the interior parts of our continent abound with salt springs, yet I cannot find that the Indians used salt in their diet till they were instructed to do so by Europeans."

Sylvester Graham tells us (*Lectures*), Mr. Wm. Bryant, of Philadelphia, who went with a company of 120 men, under the U. S. Government. beyond the Rocky mountains, to conduct to their far Western homes, the Indian chiefs who were brought to the seat of government by Lewis and Clark, says that for more than two years they lived as Indians did, without tobacco, narcotic or alcoholic substance and without salt. Most of these men suffered with various chronic complaints when they left the East, but all of them were restored to good health during their sojourn in the wilds of the West.

Salt is abundant in America, yet few Indian tribes knew of its existence. It was not used by any of them as an article of diet. The few that did use it, used it as a "medicine."

A Dr. Hoffman of the U. S. Army, writing in the San Francisco *Medical Press* in 1864, gives us an account of experiences he had with some of the "wild Indians" who inhabited the Western plans, as he passed, with the army over these in 1849. The Indians frequently

SALT EATING

visited their camp. He says: "On many occasions, I myself have offered them some surplus articles of food left by us after our meals. Soups and meats cooked in the usual way and seasoned with salt, they would invariably refuse, after tasting, saying in their own language, it was not good. Of the same kind of meats cooked without salt, they would eat heartily and with gusto. Bread, hard bread, crackers, etc., they would also eat, but anything they could taste salt in they would invariably refuse." He says that even when they were hungry they would refuse foods in which they could taste salt. "In other bands (of Indians) that we saw, it (salt) is an article of medicine rather than an article of food."

Describing these men he says: "A more athletic, hearty, stout and robust class of men cannot be found in the world than these very Indians of whom I am writing, who never used this article (salt) in any shape. Many of them are more than six feet high, others of medium size, and they will endure more hardship, stand more fatigue, have better lungs, suffer less from sickness, live longer, on a general average, than the white race, who have all conveniences."

The historian, Prescott, tells us that it required the lapse of several generations after the conquest of Mexico to reconcile the Tlascalans, "a bold and hardy peasantry," of Mexico, to the use of salt in their food. The Indians of Northern Mexico still use no salt in their food. Those of the Hudson Bay district and a few isolated regions still thrive without salt.

If Hudson Bay Indians are forced to eat salted meat, they first soak it over night in an abundance of water. They then add fresh water and boil it for an hour. They pour this water off and add fresh water and cook again.

Vilhjalmar Stefanson found the Esquimaux to be very healthy, yet none of these peoples ever use salt. Indeed Stefanson tells us that they greatly dislike it. The Siberian natives have no use for salt. In Africa most Negroes live and die without ever hearing of this "essential of life." In Europe for long periods salt was so expensive that only the rich could afford it.

About 1912 I gave up the use of salt. Up to that time I had been a heavy user of salt. At first I missed it from my foods. After a time I did not relish foods in which I could detect the taste of salt. I enjoy the fine delicate flavors of the foods much more than I ever enjoyed the flavor of salt. I have never missed salt after the first weeks after giving it up. I have never had a craving for it. My health has not suffered in any manner from lack of it.

I have brought up three children — ages 23, 20 and 17 — without salt. Their mother did not take salt before and during pregnancy nor during lactation. These children have been reared from conception without salt. They are well developed, strong and healthy and brimming over with energy and enthusiasm. Although they were reared as vegetarians, who are supposed to need salt most of all, they have not needed salt.

Since the time Graham started his crusade and condemned the use of salt along with all other condiments, literally hundreds of thousands of people in America have discontinued the use of salt, many families of children have been reared without it, and no harm has ever come from abstinence from this "essential of animal life."

For more than twenty years I have excluded salt from the diets of my patients and have watched them get well without this supposed-to-be indispensable article of "diet." Some of these patients have not returned to the use of salt after leaving my care. Some of them have reared their children without it. Nowhere has any evidence of any harm from a lack of salt been observable.

Why, with all the historical, observational, empirical and experimental evidence that is available bearing on this subject, will men continue to declare that "salt is essential to animal life"? Why will they ignore the facts and cling to a superstition?

VEGETARIANS DO NOT NEED SALT

Bunge believed that salt is essential with vegetable foods to counteract the excess of potash. This notion was exploded by Renmerich and Kurz, who, by careful experiment, showed that salt does not have the effect Bunge attributed to it.

Bunge was a German chemist, who lived more than eighty years ago. He stated that vegetarians need and crave salt, whereas meat eaters need and crave it less. The theory was based on a misconception of "biochemistry" and not upon observations of vegetarians. As a rule, to which there are many exceptions, vegetarians abstain from salt and these abstainers experience no craving for salt. There is never a need to eat common table salt.

Vegetarians who crave salt are those who so prepare their vegetables that the organic salts that exist so abundantly in them are lost. All of the organic salts are soluble in water, and when the

SALT EATING

vegetables are boiled and the water thrown away, there is naturally a craving for salt — not, however, for common table salt, but for the organic salts of foods. There are thousands of vegetable feeders who not only do not have a craving for salt but who positively loathe it.

Prof. Morgulis, who accepts the antiquated notion of Bunge, that vegetarians and vegetable eating animals crave and must have salt, admits, at the same time, that "the lack of common salt in the food, of itself, has no ill effects on the general metabolism or on the digestive function." He points out that there is a much greater excretion of chlorine through the urine during the early part of a fast than in the latter stages, and says, "it is certain that most of this chlorine comes from the salt added as condiment to the food."

He tells us that when Grunewald kept rabbits on a diet practically free from chlorides, "the elimination of chlorides in the urine ceased almost at once," but no ill effects were, otherwise, observed. He adds that when "diuretin was administered after the excretion of chloride stopped as much as one gram of chloride was caused to be eliminated, and if the dosage was repeated several times symptoms of toxemia appeared such as extreme muscular weakness, trembling, paralysis of hind limbs which soon also extended to the anterior of the body and which, in a few days, resulted in death. The chlorine content of the blood actually diminshed 50 and in some extreme cases even 75 per cent."

Diuretin (theobromin sodiosalicylate) is a poisonous powder or drug given to increase the flow of urine. The experiment described above proves that chlorine is extracted from the tissues of the body in neutralizing and expelling it. This loss of chlorine, from the organic compounds of the body, resulted in death. This does not prove that oridanry table salt is valuable to the body. The statement by Prof. Morgulis that "this effect was produced entirely through the withdrawal of chlorine from the tissues and not by the diuretin itself, since this had no effect whatever when administered in conjunction with sodium chloride" does not prove that we need table salt, it only proves that we should not take diuretin. For, while diuretin may combine with inorganic salt and, while this may save the cell-chlorides, it by no means follows that inorganic salts of chlorine are of use to the tissues of the body. The body can utiilze sodium and chlorine only when received from foods in organic combinations.

Prof. Morgulis repeats the old myth about animals craving salt and seeking salt licks and says, "hunters of deer, for instance, have always exploited this instinct, waiting for their game near the salt licks." Hunters have, also, always exploited the instinct of the ostrich to hide itself from danger by burying its head in the sand, waiting for their game near the sand dunes. The ostrich never runs his head in the sand and the deer never seeks the "salt licks" and huntrs do not even know where the "salt licks" are. This salt lick myth is like the vegetarians' craving for salt. The few vegetarians who use salt, use it sparingly. Most vegetarians do not use salt — most meat eaters use it freely. I do not know why "orthodox" men continue to lie about vegetarians. They cannot plead ignorance of the fact, for the facts are obtainable and it behooves a man of science to obtain the facts before he writes.

SALT INDUSTRY MODERN

Colburn says: "It should not be overlooked that the manufacture and distribution of salt as an article of commerce is a thing of history, and has attained its enormous dimensions within the past century and a half. It is inconceivable that in past times the population of the world, made up as it was largely of pastoral and nomadic people inhabiting the interior of the great continents, should have supplied themselves with salt as an ingredient of food as we do. The omission of any mention of it in the older chronicles and even among the more perfect records of the classics, except at the luxurious tables of the rich, goes to confirm this supposition."

SALT INJURIOUS

It is everywhere admitted that taken in large doses sodium chloride is an "irritant poison." In smaller doses it is said to be a beneficial stimulant. This is a medical delusion. Stimulation and irritation are identical phenomena. The only difference between the *stimulation* of small doses and the *irritation* of large doses is that of degree, not of kind. Farmers use salt as an insecticide.

It is generally known that salt is commonly proscribed by reg ular physicians in diseases where elimination is impaired. This is especially so in kidney disease. Physicians employ a salt-free diet in epilepsy, in Bright's disease and often in tuberculosis, because of its deteriorating influence upon the nerves, kidneys and lungs. I can discover no reason why the detrimental influence should not be eliminated in all states of disease and in health, as well.

SALT EATING

Some individuals are said to be "allergic" to salt in the usual quantities eaten. So strong is the delusion that salt is indispensible, these people are not advised to discontinue its use, but to use it in reduced quantities.

Salt is a powerful irritant. A small bit put into the eye or a cut will reveal its irirtating power. Put into a cut or wound it causes a sharp pain. Taken into the body it has the same effect upon the tissues and nerves.

Salt is everywhere met with vital resistance — this resistance constituting its so-called "stimulating" effect. A teaspoonful of salt given to a child or to a non-user increases the heart beat ten or more beats a minute. A teaspoonful dissolved in a glass of water and swallowed, if the sensibilities of the stomach have not been too greatly impaired by the previous use of salt, will occasion vomiting. Or, much mucous is poured into the stomach to protect its delicate lining and the salt is flushed into the intestine, where more protective mucous is poured out upon it and it is hurired along to the colon and expelled. It occasions a diarrhea. In either case, it is hurriedly expelled from the system, because the organic instincts recognize that it is wholy innutritious and indigestible and an irritant.

All irritants "act" as "stimulants." The repeated use of any irritant results in debility and atony, these devloping in a degree commensurate with the irritating effect of the substance. Such irritation or "stimulation" is wasteful of vitality and is never justifiable.

If salt is taken in small quantities, it is not met by such a violent reaction. Part of it finds its way into the blood, to be eliminated by the skin and kidneys. It is excreted as salt, having undergone no change in its passage through the system. The sweat of the salt eater is salty, it tastes of salt. The writer has many times seen the shirts of salt users, who were laboring hard in the heat of summer and sweating profusely, become stiff with salt. Salt could be seen upon the shirt, which smelled of brine. Such sweat is irritating to the skin and its glands. The sweat of the non-user is not so salty, and does not taste so strongly of salt.

It has long been observed that salt aggravates some conditions of organic deterioration, this being due to the inhibition it places upon the elimination of certain of the metabolic wastes of the body. For example, in Bright's disease, salt increases the edema (dropsy). Mayer mentions salt as one of the causes of war-malnutritional-edema.

Berg agrees with him. In rheumatism or eczematous conditions the so-called "salt-rheum" is increased. Dr. Haig, of England, proved that the elimination of uric acid is impeded by salt. It increases blood pressure and acts as a stimulant. Its anti-vital properties make it an excellent embalming or pickling agent. Along with oils and spices, the ancient Egyptians used a salt solution in their mummy-wrappings to preserve the bodies.

"Salt dissolved in water in a certain proportion and taken internally before breakfast, cleanses the intestines," says one author. This only means that salt is an irritant and that taken in this way it induces rapid peristalsis — a so-called laxative effect. This very effect proves its unsuitableness for human consumption. It is also due to this irritating effect that salt is used in various baths to "stimulate" the skin. *Stimulation is excitement.* I recall one patient to whom a "salt-rub" was so "stimulating" that it left him exhausted and depressed for the remainder of the day.

SALT DEPRAVES SENSE OF TASTE

Salt causes a decay of the sense of taste until it is no longer capable of appreciating the final delicate flavors of foods and loses its power of discrimination. The use of salt, the same as the use of spices, etc., depraves the sense of taste and weaknes or utterly destroys our powers of discriminating between the various food substances eaten. Salt is used in many eating places in unusually large amounts with the object of concealing lack of flavor in inferior or spoiled foods. The one who habitually uses salt does not relish his food if no salt has been added. It is true, also, that the longer the use of salt is continued the more salt is required to produce the desired effects. Salt disguises the natural taste of food, thereby, hindering the precise adaptation of the digestive juices to the nature of the food eaten. It cannot, in any true sense, improve or aid digestion, as is often claimed. Rather, it interferes with the normal action of the digestive organs and impairs their powers and sensibilities. It always, in proportion to the freedom with which it is used, diminishes gustatory enjoyment.

The sense of taste is not only a very important and necessary factor in adapting the digestive juices to the food eaten, but it is also a guide to the amount of food to eat. A perfectly normal taste is a perfect and reliable guide as to when to cease eating, providing one is eating natural unseasoned food. A perfectly normal taste is rare. If, however, the taste is "stimulated" and confused by rich spices and condiments, dressings and flavorings, it cannot serve this true function. Salt is an equal offender in this respect with these other articles.

Although the writer was once addicted to the heavy use of salt, and did not enjoy his meals without additions of salt crystals, he has not used salt for over thirty years and does not relish food containing even small quantities of salt. My wife and children do not employ it, the children never having tasted it. I do not feed it to my patients in my institution.

When patients are first deprived of salt they have the same experience I had when first I discontinued its use — the food tastes flat, insipid, dead. Only a short time passes, however, and then the foods yield many fine, delicate flavors, which taste a thousand times better than salt.

Salt is said to make foods more palatable. It is said that "unsalted or feeblly salted foods are extremely insipid. Only those who are compelled to eat such foods for a considerable time can realize how indispensable ordinary salt is to all of us. In the case of patients whose appetite is already affected by illness, severe restriction of ordinary salt becomes a fearful hardship. Sooner or later it undermines the patient's desire for food and he may be seized by an unaccountable aversion to eating and at times may decline any food."

It is said by those who eat conventional foodless foods prepared in conventional ways that the amount of "natural salts" contained in foods are not sufficient to render these foods palatable. Therefore sodium chloride must be added. This is not the fault of nature's products, but of the manufacturer's and the cook's arts. It is folly to rob the foods of their tasty, usable, organic salts and then add to them a useless irritant.

One author tells us that "one reason for the unixersal use of salt for seasoning foods is that it sharpens the sense of taste and therefore brings out the characteristic flavor of different foods and thus gratifies the palate." It would be difficult to put more fallacy into one short sentence than this author has succeeded in getting into this sentence. Salt is not, and never was, universally used to season foods. It does not sharpen the sense of taste, but blunts it. It does not bring out the flavors characteristic of the various foods, but smothers them. The salt eater tastes the salt rather than the food. Salt does not gratify the palate of any save the man who has cultivated the salt-eating perversion.

Adding salt to apples, canteloupes, watermelons, tomatoes, cucumbers, celery and other delicious foods, as is done by many salt eaters, smothers the fine delicate flavors in these foods — flavors that are as superior to that of salt as day is to night — and serves no useful purpose.

NO NORMAL CRAVING FOR SALT

One author says: "Another reason is that the body absloutely needs some salt for various purposes and this need causes a craving for it." This craving for salt is pure fiction. It exists only in the imagination of salt eaters. If these people will do without salt long enough to recover from their perversion, they will discover that both the need and the craving for salt are fictions. He says: "The craving for salt is so deeply rooted in human beings that no other condiment is able to replace salt satisfactorily."

The amount of salt used by peoples and individuals is in no sense correlated with any need for salt, but with custom and individual taste.

He says: "Children take much less salt than adults, not only because they eat less food but also because their craving for salt is considerably less." Young smokers also *crave* less tobacco than hardened perverts. The salt-eating habit is progressive. Increasing dullness of the sense of salt, caused by salt using, calls for increasing quantities of salt to give the desired taste to the food.

SALT RETARDS DIGESTION

Salt-eating is often advocated on the ground that it aids digestion. It is even said to be essential to the formation of gastric juice. Strange is it not, if this is true, that carnivorous animals do not seek and eat salt?

Sylvester Graham says: "It is a little remarkable that some have contended for the necessity of salt as an article in the diet of man, to counteract the putrescent tendency of animal food or fresh meat, when there is not a carnivorous animal in Nature that ever uses a particle of it, and few if any of the purely flesh-eating portions of the human family ever use it in any measure or manner and most of the human family who subsist mostly on vegetable food wholly abstain from it."

SALT EATING

The *stimulating* influence of salt upon the flow of saliva is well known. It is employed in some institutions in the form of a bath as the "salt-rub," because of its "stimulating" effect. The saliva poured out when salt is taken is an inactive juice mixed with much mucus.

Salt retards gastric digestion. Three parts of salt added to one thousand parts of gastric juice will, as shown by Linossier in 1900, retard protein digestion to the same extent as does the reduction of the amount of pepsin by 40 to 50 per cent. This is about the amount of salt consumed by the average person in an ordinary meal.

The genuinely absorptive work of the villi that line the small intestines can be understood only if we realize that it depends upon a selective absorption — the digested food is secreted into the blood; there is no mere osmotic passage of food through the intestinal wall. It must be that salt has a paralyzing effect upon the function of the villi, also, so that it hinders the absorption of food. It would be valuable to know how much of the reported failure of certain individuals to absorb vitamins is due to the large quantities of salt they habitually use.

SALT IMPAIRS NUTRITION

At all times under normal physiological conditions, fluid is continually passing from the blood into the tissues and from the tissues into the blood. Held in solution in this fluid is the food materials and waste of the body. The transudation of fluid is not a mere filtration; it is no mere process of osmosis. On the contrary, it is due to secretory activities on the part of the endothelium (lining of the blood vessels) which incorporates such substances in solution, both from the blood and from the tissues, and selectively passes them on to the other side. Sodium chloride has a paralyzing effect upon the secretory activities of the vascular endothelium, thus interfering with the exchange of nutritive substances and waste.

SALT IMPAIRS EXCRETION

The tissues of the body are adapted to a specific osmotic pressure and as soon as this pressure is exceeded, the substance responsible for the excess is automatically excreted by the kidneys. When this rise in osmotic pressure is due to salt eating the process of excretion is not normally carried out due to the inhibiting effect of salt upon kidney function. Both sodium and chlorine hinder the normal excretion of water by the kidney cells.

The genuine regulatory work of the kidneys can be realized only if we recognize that it depends upon a *selective excretion*. Salt paralyses the selective excretory action of the kidneys in the same way that it paralyses the selective secretory activity of the endothelial lining of the blood vessels. The excretion of salt by the kidneys is always a tardy process, the salt itself, actually retarding kidney function, although at the same time raising the osmotic pressure throughout the body.

One of the body's regulatory apparatuses is its ability to store toxins and unusable materials in the comparatively inactive tissues —bone, cartilage, connective tissues — pending its elimination at a more favorable opportunity. A favorite site for such deposits is the subcutaneous connective tissue. In heavy salt eaters, especially those with impaired kidneys, a hidden edema (dropsy) and sometimes an edema that is not hidden results from the storing of diluted salt in the subcutaneous tissue. The salt is diluted with water and is held in solution. Some of it escapes in the sweat but much of it remains in the body. Storage of this unusable substance in the less active tissues removes it from the circulation and prevents it from damaging the more vital organs of the body.

A number of competent observers have shown that the isolated administration of water does not promote the retention of water, and the isolated administration of sodium chloride does not promote retention of this salt. Only when these are taken together is there retention of both water and salt. Thus the present practice of taking salt tablets and drinking lots of water (salt creates a demand for more water) assures retention of both. Nothing but harm can come from the practice.

Profuse sweating eliminates much water and some of the salt; much salt is deposited in the clothing and left there as the water evaporates. The salt is not all evaporated and the artificial thirst produced by the salt results in re-introducing an excess of water. The profuse sweating thus produced is enervating.

The use of salt with considerable quantities of water leads to polyuria (frequent urination), while the blood at the same time becomes hydræmic — containing an excess of water. Although urination is frequent under such conditions, only small quantities of water are passed at a time. The frequent urgent desire to void urine is due to a partial paralysis of the sphincter vesicæ, produced by the salt.

"Salt-spitting," that is a salty saliva with spitting, is frequently seen in salt users who discontinue its use. This is, no doubt due to the rapid elimination of salt from the tissues that has accumulated therein over a long period of time.

POLYURIA IN VEGETARIANS

Individuals just beginning a vegetarian diet are often prone to season their foods strongly. In these there is likely to be delayed excretion, due to the inhibiting effect upon the kidneys, so that they are forced to rise several times a night to void urine. As the salt is eliminated from the diet the delayed action of the kidneys gradually ceases, *nocturnal diuresis* diminishes and day-time urination increases.

This same frequency of urination is often seen in those who adopt a vegetarian diet and exclude salt therefrom. Here the explanation seems to be that the increased intake of bases permits the body to begin the work of excreting the accumulated salt. The frequent urination continues until much of the stored sodium chloride is eliminated.

The tears of the salt user are salty and are irritating to the eyes. The tears of the non-user are not salty and are not irritating. It cannot be possible that nature intended that the tears, which are intended to lubricate and cleanse the eyes, should be irritating to these. Salty tears must be regarded as part of the process of eliminating salt from the body.

The excretion of common salt is a slow business and in persons who have habitually consumed quantities of this crystal, months or years of abstinence from its use must elapse before the deposits of salt are excreted.

SALT IN MALNUTRITIONAL EDEMA

Ship dropsy was the term applied to malnutritional edema when it developed, as it frequently did, in sailors and passengers, on the old-time sailing vessels. These people were at sea for long periods and their diet was composed of hardtack, salt meats and other salted foods and water. They lacked all fresh foods. Prison dropsy was the term applied to the same condition when it developed, as it commonly did, in prison inmates on a similar diet. Famine dropsy was the term used to designate malnutritional edema developing in famine victims, whose diet, also, was of a similar kind with plenty of salt.

Sodium chloride has a paralyzing effect upon endothelial activity. Edema can be induced by large quantities of salt. Ship dropsy, famine dropsy, malnutritional edema may be due, as much to the ingestion of large quantities of salt (coincident with a lessened intake of bases) and water as to the actual food deficiencies. Where edema develops in one whose diet contains common salt there will always be retention of this substance in the blood.

Berg says: "As a matter of experience, all observers are agreed that in malnutritional edema there is a retention of sodium chloride by the body, and that when the edema subsides there is a profuse excretion of the salt. Burger noted that when the edema was setting in, there was marked craving for sodium chloride, although as much as 12 grammes were consumed daily. The explanation doubtless is that during the onset of malnutritional edema, as during all the maladies dependent upon an ill-balanced diet, there gradually arises a loss of appetite, and sometimes a positive loathing for food, the patient attempts to stimulate appetite by over-seasoning the food."

It would be difficult to determine how much of this dropsy is due to dietary deficiency and how much is due to the large use of salt. There can be no doubt that the salt contributes greatly to the aggravation and production of the dropsy, if not to the more serious symptoms. If the plain implications of the loss of appetite and repugnance to food were heeded and food abstained from, instead of forcing the appetite (not hunger) with salt, the dropsy would be readily eliminated and chemical balance restored in the body. The fact that sodium chloride has a paralyzing effect upon the activities of both the kidneys and the ureters has been known for more than fifty years.

SALT AND HEAT

Supplying salt tablets to men in industry who are subjected to great and prolonged heat was extensively practiced for years. The same foolish practice was carried on by the U. S. Army during the recent murder-fest. Many industries have now abandoned the practice and are supplying their men with candy instead. Many men in the Army refrained from using their salt tablets and these report that they fared better than those who did eat the salt. The practice of giving men salt tablets when they are subjected to great heat has neither sense nor science to support it.

It was claimed by the U. S. Army medics that the use of salt by troops when subjected to hardships under extreme heat was to stabilize the amount of "natural" salt in the body. The use of salt by troops was to protect the men from sun-stroke, although many salt-eating soldiers did have sun-stroke when in high temperatures. One soldier wrote me: "I actually saw men fall on their faces from sun-stroke, although they ate salt."

In view of the known facts that both man and animals can live and maintain the highest degree of health and development and live to advanced ages without salt, that salt is not metabolized in the body, but is excreted in the same form in which it is consumed, that salt exerts an inhibiting influence upon certain functions of life, and that inveterate salt eaters can discontinue its use abruptly and permanently, not only without harm, but with positive benefit, how can it longer be maintained that this irritant is necessary or beneficial? That the use of salt does not add to the pleasures of life, but does, on the contrary, detract from these, will be asserted by all who have given up its use.

OTHER SALTS

In concluding this chapter a few words about other salts in common use will be of value to the student. Soda, saleratus, etc., destroy the vitamins in food, destroy the pepsin of the gastric juice and neutralize the hydrochloric acid. They "act" in the same manner as do all other inorganic alkalies when introduced into the body.

The vegetized salts, vegetable salts, celery salt and other such products sold in the Health Food stores at high prices is just common salt with powdered vegetables added. They should be abstained from.

Most baking powders are made of bicarbonate of soda and bitartrate of potash. The baking process results in the formation of rochelle salts from these. Rochelle salts is a laxative drug, for which there can certainly be no need. Prof. A. E. Taylor, of Philadelphia, says: "We must not, however, be oblivious to the fact that a saline cathartic residue results from the reaction of every form of baking powder now commonly employed."

Rochelle salts "act" by irritating the lining membrane of the intestine, proudcing thereby a demand for fluid to wash away the irritation. The general system gives up some of its fluids which are poured into the intestine. The lack of water thus produced renders the subsequent state of the intestine dryer than ever. The daily use of such laxatives must be a common cause of chronic constipation. Rochelle salts produce nephritis in animals and are probably a prolific source of this trouble in man.

Fruitarianism and Vegetarianism
CHAPTER XVII

Prior chapters have made clear the superiority of the all-plant diet over the flesh diet or over the conventional mixed diet. A few things, however, remain to be said. In nature it is obvious that in "temperate" climes, at least, animals that rely upon the surplus stores of plants for their winter food have infinitely greater chances of survival than do the predacious animals who must rely upon the kill for their sustenance. The plant feeding animals thus have a great advantage over the flesh eaters. This advantage extends to many other features of life which need not be discussed here.

I do not intend to enter into any lengthy discussion of comparative anatomy and physiology at this place, but will content myself with saying that every anatomical, physiological and embryological feature of man definitely places him in the class *frugivore*. The number and structure of his teeth, the length and structure of his digestive tract, the position of his eyes, the character of his nails, the functions of his skin, the character of his saliva, the relative size of his liver, the number and position of the milk glands, the position and structure of the sexual organs, the character of the human placenta and many other factors all bear witness to the fact that man is constitutionally a frugivore.

As there are no pure frugivores, all frugivores eating freely of green leaves and other parts of plants, man may, also, without violating his constitutional nature, partake of green plants. These parts of plants possess certain advantages, as has been previously ponited out, in which fruits are deficient. Actual tests have shown that the addition of green vegetables to the fruit and nut diet improves the diet.

The vast majority of the human race have at all times been wholly or largely plant feeders. Human tribes that have lived exclusively upon meat and other animal foods have been exceedingly rare or non-existent. Even Eskimo tribes eat some twenty-four different kinds of mosses and litchens, including cloudberry, barberry, crowberry, reindeer moss and other plants, that grow in the arctic.

It is probable that more meat is eaten by man today than at any previous period in his history. Civilization is based on vegetarianism — on agriculture and horticulture. Tribes that depend on hunting and herding do not remain stationary and do not build civilizations.

"When I go back," says Higgins in Anacalypsis II, page 147, "to the most remote periods of antiquity which it is possible to penetrate, I find clear and positive evidence of several important facts: First, no animal food was eaten, no animals were sacrificed." Origenes has left us the record that "the Egyptians would prefer to die, rather than becomes guilty of the crime of eating any kind of flesh.

Herodotus tells us that the Egyptians subsisted on fruits and vegetables, which they ate raw. Plinius confirms this statement. Harold Whitestone, in his *The Private Lives of the Romans*, says: "Of the Romans it may be said that during the early Republic perhaps almost through the second century B. C., they cared little for the pleasures of the table. They lived frugally and ate sparingly. They were almost strict vegetarians, much of their food was eaten cold, and the utmost simplicity characterized the cooking and the service of their meals."

It was only after the conquest of Greece that the Romans altered their table customs and became a luxury-loving, meat eating people. Even then the poorer classes lived frugally and, as Whitestone says, "every schoolboy knows that the soldiers who won Cæsar's battles for him lived on grain which they ground in their handmills and baked at their campfires."

Isis, one of the best beloved of Egyptian goddesses, was thought by them to have taught the Egyptians the art of bread making from the cereals theretofore growing wild and unused, the earlier Egyptians having lived upon fruits, roots and herbs. The worship of Isis was universal throught Egypt and magnificent temples were dedicated to her. Her priests, consecrated to purity, were required to wear linen garments, unmixed with animal fibre, to abstain from all animal food and from those vegetables regarded as impure — beans, onions, garlic and leeks.

Island tribes have existed who had no access to flesh food and there are several peoples who abstain from meat on religious grounds. We find this so in China, India, Turkey and among the Essenses in Ancient Palestine. The Spartans were forbidden to eat meat and, like the priests of Isis, were forbidden to eat beans. There are sects in India the members of which are still forbidden to eat beans.

FRUITARIANISM AND VEGETARIANISM

Hindhede has shown that on the whole health and length of life are greater among vegetarian than among meat eating peoples. McCarrison has shown that the better nourished fruit-eating Hunzas of North India are the equal in health, strength, freedom from disease and in length of life of any people on earth.

Vegetarian athletes have won honors in more than one field. Indeed where great endurance is required they almost always win. Many thousands of invalids have turned from a mixed diet to a vegetarian or fruitarian diet and have, thereby, saved their lives, even where they were unable to restore themselves to vigorous health.

A surgeon on the staff of the Bone and Joint Hospital, New York City, who has had a wide experience among vegetarians, told me that vegetarian women give birth to their babies very quickly, "drop them like animals" with but little pain, and recuperate very quickly. He added that when he gets a call to attend a childbirth in a vegetarian woman, he wastes no time, but rushes to her bedside and frequently arrives only to find the baby born before he gets there. He also stated that wounds heal more quickly in vegetarians than others. The surgeon, himself is not a vegetarian.

A surgeon here in San Antonio, who has handled deliveries for several mothers that the writer has cared for through their pregnancies, once remarked to me: "When I am called to care for a parturient woman that you have fed I know there are going to be no complications and everything will go as it should, but when I am called to care for a woman who eats in the conventional way, I never know what will happen."

Professor Richet found that fruits and vegetables do not induce serum diseases (anphylaxis), while flesh foods do and interprets his findings to mean that nature vetoes certain proteids, chiefly animal, as unsuitable. Certainly no meat, meat juice or eggs should ever be fed to a cihld under seven or eight years of age. It has no power to neutralize the poisons from these until this time.

Auto-intoxication and liability to infection are less in vegetarian and fruitarian than in animal feeders; many of the latter scarcely defending themselves at all, but tamely submit to parasitic imposition.

Tacitus tells us that the ancient Orientals refused to eat swine flesh because they were afraid of contracting leprosy if they consumed the animal that served them as a scavenger. Bacon is particularly resistant to the digestive secretions, its fat markedly slowing down gastric digestion.

Bouchard found that solutions prepared from the stools of meat-eaters are twice as toxic as those prepared from the stools of non-flesh eaters. Herter, of New York, observed that animals are killed quickly by solutions from the stools of carnivorous animals, but do not die of similar solutions prepared from stools of herbivorous animals.

It is quite evident that the greater toxicity of decomposed flesh foods would give rise to more severe types of diseases, should the putrefaction occur in the stomach and intestine, where absorption can occur. This perhaps accounts for the frequent devlopment of cancer and other serious pathologies in meat eaters.

In his Presidential Address before Section 1 of the British Association, 1913, Prof. Gowland Hopkins pointed out in connection with certain important proteid reactions, that the carnivore behaves differntly to the herbivore, the latter showing greater powers of synthesis and defense. As regards purity, stability and reliability, plant substances offer to man proteins and carbohydrates that are superior to those derived from flesh foods. It is known that in fruit and nut eating natives wounds heal much more rapidly than they do in flesh-eating Europeans.

There is evidence to show that vegetarians and fruitarians live longer than flesh eaters. Advocates of the flesh diet attempt to counter this evidence by pointing to the short life-span of the peoples of India. In doing so they ignore all of the other factors of life that help to determine length of life. India is a land of immense wealth and the home of one-fifth of the world's population. She possesses natural resources rivaling those of the United States. But these resources are undeveloped, the wealth is in the hands of a very few, while her millions are poverty-stricken. India is ruled by foreign exploiters who take from her a great share of what should be used to clothe, feed and house her teeming population. Ninety per cent of her people are illiterate, only thirty nine per cent of her people are well nourished while 80,000,000 of them are perpetually hungry. Besides all this, India is a land of filth — sanitation is little regarded. Under similar conditions of filth, poverty, overcrowding, ignorance, hunger and malnutrition meat eating Europe during the Middle Ages had a much shorter life span. This contrast of meat eaters with vegetarians living under similar conditions presents a brighter picture for the vegetarians.

The unfitness of certain classes of subsatnces as foods is evident from the frequency with which anaphylactic phenomena follow their use. The more closely these substances resemble the flesh of the body the more unfit are they as foods. Thus flesh is the worst offender, eggs are next and milk is last. Cancer and anaphylaxis have much in common inasmuch as they are both due to protein poisoning. Indeed, chronic latent anaphylaxis may be the long sought cancer virus.

Although cancer is a meat-eaters disease, we do occasionally hear of a vegetarian dying of cancer. In nearly all such cases the vegtarian is descended from meat-eaters and became a vegetarian late in life. In such cases the inherited diathesis is simply too strong to be countered by the haphazard food reform so often resorted to. Many cf these "vegetarians" are really so in name only, eating fish, chicken and other flesh "non-meats" regularly.

The man or woman who becomes a haphazard or a partial vegetarian and then only after some serious impairment of health has forced the change, a kind of eleventh hour repentence, will not always find salvation.

A pretty picture of how "vegetarians" are made to have cancer is presented in Dr. (M.D.) Louis Westerna Sanborn's account of cancer among the "vegetarian" Italians of Sambucci. Incidentally, in the course of his account, he makes it known that these "vegetarians" are pork-eaters and wine-bibbers — habits that have persisted since the days of ancient Rome. If the foes of vegetarianism are forced to hold up such examples of cancerous "vegetarians" in their efforts to show that vegetarians do have cancer, they are, indeed, driven into hiding.

I agree with Dr. John Round that the vegetarian argument, like the cause of temperance, has suffered from its friends. Pointing out that cancer-increase synchronises with the advance of meat eating, he says: "Amongst the Polynesians and Melanesians cancer is almost unknown, and these races are practically vegetarian; in Egypt cancer is seldom or never found amongst the black races; in South Africa the Boers and Europeans are largely meat-eaters and suffer frequently from cancer, whilst the natives who are largely vegetarians seldom so suffer."

We have been told that the meat-eating Eskimo is remarkably free from cancer and we have thought that this is due to their usually short life — they do not live long and die before the cancer stage develops. But Prof. Fibiger, writing in the *Lancet* (London) April 5, 1924, says that cancer affects Eskimos with approximately the same frequency as Europeans.

Much has been written about the failure of vegetarianism and it must be admitted that it has often appeared to fail. Most of the criticisms of the vegetarian diet have, however, missed the real reasons for the apparent failure.

Vegetarians are prevented from adopting a real food reform because they have the erroneous idea that the rejection of meat is all that is required to carry them into the dietetic heaven. They do not know that a vegetarian diet may be even more dangerous than a properly planned mixed diet. Indeed, the eating of most vegetarians is so abominable that one cannot blame people for not following them.

The diet of the vegetarian is often inadequate. One man who has had quite a vogue in America in recent years advocates a fat-free, starch-free, protein-free diet. His own emaciated condition speaks well for the evils of such an inadequate diet. The late Arnold Ehret advocated an inadequate diet. Others go to the opposite extreme. They accept the high-protein standard of "orthodox" medicine and consume large quantities of bread, cereals and pulses because these are rich in protein. A cereal and pulse diet with a deficiency of green foods and fresh fruits is obviously inadequate. It is deficient in alkaline elements — yields an acid-ash — and vitamins.

Plant-feeders will always consume green vegetables if they can procure them and in the green parts of plants, vitamins and minerals are present in their active state and in favorable quantities. So-called graminivorous animals become ill, breed badly, and rear fewer young, if they cannot get green leaf food in addition to grains.

Fruits and green vegetables were abundant in the diets of the Romans, Spartans and Egyptians and are plentiful in the diet of the Hunzas. Today the average Chinaman eats five timse as much green foods as the average American. Green foods make up the greater part and during some seasons of the years, the whole diet of all vegetarian animals.

FRUITARIANISM AND VEGETARIANISM

Dr. Densmore strongly condemned the old vegetarian diet, made up largely, as he said, of "soft, pulpy, starchy food, spoon meat," not alone because of the excess of starch and protein it contained but because they do "not involve mastication, the secretion of saliva in the mouth" is "not stimulated."

Saliva flows in response to a variety of substances — dry bread, or other dry starch, powdered dry flesh — but not in response to fresh raw flesh, moist bread or other watery substances. Mushes, boiled cereals, soups, purees, etc., do not excite the flow of saliva. There is no efficient digestion of soft, sloppy meals. The vegetarians of forty years ago consumed too much indigestible mush.

Densmore asserted the "unwholesomeness of a bread diet and cereal diet." He said "I do object to bread, cereals, pulses and starchy vegtables because of the predominant proportion of starch contained in them; but I also object to these foods; **** because their nitrogen is distinctly difficult of digestion, and the cause of unnecessary waste of vitality."

Wrong combinations also aid in wrecking the health of many vegetarians. Except for the absence of flesh foods, their meals are often as varied and their combinations as inharmonious as those of mixed diet eaters. Conservative cooking and correct food combining were unknown to the older vegetarians, but there is no excuse for present-day vegetarians to repeat these older mistakes.

The prejudice in the minds of many that vegetarianism means weakness is the outgrowth of the fact that with rare exceptions, only invalids of some sort take up vegetarianism. They are people whose stock has suffered through the indulgence of their ancestors and through their own indulgence and who now turn to vegetarianism as a means of saving their lives. They are people who have been made thoughtful through suffering and are only beginning to mend.

Vegetarianism has not failed. On the contrary, it is the one outstanding success of human and animal history. Meat eating is the great arch-type of failure as the same history testifies.

Nature's Food Refinery
CHAPTER XVIII

Foods, as we receive them from the bountiful hand of Nature, are not fitted for entrance into the blood and lymph or for the cells. They must undergo a disorganizing and refining process by which the structure of the food is broken down and the useful is separated from the useless in food. This process is called digestion.

The process by which apples, corn, beans, celery, are transformed into blood, bones, nerves, muscles, skin, hair and nails, is both complicated and intensively interesting. Digestion, the first step in this wonderful process, is the process by which food is prepared (in the mouth, stomach and intestines) for absorption into the blood and lymph to be used by the body. Digestion is carried on partly by mechanical, partly by chemical means.

ENZYMES

The chemical part of digestion is performed by a series of digestive juices, alternating between alkalies and acids. The active principles in these juices or fluids are ferments known as enzymes. All true digestive juices contain enzymes. These are substances which possess the power of instigating chemical reactions, without themselves being transformed or destroyed in course of the process. Strictly speaking, an enzyme is an organic compound formed by a living cell, while other substances which bring about chemical changes are called by the broader term, catalyzer. An enzyme is simply a special kind of catalytic agent, or a catalyst produced by a living organism.

Digestive enzymes bring about chemical changes in the food eaten. They are known as protein-splitting or proteolytic, fat-splitting or lipolytic, and starch-splitting or amylolytic, according to the type of food-stuff upon which they act. They are specific in their action, by which is meant, they are not capable of inciting several different reactions but each enzyme acts upon but one class of food. If a digestive juice affects two distinct types of food it is considered to contain two enzymes. Enzymes are destroyed by heat short of boiling and are prevented from acting by cold, although as a rule this does not prevent them from resuming their activity upon being warmed. The enzymes in the human body are most active at body temperature (about 98°F.) and begin to break down at a higher temperature. Fever prevents their action.

If they are compared with other chemicals a very striking peculiarity is disclosed. This is, enzymes are not used up in proportion to the work they do. If one is pouring hydrochloric acid upon iron to make hydrogen gas he is forced to continue pouring the acid if he is to continue evolving the gas. But if starch is being converted into sugar by pytalin the amount of sugar formed depends less upon the amount of saliva present than upon the time the enzyme acts upon the starch. A small amount of digestive juice, containing a much smaller amount of enzyme, may, under favorable conditions, act continuously with but the most gradual loss of power.

SALIVARY DIGESTION

Digestion begins in the mouth where the food is subjected to the mechanical process of grinding to break it up into smaller particles thus enabling the digestive juices to get at the food more readily. This also aids in mixing the salive of the mouth with the food. (Chewing or mastication is the only conscious work of digestion and all the subconscious processes depend upon how well this has been performed.)

Simultaneously with the chewing of the food the digestive juice of the mouth is poured out upon and thoroughly mixed with it. Saliva, as it is called, is a colorless, tasteless ropy fluid secreted chiefly by the parotoid, submaxillary and sublingual glands. Secretions from the bucal, palatine, lingual, molar and tonsillar glands also contribute to the saliva. In man it is normally alkaline in reaction, although, during fevers, while fasting, when there are digestive disturbances, and between midnight and morning it may become acid. About 1500 grams, or between one and two quarts are secreted in twenty-four hours.

Its secretion is not a simple filtration due to blood pressure but is accomplished by the action of the cells composing these glands. In common with all the cells of the body, these exercise a selective power by which they select from the blood stream the elements needed in the manufacture of saliva and reject the rest. The salivary glands are under nerve control which secures coordination.

The active principle in saliva is an enzyme known as pytalin which acts upon starches (polysaccharides), converting these into a form of sugar known as dextrines (disaccharides).

If saliva is put into a test tube with starch it will convert this into sugar. At low temperatures this process goes on slowly, the velocity increasing as the temperature increases until it reaches its maximum at about 37°C. Above this temperature the velocity again decreases, the enzyme being destroyed at about 70°C.

Pytalin is lacking in the saliva of all carnivorous and some other animals. In these the saliva is not a true digestive juice, but acts, solely to moisten the food thus enabling the animal to swallow it.

Pytalin is not present in the saliva when food that does not contain starch is taken into the mouth. The tongue contains various sets of taste buds among which are proteid and starch buds. The function of taste not only affords us pleasure, but is an all important element in the subconscious process of digestion. Particularly it serves to stimulate the flow of the digestive juices, especially those of the stomach, and to suit their character to the food eaten. The nerve impulses set into motion by the taste of foods set the mechanism into action necessary to digestion. The character of food eaten determines, through the taste buds, the character of the digestive juices released to act upon it. Saliva will be poured into the mouth but no pytalin will be present if the food eaten contains no starch. Even sugar, if put into the mouth will not occasion the release of ptyatin, although, the mouth will quickly fill with saliva.

Edinger showed by experiment that potassium rhodanate is the antiseptic principle in saliva. He found that three parts of saliva to the thousand will kill the "bacilli of cholera morbus" in one minute, while nine parts to the thousand will kill diptheria germs in the same time. Here is a constantly produced antiseptic powerful enough to destroy any germ, yet harmless to the body. Chew your food well and the saliva will aid in preventing decomposition. A pint of human saliva was collected and exposed in an open jar to the sunshine and heat of June, July and August, and at the end of the experiment showed no sign of infection or disintegration.

Pytalin is destroyed by acid in a minute percentage. Tannic acid in tea and coffee interferes with the digestion of starch. Drug ācids do likewise. *One half of one per cent of acid stops the action of pytalin.*

Tart (acid) fruits taken with starches completely neutralize the alkalinity of the saliva, the only secretion in the body able to initiate the digestion of starches, and paralyzes the ptyalin. Besides being wet, they are also acid and thus there is both a mechanical and a chemical reason why they should not be taken with cereals or other starch.

After food is masticated it is swallowed and enters the stomach where the work of digesting the starch continues until sufficient gastric juice has been poured into the stomach cavity to render its contents acid.

Dr. Cannon of Harvard University Medical School, demonstrated that if starch is well-mixed with saliva, it will continue to digest in the stomach for up to two hours. If proteins, which require an acid stomach juice in which to digest, are eaten at the same meal, nature deluges the food in the stomach, including the starch, with acid gastric juice which neutralizes the alkaline saliva and destroys the ptyalin, and starch digestion ceases shortly.

When starches are soaked with any kind of fluid – water, milk, fruit juices, etc. – very little saliva is poured out, no matter how long one chews them. Dry starches excite a copious flow of saliva rich in ptyalin. Dry starch increases in bulk upon being masticated; soaked starch does not. Dry starches, taken into the mouth with fruits, milk, water, coffee, or tea, etc., do not excite the flow of saliva.

If starches are to digest, they must be eaten dry. Starches put into soup are never digested. When starches are not digested they lie in the stomach and produce much trouble. Soaked starches are also likely to be swallowed without chewing. Unmasticated starches, even if they were insalivated would not digesst. Boiled starches do not digest.

Experiments carried on by the Defensive Diet League showed that oatmeal is never digested in the stomach. The same was shown to be true of every other cooked and soaked cereal. The stomach does not digesst starches – does not secrete a starch digesting fluid – and when starches are soaked so that they do not receive saliva and ptyalin, they cannot be digested in the stomach.

GASTRIC DIGESTION

Movements of the stomach slowly mix the food with gastric juice. This is a clear, colorless fluid, strongly acid in reaction and possessing a characteristic odor. It is secreted by about five million microscopic glands situated in the walls of the stomach, and contains an enzyme known as pepsin which acts upon proteins and acts only in an acid medium. Besides pepsin, it contains two other enzymes — renin, which coagulates the casein of milk, and gastric lipase, a fat-splitting enzyme. It also contains mineral matters and hydrochloric acid (commonly known as muriatic acid and used as a solder-in acid) which is very powerful and literally eats to pieces the food it permeates. It would soon destroy the stomach except for the fact that its walls are continually protected by an alkaline secretion. This alkaline bath in which the stomach is kept is analogous to the water bath some furnaces have to be kept in to prevent them from melting.

Gastric Secretion: Gastric Secretion is divided into:

(1) Continuous secretion: Gastric secretion seems to be continuous, but the juice secreted in an empty stomach is less acid than that produced during digestion. Continuous secretion is absent during fevers, gastritis and other gastric inflammations. (Fasting is indicated.)

(2) Appetite juice: Gastric juice is poured out in response to hunger and the sight, smell, taste and thought of food. Miller and others have shown that the sight of food is a more powerful stimulus to gastric secretion than odor. It is more important that food is pleasing to the eye than to the nose. Unpalatable food produces little or no appetite juice, though it may ultimately be well digested. It is important that our food be palatable — that we relish it. When the tongue is coated, so that food flavors cannot be appreciated by the nerves of taste, the gustatory reflexes are destroyed, appetite juice is not formed and digestion is suspended. (A fast is indicated.) Appetite juice is either greatly diminished or entirely absent in gastritis or any inflammatory disorder of the gastric mucosa, as well as in fevers. It is also stopped by pain and strong emotions, and by fear and anger. (Fasting is indicated.) Worry and mental strain cause delay in the secretion of appetite juice and hinder digestion.

(3) Chemical Secretion: Gastric juice is poured out in response to the presence of food and to by-products of the process of digestion — particularly by gastrin, a hormone formed when protein is brought into contact with normal gastric juice. Chemical secretion is arrested by fever, especially by high fever. The injection of gastrin under the skin or into the vein of a healthy subject causes an

active secretion of gastric juice. This does not occur if fever is present. (Fasting is indicated.)

Gastric juice is the product of six different sets of glands.

Three sets of glands secrete enzymes — pepsin, lipase and renin or chymosin.

One set secretes mucus.

One set secretes hydrochloric acid.

One set secretes a serous fluid, termed diluting juice, which serves to regulate the acidity and digestive activity of the juice.

About three pints of gastirc juice are secreted in twenty-four hours. About one and a half pints are required to digest a hearty dinner. The normal stomach produces about two thirds of an ounce of hydrochloric acid in twenty-four hours. The amount varies with the food eaten.

The amount of pepsin contained in a pint and a half of gastric juice produced in twenty-four hours is about seven and one-half grains. About four grains of pepsin are contained in the twenty or more ounces of gastric juice required to digest a hearty dinner, or enough to digest two-thirds pound of egg white, or three and a half pounds of dried albumen. The daily production of pepsin is sufficient to digest four or more times the amount of protein required by the body. Undigested starch tends to absorb pepsin and interferes with gastric digestion.

Pepsin is not active except in the presence of hydrochloric acid. Excessive gastric acidity prevents the action of pepsin — excess acid destroying the pepsin. Drug acids and fruit acids also demoralize gastric digestion.

The acidity of gastric juice is determined by the food eaten. Meat causes the production of a gastric juice similar to that in dogs. Pavlov, Rehfus and Hawk have shown that animal foods call for stronger acid juice than vegetable foods — the average acidity of beef is 120, eggs 80, vegetables 70. Milk calls for greater acidity than eggs, bread and cereals the lowest degree.

The secretion of gastric juice is in response to the higher centers, as these are set in motion by the taste and odor of food, and is poured into the stomach in advance of the food. It is poured out in response to substances requiring its action and variously modified to meet the requirements of various kinds of foods. If starch or other non-protein foods are eaten a gastric juice will be secreted which differs from that poured out upon proteins. As previously noted the taste lends aid in regulating its secretion, as do also the sight and smell of food.

Food taken into the mouth causes a flow of gastric juice, even if the food is not swallowed. Eager desire for food will do the same. But no amount of chemical and mechanical stimulation of the buccal membranes is capable of reflexly exciting the nerves of the stomach.

Gastric juice is not poured out in response to the presence of acid in the mouth. Salines, bitters, pepper, mustard, etc., taken into the mouth, do not result in the secretion of gastric juice. Mechanical and chemical stimulants applied to the mouth and its glands do not occasion any gastric flow.

The old fallacy that salt, pepper, mustard and other condiments and bitters aid or stimulate digestion is thus seen to be false. Active digestive juices are secreted only in response to and are modified to meet the requirements of the food substances requiring their action. Any juice that could possibly be excited by catsup, for example, after it reaches the stomach, wuold not be adapted to the digestion of meat, eggs or other substances upon which it is used. The precise and specific adaptation of the digestive juices to the particular food to be digested, renders it impossible that any "aid to digestion" can improve digestion in any way.

Carlson showed that bitters do not increase gastric secretion. Reichmann and Schoeffer showed that bitters actually lessen gastric secretion. Bitters hinder and do not aid digestion. Bitters taken into the mouth diminish the hunger contractions, as do other "stimulants" applied to the oral membrane.

Alcohol seems to increase gastric secretion, but the alcohol precipitates the pepsin thus destroying the activity of the juice.

In his classical research for the Committee, Prof. Chittenden, of Yale, showed that wines, as well as strong drinks, are decidedly detrimental to digestion. He showed that alcohol increases the flow of gastric juice, but found that an equal amount of water would increase gastric secretion equally as much. Upon further investigation it was found that the secretion induced by water possessed much more powerful digestive properties than that induced by alcohol.

The secretion of hydrochloric acid is only temporarily increased, after which its secretion is diminished, while the alcohol hinders the formation of pepsin. It also causes the mucous glands to pour such large quantities of alkaline fluid (mucus) into the stomach that this upsets gastric digestion.

It has been definitely established that tea and coffee both retard gastric digestion. Coffee is considered to have less effect than tea, providing they are both of the same strength. Since, however, coffee is customarily used in a stronger infusion than is tea, the effects of coffee in actual practice are about the same as those of tea. Their inhibiting effects are largely due to their modifying influence on the chemical processes of digestion.

The effects of these two poisonous infusions do not end with retarding the processes of digestion. They affect the stomach itself. Tea in particular, rich in tannic acid, and other astringent agents, acts as a strong irritant to the lining membrane of the stomach. Caffeol, and other substances produced by the roasting of coffee, are greater irritants even than tea. Chronic gastric catarrh and other disorders of the stomach may easily be produced and maintained by the effects of these two popular drinks.

Aside from these effects upon the stomach and the effects upon the nervous system and kidneys, produced by these two drugs, they undoubtedly affect the intestine and colon as well. There are many people upon whom coffee produces a laxative effect and this indicates that its irritating effects extend to the intestine and colon. Perhaps they also retard intestinal digestion.

As de-caffeinized coffee is not decaffeinized, and since, if it were, the coffee would still possess its tannic acid, caffeol and other poisons, and would in addition to its other effects, continue to retard digestion and injure stomach and kidneys, there seems to be no rational excuse for continuing its use.

In the well-known experiments upon Saint Martin it was found that a piece of metal could be introduced into the stomach but it would not occasion any flow of gastric juice. If, however, someone entered the room with a platter of steaming steak, the instant the man's eyes fell upon this the gastric juice would begin to flow into the stomach. When no gastric juice was needed none was supplied. Pavlov, introduced into the stomach of a sleeping dog (through a fistula) 100 grams of flesh. After an hour and a half the flesh was withdrawn by means of a string that had been tied to the meat. The loss to the meat was only six grams. This same amount of meat (100 grams) was again introduced into the stomach through the fistula, after the dog had been allowed to see and smell the meat. Under these conditions the weight of the meat was reduced by 30 grams in the sâme time. The reader will readily perceive the importance of such facts in diet. They teach us that food must be seen, smelled and tasted if digestion is to proceed normally. But the food must not be so disguised by condiments, spices, etc., as to deceive the senses as this will hinder the setting into motion, through the nerves, of the mechanism necessary to digestion.

The flow of gastric juice into the stomach is apparently in advance of the actual arrival of food and seems to be proportioned to the pleasure afforded by eating. This should teach us that the pleasure we derive from eating is only a means to an end, not the end itself.

The secretion of gastric juice is hastened and retarded by a number of factors the chief of which are here given:

Accelerated by
(1) Hunger
(2) Pleasurable taste
(3) Sight and smell of food
(4) Thought of food
(5) Joy, happiness, etc.
(6) Effects of food on lining of stomach
(7) Ingestion of water
(8) Secretagogues arising as by-products of the process of digestion

Retarded by:
(1) Fear, worry, anxiety, anger and other destructive emotions
(2) Failure to taste food
(3) Absence of hunger
(4) Lack of proper salivary digestion
(5) Pain, fever, etc.

Pepsin, the protein-splitting enzyme of the gastric juice, converts proteins into peptones. Beyond coagulating the casein of milk, renin appears to have no other function. Gastric lipase has but little effect upon fats.

Pavlov, the renouned Russian physiologist, has shown (see his *The Work of the Digestive Glands*) that the first secreted portions of the gastric juice are not always stronger in digestive power than that secreted an hour or so later. The strongest juice is poured out when it is most needed — when the quantity of food is large and when its structure is coarse. His experiments have proved that each kind of food calls forth a particular activity of the digestive glands and that the powers of the juice vary with the quantity of the feeding. Khizhin, one of his co-workers, performed experiments which have shown that feeding mixed diets, or separated administrations of milk, bread and meat, calls forth each time special modifications in the activity of the gastric glands. The secretion response is not "limited to the powers of the juice but extends to the rate of its flow, and also its total quantity." This proves that the character of the food not only determines the digestive power of the gastric juice, but also its total acidity. The acidity is greatest with meat and least with bread.

Prof. Pavlov says: "On proteid in the form of bread, five times more pepsin is poured out than on the same quantity of protein in the form of milk, and that flesh nitrogen requires more pepsin than that of milk. These different kinds of proteids receive, therefore, quantities of ferment corresponding to the differences in their digestibility."

Comparing equivalent weights, Pavlov found that flesh requires the most and milk the least amount of gastric juice;but comparing equivalents of nitrogen, he found that bread needs the most and flesh the least juice. The gland work per hour is almost the same with milk and flesh diets, but far less with bread. The last, however, exceeds all the others in the time required for its digestion, and consequently, the flow of juice is somewhat prolonged.

"Each separate kind of food," he says, "determines a definite hourly rate of secretion and produces characteristic limitations in the powers of the juices. Thus with a fish diet, the maximum rate of secretion occurs during the first and second hour, and the quantity of juice in each being approximately the same. With a broad diet, we have invariably a pronounced maximum in the second hour; and with milk a similar one during the second and third hours."

The acidity of gastric juice is determined by the food eaten, by the length of time that has elapsed since the food was consumed, and by the familiarity or unfamiliarity of the system with the food. Physicians persistently ignore these facts in making gastric tests and in feeding in hyper- and hypo-acidity. They invariably feed foods in hyper-acidity that increase the acidity and feed foods in hypo-acidity that decrease acidity. They make the same mistakes with regard to pepsin, for what is true of hydrochloric acid is true also of the secretion of pepsin.

"On the other hand," says Pavlov, "the most active juice occurs with flesh in the first hour; with bread in the second and third; and with milk in the last hour of secretion. Thus the period of maximum outflow, as well as the whole curve of secretion, is characteristic for each diet."

Pavlov also says: "The work of the gastric glands, in providing juice for the different food stuffs, must be recognized to be also purposive in another sense. The vegetable protein of bread requires for its digestion much ferment. This demand is supplied less by an increase in the volume of the juice than by and extraordinary concentration of the fluid poured out. One may infer from this that it is only the ferment of the gastric juice that is here in great requisition, and that *large quantities of hydrochloric acid would be useless, or possibly injurious.* We see from the following, that during gastric digsetion of bread, *an excess of hydrochloric acid is actually avoided.* The total quantity of juice secreted on bread is only a little larger than that secreted on milk. It is distributed, however, over a much longer time, so that the mean hourly curve of juice with the bread diet is one and one-half times less than after taking milk or flesh. Consequently, in the digestion of bread but little hydrochloric acid is present in the stomach during the period of secretion. This harmonizes well with the facts of physiologic chemistry, namely, that the digestion of starch is impeded by an excess of acid.

"From clinical observation, we know further that, in cases of hyperacidity, a large part of the starch of bread escapes unused from the gastro-intestinal canal, while the flesh is excellently digested."

Are we not fully justified, by these facts, in assuming that the variations observed in gland activity during the course of digestion have some essential meaning? Each kind of food produces a special curve of secretion, and there must be a definite purpose for it, and a special significance to the secretory reaction. Pavlov holds that the work of the digestive glands, while elastic, is at the same time specific, precise and purposive. These facts are useful in working out proper food combinations, as we shall see later.

There are foods, like the starches, which, so far as stomach digestion is concerned, can only be digested in an alkaline medium—saliva—and others, like the proteins, which can only be digested in an acid medium — gastric juice — and if eaten together, interfere with the digestion of each other. We are justified in calling these incompatible foods.

From these facts it becomes obvious that the digestion of carbohydrates and of proteins is quite different. Indeed they are almost incompatible, for the requirements of each are so different that, when taken together, one forestalls the proper gastric digestion of the other. Another important observation should be taken into consideration at this point. Carbohydrates, proteins and fats are always mixed in the diet of most people. Fats have no stimulating effect on the gastric glands; whether the oil or fat is consumed before a meal, during the meal, or after the meal, an inhibitory influence upon gastric secretion becomes apparent immediately. If consumed after the meal and the gastric juice has begun to flow, it exerts an inhibitory influence which lasts usually for one or two hours.

Fat depresses, or inhibits, the normal activity of the secretory processes and this inhibitory effect while, perhaps partly mechanical, is for the most part chemical, as is shown by the results of administering milk with an increased amount of fat. The amount of juice secreted upon cream is less in amount and weaker in power than the small amount of weak juice poured out upon milk.

Nor is the effect of fat on the secretion of gastric juice limited to the depression of the flow of the gastric juice. Its preventive influence may last from one-half to two hours; only to be followed in the third hour, if the meal of fat be at all large, by a renewed secretion of gastric juice. This late secretion is much prolonged and furnishes a considerable quantity of gastric juice and it seems to be an explanation for many cases of hyperacidity which follow the taking of oils, butter fats and meat fats with a protein meal.

Bile precipitates pepsin, so that its presence in the stomach stops protein digestion even though the contents of the stomach remain acid. (Fasting is indicated in such cases). Trypsin (pancreatic) digests pepsin so that its action does not long continue in the intestine. Bile also stops its action, as does alkalinity.

INTESTINAL DIGESTION

When the work of digestion is completed in the stomach the food is poured through the pyloric orifice into the small intestine where it undergoes further changes.

In negroes the small intestine is shorter and the large intestine longer than in the white man of similar build. There are also differences due to sex — extremes in males running from 15 ft. 6 inches to 31 feet, 10 inches and in females, from 18 feet 10 inches to 29 feet 4 inches. The tall thin type of person, with trunk of small circumference, has a shorter intestine than the heavy rugged type.

There are three digestive juices which are poured into the intestine — bile, pancreatic juice and intestinal juice; all of these are alkaline in reaction.

The pancreatic juice is secreted by the pancreas and enters the intestine just below the union of the stomach and duodenum or upper portion of the small intestine. This juice, the secretion of which is excited by the action of the acid contents received from the stomach upon the walls of the intestine, is poured out about the time the contents of the stomach pass through he pyloric valve.

Pancreatic juice contains four enzymes. One of these known as diastase or amylase resembles ptylain and continues the work of digesting starches and sugars, converting these into a form of sugar known as monosaccharides. It is not destroyed by the acid contents of the stomach as is ptyalin. A second, known as trypsin, is a protein-splitting enzyme, but unlike pepsin, does not require the cooperation of an acid to accomplish its work. In fact, it is destroyed by a strong acid. By its action the peptones are converted into amino-acids. The third enzyme known as liapase causes fat to undergo cleavage forming fatty acids and glycerine. The fourth, chymosin, or pancreatic renin, coagulates milk.

Pavlov discovered that the pancreatic juice, as it leaves the pancreas, has no appreciable action upon proteins, but becomes rapidly active when a small quantity of the intestinal juice, which Pavlov has called enterokinase, which converts the inactive trypsinogen, from the pancreas, into active trypsin. Pavlov regarded enterokinase as itself an enzyme. Active trypsin in the pancreas and pancreatic duct might destroy these organs. Nature seems to have safeguarded the body by arranging that it cannot become active until it is in the presence of food in the intestine, where it is activated by the enzymic effect of the intestinal juice upon it.

Considering the pancreatic secretion, we find the same marvelous adaptation of the digestive properties to the class of food to be acted upon. Each kind of food calls for its own particular kind of juice. The character of these juices is often the direct opposite of that seen in the stomach. In the stomach the weakest juice is poured out upon milk and the strongest upon meat; in the duodenum the weakest juice is poured out on flesh and the strongest on milk. This statement, of course, has reference to the protein-splitting character of the juice.

With regard to the starch-splitting enzyme, this is present in greater quantity in the "bread juice" and in lesser quantity in "milk juice." The fat-splitting enzyme is very scarce in "bread juice" abundant in "milk juice," and intermediate in "flesh juice." "The work of the pancreas, like that of the gastric glands," to quote Pavlov, "is specialized both as regards the quantity and property of its juice, and the rate of its progress which the secretion takes for the different classes of food."

The second of the juices poured into the intestines is bile or gall. This is secreted by the liver and enters the intestine at about the point where the pancreatic juice enters. Its secretion goes on continuously but is accelerated after meals. It contains no enzyme and is, therefore, not a true digestive juice; but acts chiefly by producing a favorable environment for the action of the pancreatic enzymes. If it is prevented from entering the intestines, the ability to digest and absorb foods, particularly fats, is reduced. Bile increases the solubility of the fatty acids by emulsification, accelerates the action of the pancreatic liapase, stimulates intestinal activity, counteracts putrefaction, and assists in the union of water and oils.

Bile, secreted in the liver and conveyed by a duct to the duodenum, is not regarded as a true digestive juice because it contains no enzyme. But by alkalizing the acid bolus from the stomach, when this enters the duodenum, it provides a suitable environment for the operation of the pancreatic and intestinal enzymes. The hydrochloric acid, of the stomach, upon entering the intestine, acts as a powerful stimulus to the flow of pancreatic juice, intestinal juice and bile, but is antagonistic to the action of their enzymes. The bile counteracts the acid and produces a favorable medium for the action of these enzymes.

Bile is a powerful disinfectant and prevents putrefaction in the intestine. It also serves to prevent the formation of gas and helps to maintain the alkalinity of the intestine.

The third or intestinal juice is secreted in abundance by small glands in the walls of the small intestine. It contains an enzyme known as crepsin which cooperates with trypsin in the final stages of protein digestion. This juice also completes the preparation of carbohydrates for entrance into the blood.

Intestinal juice—succus-intericus—is elaborated by many microscopic glands embedded in the walls of the intestine. There are four kinds of glands which secrete intestinal juice—Crypts of Lieberkuhn, Brunner's glands, solitary glands and Pyer's patches or glands. The glands of Lieberkuhn secrete an intestinal juice containing several enzymes—erepsin (Proteolytic), lactase, invertase, (Amolytic), Maltase (Amolytic), and lactase which digests milk sugar. Brunner's glands secrete a juice containing the enzyme, enterokinase, which, acting upon the trypsinogen of the pancreatic juice, as it enters the duodenum, converts this into the powerful protein-splitting enzyme, trypsin. Chymosis, which coagulates milk, is also contained in succus-interucus.

Having considered the processes of digestion let us now get some idea of the work accomplished by these. Frist, it is a refining process, breaking down the structure of the food and separating the nutritive portions from the waste or useless parts. Second, it splits up the large and complex molecules of food into smaller, less complex ones, in this way adding to the diffusibility of the food. Diffusibility is the capability of spreading and enabling substances to pass through ordinary membranes. Lastly, it standardizes our food. By this we mean it obliterates many of the characteristics of the various foods consumed and gives us, finally, practically the same set of products whatever the meal eaten. From the many strange and foreign compounds that are taken into the mouth, as food, are formed a few acceptible compounds.

When, finally, the work of digestion is completed in the intestine the carbohydrates have been reduced to a form of sugar known as monosaccharides, the fats have been converted into fatty acids and glycerol and the proteins have been reduced to amino-acids. Water and salts undergo no change. The waste portions of the food are separated from the usable portions and are sent on into the large intestine or colon to be expelled.

While fats, starches, sugars and proteins undergo several changes in the process of digestion, the mineral elements of our food are absorbed unchanged. They do not require to be digested.

INDIGESTION

So long as the body is normal, the digestive secretions are sufficient protection against the fermentation and putrefaction of food, which would otherwise be set up by microbes. If, however, the vital powers are lowered so that the secretions are deficient in quality or are insufficient in quantity, or, if there is disease, which impairs the digestive powers, bacterial fermentation sets in and we have indigestion. The fermentation produces toxins of various kinds, which, when absorbed into the blood and lymph, serve to poison the body. Some of these poisons are the ptomains and leucomains; phenol, cresol, leucin, tryson, ammonia, sulphurated hydrogen, fatty acids, oxalic and uric acids, alcohol and the xanthin bodies. Of these, indol is the most easily absorbed and is most readily recognized in the urine.

The chief causes of gastro-intestinal indigestion are overeating, enervation and bad food combinations. Enervating influences are anything that lowers nerve force and include such things as overwork, underwork, extremes of cold and heat, use of stimulants, sexual excesses, etc. Anything that enervates lessens digestive power and becomes an indirect cause of indigestion.

Overeating overworks the digestive organs, as well as introduces more food into the system than is needed. Food eaten in excess is bound to accumulate as waste and decompose as poison.

Other things being equal, digestion is more efficient when but one food is eaten. A single article of food will digest more quickly and perfectly than will the same food if mixed with other foods. The more foods one takes together, the less efficient is the process of digestion.

From the differences in the results of fermentation and those of digestion, it should be apparent that, although, the enzymes are spoken of as ferments, they do not produce fermentation. Rather, the digestive juices and their enzymes act as powerful solvents—for (and keep this fact in mind), digestion reduces food-stuffs to the diffusible state without depriving them of their organic qualities, while fermentation renders them diffusible by reducing them to the inorganic and, therefore, useless state. Digestion is solution; fermentation is disintegration.

The Digestibility of Foods
CHAPTER XIX

Many misconceptions about the digestibility of different foods exist, not alone in the minds of laymen, but also in the minds of those who are supposed to know. Studies of this subject have largely centered on the emptying time of the stomach after various foods have been eaten and the amounts of the various foods that are digested as shown in the stools. As both the emptying time of the stomach and the amounts of undigested foods that appear in the stools are affected by a number of factors, it is obvious that a large margin of error is provided for.

A food is likely to be classed as difficult of digsetion merely because it remains in the stomach longer than other foods, whereas, it may not be difficult to digest at all. The process of digestion may merely be different and call for different timing of the digestive secretions. We know, although it is commonly ignored, that the time a food remains in the stomach is determined, not by the ease or difficulty of its digestion, but by the nature of the digestive process required to digest a particular food. A food that digests in the stomach in four hours is not necessarily more difficult to digest and does not demonstrably use up more energy, than one that digests in one hour. The digestive process is simply different. A food may be classed as not very digestible merely because much of it is passed out in the stools in an undigested state, whereas, the undigested food may appear in the stools because the person to whom it is fed is unaccustomed to eating it and has not learned to digest it, or because it was fed in combinations that prevented its digestion, or because of fatigue, or from other causes. A food that is well-digested by one individual at one time under a given set of circumstances may be poorly digested by the same individual at another time under different conditions.

After making hundreds of digestion experiments Prof. Atwater computed the average coefficients of digestibility of the proteins, fats and carbohydrates in the main groups of foods used by man as part of a mixed diet to be as shown in the following table:

The Digestibility of Foods

Average Coefficients of Digestibility of Foods When Used in Mixed Diets (Atwater)

	Protein	Fat	Carbohydrates
Animal foods	97	95	98
Cereals and breadstuffs	85	90	98
Dried legumes	78	90	97
Vegetables	83	90	95
Fruits	85	90	90
Total of Food Average Mixed Diet	92	95	98

These figures, which differ in certain particulars from later findings, reveal less differences between the digestibility of various foods than are popularly supposed to exist. Prof. Sherman makes a remark that the table cannot sustain. He says that "it is noteworthy that the coefficients of digestibility are less influenced by the conditions under which the food is eaten and vary less with individuals than is generally supposed." That individual variations are not, on the whole, very great, I believe to be true; but that the conditions under which food is eaten influences the digestion of the food but little, I am sure is a statement that cannot be sustained.

The figures in Prof. Atwater's table are averages. They do not show individual variations, nor do they show differences under different conditions. They are averages compiled from digestion of food by various individuals under different conditions. It is more than likely, also, that the variations in the conditions under which foods were eaten in his experiments were not great. The digestibility of a food is one thing and is not influenced by the conditions of the individual; the digestive ability of the individual is quite another thing and is markedly influenced by the varying conditons of the individual.

Atwater did not take into account, in his experiments, the findings of Pavlov that the ability to digest a particular kind of food may be increased or decreased by eating that food or by refraining from eating that food. So far as I can find, no other experimenter has taken this fact into consideration. From Pavlov's findings it is obvious that a vegetarian would not have much flesh-digesting ability. This, no doubt, accounts, in large measure, at least, for the distress experienced by vegetarians when they stray from the fold and indulge

THE SCIENCE AND FINE ART OF FOOD AND NUTRITION

in a flesh meal. No doubt, part of their distress is of psychologic origin. On the other hand the man who regularly and habitually consumes nuts as a part of his diet will have greater nut-digesting ability than the man who seldom or almost never eats nuts. It is well-known that many people have trouble with spinach. Repeated tests have shown that if these people are fed spinach daily for a brief period, they acquire the ability to handle it without difficulty. I have seen two people in whom milk did not even coagulate, but was passed out quickly in a fluid state as it was swallowed. In these two individuals, the milk was expelled by the colon within three minutes after it was swallowed. As they were not kept on milk I had no opportunity to learn what adjustments they were capable of. I doubt that they secreted any renin, although the rapidity with which the milk was expelled would indicate that there were also other troubles.

Body chemistry is, to a large extent, determined by food. Physiology bears out the statement that a particular feeding habit produces particular enzymes or modifications of enzymes, a particular composition of the body fluids and glandular secretions and particular nerve developments. Feeding habits are cumulatively affective and provide the soil for metabolic responses. Perhaps in no other function is the change in enzymic action so obvious and in no other function is it so quickly apparent as in the function of digestion.

There is a tendency in all living tissues to enter into a condition of a more or less stable nature, when under the influence of forced work or its opposite. Pavlov found this same to be true of the digestive secretions. For example, in feeding animals, it was found that when the diet is altered and the new diet maintained for a length of time, the enzyme-content of the juice becomes, from day to day, more and more adapted to the requirements of the new food.

A dog fed for weeks on nothing but milk and bread, was placed on an exclusive flesh diet, containing more protein and scarcely any carbohydrate. The ability of the digestive juice to digest protein increased day by day, until it reached its maximum strength, while its amylolytic (starch-splitting) power progressively declined. A dog so fed showed "even after the lapse of three days" "that the proteid ferment tended to increase, while the starch ferment declined." This change has been noted for as long as up to tewnty-three days.

THE DIGESTIBILITY OF FOODS

Reversing the process, a dog fed exclusively upon a flesh diet, was placed on milk and bread and its pancreatic juices observed. The protein--digesting power of the juice dcreased progressively, until, after sixty-six days on the bread and milk diet, the whole of the pancreatic juice secreted in twenty-four hours was collected and it was found that "the digestive power for proteid is absolutely nil." Meanwhile the starch-digesting power had increased.

In some dogs the changes in the caracter of the pancreatic juice begin to manifest themselves soon after the change of diet, while, in the other dogs, the changes are slower. In this latter type, an abrupt change from one type of diet to another type of diet often produces serious illness — a curative crisis. If a sudden and radical change from the conventional diet to a new one did not result in some systemic reactions we would feel that the new diet was of the same character as the old one and expect no beneficial results threfrom.

These things are of importance, not alone in showing that the type of juice adapted to the digestion of one type of food is practically valueless in digesting another type of food, but, also, in showing that the longer one type of food is eaten, the more efficient will digestion become. The way to learn to digest a food that is difficult for us to digest, is to continue to eat it. If pepsin or hydrochloric acid is lacking in the diet, not abstinence from, but indulgence in proteins will increase these. There are, of course, limitations. Overstimulation will have the opposite effect.

Many people have difficulty in handling spinach, but just as "practice makes perfect" in other works, so, persistence in eating spinach will build up the power to digest it. This fact has been demonstrated in hundreds of cases. This rule is applicable to all articles of food.

We tend to seek foods easy of digestion. This practice undoubtedly weakens our powers of digestion. A true digestive athleticism would seek to build up the powers of digestion by an intelligent employment of foods requiring more and not less work in digestion. Pampering the digestive system undoubtedly makes a molly-coddle of it. I do not mean to sanction abuse of the digestive system — this is another thing.

Examining the stools to determine how much of a food passes undigested does not determine the digestibility of a food, not at least, until the individual has been fed upon the food under investigation long enough to acquire maximum power to digest it. It is also essential, in determining the digestibility of a food, that it be fed in combinations that do not interfere with enzymic action. Starch that may be freely digested will show up in the stools as undigested starch if eaten with acids or wtih proteins.

The vegetarian soon acquires the power to digest and metabolize his new diet. No doubt, too, this power is hereditary. Reinheimer says "that the inheritance of chemical properties which are of great importance for the production of form actually takes place is now as well known as that of morphological properties." From limited observations I am convinced that a child relishes most and digests best the type of foods upon which the mother fed during pregnancy.

Digestive speed and efficiency vary with individuals and with circumstances. However, in general, foods leave the average stomach about as follows: — fruits, vegetables, bread, eggs, lamb, beef, pork, chicken, nuts, guinea hen. Carbohydrates usually leave the stomach rapidly, proteins remain longer. Foods requiring longer time for gastric digestion are not necessarily harder to digest; it is often merely that the process of digestion is different.

Foods requiring longer time to digest remain in the stomach longest. Beef requires but slightly longer to digest than lamb. Chicken requires longer than pork despite all of the fat of the latter.

Red beets pass through the stomach rapidly. So do asparagus, raw tomatoes, lettuce (unless delayed by the usual dressings), and most vegetables low in protein and starch. Vegetables containing much starch are held up for more thorough digestion. Low protein vegetables leave the stomach with little change. Raw cabbage leaves the stomach more quickly than cooked cabbage, a thing most people know. Baked beans are slow to leave the stomach. Spinach is slow, compared with other vegetables.

Eggs and milk go more slowly than eggs alone. Old eggs require more time in the stomach than fresh, or even cold storage eggs. Boiled eggs remain in the stomach longer than raw ones. Scrambled eggs remain longer still. Raw egg whites leave the stomach rapidly. Egg white does not encourage gastric secretion, unless taken with orange juice, and is poorly digested and badly assimilated.

Raw milk leaves the stomach slowly. Pasteurized milk more slowly and boiled milk still more slowly. Milk rich in fat leaves the stomach more slowly than milk low in fat content. Buttermilk stimulates gastric secretion.

Bacon digests slowly and, perhaps due to its fat, lowers stomach acidity. It is difficult for most people to digest. Fat markedly inhibits gastric secretion and the movements of the stomach and slows down digestion.

Foods are not digested when they have passed out of the stomach. A large part of the work of digestion takes place in the intestine.

We learned in the previous chapter that such things as coffee, tea, bitters, etc., cause an early emptying of the stomach without, in any way, shortening their digestion time. In other words, foods may be sent out of the stomach before gastric digestion is complete.

Mental Influences in Nutrition
CHAPTER XX

In Vol. I it was learned that an emotion is a complex of reflexly aroused nerve-muscle-gland reactions and that the nervous, muscular and glandular reactions in certain emotional states are such as to inhibit or suspend certain functions — digestion and excretion, for example — while other of these reactions favor the performance of these functions.

Bad news cuts off a hearty appetite. Grief may suspend the appetite for days. Ordinary mental processes do not so greatly influence hunger, but fear, joy and other emotions temporarily abolish the sensation. The so-called destructive emotions abolish not only hunger but also the so-called "hunger contractions" of the stomach and the secretion of digestive juices.

The digestive secretions are, to a great extent, influenced by the emotions. While I do not intend to treat of such matters in detail at this place, we need to know that moods and emotions profoundly influence the secretions of all the glands of the body and, therby, extert a tremendous influence upon the whole of the nutritive processes.

Psychic secretion is that part of the digestive juices which flows in response to one's mental states and emotions and sense pleasures. The flow of the salivary and gastric juicse is influenced by so-called psychic factors. The sight, smell or anticipation of a meal will cause these secretions to be poured out. The stomach "waters" as does the mouth. The taste of food, even where the food never reaches the stomach, will cause the gastric juice to be poured out. People in a state of mental exhiliration, who are joyous and happy, or who experience a feeling of well-being, have better digestion than others. The so-called psychic secretion lasts about thirty minutes and constitutes approximately twenty per cent of the total amount of gastric juice.

Strong emotions like rage, fear, jealousy, worry, etc., and all intense mental impulses immediately stop the rhythmic motions of the stomach walls and suspend the secretion of the digestive juices. Fear and rage not only make the mouth dry, they dry the stomach as well. Pain impairs the secretion of the gastric juice, stopping entirely the psychic secretion. Not only do all strong "destructive" emotions inhibit the delicately regulated psychic secretion, but even too great joy will do likewise.

Nervously depressed people have poor psychic secretion and are usually chronic dyspeptics. Observations made on mental patients, particularly those suffering from the so-called *maniac depressant psychoses,* have shown that their psychic secretions are poor or negligible. Even a normal man who was about to take an examination, about which he had doubts about his ability to pass, required to digest and send a meal out of his stomach, two hours longer than under normal circumstances.

Worry, fear, anxiety, apprehension, excitement, hurry, fretfulness, irritableness, temper, despondency, unfriendliness, a critical attitude, heated arguments at meals, etc., prevent the secretion of the digstive juices and other secretions of the body and cripple not only digestion, but the whole process of nutrition.

Mental excitement results in the same weakening reactions upon the body as do intoxicants. It occasions the same degeneracy and loss of vital reserve as do alcoholics. Corrosive worries, burning thrills, the searing fires of uncontrolled emotions, freezing fears and similar mental and emotional states lower vitality, weaken digestive power and leave the food in the digestive tract a prey to microbes.

None of us go through life without repeated shocks, emotional unheavals, worries, periods of anxiety and of irritation. But the average man and woman is usually able to throw these off in a brief period. The fact that one is not able to throw them off quite readily, shows that there is something wrong.

A few years ago I put forth the theory, based on my experience, that worry, fear, shock, etc., seldom or never produce disease in the really healthy, because these are able to throw off such states before serious damage is done. This theory was reproduced in my *Food and Feeding,* in 1926.

In 1928 Dr. P. E. Morhardt, of Paris, reported the results of his long continued studies of nutrition and mental factors. He found that such emotional shocks as the loss of a loved one, loss of fortune, etc., become disease-producing because the body is in a state of "vegetative and nutritional unbalance" at the time. Such shocks are survived by the really healthy with a minimum amount of injury and leave no bad effects. They frequently result in permanent troubles in those whose health, particularly their digestive health, has been neglected.

Diabetes is given as an example of "nutritional unbalance" which leaves the nervous system in no condition to bear up under strain or shock. Other weaknesses resulting from haphazzard eating and neglect of the body produce the same effects upon the brain and nerves, so that the first "emotional upheaval" greatly aggravates the condition and produces more serious troubles. Often the mind itself, already affected by the previous nutritional unbalance and toxemia, becomes deranged.

In dealing with sugar in the urine, in diabetes, Dr. Cabot says: "As soon as marked worry comes to the patient's life, up goes the sugar when it has been scanty or absent before." The noted surgeon, Crile, gives us the dictum: "When stocks go down, diabetes goes up."

Shock, as from a wound or an operation, will cause sugar to appear in the urine. Apprehensiveness and "nervousness," or excitement do likewise. Worry, as from financial loss, is a common cause of functional glycosuria (sugar in the urine). An argument is frequently responsible for an increase in blood-pressure, gastrointestinal (digestive) disorders, gall-bladder troubles (these being outgrowths of the digestive derangements), and acute exacerbations of diabetes.

Every mood or emotion reacts upon every cell and every function in the body. Destructive emotions create discord in the physical functions of the body. "The angry man sends a torrent of rage into his own constructive cell-world," as Dr. Gibson expresses it, and disrupts the orderly working of his cells, and "previous tissue structures, once pillars of vital strength, are reduced to ruin and ashes."

Dr. Geo. A. Molien, of Denver, reports that many surgical operations may be avoided if the mental and nervous factors in the cases are corrected. He cites several cases in which operations had been advised but refused, the patients completely recovering from ailments diagnosed as gastric ulcer, appendicitis, pancreatic and intestinal disturbances and from persistent vomiting, after mental and emotional relief were secured.

Dr. Weger recalls a case cited by Cannon, which came under the care of Dr. Alvarez, of a man who suffered with persistent vomiting, having begun when an income tax collector threatened the man

MENTAL INFLUENCES IN NUTRITION

with punishment if he could not explain a discrepancy in his tax statement. The vomiting ceased as soon as the matter was straightened out, Dr. Alvarez, himself, going to the tax collector, as a therapeutic measure, to iron out the difficulties.

Dr. Weger calls attention to an experience that we have had many times. He says: "In my own institutional practice, it has come to be known among the staff that there are an unusual number of adverse digestive reactions during the twenty-four hours between noon of Sunday and noon of Monday. Patients ordinarily receive more visitors on Sunday afternoon than on any other day. Some relatives or friends bring disconcerting or depressing news. Some visitors have an unhappy effect on the patients, disturbing them by rude approach, incessant talking, a harsh, jarring tone of voice, or by the subject discussed. Unhappy situations are frequently recalled, even though the suggestion be inferential. Then again, there are patients who are worked up several days in advance in anticipation of the visit of a husband, wife, brother or sweetheart. Sunday afternoon passes without the expected visit; the emotions evoked by anticipation, impatience, uncertainty, anxiety and disappointment may for some persons be just as harmful as too much visiting is for others. As evening approaches, digestive discomforts become noticeable. Some patients have a feeling of weight in the stomach; others, gas in the bowels, some become nervous; others have headache; and some persons have a combination of these symptoms." — *Genesis and Control of Disease*.

I have seen similar results from the receipt of a letter bringing unpleasant news, or from the failure to receive an expected letter. A patient of mine, who had two checks returned by her bank, was so upset that not only was her digestion greatly impaired, but all of her symptoms were made much worse. Although the matter of the checks was quickly straightened out, the patient did not get over the effects of the incident for three or four weeks. Another case became worked up almost daily because she was away from her husband. The arrival of her father and her son brought emotional peace for the week they were present and during this time she had no digestive troubles and nervous symptoms. When they left, her emotional upheavals began again and her digestive and nervous troubles were renewed. A third case suffered with fear of hell because a medieval-minded preacher had told her she was doomed to hell, as an adultress, due to the fact that she had married again while her divorced husband was still alive. Such fears troubled her digestion and her sleep.

Dr. Weger says: "In my opinion, at least two-thirds of the patients who complain of gastric and intestinal discomfort in varying degrees of intensity are the victims of emotional unbalance." Omitting cases of cancer, ulcer and actual organic diseases of these structures, and assuming that the patients have been correctly fed, as regards amounts and combinations, I would say that more than two-thirds of such patients are victims of emotional unbalance.

Dr. Weger continues: "Our routine in such cases is to use the stomach tube at once and have the patient miss supper. Almost invariably the debris that is returned by the lavage is undigseted food, sometimes the entire noon meal. A light meal that should have been in the intestines in four or at most five hours, may be found in the stomach eight or ten hours later if the attendants are not appraised of the discomfort and measures of relief instituted earlier. If the patient does not report the discomfort and takes supper, both meals may frequently be washed out of the stomach the following morning. The less soluble foods, those that contain considerable roughage, usually constitute the bulk of that which is returned. The inference is that in these motility may have been more profoundly impaired than the secretion of gastric juice. The question has, however, not been accurately determined. It is quite possible that certain types of patients will have more decided disturbance of motility while others will have impairment of secretions."

These phenomena also occur to a slight degree in those who are fearful and worried about their diet. Those who anticipate trouble from their meal, who eat in fear and trembling and who are anxious about the outcome, will be sure to have trouble for these things inhibit to some degree the normal operation of the nutritive processes.

It is also quite probable that the length of time that elapses after the meal is taken before the bad news, disquieting visitor, etc., arrives, may determine whether chiefly roughage or the whole meal will be found in the stomach. The secretions, once they are poured out upon the food in sufficient quantity, will continue their work despite the effects of the patient's emotions upon gastric motility or upon the secretory glands.

MENTAL INFLUENCES IN NUTRITION

I do not favor the use of the lavage and find that most of these symptoms are nervous and mental rather than the effects of the food laying in the stomach. There is no reason why a little undigested food in the stomach should, of itself, cause distress, for the stomach is designed to receive and hold undigested foods. The discomfort will be relieved by the lavage. It will also be relieved, in most cases, by a hot pack placed over the stomach, with the food left in the stomach. I believe that the lavage secures relief from the discomfort in the same manner that the pack does and not merely because it empties the stomach. Some nervous states (not cases of ulcer) have pain and discomfort in the stomach only when it is empty and not when it is full.

Some of these cases are relieved by a little kindly encouragement or by intelligent sympathy. In other cases the discomfort passes off in a short time without the lavage, pack or suggestive treatment. In others, a little manipulation of the abdomen suffices to give complete relief. I do not favor the manipulation and mention it here only in illustrating my thought.

A lavage is a severe tax upon the patient and its frequent use, and this would be necessary in a certain type of patients, cannot but injure the patient. I have given many lavages in the past, but I employ them no more.

The practice of having the patient miss the meal or several meals if necessary, has my enthusiastic endorsement and has been my practice for years. It is a natural and an instinctive procedure, where instinct is permitted to hold sway.

Many times I have observed angry and frightened animals refrain from eating until, after the passage of considerable time, these emotional states had passed off. I have seen cows frightened and abused by angry milk-men and have seen them cease eating and not again resume eating for an hour or more after the milk-man had departed.

It is true that under the same circumstances many civilized men and women that also refrain from eating, find, indeed, that they lack all desire for food, but it is also too often true that many men and women will eat large meals under these and similar circumstances. Psychic and vital hygiene demand that under conditions of emotional stress eating should be refrained from. Every one of my readers will enjoy better health in the future if they follow the example of the young grief-stricken lady who, thinking that she had been deserted by her lover, did not eat for three days, saying, when the lover returned, that she could not eat, and refrain from all food until emotional calm is restored.

Noise while eating disturbs digestion. Noise, and "jazz" both reduce salivary and gastric secretion nearly one-half. Noisy crowds, excitement and the emotional stress these occasion inhibit and derange digestion. Quiet, cheerful surroundings, with congenial companions enhance digestion.

Enjoying Our Food
CHAPTER XXI

The man who "lives to eat" has been roundly condemned so much and so often that he needs no added censure from my pen. I believe that we should enjoy our food. Indeed, I believe that he who derives the greatest possible pleasure and enjoyment from his food, will have better health than the man who does not enjoy his meals. I have no patience with the doctrine of anti-naturalism that prevailed during the Middle Ages, and remnants of which still prevail — that all pleasures are evil. I do not regard a state of chronic misery as man's natural state nor loud groans as evidence of piety.

Buckle's *History* tells us of the reign of mediæval anti-Natural madness: "A Christian must beware of enjoying his dinner, for none but the ungodly relish their food." It is not difficult to understand why such a religion had to be propagated by the sword and men and women could be held to the straight and narrow path only by the persuasive power of the thumb-screw, rack and the iron virgin. The Greeks and Romans had no difficulty in propagating their joyous Nature-worship.

I believe in Epicurianism in its true meaning, in its higher sense. With Mr. Macfadden I say that "there is no natural pleasure, or natural appetite, or natural desire that was not created for a particular health-giving purpose, the following of which will add strength to the body; and the sin, the evil, lies not in commission but in omission. Cultivate Nature, natural appetites, natural desires; develop the delicacy of intuition which will enable you to interpret and follow their dictates as nearly as it lies in your power, and you will be a stronger and nobler specimen of manhood because of this."

I believe in sensualism in its true sense and not in the degraded sense with which theologians have invested the term. I believe in enjoying the pleasures of the sense of taste and I am convinced that the sense of taste is one of the most important of all man's faculties.

The gourmand who stuffs himself on three meals a day and who cultivates perversions of the sense of taste, by his use of condiments, to "stimulate" his jaded appetite, does not enjoy his food. He does not know the pleasures of taste. The "dulled, intermittent sensations" he secures from over-stimulated nerves, do not compare with the intensity of pleasure derived from natural foods, by one whose nerves are keenly alive with power and are able to sense the fine delicate flavors of foods, as only those can who have keen appetites.

Of course, it is not the merely incidental pleasures of eating that makes for health and happiness, but the ability of the food eaten to properly meet the demands of the body for nourishment. But the role of pleasure in eating must not be underestimated.

Tasting and enjoying your food actually forces you to linger longer over each mouthful and holds you back from "hurrying through the meal by the gorging process," as Horace Fletcher so ably showed.

The fact that a coated tongue prevents the normal appreciation of the flavors of food, prevents the establishment of gustatory reflexes and through these prevents the secretion of appetite juice, should show the great importance of enjoying our food.

Much pleasure may be derived from eating, but man, in his much vaunted civilization, when he comes to eat, is prone to shovel his food in with one hand while figuring up his accounts or reading the newspaper with the other. The result is that, while he derives no happiness from these other things, he derives much misery from his wrong eating.

The highest enjoyment from eating must await upon hunger. A keen hunger and the ability to heartily enjoy the food eaten is a sure indication that there will be produced a full supply of the requisite digestive juices. The more one enjoys his food and the more completely he extracts the taste of every mouthful before swallowing it, the more freely does the gastric juice flow and, consequently the more prompt and efficient will be gastric digestion.

The pleasures of development come not from the dissipation and over-indulgence of desire, but in cultivating self-control and in using one's powers in the most perfect harmony with the interests of his body and mind.

There is a limit to the powers of the digestive glands. They cannot secrete sufficient juices and enzymes to perfectly digest three "square meals" a day. Neither can one who consumes such meals always be sufficiently hungry at meal time to thoroughly enjoy his meal. He not only eats beyond his digestive capacity but he does not have the flow of "psychic secretion" that comes from an eager desire for and a keen relish of food. The gastric and other juices cannot be supplied in sufficient quantity and of requisite strength when over eating is habitually practiced.

It is part of the function of the mouth to regulate the functions of the other organs of digestion. To secure this regulation it is essential that the food be thoroughly chewed and its taste fully developed. The most delicious flavors of foods are developed by long chewing, which permits sufficient time for the saliva to act upon the foods.

The recognition of the gustatory properties of food by the nerves of taste, through reflex centers in the brain, prepares the stomach, liver, pancreas and other digestive organs for their work. The longer food is retained in the mouth and the more thoroughly it is chewed, the larger the amount of gastric juice will be present in the stomach to digest it, and the better adapted to the digestive requirements of the food will be the juice.

Tasting food, in some way not yet fully understood, regulates the process of nutrition by cutting off the appetite for one food principle after another as the body has received a sufficiency of each particular item. The sense of taste is an instinctive regulator of nutrition and, when normal or unperverted, is a dependable guide in determining the quality and quantity of food needed — provided one eats natural foods and does not disguise these with dressings and condiments.

That there exists differences in the powers of taste of different individuals is common knowledge. It was recently announced from the laboratories of the Carnegie Institution, that a certain chemical is tasteless to some people and has the bitter taste of quinine to others. Such defects in the sense of taste are analogous to color blindness and tone deafness.

The prevailing theory of taste is that there is a very limited number of tastes — sweet, acid (sour), salt, bitter and perhaps two or three others — and that other flavors are combinations of taste and smell. If this is true, how important, in view of our knowledge of the relation of the taste of food to good digestion, becomes the odor of our food and the practice of enjoying its varied aromas.

The absence of ability to perceive a particular taste may be due to paralysis, or failure of development of certain nerve fibers, or of the taste buds. There is another and more commonly observed defect of the sense of taste, to which I have given the name *Gustatory Infantilism*.

By gustatory infantilism I mean the persistence, in the adult, of childish taste characteristics. The taste-range of the child is very limited. After he has attained a certain age it is very difficult to induce him to taste a new or unaccustomed food. He makes up his mind, in advance of trying it, that he does not like it and if we succeed in inducing him to try the food, he usually decides, after sampling it, that it is not good.

With the coming of puberty the taste-range begins to widen and continues to widen throughout adolescence. Milk, if it has not already been rejected, is likely to become distasteful and many articles of food which were not relished before are eagerly sought after. A new and broader nutritional equilibrium is established with a greater food-variety as its basis.

There are people in whom these pubertal and adolescent changes do not progress to any great degree. Their sense of taste does not broaden. They carry their childish dislikes with them into adult life. As in the case of the child, it is difficult to induce these unfortunate people to try new and unaccustomed foods and, like the child, they decide before tasting the food that they do not like it after they have eaten it.

I do not know all the factors to which this defective taste development may be ascribed, but I believe that in certain people, at least, it is due to a lack of a wide variety of foods during the period when their sense of taste should normally have expanded. I have observed the frequent occurrence of this condition in people from the more northerly regions, where the available variety of foods is very limited.

I am convinced from experience with such cases, that the condition may be largely if not wholly overcome, in the majority of cases, if the sufferer will attune his or her mind to the reform effort and make an honest attempt to cultivate and educate the sense of taste. Often such persons will not do this. There are a half dozen articles of food they relish and they refuse to try to cultivate a taste for more. Perhaps in such cases there is more than the usual degree of intellectual infantilism.

Absorption of Food
CHAPTER XXII

Before food can be of any value to the body it must be carried to the cells. In order to do this, it is necessary that it be removed from the intestinal canal and be taken up by the blood and lymph. The process by which this is accomplished is termed absorption.

Some absorption takes place in the stomach and a small amount, chiefly of water, takes place in the colon, in the cecum, to be exact. The small intestine, due to its peculiar structure is specialized for the work of absorption. The greater part of the food is absorbed from this.

Some part of the process of absorption may be explained by the laws of diffusion and osmosis, but only a small part of it may be so explained. We are forced to make due allowance for the fact that the cells lining the small intestine are living. The walls of the intestine do not behave like a dead membrane. Every epitheliel cell lining the digestive tract is in itself a complete organism, a living being, with the most complete function. These exercise a selective capacity by which, in a normal condition, they permit the absorption of good food and prevent the absorption of a whole series of poisons which are readily soluble in the digestive juices. Absorption is a physiological, not a physical process; one of active selection and absorption and not mere osmosis.

This is well illustrated by the following well known facts. Certain substances which are rated by ordinary standards as highly diffusible are not permitted to pass through the intestinal lining. Magnesium sulphate (epsom salts) and grape sugar will serve as an excellent example of this. When a test is made with parchment or any ordinary membrane the sugar is found to be less diffusible than salt. In the intestine this is reversed. The sugar is readily absorbed while the salt is excluded almost entirely.

This selection of the good and useful and rejection of the injurious and useless is done by the cells lining the walls of the intestine as these take up the food from the intestine and secrete it into the blood stream.

Some of the salts seem to be absorbed from the stomach. However, most of these together with the monosaccharides, aminoacids, fatty acids and glycerol are absorbed from the small intestine. By this is meant that these compounds disappear from the intestine. It by no means follows that they enter the blood as such. It seems probable that they undergo some changes during their passage through the cells. This is known to be true of the fatty acids and soap for these are changed in their passage through the cells and enter the blood as neutral fat.

Proteins belonging to one class of animals will not nourish another class of animals if injected directly into the circulation without undergoing digestive changes. The protein (albumen) of an egg, if injected directly into the blood, acts as a poison and is immediately expelled. The proteins of nuts, wheat, cheese or milk, mutton, beef, eggs, chicken, etc., are all different and distinct but each and all of these may be used to nourish the human body. Before they can be used, however, they must first be converted into a particular class of proteins. If they are not so converted they not only do not nourish the body, but if they are forced into the blood stream they act as real poisons.

In spite of the many changes the proteins of the various foods undergo in the stomach and intestine they still remain the protein peculiar to those foods — eggs, beef, mutton, beans, etc. During their passage through the intestinal walls these proteins undergo some change (of a nature wholly unknown) which fits them for entrance into the body. For no sooner than these have passed through the intestinal wall into the circulation, than their nature is changed. They are now "human proteins."

This is of sufficient importance to justify a little further explanation. The protein molecule in the chyle, as it exists in the lumen of the intestinal canal, is known as peptone. It is a highly toxic substance in this form, yet it is the only form in which protein can be absorbed by the intestinal mucous membrane and passed on to the blood. As it passes through the cells of the intestinal wall the peptone undergoes further changes. It loses its toxicity and appears in the blood in one or another of at least three forms: namely, serum albumen, serum globulin and fibrinogen.

These proteins undergo further transformation in being built into cell substance. No one knows how many forms of protein can be produced by these transformations, nor can they always be fully

ABSORPTION OF FOOD

identified with chemical accuracy for they often exist in very minute quantities.

Once the food is in the blood stream it is carried to all parts of the body to nourish the cells and to be used for the various purposes which food serves. Food material may be conveyed directly to the liver, or it may be carried through the lymphatic system. It appears, as a general rule, that proteins and fats are conveyed directly to the liver, while the carbohydrates are sent by the other route. When the food reaches the cell it is subjected to still further changes which are apparently due to enzymic action, before it is finally incorporated by the cell.

Uses of Food
CHAPTER XXIII

If the processes of digestion seem complex and but little understood the processes of nutrition are much more so. While nutrition is claimed to be purely chemical, it is acknowledged, by even the most materialistic, to be different in many ways from the other chemical processes known to us. This is particularly true of the final stages of the process by which the pabulum is transformed into living tissue. By this final act dead matter is raised to the plane of living matter.

Even Prof. Chittenden was forced to acknowledge that this "involves a chemical alteration or change akin to that of bringing the dead to life"; while Dr. Charlton Bastian, F.R.S., London, argued that these facts of nutrition, particularly those of the plant, in which inorganic matter is converted into the organic substances of the plant, prove to us the possibility of the creation of life from non-living. All of which shows, that ,while the digestion of food materials and their conversion into living tissues is considered to be purely chemical, these are far different from any chemical actions and reactions known to the laboratory, even though the chemist may be able to discover no difference. It cannot be disputed that if the substances are the same and the processes and changes are identical the products would be, to say the least, very similar. But no chemist can even imitate the work done by plant and animal nutrition. The great mystery of nutrition is still unexplained. We can no more explain today how food material is changed into living human flesh and blood than could the lowest savage of a thousand years ago.

It is certain, however that many of the changes the food undergoes after being absorbed are due to the action of enzymes. For example there is autolytic arids, found in the tissues generally, which split the amino-acids, into simpler compounds. Then there are guanase found in the thymus, adrenals and pancreas, which changes guanin to zanthin; adenase found in the pancreas, liver, lungs, muscles, etc., which causes oxidation, as of hypozanthin to xanthin, and of xanthin to uric acid. No effort will be made at this place to take these matters up in detail. The reader who may be interested in pursuing these still further is referred to any of the standard works on nutrition. We must devote our attention to the use of foods.

Let us begin with the proteins, since these have been the subject of more discussion than any other part of our food, and are considered, by "orthodox" scientists, to be the most important of all elements of our food. All this came about as a result of the mistakes of the early physiological chemists, particularly Liebig and Vogt of Germany. These found that muscle is almost pure protein and water and Liebig thought we should eat muscle to make muscle. Of course, the cow eats grass not muscle, out of which she makes the muscle Liebig would have us eat, but this simple fact was overlooked.

Voight followed Liebig with a series of experiments on dogs. This was about 1860. With these he thought he had succeeded in proving the great physiological importance of protein. It was assumed that muscular activity is due to the oxidation of the cells themselves. It was a case of mistaking the "machine" for the "fuel;" yet, on the basis of this assumption Voight, with the aid of his dogs, estimated that the average man requires about 118 grams of protein daily. He seems later to have reduced this standard by nearly one half, but no one took the reduction seriously.

The Voight standard is now known to be much too high. Protein leaves the body through the kidneys in the form of urea. In fact, the composition of the urine depends more upon the protein (nitrogen) intake than upon anything else. By measuring the excretions and comparing these with the food consumed, it is possible to tell whether less protein or more protein is being lost than is being consumed. Examinations of the urine under almost all conceivable conditions of life and activity, have shown that in the healthy adult the nitrogen intake and output is balanced, providing, of course, the intake is not less than the actual needs of the body.

No matter how much nitrogen one consumes above the body's requirements, the organism always responds in the same way. That is, it sets aside for excretion, all surplus nitrogen. So unless the nitrogen intake is less than the body's requirements, the balance is usually struck between income and outgo. Exceptions to this are during growth, following a protracted fast, convalescence after wasting illness, and pregnancy and lactation, during which periods the body excretes less nitrogen than is consumed; and during some diseases in which there is a rapid breaking down of tissue and consequently more nitrogen is excreted than is consumed.

The body does possess the ability to store protein although compared with its ability to store carbohydrates and fats, this ability is very limited. Surplus nitrogen is carried in the blood at all times.

For growth and reproduction, larger quantities of protein are, of course, requisite, and it is even more desirable in that case that the proteins should be of high biological value. In growing children and youths the protein requirements exceed that of the adult by 50% to 100%. Pregnant and nursing women require considerably more protein than adult males or adult non-pregnant and non-lactating women.

Repeated examinations of the urine have disclosed the fact that the proportions and quantities of the urinary constituents are modified by exercise or physical labor very little. This means that protein decomposition is not materially increased by physical effort and leads to the conclusion that the protein requirements of the average healthy man or woman are no greater, while engaged in manual labor, than while engaged in mental effort.

For years the "orthodox" scientific world held tenaciously to the high protein standard set by Voight. Although Hershfeld had, in 1887, by a series of tests, placed the protein standard at 47 grams, the orthodox chemists never accepted his standard and the low protein diet did not attract much attention until Horace Fletcher startled the scientists out of their lethargy some years ago. Since then, much evidence has been accumulated by the progressive members of the scientific world, showing that protein is not so valuable as formerly supposed. In fact, the evidence is strongly in favor of the statement that protein — and certainly excessive protein — is a physiological burden and destroys health.

The experiments of Hirshfeld have already been referred to. He was a young man of 24 years and performed heavy labor, weight lifting, mountain climbing, etc., on a diet containing less than half the protein that was thought to be necessary. He lost neither weight nor strength, while the "nitrogen balance" showed that he did not lose body protein. Dr. Hindhede says of his work: "It is strange, indeed, that Hirshfeld's investigations have been allowed by science to drift almost into oblivion. He was a young man

USES OF FOOD

(twenty-four) who could make little impression against the weight of Voight's authority."

In 1913 Berg pointed out that when the conditions are in other respects optimal, the amount of protein requisite to maintain body-weight is far smaller than hitherto has been supposed. Boyd, in America, using meats as the source of protein, estimated the minimal daily amount of protein requisite to maintain body weight as 30 grammes. Berg under more accurately adjusted conditions estimated the requirements to be 26 grammes of meat protein. Rose, providing a better supply of alkalies, found the meat protein minimum to be 24 grammes. Sherman places the requirements at 30 to 50 grammes.

Hindhede raised four athletic and wide-awake children on a diet so low in protein that it has been said, "it would frighten a cooking school teacher into blind staggers." He has proved that a high protein diet is not required by growing children.

But this was not the end. Hindhede found that the excess proteins, after entering the blood, underwent decomposition and recomposition giving as a result nitric acid, phosphoric acid and sulphuric acid. There was also an excess of uric acid and ammonia compounds. He contended that in order to neutralize the acids formed by the decomposition of excess protein, the body was forced to give up its mineral salts. Thus the teeth, bones, cartilages, nails, hair, etc., were leeched of these elements.

These powerful acids destroy the liver and kidneys to such an extent that one may safely say, no man ever died of uremia whose kidneys had not been, for years, gradually destroyed by the powerful acids resulting from excessive protein intake.

It was long thought that muscular tissues are oxidized or decomposed in the development of muscular power and that they are rebuilt from food, particularly protein. This, if true, would have given rise to even larger protein requirements than the standards called for. Anyway, during these years we have been feeding upon beef steaks, eggs and other high protein foods, all the while claiming that we did not want to suffer from malnutrition and become lean, pale, individuals like the vegetarians, nor did we want to rear dwarfed offspring like the rice-eating Japs and Chinese.

The life insurance companies have discovered that the lean folks (the skinny) live about twenty years longer than they should. Every schoolboy knows that the Japanese Jenrikska men pull beef-fed Englishmen through the hills and mountains of Japan at the rate of about forty miles a day. Several years ago a seventy-mile walking race was staged in Germany. There were eight vegetarians and fifteen meat eaters. The first six men in were vegetarians. Most of the meat eaters never finished the race. Dr. Hindhede says: "A diet low in albumen increases endurance. I have never heard of a great meat eater winning a long distance race."

That the protein requirements of growing animals is not high is shown by the fact that milk, the natural food of young animals, is very low in protein, when compared to meat or eggs. Cow's milk, for example, is about three and one-half per cent protein. The calf is a very active and rapidly growing animal, in fact, of more rapid growth than the human infant. As the calf grows older, it adds grasses to its diet and these are much lower in protein content. The cow will, from grasses alone, secure all the proteins required for her and her calf, both during pregnancy and during the period of lactation.

Milo Hastings says in *Physical Culture* for March, 1916: "The human youngster grows so slowly, after the first year or two, that the amount of protein needed for growth is so small in proportion to the other elements of the diet needed for heat and energy that the active child eating a diet of cereals, fruits and vegetables in sufficient quantities to keep up childish activity, must of necessity consume more protein than is needed or can be utilized in growth.

"A young pig may gain a pound a day, but a young human rarely gains an ounce a day. In fact it takes him fifteen years to gain a hundred pounds. Eggs are about the same composition as the human body, and if for fifteen years a child ate no protein but that contained in one egg a day he would have eaten six times the protein equivalent of his own body. One sixth of an egg a day supplies the growth protein for the human youngster. On the plan of rearing young America on two pounds of meat, milk, eggs, legumes and cheese and bread a day, which plan our orthodox food chemistry prescribes, the growing child must pass through his liver and kidneys and utterly waste enough protein to build about five thousand pounds of human flesh.

"This thing figured out becomes a farce. The stuffing process of raising children is better suited to make pigs that would gain three hundred pounds of flesh in a year. Nature needs eighteen years of experience to bring a human brain to maturity, and so she provided a trap door through which to dump out the pig diet and keep us human still. How much physiological harm the dumping process works upon the child's organism we do not yet know — probably much less than most of you, after reading these lines, will imagine. The adaptability of our physiological machine is a never ceasing source of wonder."

It is evident that there is no danger of anyone ever consuming too little protein. In fact, this is just what Hindhede found in his studies of the dietetic habits of nations. He found that in the degree to which a nation lived on a low protein diet, in that degree did they suffer less from disease. During World War I, his opportunity came to demonstrate on a large scale, the truth of his findings. He was made food administrator over Denmark. His experiment involved a whole nation of millions of people and covered a period of three years. No other investigator had ever had such an opportunity. He reduced the death rate in Denmark forty per cent in one year's time by diet alone. He employed a low protein diet. He concludes that the average adult human body may require twenty grams of protein daily, but that the requirement may be even less than this. His assistant, Dr. Madsen, used an experimental diet containing but twenty-one grams of protein, with only favorable results.

Both Berg and Abderhalden have shown that the assertion that meat protein is the most valuable of all forms of protein cannot be accepted as a positive fact as regards the protein of individual muscles, but only as regards the aggregate proteins of the animal body used as food. Berg showed that the aggregate protein of eggs, cow's milk and to some extent that also of potatoes, are more efficiently utilized than meat protein. It is only fair to add that in Berg's experiments the meat was given with an excess of acids, whereas, Rose found that when an excess of alkalies is supplied the proteins of meat are approximately as valuable as those of milk.

Turning now to carbohydrates, let us state in a general way their uses in the body. They are used chiefly in the production of heat and energy. At least this is the orthodox theory. Instead of, as formerly held, the muscle cells being consumed in muscular activity, it is now asserted that sugar (glycogen or muscle sugar) is oxidized in the cells giving rise to enrgy. Fat is an available second choice. The monosaccharides are converted into glycogen in the liver.

The body stores up carbohydrates and does not eliminate all of the excess supply, as is the case with proteins. Some of these are stored in the liver as glycogen, some in the muscles as muscle sugar, while some is converted into fat and stored as such. It is only after this is done that any excess is eliminated.

We hear much of starch poisoning these days. Hindhede found that starch poisoning was seldom, if ever, met with among those people whose diet is predominantly carbohydrate, if they lived on natural instead of denatured starches and sugars. Starch poisoning, by denatured carbohydrates is due to the fact that these have been robbed of their minerals and vitamins and this causes them to leech the tissues of their salts. It also leads to carbohydrate fermentation.

To illustrate what we mean by denatured carbohydrates leeching the tissues of their mineral constituents, let us look for a minute at the process of sugar manufacture. Nature has placed in the natural sweets enough of the organic mineral elements, and water and oxygen, to satisfy their "desire" for these elements. In the process of manufacture of commercial sugar, these other elements are extracted, giving "free" and "unsatisfied" sugar. So great is the affinity of sugar for iron that it must be made in copper kettles, as it abstracts the iron from kettles and literally "eats" holes in them. In the body the denatured starches and sugars do likewise. They leech the tissues of their mineral salts. "Free" sugar also has an almost insatiable "desire" for oxygen and calcium.

Carbohydrate fermentation gives rise to carbon dioxide, alcohol, acetic acid and water and results in chronic auto-intoxication, which resembles, in every way, the symptoms of chronic alcoholism. The alcohol produces chronic irritation in the system and results in the formation of scar tissue. Previous to the formation of the scar tissue there are the usual disturbances caused by irritation. It also causes capillary congestion which result, in turn, in atrophy of brain and muscles. The irritation of the mucous surfaces results in the overproduction of mucous giving rise to catarrh.

Fats follow about the same course in metabolism as carbohydrates. These are oxidized to supply heat and energy.

The body is said to have no method of storing mineral salts as in the case of carbohydrates. Yet a fixed amount is kept suspended in the blood. After a fresh meal, there may be an excess in the blood, but this excess is promptly eliminated. The body can and does conserve and save its minerals when there is a scarcity of these. For example, the iron in the seven million cells that perish every second, from wear, is recovered, stored in the liver and spleen, and used in rebuilding the blood.

Vitamins are not employed as foods, but as aids in assimilating foods. A reserve of these is stored in the liver and other glands, fat, etc.

After foods have been metabolized they are excreted from the body through the lungs, liver, kidneys and the walls of the colon. Each organ of elimination has its own peculiar work to perform although reciprocity is not lacking. Acids are eliminated chiefly by the kidneys and lungs, carbonic acid gas being the principle excretion of the lungs. Alkalies are eliminated through the kidneys and walls of the intestinal canal. Calcium, magnesium and an increased acid-intake results in increased acid-elimination by the kidneys; whereas an increased alkali-intake results in an increased alkali-elimination by the colon. Insignificant quantities of salts and urea are eliminated through the skin.

How Much Shall We Eat?
CHAPTER XXIV

The question of how much to eat has engaged the attention of many able men and women, but the question has not been answered. The so-called scientists have figured out our requirements in calories. This I have already shown to be a fallacy. Most people advocate eating all the appetite calls for. But appetite is a creature of habit and can be trained to be satisfied with little food or to demand enormous quantities. The business of creating gluttonous appetites begins in infancy when infants are stuffed day and night. Dr. Page proved that an infant may be taught to guzzle day and night, or to content itself with two to four meals a day.

Dr. Clendening tells about how the scientists discovered how much food one requires. He then says that the discovery of these things did not alter the amount of food a given individual of given age, dimensions, and activity eats, and then he adds: "That amount is regulated very delicately by the individual's appetite and some curious, inner instinctive mechanism about which we understand very little."

If he understood very much about it he would know that the whole statement is false. Appetite is largely a creature of habit and the eating habits of individuals vary much more than do the shapes of their noses. There are many more peoples who over-eat than Dr. Clendening's statement would indicate. On the other hand the doctor himself remarks that "few diatribes on overeating point out the harmful consequences of under-eating. Yet these are quite real." It would really seem that perhaps appetite and the "curious, inner instinctive mechanism" fail to work at times.

TWO MEALS A DAY

Major Austin says: "Truly, popular tastes and prejudices are rooted more in social habits than in basic physiological demands." It should be known that the three-meals-a-day custom is really a modern one, and is not universally practiced even today. So far as history records none of the nations of antiquity practiced it. At the period of their greatest power, the Greeks and Romans ate only one meal a day. Dr. Oswald says: "For more than a thousand years the one-meal system was the rule in two countries that could raise armies of men every one of whom would have made his fortune as a modern athlete — men who marched for days under a load of iron (besides clothes and provisions) that would stagger a modern porter." He also says, "The Romans of the Republican age broke their fast with a biscuit and a fig or two, and took their principle meal in the cool of the evening." Among the many things that have been offered as an explanation for their physical, mental and moral decline has been their sensuous indulgence in food which came with power and riches. Whatever other factors may have contributed to bring about their decline (and certain it is there were many factors) there can be no doubt that their excessive indulgence in the pleasures of the palate contributed its fair share.

Herodotus records that the invading hosts (over five millions) of the Persian general Xerxes, had to be fed by the conquered cities along their lines of march. He states as a fortunate circumstance the fact that the Persians, including even the Monarch and his courtiers, ate one meal a day.

The Jews from Moses until Jesus ate but one meal a day. They sometimes added a lunch of fruit. We recall reading once in the Hebrew scriptures these words (quoting from memory): "Woe unto the nation whose princes eat in the morning." If this has any reference to dietetic proctices it would indicate that the Jews were not addicted to what Dr. Dewey called the "vulgar habit" of eating breakfast. In the oriental world today extreme moderation, as compared to the American standard, is practiced.

Dr. Felix Oswald says that "during the zenith period of Grecian and Roman civilization monogamy was not as firmly established as the rule that a health-loving man should content himself with one meal a day, and never eat till he had leasure to digest, i.e., not till the day's work was wholly done. For more than a thousand years the one meal plan was the established rule among the civilized nations inhabiting the coast-lands of the Mediterranean. The evening repast — call it supper or dinner — was a kind of domestic festival, the reward of the day's toil, an enjoyment which rich and poor refrained from marring by premature gratifications of their appetites."

A sixteenth century proverb says, "To rise at six, dine at ten, sup at six and go to bed at ten, makes a man live ten times ten."

Katherine Anthony informs us that the average English family adopted the habit of eating three meals a day during the reign of Queen Elizabeth. Andrew Borde, a physician who lived during the reign of Henry VIII, wrote that: "Two meals a day is sufficient for a rest man; and a laborer may eat three times a day; and he that doth eate ofter lyveth a Beestly lyfe." Salzman's *English Life in the Middle Ages*, tells us that: "Breakfast as a regular meal is little heard of, though probably most men started the day with a draught of ale and some bread."

"Barely two centuries ago," says Major Austin, "the first meal of the day in England was taken about noon. Breakfast was an unrecognized meal and it originated in the practice of ladies taking an early dish of chocolate before rising. The ancient Greeks — the finest of people, physically and mentally, that ever lived — ate but two meals a day. The same was true of the ancient Hebrews and it is the custom of some of the best fighting races in India today."

The Countess of Landsfeld, writing in 1858, describes the eating habits of the English upper class of that time in these words: "After this meal comes the long fast from nine in the morning till five or six in the afternoon, when dinner is served." This would indicate that the two-meals-a-day plan had survived in England up to that time.

The adoption of three meals a day, in England, came along with the increasing prosperity of that country. Indeed it may be stated, as a general rule, that the quantity of food eaten in any country in all ages, has depended more upon their economic envornment than upon their nutritional needs. Wealth and plenty have brought increased food consumption. In Ancient Rome these factors resulted in the eating of many meals a day, the eater taking an emetic immediately after finishing his gustatory enjoyment and then repairing to the vomitorium, after which he had another meal.

Plutarch must have had such practice in mind when he wrote: "Medicinal vomits and purges, which are the bitter reliefs of gluttony are not to be attempted without great necessity. The manner of many is to fill themselves because they are empty, and again, because they are full, to empty themselves contrary to nature, being no less tormented with being full than being empty; or rather they are troubled at their fullness, as being a hindrance of their appetite and are always emptying themselves, that they may make room for new enjoyment."

A former patient of mine, who spent two years among a tribe of Indians in South America, informed me that these people ate their first meal of the day, after the hunters returned from the hunt. They would leave for the hunt about nine o'clock in the morning and return when they had secured enough game for the tribe. If the hunt failed, as it sometimes did, they had no meal in the morning. Dr. Oswald quotes a Rev. Moffat as saying that the Gonaque Hottentots are nowadays incommoded by a five day's fast, and get along on an average of four meals a week.

Major Austin says: "Experience has shown that in the past, two meals a day met the demands of appetite in *all* fully grown individuals — men and women, including expectant mothers."

THE DAY'S HEAVY MEAL

I do not agree with those who insist that the morning meal should be the chief meal of the day. If digestion is to proceed normally almost the entire attention of the system must be given to the work. Blood is rushed to the digestive organs in large quantities. There is a dilatation of the blood vessels in the organs to accomodate the extra supply of blood. There must be a consequent constriction of the blood vessels in other parts of the body in order to force the blood into the digestive organs and to compensate for their own loss of blood.

But if the brain and muscles are to work they, too, require an increased blood supply. In order to supply them there is a dilatation of the blood vessels in the brain or muscles and a contraction of the blood vessels in the viscera. Every part of the body cannot be supplied with extra blood at the same time. If one part gets an extra supply some other part must get less.

The same is true of the nervous energies. Organs that are working must be supplied with nerve force. If one is engaged in mental or physical effort his nervous energies are diverted from the digestive organs and digestion suffers.

The animal in a natural state lays down and takes a rest, perhaps some sleep, after eating a meal. Some years ago an experiment was made by feeding a dog his usual meal of meat and then taking him for a fox hunt for a few hours. The dog was then killed and the stomach opened. The meat was found to be in the same condition as when eaten. Another dog fed at the same time and left at home to rest had completely digested his meal.

The dog in the chase was using all his blood and nervous energies in running. Digestion simply had to wait. In spite of the fact that this principle is well known, there are still many, who pose as diet experts, who advise that the heartiest meal of the day be taken in the morning. The reasons given are (1) The body after a night of sleep is better able to digest the meal than in the evening after the day's work is done, and, (2) The food eaten at this time will supply energy for the day's work.

It is true that we have more energy after the night's rest than after the day's work. It is not true, however, that the digestive organs have rested during the night. It is also true that real hunger is not produced by a night of restful repose and to eat a heavy meal in the absence of hunger would be contrary to the first law of trophology. All of this aside, the digestion of a meal eaten in the morning would have to wait upon the other work. We can force our mind and muscles to act and thereby withdraw the blood from the stomach but the stomach cannot force these other organs to cease their activities and permit the blood and nerve force to be sent to it.

If food supplies energy, it can do so only after it is digested and absorbed. Under normal conditions the digestion of a meal in both the stomach and intestine requires from ten to sixteen hours. If one is working, either mentally or physically much longer time is required. Food taken in the morning could not, therefore, supply any energy for the day's work. On the contrary if the food is to be digested, that part of the energy required to do the work of digesting it is taken from the day's work. Anyone who will test this out may soon satisfy himself of the correctness of this principle. Let him give up the morning meal for a few weeks and note the results.

The morning meal is best omitted altogether. At most it should consist of an orange or unsweetened grape fruit. The noon meal should be very light. The evening meal should be the heaviest meal and should be taken only after one has rested a little from his day's toil.

During sleep the blood is withdrawn from the brain and muscles. So, also, nerve force is withdrawn from the muscles. The viscera receive the blood and much of the nerve force. Digestion may proceed without hindrance. If one is sleeping there are no fears, worries, anxieties, etc., to interfere with the work of digestion.

Of course, if one has had a full meal for breakfast and a full meal for noon he has already had too much food and will be very uncomfortable if another full meal is taken in the evening. Three dinners in one day are two too many. But this is the popular practice, especially among the laboring classes. As a result, they become old and stiff and worn out early in life.

HURRIED EATING

If one goes into a restaurant in the early morning in any one of the larger cities and observes the clerical and professional world breakfasting he at once discovers one of the reasons why there is so much inefficiency, weakness and disease among this class. They may be seen in large numbers eating a breakfast of eggs and toast or rolls, with coffee. No time is taken to properly masticate the food. It is washed down with coffee, while the "eater" nervously fingers the pages of the morning paper.

Atfer a breakfast of this kind they rush off to their work and get through the morning some way. It is from this class that we get most of our patients.

Eating should be done when there is leisure to digest. Any other plan is unnatural and contrary to all the laws of physiology.

GLUTTONY

"No man ever ate too little," declared Dr. Oliver Wendell Holmes Surfeiting has destroyed more lives than starving. For everyone who suffers from underfeeding there are ninety and nine who suffer from gluttony. The markets of the world are glutted with foods of all kinds, as they never were before in the world's history. Their abundance, tempting variety and comparative cheapness, coupled with the many means employed to whip up an overstimulated and sated appetite to "fresh indulgence in the tempting, but life-withering concoctions of extravagant cooking, with its embalmed preserves, alcoholized liquids, crystalized fruits, frozen creams, aniline dyed dainties, and the constantly increasing nondescript menaces known as pies, puddings and French pastries — there is certainly a tremendous need for instructing the people in what not to eat."

Many people are like clams — mostly liver and stomach; or, perhaps I should say they are like worms — all gut. Dr. E. E. Keeler says in *Here's How Health Happens*: "The stomach according to the clam and some other people, is a bag of an indefinite expansive capacity useful to hold any old thing that the palate may enjoy and as much of the commodity as may be obtained." We are lured to our doom by our appetites; yet, surely we cannot take every appetite and any and every association for normal. "Accustom your appetite to obey reason with willingness," advised Plutarch.

The philosophers of antiquity prided themselves on their frugal habits, which ranked, next to godliness in their estimation. Lycurgus, the Spartan, was more fearful of excess in the quantity rather than excess in the quality of the food of his countrymen.

Here in this country intemperate eating is one of our universal faults. Almost all of us are guilty of it, not merely occasionally, but habitually and almost uniformly, from the cradle to the grave. Even the sick are urged to eat, in many instances to gorge themselves, in spite of the loudest warnings and strongest protests of nature.

Habits of eating are usually acquired in infancy and are cultivated, nourished and developed throughout childhood and youth. They do not tend to correct themselves spontaneously. They continue with us as imperious masters, calling as loudly as ever for gratification. A dyspeptic, eating three to six meals a day, is always craving food; though overeating he is literally starving to death. It would be an astounding revelation to many doctors and dyspeptics to watch a fast in such cases and see how quickly the abnormal appetite rights itself and how rapidly the nutritive processes improve.

We teach, hire, bribe, coax, tempt and coerce our children into overeating from the very day of their birth. Helpless infants are stuffed until nature is compelled to get rid of the excess by drooling, vomiting, diarrhea, excessive urination and, finally by febrile and eruptive processes. We coax them to eat more and more and deliberately cultivate gluttony in them. At school they are fed milk and candy between meals. The result is that we are among the greatest eaters in the world. Wm. J. Bryan is our national idol.

Gluttonous indulgence in reckless food-mixtures has produced more disease and suffering than strong drink. The immediate effects of gluttony may be masked by a good digestion, but ultimately it is fatal to strength and manhood and results in premature death. Many are lured to their doom by their appetites.

Gluttony, especially the common overindulgence in incongruous food mixtures, leads to gastro-intestinal fermentation and putrefaction, with the resulting poisoning from this source. This leads to the destruction of the body's reserves which are designed for the preservation of health and strength until a ripe old age is attained.

Temperate eaters have good digestion and are never aware that they have stomachs, while heavy eaters are always faint, thirsty, bloated, troubled with acidity, eruptions, diarrhea, constipation or some other disorder of the digestive system. Hoggishness causes all kinds of disorders that we attempt to remedy by various kinds of magic, but continue to practice the hoggish eating.

I strongly suspect John F. Flood, Secretary of the Pittsburgh Health Club, of being the author of the statement that "A man makes a perambulating sewer of himself and regularly carries about with him a mass of putrefying flesh and fermenting starches, etc., and then when he gets the jim-jams, we talk about mental attitude. Gosh! It's thrilling to hear them spout! °°° Unfortunately, they will do anything but give up their physical bad habits, especially those of atrocious eating. °°° Now let us go into the silence, place our hands on our knees, be still and believe ourselves well. That vicious mixture of meat, potatoes, bread, butter, coffee, pie, candy will then sweetly digest. Keep a sweet disposition, Pollyanna yourself and everything will come out all right in the best of all worlds. °°°

"Someone whispers: 'Oh, I don't care, the going into the silence and accompanying bunk, pardon me, the accompanying soothing syrups, help me.'"

I am convinced that the habit of eating denatured foods is a chief cause of over eating. These foods do not completely nourish the body and, therefore, do not satisfy the demands of hunger, unless consumed in large quantities. Great variety at a meal also overstimulates the sense of taste and leads to over eating. Spices and condiments have the same effect. It is really difficult to overeat when one is eating unseasoned foods.

"Sunk into the degenerating grip of gluttony, their mental attitudes become transposed into its corresponding physical attitude — that of the groveling swine. Every individual who is a slave under his appetite, — be he vegetarian, fruitarian or carnivorian — who eats for the mere sake of appetite and sensuous indulgence, is a glutton in his nature, an egotist in his motive and a swine in his attitude.

"While gluttony may give rise to an appearance of health and strength in the rounded out tissues, it will never produce the firm, strong, wiry, enduring energies of the individual who submits his system to the strengthening and beautifying discipline of self-control and refined dietetic reserve."

It is time for us to learn that we are not "in tune with the Infinite" so long as we are regularly transgressing any of the laws of life. Nature does not sanction any form of intemperance. A league of temperate eaters would certainly find a large field for reform.

Health and serviceability demand that an organism shall possess all that is necessary but no more. Redundancy beyond a reasonable reserve for emergency, is unwholesome and becomes an impediment to physiological efficiency. Moderation is a symbiotic virtue. Ruskin stressed his contention that the increase of both honor and beauty is habitually on the side of restraint. This goes for restraint in eating too.

Exhuberance of nutriment, as of many other good things, is more often a curse than a blessing. Overfeeding on "rich" foods wears out the vital powers through over-stimulation, overworking the digestive organs, the heart, the endocrine system, and the emunctories, by the strain placed on them and gives rise to intoxication through the poisons which these foods generate.

Much poisoning in infusorians has been found to be due to intensive nourishment. It needs only a short fast to restore the animals to youth. In higher animals, also, "brief hunger has a beneficial effect." Bees easily become debauched by a surfeit of food and render themselves liable to "disease." A reduction of surfeit is essential to the most vigorous manifestations of vitality.

The fact that the organism is unable to exist without the vital purifier, the cortex of the suparenal glands, should convince us of the harmfulness of overeating with its resulting intoxication. Excess is fatal to healthy action.

Over-feeding of invalids in an effort to give them health and strength is still a popular procedure. How often do we see this fail. How frequently, indeed, do we see increases of strength and gains in weight follow upon a reduction of surfeit. Many invalids will be killed outright by over-feeding who would recover if fed barely enough food to sustain the most essential vital activities while resting. I have watched more than one invalid, whose life was despaired of, gradually grow stronger and finally recover, while being fed a *starvation diet.* Overfeeding of such patients accounts for many needless deaths each year.

NOTED GLUTTONS

Noted gluttons are many; only a few of them can be noticed her. Samuel Pepys lists as his typical dinner: "a dish of marrow bone, a leg of mutton, a loin of veal, three pullets, two dozen larks, a great tart, a neat's tongue, anchovies, prawns and some cheese."

Charles V was a glutton of no small capacity. An historian of the time tells us that he would breakfast at 5 A.M. on an entire fowl stewed in milk. He had dinner at noon with at least twenty dishes. Two suppers were eaten — one at 5 P.M., the other at midnight. Although he suffered persistently with gout and indigestion he insisted on a feast for and with all the visiting nobles.

Samuel Johnson, literary man and dictionary maker, who lived in the eighteenth century, was a notorious glutton and food drunkard. Queen Elizabeth is said to have begun her day with enormous helpings of mutton stew, beef, veal, and chicken.

The French kings and nobility were as gluttonous as the English. They were wedded to the ancient philosophy of Epicurus: "eat, drink and be merry, for tomorrow we die." Even after the kings had passed, we find Napoleon possessed of an appetite that knew little bounds. Though, as one authority puts it, "he frequently stupefied himself with food," there were times when he was abstemious.

In Colonial America the upper classes — the landed gentry and the aristocracy — regarded "good feeding" as an evidence of physical prowess. A Frenchman who visited a Virginia home describes a "simple" luncheon of "corned beef, stewed goose and leg mutton; with vegetables of every kind — all washed down with generous libations of hard cider."

"He aged," writes Frank Parker Stockbridge, of Bryan, in *Current History,* for Sept. 1925, "but he retained *** his gargantuan appetite until the last. A teetotalar by conviction, he was the most intemperate of feeders. To see Bryan devour a large platter of sour kraut and frankfurters, served originally for four men, and call for another helping, as I saw him do one hot day in St. Louis, was a liberal education in gastronomics."

Bryan was a food inebriate. He had been food poisoned for many years. His advocacy of temperance did not extend to food and eating. Sloane Gordon, a newspaper correspondent, who accompanied Mr. Bryan on all his great campaign tours and on many other lesser excursions, says of him: "It is probable that few more intemperate men ever lived. Not in drinking but in eating." Writing in the *Chicago Herald and Examiner*. After Mr. Bryan's death, Mr. Gordon describes a "breakfast — a breakfast mind you — " as follows:

"Cantaloupe was first served. Bryan ate a whole one — an immense yellow-meated melon. It was in the Fall season — early Fall — and quail were on the bill of fare. Bryan ate two. Virginia ham and eggs followed. Bryan ate almost ravenously of this delicious ham in large portions and consumed not less than six eggs, *** when batter cakes were served, *** the commoner disposed of a plateful, swimming in butter and then accepted a second helping and got away with that.

"Numerous cups of coffee, potatoes and side dishes of various kinds accompanied the cantaloupe and the ham and eggs and the rest of it. ***"

Tom L. Johnson, the celebrated single-taxer, himself a hearty eater, once remarked, "I guess I'm a glutton, but if I am one, William J. Bryan is two of them."

There has been much wasted speculation about what killed Bryan. The true cause of his death is so patent that everyone, who is not wilfully blind, may see it. Bryan dug his grave with his teeth. He shoveled in enormous quantities of food in the most reckless combinations. He may never have taken a drink of alcohol in his life, but he manufactured it in great quantities.

Bryan had diabetes. Professor Scopes tells us that at a banquet, attended by both the prosecution and the defense of the great Tennessee side-show, Bryan refused all sweet foods, all foods containing sugar, because of his diabetes, but ate more potatoes than an Irish paddy. He ate a very hearty meal an hour or so before his death.

He had hardening of the arteries. I do not know whether he died of "heart failure" or of "appoplexy"; but I do know that, whichever of those was given as the cause of death, he was killed by gluttony. He worked his body to death with intemperate eating. He poisoned himself with alcohol and other toxins generated in his stomach and intestine. He ate enormous quantities of denatured, acid-forming foods in combinations that made digestion impossible. His reserves were consumed, his tissues weakened and his organs imparied.

Graham began his carrer as a temperance lecturer in Pennsylvania, in 1830. He soon discovered that temperance should not be limited to drink. For, even the most thirsty could not live by drink alone. He saw that intemperance in food was as potent to make men gross and diseased as drink. Indeed, it was his thought that if drunkeness had slain its thousands, gluttony had certainly slain as many more.

It would be difficult to estimate the extent to which the people of Graham's day over ate, but gormandizing was certainly one of the favorite indoor sports. Were Graham living now he would probably think that most of our people are temperate eaters by comparison. Over-indulgence in meats and starches was very common then, even as it is now. The "old timers" had a capacity for roasts and barbecues. An old cook book warned husbands that should they bring home some of their gentlemen friends for dinner, unannounced, not more than two or three kinds of meat could be expected. It is not certain how many meats were served if the company was properly announced, but the menus of ceremonial banquets shows that it was not unusual to serve as many as thirty or more kinds of meat, including fish, at one occasion.

Leisurely pre-civil war gentlemen sometimes sat at the table for as much as seven hours at a stretch imbibing meats and wines, to be followed by gout and other of the ills that were considered as the marks of "good living." In contrast to this, ancient philosophers prided themselves on their frugal habits, which ranked next to godliness in their esteem.

Physical workers think they must eat an abundance of food, especially of the kinds that are said to "stick to the ribs," in order to produce and maintain the strength and endurance required in their work. Most athletes hold to the same view.

That all of these ideas are false has been demonstrated over and over again. Overeating by athletes and physical workers is one of the chief causes of premature ageing in these classes. Perhaps the most signal demonstration in modern times of the ability of the body to build and maintain Herculean strength and great endurance on little food, was given by Prof. Gilman Low when he established the phenomenal record of lifting one million-six-thousand (1,006,000) pounds in thirty five minutes and four seconds, after a period of training on one meal a day and less. This lift was accomplished by lifting 1000 pounds 1,006 times in the time specified. This feat was accomplished after two months of training on a diet on which the average stenographer would "starve to death." For the first five weeks he ate one meal a day, almost wholly of uncooked foods, having meat only twice during this period. His diet consisted of eggs, wholewheat bread, cereals, fruits, nuts, milk and distilled water. During the last three weeks of his training period he ate only four meals a week; the last meal was consumed eleven hours before the lift. In fifty-six days of training for this lifting Low ate forty-seven meals.

Mr. Low lost five and three-quarter pounds during the thirty-five minutes. Fifteen minutes later, he lifted one ton forty-four times in four minutes. It is particularly instructive that Mr. Low had previously attempted the big feat after training on two meals daily and had been compelled to quit, after reaching a little more than the half-million mark, due to sore distress and dizziness. See, also, Vol. III.

Fasting men, when active, lose an average of about one pound a day. As these fasters are consuming all (or more) water than the body demands, the loss must be regarded as true body loss. This would indicate that sixteen ounces of actual nutritive matter (food exclusive of bulk or waste) represent about the actual daily needs of the body. This does not mean sixteen ounces of dehydrated nutritive substance.

The amount of nitrogen or protein in the pound of daily loss is very small and should further confirm what has been said about our need for only a small quantity of protein. Due to mineral conservation by the fasting body, the daily mineral losses during the fast probably do not represent the actual daily need for these. Activities are rarely as great during the fast as when eating and the daily carbohydrate requiremnt is slightly greater than the fasting losses indicate. Nutritive redundancy, more especially a redundancy of protein, tends to overflow into reproductive channels and manifest itself either in wasteful sexual activities or in redundant and inferior multiplication.

WORKING-CLASS IDEALS

Through the ages the working classes, which have always constituted the greatest portion of any population (at least, this has been so until today, when the working class has been transformed into the shirking class), the slaves, endentured workers, serfs, and free workers have been forced to live more or less abstemious lives. Only the wealthy and the nobles were able to overindulge in food and other substances to any great extent, except, perhaps, on special occasions, when the slaves and workers were indulged. This has not been due to any essential difference between the noble hogs and the working hogs. Whatever virtue of temperance the working class has possessed has grown out of necessity, or, what is perhaps more accurate, out of the economics of scarcity that existed.

Always desirous of aping their "betters" in all things, the workers have always been discontented because they were unable to indulge in all the vices of the "upper class." When white bread was so high in price that only the well-to-do could afford it, they bemoaned their lot because they had to eat black bread. The poor fools have always wanted to emulate the famous gluttons of history.

When we read that a Roman feast would last for days, the guests reclining at a table, and thrusting a finger or feather down their throat to induce emptying of the stomach, when surfeited, so that they might begin eating all over again, we are not to understand that the Roman working class and Roman slaves ever had either the food or the leisure time to indulge in such destructive practices. Only the parasitic class could do so. It is unfortunate that the ideals and practices of the parasite tend to become the ideals and practices of the workers, so that, even, those who think they want to revolutionize the world do not want a revolution — they want only to alter conditions so that all can "enjoy" the indulgencies of the parasites.

It would be a serious mistake to conclude from the examples of Charles V, Pepys, Johnson, Elizabeth and others that the British working class had an abundance of food or that they had midnight meals, or to conclude from the eating habits of the French kings and Napoleon that the French working class ate large quantities of food. Had they been able to eat in this way, the French revolution would never have occurred. Let us not think that the slaves, either white or black, and "poor white trash" of Colonial America ate luncheons such as the one described by the French visitor.

THE SCIENCE AND FINE ART OF FOOD AND NUTRITION

The records of the old gluttons make frequent references to huge portions of ginger, red pepper, nutmeg, cloves and other condiments, which were consumed before and during each repast. These irirtants were formerly so high in price that the working class could not afford such luxuries. Today they are so abundant and so cheap that almost everybody employs them. There is little danger of a revolution so long as the *working class* can have these luxuries, plus beer and white bread. The Russians had only black bread before the 1918 revolution — they are now demanding and getting white bread. Russian life is "improving"! The old records also make frequent references to gastritis, peptic ulcers, gout and even gastric cancer. Napoleon died of cancer of the stomach. These are luxuries, too, that the working class has always aspired to "enjoy." Neither the workers nor their leaders know anything about what living should be. Their cry of "abundance for all" is really a demand for surfeit.

The repeal of the prohibition law in this country was not accomplished so much by the millions spent by the brewers and distillers, nor so much by any public or official opposition to gangsterism, which was falsely blamed on prohibition, nor, even, so much by the fact that women voted for repeal, as it was by the demand of the workers that they be permitted to drink if the men of wealth were to be permitted to do so. It was a rank injustice to permit the predatory groups to drink and withhold the poisonous concoctions from the workers. John L. Lewis wanted his miners to have beer. He can control them better that way. To avoid a revolution give the workers beer and circuses.

A man's value lies not so much in what he possesses in health, strength and life, as in the use he makes of these things. He may recklessly and wantonly squander his physiological reserves until like the spendthrift who soon becomes financially bankrupt, he reaches middle age in a condition of vital bankruptcy.

How to Eat
CHAPTER XXV

One should always seek to eat at such times and under such conditions that will insure the best results in digestion. Some things enhance digestion while others impede it. The first rule in any truly natural system of feeding should be:

I. EAT ONLY WHEN HUNGRY

If we do this we eat only to supply the demands of the body. We cannot repeat too often the admonition, do not eat if not hungry.

If this plan were followed the present three meals-a-day plan would end. Also the practice of many of eating between meals and in the evening before retiring would cease. For most people real hunger would call for about one meal a day, with occasionally some small amounts of fruit during the day.

Hunger is the "voice of nature" saying to us that food is required. There is no other true guide as to when to eat. The time of day, the habitual meal time, etc., are not true guides.

Although genuine hunger is a mouth and throat sensation and depends upon an actual physiological need for food, muscular contractions of the stomach accompany hunger and are thought by physiologists, to give rise to the hunger sensation.

Carlson, of the Chicago University, found that in a man who had been fasting two weeks, these gastric "hunger" contractions had not decreased, although there was no desire for food. The same has been observed in animals. Indeed these contractions are seen to increase and yet they do not produce the sensation of hunger. I do not consider these so-called "hunger-contractions" as the cause of hunger. Real hunger is a mouth and throat sensation.

But there is a difference between hunger and what is called appetite. Appetite is a counterfeit hunger, a creature of habit and cultivation, and may be due to any one of a number of things; such as the arrival of the habitual meal time, the sight, taste, or smell of food, condiments and seasonings, or even the thought of food. In some diseased states there is an almost constant and insatiable appetite. None of these things can arouse true hunger; for, this comes only when there is an actual need for food.

One may have an appetite for tobacco, coffee, tea, opium, alcohol, etc., but he can never be hungry for these, since they serve no real physiological need.

Appetite is often accompanied by a gnawing or "all gone" sensation in the stomach, or a general sense of weakness; there may even be mental depression. Such symptoms usually belong to the diseased stomach of a glutton and will pass away if their owner will refrain from eating for a few days. They are temporarily relieved by eating and this leads to the idea that it was food that was needed. But such sensations and feelings do not accompany true hunger. In true hunger one is not aware that he has a stomach for this, like thirst, is a mouth and throat sensation. Real hunger arises spontaneously, that is without the agency of some external factor, and is accompanied by a "watering of the mouth" and usually by a conscious desire for some particular food.

Dr. Gibson says that, "The condition known as appetite, *** with its source and center in nervous desire, and its motive in self-indulgence, is a mere parasite on life, feeding on its host — the man himself — whose misdirected imagination invites it into his own vital household; while hunger, on the other hand, is the original, constitutional prompter for the cell-world calling for means to supply the true need and necessities of man's physical nature. *** Appetite does not express our needs, but our wants; not what we really need, but what we think we need. It is imagination running riot, fashioning out of our gluttonous greed an insatiable vampire which grows with our wants, and increases its power until finally it kills us unless we determine to kill it. *** As long as our attention is absorbed in the pleasures of the table, in the gratification of eating for its own sake, and in the introduction of new combinations to bring about stimulating effects, we are increasing the power of our appetite at the expense of our hunger."

The hungry person is able to eat and relish a crust of dry bread; he who has only an appetite must have his food seasoned and spiced before he can enjoy it. Even a gourmand is able to enjoy a hearty meal if there is sufficient seasoning to whip up his jaded appetite and arouse his palsied taste. He would be far better off if he would await the arrival of hunger before eating.

There is no doubt of the truth of Dr. Geo. S. Weger's thought that *appetite contractions* in the stomach are often excited by psychic states, as influenced by the senses." Appetite contractions thus aroused, are of distinct advantage in digesting a meal if they are super-added to pre-existing hunger contractions. We know that these psychic states increase the flow of the digestive juices — make the stomach "water" as well as the mouth — and enhance digestion.

Dr. Claunch says, "the difference between true hunger and false craving may be determined as follows: when hungry and comfortable it is true hunger. When hungry and uncomfortable it is false craving. When a sick person misses a customary meal, he gets weak before he gets hungry. When a healthy person misses a customary meal, he gets hungry before he gets weak."

If we follow the rule to eat only when truly hungry, those people who are "hungry" but weak and uncomfortable would fast until comfort and strength returned. Fasting would become one of the most common practices in our lives, at least, until we learn to live and eat to keep well and thus eliminate the need for fasting.

There are individuals who are always eating and always "hungry." They mistake a morbid irritation of the stomach for hunger. These people have not learned to distinguish between a normal demand for food and a symptom of disease. They mistake the evidences of chronic gastritis or of gastric neurosis for hunger.

Hunger, as previously pointed out, is the insistent demand for food that arises out of physiological need for nourishment. Appetite, on the other hand, is a craving for food which may be the result of several different outside factors operating through the mind and senses. Anything that will arouse an appetite will encourage one to eat, whether or not there exists an actual need for food.

Hunger may be satisfied and appetite still persist, a not unusual thing. Our many course dinners, with everything especially prepared to appeal to the taste and smell, are well designed to keep alive appetite, long after hunger has been appeased. No man is ever hungry when he reaches the dessert, so commonly served after a many course dinner. Few, though filled to repletion and perhaps uncomfortable in the abdomen, ever refuse to eat the dessert. It is especially prepared to appeal to appetite. This style of eating necessarily and inevitably leads to overeating and disease. Too many articles of food at a meal overstimulate and induce overeating.

Hunger and the sense of taste are the only guides as to the quantity and character of food required. If we eat when we are not hungry, and if the delicate sensibilities of taste have been dulled and deadened by gluttonous indulgence and by condiments, spices, alcohol, etc., it ceases to be a reliable guide.

The unperverted instinct of hunger craves most keenly the food that is most needed by the body and the unperverted taste derives the most pleasure and satisfaction out of the food or foods demanded, and will be satisfied when we have consumed sufficient of such food or foods to supply the body's needs. But, if we have been in the habit of crowding the stomach when there is no demand for food, just because it is meal time, or because the doctor ordered it, and we know no other indication that enough food has been consumed, than that the stomach can hold no more, we are headed for disaster. The existence of a natural demand for food indicates that food is required by the body and that the organs of the body are ready to receive and digest it. Eating when there is no time, or as a social duty, or because one has been able to stimulate an appetite, is a wrong to the body. Both the quality and quantity, and the frequency of meals should be regulated by the rules of hygiene rather than by those of etiquette and convenience.

ANOREXIA

Anorexia is a loss of appetite. There are many conditions in which a temporary loss of desire for food is quite normal. Such, for example, as after great fatigue, from strong emotions, as grief, anger, etc., in acute and, usually, chronic disease, and after eating. Hysteria and certain mental states often give rise to a loss of appetite. No food should be taken so long as there is no desire for food.

Rule 2. *Never eat when in pain, mental and physical discomfort, or when feverish.*

If eating is followed by bodily discomfort or by gastric and intestinal distress, do not eat until comfort has returned. This rule is universally followed on the plane of instinct.

Pain, fever and inflammation each and all hinder the secretion of the digestive juices, stop the "hunger contractions," destroy the relish for food, divert, the nervous energies away from the digestive organs and impair digestion. If pain is severe or fever is high all desire for food is lacking. If these are not so marked a slight desire may be present, especially in those whose instincts are perverted. Animals in pain instinctively avoid food.

As physical distress acts in the same manner as the psychic states, in inhibiting the flow of digestive juices and in preventing the hunger contractions, we have in this the physiological basis for our rule not to eat when in pain and physical discomfort.

The absence of hunger in fever has been shown to be associated with the absence of hunger contractions. This should indicate the need for fasting. Any food eaten while there is fever will only add to the fever. The fact that a coated tongue, which prevents the normal appreciation of the flavors of food, prevents the establishment of gustatory reflexes and, through these, the secretion of appetite juice, should show the great importance of enjoying our food. The feverish person needs a fast, not a feast.

The less vitality one has, the less variety and the less quantity of food the body can take care of. The practice of stuffing the weak and the sick, to "build them up," is ruinous.

"Psychic secretions" are absent or nearly so in states of mental depression. This, then, is the physiological basis for our rule not to eat when in mental distress.

In the chapter on digestion it was learned that certain mental states enhance digestion while others retard and impair the process. The illustration is an old one, of the person, who sits down to enjoy a hearty meal, after a hard day's work. He is ravenous and enjoys his food. Just as he is about to begin eating some one brings him news of the loss of a loved one through death, or of the loss of a fortune. Instantly all desire for food is gone.

The body needs all its energies to meet this new circumstance, and it requires much energy to digest food. Food eaten under such conditions is not digested. It will ferment and poison the body.

A very interesting experiment once performed upon a cat will be of aid to us here in making this rule clear. The cat was fed a bismuth meal after which his stomach was viewed by means of the X-ray. The stomach was observed to be working nicely. At this point a dog was brought into the room. Instantly, fear "seized hold" of the cat. His muscles became tense and motionless, his hair "stood on end." The stomach was viewed a second time and seen to be as tense and motionless as the voluntary muscles. Digestion was at a standstill. The dog was taken from the room whereupon the cat became calm and settled, with the result that the stomach resumed its work.

"Anger, hatred, envy, grief, fear, doubt, anxiety," says Mrs. Viola Mizzell Kimmell, in her *Right Eating a Science and a Fine Art,* "are all deadly foes to the digestion of the most hygienic meal ever eaten. Even an ecstacy of delight or love drives hunger away and robs the digestive organs of the blood and energy needed for their work. Leisure, peace, quiet, are the ideal attributes of one during the entire process of digestion, if one eats in order to live a comfortable, efficient, clean life."

Scolding, nagging and quarreling at meals is ruinous to health. In many homes all of the petty disputes and differences of the day are pent up and reserved to be released in a torrent of irritability and nagging at the evening meals.

Every care and mental disturbance should be removed. Worries, fears, envies, jealousies, domestic misunderstandings, with their injured feelings and emotional strains, should be excluded from the dining room.

No unkind word should ever be uttered at the dining table. A harsh look that brings fear or anxiety is out of place at meal time. The gastric secretions are at the mercy of the emotions. "Joy exhilirates digestion; gloom depresses or vitiates it," says Dr. Gibson. Mince pie with cheer will be better digested than an apple with pessimism. A fault-finding, envious, jealous atmosphere at the table has a more ruinous effect upon digestion than most drugs. It is the height of folly to feed mentally distressed or emotionally taxed patients.

Also, don't worry about your food. Don't become a "diet bug." Eat and forget. *Keep your mind out of your stomach.* It is the most indigestible thing of which I know. If you have eaten something you should not, or if the combination was wrong, it will not help but will make matters worse to worry about it.

Rule 3. *Never eat during or immediately before or after work or heavy mental and physical effort.*

The ancient Roman proverb, "a full stomach does not like to think," may be expanded by adding, "nor to plough." Leisure time for digestion is important. Dr. Oswald well says: "Every hour you steal from digestion is reclaimed by indigestion."

As a mere matter of habit, the mind will stray to the dining room when the wonted meal-time comes around even if genuine hunger does not return with that hour, but if the hour is permitted to slip by without eating the matter is soon forgotten and the supposed desire for food ceases.

The choice of fixed hours for eating is of much less importance than to *never eat till you have leisure to digest*. We cannot digest and assimilate our food while the functional energies of our system are engaged in other duties. After a hearty meal animals retire to a quiet hiding place and the "after-dinner laziness," which follows a heavy meal is simply nature's admonition to us to follow their example and rest also. The idea that after-dinner exercise or after-dinner speeches promote digestion is a pernicious fallacy.

Normal digestion requires that almost the entire attention of the system be given to the work. Blood is rushed to the digestive organs in large quantities. There is a dilatation of the blood vessels in these organs to accomodate the extra supply of blood. There must be a coetaneous constriction of the blood vessels in other parts of the body in order to force the blood into the digestive organs and to compensate for their own loss of blood.

The functions of digestion cannot be performed without a large supply of blood and nervous energy. The period of comparative lassitude, which follows a hearty meal, is proof that this supply of blood and energy is at the expense of the rest of the organism.

Man is so constituted that he can do well, only one thing at a time. A hearty meal makes him stupid because all of his available energy is employed in the effort to digest such a load. Eating is a business in itself. It should be divorced from all other mental and physical activity. No meal should ever be eaten until after the body has had sufficient mental and physical rest to gain "physiologic poise" and readiness for digestion.

Dr. Cannon tells us that in extreme fatigue, the rhythmic contractions of the stomach fail to occur either in animals or in man. Being "too tired to eat" is a commonly observed fact and the laboratory has shown that this absence of the sensation of hunger, with, usually, a distaste for food, is co-existent with an absence of the hunger contractions of the stomach. This is the physiological basis for our rule to rest before eating.

In an article on "Gastric Juice and Prevention of Enteric Fever and Cholera," published in the *Journal of the Royal Army Medical Corps*, Feb. 1916, Major Reginald F. Austin presented evidence to show that both officers and enlisted men rendered themselves liable to develop dysentery, cholera and enteric fever by eating when they were fatigued and had no appetite. Hearty eating when one is very tired from either mental or physical work is likely to be followed by indigestion, malaise and incapacity for work, due to a deficiency of active gastric juice under these conditions. Rest and especially sleep, is more important, under such circumstances, than food. After relaxation and rest have been had one may eat.

No food should ever be eaten immediately before or after bathing. No food should be eaten until one is fully rested from fatigue or exercise whether mental or physical. No food should be taken during or immediately preceding work, vigorous exercise or study.

Rule 4. *Do not drink with Meals.*

This is a very important rule and should be adhered to strictly. It has reference to the use of water, tea, coffee, cocoa or other watered drinks while eating. Milk is a food, not a drink.

Animals and so-called primitive peoples do not drink with their meals and there is every reason to consider this instinctive practice to be best.

Laboratory tests have determined that water leaves the stomach in about ten minutes after its ingestion. It carries the diluted, and consequently weakened, digestive juices along with it, thereby interfering seriously with digestion. It is often argued that water drinking at meals stimulates the flow of gastric juice and thereby enhances digestion. The answer to this is (1) It is not the natural way to stimulate the secretion of digestive juices and results sooner or later in an impairment of the secretory power of the glands; and (2) It is of no value to digestion to increase the secretion of digestive fluids, only to have them carried out of the stomach, into the intestine, before they have had time to act upon the food.

Water taken two hours after a meal enters the stomach at a time when the gastric juice is there in abundance and the reactions are proceeding nicely. The water sweeps these on into the intestine and retards digestion. Take your water ten to fifteen minutes before a meal, thirty minutes after fruit meals, two hours after starch meals, and at least four hours after protein meals.

Drinking at meals also leads to the bolting habit. Instead of thoroughly masticating and insalivating his food the one who drinks with his meals soon learns to wash it down half chewed. This practice should be avoided at all costs. Milk is a food and should be slowly sipped and held in the mouth until thoroughly insalivated before swallowing. No other food should be taken in the mouth with the milk. Thoroughly chew, insalivate and taste all food before swallowing. Food that is treated in this way can be swallowed without the aid of a liquid.

Cold drinks, water, lemonade, punch, iced tea, etc., that are often consumed with meals, impair and retard digestion. Cold stops the action of the enzymes which must wait until the temperature of the stomach has been raised to normal before they can resume their action. When the cold drink is first introduced into the stomach this is shocked and chilled. After it is sent out of the stomach and the reaction sets in, there is a feverish state resulting in great thirst. Ice cream acts in these same ways. Eating ice cream is like putting an ice pack to the stomach.

Hot drinks weaken and enervate the stomach. These destroy the tone of the tissues of the stomach and weaken its power to act mechanically upon the food. The weakening of its tissues in this way often helps in producing prolapsus of the stomach.

Extremes of heat and cold interfere with the secretion of the digestive juices. The functional powers of the secretory glands are at their highest when working in a temperature conforming to that of the normal body temperature, or at least, when the temperature does not exceed 100 degrees.

Water in coffee, tea, cocoa, lemonade, etc., is water still. These drinks also stimulate the appetite and lead to overeating. Aside from this, the first three named each contain powerful poisons that act as excitants. Their habitual use impairs digestion, wrecks the nervous system and injures the kidneys. The coffee and tea user, as a rule, perspires excessively in summer.

A splendid rule for drinking is to *drink all the water desired ten to fifteen minutes before meals, thirty minutes after fruit meals, two hours after starch meals and four hours after protein meals.*

Rule 5. *Thoroughly masticate and insalivate all food.*

Food that has been completely broken up by chewing, is readily accessible to the digestive juices but foods that are swallowed in chunks require much longer time for digestion. Much energy may be saved in the digestive process if we but take a little time and chew the food. Besides this, swallowing food without chewing it leads to overeating, hurried eating and all the train of digestive evils that arise from these.

Starches and sugars that are washed down with water or coffee, will be certain to ferment and give rise to acids which will make life miserable for the one who is foolish enough to eat in this manner. When starches and sugars are bolted, fermentation follows, even though there is no fault with the combination. This occurs because the food is not insalivated and there is no provision in the stomach for the digestion of these foods. Proteins do not require as much chewing as starches.

QUANTITY AND BULK

I believe that Nature "intended" man to eat well when he does eat. I do not believe in the "little-food-at-a-meal" practice, or the "little-and-often" practice. Digestion is not wholly a chemical process. It is partly mechanical. The normal healthy stomach is a muscular bag possessed of considerable contractile and expansile power. The experiments of Cannon and others showed that the stomach cannot properly grasp the food, turn it about and mix it with the digestive juices and, then, pass the mass on into the small intestine unless there is a certain minimum of food in it. A certain amount of bulk, not merely in the food itself, but also in the residue remaining after digestion, is essential, not merely to good stomach digestion, but to good intestinal digestion as well.

Concentrated nourishment – foods that leave little residue –, eating "little and often," broths, liquid diets, etc., are not ideal diets and dietary practices. They may be used temporarily in a few diseased states, but even here they are, for the most part, seldom best.

Correct Food Combining
CHAPTER XXVI

Physicians prescribe, cooks prepare and people eat all manner of combinations of food, without the slightest regard for the physiological limitations of man's digestive system. It is the general view, lay and professional, that the human stomach should be able to digest about any number and variety of food substances that may be put into it at one time.

Digestion is governed by physiological chemistry but the so-called food scientist continues to disregard this fact. He writes out his menus without the slightest thought of the decomposition that his jumbled mixtures are certain to cause in the digestive tracts of his patients. He never thinks of the fact that he is actually poisoning those who pay him for advice and instruction.

Certain physiological limitations of the digestive glands and of the digestive enzymes and juices should be considered in planning a meal for either the well or the sick. With a knowledge of these limitations at hand, we are in a position to plan a dietary which will adjust itself to the physiological limitations of the digestive glands and their secretions.

Not what we eat but what we digest and assimilate adds to our health, strength and usefulness. An unhampered or unimpeded digestion may be guaranteed only to the extent to which we guard our stomachs against food combinations and mental and physical conditions which disturb and impair digestion. A stomach that is reeking with decomposition will not supply to the body the "calories" and "vitamins" originally contained in the food eaten.

The specific action of the digestive enzymes, the careful timing of their secretion and the adaptation of the strength and character of the digestive secretions to the character of the food upon which they are to act was seen in our study of the processes of digestion. The more these facts are studied, the more it appears to be utterly impossible to digest the conglomeration that makes up the usual meal of the average man or woman.

In this chapter it is intended to shed more light upon the principle that the digestion of different foods requires special adaptations in the digestive juices. This is true in man, in animals, in plants. Suppose we begin with the carnivorous plants.

Carnivorous plants are of three general types—namely, (1) plants with an adhesive apparatus with which to catch their prey, such as Drosophyllum Lusitanicum, (2) plants which show movements in the capture of their prey, as Pinguiculavulgaris (Butterwort) and Drosera Rotundifolia (Sun-dew), and (3) plants with traps for the capture of insects, as Nepenthatceoe (Pithcer Plants), Cephalotus Follicularis, Lathroea Squamaria (Toothwort), Dionacea Muscipula (Venus' Fly-trap), Utricularice Neglecta (Bladderwort), etc.

The leaves of the first class, of which Drosphyllum, which grows in Portugal and Morocco, is representative, are covered with a viscid and very acid substance, secreted by the glands in the leaves and flower stalks. The drops of secretion are readily removed from the leaves but are replaced with great rapidity, the glands being able to secrete large quantities of acid juice.

An insect alighting on the leaf becomes clogged by the viscid secretion adhering to its legs and wings. Crawling on, as it is unable to fly, it is soon bathed in the acid fluid, and sinks down dead. It is not uncommon to see a plant covered with the refuse of dead insects, which have been exhausted of their nutriment, while, at the same time, there are numerous recently alighted insects struggling to get away.

Experimenting with these plants, Darwin found that their secretion is absorbed in about an hour and a half if a proteid is placed upon them; no absorption can be detected when small bits of glass or charcoal are used in the same way. Unlike many of the carnivorous plants, Drosophyllum does not secrete very much more fluid after stimulation by albuminous substances, but the fluid becomes more acid and contains more ferment.

Butterwort, in addition to secreting a viscid fluid, with which to catch its prey, also curves up its leaves on the prey in digesting it. Soon after an insect is captured, the glands in contact with it (none of the glands except those in actual contact with the insect secret the digestive fluid), pour out a large quantity of fluid, which is more viscous and strongly acid in reaction, the previous secretion having been neutral. Although fragments of grass, placed on a leaf of this plant, occasion a slight degree of incurvation, which begins as soon as does incurvation following the capture of an insect, it does not last long and is not accompanied by any secretion. The secretion of the glands of this plant is neutral in the fasting state, but shortly after stimulation with a nitrogenous substance becomes acid and contains an enzyme with an action similar to that of pepsin.

A close parallelism exists between the digestive power of Drosera and that of the mammalian stomach, both of which are able to digest vegetable as well as animal proteins. The secretions of Drosera digest those same substances — albumen, milk proteids, fibrin, etc.,— that are digested by hydrochloric acid and fail to digest those substances — cellulose, epithelial cells, mucin, starch, oils, etc., that gastric juice fails on. The digestive process is stopped in both by the addition of an alkali — such as soda — and recommences on the further addition of acid. In both, the enzyme requires the presence of an acid to activate it.

Darwin's experiments with these plants showed that while digestible nitrogenous substances excite the secretion of an active juice, indigestible substances, even if nitrogenous (with the exception of ammonium salts) only occasion an increased secretion of an acid but inactive fluid.

Venus' Fly Trap, which closes up on its prey, pours out an active juice with which to digest it. Unlike the glands of Drosera, the glands of this plant do not secrete before stimulation, nor do they act unless the stimulant is nitrogenous and soluble. The secretion is acid and contains a peptic ferment. It is also strongly antiseptic.

I need not consider more of the many types of carnivorous plants that exist and have been studied. In general we may say that during the "fasting" state, the digestive secretions of all carnivorous plants are either neutral, or are but mildly acid in reaction; but, that when digestible nitrogenous substances are placed upon them, the secretion becomes strongly acid and contains an enzyme, previously absent, which acts upon proteins as does pepsin. If non-nitrogenous substances are placed upon the leaves there may or may not be an increased secretion. If the secretion is increased, it may be acid, but will contain no enzyme.

In the case of the nitrogenous substances, the juice contains active digestive properties, which have the same action on protein substances as does pepsin; while with indigestible bodies, even if nitrogenous, and in the case of all non-nitrogenous substances, these active digestive agents are absent. We note here a precise adaptation that is seen in all forms of life.

There is not only a difference in the character of the juice poured out upon different substances; there is also a marked difference in the amount of fluid poured out and in the length of time it is secreted. There are also marked differences in the physical behaviour in these plants towards the various substances. When protein is placed upon the leaves of some plants, the incurvation of the leaf is often great enough to completely envelop the bodies and lasts until digestion and absorption are completed. But if bits of glass are dropped on their leaves, a certain degree of incurvation occurs, but it is not accompanied with any secretion and does not persist.

Dr. N. Phillip Norman, Instructor in Gastro-enterology, N. Y. Polyclinic Medical School and Hospital, New York City, says: "In studying the action of different enzymes, one is struck by Emil Fisher's statement that there must be a special key to each lock. The ferment being the lock and its substrate the key, and if the key does not fit exactly to the lock, no reaction is possible. In view of this fact is it not logical to believe the admixture of different types of carbohydrates and fats and proteins in the same meal to be distinctly injurious to the digestive cells? If since it is true that similar, but not identical, locks are produced by the same type of cells, it is logical to believe that this admixture taxes the physiologic functions of these cells to their limit."

The digestive juices are complex and elaborately contrived fluids. The work of the digestive canal is beautifully performed and most carefully adapted to the work in hand. For each set of raw materials, a suitable combination of digestive secretions, with special properties, are required and are, therefore, produced. The digestive glands are able to vary their work considerably, not alone with respect to the quantity of juice secreted, but also with respect to the properties of the juice.

There is more water or less water, a higher degree of alkalinity, or acidity, a different degree of concentration of the enzyme or a total absence of enzyme, as required by the different classes of foods and as required at various stages of the process of digestion of one kind of food.

All of these separate conditions of juice activity are not without their importance, although they are wholly disregarded by "orthodox" dietitians and by the physicians and practitioners of all schools.

Physiologists usually gloss over these facts, so that the student of physiology is not impressed with their practical importance.

It is clear that the character of the juice corresponds with the requirements of the food to be acted upon. Carbohydrate foods receive a juice rich in carbohydrate-splitting enzymes, protein foods receive a juice rich in protein-splitting enzymes, etc. This alteration of the juice extends both to its strength and to the absolute quantities of the ferment, just as we saw it do in the case of the carnivorous plants. So different in character are the specific secretions poured out on each different kind of food, Prof. Pavlov speaks of "milk-juice," "bread-juice," "flesh-juice," etc.

Based on our knowledge of the chemistry of digestion, briefly presented in this and the chapter on digestion, I present the following rules. These rules have been carefully tested in practice by the writer and many others and have stood the test of experience. They should be followed by well and sick alike.

ACID-STARCH COMBINATIONS

1. *Never eat carbohydrate foods and acid foods at the same meal.*

Do not eat bread, potatoes, or peas, or beans, or bananas, or dates, or other carbohydrates with lemons, limes, oranges, grapefruits, pineapples, tomatoes or other sour fruit.

The enzyme, ptyalin, acts only in an alkaline medium; it is destroyed by a mild acid. Fruit acids not only prevent carbohydrate digestion, but they also favor their fermentation. Oxalic acid diluted to one part in 10,000 completely arrests the action of ptyalin. There is enough acetic acid in one or two teaspoonfuls of vinegar to entirely suspend salivary digestion.

Dr. Percy Howe, of Harvard, says: "Many people who cannot eat oranges at a meal derive great benefit from eating them fifteen to thirty minutes before the meal." But Dr. Howe does not appear to know why these people cannot take oranges with their meals. I have put hundreds of patients, who have told me that they could not eat oranges or grapefruit, upon a diet of these fruits and they found that they could take them. Such people are in the habit of taking these foods with a breakfast of cereal, with cream and sugar, egg on toast, stewed prunes and coffee, or some similar meal.

Tomatoes should never be combined with any starch food. They may be eaten with leafy vegetables and fat foods. The combination of citric, malic and oxalic acids found in tomatoes, (which are released and intensified by cooking), is very antagonistic to the alkaline digestion of starches in the mouth and stomach. They should not be used on salads at a starch meal.

The physiologist, Styles, runs from the practical application of our knowledge of the chemistry of digestion by saying: "If the mixed food is quite acid at the outset, it is hard to see how there can be any hydrolysis (enzymic digestion of starch) brought about by the saliva. Yet we constantly eat acid fruits before our breakfast cereal and notice no ill effects."

That we "notice no ill effects," from such acid-starch combinations, is true only of those who give no attention to the matter. All students of food combining know that this combination does produce ill effects. Stiles would, of course, say that these ill effects are due to germs.

He continues: "Starch which escapes digestion at this stage is destined to be acted upon by the pancreatic juice, and the final result may be entirely satisfactory." It is true that the starch will later be acted upon by the pancreatic and intestinal enzymes, providing it has not previously been acted upon by bacteria, the thing that usually occurs, giving us gas and a sour stomach and the notion that: "I cannot eat oranges or grapefruit. They give me gas."

Assuming, for the sake of argument, that no fermentation occurs, are we to assume, also that salivary digestion is of so small consequence that we can afford to dispense with it altogether? I do not think so and Stiles himself hints the same, when he adds: "Still it is reasonable to assume that the greater the work done by the saliva, the lighter will be the task remaining for the other secretions and the greater the probability of its complete accomplishment."

In cases of hyperacidity of the stomach there is great difficulty in digesting starches. Much discomfort is caused by eating them. They ferment and poison the body. Acid-starch combinations are very rare in nature — the sour apple coming nearest to being such a combination.

The highest efficiency in digestion demands that we eat in such a way as to offer the least hindrance to the work of digestion and not that we seek flimsy pretexts for continuing our customary haphazard eating. We should make the best use of our knowledge of the chemistry and physiology of digestion and of the limitations of the digestive enzymes and not try to ignore this knowledge altogether. This is particularly important in diseased states and in cases of crippled digestion.

Is it true that the pancreatic juice will digest starch when the first step in the process has not been made by the ptyalin? It is asserted by some that ptyalin is the only agent in the body capable of initiating the digestion of starch. Whether or not this is true, certainly salivary digestion is not to be regarded as unimportant. For, when it fails to occur, fermentation is practically certain to take place.

PROTEIN-CARBOHYDRATE COMBINATION

2. *Never eat a concentrated protein and a concentrated carbohydrate at the same meal.*

This means do not eat nuts, meat, eggs, cheese, or other protein foods at the same meal with bread, cereals, potatoes, sweet fruits, cakes, etc.

In the ancient Hebrew writing (Exodus) we read: "And Moses said °°° Jehovah shall give you in the evening, flesh to eat, and in the morning, bread to the full, °°° and Jehovah spake unto Moses saying °°° at evening ye shall eat flesh, and in the morning ye shall be filled with bread." This statement from *Exodus* is one of the earliest records of the practice of eating proteins and carbohydrates at separate meals. Perhaps this indicates that this was the custom of the time in which the book of *Exodus* was written. Was it the custom of the Hebrews only, or did they acquire this practice from the Egyptians among whom they are supposed to have spent some four hundred years and from whom they had just escaped? Some scholars insist that the books attributed to Moses were written at a later date, after the Hebrews were released from Babylonian bondage. Did they acquire the practice from the Babylonians? Unfortunately, historians have supplied us with little information about the living habits of the past.

The Bible story does not tell us anything of the origin of this custom, nor how long it had been in existence, but the fact that in that story it is invested with divine sanction may be taken to indicate how firmly fixed was the practice and how important it was considered among the Hebrews of the time. I do not pretend to know how widespread this practice may have been, nor how long it may have been practiced; but there is evidence that it was also a practice among the Greeks. In an article in *Your Physique,* Sept. 1946, David P. Willoughby, a leading authority on physical education, tells us that "the regular diet of pugilists and wrestlers of antiquity "consisted mainly of meat — preferably beef, pork, or kid — and bread. Meat and bread were not to be eaten at the same meal." Here is a practice of keeping proteins and carbohydrates apart in eating that has a sound physiological basis.

Remnants of the practice still exist among Mediterranean peoples. When an Italian working man makes a meal on a loaf of black bread and a few pieces of garlic, he may be following an ancient practice, that, so far as we know, may go all the way back to the instinctive practices of our primitive ancestors.

The Earl of Sandwich is credited with having invented the sandwich — a modern dietetic abomination. The hamburger, a similar abomination, is also a modern dietetic innovation. Egg sandwiches, cheese sandwiches, ham sandwiches and similar protein-starch combinations are of recent origin. Dr. Tilden used to say that Nature never produced a sandwich. How true are his words!

The digestion of carbohydrates (starches and sugars) and of protein is so different, that when they are mixed in the stomach they interfere with the digestion of each other. An acid process (gastric digestion) and an alkaline process (salivary digestion) can not be carried on at the same time in an ideal way in the stomach. In fact, they cannot proceed together at all for long as the rising acidity of the stomach contents soon completely stops carbohydrate digestion and this is followed by fermentation.

Marshall showed that undigested starch in large amounts in the stomach absorbs pepsin and thus prevents the acid from entering into combination with the proteins and so increasing the free hydrochloric acid.

Tests made in this country are said to have revealed that the eating of starches and proteins together delayed the digestion of protein but four to six minutes — an insignificant delay, if true. But Marshall's showing would lead us to think that protein digestion would be longer delayed, or that it may not be well digested at all.

Arthur Cason, M.D., D.P.H., F.R.S.A. (Lond.), writing in April 1945 *Physical Culture* mentions two groups of experiments made by him and his aids which showed that the eating of protein and carbohydrate at the same meal does retard and even prevent digestion. He made control tests in which were recorded digestive rates for each and a final analysis of the feces was made. He says "such tests always reveal that the digestion of proteins when mixed with starches is retarded in the stomach; the degree varying in different individuals, and also in the particular protein or starch ingested." He adds: "An examination of the fecal matter reveals both undigested starch granules and protein shreds and fibers, whereas, when ingested separately, each goes to a conclusion."

Cason's findings are more in line with what we would expect from Marshall's showings. It may be that the "tests" made in this country took into consideration nothing more vital than the emptying time of the stomach — a fallacy in the study of digestion that has been exploded in a previous chapter.

Beans contain about 25% protein and approximately 50½% carbohydrate or starch. This doubtless accounts for their difficult digestion and the readiness with which they ferment. Prof. McCollum says that navy beans have a peculiar and indigestible carbohydrate. But McCollum knows nothing of combinations. Beans are a "bread and meat" combination and each of their two principle constituents requires entirely different processes for digestion. The starch of the bean lies in the stomach while its protein is being digested and, except under the most favorable circumstances, ferments, producing gas and toxins. Because of their complex character, dry beans, a protein-starch combination, tax the digestive powers more than simpler foods; but the gas, discomfort and other trouble that so commonly follow eating them are not due so much to the beans themselves as to the company they keep. Baked beans are preferable to beans that are boiled and taken saturated with water. If taken thus relatively dry, well chewed, and eaten in proper combinations, beans are readily digestible.

Candy, sugar, etc., greatly inhibt the secretion of the gastric juice and markedly delay digestion. Consumed, a large amount at a time, candy is very depressing to stomach activity.

Whatever may be true with reference to the effects of the starch-protein combination upon the digestion of protein, it is certain that this combination is disastrous to starch digestion. There is no doubt that the gastric juice destroys the ptyalin of the saliva and stops salivary digestion.

The physiologist, Stiles, says, *Nutritional Physiology*; "the acid which is highly favorable for gastric digestion, for example, is quite prohibitive of salivary digestion." He, however, in common with all other physiologists, makes no practical application of this fact in feeding the well or the sick. He says of pepsin, "the power to digest proteins is manifested only with an acid reaction, and is permanently lost when the mixture is made distinctly alkaline.

The conditions which permit peptic digestion to take place are, therefore, precisely those which exclude the action of saliva." He sees no reason, however, why we should eat foods requiring salivary digestion at meals separate from those at which we eat foods requiring peptic digestion. Indeed, he declares of the salivary enzyme, ptyalin, "the enzyme is extremely sensitive to acid. Inasmuch as the gastric juice is decidedly acid it used to be claimed that salivary digestion could not proceed in the stomach. But it has come to be recognized that when a large mass of food is introduced into the stomach within a short time the gastric juice penetrates it rather slowly. A few minutes after the completion of a meal we may picture the stomach contents as being acidified near the surface, the acid slowly making its way inward, but having a neutral or even alkaline central portion. Salivary digestion will be continued in the steadily diminishing region not yet reached by the acid, and will cease only when the gastric secretion from one wall of the stomach meets that from the other."

This effort to escape the practical application of the physiological limitations of the digestive enzymes might have some merit, if we were in the habit of swallowing our food en mass, and not small amounts at a time. At the same time, the alkaline saliva must impede the work of pepsin, a thing that would be reduced to a minimum if proteins, which require little insalivation, were eaten alone. (It is not true that gastric juice is decidedly acid. It is sometimes strongly acid, sometimes very weakly acid, depending upon the character of food eaten). Why spend years in the study of physiology if we are to forget it immediately and disregard the practical applications that may be made of our knowledge of physiology.

Milo Hastings objects that laboratory feeding experiments have disregarded food combinations and have given attention to the diet as a whole. This objection has little weight. It is quite obvious that the laboratory has not given us the last word on feeding and Mr. Hastings is in no position to say that if and when combinations are tested in the laboratory the experimenters will not obtain better results than now in their feeding experiments.

Certainly foods requiring an alkaline condition for their digestion should not be eaten with foods necessitating an acid condition for their digestion. Foods requiring an alkaline condition for digestion should not be eaten with acids.

Stiles continues: "Any rotation of the contents would probably bring about an earlier distribution of the acid and arrest of starch digestion. No such rotation seems normally to occur." While there may be no rotation of the contents of the stomach, there is certainly considerable movement in it and this serves, as Stiles himself bears witness, to mix the semi-fluid foods. He talks of the food in the stomach as though it were more or less a solid mass through which the digestive juices must pass by osmosis; whereas this mass of chewed food, food juices, saliva and usually water, is a semi-fluid mass in constant to-and-fro motion. Assuming that he is right, there would still be interference with salivary digestion in those starches on the outside of the food-mass.

V. H. Mottram, professor of physiology in the University of London, says in his *Physiology* that it is in the distal end of the stomach that the churning movement mixes the food and gastric juice and no salivary action is possible. Now gastric juice digests protein and saliva digests starch. Therefore, it is obvious that for efficient digestion the meat (protein) part of a meal should come first and the starchy part second — just indeed as by instinct is usually the case. Meat precedes pudding the most economical course of procedure."

Mottram at least recognizes the fact that an acid gastric juice destroys ptyalin and stops starch digestion, even if he tries to squirm out of any rational application of the fact. Instinctively, as observed in the eating habits of wild animals (and of domestic animals also, where they are permitted to choose their own foods) proteins and carbohydrates are eaten at separate meals, not protein first and starch last. It is customary to eat meat, eggs, cheese, etc., and bread together. Watch a man eating a hamburger and see if he is instinctively taking his meat at the first part of his meal and his starch last. We can only assume that Prof. Mottram does not want to be classed as a "faddist," else he would not have resorted to this obvious "dodge" to escape the logical application of the facts of digestive chemistry he had presented.

Tilden, who was once a professor of physiology in a medical college, remarked: "Educated (scientific) M. D.'s, have known all about the chemistry of digestion, because their bosom companions, the Ph. D.'s, have overworked their laboratories, and particularly their glass stomachs (the immortal test-tubes), to serve their doctor friends." It is unfortunate that the physiologists have been so anxious to justify conventional eating practices and so unwilling to make any practical applications of the factors of digestive chemistry in eating. Had the physiologists not been derelict of their duty, our eating practices of today might be far different.

One objection to this rule of food combining often made is that the stomach is always acid. This assertion is made in obvious disregard for the facts of digestive chemistry which we have already learned. We know that the type of juice that is poured into the stomach is determined by the kind of food that is eaten.

Perhaps the most common objection made to this rule is that Nature, herself, has produced protein-starch combinations. Indeed, it is often asserted that almost all natural foods are starch-protein combinations. Alfred W. McCann reasoned that if nature combines starches and proteins in the same food there can be no harm in us combining them in the same meal. Carlton Fredericks, a biochemist, makes a somewhat similar objection to this rule. Such objections are made in obvious ignorance of the facts of digestive adaptations. The objectors should study physiology a little.

There is a marked difference between the digestion of *a food* and the digestion of a mixture of *different foods*. Let us look at the digestion of bread: here we have an almost neutral gastric juice while starch digestion is going on and, then, after starch digestion has been completed, a highly acid gastric juice is secreted to digest the protein.

Pavlov proved another thing with regard to the purposive adaptation of the digestive juices. Bread proteid requires much pepsin and but little acid. This requirement is met, not by an increased flow of juice, but by an extraordinary concentration of the juice secreted. Acid inhibits the digestion of the starch of the bread and so an excess of hydrochloric acid is avoided. It is obvious, from these facts, that the eating of a bread and meat combination is exceedingly unphysiological. Yet this simple practical application of our knowledge of the complex process of digestion is constantly ignored.

If wheat is eaten alone (a monotrophic meal), there will be secreted a juice poor in hydrochloric acid but rich in pepsin. This juice will be poured out over a long period of time. Thus starch digestion and protein digestion go on concurrently. If meat and bread are eaten together much hydrochloric acid is poured out, so that starch digestion is suspended. If we eat but one food at a meal, nature can adapt her digestive juices to the food; but if we are going to eat several foods at a meal, this adaptation is impossible, unless the food is properly combined. At that, cereals and pulses, which represent protein-starch combinations, sweet potatoes, a sugar-starch combination and sour apples, an acid-starch combination, are prone to produce fermentation.

Dr. Richard C. Cabot, of Harvard, says: "When we eat carbohydrates the stomach secretes an *appropriate* juice, a gastric juice of different composition from that which it secretes if it finds proteins coming down. It is one of the numerous examples of choice or intelilgent guidance carried on by parts of the body which are ordinarily thought of as unconscious and having no soul or choice of their own."

This statement of Cabot's presents a fact of physiology. It is borne out by Pavlov's showing that each kind of food calls forth a particular activity of the digestive glands. The digestion of starches and proteins is so different that when these foods are eaten together, they interfere with the digestion of each other. The acid poured into the stomach to digest the protein prevents starch digestion.

To a single article of food that is a starch-protein combination the body can adjust its juices, both as to strength and timing, to the digestive requirements of the food. But when two foods are eaten with different, even opposite, digestive needs, this precise adaptation of juices to requirements becomes impossible. If bread and flesh are eaten together, instead of an almost neutral gastric juice being poured into the stomach during the first two hours of digestion, a highly acid juice will be poured out immediately and starch digestion comes to an almost abrupt end. (Please note that carnivores in nature never mix carbohydrates with their meat.) Thus it is apparent that Frederick's statement that "the body is equipped to handle carbohydrates and proteins simultaneously with great efficiency" is not accurate and is based on ignorance of the facts of physiology.

It is true that the natural combinations offer but little difficulty in digestion, but neither the food factories nor the cooks have been able to produce protein-starch combinations capable of digestive completion. What nature has combined, nature can digest. What man may combine, she often finds indigestible. Dr. Tilden was eternally right when he repeated on more than one occasion that nature never produced a sandwich.

PROTEIN-PROTEIN COMBINATION

3. *Never consume two concentrated proteins at the same meal.*

Do not eat nuts and meat, or eggs and meat, or cheese and nuts, or cheese and eggs, etc., at one meal. Do not use meat and milk or eggs and milk or nuts and milk at the same meal. Indeed, milk, if taken at all, is best taken alone. Dr. Gibson well expresses it thus: "The best way with milk is either to take it alone or leave it alone." An exception may be made to this in the case of acid fruits. The popular superstition that lemons, berries, cucumbers, etc., with milk is dangerous has no foundation.

Two proteins of different characters and different compositions, calling for different types of digestive juices and these juices of different strength and character and pouring into the stomach at different times, should not be consumed at the same meal. One protein at a meal should be the rule.

There is protein in everything one eats, but in most foods there is such a small amount that we ignore it in combinations. All the rules for combining foods should be recognized as applying only to the concentrated starches, sugars, fats and proteins.

It is objected that since the various proteins differ so much in their amino-acid content and the body requires adequate quantities of certain of these it is necessary to consume more than one protein at a meal to secure adequate protein. Most people eat three meals a day or twenty-one meals a week. A great many of these eat between meals so that they eat many more meals a week. I can find no logical necessity for cramming them all into the stomach at one sitting. An ample variety of protein foods may be eaten by consuming different proteins at different meals.

Is there no significance in the fact that the strongest juice is poured out upon milk in the last hour of secretion? Do Orthodox Jews not follow a physiologically excellent practice when they refrain from eating milk and flesh together? Eggs require different timing in secretion than do either meat or milk. Should they not be eaten separately from flesh and milk? Perhaps the ruinous consequences of over-feeding tubercular patients on milk and eggs is at least partly explained by this indigestible food mixture.

PROTEIN-FAT COMBINATION

4. *Do not consume fats with proteins.*

This means do not use cream, butter, oil, etc., with meat, eggs, cheese, nuts, etc.

Fat depresses the action of the gastric glands and inhibits the pouring out of the proper gastric juices for meats, nuts, eggs, or other protein. Fats mixed with foods delay the development of appetite juice and diminish its quantity. The presence of fats in the stomach diminishes the production of chemical juice. Fatty acids lessen the activity of the gastric glands, lessen the activity of the gastric juice and lower the amount of pepsin and hydrochloric acid and may lower the entire digestive tone more than fifty per cent. This inhibiting effect can come even from fats in the intestine. Oil introduced into the rectum decreases the amount of gastric juice, though it does not alter its quality. (Oil enemas are bad.)

One of my correspondents, a very careful student, a professor of anatomy in one of the country's leading universities, suggests that fat and starch is a poor combination. Among other reasons which he offers is this one, which strikes me as having some weight: "According to Cannon, *** fats remain long in the stomach when taken alone and when combined with other food-stuffs markedly delay their exit through the pyloris. Under normal circumstances starches are retained in the stomach a relatively short time. By delaying the passage of the starch from the stomach into the intestine, due to the presence of the fat, we are affording excellent opportunity for fermentation, especially in the case of those who are enervated or otherwise possess weak digestive powers."

I fully agree with this student, W. R. Beard, of Columbus, Ohio, when he says: "At best, food combining, especially concentrated types, is a questionable experiment and an outgrowth of human ingenuity and of questionable merit." The less complex are our food mixtures, the simpler are our meals, the more efficient may we expect digestion to be.

Mr. Beard says that it has been his experience that the amount of fat taken with starch need not be great to cause fermentation. I have not personally observed this, but it may be an oversight on my part, that is, I may have attributed the resulting fermentation to something other than the combination.

Pavlov points out on the other hand, that fat and starch — bread and butter — is less difficult to digest and explains that, "bread requires for itself, especially when calculated per unit, but little gastric juice and but little acid, while the fat which excites the pancreatic glands' insures a rich production of ferment both for itself and also for the starch and protein of bread." In dealing with the influence of the fat-starch combination upon digestive secretion, he comes very near to a recognition of the principle of incompatibility of foods. He says: "There is no struggle in this case between the several food constituents, and therefore no one of them suffers." It will be noticed that a fat-starch combination is not only good in the stomach, but equally good in the intestine.

ACID-PROTEIN COMBINATION

5. *Do not eat acid fruits with proteins.*

This is to say, oranges, tomatoes, lemons, pineapples, etc., should not be eaten with meat, eggs, cheese or nuts.

Prof. Pavlov positively demonstrated the demoralizing influence of acids, both fruit acids and the acid results of fermentation, upon digestion. Acid fruits by inhibiting the flow of gastric juice — an unhampered flow of which is imperatively demanded by protein foods — seriously handicaps protein digestion and results in putrefaction. Nuts and fresh cheese are about the only protein foods that do not quickly decompose under such conditions and these have their digestion delayed. Acids do not inhibit the flow of gastric juice anymore or any longer than does the oil of nuts or the cream of cottage cheese.

Instead of orange juice, grapefruit juice, pineapple juice, etc., assisting in the digestion of proteins when taken along with these as is taught in certain quarters, these acids actually retard protein digestion.

So-called health specialists and dietitians, who ignore this fact, and continue to recommend sour salad dressings and acid fruit drinks at meals, are unworthy of the trust placed in them by those who seek their advice. Lemon juice, vinegar, pickles, etc., when mixed with the food, serve as a check to hydrochloric secretion. Just as acids interfere with the secretion of hydrochloric acid, so sodium or alkali interferes with pepsin secretion and lowers gastric acidity.

I have not been able to find any evidence that acids other than hydrochloric acid activate pepsin. At any rate, there is no need for additional acids as the stomach is capable of supplying all the acids required to provide a favorable medium in which the pepsin can act and supply this at the right time. Additional acids rather than helping in the digestion of protein hinder or suspend the secretion of digestive juice. Gastric juice is not poured out in response to the presence of acids in the mouth and stomach.

Milk and orange juice, while by no means an indigestible combination, is far from a good combination. Orange juice and eggs form an even worse combination. Pineapple juice and flesh is equally as bad. Pineapple juice does not digest flesh. It is well to bear in mind that flesh is not digested by acid but by pepsin. The hydrochloric acid of the stomach supplies the proper environment for the action of pepsin.

SUGAR-STARCH COMBINATION

6. *Do not consume starches and sugars together.*

Jellies, jams, fruit butter, sugar, honey, syrups, molasses, etc., on bread, cake, or at the same meal with cereals, potatoes, etc., or sugar with cereal, will produce fermentation. Hot cakes with honey or syrup is an abomination.

The practice of eating starches that have been disguised by sweets is also a bad way to eat carbohydrates. If sugar is taken into the mouth it quickly fills with saliva but no ptyalin is present. Ptyalin is essential to starch digestion. If the starch is disguised with sugar, jellies, jams, syrups, etc., the taste buds are deceived and carbohydrate digestion is impaired. Monosaccharides and disaccharides ferment quicker than polysaccharides and are prone to ferment in the stomach while awaiting the completion of starch digestion.

Sweet fruits with starch result in as much fermentation and the same fermentation products, as does sugar, jellies or syrups. We do not feed these with starches. Wm. Henry Porter, M. D., in his book, *Eating to Live Long*, says that eating fruits is "one of the most pernicious and reprehensible of dietetic follies," but even he admits that fruits eaten without other foods are all right. He claims fruits prevent digestion of the other foods. He only needs to understand food combining.

For the reason that fruits of all kinds should not be combined with other foods, we must condemn as violations of the neuro-chemical laws of digestion the ever-increasing number of fruit-breads — raisin-bread, fig-bread, prune-bread, banana-bread, fruit in coffee-substitutes, etc. These things have but one excuse for existence — they induce the eater to take more bread and thus result in the sale of more of this food .They produce indigestion in everyone.

An inactive saliva is poured out abundantly upon dry or powdered meat, to moisten it and aid in swallowing; but no saliva is poured upon fresh meat. Similarly, much saliva, active in this case, is poured out upon dry starch, both to moisten and digest it; but no saliva is poured out upon boiled or soaked starch.

It has been known since Beaumont made his experiments, that pieces of metal, stone, etc., placed in the human stomach, do not excite the secretion of gastric juice. It is also true that non-starch substances, although they may occasion the secretion of copious amounts of saliva and may be well chewed, do not excite the production of an active digestive juice in the mouth. Even in the case of sugar, a carbohydrate, no ptyalin is secreted when this is eaten. To eat of sugar, white or brown, jellies, jams, honey, syrups and molasses, sweet fruits, etc., with bread or other starch is to invite fermentation.

Major Austin says: "foods that are wholesome by themselves or in certain combinations often disagree when eaten with others. For example, bread and butter taken together cause no unpleasantness, but if sugar or jam or marmalade is added trouble may follow. Because the sugar will be taken up first, and the conversion of the starch in the bread into sugar is then delayed. Mixtures of starch and sugar invite fermentation and its attendant evils."

Most of us are aware that no digestion of sugar, syrup, honey, etc., takes place in the mouth and stomach. Such being the case, why should sugars of any kind be delayed in the stomach awaiting protein or starch digestion. Fermentation is inevitable when this is done.

Sugar with starch means fermentation. It means a sour stomach. It means discomfort. Those who are addicted to the honey-eating practice and who are laboring under the popular fallacy that honey is a "natural sweet" and may be eaten indiscriminately, should know that this rule not to take sweets with starches applies to honey as well. Honey or syrup, it makes no difference which, with your hot cakes, honey or sugar, it matters not which, with your cereals, honey or sugar to sweeten your cakes, — these combinations spell fermentation. White sugar, brown sugar, "raw" sugar, imitation brown sugar (that is, white sugar that has been colored), black strap molasses, or other syrup, with starches means fermentation. Soda will neutralize the resulting acids, it will not stop the fermentation.

STARCH-STARCH COMBINATION
7. *Eat but one concentrated starch food at a meal.*

CORRECT FOOD COMBINING

The rule to consume but one starch food at a meal is probably more important as a means of avoiding overeating of starches than as a means of avoiding a bad combination. While overeating of starches may lead to fermentation, there is no certainty that the combination of two starches will do so.

It is insisted by many that the digestive organism has need of and invincible affinity for one form of starch at any particular time. If two or more starches are eaten at the same time, at the same meal, one or the other will be selected for digestion and assimilation and the other permitted to go untouched in the stomach, not only without itself being passed on to digestion in the bowels, but also retarding the digestion of other foods, with fermentation, sour stomach, belching, etc., as the certain result."

There is only one kind of starch, but starchy foods differ greatly. It may be true that the starch-splitting enzymes manifest a preference for one starchy food, although I have been unable to find any physiological ground for the statement, nor have I seen fermentation result from eating two starches where they were each consumed in small quantities. I think the chief reason for not eating two starches at the same meal is to avoid overeating of starches.

Certain biochemists say that when you have taken bread and potatoes you have exhausted your starch-license. *Hygienists* advise but one starch at a meal, not because there is any conflict in the digestion of these foods, but because taking two or more starches at a meal is practically certain to lead to overeating of this substance. We find it best, and this is doubly true in feeding the sick, to limit the starch intake to one starch at a meal. People with unusual powers of self control may be permitted two starches, but these individuals are so rare, the rule should be: *one starch at a meal.*

Writing facetiously of rules for eating carbohydrates, Carlton Fredericks says: "Don't serve more than two foods rich in sugar or starch at the same meal. When you serve bread and potatoes, your starch-license has run out. A meal that includes peas, bread, potatoes, sugar, cake and after dinner mints should also include a Vitamin B Complex capsule, some bicarbonate of soda (other than that used on the vegetables), and the address of the nearest specialist in arthritis and other degenerative diseases."

For more than forty years it has been the rule in *Hygienic* circles to take but one starch at a meal and to consume no sweet foods with the starch meal. Sugars, syrups, honeys, cakes, pies, mints, etc., have not been tabu with starches. We do not say to those who come to us for advice: If you eat these foods with your starches, take a dose of baking soda with them. We tell them to avoid the sugars with the starches and thus avoid fermentation that is almost inevitable. In *hygienic* circles it is considered the height of folly to take a poison and then take an antidote with it. We think it best not to take the poison.

TAKE MELONS ALONE
8. *Do not consume melons with any other foods.*

Watermelon, muskmelon, honeydew melon, pie melon, casaba melon, cantaloupe, and other melons should always be eaten alone.

I know of no physiological reason for this rule. We do know that these foods decompose very quickly in the stomach and are almost sure to cause trouble if eaten with other foods. If eaten alone — a meal made of them — so that they are quickly passed out of the stomach they form excellent and delightful foods. People who complain that melons "do not agree" with them will find that if they eat them alone — but not between meals — they can enjoy them without an aftermath of discomfort. Because of the ease with which melons decompose they do not combine well with any food, except, perhaps, with certain fruits. We always feed them alone, not between meals, but at meal time.

TAKE MILK ALONE
9. *Milk is best taken alone or let alone.*

Milk is the natural food of the mammalian young, each species producing milk peculiarly and precisely adapted to the various needs of its own young. It is the rule that the young take the milk alone, not in combination with other foods. Milo Hastings once objected that calves will take milk and a few minutes later eat grass. But we are not to forget that the calf has a few more stomachs than we have and can do this without difficulty.

Milk acts as a gastric insulator. Its cream inhibits the outpouring of gastric juice for some time after the meal is eaten. Milk does not digest in the stomach, but in the duodenum, hence in the presence of milk the stomach does not respond with its secretion. This prevents the digestion of other foods introduced along with the milk. Perhaps milk could be taken with starch, if we took pure starch, but no starch food is pure starch. The use of acid fruits with milk does not cause any trouble and apparently does not conflict with its digestion.

COMBINATIONS IN THE INTESTINE

Bearing in mind the facts known about intestinal digestion it seems probable that proper combinations are important even in intestinal digestion. In other words, a properly combined meal is properly combined throughout the whole course of the digestive tube; while an improperly combined meal is probably wrongly combined throughout the whole course of digestion. A few facts may help to make this clear. Prof. Pavlov says, "the existence of fat in large quantities in the chyme restrains in its own interest the further secretion of gastric juice, and thus impedes the digestion of proteid substances; consequently a combination of fat and proteid-holding food is particularly difficult to digest."

While the processes of digestion in the intestine all take place in an alkaline medium and it seems logical to assume that combinations make little or no differences in the intestine, Dr. Cason says, in an article previously quoted from, that "the digestion of starches in the small intestine when accompanied by proteins produces a distinct stasis." This would indicate delayed digestion.

It seems certain that the putrefaction and fermentation that begins in the stomach as a consequence of wrong combinations will continue in the intestine. Good salivary and gastric digestion would seem to be essential to good intestinal digestion.

I append the accompanying chart, as a guide to food combining, which is modeled after one designed by Dr. Weger. I have made certain additions to the chart and have disagreed with him in a few minor particulars. My reasons for disagreeing with him are based both on physiological principles and experience. His chart does not include melons and fats and does not differentiate between sour or butter milk and sweet milk. These have been added to my chart.

Combinations marked good are good for the weakest digestion.

Combinations marked fair are permissible if digestion is unimpaired.

Combinations marked poor should never be employed unless digestion is at its highest.

Combinations marked bad should not be employed by even the strongest digestion.

Salads should contain no starch, such as potatoes; no proteins, such as eggs or shrimp; no oils, such as olive oil or dressings containing oil; no acids such as vinegar or lemon juice. Salt should also be omitted.

Sugar, syrup molasses and honey have been left out of this chart because they combine badly with all foods and also because they are best not eaten.

A second food combining chart is presented which may prove more helpful to some of my readers. By studying the two charts, it is easy to find the foods that do combine with each other. Making use of these facts of combination, the following plan of eating for three meals a day is suggested:

Breakfast: Fruit. Any fruit in season may be used. It is suggested that not more than three fruits be used at a meal, as, for example, grapes, well ripened bananas and an apple. It is well to have an acid fruit breakfast one morning and a sweet fruit breakfast the next. In season breakfast may be made of melons. In the winter months, one or two dried fruits such as figs, dates, raisins, prunes, etc., may be substituted for the fresh fruits. A winter breakfast of grapes, figs and pears will be found ideal.

Noon meal: A large raw vegetable salad of lettuce, celery, and one or two other raw vegetables plus avocado and alfalfa sprouts or nuts and seeds. As an alternative, a vegetable salad (omitting tomatoes from this salad), one cooked green vegetable and a starch.

Evening meal: A large raw vegetable salad (if nuts or cottage cheese are to be used as the protein, tomatoes may be used in this salad), two cooked non-starchy vegetables and a protein.

Fat meats, sour apples, beans, peanuts, peas, cereals, bread and jam, or hot-cakes and honey or syrup, are notoriously slow in digesting and are frequent sources of discomfort and putrescent poisoning. Much of this is well known to the layman, all of it may be known to the careful observer. The intelligent person will not lightly cast aside such facts but will use them as guides in eating.

"Occasional indulgence in any old food combinations will not do great harm," says Major Austin. "It is not what we do occasionally that matters much but what we do habitually that tells in the long run.

"It is certainly everyone's duty to have the courage of his convictions, but a cause is not benefitted by unreasonable advocates. So when at a friend's table do not deliver a homily on food combinations, and critically select and refuse, causing the host embarrassment. Take what is offered, and do not think about it unless sick or uncomfortable; then do not eat. No one should eat when seedy or out of sorts—no, not to please anyone."

	Protein	Starch	Fat	Sweet Milk	Sour Milk	Non-Starchy Vegetabels (cooked)	Salad or Raw Green Vegetables	Acid Fruits	Sub-Acid Fruits	Sweet Fruits (Dried)	Melons
Protein	bad	bad	bad	bad	bad	good	good	poor*	bad	bad	bad
Starch	bad	good	good	bad	bad	good	good	bad	bad	good	bad
Fat	bad	good	good	fair	fair	good	good	good	good	good	bad
Sweet Milk	bad	bad	good			poor	poor	fair	fair	bad	bad
Sour Milk	bad	bad	good			poor	poor	fair	fair	poor	bad
Green Vege.†	good	good	good	poor	poor	good	good	poor	fair	poor	bad
Sub-Acid Fruits†	bad	bad	good	fair	fair	poor	poor	good	good	good	fair
Acid Fruits	bad	bad	good	fair	fair	fair	fair	good	good	poor	fair
Sweet Fruits‡	poor	poor	good	poor	fair	poor	poor	poor	good	good	fair
Melons	bad	bad	bad	bad	bad	bad	bad	bad	fair	fair	good

*Acid fruits are fair with nuts. †Raw or cooked. ‡Dried.

CHART "A"—GENERAL FOOD COMBINING CHART

COMMON FOODS	COMBINE BEST WITH	COMBINE BADLY WITH
Sweet fruits (Sub-and non-acid)	Sour Milk	Acid Fruits Starches (Cereals, Bread, Potatoes) Proteins, Milk
Acid Fruits	Other Acid Fruits Fair with Nuts Fair with Milk	Sweets (all kinds) Starches (cereals, bread, potatoes) Proteins (except nuts)
Green Vegetables	All proteins All starches	Milk
Starches	Green Vegetables Fats and Oils	All Proteins All Fruits Acids, Sugars
Meats (all kinds)	Green Vegetables	Milk, Starches, Sweets Other proteins Acid Fruits and Vegetables Butter, Cream, Oils
Nuts (most varieties)	Green Vegetables Acid Fruits	Milk, Starches, Sweets Other proteins Butter, Cream, Oils, Lard
Eggs	Green Vegetables	Milk, Starches, Sweets Other proteins Acid Foods Butter, Cream, Oils, Lard
Cheese	Green Vegetables	Starches, Sweets Other proteins Acid Foods Butter, Cream, Oils, Lard
Milk	Best taken alone Fair with Acid Fruits	All proteins Green Vegetables Starches
Fats and Oils (Butter, Cream, Oils, Lard)	All starches Green Vegetables	All proteins
Melons (all kinds)	Best eaten alone	All Foods
Cereals (grains)	Green Vegetables	Acid Fruits All proteins All Sweets, Milk
Legumes Beans and Peas (except green beans)	Green Vegetables	All proteins All Sweets, Milk Fruits (all kinds) Butter, Cream, Oils, Lard

CORRECT FOOD COMBINING
CHART "B"—DETAILED FOOD COMBINING CHART

Nonstarchy & Green Vegetables
(See More Complete List)

Lettuce	Cucumbers	Greens (Kale, etc.)	Okra
Celery	Sweet Peppers	Summer Squash	Kohlrabi
Celery Cabbage	Cauliflower	Eggplant	Green Corn
Cabbage	Broccoli	Turnips	Green Beans
	Brussels Sprouts		

Protein	Protein/Starch (Combine as Starch)	EAT NONSTARCHY & GREEN VEGS. With *EITHER* PROTEIN or STARCH DO NOT COMBINE PROTEIN & STARCH	Starch	Mildly Starchy
Nuts	Beans		Potatoes	Carrots
Seeds	Peas		Sweet Potatoes	Beets
Olives	Lentils		Yams	Rutabaga
Cheese	Peanuts		Mature Corn	Winter Squash
Eggs	Coconuts		Jerusalem Artchks.	Pumpkin
Flesh Foods	Chestnuts		Parsnips	Edible Pod Peas
	Wild Rice		Salsify	Globe Artcks.
	All Grains			Water Chestnuts
				Sprouted Grains

DO NOT COMBINE VEGETABLES, PROTEINS OR STARCHES WITH FRUITS

Except: Nuts with Citrus —Fair Combination
Lettuce & Celery with Fruit —Good Combination

Acid Fruits	EAT SUBACID FRTS. With *EITHER* ACID OR SWEET FRUITS DO NOT COMBINE ACID FRUITS & SWEET FRUITS	Sweet Fruits
Citrus		Bananas
Pineapples		Persimmons
Strawberries		Thompson Grapes
Pomegranates		Muscat Grapes
Sour Apples		All Sweet Grapes
Sour Grapes		All Dried Fruits
Sour Peaches		
Sour Plums		
Sour Cherries		

Subacid Fruits

Sweet Apples	Subacid Grapes	Apricots	Blueberries
Sweet Peaches	Pears	Sweet Plums	Raspberries
Sweet Cherries	Papayas	Cherimoyas	Blackberries
	Mangos	Fresh Figs	

Tomatoes: Use with Green & Nonstarchy Vegetables & Protein
Avocados: Best with Salad
      Fair with Subacid Fruit or Starch
Melons: Eat Alone

CHART "C"—SIMPLIFIED FOOD COMBINING CHART
Also See Previous Page: DETAILED FOOD COMBINING CHART

Eat
NONSTARCHY & GREEN VEGETABLES
With

Either PROTEINS	Or	STARCHES
Nuts & Seeds	← DO NOT →	Peanuts
Olives	COMBINE	Coconuts
Cheese		Chestnuts
Eggs		Wild Rice
Flesh Foods		Grains
		Starchy Vegs.
		Mildly Starchy Vegs.
		Legumes

Eat
SUBACID FRUITS
(All Fruits Not Sweet or Acid)
With

Either ACID FRUITS	Or	SWEET FRUITS
Citrus	← DO NOT →	Bananas
Pineapples	COMBINE	Persimmons
Strawberries		Sweet Grapes
Pomegranates		Dried Fruits
Sour Tasting		
Fruits		

DO NOT COMBINE VEGETABLES, PROTEINS
OR STARCHES WITH FRUITS
Except: Nuts with Citrus —Fair Combination
Lettuce & Celery with Fruit —Good Combination

Tomatoes: Eat with green and non-starchy vegetables and protein
Avocados: Best with Salad
　　　　　Fair with Subacid Fruit or Starch
Melons: Eat Alone

CORRECT FOOD COMBINING

CHART "D"—PROTEINS

Nuts		Seeds
Pecans	Macadamias	Sunflower Seeds
Almonds	Pistachios	Sesame Seeds
Brazil Nuts	Pignolias	Pumpkin and Squash Seeds
Filberts	(Pine Nuts)	
Hazelnuts	Indian Nuts	
English Walnuts	Beechnuts	
Butternuts	Hickory Nuts	
Heart Nuts		
Black Walnuts		
Cashews (not really a nut, but classified as a nut)		

Other Plant Proteins	Low Protein
Soy Beans (fresh, dry or sprouted)	Avocados (may also be classified as a fat and as a neutral fruit)
Sunflower seed sprouts	Olives
Lentil sprouts	Milk (not recommended)
Garbanzo sprouts	

Green Vegetable Proteins** (Combine as Starch)	Starchy Proteins** (Combine as Starch)		
Peas in the Pod	Beans	Peanuts	ALL GRAINS:
Lima and other Beans in the Pod	Peas	Chestnuts	Wild Rice Wheat
Mature Green Beans in the Pod	Lentils	Coconuts	Rice Rye
Mung bean sprouts*			Buckwheat Barley
			Millet

Sprouts (contain significant amounts of protein, esp. in early stages)	Animal Proteins
	Cheese (raw milk or unprocessed)
	Eggs (not recommended)
Soy Sprouts — Combine	All Flesh Foods (except fat) (not recommended)
Lentil Sprouts — As	
Sunflower Seed Sprouts — Protein	
Alfalfa Sprouts (may be combined as green vegetable)	
Mung bean sprouts*	
All Seed, Bean & Grain Sprouts	
Combine seed and bean sprouts as protein—(except alfalfa)	
Combine grain sprouts as mildly starchy	

* Mung beans sprouted to green leaf stage—green vegetable starch/protein
** Classified as Starches for Purposes of Food Combining

THE SCIENCE AND FINE ART OF FOOD AND NUTRITION

CHART "E"—STARCHES

Starchy Proteins
(Classified as Starches for Purposes of Food Combining)

Peanuts	Dry Beans	Lima & Other
Chestnuts	Dry Peas	Beans in the Pod
Coconuts	Lentils	Mature Green
	Peas in the Pod	Beans in the Pod

Wild Rice	ALL GRAINS	Oats
Brown Rice	AND	Wheat
Buckwheat	ALL FOODS	Rye
Groats	CONTAINING	Barley
Millet	GRAINS	

Starchy Vegetables

White Potatoes	Jerusalem Artichokes
Yams and Sweet Potatoes	Parsnips*
Mature Corn	Salsify (Oyster Plant)*

Mildly Starchy Vegetables

Carrots	Winter Squash (acorn,
Globe Artichokes	butternut, hubbard,
Beets	banana, etc.)*
Rutabaga	Pumpkin*
Edible Podded Peas	Water Chestnuts
	Sprouted Grains

NOTES:

*Parsnips (17.5% starch) and salsify (18%) are sometimes listed as mildly starchy or even non-starchy vegetables, but since they contain as much starch as the potato (17.1%) they should properly be classified as starchy.

Winter squash (12.4%) and pumpkin (6.5%) are shown on some charts as starchy, but their starch content is quite a bit lower than potatoes (17.1%). I would consider them mildly starchy (or you could consider winter squash as borderline).

Cauliflower is sometimes listed as mildly starchy, but, with a starch content lower than broccoli (5.9%) and Brussels sprouts (8.3%), it properly belongs in the non-starchy category.

CORRECT FOOD COMBINING

CHART "F"—NON-STARCHY AND GREEN VEGETABLES

Lettuce	Rappini (similar to broccoli)	Eggplant
Celery	Brussels Sprouts	Green Corn (if not mature, and if eaten less than two hours after picking)
Cabbage (young, sweet)	Kale	Green Beans (young & tender)
Celery Cabbage	Collard Greens	Zucchini
Cucumber	Dandelion Greens	Yellow Crookneck Squash and all other summer squash
Cauliflower*	Turnip Tops	Chayote
Escarole (if not bitter)	Mustard Greens (if young & mild)	Bok Choy
Endive (if not bitter)	Okra	Alfalfa Sprouts
Sweet Pepper	Kohlrabi	
Broccoli	Turnips	
Spinach	USE SELDOM IF AT ALL—TOO HIGH IN OXALIC ACID (A CALCIUM ANTAGONIST)	Beet Tops
Swiss Chard		Rhubarb

Bitter Cabbage, Endive, Escarole—should not be used—contain concentrated acids and irritants

Parsley	Contain Mustard Oil	Onions
Watercress	Irritant foods (unless very young and sweet)—should not be used often or in large quantities	Leeks
Chives		Radishes
Scallions		Garlic
		Mature Mustard Greens

FATS

RECOMMENDED FATS: Edible Seeds, Nuts and Avocados (Protein/Fat Foods)

These Fats NOT Recommended

Butter	Not recommended for regular use.
Cream	Used occasionally by some Hygienists.

Olive Oil		Oils are used occasionally by some Hygienists.
Sesame Oil		Use unrefined Cold Pressed Oils, preferably stable oils like olive and sesame oil, less likely to be rancid.
Sunflower Seed Oil	ALL OILS	
Corn Oil		
Peanut Oil		Oils are fragmented, concentrated foods, and are best omitted.
Cotton Seed Oil		
Safflower Oil		

All Meat Fats (not recommended)

Butter Substitutes (not recommended)—Oleomargarine and the hard white hydrogenated "vegetable" shortenings commonly used in frying and baking are particularly pernicious substances, which the body is not equipped to handle.

(Fats delay digestion—may take up to four to six hours.
The need for fat is small, and the best sources are whole foods like nuts and avocados.)

*Cauliflower is sometimes listed as starchy, but with a starch content (5.2%) lower than broccoli (5.9%) and Brussels sprouts (8.3%), it properly belongs in the non-starchy category.

THE SCIENCE AND FINE ART OF FOOD AND NUTRITION

CHART "G"—FRUITS

SWEET FRUITS

		Dried Fruits
Bananas	Dates	Apples
Persimmons	Figs	Cherries
Thompson Grapes (Seedless)	Raisins	Bananas
Muscat Grapes	Prunes	Litchi "Nuts"
All Sweet Grapes	Apricots	Carob
Fresh Figs	Peaches	All Dried Fruit

Some unusual or tropical fruits not listed—Sweet taste is a good indication of their classification.

SUBACID FRUITS

Sweet Apples (Delicious)	Papayas	Blueberries
Sweet Peaches	Mangos	Raspberries
Sweet Nectarines	Apricots	Blackberries
Pears	Fresh Litchi "Nuts"	Mulberries
Sweet Cherries	Sweet Plums	Huckleberries
Some Grapes (Neither sweet nor sour)		Cherimoyas

Some unusual or tropical fruits not listed.

ACID FRUITS

Oranges	Kumquats	Limes
Grapefruit	Loquats	Sour Apples
Pineapples	Carambolas	Sour Grapes
Strawberries	Loganberries	Sour Peaches
Pomegranates	Gooseberries	Sour Nectarines
Lemons	Cranberries (not recommended—they contain benzoic acid)	Sour Plums
Kiwi Fruit		Sour Cherries

Tomatoes—Acid Fruits, without the sugar content of other acid fruits. Used with vegetable salad or any green or nonstarchy vegetables, but not at a starch meal. May be used with nuts or cheese, but not with meat, milk, or eggs.

Some unusual or tropical fruits not listed—Acid (or Sour) taste is a good indication of their classification.

MELONS

Watermelon	Muskmelon	Banana Melon
Honeydew Melon	Casaba Melon	Persian Melon
Honey Balls	Crenshaw Melon	Christmas Melon
Cantaloupe	Pie Melon	Nutmeg Melon

SYRUPS AND SUGARS

Brown Sugar	Maple Syrup	
"Raw" Sugar	Cane Syrup	None of these substances are
White Sugar	Corn Syrup	recommended.
Milk Sugar	Honey	

RESULTS OF WRONG COMBINATIONS

The continuous struggle with indigestible food mixtures and with the poisonous products of their bacterial decomposition sooner or later wears out the body, for it is a break on the process of nutrition that involves a prodigious waste of the vital forces and draws upon physiological reserves which have been set aside for future use.

What are those acid eructations (belchings) that so commonly follow meals of meat and bread, starch and milk, fruit and starch, sugar and starch, and other combinations we condemn? Are they symptoms of good digestion? There is gastric distress ("heart burn"), gas and eructations that cause throat irritation, mucus flow and coughing. The eructations are often so acrid, they cause burning of throat and nose.

Feed these people correctly combined meals and their fermentation with gas and eructations end. Physicians and others who scoff at food combining would show more intelligence if they would study the effects of the indigestible mixtures they prescribe and cease wasting time ridiculing those who are attempting to teach the people sane eating practices. While they sit and scoff the world moves on and leaves them.

Physicians, druggists and patent medicine manufacturers are kept busy supplying the demand for drugs to relieve the discomforts that grow out of wrong food combinations. Millions of dollars are yearly spent for alkalizers, laxatives and anti-gas remedies. Tons of Alkaseltzer, Tums, Bell-Ans, bicarbonate of soda, charcoal, milk of magnesia, syrup pepsin, etc., are swallowed yearly by the American public. Physicians prescribe as many more tons of drugs for the relief of abdominal discomfort.

Fermentation and putrefaction is so well nigh universal in the digestive tracts of our people that many physiologists and physicians have come to look upon the sub-diaphramatic cess-pool as normal. The fermentation and putrefaction is present in the digestive tracts of those who experience no discomfort in the abdomen. These people who experience no abdominal distress will swear that their bad combinations do not bother them.

One of the two chief reasons for careful eating is to prevent fermentation and putrefaction of food. One of the greatest causes of gastro-intestinal decomposition is wrong food combining. It is difficult to exaggerate the clinical picture resulting from the reeking decomposition which begins in the stomach and continues in the intestine as a result of food-mixtures which are all but indigestible.

Must I emphasize that the products of bacterial decomposition of food-stuffs are the same when the decomposition occurs in the stomach as when the food rots outside the body. The putrescence arising in the digestive tract is no less hostile to life and health than when it arises in a swill barrel.

Let us notice an average meal consumed in the average home. It consists of bread, meat, potatoes, perhaps a soup or pie or a dessert of gelatin or ice cream or canned or stewed fruit, and one or more green vegetables. There are the usual gravies and sauces, sugar and cream, catsup, mustard, salt, pepper, and milk, tea or coffee. Indeed, the purpose of eating seems to be to see how great a variety of heterogeneous substances can be put into the stomach at one time. Of course, no digestive system was ever designed to digest such an unholy combination of foods, slops and "relishes." The stomachs of those who eat such meals have been converted into swill barrels and garbage cans. Fermentation and putrefaction are inevitable.

Did you ever notice a garbage barrel; the great variety of substances in it — meats, eggs, several kinds of vegetables and fruits and scraps from the table, coffee and other substances. What a lot of putrescence results when it begins to decompose! Now think of all the putrescence that will develop in your alvine canal, when a similar mixture of food substances undergoes bacterial decomposition therein. Can you imagine good health resulting from such eating? Do you marvel that people are sick?

All the secretions of the digestive tract — saliva, hydrochloric acid, bile, pancreatic juice, intestinal juice — are antiseptic, or bactericidal. Gastric juice possesses an anti-fermentative power to prevent bacterial decomposition in food. The same is true of bile. The hydrochloric acid of the stomach, together with pepsin, the trypsin of the pancreatic juice and perhaps the intestinal juice are normally very destructive to germ life, digesting germs as readily as meat or bread. They resist and prevent bacterial decomposition in this garbage and attempt to digest it. But complete success in either of these efforts is impossible. Digestion cannot be perfect and more or less bacterial decomposition is inevitable. Such eating is better designed to poison than to nourish the body.

The American breakfast of grapefruit and sugar followed by baked apples, or stewed fruit or jam, and completed with coffee and sugar, perhaps eaten hurriedly, while nervously fingering the morning paper, and topped off with a cigarette, is sending millions to the doctors of all schools and ushering many thousands into premature graves.

Orthodox (?) food scientists and their trailers in medical ranks thought that with the discovery of "calories," they had found the master key that would unlock all the mysteries of human dietetics. Basing their work on the calorie standard, physicians would prescribe a diet for a patient about like the following:

Lamb stew with vegetables (400 calories), mashed potatoes (175 calories), sliced tomatoes (100 calories), strawberry shortcake and cream (160 calories), or ice cream (200 calories), a glass of buttermilk (130 calories), stewed prunes (150 calories); this constituting 1115 calories or approximately one-third the estimated required 3500 calories.

Wtih the "discovery" of "vitamins" the same foolish mistake is being repeated. The most deficient and one-sided diets are fed and then small quantities of supposed vitamin-rich substances — orange juice, tomato juice, cod-liver oil, yeast, etc. — are fed in a vain endeavor to render such diets adequate.

The calorie was a fetish. The vitamin has become the same. The older food specialists completely overlooked the important fact that the patient did not secure his calories from his food unless he digested and assimilated it. He fed his patients the most incongruous and indigestible mixtures, which set up fermentation and decomposition, and this completely changed the character of the food and as completely altered its relations to the body and its welfare.

The present day food specialist, feeding vitamins instead of calories, makes the same mistake. He feeds his patients abominable mixtures of soup, potatoes, pies or puddings, preserves, ice cream, coffee, or tea and then, "balances" it up with a teaspoonful of orange juice or a dose of grease of the cod-liver.

Such mixtures as this and the one described before will take on decomposition and turn out such products as carbonic acid gas, alcohol, ammonia, bacterial acids, etc. In order to neutralize, isolate and eliminate these poisons the body will be forced to draw upon its precious vital reserves. Such food mixtures not only do not yield up their calories and vitamins to the body in full measure, but they rob it of its reserves. For, when poisons accumulate in the body beyond its ordinary powers to neutralize and eliminate, its reserves are called upon and expended in freeing the body of the toxins.

The only reason that the great mass of poisons which arise out of the decomposition of our foods in our digestive tracts do not result in speedy death, is that nature has provided us with constitutional reserves with which to resist the recurrent accidents and emergencies of our daily lives. These reserves are especially intended to meet the needs of old age, when the forces of life are feeble and the self-regenerative powers of the body are impaired.

If the body's reserves are carefully hoarded they will carry us well beyond the hundred-year mark with youthful enthusiasm and zest. Their depletion is one of the most common calamities of modern life. The alkaloids and alcohols, with which gastro-intestinal decomposition charges our bodies, rob us of our reserves, greatly weaken our vital resistance and sooner or later produce a state of physiological collapse. We permit the silent, continuous leakage of our vital reserves until, by its sapping influence, we are brought below the line of safety. Our powers of repair and restitution are bankrupted and we are unable to "come back."

Effects of Cooking
CHAPTER XXVII

Speculations upon the origin of cooking are, perhaps futile. I have suggested that it may have developed out of ancient black magic — that it was an effort to impart the magic properties of fire to food. Certain it is, man did not cook his foods until after he learned to use fire and it was probably long thereafter, before he cooked much of it.

Someone has said: "God made man and the Devil made cooks." A British writer says: "Just try to imagine what a powerful lever the Devil possessed when he invented cooking and persuaded the primitive savages to seek after extraneous foodstuffs which could only be eaten if they were softened and made tasty by means of heat." Accepting the Devil as merely the personification of evil, he is undoubtedly the Father of Magic.

Simple prolonged heating of foodstuffs, especially at a high temperature and doubly so in the presence of water, either that contained in the foods themselves, or that added in the process of cooking, certainly results in a number of important changes in the foodstuffs which render them less and less valuable as foods. Even those foods that are regarded as fairly *thermostable* are certainly damaged by prolonged heating so that a diet that may be adequate in the uncooked state may be very inadequate after being thoroughly cooked. (High degrees of heat in the presence of water produces *hydrolysis*.)

At about 145 degrees Fahrenheit certain properties of plant life are destroyed. A leaf of cabbage, for example, if immersed in water that can be easily borne by the hand, will wilt, showing that part of its cellular life is destroyed at that low temperature. The heat to which such foods are subjected in cooking may be increased or prolonged until all the properties of the plant are destroyed. Many articles of food which are baked in an oven are subjected to a very intense heat ranging from 300 degrees F. to 400 degrees F. Much of their food value is destroyed, thereby. Bread that is browned in an oven is half-destroyed, being partly charcoal, tar, and ashes. If it had been left in an oven twice as long it would have been entirely destroyed. At every step in the process of cooking from the time the food is put in or upon the stove until it is entirely destroyed, if it be permitted to cook that long, destructive changes take place that impair its food value and unfit it for use by the body. I propose here to discuss the most important of these changes in the following order:

(1) *Cooking coagulates (hardens) the proteins of milk, eggs, meat, etc., making them tough and, with the exception of egg protein, less digestible, while impairing their food values.*

Protein digestibility is decreased by cooking, except in the case of egg whites. If egg white is just curdled it is rendered more easily digestible — if it is boiled hard it is made difficult of digestion. Meat protein is hardened at 160° F. Meat is more easily digested raw than cooked. Milk protein is coagulated at 145° F. and becomes less digestible than raw milk.

Sensitive amines are supposed by some to be saponified by heat, especially in the presence of water. Becoming a bit technical, for which I apologize to my lay readers, the amine group is replaced by the hydroxyl group in the foodstuffs and it has been shown that the hydroxides cannot be reaminised by the animal body. This means that the protein has been reduced to useless substances. It is said that while among the synthetic amines there are many which, owing to peculiar structural conditions, the amine group is readily detachable, no such substances are known among the natural amines. This is not wholly true, for it is known that water in which meat has been boiled contains more ammonia than was demonstrable in the meat. There is unquestionably a splitting off of certain amines. To assume that this has no bearing on nutrition in the absence of direct proof of such effect does not seem to me to be justifiable.

When either cystin or cystein are heated in the presence of water the sulphur is split off so that, as Berg says: "both cystin and cystein are ° ° ° rendered valueless for nutritive purposes, inasmuch as sulphydration cannot be affected in the animal body." He says that this decomposition of the sulphhydril group of amino acids by heat in the presence of water "does actually occur."

I quote the following from *Vitamins* by Ragnar Berg: "the experiments of Francis and Trowbridge and those of Trowbridge and Stanley have shown that when meat is boiled even for a comparatively brief period, organic phosphates are transformed into inorganic."

EFFECTS OF COOKING

Berg says: "Besides the sulphur group, we have reason to suppose that the food contains other groups of substances wtih a readily modifiable composition. °°° We are, however, certain that the proteins, and especially the neucleoproteins, contain *thermoliable* mixed-organic compounds." He mentions certain phosphates that are rapidly transformed by the cooking process and points out that while the body is capable of taking the more complex phosphates and reducing them to lower stages, it is unable to reverse the process. Only plants can do this.

Simple prolonged heating of foodstuffs, especially at high temperatures or under pressure, produces the following effects:
1. The disaminisation (deaminization) of vitally important amine compounds.
2. The decomposition of similar sulphur compounds (and perhaps of substances belonging to other unstable groups.)
3. The metamorphosis of metaphosphates and pyrophosphates into orthophosphates.

The first two of the above listed effects renders it impossible for the foodstuffs to be assimilated to form cell-substance, for the unstable groups in the food mixture will have been destroyed.

In considering the evils that may flow from deaminization of proteins (or of amino acids) by the cooking process, it is probably important that we think primarily of the effects of cooking upon the essential amino acids. Berg's conclusion, however, after reviewing the evidence, is that deaminization is not as important as the change of organic phosphates into inorganic.

Prof. Charles Richet, of the Paris Academy of Sciences, fed raw beef juice to tubercular patients and reported excellent results from this diet. He concluded however, that cooking meat interfers with the perfect assimilation of it that might otherwise occur. *Rare beef has no vitamin value and its iron is said to be very poorly utilized by the body.* This is probably not so of the iron in raw beef.

The British sociologist, Anthony Ludovici, recounts an instructive experience with cats. He bred cats for the purpose of studying the process of birth. He discovered that cats actually enjoy the process of birth, that they purr while their kittens are being born. Mr. Ludovici realizing that animals never cook their foods, took it for granted that his cats should have raw meat. Then, on one occasion, he was called away to the country and left one of his female cats in the care of some friends. When her kittens were born shortly after his return, her flanks heaved helplessly for several hours and she groaned almost like a human being. He despaired of her ever delivering her kittens. Inquiry revealed that his friend had fed the cat on cooked meat, vegetables, bread and milk and milk puddings. Further investigation revealed that not merely the happiness of cats during parturition but of other animals also, is inseparably connected with optimum condition during gestation − pregnancy. He found he was able to produce pleasurable or painful parturition at will by feeding his cats in different manners and keeping them indoors or outdoors. He discovered that he could do the same thing with bitches and, upon inquiry among shepherds, discovered the same thing among sheep. He tells of difficulties among cows and horses fed in certain very unwholesome ways. I have never seen difficulty in cows, and I have watched the birth of many calves, but these cows were supplied with good pasturage and were outdoors all through gestation. Not merely raw flesh foods, but uncooked foods of all kinds, are best for food.

In Vol. 39 (pages 21-31), 1939 of the *Transactions of the American Therapeutic Society,* F. M. Pottenger, M. D., and D. G. Simonsen recount the results of some experiments which they performed with cats. For a lengthy period of time they fed two groups of cats on similar quantities of meats and vegetables. The only difference between the diets of the two groups was that the meat of one group was uncooked, that of the other group cooked.

These men report that all the cats that received the uncooked flesh led normal lives, appeared perfectly healthy and were able to reproduce themselves throughout the length of the experiment which ran through several generations. On the other hand, none of the cats fed cooked meat were able to maintain good health for any length of time, nor were some of the second and third generations able to reproduce. All of the cats eating cooked flesh developed very serious troubles, such as softening of the bones, including those of the skull, bowed legs, rickets, curvature of the spine, paralysis of the legs, thyroid abscesses, convulsions, cyanosis of the liver and kidneys, enlarged colon, degeneration of the motor nerve ganglion cells throughout the spinal cord and brain stem, with some cells affected in the cerebellum and cerebral cortex.

The reader's attention is directed to the cumulative effects of this diet. A diet that seems adequate in one generation may turn out

EFFECTS OF COOKING

to be very inadequate if carried out through a few generations. It should not be thought that because a particular mode of eating seems adequate for an individual that it will not produce serious results in the children or grandchildren. Long ago it was said: "The fathers have eaten sour grapes and the children's teeth are set on edge."

(2) *Cooking alters the fats in food rendering them less digestible and converting some of them into poisons.*

Fatty emulsions tend to break down when exposed to heat, while fats exposed to high temperatures are made less digestible. The application of heat to fats and oils of all kinds develop free fatty acids which are not only non-assimilable, but are often poisonous.

(3) *Cooking causes a great loss of the soluble minerals in the food.*

It has been shown that when meats are boiled, from 20 to 67 per cent. of their salts are found in the broth. When these are baked 2.5 to 57.2 per cent of the mineral is found in the drippings of the meat. The meat is already predominantly acid-forming, before it is subjected to these processes.

When potatoes are peeled and soaked in cold water before boiling 38 per cent. of their mineral matter is lost. Green vegetables, when boiled and the water in which they are boiled is poured off or rejected, lose practically all of their soluble minerals. White flour, denatured corn-meal, polished rice, and all other denatured or demineralized foods have lost most of their minerals. Beans and peas, cooked in the usual manner lose much of their mineral content.

Prof. Snyder showed that 100 lbs. of cabbage contains 7.5 lbs. of solids, more than one-third of which — 2.50 or 3 lbs. — are lost when cooked in water. Spinach has a solid content of 10%, of which, nearly one-fourth is lost when cooked in water. Carrots cut into small pieces and cooked in water lose 20% to 30% of their weight. If rice is boiled and the water poured off, it loses so much of its valuable nutriments that Native Indian soldiers preferred to drink the liquid and leave the rice for the British.

Milo Hastings writing about some cooking experiments conducted in the laboratory of the department of agricultural chemistry of the University of Wisconsin, says:

"In this interesting investigation sixteen kinds of vegetables were cooked in three different ways. One lot of each vegetable was boiled in enough water to cover the cut up vegetables. A second lot was cooked in twice as much water. A third lot was steamed without coming in contact with the water except such water as would collect on the vegetables by the condensation of steam.

"The raw vegetables and those cooked in these different fashions were all carefully analyzed for the total amount of food elements, of protein and of calcium, magnesium, phosphorus and iron. The results showed that all food elements are lost to a much greater extent in boiling than in steaming.

"The general average of loss of total nutriments was three times as great in boiling as in steaming. The loss was naturally greater from the leaf vegetables than from the root vegetables. Cabbage seemed to suffer more than any other type of food in the experiment. The reason for this is that cabbage, when cut up for cooking is cut across the leaf structure. Spinach suffers less because the leaves are cooked whole. Cabbage cooked in the larger volume of water lost 60 per cent. of its total dry matter, 62 per cent. of its protein, 72 per cent. of its calcium, 60 per cent. of its phosphorus and 67 per cent. of its iron. In other words, when one eats cooked cabbage, he is getting only a third of the value of raw cabbage, to say nothing of the destruction of the vitamins. Even the steaming process of cooking cabbage gives none too good a record, as this showed losses of from 22 to 43 per cent. of the above listed food elements.

"In the case of spinach the loss of iron is of especial interest as spinach is the richest known source of food iron. Boiling in enough water to cover showed a loss of 43 per cent. of the iron in spinach. Cooking in twice that much water showed a loss of 57 per cent. of the spinach iron. Steaming showing a loss of 25 per cent. of the iron.

"Not all foods showed such large losses from the cooking, thus potatoes, even though pared showed only 9 per cent. loss of total food in boiling and only 4 per cent. loss in steaming.

"This investigation will certainly help to explain why the ordinary boiled vegetable dinner, such as is served in the unprogressive restaurants, is such a flat tasted and washed out affair. Nearly half of the valuable mineral elements have probably been poured down the sewer along with the dish water. Clever cooks make sauces for such washed-out vegetables that may compensate for the loss in tastiness of the natural ingredients, but only intelligent cooks try to prevent such losses."

Berg says: "the mere steaming of vegetables for five minutes dissolves out so large a proportion of the inorganic bases that the residue contains an excess of acids. Simultaneously the vitally important complettins (vitamins) are entirely dissolved out of the vegetables."

(4) *Cooking destroys the elementary plant form, tearing down its structure, changing its composition and bringing about certain destructive changes in the element-groupings in all foods, returning part of these elements, especially the organic salts, to their inorganic and, therefore, useless state, so that a large part of their mineral content is lost.*

Plant processes take the unorganized elements of the earth and air and organize these into related compounds, which, then, become available for animal life. Without vegetation there could be no animal life, for the reason that soil and rock are not available substances for animal replenishment. This being true, it is only natural to conclude that once plants have organized these elements into forms available for animal sustenance, any process which returns them wholly, or in part, to their primitive condition renders them, to that degree, unfit for food, and more or less disease producing. That cooking brings about more or less oxidation and disorganization in every oxidizable substance in foods of all types, admits of no doubt. When nutriment has been oxidized in the body, the resulting "ashes" cease to be usable and are eliminated. What reason have we to believe that food oxidized outside the body is more fit for use? Ralph E. Sunderland, chemist and food scientist, declares oxidation to be the chief destroyer of foods and explains the matter thus:

"The same elements (the sixteen chemical elements composing the human body), are the component parts of technically 'fertile' soil in which they are present in inorganic form and as such are not assimilable by the human body, else we could look directly to the soil for our substance. In order to convert these inorganic elements or minerals into a form which can be assimilated by the human body it is necessary for nature to create from the soil vegetation in which these same elements are present in organic form. In vegetation they remain organic until, by oxidation, they return again to their original inorganic form ready to produce more vegetation.

"True food is totally organic substance. If that organic substance is permitted to become, to any degree, inorganic, it simultaneously becomes to that degree useless as food.

THE SCIENCE AND FINE ART OF FOOD AND NUTRITION

"All organic minerals oxidize when they come in contact with oxygen and moisture. That is, they thus become inorganic again. In ordinary room-temperature the process of oxidation proceeds; but in the presence of heat oxidation is very greatly increased. Therefore, the cooking of vegetation in the presence of the oxygen of the air — the condition under which all home cooking and most commercial cooking occurs — changes a large part of what was organic and useful as food into inorganic oxides which cannot be assimilated by the human body."

French investigators found that when milk is boiled the complex calcium-magnesium carbono-phosphate it contains, is decomposed and precipitated in an insoluble form. This means that a natural organic salt which is directly assimilable and available for immediate bony growth, is changed into a form almost impossible of assimilation.

McCollum and Parsons in this country, found that the precipitated salts cling to the walls of the vessel or container so that part of them are actually eliminated from the milk. The excess of bases in the milk is thus greatly reduced. As this excess is low in even the best of milk, the double robbery of alkalies occasioned by boiling has grave consequences.

It is a fact, therefore, that the longer foods are cooked and the higher the temperature to which they are subjected, the more oxidation takes place and the greater is the destruction of the food. I may add, also, that efforts to cook out of the presence of the oxygen of the air, though not as destructive as the common forms of cooking, produces great ruin to the food. Cooking onions, cabbage, cauliflower, etc., oxidizes the sulphur. These foods should never be cooked.

(5) *Cooking renders starches less digestible and more prone to fermentation.*

Cooked starches are said, by many, to be easiest of digestion. Toasted bread is said to be dextrinized. Are these things so? It has long been known that animals digest raw starch best and that they do not fare well on cooked foods. Farmers quit cooking food for their animals years ago. Milo Hastings says:

"Closely akin to the idea of predigesting cereals by roasting and toasting them are the old notions that raw starch is indigestible and that all home cooked starchy foods need very long, tedious periods of cooking. This idea was almost universal a generation ago and is probably still taught in school text-books, which are usually a generation behind.

"I got suspicious of the idea that humans couldn't digest raw starch when I was in college and read about experiments in cooking grain for farm animals, in which the scientists proved that the cooked foods were less digestible than uncooked foods — for animals.

"The human food teachers came back by saying that man's digestive system has been changed by long ages of cooking and had lost the power to digest raw starch. So I tried it, and did my college thesis with a series of experiments on the digestion of raw versus long cooked cereal starches. I found out that my own particular digestive organs worked just like the pigs' and cows'. Worse yet for the popular theory, my mother insists that I wasn't descended from raw turnip eaters, but that our folks came over in the next ship after the Mayflower and had been cooking as long as the rest of them."

The Department of Agriculture, in Washington, conducted experiments which revealed that raw corn, rice and other starches are digested in amounts up to eight ounces, daily. Raw potatoes showed digestibility of seventy-eight per cent.

Kellogg, Langworth and Devel have each shown that raw starches digest quite easily. The Scotch Highlanders have, from time immemorial, eaten their oatmeal simply scalded. Hon. W. N. Beaver for many years a magistrate in Papua, New Guinea, says that the natives of Kiwai formerly ate their rice raw.

Raw cabbage digests in two hours whereas it requires four hours for cooked cabbage to digest. As almost everybody has difficulty with cooked cabbage and almost nobody has trouble with raw cabbage these differences are common knowledge.

High temperatures are required to change most sugars although the sugar of milk is changed in pasteurizing.

Actual feeding tests have shown that the brown crust of bread has less food value than the soggy inside. In other words the most thoroughly cooked portions of food (any food) are less valuable as food than the less cooked portions.

The facts are that cooking renders starches less digestible, while boiling them so that they are saturated with water, prevents all salivary digestion. Very little dextrinization of starch is produced by cooking. It is the office of the salivary enzyme *(ptyalin)* to perform this work and we profit by permitting salivary digestion to digest our starches. Toasting bread charcoalizes rather than dextrinizes it.

(6) *Cooking destroys the vitamins in foods and impairs or completely destroys their anti-neuritic, anti-scorbutic, etc., factors.*

Before vitamins were ever heard of and before it was found that cooking destroys or impairs vitamins, the advocates of eating all foods raw held that, besides the ordinary chemical elements in foods, there was something else which they termed life, which was destroyed by cooking. For example, Prof. Byron Tyler had an article in *The New York Herald,* Sunday, October 14, 1900 entitled "Cooked Food is Humanity's Greatest Curse," in which he proclaimed that "cooked food is dead food." That these men were right in principle is now undoubted. The "life" of foods was undoubtedly those qualities now called vitamins.

Raw food advocates also contended that man cannot use inorganic substances and that cooking returns food elements to their inorganic state. The change in the meaning or use of the word organic has resulted in much confusion, but the truth announced by our predecessors is unimpaired and cooking does, as they claimed, both disorganize food and return part of it to its inorganic (as they understood the term) state, thus making it useless to the body. There can be no doubt about this.

Although reports on this conflict considerably, cooking undoubtedly destroys vitamins. Berg says: "Since the complettins (vitamins) C and B and the anitneuritic D are readily soluble in water, they are dissolved out in the first boiling."

Vitamins are very delicate and unstable things and are lost and destroyed in many ways. Foods that are cooked and held over to the next meal lose some or all of their remaining vitamins. Dried foods have lost much of their vitamins in the drying process. Canned foods that are cooked and stored in the warehouses lose their vitamins. Canned foods and dried foods have very little to no protective power.

There are many methods of cooking. How much of the vitamin content of a particular food is lost in cooking depends upon: 1. the method of cooking employed; 2. the temperature to which the food is subjected; 3. the duration of the cooking time; 4. the abundance or relative abundance of oxygen that reaches the food while it is cooking; 5. the pressure to which it is subjected; 6. the presence or

EFFECTS OF COOKING

absence of light; 7. how much the food is cut up before being cooked; and 8. the kind of vessel in which it is cooked.

Riboflavin is destroyed in appreciable amounts when meats and vegetables are cooked in the presence of light. This vitamin is lost to but slight degree when the foods are cooked in the dark or in a closed container. The loss of pantothentic acid from cooking is moderate to slight in vegetables but is up to one third in flesh foods. Pyrodoxin losses are moderate for flesh, much smaller for vegetables and it is claimed that the amount of this vitamin is increased by cooking in a few vegetables. Cooking causes a very high loss of biotin from flesh, even as high as 72 per cent. Its loss in vegetables is reported by some investigators to be only "moderate to negligible." When vegetables are cooked they lose as high as 59 per cent of their inositol. Flesh foods loose less of this vitamin. Folic acid losses in cooking are very great for most foods. From one-third to one-half, even as much as two-thirds of niacin is lost from meats in cooking. Some investigators deny this, saying the loss of this vitamin is slight. Perhaps these differences of opinion grow out of the use of different methods of cooking in making their tests.

Studies of the foods served to patrons of restaurants have shown that the average loss of vitamin C from vegetables is 45 per cent; of thiamin is 35 per cent. Heat and cooking them in water and throwing away the water accounted for these losses. An additional loss of about 15 per cent of vitamins occurs when the vegetables are held for long periods on the steam table before serving them. Restaurant eaters are advised to concentrate on raw vegetables and to eat early before foods have stood for prolonged periods on the steam table.

Cooking foods under high pressure is rapidly destructive of their vitamins. Prolonged cooking is also very destructive of vitamins.

Quick-cooked vegetables lose less of their vitamins and minerals. The longer they are cooked and the longer they stand after cooking, the more of their value they lose. They should be eaten soon after cooking is completed.

Cooking green soy beans causes a loss of 48 per cent of their vitamin C. Sprouted soy beans lose 70 per cent of their original content of C. Thiamin and carotine are also lost in the processing and cooking of soy beans.

The antiscorbutic qualities of milk are more or less completely lost if the milk is pasteurized, boiled, condensed or dried. Dried quickly at a high temperature milk seems not to lose its antiscorbutic qualities, but it loses in food value in other ways. When it is boiled its antineuritic powers are destroyed even more rapidly than its growth-promoting powers. Barnes and Hume showed that the drying of milk reduces its antiscorbutic efficiency to about two-fifths the original. The impairment of the antiscorbutic qualtities of milk by the condensing process is great enough that young monkeys, fed on a diet of condensed milk, develop infantile scruvy. Typicail scurvy is produced in adult monkeys and guinea pigs by this same diet.

Hess and Unger found that the most actively antiscorbutic vegetables lose their efficacy upon drying. The excess of bases and the water soluble antiscorbutic vitamin C are leached out of the vegetables by the bleaching process. Soldiers fed on preserved vegetables develop scurvy. An outbreak of scurvy in a Rummelsburg orphanage was referred by Muller to the use of dried vegetables and pasteurized milk. Fresh vegetables resulted in recovery. When soup-tablets and dried vegetables predominate in the diet, malnutritional oedema develops. Canned or preserved fruits and vegetables lose their antiscorbutic qualities.

Heating white cabbage impairs its antiscorbutic quality while twenty minutes of boiling the juice of cabbage notably reduces this quality; an hour's boiling completely destroying it.

According to Givens and McClugage, finely minced raw potatoes may be boiled for fifteen minutes without appreciably affecting their antiscorbutic qualities, but these are greatly impaired by one hour's boiling. Quick cooking of foods at a high temperature brings about less damage to the food than prolonged cooking at a low temperature.

In the case of seeds, such as nuts, beans, peas, grains, etc., the germinating principle is destroyed so that cooked seed will not germinate.

The following account of some experiments with raw and roasted corn was published during World War I: "In order to find out the place of maize in war bread two French physicians carried on extensive feeding experiments with pigeons. They reached the conclusion that highly milled maize is responsible for at least three deficiency diseases.

"Weill and Mouriquand published the results of some experiments on the practicability of maize as the chief constituent of bread and the possible relations between maize diet and pellagra. The authors had already shown that decorticated (hulled) cereals, grain and legumes when fed to pigeons and fowls as an exclusive diet lead to paraplegia, paralysis and death. The cause of the latter is believed to be the depreciation of a ferment contained in the cortex of the grains, which is as essential to nutrition as sufficient calories, protein and mineral matter.

"The authors fed whole maize to a pigeon aged six months as the sole diet for a period of 240 days. The bird, shut up in its cage showed great activity and vigor. Control pigeons living exclusively on entire wheat, barley, rice and oat grains were well nourished and vigorous.

"When a mixture of whole grains was heat sterilized (120 degrees Centigrade), the birds survived ninety days and died paralized, but a certain addition of raw grains prevented beriberism. One-third part of raw grains appears to give perfect protection.

"Pigeons were now fed on decorticated, highly milled maize. The latter was refused and the birds were artificially crammed with it. After a period of sluggishness flight became impossible (thirty-third day) and death, preceded by paralysis, soon followed. Emaciation had also taken place. Hence, both cooking and decortication deprive the grains of vitamins or ferments."

Berg points out that a mixture of equal parts of soy bean, wheat, wheaten bran, sun-flower seeds, hemp seeds, and rye meal (a mixture which is perfectly adequate in the crude state), proves conspicuously inadequate after it has been made into a paste with water and then baked.

In his experiments with monkeys McCarrison showed that cooked foods, the same as deficient and ill-balanced foods, produce, within a short time, diarrhea, or actual dysentery. The monkeys so fed lost appetite, developed anemia, unhealthy skin, loss of body weight and all the vital organs began to atrophy. He pointed out that "among the pathologic processes resulting from deficient and ill-balanced food are the impairment of the protective resources of the digestive tract against infection," and added that "there is good reason to believe that the prolonged use of moderately faulty food will lead to these results as certainly as the less prolonged use of more faulty food."

(7) *Cooking drives off part of the food into the air as gasses.*

That the cooking of milk, even pasteurizing it, greatly impairs its food value is well known. Eggs and vegetables, like cabbage, cauliflower, onions, etc., rich in sulphur, have their sulphur oxidized. They should never be cooked. Phosphorus is also oxidized. The iron in food is ruined as food.

Iodine and manganese are oxidized at low temperatures.

Cooking produces changes in the sulphur content of eggs that cause it to form gas in the intestine of many who eat them. This gas is not only offensive, it is harmful.

(8) *Cooking changes the flavor and odor of foods and renders them less palatable.*

It is often argued that cooking adds to the palatability of food. This is, at least, not true with most foods and we have noticed that the others are not palatable after being cooked unless they have been flavored, spiced, sweetened, peppered, salted, etc., or have had mustard, casup, horseradish, or some form of dressing added. The fact is we are always kidding ourselves into believing that the things we are in the habit of doing are the very things we should do; that the things we have learned to like are the things that are best for us, and we consciously or unconsciously resist any proposed change, even, if there are plenty of evidences that the change would be for the better.

The relish for food is often a mere matter of habit. Those accustomed to eating cooked foods find they do not relish certain foods in their uncooked state. This calls for a reeducation of the sense of taste.

(9) *Cooking food wastes much of its food elements and renders it less nutritious.*

This is quite contrary to the popular notion. However, as we have just seen, cooking robs food of much of its value and adds nothing to it. It does not increase, but in most cases decreases, its digestibility.

The United States Department of Agriculture's Bulletin, No. 22, says: "Ladd, while connected with the New York State Station, reported analysis of cooked and uncooked clover, hay and corn meal and determination of digestibility of the same. These showed that the percentage of albuminoids and fat and the relative digestibility of the albuminoids were more or less diminished by cooking. The experiments made by our experiment stations in preparing food have been mostly with pigs. At least thirteen separate series of experiments in different parts of this country have been reported on the value of cooking or steaming food for pigs. In these cooked or steamed barley meal, corn-meal, and shorts; whole corn, potatoes, and a mixture of peas, barley and rye have been compared with the same food uncooked (usually dry). In ten of these trials there has not only been no gain from cooking, but there has been a positive loss, i. e., the amount of food required to produce a pound of gain was larger when the food was cooked than when it was fed raw, and in some cases the difference has been considerable."

Was not Dr. Oswald right, then, when he declared: "For even the most approved modes of grinding, bolting, leavening, cooking, spicing, heating and freezing our food are, strictly speaking, abuses of our digestive organs." And not of our digestive organ only, but of the whole body. Cooking is the oldest and most widely used method of denaturing our foods.

TARS

Tars are complex heterogeneous substances that are derived from a variety of sources. Any organic compound that is subjected to great heat, as in frying or roasting, undergoes decomposition with the formation of highly complex black tar. Most people are familiar with the tar formed in the burning of tobacco in cigarette, pipe and cigar. The bowl of the pipe and the pipe stem become clogged with the sticky, and foul smelling stuff.

Tar forms in coffee while it is being roasted; it forms in the cereals, beans and fruits when these are roasted in making coffee-substitutes. Coffee drinkers and drinkers of coffee substitutes daily take tar into their bodies just as the smoker gets tar into his mouth, throat, lungs and blood.

THE SCIENCE AND FINE ART OF FOOD AND NUTRITION

If potatoes, beans, peas, etc., become dry in cooking and get scorched, tar forms. Scorched toast has tar in it. In frying potatoes, eggs, meat and other foods tar is often formed unless great care is exercised not to overheat these foods. Meats roasted in an oven that is too hot get black on the outside. Tar is formed.

Tar is an irritant. It is one of the irritants that is known to result in the formation of tumors and cancers. It would be profitable to know what percentage of the tumors and cancers that exist today owe their origin to the tars taken into the bodies of almost everyone who eats cooked foods and drinks coffee or coffee substitutes. Living in smoky cities and inhaling the smoke takes tar into the lungs. This as much as tobacco smoke, may contribute to the production of cancer of the lungs.

COOKING AND DIGESTIBILITY

The manner in which foods are cooked alters their digestibility. Cabbage, for example, cooked in one way is easily digested; cooked in another manner is almost indigestible.

Much of the indigestibility of cooked foods results not so much from the cooking, *per se*, as from the mixtures that are jumbled together to cook. Take the Southern practice of cooking beans, greens, cabbage, etc., with a large piece of fat, salt bacon, as an example of concocting indigestible mixtures; or the method of frying potatoes (starches) in fat.

COOKERS

The waterless cooker is the best cooker that has been devised. This should not be confused with the pressure cooker. Rapidly growing in popularity, this expensive and dangerous (they sometimes explode) pressure cooker is the worst cooker ever invented. Cooking foods under high pressure rapidly destroys their vitamins. The old fireless cooker that cooked foods at a low temperature over a long period, was a very destructive cooker. Frying pans and boilers are among the worst cooking utensils. Several different types of waterless cooker are available. The reader may choose his own. I have no prejudices against the aluminum cookers, but if the reader is afraid of this form of cooker, the stainless steel cooker is very efficient.

EFFECTS OF COOKING

FROZEN FOODS

Frozen foods are new but are rapidly becoming very popular. The deep-freeze refrigerator that enables people to freeze their foods in their own homes, is also becoming popular. Is this the great boon to mankind that the promoters of the frozen food industry claim?

Some foods are completely ruined by being frozen. Frozen lettuce, frozen bananas, frozen oranges and many frozen greens are completely unfitted for use as food. It is inevitable that all foods shall be more or less damaged by the freezing process, despite the claims to the contrary. Quick freezing does cause loss of some of the vitamins. Although it is common to deny that freezing causes a loss of vitamins, it is readily admitted by the defenders of the process that the process of thawing out the foods before using them causes considerable vitamin losses. If, then, they are cooked, there are greater losses. Frozen foods should be used when fresh foods are not available, yet I see people buying frozen corn or frozen strawberries, etc., while these foods are in season.

Uncooked Foods
CHAPTER XXVIII

The *Journal of Health* in its issue of May 1833 and the *Moral Reformer* June 1835, affirmed as a general principle that no person, whether gentleman, farmer or tradesman, woman or child, could eat to advantage, or even with impunity, vegetable matter which had not been softened and changed by cooking processes.

People were not only afraid of plant foods in those days, but they were especially afraid of them in their uncooked or natural state. It was a day of much cooking — vegetables were par boiled and then boiled again. The water in which they were par boiled was thrown away. Little was left for the eater but an almost foodless husk which had been reduced to a mush that required practically no chewing.

Graham on the other hand, laid down the principle that man's "physiological interests would be best sustained by those vegetable products which require no culinary change, or cooking." He thought that cooking not only reduces the value of the foods, but that it actually reduces the digestive powers of those who eat cooked foods. Then he said: "It may therefore, be laid down as a general law, that all processes of cooking, or artificial preparations of food by fire, are, in themselves, considered with reference to the very highest and best condition of human nature, in some degree detrimental to the physiological and psychological interests of man."

Cooking, the most universally employed process of denaturing our foods, is in every way injurious to foods and to man. Whether we cook plant substances or animal products, cooking is ruinous to the properties of the food. The fluids of the plant are, in great part, lost in cooking. With these go the minerals and vitamins of the plant. With them also go the natural flavors and aromas of the food. The nutritive value of foods are impaired or destroyed by cooking and their digestibility is lowered.

We must tap the richest sources of vitality which Nature posseses and turn them to valuable account. We must supply ourselves and our children with superior nutritive substances and these can only come from nature. Not to the chemist, nor to the food manufacturer, must we go for superior nutrition; but to the original source of nutrition. In nature's products are the requisites of superior nutrition. All the sources of vigor and all the means of resisting pathogenetic ("disease" producing) causes are found in natural products as these come from the hands of nature.

In fresh fruits and green vegetables and nuts, or the juices of these, are all the minerals and vitamins and high-grade proteins, and other substances needed by the growing, developing human body to bring it to a state of physical, mental and moral perfection and to maintain it in this state indefinitely.

All the virtues of foods are retained when they are eaten uncooked and they not only protect against the causes of disease, but they add to the joys of life, enhance bodily vigor, and give that strength to the sexual powers that means better offspring.

Fresh foods, green foods, whole, natural foods, unprocessed foods, unrefined foods, foods that have not lost their substances nor had their values deteriorated by heating, drying, cooking, canning, and refining processes are full of the elements of superior nutrition.

Graham wrote: "It is nearly certain, as I have already stated, that the primitive inhabitants of the earth ate their food with very little if any artificial preparations. The various fruits, nuts, seeds, roots, and other vegetable substances on which they subsisted, were eaten by them in their natural state, with no other grinding than that which was done by the teeth."

It is obvious to even the least intelligent that animals in a state of nature subsist exclusively and entirely on an uncooked dietary. It is equally as obvious that man subsisted entirely and wholly on uncooked foods before he learned the use of fire. We have no means of knowing how long man lived on the earth before some enterprising young genius learned to make fire, nor how long it was thereafter before he began to apply fire to his foods. I think that we will not go wrong in assuming that the use of fire has persisted but a moment in his history.

Prof. Jordon, of the University of Chicago, says that the people of the stone age were unacquainted with the art of cooking, but ate their foods in their natural state. Animals and, to a large extent, so-called primitive peoples, take their food directly from the hands of nature and eat it unchanged.

The so-called primitive tribes live largely or wholly upon uncooked foods. The Esquamaux will catch a fish and eat him without taking the trouble to first put him to death. He will kill a walrus and feast off his fresh warm flesh at once. The Hawaiian will wade out into the sea with his harpoon or spear and dive down and spear a fish or catch some other sea creature, come up and eat him without troubling to first get onto the shore. Some African tribes will catch a grass hopper or beetle off a tree and eat it whole on the spot.

The fact that primitive man ate his foods uncooked is evidence that raw foods are adequate to support life. Indeed there is much evidence to show that certain qualities possessed by raw foods are indispensible to life. It is quite probable that the enzymes of raw foods are of use to the body. Research may show that plant enzymes are the sources of animal enzymes.

My esteemed friend and erstwhile co-worker, Dr. B. S. Claunch, said in an excellent talk on *How Disease is Built*, delivered at Sorosis Hall, San Francisco, Dec. 10, 1922: "Thre are nearly 700,000 species of animal life, and everyone of these species except man — the highest — lives exclusively on live, uncooked, organic food. No other animal except man eats devitalized foods that have been rendered inorganic —reduced from their organic structure to dead, inorganic substances. °°°" "As I stated before, animals of every kind live on uncooked food with the exception of man. Incidentally, man is the only species in the entire animal kingdom that is sick, with the exception of a few that have their diet prescribed for them by man — domesticated animals. They are sick the same as man, because man supplies their food and directs their eating habits instead of permitting them to select their own foods.

"Cooking foods and processing them — refining, sterilizing, preserving, pickling, flavoring and coloring — all tend to devitalize them. When such substances are eaten — these are practically the only kinds obtainable today in the modern eating places — about one-fourth in unchanged. The nourishment obtained from the one-fourth keeps you alive for a few years; the poison you get from the other three-fourths keeps you sick most of the time."

Not a single truth in these statements of Dr. Claunch's is injured in any way by the fact that he has repudiated them. No truth is impaired by the desertion of its advocates. The fact that Dr. Claunch now advocates, or did, for a while, advocate an almost exclusive meat diet, and this well cooked, does not alter the fact that *homo (SAP)iens* is the only species on earth which eats cooked food. Nor does it change the fact that cooking and processing foods injures

UNCOOKED FOODS

and impairs them. When a man changes his mind it does not change the facts.

Cooking utensils only made their appearance a few thousand years ago and for a long time only some foods were cooked. During the Dark Ages the Black Art of Cooking was "improved" and popularized and the custom of cooking spread to such an extent that those who ate uncooked foods came to be looked upon as savages, but little above cattle. Cooking became popular during the thousand year reign of anti-naturalism, which cost the human race so much and yielded so little, and was popularized by the anti-natural dogmas of that time. The germ theory gave an added reason for thoroughly cooking everything we eat, for it taught us to thus kill the "pathogenic microbes" in and on our foods.

Graham declares: "If man subsisted wholly on uncooked food, the undepraved integrity of his appetite, his thorough mastication and slow swallowing, and his simple meal, would greatly serve to prevent over-eating, and thus save him from the mischievous effects of one of the most destructive causes operating in civic life. *** Whatever may be the kind of food on which man subsists when the artificial preparation is made as far as possible in accordance with the physiological laws of constitution and relation established in his nature, and is of simple character which leaves the proportions of nutritious and innutritious properties as nature combined them, or in the general average conforms in this respect to nature, and effects little change in the nutritious principles, and retains the natural requisition for the function of the teeth, and thus secures the proper chewing of the food, and the mixing of it with the solvent fluid of the mouth, and the swallowing of it slowly, the artificial process of preparation militates very little, if at all, against any of the physiological interests of the body. But if the preparation concentrates the nutriment properties, and destroys the true proportion between the bulk and nourishment, and effects improper changes and combinations in the nutriment elements, and does away with the necessity for mastication, and presents the food in too elevated temperature and enables us to swallow it too rapidly with little or no exercise of the teeth, and without properly mixing it with the saliva, the artificial process of cooking is decidedly and often exceedingly inimical, not only to the physiological interests of the alimentary organs, but the whole human system. And let it ever be remembered, that, as a general rule, the process of cooking, when regulated in the very best manner, cannot so perfectly adapt the substances which it is necessary to cook, to the physiological properties and powers of the human body, as to render them equally conducive to the highest and best conditions of man, with those substances which are naturally adapted to the alimentary wants. And, therefore, as already stated, all processes of cooking, or artificial preparation of food by fire — considered in reference to the very highest capabilities of human nature — must be regarded as in some measure an evil."

Inherent in Graham's views and principles, though in the very nature of things, this could not have been known at that time, was the saving of the minerals and vitamins of foods by eating them as nature produced them without, first, processing, refining and cooking them. No doubt it was this fact that led Prof. Stiles to declare, when the discovery of vitamins was first announced, that it was merely a re-statement of Graham's views.

We do well to remember that chemistry was a young science or hoped-to-be-a-science, and food chemistry was not yet born when Graham penned these lines. He covered all the ground in a general, and in some particulars, a vague way, which we of today, with greater knowledge, are permitted to cover more in detail. But it is a standing monument to the genius of the man that, with all our increased knowledge of foods and their relation to the body, we can only bow to him and say, "Yes, Mr. Graham, you are right." For Graham's book, now nearly a hundred years old, is up to date, and in some respects, he is ahead of us yet. If you want to know nature cure, read Graham. If you want to know natural hygiene, read Graham. If you want the newer knowledge of nutrition, read Graham. His was a master mind. He saw clearly then what the orthodox world is just beginning to see.

Graham said: "If man were to subsist wholly on alimentary substances in their natural state, or without any artificial preparation, by cooking, he would be obliged to use his teeth freely, and by so doing not only preserve his teeth from decay; but at the same time and by the same means, he would thoroughly mix his food with the solvent fluid of his mouth. *** Again, if man were to subsist wholly on uncooked food, he would never suffer from the improper temperature of his aliment. *** If man were to subsist entirely on food in a natural state, he would never suffer from concentrated aliment *** If man subsisted wholly on uncooked food, he would not only be preserved from improper concentrations, but also from pernicious combinations of alimentary substances *** it is uncontrovertable that the alimentary organs of man and of all other animals can digest one kind of food at a time, better than a mixture of different kinds. ***"

If we cut this up we find that:

(1) Uncooked food, requiring more chewing, supply the teeth with much needed exercise.

(2) The necessary chewing insures proper insalivation.

(3) Uncooked food would preserve the teeth and stomach from the injury produced by hot foods.

(4) Uncooked foods would possess the proper proportion of "nutritious and innutritious (bulk) matter" to which "the anatomical construction and physiological powers of the alimentary organs of the human body are constitutionally adapted."

(5) Uncooked foods tend to prevent "pernicious combinations."

(6) Mono-trophic meals are the most easily digested.

Today we may add the following other virtues of the uncooked diet:

(7) Uncooked foods possess their vitamins and complettins, enzymes, salts, acids, carbohydrates, proteins and fats in the organic and unimpaired state in which nature produces them.

(8) The necessity for chewing them insures tasting them to the fullest, and this assures proper adaptation of digestive juices to the character of the food.

(9) Chewing and tasting the food tends also to prevent over eating.

(10) Uncooked foods are not so easily adulterated as are the canned, pickled, embalmed foods so largely eaten today.

(11) Uncooked foods do not ferment so rapidly.

(12) Uncooked foods, if spoiled, cannot be "camouflaged" and passed off on us as good food, as cooked foods can be.

(13) The uncooked diet saves time, food and labor in preparation.

Graham and his co-workers had placed great emphasis upon the value of fruits, vegetables and whole grains in their natural, *i.e.*, unprocessed and uncooked, state. The "raw food movement" may rightly be said to have been started by Graham. Though it never made great headway until after the discovery of the value of minerals in food and, later, the discovery of vitamins. There were three thousand "raw fooders" in Chicago alone in 1900.

Uncooked fruits, nuts, vegetables and whole grains were not merely "protective" foods to Graham, Trall, Allcott, Densmore, Page and others; they were nutritive; indeed they represented the best and highest form of nutritive material. Dr. Trall proclaimed (1860) all fruits and vegetables to be protective, by which he did not intend to detract from their nutritive qualities. The world has been a long time discovering what Graham knew — namely, that cooking impairs or destroys the protective and nutritive values of foods.

It is almost axiomatic that fruits, nuts and vegetables are the only foods that can be relished raw. Other foods hardly belong to man's natural diet. Buying fruits and vegetables to provide minerals and vitamins for yourself and your family and then destroying the vitamins and extracting the minerals and throwing these away in the process of preparing them fails of its purpose. Only when you eat your fruit uncooked and consume big salads of uncooked vegetables can you be sure of obtaining a sufficient supply of minerals and vitamins.

The "orthodox" medical world became so frightened over germs a few years after Graham's death that they insisted on thoroughly cooking everything, to destroy germs; while their preoccupation with the calorie value of foods caused them to deny that fruits and vegetables have any food value. No wonder Prof. Stiles saw in the vitamin announcement, a re-statement of Graham's principles.

The nearer their natural and unchanged state our foods are eaten the better for us. The natural "affinity" existing between the needs of our cells and the nutritional elements in natural foods supplies us with an infallible guarantee that we will get the needed salts, vitamins, and other food elements from natural foods. All true foods are more tasty "raw"· than cooked. Cooked food, sans seasoning, are flat and insipid, as well as less nutritive.

Eugene Christian says: "We have in this country hundreds of articles of food which can be most advantageously used without cooking; yet the cook intrudes his art, bakes, boils, stews, broils, and heats these things, until their original elements are wholly changed, until many of them are rendered almost totally valueless.

"Thus robbed of their elmentary and delicious flavors, the cook endeavors to make them appeal to the sense of taste by mixing, jumbling together, spicing, and using decoctions called extracts, the properties of which he knows absolutely nothing, until the original substance is so disguised that it cannot be recognized in taste, color and flavor."

In one of his splendid *Health and Diet Bulletins,* Ralph E. Sunderland says: "These are true foods because their original organic nature has not been changed, by oxidation, to inorganic status. Only organic substance is food. No inorganic substance is food because it is not assimilable in the body. This is a law. Every cooking process which involves exposure of the original organic food substance to the oxygen of the air fosters oxidation. This is true whether the cooking is done at home or in some factory. There must be life in food. Life in food is expressed only by its organic nature or condition. There is no life in oxidized (inorganic) substance. Upon this foundation all scientific diet teaching must rest."

RAW OR UNCOOKED?

In its original sense "raw" meant "unfinished." We speak of "raw materials" and the "finished product." It originally had no reference to cooked or uncooked foods. Custom, however, or usage makes language and since usage now sanctifies the use of the word "raw" in the sense of "uncooked" we shall accept this usage and so employ the word in this book. But let us keep ever in our minds that nature finishes or perfects her foods and they require no fixing to complete them.

"Foods that have been ripened and brought to a state of maturity by nature cannot consistently be called 'raw'," says Eugene Christian. "Think of applying this ugly word to a luscious bunch of purple grapes swinging to and fro in bowers of green. Or to a hickory nut that has ripened in the top of a mountain tree, whose life-giving properties have been filtered through a hundred feet of clean, white wood. Or to a delicious apple, or peach, reddened, ripened and finished — nursed in the lap of nature, rocked in her etherial cradle, and kissed from the odorous blossoms of infancy on to maturity by the soft beams of the life-giving sun, ready for use; they are perfect, they are not raw, they are done; and when they are cooked they are undone. They are as far removed from their finished condition as if they were green or but half grown."

DEFENSE OF COOKING

Cooking is claimed to be a predigesting process; it renders foods more digestible and thus saves the energies of the body. We are advised to avail ourselves of the advantages of this "pre-digesting" process. Invalids are especially admonished to eat well-cooked, toasted, dextrinized, etc., foods.

It has been previously shown that cooking does not pre-digest our foods. With rare exceptions, such as that of egg white, foods are rendered less digestible by cooking and all of them are rendered less nutritious.

But if this claim were true, there still seems to be no reason why we should cook our foods. Why we should substitute the wasteful processes of cooking for the conserving processes of digestion.

We should certainly avoid "pre-digested" foods. Our organs of digestion are made to perform the work of digestion and we should look with much suspicion upon all substitutes for these. If we do the work of the digestive organs for them, we weaken them and their functions. I do not believe that we can strengthen a weak digestion by eating so-called predigested foods, any more than we can strengthen a weak arm by refusing to use it.

The digestive juices are the natural food solvents and instead of weakening these by resort to half-foods, so-called pre-digested foods, and by resort to drugs and various "aids to digestion," we should correct the causes of impaired digestion and feed naturally.

If there is a need for rest of these organs and functions, give them a rest; but do not try to do their work for them. To "nourish" a sick body on "pre-digested," denatured products will not produce health and strength.

ECONOMY OF UNCOOKED FOODS

A raw food diet saves time, labor and money. It is estimated, and the estimate is probably approximately correct, that "as compared with cooked, it only takes about half the quantity of uncooked food to sustain life." The digestibility of foods is not increased by cooking; but their food values are greatly reduced. Cooked foods do not nourish the body as well as uncooked foods. It is impossible to nourish the body on a diet consisting exclusively of thoroughly cooked foods. We subsist largely on the uncooked foods in our diet and on the uncooked or but partially cooked portions of our cooked foods. Cooking renders a large part of food valueless as food. He who lives on uncooked foods may, therefore, live cheaper at the same time he lives better.

The Esquimaux, in his remote haunts, lives largely on a flesh diet. He eats practically the whole of the animal and eats it raw. He catches up a fish out of the water and eats it "blood-raw" with as much relish as his civilized brother eats a piece of candy. But where he attempts to live on a diet of cooked meat, his health and strength fail and he becomes diseased.

The un-fired diet eliminates entirely the fuel bill in as far as this relates to cooking. But of greater importance than this is the saving of the time and energy of women. "When the house is provided," says Dr. Christian, "and the woman who has dreamed of a true home is settled therein, it gradually dawns upon her that instead of being a queen, she is an imprisoned vassal. She finds she must stand over a minature furnace for an hour in the morning and breathe the poisonous odor of broiling flesh, and spend another hour among the grease and slime of pots and dishes, instead of occupying that time walking in the life-giving sunlight and drinking in nature's purifying air.

"She soon realizes that the fires of the morning are hardly out until those of the noon are kindled and the labors from luncheon often lap into the evening, and those of evening far into the night. The throne over which she dreamed of wielding the queenly sceptre has been transformed into a fiery furnace, gilded with greasy pots and plates, blood and bones, over which she has unfurled the dishrag, and by the common custom of her country, it waves over her helpless head as an ensign of her rank and profession, under which she is really a slave."

She is forever washing dishes, greasy dishes, in the sink. She spends six to eight hours a day preparing meals and washing dishes. The realization of this great waste of human time and labor was forcibly brought home to me during World War I. I served for seven months in a kitchen where we fed over two hundred men three times a day. We had a mess sergeant, several cooks, a dining room orderly and several kitchen police. The work started before dawn when the other soldiers were all asleep and ended late in the evening about the time the other men were ready to retire. We spent our time spoiling good food or further spoiling foods that had already been greatly spoiled at the factory or cannery, and in washing greasy pots, pans, dishes, etc. An army of men was required to feed the army.

Hotels, restaurants and house-wives have spent ages in competition with each other to see which could prepare the greatest variety of tempting, but foodless dishes, with which to tickle the palates, usually the perverted palates, of the eating world. I am not alone, however, when I say that experience has shown that men are usually more willing to accept a dietary reform than women. Women want to "fix" things and mix things and prepare that which appeals to the eye. For ages the kitchen has been the chief meidum of expression for her and it was through the art of cooking that she expressed herself. She finds it hard to break away from her traditional channels of expression. Dietary reform is greatly handicapped by the opposition of those who would profit most by it.

OBJECTIONS TO THE UNFIRED DIET

It is frequently objected that "prolonged maintenance of the body in a state of health and fitness on a diet of raw foods is possible only when the foods are judiciously chosen." The same is true, but to a greater extent, of cooked foods.

Dr. Kellogg says: "A person who desires to live upon a raw diet, in arranging his bill of fare cannot base his selection upon the supposition that all raw foods are complete nutriments, but must possess a sufficient knowledge of the newer facts pertaining to nutrition to enable him to make such combinations of food stuffs as will constitute an aggregate complete in all the elements required for perfect nutrition and in adequate quantities."

This fact is equally true if one is going to eat a diet of cooked foods. The cooked diet must also be made up of "such combinations of foodstuffs as will constitute an aggregate complete in all the elements required for perfect nutrition and in adequate quantities." I know of no one who claims or supposes that "all raw foods are complete nutriments." But the newer facts of nutrition prove beyond a doubt that it is much easier to be properly nourished on a raw than on a cooked diet.

There never was a time when any portion of the human race lived almost entirely on cooked foods, nor was there ever a time, until within very recent times, when a large part of the race subsisted chiefly on cooked foods.

Well does Adolph Just say in his *Return to Nature,* "If you are well and would keep well, why not listen to Nature's appeal? Think you; were there no fine men and women roaming about the earth thousands and thousands of years even before the discovery of fire, and before either the first chef or medico was evolved? Will you believe that nature, at the outset, overlooked the matter of man's health, and that he remained an outcast in the plan of things, until, by his own wit, pills, drug-lists, and patent foods had brought him his salvation? Man's food was sun-cooked in those ancient days, and the sun cooks our food at the present time. Artificial cooking is no blessing to mankind. It may be accepted as an axiom that cooking kills; and there is a vast variety of natural foods — beautiful, sweet-scented, and delicious — on which we may draw both for our sustenance and for the mere pleasure of the palate."

An objection has been raised to the use of uncooked foods in Northern climates because the "shipped-in green-picked fruits and sprayed vegetables come devitalized during the winter season." That the people of the North do not always have access to the best of green or fresh foods in the winter months is true enough, but this is all the more reason why they should consume them in the uncooked state. Cooking these fruits and vegetables wilts and devitalizes them still more. Cooking them renders them less nourishing than they are when purchased. The less suited are these foods for nutritive purposes the greater is the need to avoid further reduction of their nutritive values. It is necessary to preserve to the utmost, all the food values they possess and not destroy them in any manner whatsoever.

Rather than a "good five cent cigar," what this country needs is a great teacher, one who, with the eyes of a superior being, can see the roots of our troubles, the causes of men's perennial lassitude, constant seeking after stimulants, the causes of their deterioration, weakness, decrepitude, impotency and suffering; one who possesses a deep knowledge of the secrets of nature, who knows the almost magic virtues of fresh fruits, uncooked vegetables and nuts, and who can stir our people as no man ever stirred them before.

Piles of shattered pottery, superfluous stew pans, crushed baking ovens, and the ash-heaps left from the burning of "food" factories, refineries, etc., would be found in the wake of such a saviour of our nation. Our people must be made drunk with enthusiasm and wild with eagerness for a new life based on a new and superior nutrition. The man who can stir this nation to its roots and bring it back to a pristine state of health and perfection will deserve to rank among the world's greatest men.

Salads
CHAPTER XXIX

Horses cannot exist on a diet of grains alone. They need an abundance of green food (grass) along with their grains. Grass is their salad. Worn-out horses placed on salad (the grass in the pasture) and permtited to roam at pleasure soon get to racing, rearing and kicking just from exuberance of spirits.

Bamboo shoots, young, tender and easily digested, form a large part of the diet of the gorilla and other anthropoid apes. These form for the apes, a wonderfully appropriate vegetable salad. Such shoots, or the ordinary, softer green vegetables and roots, taken as salads, are essential to good nutrition, the finest development and the highest degree of health in man.

Gramnivora in nature do not live exclusively on grains, but have great liking for young and tender green stuff, being especially fond of the fresh shoots of newly germinated plants. Many worms, insects, snails, etc., do the same. Go where we will, the need for the young green plant is evident.

Until the chemists discovered vitamins no one, except the students of nature and natural feeding practices, knew just why the gentle old family cow would occasionally smash fences to get into the growing corn or across on the other side where the grass was green or the alfalfa was deep. Give the old cow access to plenty of green vegetation and an abundance of grains and she will eat heaviest of the green vegetation. It was not known until recently why children would snitch apples or other fruit while the owner's back was turned. The instincts that drives all animal life to seek elemental needs were not understood and could not be understood under the older dietary theories.

Man requires his daily supply of green grass as much as does the horse, cow, ape, bird, etc. Not the small salad (two leaves of wilted lettuce, a thin slice of a half-ripened tomato, a radish and a spoonful of foul-tasting dressing) served in the restaurants, but a large bowl of salad each day is required by every one. Since the days of Graham the people of this country have learned to eat a lot of fruits and vegetables, but we could well afford to eat more.

SALADS

Vitamins are just now the only food elements that occupy the mono-idead minds of the gum-willies, just as the calorie was once the god of their worship, just as dextrinized bread was once the one great idea in their feeble heads. If the medical man condescends to notice minerals at all he is likely to prescribe calcium lactate, citrate of iron, and other inorganic salt preparations and ignore the organic salts of fruits and vegetables.

Under the tutelage of the *Hygienists* the people learned to eat raw foods in spite of the dire warnings of the profession. Soon raw lettuce and celery were served in the hotels and restaurants and in the dining cars on the trains. In the homes of the country raw foods were growing more popular. Everywhere more and more of such foods were raised and marketed. Today thousands of train loads a year of lettuce are shipped all over the country. The same is true of celery and other foods. Raw foods are eaten today, of all places, in the homes of the physicians, themselves. What's more, instead of the people dying from typhoid and other "germ disease" as a consequence of eating these "indigestible," "foodless" and germ-laden foods, they actually recovered from diseases that the medical profession had pronounced *incurable*. Something had to be done. They sent their researchers to the laboratories to find out why the "quacks" were successful where they failed miserably. These gentlemen soon came up with the discovery that these raw fruits and vegetables are richly supplied with vitamins and that these vitamins are responsible for the recoveries. Wonder of wonders! These vitamins enabled physicians to so far forget their bacteriophobia that they actually ventured to eat a leaf of raw lettuce! Some of them actually ate apples that had not been baked.

Fruits and vegetable salads provide in delicious form the mineral and vitamin-bearing foods so essential to good nourishment. Instead of emphasizing fresh fruits and raw vegetables, the medical man and his satelites in the various schools of so-called healing, together with the professional dietitians and the bio-chemists, are likely to emphasize liver, liver extract, cod-liver oil, halibut liver oil, kidney, milk, eggs and yeast. He will also prescribe synthetic "vitamins."

So far as the medical profession as a whole is concerned and so far as the general public is concerned, there is an inexcusable lag between accumulated and proven facts and principles of nutrition and the actual use of this knowledge. The newer knowledge of nutrition is not much used by the people and their physicians. In the hospitals physicians are still feeding their patients as they did fifty years ago. The printed diets they give to their patients are not based on proven dietary principles and are in almost every instance inadequate.

Up until very recently the medical profession advised the people never to eat raw vegetables or raw fruit, because of the germs on these. But a few years ago a real "scientific" physician would scarcely have dared hold a head of lettuce in his hands without rubber gloves, if, indeed, he could have been induced to touch it, or even go into the same room with it. All of a sudden they made the discovery that raw vegetables and fruits carry vitamins and that it is the vitamins in these foods that restore health and prevent sickness.

The medical profession had urged — even coerced — the people to "eat plenty of good, nourishing food," not germ-infested vegetables, and had overworked the underweight bogey so long that the frenzy caused by food debauchery had to be counteracted. At medical meetings a few physicians began to speak out against the "meat, bread, potato diet" with its accessories, such as "sweet desserts, butter, cream, sugar and mayonnaise, which conduces to degenerative diseases."

Will physicians urge people to eat raw vegetables and fruits, will they urge a large daily salad of raw vegetables? They will not. There are too many people who could trace this advice to its origin and this would embarrass the "scientific" crowd. They will have the chemists analyze the quintessence of life out of all foods and label it vitamin and urge the people to have their vitamin pills each day. They will classify their extracted and synthetic vitamins along with pepsin, inglucin, insulin, calories, gland extracts, etc. They will continue to advise food-drunken humanity to: "Eat as you please; food, tobacco and other habits have nothing to do with health."

The profession has learned how to talk loud and long about many things. Their loquacity is an acquired habit. Their effort is to see how much they can say about something of which they know nothing. Their long-winded talk about vitamins, food blends, diet, etc., may lead the layman to believe they know something about nutritional science. It is a mistake. Food knowledge has not penetrated beneath the epidermis of the profession and everyday physicians may be heard to advise patients to eat whatever they please; that food has nothing to do with health.

SALADS

The thousands of acres of vegetables in cultivation in this country, the mile upon mile of fruit orchards that exist to supply an ever growing demand for fruits — these things did not result from the work of the regular physicians, but from the efforts of the "irregulars," the fanatics, faddists, quacks. These men educated the people into a knowledge of the value of these foods at a time when the regular profession was declaring that such foods were without food value and were dangerous in their raw states beacuse of the germs they carry. The medical profession gave no attention to diet until popular sentiment compelled them to stop fumigating long enough to at least give lip service to the subject.

The ignorant person may continue to neglect these foods, referring to them as "rabbit foods," but intelligent people are no longer misled by such disparaging expressions. Their value and the necessity for consuming them daily are no longer doubted.

The old style of eating caused dullness and drowsiness in people. It caused them to develop diabetes, Bright's disease, tuberculosis, gastric ulcer, hardening of the arteries, appoplexy, gall-stones, etc. For the distress caused by such eating, our fathers took bitters, pepsin, and baking soda. The newer style of eating results in diabetes, tuberculosis, heart disease, hardening of the arteries, gastric ulcer, nervous diseases, etc. For the distress caused by present-day eating, people consume tons and tons of alkaseltzer, Bell-ans, Tums, baking soda.

WHAT IS A SALAD?

Salad is from the Latin meaning salt and true salads are abundant in organic salts. They are also abundant in vitamins. They are of prime importance and should not be neglected. Such salads as potato salad, shrimp salad, etc., are not to be classed with green vegetable salads and are not substitutes therefor. Fruit salads are usually made of canned fruits, hence are not true salads. Cooked salads do not serve the true function of a salad. A macaroni salad is a travesty on the fair name of salads.

Dr. Maurice Shefferman very appropriately calls potato salad, tuna fish salad, salmon salad, chicken salad and like concoctions, "unreal salads." He says they are "concoctions" devised by "old-time tea-room operators" that have been appropriated by the restaurant and drug-store counters. He says a restaurant owner once told him: "You can make a much better chicken salad out of pork than you can from veal."

The restaurant and drug store salads commonly consist of a small quantity of tuna or salmon or some similar substance, with chopped celery, cole slaw, and mayonnaise, a couple of leaves of wilted lettuce, vinegar, salt, with, often, the addition of various spices. French dressing may be used instead of mayonnaise.

The usual vegetable salad served in hotels, restaurants and drug stores consists of two leaves of wilted lettuce, one or two thin slices of a half-ripe tomato, a spoonful of greasy dressing and a radish or a pickled olive. Such a salad is not worthy the name and, even if it were good, would not meet the salad needs of a canary. The *Hygienic* rule for eating salads is to eat a tubful of it.

A few simple rules for salad making should be observed:

1. *Salads should be made of fresh vegetables*. If these can be had direct from the garden, this is better. In purchasing vegetables in the market for salads, choose the freshest and crispest vegetables obtainable. Wilted and shrunken vegetables have lost both palatableness and food value.

The green, outer leaves of plants—those parts that are exposed to the sunlight in growing—make the finest salads. Leaf lettuce is superior to head lettuce. Green celery is superior to white. Lettuce, celery, cucumbers, tomatoes, sweet peppers, etc. make excellent salad vegetables.

2. *Salad vegetables to be avoided*. Spinach, swiss chard, beet tops, and rhubarb should be seldomly used if at all because of their high content of oxalic acid, a calcium antagonist. Bitter cabbage, endive and escarole should also be avoided because of their concentrated acids and irritant contents. Parsley, watercress, chives, scallions, onions, leeks, radishes, garlic, and mature mustard greens should similarly be avoided as irritants, most containing mustard oil.

3. *Vegetables and fruits used in salads should be well cleaned*. Products, such as apples, that have been sprayed with arsenic, should be carefully washed and dried. Delicate green leaves, after washing, should be permitted to dry slightly before using. Carrots, beets, etc., should not be scraped, or peeled before using, but should be carefully scrubbed with a brush.

4. *Salad vegetables should not be broken, diced, hashed, cut, sliced, etc*. This causes vital losses by oxidation.

While we have long observed that foods lose their palatableness and undergo obvious changes upon being cut, sliced, shredded, etc., as a result of oxidation, only recently has it been shown that these measures, so popular with those who like their salads shredded and their peaches sliced, cause a loss and destruction of vitamins.

SALADS

The results of some of these latest tests will help us to appreciate the value of natural foods in their natural state.

Analyses for vitamin C showed that approximately 10% of this is lost during the six minutes required to shred the cabbage and an additional loss of 4% occurs in the 10 minutes required to mix a dressing for the salad. The additional loss when the cabbage was chopped rather than shredded was 4%. The finer the cabbage is shredded or chopped and the longer it stands before being eaten, the greater is the loss of this vitamin.

Dr. Fredrick F. Tisdall of Toronto, Canada reported astonishing losses of vitamin C from foods as a result of processing. His report was made before the American Institute of Nutrition. He says the mere act of grating either raw apples or raw potatoes causes a complete disappearance of vitamin C. The mere act of chewing these foods causes the destruction of half their vitamin C. "Thank God for the tomato and the orange!" he exclaimed. "They don't act in the same way."

Other investigators reported comparable losses from other foods. For example, when Savoy cabbage is chopped it loses much of its *ascorbic acid*. Even the type of chopper makes a difference. One chopper destroyed thirty per cent of this vitamin in a few minutes, while a different type of machine destroyed sixty-five per cent.

Recent reports state that two British scientific workers, Doctors Frank Wokes and J. G. Organ, of Kings Langely, England, have discovered that vitamin C is destroyed by ascorbic oxidase – ascorbic acid oxidase. Ascorbic oxidase is produced in large amounts when fresh fruits and vegetables are cut. The report tells us that "being set free, through cutting, the oxidase attacks vitamin C contained in these chopped up vegetables and fruits." Then it also reports that "In tomatoes, for example, the oxidase is present in the skin. If a tomato is sliced into large pieces much less oxidase is freed than if the pieces are small."

The "report," as it comes to us through the newspaper, is a bit confused or garbled. We interpret it to mean that oxidase is present in certain parts of the fruits and vegetables and is released in the shredding and cutting processes and mixed with the general substance of the food. Coming in contact with vitamin C the oxidase causes it to unite with oxygen – the familiar process of oxidation – and, thus, destroys the vitamin C.

The British investigators found that when lettuce is shredded it loses 80 per cent of its vitamin C in one minute. Using oranges, cabbages and other fruits and vegetables in these experiments they found the same thing. They found that ripe tomatoes lost much less vitamin C than did the green ones on being chopped into small pieces. In all green leafy vegetables destruction of vitamin C was very marked. It was found that mincing of fruits and vegetables is harmful in that it deprives the body of vitamin C.

From these findings it is evident that foods lose more than color and flavor when they are chopped, grated, ground or mashed in the preparation of salads and juices, or in being cut up for cooking purposes.

These facts are expected to result in a complete re-examination of all of our vitamin-food standards. Heretofore these standards have been concerned only with the amount of vitamin in the food. They have taken no account of the actual amount of vitamin that reaches the body. The destruction of vitamins by processing and cooking, and by chewing, has been more or less ignored, especially in practice.

There is nothing new in the discovery that cutting fruits and vegetables into small pieces and permitting the air to reach them, results in oxidation. That the foods undergo changes in color, flavor and odor is apparent to all. These changes are results of chemical changes in the foods and these changes result largely from oxidation.

In 1928 when, Dr. Shelton's Health School was founded, the rule was instituted that fruits and vegetables are not to be shredded, diced or cut into small pieces and this rule is rarely varied from. Fruits are served whole, even tomatoes are served whole, or in large pieces. We have avoided oxidation of foods as much as possible. Our refusal to grate salads, slice peaches and to follow the fad of extracting juices from vegetables here at the Health School has been fully justified by the results of these experiments.

Much of the damages of foods that result from cooking are due to oxidation — heat instead of oxidase being the catalytic agent — and we have at all times served most foods in their natural or uncooked state. Every real advance in knowledge of foods confirms the wisdom of our "return to nature" in diet.

To compensate for the lack of vitamins in our conventional cooked and over cooked diet we are offered vitamin concentrates and synthetic vitamins. These things are of little to no value, are expensive and fail to compensate for all of the food losses caused by cooking.

How much better and simpler would be the use of raw foods! Better nourishment for less money and costing less time and effort in preparation may be had from raw foods. If you do not want to completely abandon cooked foods, if you still desire a baked potato or steamed spinach, make up your diet of at least three-fourths uncooked foods. Have a large raw vegetable salad with each protein and each starch meal. Do not skimp on the salad. Eat a tub of it.

4. *In making fruit salads, the fruits should be used whole or cut into large slices.* No sweetening substances should be added. Apples, peaches, etc., when sliced soon become brown and undergo a change of taste from oxidation. They also lose vitamins.

5. *Vegetables to be used in salad making should not be soaked in water.* They should be carefully picked and thoroughly cleaned, care being taken not to bruise them in these processes. Soaking them in water leeches minerals and vitamins from them and reduces their value as foods.

6. *Make salads simple and do not try to put the whole garden into a salad.* The object in making a salad is not to try to see how many ingredients can be jumbled together. Salads should be simple and composed of but few ingredients. Three ingredients should be the limit. The practice of cutting up, shredding and otherwise wrecking a dozen or more articles of food and mixing them all together in a salad is pernicious. The loss of vitamins from such a salad, by oxidation, makes such a salad incompetent to serve the purposes for which salads are eaten. Salads may be simply prepared and yet served in ways to tempt the most fastidious tastes. They require a minimum of activity in the kitchen.

7. *Salads should be made pleasing to the eye*, but at no time should nutritive value and wholesomeness be sacrificied to artistic appearance. Salads should be daintily prepared, beautiful and appetizing when seen, and fresh and crisp to eat. But the value of the foods making up the salad should not be sacrificed to eye-appeal as is so often done. Important as is eye-appeal, it is not as important as wholesomeness and nutritive value. If the eater is truly hungry he will scarcely notice the occasional lack of eye-appeal.

If garnishing is required a small amount of cress, parsley or cabbage may be used for this purpose. The addition of a radish or two or of a few sprigs of mint to a salad is not objectionable from the *Hygienic* standpoint. Adding pickled olives is objectionable.

8. *Do not violate the rules of food combining within the salad or with the salad and the rest of the meal.* A tomato salad with a starch meal violates the rule not to take acids with starches. Lemon juice on a salad taken with a protein meal violates the injunction against taking acids and proteins together.

The addition of cheese or nuts to salads is permissible only if these foods are to form the protein part of the meal. If eggs are to be added to a salad this should be done only when eggs are to be used as the protein at a protein meal.

Most published salad recipes, even those carried in the health journals and in books on nutrition, are unhygienic concoctions. Here is a sample taken from the pages of a magazine devoted to diet:

VEGETABLE SALAD

3 medium sized carrots.
1 cup tiny — cooked peas.
1 cup shredded cabbage.
1 cup grated hard boiled eggs.
2 teaspoonfuls vegetable salt.
1 cup lemon vegetable jelly.

With what kind of a meal can such a concoction be beaten? Why the salt? Why the cooked peas? Why spoil the cabbage by shredding it? Why the hard boiled egg? The true *Hygienist* will steer clear of such unwholesome concoctions. This salad is a whole series of bad combinations within itself and will not combine with either a protein or a starch meal.

9. *Do not use salt, vinegar, lemon juice or dressing of any kind on a salad.* Salad dressings are comparatively very new things in the arts of the cook and are for the most part abominations. No intelligent person acquainted with the first principles of nutrition will ever be guilty of using them. They almost invariably form incompatible combinations with other parts of the meal.

Salad dressings, made of olive oil, or soy oil, and lemon juice (with sometimes the addition of egg-yolk; at times, honey is also added), are not wholesome additions to a salad. Both the fat and the acid inhibit protein digestion, while the acid inhibits starch digestion. The natural flavors of foods are much more delicious than

SALADS

the taste of the dressing. No one who desires the best of digestion will violate the laws of correct food combining by using so-called "health-dressings."

HOW TO EAT SALADS

When Dr. Tilden initiated the daily salad habit (this was back in the 1890's) the practice was vigorously condemned by the medical profession. Today many physicians and most nutritionists are advising the daily salad without giving credit where it is due. My own view is that two salads a day should be eaten — one with the starch meal the other with the protein meal.

The bio-chemist, Carlton Fredericks, advises taking vitamin capsules with starch. For more than forty years it has been the practice in *Hygienic* circles to take a large raw vegetable salad (leaving out tomatoes or other acid foods) with the starch meal. The salad has been a very large one, measured by ordinary standards, and made up of fresh uncooked vegetables. This salad carries an abundance of vitamins and minerals. The vitamins in these vegetables are the real genuine articles and no chemist's imitations of the real thing. No just-as-good substitutes for vitamins have ever satisfied the *Hygienists*. We take the real article or nothing. His capsule-eating is a commercial program and belongs to the drug fetish.

Mr. Fredericks, himself, points out the complementary action of the vitamins. We need, not just the vitamin B complex, but all vitamins. A large raw vegetable salad supplies several known vitamins and those that may exist but have not yet been detected. Vitamins not only cooperate with each other in the nutritive processes, but they also cooperate with the minerals in the body. These are supplied by the vegetable salad. To take vitamin preparations that are combined with calcium or iron or other minerals will not answer the purpose. These minerals are in non-usable forms. There is no better source of food substances than the plant kingdom — the laboratory and the chemist have not yet been able to concoct acceptable foods.

SAMPLE SALADS

"Recipes," says Leslie Powel, a British Natural Therapist, "are ten a penny, and most of those met with through the ordinary channels give the food-conscious person a sense of dismay. They are so often an offense against Nature, things of elaborate artifice, inviting acts of culinary sabotage, and leading in all probability to digestive derangement." He adds, "usually it will be found that the healthfullest recipes are also the simplest; we make food an unnecessarily complicated business for much of the time, without gaining much, if anything, in epicurean pleasure."

The following recipes for salads are not intended to exhaust the list of delightful salads that may be made. They are intended, rather, to serve as models or guides by which the intelligent student of nutrition may make his own salads. Many combinations of vegetables are possible in salads. These recipes for salads are simple, conforming to the principles of correct combining which should be observed in making all salads.

1	large dish red leaf lettuce	1	large dish Boston lettuce
1	whole tomato	3	stalks of green celery
1	sweet pepper	1	medium size cucumber
1	bunch of parsley (if young and sweet)	1	large sweet red pepper
		1	large dish of butter lettuce
½	head of lettuce	1	ripe tomato
1	whole tomato	1	whole cucumber
3	stalks of celery		
		½	head of Romaine lettuce
1	large dish green leaf lettuce	3	stalks of green celery
1	whole ripe tomato	¼	head of cabbage
1	stalk of French endive (if not bitter)		
		¼	lb. dandelion leaves (if young and sweet)
1	large dish of salad bowl lettuce	2	small carrots
3	stalks of green celery	1	large dish bibb lettuce
1	medium sized cucumber, whole		
		1	large dish red leaf lettuce
1	head of endive (chicory)	1	whole cucumber
1	sweet pepper	1	stalk French endive (if not bitter)
3	stalks of green celery		
¼	head of cabbage	¼	head green leaf lettuce
1	whole ripe tomato	1	bunch of water cress
3	stalks of green celery	3	stalks of green celery
¼	head of cabbage	1	large dish Romaine lettuce
3	stalks of green celery	1	large ripe tomato
3	whole carrots	3	stalks celery

SALADS

Boston lettuce	Bibb lettuce
Cabbage	Cabbage
Sweet pepper	Sweet pepper
Red leaf lettuce	Green leaf lettuce
Fresh Corn	Chinese cabbage
3 stalks celery	Cucumber

FRUIT SALADS

As before stated, fruit salads are best made of whole fruit. The following salads are excellent:

Plums	Plums
Cherries	Peaches
Apricots	Apricots
Peaches	1 large pear
Plums	1 apple
Cherries	Grapes

If a fruit is cut for a salad, it should be cut into large pieces to avoid oxidation as much as possible and eaten immediately. It should not be cut and permitted to stand for long periods before eating. The following salads of cut fruits may be used. They may be eaten with four ounces of nuts, or, if you are not a total vegetarian, four ounces of cottage cheese. A large fruit salad and the four ounces of nuts or cheese should make a meal. Do not eat the sweet fruit salads with nuts or cheese. Either make a fruit meal of these salads, or take a glass of sour milk or buttermilk with them.

Sliced oranges	Sliced pineapple
Cut tart apples	Sectioned grapefruit
Lettuce leaves	Lettuce leaves
Sliced apples	Sliced bananas
Cut Pears	Sun-dried (or fresh) figs
Celery	Pear or apple
Lettuce leaves	

Diced Avocados
Sliced cucumbers
Lettuce leaves

Sliced oranges
Sectioned grapefruit
Sliced tart apples
Lettuce leaves

Sliced peaches
Whole apricots
Plums
Lettuce leaves

Sliced bananas
Cherries
Sweet grapes
Lettuce leaves

Conservative Cooking
CHAPTER XXX

Foods are prepared by Nature. She turns out a finished product. There is no need for further preparation. But we have become so artificial in our habits and in our thinking, that a few words of caution are needed.

The less "preparation" foods have undergone, the better and more wholesome they are as foods. The more simple the method used in preparing them, the more valuable they are. As well try to improve the rose by paint or perfume as to try to improve nuts or fruits by cooking. How foolish to cook a peach or an orange and then try to hypnotize yourself into believing that you have improved its delicious flavor or increased its dietetic value!

The modern kitchen is a mass of unnatural and anti-natural things and processes. We have forsaken the natural and have developed our present methods of preparing foods in a hap-hazard and thoughtless way.

Every man and woman should possess a clear understanding of the "complexities and possibilities of modern public cooking," together with a full knowledge of the "significance or the insignificance of the digestive appeals, the safety or unsafety of its unprincipled combinations, and the imperative necessity of moral power, backed by the will, to control the demands of a false, because overstimulated, appetite."

The first step in improving the methods of cooking foods was made by Mr. C. Leigh Hunt Wallace, an English vegetarian and editor of the *Herald of Health*. This journal was the official organ of the Physical Regeneration Society, of which Mr. Wallace was leader. This society opposed drugs and vaccines of all kinds and stood for living reform. In their "General Rules for the Maintenance of Health," I find these words: "all vegetables shall be stewed in their own juices or served with the water in which they are cooked in the form of sauce or gravy. Or they may be steamed or baked, but in whatever way they are prepared, all their natural salts and flavors must be conserved." Mr. Wallace called this "the conservative system of cooking."

Much of our over praised cooking consists in boiling the minerals out of our foods and pouring these down the drain pipe and conservative cooking seeks, among other things to conserve these minerals. Vegetables, even potatoes, should never be boiled. The old method of par-boiling vegetables and throwing the water away carried away practically all of the soluble salts and vitamins.

Open-vessel-cooked foods are largely devitalized, with the oxygen so combined that it is valueless. The vitamins are destroyed and the mineral salts are disarranged or lost. The waterless cooker is less objectionable in these respects.

Rapid cooking at a high temperature produces less damage, while low heat long continued, causes more damage to food. For this reason the "fireless cooker" and other forms of slow cooking are least desirable. Cooking done under steam pressure quickly destroys all vitamins in our food.

CHOOSING FOODS

Wilted lettuce is poor food. The same is true of celery and other vegetables. Fresh foods are best. The tops should be cut from beets, turnips, radishes, etc., as these, when wilting, extract the best elements from the roots.

The mere wilting of vegetables impairs their value as food. Dr. Howe says, "Vitamins of the greatest importance are found in the green leaf vegetables as they come fresh from the gardens, but at least one of the most important of these vitamins is either killed or greatly reduced in efficiency if such vegetables wilt or are kept in cold storage. This does not mean, however, that the cold storage process is not a very valuable means of storing some forms of food.

"A knowledge of what wilting or storage will do to these tender vegetables is not confined to man. In fact, the animal knew it first. If we place fresh lettuce and either wilted or storage lettuce at the same time before the animals in our laboratory, not only will they neglect the wilted lettuce for the fresh, but they seem to feel that the wilted lettuce is suitable only for bedding and they contentedly trample or crunch upon it while eagerly devouring the fresh."

Wilted lettuce, wilted celery and other wilted vegetables are poor foods. Foods that are shipped long distances lose much of their food value. Fresh foods are always best. Canned vegetables and fruits lose much of their value by standing for a long time in the

CONSERVATIVE COOKING

cans. The acid fruits seem to be an exception to this, at least they do not lose their quality as early as do other foods.

PREPARATION

Never soak vegetables in water for this extracts valuable elements from them and leaves them tasteless and worthless. Lettuce and celery should not be crisped in this way. Vegetables should be washed quickly, care being taken not to bruise them. They may then be wrapped in a damp cloth or wrapped in paper to protect them and placed in the refrigerator or in the fresh air to become crisp. No vegetable should ever be permitted to stand, even for a moment, in water. If they are permitted to stand in water they will be robbed of their precious minerals, which will be absorbed by the water, and you will only eat impoverished vegetables.

FRUITS AND NUTS

Nuts should never be cooked or roasted.

Fruits should never be cooked. This applies with equal force to dried fruits. Dried prunes, figs, peaches, pears, apples and other dried fruits should be carefully washed and then have enough warm water poured over them to cover them well but not enough to float them. Cover the vessel and let them stand over night. When serving, the water in which they have been soaked, being full of the salts of the fruit, should be served with them. No sugar should be added. Fruits thus prepared are much more pleasant than cooked fruits and are also much more easily digested. It requires a better digestion than most people have to digest cooked fruit. Better not try it.

LEAFY VEGETABLES

Vegetables should be cooked in their own juices with barely enough water to prevent burning and their juices served with them. When spinach, for example, is boiled and the juice is not eaten most of the soluble salts go down the drain pipe. They are lost.

The more food is cooked the deader it is. It should be eaten raw or slightly cooked. Thoroughly cooked − "dead" − foods may build the body but they can never vitalize it.

Leafy vegetables should never be steamed or cooked until they change color. Cook vegetables as short a time as possible, to preserve the living essence as far as possible, and then eat soon after cooking. Do not cook vgetables ahead and let them stand for hours before eating. Twice cooked vegetables have less food value and are less digestible than once cooked vegetables.

The lowly turnip green, so popular throughout the south, as attested by the words of the song: "Cornbread, buttermilk and good old turnip greens," is a rich source of calcium, iron and other minerals. The stems of the green are also fair sources of calcium, though containing less iron. The total ash of this green is important. But when parboiled and boiled for long periods, most of its value is lost.

Cabbage and onions have their sulphur oxidized by the usual methods of cooking them. Small heads of cabbage or small onions may be placed whole in a waterless cooker and cooked whole.

TUBERS AND FRUITING PLANTS

Carrots, beets, turnips and other tubers, also squash, tomatoes, etc., should not be pared and cut up before cooking. Scrub them thoroughly with a brush and cook them whole. Serve and eat whole, flavored with a little butter or oil only.

Potatoes should always be cooked in their skins and the skins eaten. Bake them 40 minutes in a very hot oven, or steam them in a waterless cooker.

ANIMAL PROTEINS

Eggs should be soft-boiled, coddled or poached.

Meats are best baked or broiled under the flame to retain their juices. The juices of the meat should be served with it. Fish may be steamed or baked. No meat should ever be fried. "Frying turns meat into an alkaloid," a poison, says Dr. Gibson.

CEREALS

Cereals should be served dry. They should not be boiled. They may be steamed or scalded and served with a little butter or cream — but not with sugar or milk. Stale bread is better than toasted bread.

SOUPS AND GRAVIES

Soups, which are usually swallowed without mastication, are bad foods. They are especially bad when starch is added to them. Starch, flour, tapioca, rice, etc., should never be added. Okra added to soups thickens them nicely and is not objectionable.

Gravies are objectionable and should not be prepared.

ADDITIONS TO FOODS

Butter, cream, or oil served on vegetables should be added when serving and not while cooking. Fats should never be cooked.

All the vitamins are quickly destroyed by baking soda or other alkali added to the food. The fats, grease, salts, soda, acids, sugar, spices and pungent extractives so freely used in modern cookery, not only stimulate to overeating, but actually interfere with the digestive processes.

Acids added to food not only interfere with digestion but cause much trouble. Dr. Leedon Sharp (M.D.), of Intercourse, Pa., says that when a girl comes to the doctor complaining of "that tired feeling," "want of energy," "lack of pep," precarious appetite, chronic constipation and some menstrual irregularities, even if "apparently robust, often times over weight and having rosy cheeks;" if she answers "I love them" to the question "do you like pickles?", chlorosis may be diagnosed whether or not the peculiar greenish hue of the skin is presented. Blood examination, he says, will show the red cell count to be about normal with no increase in white cells, but with hemoglobin as deficient in some as 40 to 50 per cent.

Bleached vegetables are inferior in food value to green vegetables. Their value decreases in proportion to the time required to bleach them. The bleaching process robs them of vitamins and bases.

DRIED FOODS

Dried foods, other than dried fruits, are now on the market. Milk, vegetables, and meats are often dried. It has been the theory in the past that this deprived the foods of nothing but their water. This is now fully proved to be not so. Barnes and Hume have shown that milk dried by the ordinary processes loses about two-fifths of its antiscorbutic efficacy. Hess and Unger state that the most actively antiscorbutic vegetables lose their efficacy when dried. An outbreak of Scurvy in the Rummelsburg orphanage, a few years ago, was attributed by Mueller and Erich to the use of pasteurized milk and dried vegetables. These vegetables had been bleached before drying and this made them all the worse, for in the bleaching they had forfeited their excess of bases. Heating at a comparatively low temperature, 30 to 40 degrees centigrade, is more injurious to vitamin C, than boiling for an hour.

The drying of cabbage, carrots and dandelion greatly impairs their antiscorbutic qualities. The C quality of cabbage is wholly destroyed at 110 degres centigrade. Dried potatoes are also deficient in C. Dried cabbage, when stored for two to three weeks, has its vitamin C reduced by about nine-tenth. Three months storage completely destroys its antiscorbutic qualities.

THE SCIENCE AND FINE ART OF FOOD AND NUTRITION

The outbreak of scurvy in the Bulgarian Army during the Balkan war a few years ago, developed in spite of (perhaps, as Berg insists, because of) the fact that dried vegetables were supplied as prophylactics.

Sulphured fruits are unfit for use. They are saturated with the poisonous sulphurous acid used in bleaching them. Sundried and dehydrated fruits are preferable and I am suspicious of the dehydrated articles.

Stefanson's experiences in the Arctic emphasizes the need for fresh foods and confirm the results of many experiments which show that preserved, heated and desiccated foods lose much of their value. The value of fresh, raw fruits and vegetables and the inadequacy of denatured, processed, refined, cooked, canned, dried, desiccated, preserved and embalmed foods, as revealed by experience and experiment, will remain unshaken.

Cooking, bleaching, canning, preserving and drying (with the possible exception of sun-drying) of fruits, vegetables, grains, milk, meat and other food stuffs, are all denaturing processes and have much the same results as the milling of wheat or the polishing of rice. "Since prolonged heat is in any case injurious," says Berg, "it is obvious that the drying of nutrients at a raised temperature must be extremely disadvantageous."

CANNED FOODS

Canned foods are extensively used. The canning industry is one of the largest industries in America. It yearly spends millions of dollars to increase its business and to induce people to believe that canned foods are excellent foods. Subsidized research workers, scientists, physicians and others issue statements designed to increase confidence in canned foods.

The process of canning foods has undergone a great change within recent years, so that canned goods are better today than they were some years ago. Canned goods, many of them at least, are not without real food value, but they can never be made to take the place of real foods and should never be used when other foods may be had. There are many hospitals and sanitariums which feed canned foods to patients and to children. This I consider a criminal practice. I have never fed canned foods to patients, nor to children.

We are frequently told that present day methods of canning preserves the salts of the foods and does not destroy their vitamins. That their vitamins are impaired does not admit of doubt and Berg

CONSERVATIVE COOKING

tells us "it seems undesirable to trust to the antiscorbutic efficacy of stored products. The antiscorbutic power of expressed cabbage juice, lemon juice and orange juice, seems to disappear in consequence of prolonged storage." Prolonged heating of acid fruit juices does not completely destroy their vitamin C, these qualities are lost after being bottled or canned and stored.

No method of canning is known that does not impair the salts of food and to a greater or lesser extent the other qualities of the food. Home canned foods are also bad. Professor Morgulis rightly says: "A new and serious source of malnutrition has arisen in our modern industrialized civilization. By the implacable economic forces women have been drawn away from their traditional place in the home and into the turmoil of industrial production. At the same time the factory has intruded itself into the home and has preempted much of the woman's function of preparing the family's food. The manufacture of foods dispensed in cans and all ready to be served has insinuated itself into the homes of the people to such an extent that it has become literally true that many households can now-a-days be conducted with the aid of two implements – the cork screw and the can opener. The evil of these industrial conditions is seen not only in the circumstance that the younger generation is deprived of proper maternal care, but also in the fact that owing to qualitative deficiencies, tinned goods, when these are the staple articles of diet, may produce the effects of partial inanition."

COOKING VESSELS

Many types of cooking vessels are offered the public. Cooking vessels are made of many kinds of materials. Some of these distribute heat more uniformly than others and cook the food quicker. The less vegetables are cooked, the better. They should be heated or steamed, but just enough so as not to significantly change their natural shape or color. The use of aluminum, stainless steel, or teflon is not advocated. Aluminum combines with the acids in the foods forming poisonous aluminum compounds. Stainless steel cookware contains nickel and chromium that leach into the foods when used. Teflon is highly poisonous as it contains fluorine and gives off poisonous gases under certain conditions. Opaque glassware and fine baked enamelware have no known strikes against them. Good quality enamel cookware with tight lids allow for steaming vegetables with very little water. If the enamel is chipped, however, it is best to discard it, since lead is leached into the food.

Effects of Denatured Foods
CHAPTER XXXI

By denatured foods is meant foods that have been so altered and impaired in the processes of manufacturing, bleaching, canning, cooking, preserving, pickling, etc., that they are no longer as well fitted to meet the needs of the body as they were in the state Nature prepared them.

Every trophologist knows that the old "balanced ration" was what McCarrison called it, a "deficiency ration." It was composed of four items – proteins, carbohydrates, fats and water. Numerous animal experiments have shown that, while proteins, carbohydrates and fats are food elements, they are not in and by themselves food, either when taken alone or when artificially mixed.

In the Museum of Natural History (New York), is an exhibit showing the effects of soil deficiency on plant life. These plants, all of the same kind, were reared in soils lacking some element. The exhibit has to be seen to be fully appreciated. The plants range in size from about three inches to about eighteen inches in height. Their color ranges from pale yellow to dark green. The leaves of some are broad, of others narrow. Some of the leaves are kinky. All of the plants except one is defective both in size, color and features and all except that one were raised in soil lacking some food element. For example, one was raised in a soil lacking iron, (the plant has "anemia"), another in a soil lacking potassium, another in a soil lacking nitrogen, etc.

Food is the "soil" of animals. The digestive tract represents their roots. If essential food elements are lacking in their soil (foods), they, like the plants in the experiments, fail and die. Ride along the highway with an experienced farmer and he will point out to you, as he passes swiftly by in a car, fertile soil and poor soil, by the vegetation growing thereon; but the same farmer fails to recognize that sickly and stunted children are the result of poor soil (food).

Experiments revealed that animals fed on a diet composed of purified proteins, purified starches, purified fats and inorganic salts, although they may live on these for a time, do not grow and in a short time develop various pathological conditions as a result of such

EFFECTS OF DENATURED FOODS

a "diet." If whey, or fruit juice, or vegetables are then added to the diet, the symptoms improve and the animals thrive better.

One physician sums up these results in these words: "What has been established is that a diet that contains enough *nourishment*, by all the recognized chemical standards, still fails to support normal growth and physiologic normality, if it lacks some unknown substances present in a variety of animal and plant tissues. A very little of these substances needs to be present, but there is an irreducible minimum."

Children and adults, alike, regularly consume breakfasts such as this one: Stewed prunes, a denatured cereal with white sugar and pasteurized cream, toast (white), pasteurized milk and, perhaps, bacon and eggs. Every article in this breakfast is denatured and altered chemically to a great extent. It is a predominantly acid forming breakfast and yet, the vitamin faddist will tell us only that it is lacking vitamin C or D. He will advise adding a little orange juice and cod-liver oil to make this a good breakfast. Our vitamin knowledge, where it is permitted to obscure all else, as is usually the case, certainly blinds so-called dietitians to some of the most important facts and principles of food science — *trophology*.

Except for the fresh fruits and vegetables you eat, practically everything you have on your table has had something done to it. Your milk is pasteurized, condensed, evaporated, boiled; your eggs are from hens that lay two or three hundred eggs a year and are fed on "rich" fare that produces disease in them. Your sugar is the crystalized, refined and bleached sap of cane or beet that has had all the minerals and vitamins removed from it. Your cereals are cracked, rolled, hammered, frittered, curled, flaked, ironed and even "shot from cannon," they are roasted, twice roasted, boiled, and in other ways rendered foodless. Wheat is milled, its minerals and vitamins removed, the flour is bleached and chemicalized. Its most important food elements are removed in the milling process. Your flesh foods are embalmed, smoked, pickled, salted, canned, corned, sausaged, friend, baked, broiled, refrigerated, cold-storaged and kept for long periods before being eaten. They are often drugged to give them color or flavor. Perhaps they come from sick animals. Your dried fruits are heated in drying, bleached with sulphur dioxide, stored for long periods of time and, finally, stewed and mixed with white sugar before being eaten.

THE SCIENCE AND FINE ART OF FOOD AND NUTRITION

The refining, preserving and cooking processes to which our foods are subjected destroy extraordinarily delicate and tender vital food factors. The refining and cooking processes rob foods of so much of their values that we add salt, sugar, spices, pepper and various other condiments and seasonings to them to make them palatable. Without the additions of such things they are dull, flat, insipid. Not so natural foods. Nature has placed delicate flavors and aromas in her foods that appeal to the senses of taste and smell.

A nation whose diet is made up almost wholly of such foodless foods cannot possibly be well nourished. Why go to great lengths and much trouble to build up our soils and then take everything out of the foods that the improved soils have put into them? When physicians prescribe such foods for infants and young children, for pregnant and nursing mothers and for patients they display both a lamentable ignorance of food values and a callous indifference to the welfare of children, mothers and patients. When they eat such foods themselves and feed them to their own children, they reveal that ignorance is their most prominent characteristic.

Over eighty years ago, Dr. Magendie, of Paris, starved one full pen of dogs to death by feeding them a diet of white flour and water, while another pen thrived on whole wheat flour and water. He fed another pen of dogs all the beef tea they could consume, and gave the dogs of another pen only water. The beef tea fed dogs all starved to death. The water fed dogs had lost considerable weight and would have starved also if the experiment had been continued; however, they were alive after those fed on beef tea were all dead. They were fed and all recovered.

Dogs fed on albumen, fibrine, or gelatine — the constituents of muscle — died in about a month. They can live longer than this on water alone. Dogs fed on the constituents of muscle artificially mixed, died in about the same time. Dogs fed on oil, gum or sugar died in four to five weeks. Dogs fed on fine (white) flour bread lived but fifty days.

A goose fed on egg white died in twenty-six days. A duck fed on butter died in three weeks, with the butter exuding from every part of its body, its feathers being saturated with fat. A goose fed on gum died in sixteen days; one fed on sugar in twenty-one days; two fed on starch died in twenty-four and twenty-seven days.

Dr. Page says, "Pigeons, chickens and mice will flourish on Graham (whole wheat) flour, but all will die within three weeks on white flour." A colony of mice fed on the best grade of white flour will all develop constipation in three days and die within a month. An equal number fed on whole wheat flour will flourish and gain weight.

In the process of making white flour out of wheat grain the outer coat of the grain is removed. This removes seventy-five per cent of the calcium of the wheat, much of the phosphorus, four-fifths of the iron and much of the other minerals of the wheat. The process also removes seven-eights of the thiamin and niacin, and three-fourths of the riboflavin. Much protein of the wheat is also cast aside by the milling process and the protein thus lost is of better quality than that in the heart of the wheat. Farmers feed these cast-off portions of the wheat to their horses, cows, pigs, chickens and other animals. "What fools these mortals be!"

In the milling process about thirty per cent of the wheat grain is thrown away and with it practically all of its alkaline minerals. White flour is of so little value that bugs, weevils and worms, that readily eat and do well on whole wheat flour, will not eat it except when forced to do so by extreme hunger, and then it kills them in a short time. How true is the statement that "we boast of having the whitest flour in the world. We have also the thinnest hair, and the poorest bones, teeth and nerves as a result."

Whole wheat alone, as pointed out in a previous chapter, will not sustain life in a normal manner. After a shorter or longer period the normal rate of growth slackens, unless green foods are added to the diet.

Many of the "diets" employed for experimental purposes are not worthy of the name. Rats fed on the following "diet" showed rickets in thirty days:

 White flour _____ 95.0%
 Calcium lactate _____ 2.9%
 Sodium chloride _____ 2.9%
 Iron citrate _____ 0.1%

Nobody but an ignoramus could call this a diet. The white flour it contains is the only thing in it that even remotely resembles food.

A number of diets deficient in various vitamins have been formulated by the investigators. Here is one for example, formulated by Osborne and Mendel:

THE SCIENCE AND FINE ART OF FOOD AND NUTRITION

Purified Casein ---------------- 18%
Cornstarch -------------------- 48%
Lard ------------------------- 30%
Salts ------------------------- 4%
0.3 Gm. dried yeast (for vitamin B_1)

It is obvious at a glance that this is not a diet. There is almost no food in these materials. The salts are inorganic. The starch is devoid of minerals as is the lard. The casein is *purified*, which means that it has been deprived of its salts. Vitamin A is not the only thing lacking in this "diet." Experiments with "diets" of this nature can have no practical value in enabling us to better feed ourselves, our children and our patients. It should not surprise us that subsistence on this "diet" for any length of time will stop the growth of young animals. Growth could hardly be expected to last beyond the exhaustion of the stored reserves in the bodies of the animals.

The addition of one or more vitamins to such "diets" will not render them adequate. A true diet must be composed of foods: *natural foods*. Neither of the "diets" presented above resemble even the worst diets eaten anywhere.

Here is another example of these experimental diets, fed by Dr. Percy Howe, of Harvard University: "We take soy beans (50%), rolled oats (28%), dried whole milk (10%), yeast (4%), butter (5%), agar (1%), calcium carbonate (1%), and sodium chloride (1%), mix moisten with water and bake into a hard cracker. We feed a liberal quantity of pure cellulose, in the form of filter paper, as roughage. This diet contains enough of everything to sustain life except Vitamin C, and we may be sure that no animal is going to get his living from it unless he chews hard and long."

The statement that this diet contains enough of everything, except Vitamin C, to sustain life is absolutely and unqualifiedly false. This is not a diet at all. It is a poison, if it is anything. It certainly is not a food.

Sodium chloride is common table salt and is not assimilable or usable by the body. It is excreted unchanged. It comes out in the same state it entered the body. No metabolized food does this. It is not food, but an irritant. Its addition to food, supplies no lacking element. The same is true of calcium carbonate. It is a useless inorganic salt. It supplies the body with nothing.

In trying to prove that this "diet" only lacks Vitamin C, he takes no consideration of the oxidation of sulphur and phosphorus,

EFFECTS OF DENATURED FOODS

for example, in the process of cooking. The proteins of soy beans are of a high grade, but cooking them into crackers doesn't make them any good. Take, again, the milk contents of this "diet." It is already injured when it comes to the hand of this experimenter, by the process of drying, and is still further injured in being cooked into a cracker.

The mere process of "sterilizing" (pasteurizing) milk, and this is done at a comparatively low temperature, causes the calcium-magnesium-carbonphosphate it contains (a salt indispensable to the upbuilding of bones) to break up into its constituent salts and three of these — calcium phosphate, magnesium phosphate, calcium carbonate — are practically insoluble, and their usefulness greatly impaired. There is also a partial coagulation of the milk protein, the coagulated portion being precipitated with the salts. There, is by simple sterilization of milk, a great and physiologically important reduction of the bone-nourishing salts of the milk. When still greater and more prolonged heat is applied, as in baking, there is still greater damage done to these salts and proteins. The same thing occurs with the salts and proteins of the beans, oats and yeast. The butter is rendered practically indigestible.

Is it any wonder, then, that Dr. Howe hastens to add: "No animal is going to get his living from it very long no matter how hard he chews, because if it is not changed, all the animals fed exclusively upon it will be dead in four weeks." We don't doubt it. Indeed, we would expect it. And we would expect it if we had never heard of vitamins. Animals fed on such "food" are not fed. It is not food.

We have not learned to make, nor even to imitate living substances. We know that animals are dependent upon plants for their food and cannot go directly to the soil for it. We can neither synthesize these substances in the laboratory, nor can we tear them down in the kitchen or in the laboratory in "purifying" them (extracting their salts from them) without greatly impairing their food values. It is a mistake to assume, as these experimenters do, that chemical substances constitute nourishment irrespective of their form or condition.

In these experiments they had not fed these animals upon foods at all. Nature's chemistry had been greatly altered and the breaking up of their peculiar element-groupings by the refining and cooking processes and the changing of their salts had rendered them all but valueless as foods. I strongly suspect that the "unknown substances" to which the term "vitamin" has been applied are foods — natural food. Nature gives us apples, pears, cabbage, celery, lettuce, oranges, nuts, etc., and not vitamins. The vitamin may be the peculiar chemical structure of the whole, unprocessed, uncooked food.

Uncritically referring all the evils that flow from a preponderantly denatured diet to a lack of vitamins is rank folly. Many food factors besides vitamins are lacking in these diets. Various minerals are lacking. Often essential amino acids are not present. The fats are commonly cooked and renderd useless. In the same way, referring all the improvement that follows the addition of fruit or vegetable juices to the inadequate diets to vitamins is folly. These juices contain much other food material besides their vitamins — materials that are often greatly lacking in the various denatured diets consumed by people everywhere.

Nerves and brain are rich in phosphorus. Polished rice, the classic "cause" of beri-beri is practically free of soluble phosphorus. Indeed, Berg says: "Chamberlain, Bloombergh and Kilbourne pointed out that all the nutriments known to cause beri-beri are poor in phosphorus and potassium." Schaumann has shown that directly upon the beginning of an experimental diet, the balance of nitrogen ash, and above all phosphorus and calcium, becomes markedly negative, and grows continually more unfavorable as the "disease" progresses.

"Scala," says Berg, "reproaches physiologists who are experimenting as to the causation of deficiency diseases with uncritically referring all the manifestations to the account of the complettins (vitamins) and with forgetting that the organic extracts they use in their experiments contain in addition comparatively large quantities of inorganic substances (mineral salts) which likewise exercise a powerful influence." Orange juice is given to complement pasteurized milk. It is supposed to supply vitamin C, destroyed in the milk by pasteurization. But orange juice contains several salts and organic acids, and pasteurized milk has some of its salts spoiled for use. Does the orange juice supply salts or vitamins?

Merely by adding an excess of starch or starch and fats to otherwise natural food, rich in so-called vitamins, McCarrison was able to produce in monkeys, to which he fed this food, diarrhea, dysentery, dyspepsia and gastric dilatation, gastric and duodenal ulcer, intussuception, colitis, and failure of colonic function. Starch poisoning thus caused conditions commonly attributed to avitaminosis, despite the presence of what is supposed to be an abundant supply of vitamins. If the mere addition of small amounts of vitamins to a deficient diet is enough to do all the experimenters claim it will do, these results should not have followed such feeding.

McCarrison also showed that "one cannot in practice dissociate the effects of deficient and ill-balanced foods from those of bacterial or protozoal agencies whose ravages have been made possible by faulty food." This is equivalent to saying that the deficiencies and the toxemies are so inextricably bound up that they cannot be separated.

Berg says: "Above all we have to remember that when an extract is made from uncoagulated material (uncooked foods), chiefly the bases (alkaline salts) pass into solution; whereas when the extract is made from material in which the protein has been coagulated by heat (cooked), acids predominate in the solution. This fact may in part explain the reported behaviour of the thermoliable complettins." In other words, when we are told that heat destroys vitamins, we are to understand that solutions extracted from cooked foods are rich in acids.

Many of the evidences of deficiency could easily result from a leaching of the body of its alkalies by an excess of acids, such as the loss of calcium by the bones and the failure of calcification in the growing bones.

Aulde observed that when there is either a lack of calcium or an excess of acid in the food, vitamin A has no effect. McCollum, Ewald Abderhalden, Miller and Hart have all shown that avitominosis (failure to utilize vitamins) is produced by an excess of acid in the food. Peckham found that minerals and vitamins are valuable only in the presence of each other. Aulde claims that calcium is usable only in the presence of vitamin A. Similar facts are observed by numerous investigators with regard to vitamin B and other vitamins. (Many investigators consider B and D to be identical). Some of the pathological features of scruvy especially the bone disorders, edema, tissue fragility and the liability to hemorrhage, indicate the presence of a strong acidosis. The scurvy producing diet is unquestionably deficient in bases while the antiscorbutic diet is rich in bases. It is also claimed that the salts are not assimilated in the absence of the vitamins; but this amounts merely to the fact that inorganic salts spoiled by cooking are not assimilated.

Experiments recounted by Sylvester Graham showed that the addition of wood shavings, blotting paper and other forms of foodless roughage to the diet of an animal fed certain defective diets was enough to overcome pathological conditions and restore health. Graham attributed the evils of such a diet to poisoning from gastrointestinal decomposition. This is certainly present in most, if not all cases of avitaminosis.

The multiplicity of factors in nutrition render it difficult for the laboratory research worker to assess the practical value of his findings, while his limited view is likely to cause him to over-estimate the importance of the aspect of nutrition upon which he is working. "Vitamin deficiency" may be almost anything.

Animals confined to mineral-free diets become weak, dull, listless, have fits and die. They reach a point where they refuse to eat. If they are now force-fed on the same diet, they die quicker than animals not fed at all. In these experiments the nervous system suffers most. A dog so fed showed sudden fits of madness, became weak and uncertain in his movements, trembled and showed signs of nervousness, and grew weaker and weaker until he could scarcely crawl.

A man will starve to death with just as much certainty and just as speedily, and in most cases more speedily, if he attempts to live upon foods containing only one or two elements of nutrition, as if he were totally abstaining from food. A diet of white flour and water, or white sugar and water will result in death much sooner than a diet of water only. This is due to the fact that if no food is eaten the body feeds upon its own balanced foods reserves; whereas, it has no adequate provision for meeting the exigencies created by prolonged subsistence on one-sided diets.

Milk of cows or mothers may actually be dangerous to calves or children. Cows fed on commercial feeds produce milk which causes calves to become blind, have fits and die. Hens fed in the same manner produce eggs with pale or colorless yolks, lacking in iron and other minerals, which either will not hatch at all, or will produce a chicken which will not be able to live. Cubs born of the circus lioness, fed on meat alone, are born with cleft palates, due to lack of lime.

McCarrison showed definitely that foods and combinations of foods which are inadequate and unsatisfactory in feeding animals,

EFFECTS OF DENATURED FOODS

are equally as inadequate and unsatisfactory in feeding man. If our foods do not contain enough of the right kinds of mineral salts, we simply starve to death. It does not matter how much "good nourishing food," as this is commonly understood, that we consume, if these salts are not present in sufficient quantities, we suffer from slow starvation, with glandular imbalance or disfunction, lowered "resistance to disease" and other evidences of decay.

In 1914, 4,000 men, engaged in the building of the Medina-Mamora Railway in South America, were killed by acidosis, beri-beri and tuberculosis, induced by an acid-forming diet of meats, white flour, degerminated corn meal, polished rice, tapioca, corn starch, farina, cakes, jellies, jams, glucose, sugar, syrups, lard and canned goods. The project had to be abandoned.

All around the workers in the woods, the monkeys subsisted on the fruits and nuts that grew in abundance. These were strong and healthy and free from the ailments from which the men were dying. The men, however, spurned the monkey food, just as the man in civilization refuses to eat celery, lettuce, etc., and refers to them as grass and fodder. The only members of the above crew of men who remained to tell the story were saved by a diet of acid fruits.

In 1925, twelve convicts in a Mississippi penitentiary volunteered as subjects for a dietetic test Dr. Goldberger, who made the test, wanted to prove that pellagra is caused by carbohydrate foods. These twelve men were fed on demineralized and degerminated corn products, with the result that they all developed the disease and underwent intense suffering. Some of them even attempted suicide. They were placed on a normal diet with the result that their usual health was soon re-established.

It should be carefully noted that these men were fed on denatured and not natural carbohydrates. It is extremely doubtful if such results would have been obtained if natural carbohydrate foods had been used. Certain it is that it would have required much longer time to have brought about these results. Natural, whole corn is not a perfect food. As an exclusive diet it would in time produce a "deficiency disease."

Twenty to forty days on a white flour and water diet are enough to produce death in a man, from scurvy, after days of torture, bleeding gums, swollen joints, pains and other symptoms. It may be objected that we do not confine ourselves to diets of white flour or of corn and corn products, but eat a variety of foods. Mere variety is not sufficient, as was seen in the foregoing account of the Medina-Marmora railway workers. Another very striking case, which proves that even a varied diet of denatured foods will produce the same effects as those observed to follow a denatured mono-diet occured during the world holocaust of 1914-18.

The German raider, the Crown Prince Wilhelm, after having been upon the high-seas for 255 days and sinking 14 French and British merchantmen, was forced to put into port, at Newport News, because 110 of her crew were stricken with beri-beri. The crew was dropping at the rate of about two a day. The men presented symptoms of weakness, irritability, muscular atrophy, paralysis, dilatation of the heart and pain upon pressure. Their diet had been very similar to that eaten in the average American household. It consisted of fresh meat, white flour products, canned vegetables, potatoes, sweet biscuits, cheese, oleomargarine, tea, coffee and champagne. Much fresh fruit and vegetables and whole wheat had been captured by the raider from the French and English merchantmen, but these had either been sent down to the bottom of the sea or eaten by the officers. Only the "staple" foods were retained for use by the crew. None of the officers developed the condition.

The ships physicians were unable to deal with the situation. So were the American physicians. They did not know the cause of the suffering of these men, nor what to do for them. Except for Alfred W. McCann, all or most of them probably would have perished. He prescribed for them a diet very rich in basic salts, with the result that improvement was immediate and rapid. All protein, sugar, fat and white flour was excluded from the diet. In two weeks the most severe cases were up and the men rapidly regained their health. No drugs were given. How true is Berg's remarks that, "This warship was conquered by the food preserving industry."

It will be asked: Why does not the average individual, eating a diet so similar to that eaten by the Medina-Marmora railway workers and the crew of the German raider, suffer in the same way? The answer is: He does, but not to the same extent, due to the fact that he consumes enough alkaline foods — fresh fruits, fresh vegetables, etc. — to protect him to a great extent. The steady death rate from tuberculosis, the rapid increase in nervous afflictions and degenerative diseases and our constantly lowered resistance to epidemic influences, reveal that we habitually consume too many denatured and acid-forming foods.

It is not enough that we consume even large amounts of the "protective" foods with our denatured acid-formers. This is too much like taking an antidote with the poison. We should cease taking the poison. If we offset the denatured foods with large quantities of base-forming foods, this entails a hardship upon the organs of digestion and elimination.

The lesson is plain. If we desire health, we must cease eating denatured foods. The examples given may be extreme, but conditions all around us prove them not to be exceptional. Almost everyone shows signs of the effects of denatured foods.

"Orthodox" food scientists tell us that we can eat white flour, white sugar, polished rice, etc., and "offset" the deficiencies in these by eating green vegetables and fruits. Leaving out of consideration the evident folly and waste of denaturing these foods and, then, trying to offset their factory-made deficiencies; we are still left with a big problem on our hands — that of finding room in our stomachs to put the necessary amounts of "offsetting" foods to make up the deficiencies; and also that of finding the money with which to buy these foods.

If we ate but small amounts of denatured foods, we might accomplish this. But when we take white flour, white sugar, lard, polished rice, denatured cereal products, pasteurized milk, etc., all of which are denatured, they do not balance, or offset each other. They are all lacking in the same elements. One would have to eat a tub of spinach or cabbage to "offset" the ordinary meal. Even if our diet is half denatured and half natural, the excess in the natural foods will not be sufficient to compensate for the deficiencies in the denatured half. McCann estimated that it would require the expenditure of $40,000,000,000 for "offsetting" foods, to compensate for the losses which our $2,000,000,000 wheat crop of 1919 sustained in converting it into white flour. There is not money enough in the world to buy sufficient offsetting foods, even if we had capacity to consume enough of them. There can be no sensible defense of the denaturing practice.

Those who declare that denatured, refined and "ashless" foods are all right because the growing child, the young mother, the athletic youth and working adult obtain a great variety of "offsetting" foods which balance-up these denatured foods, are greatly in error.

The great bulk of their diet is made up of white sugar, white bread, white rice, denatured breakfast foods (cereals), glucose table syrups, glucose candies, ginger-snaps, and other cakes and pies, doughnuts, soda crackers, corn meal mush, tapioca, pearled barley, ice cream, pasteurized or boiled milk, meats, oleomargarine, lard and cooking compounds. Canned fruits and vegetables, cooked foods, etc., are not offsetting foods. These foods all need to be offset and no man, woman or child can eat sufficient fruits and vegetables to offset the deficiencies of such a diet. None of these foods will nourish the body. None of them build bones and nerves. None of them build normal blood. On any or all of them animals die.

Dr. Seale Harris, of Birmingham, Alabama, in an address before the American Medical Association, said: "The sugar-fed child is one of the saddest sights in the world. Many sugar-saturated vitamin-starved Americans, that is, those who live largely on white flour bread, white potatoes, white rice. lean meats, sugar-saturated coffee, and sugar-laden desserts, with candy and soft drinks between meals, would seem to be susceptible to ulcer and other abdominal diseases in which infection plays a part."

We may concede that such a diet is lacking in vitamins — we know that it is lacking in calcium, iron, magnesium, manganese, sulphur, phosphorus, iodine, sodium, silicon and other minerals. Children and adults fed on such a diet are certainly mineral-starved. Sugar is not merely vitamin-free, it is also mineral free. Children fed as above are suffering from a dyscrasia, which has its origin in a lack of the above named elements.

How absurd the prevailing notion that a diet such as that described by Dr. Harris, may be rendered adequate by the addition of nauseous cod-liver oil, or by adding a few cakes of yeast to the diet.

McCann says: "When the phosphorus goes the iron goes. When the iron goes, the calcium goes. When the calcium goes, the potassium goes. When these substances go the vitamins go with them, leaving the starches and the gluten behind. Starches and gluten do not themselves sustain life, do not protect health.

"The food factory cannot remove any element from whole wheat or from any other cereal without also removing all the other elements. These elements are so intimately bound up with each other that when one departs all follow."

The practice of peeling certain foods and throwing away the parings is wasteful and harmful. In the indigestible woody fiber and branny cellulose of beans, peas, cereals, fresh corn and nuts, and in the skins of the cucumber, squash, tomato and similar foods, and the seeds of berries, are many solubles (mineral salts) which are yielded up to the body during their passage through the digestive tract. The salts are needed by the body and to throw them away is folly.

In the animal body the various chemical elements are distributed in varying proportions in the different tissues — the muscles are rich in proteins, the bones are rich in calcium and phosphorus. the nerves are rich in phosphorus, the blood is rich in iron and sodium. So, also, in plants, the chemical elements are variously distributed in their different structures.

In a general way potassium, sodium, calcium, iron and sulphur pass into the stems, leaves, and fruits of the plants, while potassium, phosphorus and magnesium predominate in the seeds and roots. Green leafy tops are rich in lime and other needed minerals.

In the lower portions of all vegetables is located the greatest amount of starch and the least amount of minerals and vitamins. The upper green tips of the cabbage are the seats of the greater quantity of minerals and these diminish as we move down to the thick stems. In a general way it is estimated that there are five times as much minerals and vitamins in the green, leafy tops of radishes, onions, beets, turnips, carrots, spinach, lettuce, celery, etc., as in the lower or root portions.

In seeds there is an accumulation of calcium, sodium magnesium, sulphur, flourine and silica in the outer layers, while potassium and sulphur predominate in the inner parts. The vitamins in potatoes are in their eyes and the minerals are under the skin. In grains the vitamins are chiefly in the germ and the minerals are in the outer layers.

All the elements are necessary to sustain life and no portion of the plant should be thrown away. If the grains are ground up and their midlings, bran and germ are thrown away all the vitamins and nearly all the minerals are discarded. If we dig out the eyes of the potato and peel the potato we lose practically all the minerals and vitamins.

There are very few conditions in which we must omit the coarser of these substances and for most patients and all normal individuals they should be a part of the diet. The human digestive tract is as well adapted to handling these things and can take care of them as well as can the digestive tract of the ape or the deer. Nature has not designed man for a diet of mush and does not confine him to such a diet. Indeed a mush diet proves his undoing. Freezing breaks down food both chemically and physically and impairs its food value. Rabbits and chickens will not eat frozen lettuce or cabbage. Freezing breaks down these foods to so great an extent that it is plainly visible to the eye. Ice cream, ices, sherberts, frozen fruits, etc., cannot be recommended. Iced drinks are also bad for the reason that they impair digestion.

The natural affinity existing between the needs of the cells of man's body and the nutritional elements of fruits, nuts and vegetables, is sure guarantee that the eating of natural, that is, unprocessed foods, is thoroughly safe and constructive and that it is in closest harmony with the physiological or biological requirements of the body. Vitamins, calories and other necessary food elements will be supplied as needed by such a plan, and any method of processing our foods and all attempts to reinforce their unfoldment and effects within the body must result in a disturbance of the functions and processes of life.

Dr. Gibson lists, as Life threatening foods, "Ice cream, malted milk, preparations of cocoa and chocolates, alcoholic preparations, any preparation of bran, if separated from the grain itself, any form of bottled beverages, any form of pastry containing sugar, melted butter or lard, patent-sifted flour, cream, or fruit extracts, all kinds of factory preserves, every food stuff that kitchen chemistry has changed from a healthy natural product of vegetative evolution, into a haphazard output of unscientific digestion-and-nutrition-defying food camouflage."

All processed foods should be eschewed. Any treatment of foods which alters their chemistry, or that extracts some of their essential elements, offers nothing but devitalized husks to the consumer.

Sterilizing, predigesting, malting, dextrinizing, glutenizing, pasteurizing, refining, pickling, preserving, denaturing, extracting, concentrating, diluting, emulsifying, concocting, separating, isolating, demineralizing, frying, boiling, baking, hashing, "fruiting" 'crinking," processes are injurious, both to the nutritive value of foods and to the vitality of the consumer. The doctor, the cook, the chemist and the food manufacturer should be required to keep their hands off the food outputs of nature.

EFFECTS OF DENATURED FOODS

The factories, refineries, mills, canneries, bake shops, cooks, etc., have seen to it that we get but little natural foods. Not only have they been very busy subtracting, from them their valuable mineral elements, but they have also learned to add to them many irritating, injurious and poisonous chemicals, dye stuffs, preservatives, etc., until thousands are yearly killed and many are weakened in body and mind. We are fast becoming a race of glass yes, bald heads, false teeth and wooden legs as a result. As one well known Hygienist has so truthfully remarked: "We wake ourselves with caffein, move our bowels with cathartics, coax an appetite with condiments, seek rest in nicotine, go to sleep with an opiate, and die just when we should begin to live."

Under-Nutrition
CHAPTER XXXII

Malnutrition, (Innutrition, Undernutrition) is simply poor or inadequate or defective nutrition — slow starvation. The child is undernourished or is not well nourished. Such a person may be overfed. The cases of malnutrition in those who actually do not eat a sufficient bulk of food are comparatively very rare.

Almost the whole of the American population is suffering from undernutrition. The discovery during the war that so many of the young men in this country are such miserable specimens of physical manhood occasioned a temporary interest in the subject of malnutrition, just as a similar interest in the nutrition of her young followed a similar discovery in the young men of England during the Boer war. Although, this temporary interest in the physical welfare of our future cannon-fodder waned as the patriotic fervor which gave rise to it lessened, with the passing of the war, malnutrition of our children and adults is as acute as ever if not more so. Routine examinations of school children have revealed that malnutrition is as prevalent in these as it was in the young men examined in 1917-1919 and 1933-1946.

Sir Stephan Tallents, Secretary of the Marketing Board (England) in an appeal, in the first half of 1932, for a closer understanding of matters vital to the British Empire, declared: "Research workers have satisfied themselves that whole populations — indeed a scientist told me the other day that I might safely say whole continents — are suffering from malnutrition." He lamented the fact that it takes twenty years for the results of scientific research to percolate into practice.

The United States Children's Bureau found that one-fourth to one-third of the children in this country are definitely malnourished according to medical standards. In some communities malnourishment is so common that it is hardly recognized as an abnormal condition. They found that the number of children of really superior nutrition is really very small.

While a majority of these children manage to grow up, they carry the marks of faulty nutrition with them throughout their lives. Small bones, weak, receding, deformed chins, deformities, defective teeth, undeveloped bodies, flat chests, deformed spines, poor sight, anæmia, marked susceptibility to disease, and low mentality are only some of the more obvious results of malnutrition. Here in San Antonio, among our Mexican population, one scarcely sees a single Mexican who does not present unmistakable evidences of malnutrition.

Malnutrition shows itself in a variety of ways. In young children growth is arrested, the teeth and eyes are defective, sore eyes and rickets, emaciation and deformity develop. In adults, anæmia, loss of appetite, underweight, constipation, pellagra, beri-beri, and nervous troubles result.

Malnutrition manifests itself not only in a failure to gain in height and weight but in many other ways. Indeed many malnourished children are fat, while, others are as tall as the average child of their age. A child may be normal, meaning the median or average, as far as height and weight are concerned, and still present many evidences of malnutrition.

The more common symptoms of malnutrition are a dry, delicate skin which is either pale or wax-like or else sallow, or pasty, or earthy in appearance; dry, rough hair, brittle nails; blue circles or dark hallows under the eyes, with a pale, colorless mucous lining of the eye-lids; loose skin, flabby, undeveloped muscles, round shoulders, projecting shoulder blades, fatigue posture, prominent abdomen, irritability, listlessness, inattention, "laziness," undue mental and physical fatigue, mental backwardness, a temperamental disposition, lack of natural inquisitiveness and a lessened power of concentration; the child is also likely to be finicky about his food. The undernourished child is usually underweight, although some of them are fat and flabby. Borderline conditions of malnutrition commonly pass for healthy conditions.

Dr. Hess, of Columbia University, says that clear-cut disorders are not the most common or important results of food deficiency. Lack of vitamins, he says, "generally does not bring about typical pathological states but obscure alterations of nutrition, ill-defined functional disabilities which cannot be characterized or even recognized as disease."

These ill-defined functional disabilities and obscure alterations of nutrition represent the initial beginnings and the subsequent so-called disease is only a further development of the same alterations and disabilities. It is of the highest importance that we realize that by reason of faulty diet, or other factors that impair nutrition, serious damage to the young may occur without the development of symptoms which definitely mark the condition as deficiency.

The causes of malnutrition are commonly divided into three classes: *physical, social* and *dietetic*.

The "physical causes" are diseases and various malformations. Among these are listed tuberculosis, chronic disease of the tonsils and sinuses connected with the nose, pyelitis, decaying teeth, adenoids and deformities of the jaw and nose. Chronic disease of the tonsils and sinuses connected with the nose are said to be "the most common of the diseases causing malnutrition in childhood." "Decaying teeth often cause malnutrition." "Adenoids and deformities of the jaw and nose are the most common of the deformities which produce malnutrition." Tuberculosis is not considerd a common cause of malnutrition in childhood.

Morse, Wyman-Hill say of malnutrition due to these causes: "The remedies are obvious: removal of diseased tonsils and teeth and of the adenoids, treatment of the sinuses and pyelitis, and correction of the deformities." This is a surgical program and is aimed at effects, not causes.

K. B. Rich in a report of the work of the educational authorities in the Chicago Elementary Schools, showed that the treatment of enlarged tonsils, adenoids, carious teeth, and flat-foot are ineffectual in over-coming malnutrition, although the program had been undertaken with great expectations of success. Fresh air, sunshine, exercise, and improved diet and cleanliness were then tried and these proved effective.

Decay of the teeth is due to malnutrition. So is tuberculosis. So are most deformities of the nose and jaw. The medical profession is so in the habit of getting the cart before the horse — of converting an effect into the cause — that they do it unconsciously. Take the one factor of decay of the teeth. This is so unmistakably an effect of faulty nutrition that we can hardly excuse those who say that the tooth decay causes faulty nutrition.

In the discussion of the "social causes" we usually find more evidence of intellgience, although the treatment of these seldom goes far enough, due to the fact that our universities and research institutions are controlled by big business interests and to the further fact that these same universities and research institutions are large stock holders in oil companies, mining companies, cotton mills,

UNDER-NUTRITION

etc., and are deeply interested in dividends from these. It is, therefore, more profitable to these institutions to vivisect animals, study germs, and endorse serums and surgery than it would be to tell the truth about the social causes of disease, where this might tend to decrease the incomes of these big busienss concerns.

Under social causes we find listed lack of fresh air and sunlight, too hot or too cold houses, mental over fatigue and physical over fatigue. Physical over fatigue is said to be due, usually, to too much hard play. The more than two million children, employed in poorly ventilated, poorly lighted mills, factories and sweat shops in this great land of "progress" and "prosperity" are not likely to play too hard.

There is no condemnation of the crowded slums of our larger cities where sunshine and fresh air are lacking. There is no condemnation of the low wages, high rents, and other economic factors that prevent parents giving their children the benefits of fresh air and sunshine.

Other "social causes" are insufficient sleep, due either to excitement or improper food, or to the premature abandonment of naps and rests or to not putting the child to bed early enough; too much study, neglect at home, family friction, unsuitable books and stories, too many parties, movies, long automobile rides, and too much other such excitement or improper amusement.

To these causes, let me add nagging, scolding and whipping and slapping of children, overclothing, too much handling, especially of infants, smoking by older members of the family in the house, drugs, serums, vaccines, surgical operations, etc.

"The remedy," say Morse-Wyman-Hill, "is, of course, a simple rational, not too strenuous life, without undue excitement, and with plenty of fresh air and sunshine." The remedy must go beyond this prescription. It must take the children and their mothers out of the mills and sweat shops; it must remove them from the slums and crowded tenements; it must supply these children with an atmosphere of love and kindness. It must supply them with houses that are not "too hot or too cold." It must keep them out of the hands of the surgeons and the pus punchers and serum squirters.

Under "dietetic causes" is mentioned "improper food" rather than a "lack of food." This means that the child is fed on foods that are inadequate in one way or another; that do not supply the child's body with all the needed food elements. Without indulging in the customary stereotyped chin music about "calorie requirements," "balanced diets," "protein needs," "fat needs," "accessory foods or vitamins," etc., let me say that this means that the child is fed on white flour and its products, degerminated and demineralized corn meal, denatured cereals, pasteurized and canned milk, sulphured and canned fruits, jellies, jams, white sugar, candies, ice cream, cocoa, chocolate, soda fountain slops, cooked vegetables, mashed potatoes, pies, cakes, crackers, cookies, etc., to the exclusion of fresh raw fruit, fresh raw green vegetables, fresh raw milk (preferably its mother's milk) raw nuts, and whole grains, if grains are used.

A child may be eating foods containing all the food elments required, and yet, due to indigestion from overeating or from any of the above mentioned "social causes," not be able to digest and assimilate its food. Many cases of malnutrition are due to this cause. Undernourishment from overeating is common in our oft-fed babies. Dr. George S. Weger rightly says that an: "Overcrowded nutrition means starvation, whether it be in the infant that is fed more because it cries from already having had too much, or in the adult who gluttonizes because he is drunk on food and craves more stimulation of the same sort." When parents and physicians accept this fact and act upon it, children will be more healthy and will develop more beautifully

A common, but unrecognized cause of innutrition is toxemia resulting from impaired elimination. This toxic state of the blood and lymph is back of the chronic disease of the tonsils, adenoids and sinuses, which is listed as a "physical cause" of malnutrition. Toxemia deranges and perverts nutrition. It is due to anything that overtaxes the vital or nervous powers and checks elimination.

There are all degrees of malnutrition ranging all the way from a near-normal condition where there seems to be no definite symptoms, but still the child appears to be in not quite normal condition, to a condition presenting all of the symptoms previously described and many more and worse conditions. Malnutrition lays the faulty anatomic foundation of various organic diseases in later life. The remedy is a complete overhauling of the child's life — social and dietetic. See chapter on *Feeding of Children*.

What are classed as nutritive, or *deficiency* diseases have two groups of causes — namely:

UNDER-NUTRITION

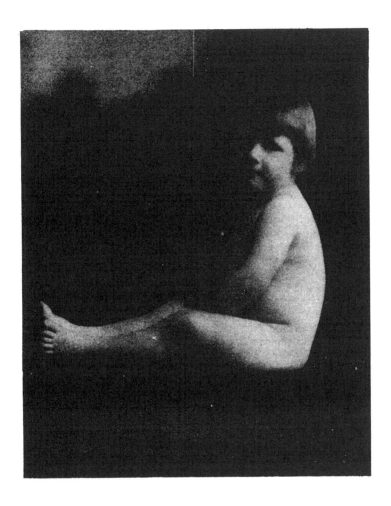

Example of Superior Nutrition

THE SCIENCE AND FINE ART OF FOOD AND NUTRITION

1. Deficiencies in diet, either in quality or quantity, usually, except in famine districts, in quality.

2. All of those factors and influences, whatever their nature and source, which render it difficult or impossible for the body to utilize the elements of its food, even though the food is perfect.

Dietitians rarely give any attention to this second group of causes. They experiment with healthy animals and seldom see any other factor than that of a studied and deliberately made dietary deficiency. They are easily misled by their one-sided, or as they call them, controlled experiments.

In dealing with children and adults let us always keep in mind that we are not dealing with controls. The life of a human being, child or adult, is much more complex than that of any experimental animal in the laboratory. His environment is more varied, his contacts greater in number, the influences to which he is subjected more numerous, and the resources of his environment greater.

Pregnant mothers that are fed on a good diet, if their nutrition is impaired by overwork, worry, fear, or other cause, will not be able to assimilate the elements of their food and their babies will be born with the "seeds" of some deficiency disease "in their bones." The babies will then be fed-up (stuffed) in an effort to force them to take on weight and their own weak nutritive machinery will be so impaired that, in spite of an adequate diet, deficiency will develop. Too much handling, drugging and any other cause that debilitates the infant and child will damage its nutrition sufficiently to bring on nutritive disease. Indeed there is an element of *nutritive disease* present in every so-called disease.

The needs of children for vitamins, salts and proteins are relatively greater than those of adults. These things are absolutely indispensible for the processes of growth and a deficiency in any one of them during the growth period has nutritional consequences. For this reason it is during infancy and childhood that most careful attention to nutrition is essential.

By slight alterations in feeding, it is possible to produce all degrees of muscular change, and "other physiological functions are undoubtedly interfered with by the same apparently small dietetic abnormalities."

Many eye troubles are blamed on the teeth, when, as a matter of fact, it would be equally correct to blame the tooth trouble on the eyes. Dr. Howe says: "Now it is apparent that both tooth and eye-trouble may have the same underlying cause! Xerophthalmia (the disease that attacked the Roumanian children because of the lack of vitamin A in their diet) is one of the first signs of vitamin deficiency in experimental guinea pigs. Running eyes occur in vitamin-deficient feeding. Many of our skulls showed decalcified areas in the orbit (eye socket) usually at the base of the teeth.

In young guinea-pig mothers on the vitamin deficient diet, many eye disturbances appeared, cloudy spots on the coatings of the eye, opacity of the lens in both eyes like cataracts. After feeding the cataract specimen with orange juice in large quantities, the trouble disappeared."

"Vitamin deficiency" may mean anything such as deficiency in health. When the diet is properly balanced with regard to minerals, there is no likelihood of any deficiency in vitamins occurring. By shortage or deficiency the "orthodox" food scientist usually means a shortage sufficient to result in some "deficiency disease." If ordinary health is maintained they are satisfied; superior health is not worth working for. We want better health than just average or so-called "normal" health. Not merely freedom from "disease," however slight, but abounding, positive health is the goal every parent should set for his or her children.

Sherman and Macleod found in their animal experiments, that a great abundance of "vitamin-rich" foods, far more than enough to eradicate evidences of deficiency, added to a diet that is fully adequate for the development of the normal size, produces a marked superiority in the appearance and condition of the animal. There is increased growth and weight, the animal matures earlier, has a longer adult life, increased reproductive power with more offspring, has a delayed senility, so that the whole life-span is increased about ten per cent. This improvement may properly be called super-health.

Hypo-Alkalinity
CHAPTER XXXIII

Acidosis is the term misapplied to a lessened alkalinity of the body fluids. The fluids of the body are normally slightly alkaline. A lowering of the alkalinity of these fluids is more properly termed *hypoalkalinity*. Acidosis or hypoalkalinity is defined as a condition characterized by a deficiency of fixed alkalies in the body, which leads to an increased production of ammonia in the urine and a high acidity.

Acidosis is not acid blood, for the blood never becomes acid during life. An alkaline blood and lymph is necessary to life and health and for the blood to even reach the point of neutrality would cause speedy death.

The normal ratio between the alkalies and acids of the body is approximately 80 to 20 — 80% alkali and 20% acid. This proportion is maintained in balance by the so-called "buffer salts" — sodium, potassium, calcium and magnesium — from which either side may draw as need arises. When this "buffer" or "balance wheel" is in normal order any excess of acids in the body is promptly neutralized. It is only when there is a deficiency of these salts that troubles may arise. A shortening of the relationship between these is wrongly termed acidosis.

The body will not tolerate any free acid for a minute, except in the stomach during the process of digestion. All acids are instantly "bound," by being combined with alkalies, to render them harmless. The body makes use of every resource at its command to preserve its alkalinity for the reason that its cells can thrive only in an alkaline medium and cannot possibly thrive in an acid medium.

Since we supply acids and alkalies to our bodies through food, the matter of a balance between acid foods and alkali or base foods is important. If an excessive amount of acid food is eaten, the blood is forced to draw upon its alkaline reserve, its "buffer salts," in order to maintain its normal alkalinity. When we have taken more acid into the body than we can "bind" without sacrificing some of the bases of the tissues, blood alkalinity falls below the normal level and we have hypoalkalinity or acidosis.

HYPO-ALKALINITY

Every food eaten leaves behind it an ash after it has been used by the body. The ash is either acid or alkaline. Eating too much acid-ash food, or eating it over long periods of time, results in storing acid-ash in the cells and in depleting the body of its alkaline reserve.

Acid-ash foods are all meats, eggs, cheese, milk (in adults), all cereals and cereal products, legumes (except in the green state), nuts, and all denatured foods of all kinds. Denatured foods have been robbed of their bases.

The alkaline-ash foods are fruits (except cranberries, prunes and some plums), all green vegetables and milk (in infants). Fats and oils are classed as neutral foods.

Severe acidosis may be produced experimentally by deficient diets, but such severe states are seldom met with in life, except in famine. Maignon has repeatedly shown that an exclusive protein diet is positively toxic even in the carnivora. Whipple, Slyke, Birkner, and Berg have shown the same thing.

The medical administration of acids, such as salicylic acid, benzoic acid, boric acid, sulphuric acid, etc., leads to a dangerous loss of bases, for these acids can be rendered harmless and subsequently eliminated only after being combined with alkaline elements. Hydrochloric acid, prescribed by physicians in supposed gastric hypoacidity, also leaches the body of its bases and aids in producing acidosis.

Free acetic acid, as found in vinegar, if consumed in quantities, may lead to symptoms of acid poisoning. It is even more injurious to health than alcohol. The body is called upon to sacrifice its bases to neutralize the acid, while it has a particularly destructive effect upon the red corpuscles and may produce anæmia.

A diet poor in bases, or food that has been robbed of its bases, has the same deleterious effects. The meat diet, as used in civilized countries, is of this type. An exclusive muscle-meat diet, when fed to dogs, will not maintain health and growth. If dogs are fed on meat from which the juices have been expressed, "emaciation ensues after a time, toxic symptoms set in, death speedily follows, and postmortem examination shows in the skeleton changes characteristic of osteomalacia and osteoporosis." (Osteomalacia is softening of the bones; Osteoporosis is the rarefication — decrease in density — of bone due to enlargement of its cavities or the formation of new spaces). Cooking meat extracts much of its juices and, where these extracted juices are not eaten, the same draining of minerals from the bones and other tissues of the eater must occur.

Flesh eating animals eat the bones of their prey, for it is here that most of the calcium of the vegetables eaten by the prey is deposited. When a man eats meat he eats only the soft parts, thus he fails to secure the calcium. Carnivorous animals also supply their need for bases by drinking the blood and by eating the internal organs and cartilages. These are consumed raw and with a minimum of loss. Berg says: "It also appears that wild carnivora consume at times considerable quantities of fruits, leaves and buds; they do this especially in the autumn, whereas in the spring they live almost exclusively on animal food."

An exclusive meat diet, like an exclusive grain diet causes a great loss of bases from the body and causes "acidosis." Benedict and Roth found that the basic turn over is much less in vegetarians than in persons on a mixed diet. An excess of bases is always desirable and is necessary to the best utilization of proteins and carbohydrates.

Acids arising from decomposition of foods in the digestive tract require to be neutralized. These, like tea, coffee, cocoa and chocolate, deprive the body of bases.

The exclusive eating of fat is also a source of acidosis; for, the free fatty acids liberated by the splitting up of fat in the intestine cannot be absorbed so far as is known. This neutralization must occur, therefore, in the intestine itself, at the cost of the alkalies of the bile as well as of the food. The unabsorbed fatty acids are eliminated in the stools in the form of sodium soap, calcium soap and potassium soap, and this soap formation robs the body of these bases.

All organic acids produced in the body and all mineral acids deplete the alkali-reserves of the body. The normal processes of life produce acids in the form of waste and the body's bases are consumed in neutralizing them. There is a constant demand for bases and the conventional diet does not supply these in adequate quantities. If our foods do not maintain the normal alkalinity of the blood and tissues, disease develops; for if there is a lack of bases, the body must withhold from neutralization some of the poisonous organic and mineral acids, so that as these gradually accumulate, an acid-toxemia results.

HYPO-ALKALINITY

Violent or long-continued emotional states and overwork result in the formation of acid metabolic end-products that require to be "bound" with bases.

"Acidosis" may be very mild and even transitory in its initial stages, and very severe and dangerous when fully developed. Between these two extremes a large number of intermediate stages may exist. Severe states of acidosis, as seen in certain diseases, develop only after the acid-toxemia has so greatly impaired the organs of the body that metabolism is greatly crippled. The attention of the medical profession has always been fixed upon the severe terminal forms of acidosis and they have ignored its initial stages. The clinical diagnosis of acidosis was made only after the hypoalkalinity had reached a far advanced and dangerous stage. They looked only for the end-point of the pathological evolution resulting from a progressive acid-saturation and alkali-depletion of the tissues.

The decline of blood alkalinity, as previously pointed out, may be due to one or more of many factors. Whether we regard it as a "rising acidity" or a "lowered alkalinity" makes little practical difference so long as we know its sources and how to avoid these.

Whether an increasing acidosis — *hypoalkilinity* — is due to the accumulation of the acid end-products of protein metabolism, or to the binding of the too great a proportion of the body's alkalies by the development of acid fermentation in the digestive tract, or to the consumption of an excess of acid-rich and alkali-deficient foods, or to the medicinal use of acids, makes no difference. The results are the same; beginning with a lowered available alkalinity and a resulting crippling of function, proportionate to the degree of *hypoalkalinity*, and progressing to serious organic disease and death.

The symptoms of *acidosis* are fatigue, headache, loss of appetite, sleeplessness, general nervousness, acid stomach (hyperacidity), acid perspiration and frequent troubles — colds and the like — and a sour disposition.

Acidosis inhibits growth in the young, depletes the bodies of adults, and lowers vitality. It imposes a tremendous handicap upon pregnancy and lactation. It predisposes to tuberculosis, cancer, pneumonia, appendicitis, measles and other "diseases."

Chronic fatigue is often nothing more than acid-toxemia and this same acid-toxemia, if not removed, will in its extension and continuation, result in premature "old age," functional and organic disease and death. The blood robbed of its normal alkalinity can not neutralize or correct the acid "fatigue products" and these are permitted to poison the body. The health, strength, youth, growth and preservation of the body depends upon a certain fixed degree of alkalinity. Old age is a disease which has not, as yet, taken on definite organic form. It is the result of auto-intoxication, that is, of retention of acid waste.

Men who have become almost fanatical about heredity assert that diet has nothing to do with length of life — it is all a matter of heredity. But if a pair of rats are fed on a diet of meat, grain and tubers, such as potatoes and beets, they will live about one year. If milk and cabbage are added to this diet, the rats live nearly three years. Food does help to determine longevity — make no mistake about that.

The noted surgeon of Cleveland, Dr. George W. Crile, says: "There is no natural death. All so-called death from natural causes are merely the end-point in a progressive acid saturation."

The cells of the body are born, pass through their regular life-cycle and are exfoliated and replaced by new ones. Whether they are replaced by normal cells or diseased ones depends wholly upon the kinds of materials out of which the new cells are created and upon what inhibiting waste is present or absent. The body is created anew daily; but if its blood and lymph are not normal the process of renewal is imperfect.

Diet Reform vs. Supplemental Feeding
CHAPTER XXXIV

We have become so artificial in our habits of thinking that it almost invariably occurs that when a discovery of the value of some type of food is made, we think immediately of some artificial way to secure the benefits of the discovery. We seem to be afraid of natural foods. Food manufacturers find us easy dupes and sell us all manners of patented foods that are guaranteed to be "just as good" as or even better than the natural product. Another group exploit sea weeds as supplements to our diet and sell enormous quantities of these unpalatable substances.

When false nutritive elements such as iron or synthetic vitamins, are added to a food of which they are natural constituents but from which they have been removed in the processing of these foods, these foods are said to be *restored*. When such pseudo-food factors are added to foods in which these elements exist naturally in sparse quantities, the food is said to be *enriched*. When elements are added which do not naturally occur in the food at all the food is said to be *fortified*. When one food is used to enrich another, the food is said to be *supplemented*. Two foods that enrich one another are said to *supplement* each other.

For the most part, *restoration, fortification* and *enrichment* of foods is a farce. The inorganic lime salts, iron salts, etc., used in these processes are non-usable; the synthetic vitamins employed for these purposes are of no value. Supplementing foods is a mere game. Since no one ever lives on but one or two foods and since no one food is of and by itself, adequate to meet the nutritive needs of man, we live upon a diet composed, at all times, of a variety of foods. We need only to make sure that the *tout ensemble* of the foods we consume meets the *tout ensemble* of our nutritive needs and should cease the parlor game of supplementing one food with another. Back to natural eating, should be our rallying cry. Are we such fools that we are going on forever removing from natural foods essential nutritive factors and then replacing them with "just as good" synthetic substances? Shall we forever bow the neck to the yoke of commercialism and a false science created by this same commercialism?

After going to great lengths to spoil nature's food products we seek to supplement them with brewer's yeast, wheat germ, black molasses and yogurt made from boiled milk. We eat white bread, white sugar, pasteurized milk, canned vegetables, etc., and expect to render such a diet adequate by the addition of cod-liver oil or other fish oil, a small amount of orange juice, or rice polishings. We cook our spinach until it is black and mushy, boil our cabbage until it is unrecognizable, peel and boil our potatoes, bake our apples and drown them in a syrup made of white sugar and then eat brewer's yeast and convert our intestinal tract into a beer vat. Or, we eat black molasses which is as efficient as brewer's yeast in producing fermentation.

Martin Frobisher, Jr., in his *Fundamentals of Bacteriology* says that yeast cells "synthesize several vitamins which are of great value in the maintenance of health" and that "yeast may therefore be taken *if the diet is otherwise deficient in these vitamins.*" But he adds that "normal foods, in good variety, including eggs, milk, butter, vegetables such as spinach and lettuce, whole cereals and citrus fruits, furnish practically everything offered by yeast, and in a more rational form."

The fact is that a good variety of natural, unprocessed, uncooked foods furnish everything offered by yeast and much that yeast does not offer. That they furnish these things in a "more rational form" hardly needs be added. Why, then, say yeast may be taken, "*if the diet is otherwise deficient in these vitamins?*" Why not resort to the more rational forms of dietary substances to make the diet adequate?

It was found by certain British and German investigators that the addition of fresh carrot juice or raw spinach juice to the diet of children suffering with severe scurvy results in recovery. The addition of fresh vegetable juices to the diet has given excellent results in many cases of malnutrition. The same is true of fruit juices. It is amusing to see the "discovery" of their value trumpeted to the world as a "brilliant medical discovery," thirty years after it was rejected by the medical profession as nonsense of the faddists and quacks. We faddists and quacks were not dismayed by their taunts and are now triumphantly right.

DIET REFORM VS. SUPPLEMENTAL FEEDING

Changes in the urine prove positively that metabolism is improved by the liberal use of fruits and green vegetables or their juices. The urine finds particularly indicate a more complete protein transformation and oxidation. The improvement in adults is not so quickly gained as in the young, but is finally by just as positive.

These juices are valuable not alone in malnutritional states in children, but also in chronic diseases in children and adults. Their excesses of bases supply needed basic salts to the body and enable it to sweep itself free of acids. But the juice of no food is as valuable as the food itself.

The child-feeding tests carried on by experimental nutritionists are merely tests of supplemental feeding. No great or radical change is made in the conventional, inadequate diet. They merely supplement the diet the children are eating, with milk or fruit juice or some other such food and compare the children so fed with those not so fed.

Many such tests have been made on animals and many on school children. A California school test compared milk, oranges and milk and oranges as supplements to the regular diets the children were receiving, with the following results:

	Expected gain in pounds	Actual gain in pounds	Percentage excess gain
No supplemental food	.54	.69	.28
Milk	.46	.95	106
Orange	.58	1.40	141
Milk and Orange	.48	1.07	122

It will be noted that oranges alone gave the greatest gain and that oranges and milk gave greater gains than milk alone, although oranges and milk did not equal oranges alone. Although this is disputed, I contend that this test shows that oranges are better supplements to the average diet than is milk. This does not mean that oranges as an exclusive article of diet is as complete food as milk as an exclusive article of diet, but merely that as a supplement to the inadequate diet conventionally fed to children oranges are superior to milk.

There are two other important particulars in which these tests are defective. First, they are never carried out over a sufficiently long period of time to give ultimate results; and, second, they deal with children *en mass* and the reports are mere averages. Individual differences are submerged. In the reports the great gains made by a few on the supplemental feeding submerge the actual losses made by others.

In reporting averages for those on the non-supplemental diet, no account is taken of the individual differences shown by the children in this group. The conventional diet is not uniform. No two families, and no two individuals, eat exactly alike. No adequate attention is given to the individual diets consumed by the children in both groups.

The children on the supplemented diet show on the average some advantage (some improvement in health or in the rate of growth) over the average of the children on the non-supplemented diet. While such experiments point to possibilities, they certain-do not establish an ideal method of feeding. Radical changes in the conventional diet and not mere supplements thereto are essential.

It is unfortunate that the discovery of the value of fruits and vegetables or their juices has not lead to a revolutionizing of our feeding and eating practices, but to an endeavor to supplement the inadequate diet now employed. There is altogether too much effort to "improve" the conventional white-flour-white-sugar-mashed-potato-diet by adding a few drops of cod-liver oil or a few spoonfuls of tomato juice or orange juice or a few powdered sea weeds.

It is urged that "even unsuitable food can be favorably influenced by the addition" of so-called "food adjuncts." Commercial houses and dietitians have been quick to take advantage of this claim. Doctors and false dietitians have used this as a barrier to true food reform. These adjuncts or accessories may be manufactured, prescribed and sold at large profits. It was shown in a previous chapter that it is impossible to eat sufficient "offsetting" foods to completely compensate for the deficiencies of a predominantly denatured diet, such as is commonly eaten in this country.

Supplements of the right kind are useful to those who are situated so that they cannot get a proper diet, or to those who are unable to digest and assimilate certain essential foods. But a really correct dietary requires no supplements. It is complete in itself and fully adequate to meet all the food needs of the body.

Today we are being offered "accessory foods" rather than food reform. Commercial firms have placed their "food accessories" on the market to be taken in doses of a spoonful or more at a time, just like drugs. The "accessory foods" are supposed to adjust an "ill-

DIET REFORM VS. SUPPLEMENTAL FEEDING

balanced diet." Why not balance the diet? We need to thoroughly revolutionize and completely reform our diet.

One house advertises that its product "is not a substitute, but is the quintessence of the green leaf in a palatable and assimilable form." This is not a dietetic, but a drug conception. No process can take the "quintessence of the green leaf" and give it to us so that it will be as valuable as the green leaf. Besides, the green leaf exists in a palatable and assimilable form.

Dr. Oswald says: "Ours is an age of extracts. We have moral extracts in the form of Bible-House pamphlets; language-extracts in the form of compendious grammers; exercise extracts under the name of gymnastic curriculums; air-extracts in the shape of oxygen-bladders, and a vast deal of such food-concentrations as Liebig's soup, fruit-jellies, condensed milk, and flavoring extracts. But, somehow or other, the old plan seems after all, the best."

Artificial food preparations are advertised to contain just the food elements required and to contain these in just the right proportions. This claim has weight only with those who do not know that the makers of the foods do not know what the right proportions of these elements are. One firm advertises that one of its "accessory foods" is "concentrated to more than 400 times the potency of the fresh, raw vegetables from which it is derived." There is no reason to believe that such concentration can be helpful. Man is correlated with and adapted to foods as Nature — the plant kingdom — produces them.

Berg says: "All artificial (food) preparations are more or less unbalanced, simply because the fundamental knowledge necessary for their manufacture is entirely lacking. Only living plants can give us all the factors necessary for the maintenance of health." He further says: "physiologically, we have not the slightest idea how many or in what proportion mineral substances are required by the human being. It is identically the same with vitamins."

Consistent with our artificial thinking habits one company that produces and sells prepared spinach juice, after supplying much unimpeachable testimony showing the great value of spinach, supplies four reasons why we should reject fresh spinach as unsuitable, and should employ their processed and inferior product instead.

The shelves of the so-called health food stores of the land are groaning under their load of bottled, canned and powdered foods and food juices; each one guaranteed to be good for dozens of so-called diseases; each one a necessary adjunct to our diet. Their minerals and vitamins are said to be concentrated so that only small amounts of them supply the deficiencies in the conventional diet.

Instead of adding bottled spinach juice, powdered sea weeds and other such inferior products to the conventional, deficient diet, we need to revolutionize our diet. The real health foods do not come in cans, bottles, boxes and capsules. They are grown in garden and orchard, are irradiated by the sun, rather than by an ultra-violet ray lamp, and are more suited to the nutritive needs of our bodies as they come, ready-made, from the lap of mother nature, than after they have been dried, powdered, canned, bottled and cooked.

Superior nutrition can come only from a fundamentally correct and fully adequate dietary and no amount of supplementary additions to our, at present, largely denatured diet can give us superior nutrition.

Beginning the Reform Diet
CHAPTER XXXV

The question, How shall I begin the new way of eating?", is asked by thousands who first become acquainted with the principles of right eating. Just how shall they begin? How shall they prepare their new dietary? Shall they change to the new diet gradually or abruptly? How much shall they eat? What reactions may they expect? These are important questions, which, unfortunately, most of the literature of the subject does not help them to answer. We have many vegetarian cook books and books filled with vegetarian recipes and menus; but too often these imitate the old diet rather than lead the neophyte into correct eating practices. These books represent a compromise with perverted tastes, false appetancies, and wrong practices. This is, perhaps, the chief reason so many vegetarians fail to realize the full benefits of the vegetarian way of life. I get mental vertigo when I go through these books and read all the recipes for making meat substitutes, mock turkey, etc. What do we need with a "meat substitute?" Either vegetarianism is a correct way of life, or it is not. Either meat is the substitute, or it is a normal part of man's diet. There can be no need to imitate the old diet if it is wrong. We need to discard the substitute and return to the original, the genuine; we need to make a complete break with the old dietary practices.

Dr. Philip Norman refers to *"The American Home Diet,"* an "excellent work" prepared by McCollum and Simonds, and says of the balanced menus" which "have been introduced with instructions for their use," that: "These meals are ordinary meals fortified with green vegetables, fruit and milk. Custom has so shackled the thought of investigators that they have not been able to break away from the bread, meat and potato type of diet. The balanced meal, therefore, is simply an improvement as regards the balance of dietary essentials. It does not take into account the physiologic process of digestion." It does not, in other words, pay the slightest regard to combinations. These "investigators" are so conservative and so shackled by custom and convention that they are afraid of radical revision of the dietary.

Hygienists are not so timid. They have not hibernated in antiquity. They are not bound by traditions and outworn customs. They long ago got rid of the meat, potato and bread type of diet. "Bread is the staff of death," declared Emmit Densmore, many years ago. Meat we have rejected for over a hundred years. Combinations we have developed.

Household hints, dietetic advice, etc., as dished up to the public, in the columns of the daily press, and, as sent out over the radio, are all designed to sell the goods of the advertisers. These pernicious pieces of propaganda encourage people to go on blindly, as they have always done, and prepare their foods to tickle their palates. The advice thus given the public is actually criminal.

I do not mean to say that the conventionally healthy cannot eat such things and maintain the conventional health standard; but I do insist that they cannot be as well with them as they can be without them. I say also that every meal of such food renders them more liable to various forms of chronic "disease."

The usual doctor-prescribed diet is not a diet at all. The average diet prescribed by the average doctor, contains the same foods, denatured and adulterated, and the same reckless combinations, which the patients have been eating all their lives, and which have built the nutritional states which form the biological ground work for the affections with which they suffer. Doctors, often oppose real eating reform for selfish reasons, and the people are so bound in voluntary or self-forged chains of slavery to the palate that they are easily taken in by the ludicrous diatribes of their natural enemies, the heresy-hunting medical high priests, and are easily induced to leave in the lurch their true helpers and benefactors, the dissenters.

What can they know of food-reform who know it only from hearsay — what can they know of food reform who have seen it only in a few isolated cases of superficial and eleventh-hour changes of eating habits?

CONFUSION EVERYWHERE

Happily trophologic knowledge increases and spreads from week to week. As time passes ever increasing numbers of people become interested in the proper care and feeding of their bodies. Unfortunately, those who are seeking increased knowledge are flooded with such a mass of conflicting theories and practices and confronted with so much disagreement between those who pose as leaders in the field of dietary science and are the loudest in trumpeting their own horns, that they often become confused and discouraged and give up in disgust.

The market is flooded with cook books and menu books, the newspapers and magazines carry innumerable menus and recipes. Food manufacturers issue free cook books, the recipes and menus of which all contain their own products as essential ingredients.

For the most part, the authors of these books and newspaper and magazine articles are busy multiplying stimulating dishes for the palsied tastes and waning appetites of gluttons. In most such works, the greatest effort of their authors seems to have been to mix and mingle together the greatest number of articles of foods, seasonings, saltings, spicings, greasings, etc., into a single dish; and jumble the greatest possible variety of heterogenous substances into the stomach at a single meal.

To counteract, therefore, to some extent at least, the misinformation and the demoralizing tendency of the ordinary cook book and the great mass of rubbish that is written on diet, and to aid the young particularly, in an understanding of the true relations of food to health, this chapter has been prepared.

AMERICAN DIET INADEQUATE

It is asserted by orthodox authorities that most of the native diets of the different races are far superior to the conventional American diet, even at is best. What a blow this must be to the smug complacency of that great mass of me-and-God physicians who assume that the American diet is an adequate diet and that any diet that radically differs from this is hopelessly inadequate.

These same authorities recognize the possibility of securing an adequate diet in a variety of ways, but they seem to overlook the important fact that the conventional American diet is inadequate, not because it is lacking in variety and amount, but because it is almost wholly a denatured diet. This failure to recognize the source of the inadequacies of the American diet leads them to say that, instead of trying to improve the diets of foreign peoples, who come to this country, by persuading these people to conform to American standards, a thing demanded by ignorant doctors, ignorant labor leaders and selfish food manufacturers (food spoilers); the "more logical procedure would be to persuade each nationality group to return to the best features of the diets of their native land."

This "more logical procedure" is not an ideal solution of nutritional problems. If the native Irish diet and the native German diet are both good, there is no reason why the German cannot eat the Irish diet and the Irishman eat the German diet. But if neither of these diets is the best possible, why not present both the German and the Irishman with the best diet instead of persuading him to eat as always? We want optimal growth and optimal health and the dietetic excellence upon which these depend.

WHAT IS DIET REFORM?

Food reform involves many changes in personal and social habits and these often come in conflict with the habits of thinking and acting of your family and associates. Unless, however, you are afraid of being lost out of the social package on the way down town, you have nothing to fear. You do not need to become a social outcast and should not do so unless you are big enough to be an outcast.

Edgar J. Saxon of England well says: "Food reform begins and ends with discrimination, choice and pleasure. Abstinence from unwholesome food is not a good beginning, and it is a very bad end. Abstinence is healthy only when it easily and invariably results from choice of something better." The emphasis should be placed on the positive side — on the side of wholesomeness, integrity, pleasure and fitness to supply the needs of the body; not on the negative side — that of mere abstinence from unwholesome foods, as essential as this is.

Food reform can take place without altering the way of feeding. White bread can be supplanted with wholewheat bread and one may then go on eating excessively of bread and eating it in all possible wrong combinations. Eating reform may and may not accompany food reform. Eating reform occurs only when one begins to eat properly.

IS YOUR BOON MY BANE?

Is it true that "one man's meat is another man's poison?" Is water one man's poison and food another's? Is calcium? Is phosphorus? Is sodium? No one makes such absurd claims, yet the foods that are said to be boons to one man and banes to another never enter the blood stream as whole foods. They are broken down in the process of digestion and enter the blood as amino acids, monosaccharides, fatty acids, minerals and vitamins. Little fish never swim around in the blood streams of fish eaters. Potatoes are not rolled through the arteries and veins like marbles.

BEGINNING THE REFORM DIET

It is protested that "we are not all constituted alike." But physiologists have not found evidence that life is as chaotic as this implies. We each start life as a fertilized ovum, pursue the same course of orderly evolution, are born with the same number and kinds of organs and with the same functions. We possess the same glands and the same digestive systems. We are composed of the same chemical elements in the same proportions. Each of us secretes the same number and kinds of digestive juices and the same digestive enzymes. Structurally and functionally, our digestive systems are so much alike that the physiologists cannot find that different constitution we hear so much about. Everything points to the conclusion that we are constituted upon the same principles, are constructed alike, have the same nutritive needs and are equipped to digest and utilize the same kinds and classes of foods.

No man has the constitution of the dog or the cow. All men have human constitutions. No one ever proclaimed that cows are so differently constituted that while some of them live well on grasses and herbs, others must have flesh-foods. No one pretends that while most lions live on flesh, blood and bones, some lions are so constituted that flesh is their poison and they must graze like an ox.

What is *constitution?* It is the composition of the body. It is the *tout ensemble* of organs and functions that constitute the body. Every organ and every function in the body of one man is subject to the same laws as are the organs and functions of the body of any other man. The laws of nature do not require one kind of practice in one man and another and opposite kind of practice in another man. Habits and circumstances that are precisely adapted to the laws of life in one man are practices and circumstances that are precisely adapted to the same laws in another man.

Because of this false doctrine that there are many kinds of human constitutions, requiring different habits and circumstances to conform to the laws of life, we are misled into all kinds of errors. "Tobacco does not harm my constitution" says one, while another confidently asserts that "coffee agrees with my constitution." Another possesses a constitution that requires large quantities of food, while another is so constituted that he requires very little sleep. There is hardly an injurious practice and indulgence in the whole long catalogue of man's abuses of himself, that is not defended by those who practice them, or indulge, on the ground that it agrees with their particular and peculiar constitution. None of them, so far as I have been able to ascertain, have ever found that jumping from the top of the Empire State Building agrees with their constitutions. But if life is as chaotic as they seem to think, there seems to be no reason why some constitutions should not be found that would need and require such jumps.

Life being what it is and natural laws being what they are, what is really and permanently best for one is best for all; and what is injurious for one, is so for all.

None of the above is to be interpreted to mean that human needs do not vary under different conditions and circumstances of life. No one would be foolish enough to declare that the three days old infant and the fifty years old man have identical needs; or that the needs of man in the tropics and his needs in frigid regions are identical. Nor are the needs of the sick and those of the healthy identical. This is not due to any change in the law, but to change in conditions. The same man has different needs under different conditions.

There are individual weaknesses and differences in resistance that call for temporary modifications of any program of living, but it is essential that the modifications comply with the laws of life. All programs or parts of programs that violate these laws are ultimately ruinous. Variations within the law are legitimate. No variations that step outside the law are ever permissible.

ATTITUDES

Your success or failure in your effort at dietary reform will hinge largely upon your attitude to your own life. You will have to form and fix new habits at the same time you uproot and cast out the old ones. This requires that you go through periods of readjustment which you will never go through except on the conditions that you really desire to go through them and that you have the trophologic knowledge essential to guide you through this period. Iron in your will is often more important than iron in your food.

Habit will accustom you to whatever is best if you "stick it out," but you must be able to resist the temptations of the lunch counters of "commercialized kitchendom" and withstand the taunts of your ignorant and misguided, though often well-meaning friends and family. Persist in your determination to form good habits as you did in forming the tobacco habit over the protests of your organic instincts, and you will certainly succeed. You can learn to like any good food which you may not now relish, even more quickly than you learned to like the taste of beer.

By a recognition of the simple rule that what is not *for* me is *against* me, it becomes easily possible to cultivate proper attitudes towards dietary practices.

ACQUIRED TASTES

Our food tends to become more and more a matter of taste and appetite, the latter trained and perverted by the cook and the chef. We eat what we like, or what has been prepared so that we will like it, or what we have cultivated a taste for, rather than what we need. We force ourselves to acquire a taste for things that are not good for us, but, which, are often positively harmful to us.

There may be intuitive dislikes or aversions to foods which should not be disregarded. But most of our likes and dislikes are so conditioned by habits that our dislike for fruit may and frequently is due simply to our habit of using tobacco. But an innate repugnance to a special dish, or even a special class of foods, may be safely indulged, so long as other foods are adequate. Abnormal antipathies may indicate constitutional abnormalities or else emotional complexes.

Whatever may be true of our dislikes, our likes are not always to be respected. As Dr. Oswald says, "a child's whimsical desire to treat innutritious or injurious substances as comestibles should certainly not be encouraged °°°°. For, it is a curious fact that all unnatural practices — the eating of undigestible matter as well as poisons — are apt to excite a morbid appentency akin to the stimulant habit. The human stomach can be accustomed to the most preposterous things—*Physical Education*, p. 61.

ACQUIRING NEW TASTES

The acquisition of new tastes is not at all difficult, not nearly so difficult as is the acquisition of the taste for tobacco, alcohol, coffee, chocolate, etc. If we go at eating reform with the same determination we employed in learning to smoke, there will be no failure. A taste for any wholesome substance may be acquired in much less time and with much less effort than can the taste for unwholesome substances.

It is easier to acquire a relish for wholesome substances than for unwholesome ones, Plutarch advised "choose out the best conditions you can and custom will make it pleasant for you." Again, "accustom your appetite to obey reason with willingness."

VARIETY: SPICE OF GLUTTONY

King Cyrus asked the ambassador of a luxurious potentate: "Do you know how invincible men are who can live on herbs and acorns?"

Simplicity should characterize the meals. A variety of foods at a variety of meals should be the rule. Too many foods at a time complicate the digestive process. Great variety always encourages overeating.

I have coined the term monotrophic meals to designate the practice of eating but one food at a time as distinguished from the mono-diet where only one food is consumed (as the milk diet) at all times. The monotrophic meal simplifies matters but is not essential if the meal is properly combined.

The strictest monodiet tends to become extremely monotonous and will not be long adhered to. Moses fed the Hebrews on a monodiet in the wilderness — a diet of *manna* — against which they were in constant rebellion.

The milk diet is an example of a real mono diet. Monodiets have certain value in various conditions, but they are by no means an ideal diet for long, regular and continued use, not alone because they are monotonous, but, also, and more importantly, because they are very inadequate.

There are other reasons why a variety of foods should not be eaten besides the fact that they induce overeating. The greater the variety of foods consumed at a meal, the more complicated and, consequently, less efficient, becomes the digestive process. Simple meals digest better and with less tax upon the digestive organs than complicated meals. Digestion is most efficient when but one food is eaten at a time. Where the limitations of the digestive enzymes are not respected, as is the case with millions, and no consideration is given to the proper combinations of foods, the more foods that are eaten at the meal the more complicated the digestive process becomes.

The reader will please bear in mind that I offer no objection to eating a variety of foods. I believe, on the contrary, in eating a wide variety of them. I am here discussing the evils of the common practice of trying to secure the whole variety at one meal. Properly managed, a variety of foods guarantees better nourishment than only a few foods.

To return to our main theme, that of overeating induced by great variety at meals, let us point out that it is practically impossible to avoid overeating so long as appetite is constantly tempted and stimulated by a great variety of foods. So long as we insist on

BEGINNING THE REFORM DIET

having a great variety of foods at the same meal, the evils of overeating will remain within us.

CRISES

Every adaptation to habits, agents and influences which are inimical to life is accomplished by changes in the tissues which are always away from the ideal. The renovating and readjusting processes that must follow a reform in living is accomplished by the tearing down and casting out of these unideal tissues. New and more ideal tissues take their places. The body is renewed.

This process of readjustment is not always smooth. Aches and pains, loss of weight, skin eruptions, etc., may result. Helen Densmore truly says that, "If it were true that, after many years of abuse, we could stop the wrong course of living and all the blessings of health follow immediately, it would be proof that this disobedience is not so bad after all."

As she says, "With the drunkard the curative action is recognized at once; all know that it is not the water that is making him ill, but the alcoholic poison which he had been before accustomed to. So mother, sister, sweetheart and friends with one accord appeal to him to keep up his courage, notwithstanding his apparently bad symptoms. How differently is the poor dyspeptic treated when he attempts to reform in diet. With one accord his friends try to prevail on him to abandon it; assure him that he is killing himself; read him tomes of medical authorities to show that he is impoverishing his blood by his 'low diet' and when he returns to the old injurious diet, just as with the dram of spirits in the case of the drunkard, the effect is to stop the curative action; he feels braced up, and this is taken as proof that he was all wrong, and the accumulation of disease commences again."

These renovating crises are seldom severe and are always followed by better health. Persistence and determination are required when they come. Most people, particularly young and vigorous ones, will make the change with very little or no discomfort.

Such are our prejudices and prepossessions, and so strong is our tendency to cling to old forms and old schools, that when these manifestations appear, as they sometimes do, even though we have been forewarned and prepared to expect them, many more fail through fear born of ignorance or lack of comprehension of these curative crises than continue with the reform.

PERVERSIONS

The appetite may be depraved to an almost unlimited extent, as exemplified in the dietetic habits of the various peoples of the earth. *Pica* is a form of perverted appetite which manifests itself in the eating of chalk, clay, sand, coal, charcoal, hair, paint, cloth, dirt, acids, cinders, ordure, fire, bits of wood, candles, paper, leaden-bullets, glass, beads, stone, knives, marbles, pieces of money and various other indigestible and non-nutritious substances. Akin to this is the eating of spiders, lice, toads, serpents, leeches, snails, etc. No doubt the eating of salt, pepper and other condiments and the use of tobacco, betel, or other such substance, should also be classed as perversions of the sense of taste.

The depraved appetite is sometimes the result of deliberate cultivation as in the use of salt, condiments and tobacco. It is sometimes a symptoms of "disease." In hysteria, chlorosis, pregnancy and certain mental and nervous ailments, the appetite often craves the most singular and disgusting articles.

Disturbed or inadequate nutrition may be at the base of much of this perversion. A lack of minerals or vitamins may give rise to a vague, ill-defined craving that causes the victim to eat anything in an effort to satisfy his craving. In pregnancy and chlorosis the abnormal cravings seem certainly to be due to nutritive deficiencies and soon yield to proper feeding. Frequent sun bathing of children is claimed to aid in preventing abnormalities of taste in them.

Dirt eating or *African Cachexia*, is a form of depraved appetite (pica) that prevails among the negro population of hot climates and appears to belong to the negro race almost exclusively. The individual so depraved experiences an irresistible craving for substances of an indigestible and disgusting character. Clay, earth, mortar, dust, ashes, chalk, slate, bricks, and shells are often devoured in enormous quantities, while food is almost wholly rejected as disgusting and worthless. The appetite seems to be wholly depraved. The condition has long been known in tropical America and has been observed in the southern part of the United States.

Of a similar character to filth eating is that perversion of the sense of taste that manifests itself in salt-eating, condiment using, tobacco chewing, snuffing and smoking, pickle eating, drinking of alcoholic and soft drinks, and the use of other such substances. None of these things supply any need in the human body. None of them are essential to normal enjoyment of food. All of them are harmful. A taste for them must be cultivated before they can be enjoyed, after which they enslave their victims as truly as the coffee habit, tea drinking or morphine using.

What Jennings called a "good physical conscience" is the sum total of an individual's unimpaired, unperverted instincts and reflexes. It may be well to impress the reader with the importance of maintaining a clear "physical conscience." The advantages of a good physical conscience are too obvious and too numerous to need or admit of a full notice here. The individual who is so fortunate as to possess one, is in much less danger of violating physical law than one who does not. If the former were to receive into his stomach but a small particle of black pepper, though ultimately mixed with his food, unperceived by him at the time, it would inflict a pang on the tender, upright sensibility, that would be remembered a long time, and operate as a caution against further transgression. Another benefit derived from a good physical conscience, is that while it guards against the admission of noxious substances into the system, it also imparts a very high relish to those plain, simple substances, that are adapted to the wants of the body."

CHANGING TO THE NEW DIET

Make the change to the natural diet as abruptly and fully as your circumstances permit.

There need be no transition period. Nothing is gained by "tapering off" of the old diet and "tapering on" the new. There is no danger in an abrupt change. The quicker and more fully you get away from the harmfulness of the latter and begin to receive the benefits of the former the more satisfactory the outcome.

Whether you abandon a stimulating diet for a non-stimulating one or abandon overeating for moderation in eating, you will at first, in almost every case, feel a want of "sufficient" food. There is likely to be faintness and a feeling of weakness. There may be a loss of flesh although, there is a frequent gain. There are often discomforts and unpleasant sensations in the stomach, headache and other symptoms that may alarm the reformer and his friends. All of these symptoms may occur while you are still taking much more than enough food to meet all the demands of your body.

But if you will continue with your efforts until the body has had time to re-adjust itself and repair the damages of the prior unwholesome food or excessive quantities of food you will not be long in realizing the actual and lasting benefits of your change of eating.

I am convinced from years of experience that the easiest way to make the transition from the old and unwholesome mode of eating to the new and *hygienic* mode of eating is to first undergo a fast. Cleansing of the system, nervous readjustment, repair of damages and fading away of cultivated and abnormal longings and cravings are much more rapid in the fast than while eating.

It is not easy for the habitual user of salt, pepper and other condiments to learn to relish unseasoned foods if he stops using condiments and goes on eating. But after a fast he finds keen relish in uncondimented foods and does not miss the condiments. He can overcome his craving for stimulating foods, coffee, tea, etc., quicker by fasting just as by fasting he can more easily and quickly get away from his cravings for tobacco, alcohol, opium, etc. Fasting not only speeds up the systemic readjustments, it makes them easier and more bearable. If the fast lasts long enough, even the old desire for large quantities of food comes to a natural end.

No reader should get the idea from this that he should put off reforming his eating habits until some time in the future, when he can find time to undergo a fast. There is no time like the present to change from unwholesome to wholesome habits and anyone can do it who is determined. It is as difficult as pictured above in only the worst cases and will become more difficult the longer the old habits are persisted in.

Young people can adjust themselves to a change of habits much more readily and in less time than old people, not alone because their bodies are more pliable but also, because they have not, as a rule, become so thoroughly enslaved to the habits that they need to break. Break your bad habits early and cultivate good ones that will sustain you in health and strength throughout a long, happy and useful life.

In the great main the difficulties that one encounters in breaking bad habits are determined by the condition of the body. The less enervated and enslaved the body, the easier the transition to good habits. For this reason, also, the sooner you abandon your imprudent eating habits and begin to cultivate habits that are in harmony with your highest and best physiological requirements, the easier will be the switch-over.

Eat simple meals of few items of food.

It is a matter of common experience that we tend to eat much less food when we take but one at a meal. If we are eating but

BEGINNING THE REFORM DIET

one vegetable we eat just so much and we are satisfied; but if we are eating two vegetables we tend to eat as much of each as we would of a single vegetable if we have only the one or the other at a meal. For example, if we are eating carrots and have consumed all we want of these, we can go back for a serving of asparagus or spinach and apparently start eating all over again. Variety is the spice of gluttony.

This common experience does not prove that we need a variety of foods to supply our demands at the time; but that a variety of foods tends to induce overeating.

This is only one of the reasons why the common habit of eating desserts at the end of a meal is an unwholesome practice. We can always eat a piece of cake or pie or a dish of ice cream or other dessert, even after we have consumed so much of other foods that we experience a sense of uncomfortable fullness. The greater the variety of foods we take at a meal the more we are likely to eat. If we have six foods in our menu we are likely to eat much more than if we have only three. We are a nation of gluttons and much of our overeating is due to the great variety of foods that are placed on our tables at each meal. This practice stimulates the appetite and the gustatory sense to the utmost at each meal.

Indeed, it is the custom to serve the foods in a regularly graduated scale of gustatory relish. Starting with the food that gives least enjoyment and gradually working up to the food that gives the greatest relish, we end by eating two, or three and four times as much food as we actually require and more food than we would take except for this stimulation of our appetites.

Having eaten all he wants of one food, the eater turns to another and still another until he has eaten several foods. Having eaten all he needs or much more, he takes as a final part of his meal, the article he relishes most. After eating two or three times the quantity of food he requires, he can still "top off" his meal with a piece of pie or cake or some other dessert.

It is the rule that our people continue to eat in this manner until appetite is so depraved and diseased that it becomes an imperious master. This is especially true of those on the conventional diet of stimulating foods. They establish a nervous "craving" for stimulation which is referred to the stomach for satisfaction and is in every way like the craving of the drunkard for his alcohol or of the morphine addict for his morphine.

A morbid appetite, thus established, which is in reality nothing but a morbid longing of enervated nerves for their accustomed stimulus, which they receive by means of food, is not satisfied when the body has received sufficient food to meet its needs, but is satisfied only when the nervous system has received enough stimulation to bring it up to its ordinary tone. When this stage has been reached it is all but impossible to avoid overeating. He is now a food addict and his appetite is a despotic, even painful master. He has a powerful and painful craving or longing of an outraged and diseased nervous system, not for food, but for the accustomed stimulant.

Normal hunger and appetite are never the despotic master that the food addict slaves for. While the addict has a depraved, diseased, despotic, intolerably painful passion; the normal person experiences a healthy, mild, pleasant desire which is never painful and outrageous and which conforms perfectly to the real wants, the physiological needs, of the body. The difference is the same as that between the "craving" of the inebriate for his alcohol and the desire of the normal man for a glass of pure water. Normal demands are never painful.

Begin the day's eating with a meal of luscious fruits.

These foods are abundant in minerals and most vitamins, contain sugars in their most wholesome and readily assimilable form and are a delight to the gustatory sense. They are easily and quickly digested and present no problem to the man or woman who must go to work soon after eating. They are usually lacking in complex albumens, most of them are low in calcium and many of them are deficient in vitamin A. Fruits are not complete foods and no one should attempt to live exclusively upon them, except for short periods for special purposes, to the exclusion of all other foods.

Fruits should be eaten in their natural state — uncooked, unsalted, unseasoned — and they should be eaten whole. It is not wise, save in certain exceptional circumstances, to extract and take only their juices. Fresh fruits are superior to dried fruits. Canned fruits are practically valueless and often are only confections.

Fruit is best eaten at a fruit meal with not too great a variety of fruits at a time. Three fruits at a meal should meet the demands of everyone.

Have at least one large raw vegetable salad each day.

If three meals a day are eaten, unless two of these are fruit meals, two salads a day should be eaten. Green leaves are indispensable to the biologic diet. Fruits will not take their places. Green leaves supply complex albumens, offering all the essential constituents of human albumen.

The simple albumens of grains, tubers, roots, and fruits either do not contain them all, or contain but inadequate quantities of essential constituents such as tryptophane, lysin, etc.

It is asserted that green leaves contain sufficient quantities of complex albumens to meet human requirements. This is so only if the leaves are eaten in large quantities as they are by the cow or horse. We lack capacity for such bulk and could acquire it only by developing a large, unsightly abdomen.

Green leaves supply the tender cellulose that gives the needed bulk to food. They supply the different essential vitamins, A, B, C, etc., are abundant in alkaline salts, iron and lime in particular, in particularly assimilable form. The green coloring matter (chlorophyll) they contain is also essential to perfect nutrition.

Salads should be raw, composed of not more than four vegetables and should be eaten without salt, vinegar, oil, lemon juice or dressing and condiments of any kind.

The following vegetables are especially adapted to salad making: cabbage, lettuce, celery, cucumbers, radishes, onions, French endive, tomatoes, cress, parsley and others. Cabbage contains ten times more lime than lettuce and is easier for most people to digest. Onions should not be used often or in large quantities. The same is true of radishes and other "hot" foods.

It was not until the "Exhibition of 1851" that salad-oil was known to any save the aristocracy of England; yet, so firmly fixed has become the habit of putting oil on salads in the short time that has since elapsed, many people cannot conceive of enjoying a salad without oil. Nevertheless, the habit should be abandoned.

Consume nuts as the chief protein supply.

Most nuts are rich in the complex albumens so essential to the building of human tissues. The proteins of practically all nuts are adequate and any slight deficiency that may exist in a particular nut will be compensated by the albumens of green leaves.

Nuts are also valuable for their rich stores of minerals and vitamins and for their easily digested oils. Most nuts also contain readily assimilable sugars.

Consume fats in moderate quantities.

Fats — butter, cream, oils, etc. — retard digestion, especially protein digestion, thereby increasing gastro-intestinal putrefaction and thus overtaxing the liver and kidneys with the resulting poisons.

Fats are best added to foods after they are cooked, not while they are cooking, and should not be taken with a protein meal.

Cook but few foods and cook these but little.

This rule is given for those readers who are not yet ready to completely abandon cooked foods. There is no doubt in my mind that an exclusively uncooked diet is the ideal. Those who are not yet ready to wholly abandon cooking must learn to cook in a way to damage foods least.

Drink pure water only.

There is but one drink — water. All other "drinks" are either foods (fruit juices, milk, etc.), or poisons (coffee, tea, cocoa, soda fountain slops, beer, wine, etc.). The coffee and tea user is likely to suffer from headaches when these poisons are discontinued. These will not persist for more than a few days and there should be no thought of returning to these poison habits.

Drink water when you are thirsty. It should not be taken with meals. Water should not be cold. Cool water is well. Drink it slowly, take all thirst demands. Do not force yourself to drink in the absence of thirst and do not get into the habit of routine drinking. Drink pure, not hard and not drugged waters.

Exclude table salt, pepper (all kinds), cloves, spices condiments and dressings from your diet.

These things have no value and serve no useful purpose in the body. They are one and all irritating. They pervert the sense of taste, retard digestion and induce overeating. Irritating condiments are potent factors in producing cancer of the stomach.

A normal person, eating natural foods and eating only when hungry, will find no need for "appetizers." The person who cannot enjoy his meal without the assistance of an "appetizer. would do well to miss the meal. Hunger is the best sauce.

Without the accustomed salt, vinegar, pepper, and other condiments, the food is likely to taste flat, dull and insipid at first. But soon the palsied nerves of taste are renewed, the thickened skin of the tongue is removed, and the eater discovers fine delicate flavors in his foods that he never dreamed were there.

Salt eaters who give up salt and return to a vegetable diet are almost sure to find that they will be forced to urinate frequently at night. As soon as the body has freed itself of its accumulated salt, this annoyance ceases.

Avoid harmful and useless vegetable and fruit substances.

Not everything in the fruit and vegetable world can be considered food. The poppy plant, nightshade, tobacco and numerous other plants are poisonous. There are numerous poisonous berries and fruits.

Vegetable and fruit substances that are in common use that are best omitted from the diet are rhubarb and cranberries. These foods contain such an excess of oxalic acid that they are more or less poisonous. There are poisonous and non-poisonous mushrooms. The non-poisonous are not foods as they are absolutely indigestible. They pass out in the stools exactly as they were swallowed. There is reason to believe that beets, also, are indigestible.

Vinegar, made by fermentation of fruit sugars, contains alcohol and acetic acid. The acid is more damaging to the liver than the alcohol. Vinegar also retards digestion.

Acid absorption, either an excess of wholesome organic acids, or the absorption of vinegar acid and drug acids, is gravely detrimental and is doubly so to those with impaired livers. Robust individuals may, without the slightest advantage to themselves, consume such things and eliminate them with only imperceptible losses of vitality. They should keep in mind that not even the most powerful constitutions can be abused with impunity.

This should not be interpreted to mean that acid fruits are not wholesome foods. The warning with reference to these foods is against excess.

There are many articles of food that both the well and the sick may eat without killing them instantly, but the problem of the trophologist is to discover what is best to eat — what will assure the highest degree of vigor and the longest life.

Sugar-cane was introduced into Europe by Alexander the Great. It was planted in the West Indies in the fifteenth century. Sugar has become an article of every-day use only within the past sixty or seventy years. Before this time its price was too high to be used except by the rich. In one of his annals, Sir Walter Raleigh gives the market price of sugar at that time at fifty shillings (about $12.00) a pound. White sugar is a "starvation food," like white flour and polished rice. It is lacking in salts and vitamins. Sugar is not an essential addition to the diet.

THE SCIENCE AND FINE ART OF FOOD AND NUTRITION

The penchant for sweetmeats which children share with monkeys and savages may best be satisfied with sweet fruits, rather than with the unwholesome concoctions of the baker's and confectioner's art.

All adulterated and denatured foods should be studiously and consistently avoided. Sugar and other products are used in equal abundance as denatured cereals. Cakes made of denatured cereals, white sugar, cold-storage eggs, pasteurized milk, coal tar dyes, synthetic flavors, poisonous baking powders, and decorated with embalmed fruit or fruit wastes are especially popular. The dietary reform needed is a radical revolution — *a complete return to nature*.

Refrain from eating left-over cooked foods from the previous meal.

Unless chilled immediately, they undergo an insidious fermentation from one meal to the next. If chilled and then warmed over the deterioration is equally as great. Economy as well as superior nutrition dictates that meals be prepared so that little or no food is left over.

Fruits that have been cut, melons that have been opened, and salads that have been shredded also decompose quickly. If more than one-day storage is planned, cover the cut surface with a plastic sealing wrap or wax paper; always remove the thin slice that was next to the plastic before re-using.

Reject canned foods.

Canned foods usually contain industrial poisons, preservatives, artificial flavorings, colorings, etc., and are often produced from inferior foods. Due to long storage they undergo much deterioration and are especially lacking in protective qualities. Some of them, especially fruits, are put up in sugar (white sugar), and others contain salt, vinegar, spices and various condiments. They are commonly overcooked.

Eschew animal foods.

Meats (fish and chicken are also meats), eggs, milk and milk products form no normal part of man's natural diet. They are certainly not essential to the highest degree of physical and mental strength and efficiency. Heavy physiological and biological penalties are exacted for continued violation of legitimacies of nutrition.

Eggs and flesh have a tendency to putrefy in the intestine. Flesh is a fruitful source of parasitic contamination. Alimentary allergy is almost wholly a reaction against foods of animal origin.

BEGINNING THE REFORM DIET

Always eat moderately.
It is easy to train yourself to eat more and more and by so doing create an imperious, but false, appetite. It is equally possible to cultivate moderation and be satisfied with only enough food to meet your needs.

Exuberance of nutrition, as of many of the other good things of life, is frequently rather a curse than a boon to the body.

Wisdom dictates that we cultivate moderation in the consumption of intelligently chosen natural foods. Choose foods of good quality, cleanse them and prepare them properly and enjoy them fully, but do not make the pleasures of eating an end and aim of life.

Heavy muscular effort and cold weather increase food needs, especially do they increase the need for fat starches and sugars. Hot weather and disease diminish the need for food. It is wise and safest to fast when ill. Drugs and artificial treatments are harmful. Only natural processes are acceptable.

Many people eat large quantities of bulk foods merely to "fill up." They are not "satisfied" unless they feel full. This is not necessary. It is not healthful. It does not improve function. We ought to get away from the idea that our main object in life is to be forever filling up and emptying out again.

The man who has been accustomed to eating stimulating foods and whose nervous system has become accustomed to this form of stimulation until there is a marked longing for stimulation, and who, then undertakes to reform his mode of eating and live upon a natural, unstimulating diet, will find this most difficult at first. His craving and longing for the customary stimulation will be very strong and hard to resist. Herein lies the danger.

Unless he exercises great caution and the most rigid self-control and self-denial, he will establish the habit of eating enormous quantities of his new foods, in his efforts to meet the "demand" of his enervated nervous system for stimulation. Overeating on the new diet will be as difficult to overcome, once the habit has become established, as was the prior habit of overeating the stimulating foods.

We tell these people, when they attempt to reform their eating habits, to eat only what food their bodies require. But we might as well tell them not to get wet while they are standing in the rain. We never supply them with a knowledge of how much food their bodies require.

Set a man down to a table loaded with good things to eat and let him have an appetite trained by years of overeating to be satisfied only after large quantities of food have been consumed, give him no valid guide to the amount of food he should eat, and where will he stop? Certainly not until he has eaten two or three times as much food as he needs. Every mouthful of food he eats convinces him that his body requires a "little more." Or, he may think that this time, at least, he may indulge in a full allowance.

His tendency is always to try 'experiment' in the wrong direction. He is more likely to attempt to see how much he can eat without killing himself immediately than he is to try to see if he can be well-nourished and satisfied on less food.

He certainly cannot depend upon his appetite; neither in the selection of his food nor in determining the amount of food to eat. For this voracious creature of habit and miseducation is both a blind and a false guide. It will lead him back to the abandoned flesh-pots and urge him, always, to eat more and more. His appetite must be re-directed and re-educated and this will call for knowledge, determination, will power and persistance.

If he depends upon his feelings and cravings he will find, like the man who attempts to abandon a long-established tobacco habit and depends upon his feelings to guide him, that his system demands large quantities of food, even the unwholesome foods he is trying to abandon. The feelings of the tobacco addict easily convince him that his system demands tobacco. He finds that he cannot do without this poison.

The immediate feelings following a change of diet determine nothing. They do reveal whether the former diet was healthful or unhealthful. No disagreeable "reactions" follow a change from one healthful diet to another healthful diet.

The true method of determining whether or not the body needs tobacco is to abstain from its use until the body has become accustomed to do without it, until it has had ample time to recover its normal tone and repair the injury done by tobacco and eradicate its effects. Having abstained this long, compare the body in its present state with its state while using tobacco. This will decide the real influence of tobacco upon the body.

In the same way when changing from the conventional eating practices to *hygienic* eating practices, the immediate feelings determine nothing. Only the final results of a long-continued experiment will reveal the real effects of the two modes of eating.

BEGINNING THE REFORM DIET

Eat your food in proper combinations.

Study carefully the chapter on food combining and make regular use of it until proper combining of foods becomes an automatic habit. Thereafter, conscious attention to the matter will not be so necessary.

It is a good plan to serve one (at most two) cooked vegetables along with a salad and a protein or starch; or, better still, serve the salad and protein or starch only and no cooked food. This kind of eating does not tempt to overeating. If a large salad is had at the beginning of the meal it tends to prevent over-eating of the more concentrated food-stuffs.

The bulk of each meal should consist of fresh fruits or fresh green vegetables. If an exclusive raw food diet is not adopted, the diet should be at least three-fourths raw. Foods should be combined properly.

Oils and acids should not be added to salads as a general thing. Acids interfere with both starch and protein digestion. Gastric secretion of hydrochloric acid is feeble or lacking when unemulsified fats are taken in the food. Vinegar or lemon juice should be omitted. Oils and acids interfere with protein digestion.

The juices of cabbage and other vegetables, added to a meal, greatly increase the gastric secretion. Not only do they cause more gastric juice to be poured out, but the enzymic content of the juice is markedly raised. Hence, the wisdom of feeding an abundance of green vegetables with protein foods. Cabbage juice actually completely neutralizes and counteracts the inhibiting effects of fat upon gastric secretion and motility and, as before stated, even small amounts of some fats slow down gastric secretion.

Fruit, notwithstanding its high value as food, if eaten with a regular meal, may cause the whole meal to become a reeking mass of decomposition. Because of the ease with which it decomposes after its investing membrane is broken, and because of its chemistry, it is best eaten as a fruit meal—acid fruits at one meal; sweet fruits at another.

Fruits require from sixty-five to eighty minutes for complete digestion. To throw such foods into the stomach with foods which require hours of digestion works havoc with the chemistry of digestion. If fruits "don't agree" with you, try eating them correctly and learn what a wonderful food fruit really is.

PLANNING MEALS

The neophyte in trophology is usually bewildered by the conflicting claims of the "authorities" and by the vast array of cleverly advertised "health foods" offered for his use. These "health foods" are "indispensable," in fact, to round out his diet and assure him of adequate nourishment. Most of the claims made for the patent foods offered as indispensable adjuncts to the diet are false. These foods are far inferior to fresh fruits and green vegetables and some of them are positively harmful.

Dietetic tricks — pep cocktails, potassium broths, horse-mint tea, etc. — are offered as miracle workers. These are mere catch-penny devices and do not possess the virtues ascribed to them. One doctor makes a great fuss over what he calls the twenty-twenty-sixty diet. It is this in name only. The name is a catch-penny device. Its promoters do not even figure out the matter or disclose how one is to figure it out for himself. Indeed, figuring it out would be impossible.

The authors of recipes and cook books know nothing of the newer knowledge of nutrition. They throw their materials together in more or less haphazard fashion according to time honored custom in preparing tasty indigestibles. Their cooking recommendations spoil much of the food in the process.

The following sample menus will be found adequate to supply the nutritive needs of the hardest worker. Chronic sufferers should eat much less. Mental workers will require less starch. By using only wholesome foods and following the rules for food combining given in a previous chapter, the reader may easily work out a great variety of menus.

The object aimed at in this book is to teach the reader the principles of trophology, particularly the principles of food combining, so that he may work out his own menus from the food at hand. Menus must change with the seasons, as foods come into and go out of season. Foods differ in various parts of the country, so that a menu prepared for one part of the country cannot always be prepared in another. The reader is urged not to live by charts, but by principles. Learn the principles and you can work out your own menus. Don't be dependent, all your life, on the menus prepared by another.

BEGINNING THE REFORM DIET

In employing the menus herewith given, bear in mind that any green vegetable may be substituted for any other in preparing menus. If the starch given in one of these menus is not available, any other starch may be substituted. If you cannot procure the protein given in the menu, any other protein may be used. Thus: if pecans are not available use almonds or Brazil nuts; if Hubbard squash is not available, use potatoes or peas; if spinach is out of season, use chard or beet greens, or kale. Making up your own menus is so simple that you should never have to puzzle over how to create your own. Vary the menus from day to day. Do not permit your diet to become monotonous.

BREAKFASTS

1. 3 oranges
2. Unsweetened grapefruit
3. ½ lb. of grapes, 1 apple
4. 2 pears, 8 sun dried or fresh figs
5. Soaked prunes, 1 apple or pear
6. 2 pears, a dish of dates or sun dried figs
7. A dish of sliced peaches, cherries or plums
8. 1 apple or ½ lb. grapes, a dish of dates or prunes
9. Watermelon
10. Cantaloupe
11. Peaches (cream, if desired), no sugar
12. Berries (cream, if desired), no sugar

LUNCHES (Noon Meal) Raw

1. A vegetable salad
   Carrots
   Beets
2. A vegetable salad
   Sweet corn
   Turnips
3. Celery
   Chinese cabbage
   Avocados
4. A vegetable salad
   Cauliflower
   Fresh corn (not canned)
5. A vegetable salad
   Carrots
   Green peas
6. Acid fruit salad
   4 ounces of shelled nuts
7. A vegetable salad
   Raw turnips
   Cottage cheese
8. A vegetable salad
   Nuts

THE SCIENCE AND FINE ART OF FOOD AND NUTRITION

DINNERS (Evening Meal) Raw

1. A vegetable salad
   Broccoli
   Nuts

2. An acid fruit salad
   Apples
   Nuts

3. A vegetable salad
   Chinese cabbage
   Avocados

4. A vegetable salad
   Cabbage
   Nuts

5. A vegetable salad
   Cauliflower
   Nuts

6. Acid fruit salad
   4 oz. cottage cheese

When vegetables are cooked in the waterless cooker they are steamed in their own juices. To avoid the clumsy statement in directing the preparation of cooked vegetables: "cooked in the waterless cooker," I shall employ the term, steamed. The reader must bear in mind that I do not have reference to the regular practice of steaming vegetables.

BREAKFASTS

1. Honeydew melon

2. Persimmons
   Dried figs
   Apple

3. ½ lb. grapes
   10 dates
   Pear

4. Casaba melon

5. Grapefruit
   Oranges

6. ½ lb. grapes
   Persimmon
   Prunes

LUNCHES (Noon Meal) Cooked

1. Lettuce, cucumber and celery salad
   Steamed Broccoli
   Baked potato

2. Lettuce and sweet pepper salad
   Baked cauliflower
   Steamed carrots

3. Lettuce and celery salad
   Cabbage
   Green peas

4. Lettuce, cabbage and cucumber salad
   Beets
   Brown rice

5. Lettuce and French endive salad
   Steamed asparagus
   Baked potato

6. Celery
   String beans and cauliflower
   Steamed carrots
   Sweet potatoes

BEGINNING THE REFORM DIET

7. Vegetable salad
   Broccoli, steamed
   Winter squash

8. Vegetable salad
   Rutabaga, steamed whole
   Kale, steamed
   Baked potatoes

DINNERS (Evening Meal) Cooked

1. Lettuce, cucumber and tomato salad
   String beans
   Nuts

2. Celery and lettuce
   Steamed Brussels sprouts
   Buckwheat groats

3. Vegetable salad
   Steamed whole cabbage
   Green beans
   Pecans

4. Lettuce, green pepper and endive salad
   Kale
   Nuts

5. Romaine lettuce
   String beans and turnip greens
   Ricotta cheese

6. Lettuce, tomato and celery salad
   Steamed eggplant
   Lentils

7. Vegetable salad
   Steamed broccoli
   Fresh green beans, steamed
   4 oz. pecans

8. Vegetable salad
   Steamed or baked cauliflower
   4 oz. English walnuts

9. Vegetable salad
   Baked eggplant, baked whole
   Steamed asparagus
   4 oz. Ricotta cheese

10. Vegetable salad
    Steamed okra
    4 oz. Brazil nuts

Those who desire to use meat or eggs may substitute these for nuts or cheese in the foregoing evening menus, except where fruit salads are used. Strict vegetarians will exclude cheese from these menus.

SAMPLE MENUS FOR THE DAY

1

Breakfast	Lunch	Dinner
Watermelon	Vegetable salad	Large raw vegetable salad
	Kale	Broccoli
	Potato	Green beans
		4 oz. shelled pecans

	2	
Breakfast	Lunch	Dinner
¼ lb. grapes	Vegetable salad	Salad (vegetable)
1 apple	Broccoli	Okra
10 dates	Potato	Summer squash
		4 oz. Brazil nuts

	3	
Breakfast	Lunch	Dinner
1 well-ripened banana	Vegetable salad	Vegetable salad
	Broccoli	Kale
1 pear	Hubbard squash	4 oz. almonds
10 figs	(baked whole)	

	4	
Breakfast	Lunch	Dinner
Cantaloupe	Vegetable salad	Vegetable salad
	Zucchini squash	Green beans
	Nuts	Fresh corn
		Avocado

WORKER'S DIET

Men who work hard, or who work long hours, insist that they require large quantities of food to meet their needs. They insist that they need foods that "stick to the ribs." They work hard and can't live on hay. Men who work hard need more food than the idlers. Men who do physical work need more food than those who do mental work. But the differences in the food needs of these two classes are not as great as they suppose. The fact is the men who so loudly proclaim their need for so much food are food drunkards. They habitually eat two, three, and four times as much food as they actually use.

They reduce their energy by their overeating and poison themselves thereby at the same time. When they miss their accustomed food stimulus and feel weak, dizzy, or have pains, they mistake these morbid symptoms for an indication that they need the great quantities of stimulating foods they actually eat. They are enervated and toxemic from overeating and mistake the symptoms of these for the normal demands of the body for nourishment.

These people suffer much, age early and die prematurely because of their overeating. Heart diseases, arteriosclerosis, diabetes, Bright's disease, cancer, etc., finish them off years before they would reach the end if they ate prudently. These are the endings of those who live by "the belly's gospel of three squares plus and go by your appetite." These people should bear in mind Graham's words: "A drunkard may reach old age, but a glutton, never."

FOOD AS A "PICK-UP"

Food is often used as a "pick-up." Stimulation and nutrition are confusedly identical in the minds of almost everybody. Unless the meal is too heavy, a "pick-up" of energy follows immediately upon eating. To eat when there is no actual need for food merely for its stimulating effect is a misuse of food.

Feeding Mothers
CHAPTER XXXVI

The vital importance of pre-natal life is beginning to receive recognition and we have begun to recognize that a woman is not necessarily physically and otherwise fit to be a mother, merely by reason of the fact that she is a woman.

In many important particulars the most important period of the physical life of an individual is the pre-natal period. It is during this period that all the foundations are laid, all the tissues and organs are formed and cellular activities are at their highest. The heart, lungs, liver, brain, nerves, eyes, ears, teeth, skin, bones, muscles, kidneys and other tissues and organs are formed and prepared for their functions during the nine months of intra-uterine life.

From a minute mass of "protoplasm" 1/125 of an inch in diameter by the orderly processes of cell multiplication, cell specialization, combination, and organization there is built up, step by step, in orderly sequence, the complete and perfectly formed infant. Food is the material out of which the body of the infant is built and this material is supplied by the mother.

Nature has made a wonderful provision for nourishing the developing embryo. In women the maternal structures directly, without the intervention of a special apparatus, supply nourishment to the fertilized ovum, which is the potential child. Very early, however, in uterine life a peculiar mechanism is formed through which passes from the mother's blood stream, to the embryonic or fetal blood-stream, the nutrient materials needed by the developing child. This structure, known as the placenta (after birth), is developed partly by the mother and partly by the child.

The placenta acts in the double capacity of pulmonary and intestinal mucous membranes; taking up both oxygen and food carried in the mother's blood. The fetus then receives its nutritive materials from the placenta. The mother does not give even a drop of her own blood to the child. The latter forms its own blood, from the food material supplied through the placenta. The function of the placenta is chiefly absorptive but partly eliminative, for through it the fetus eliminates its waste.

MOTHER-CHILD SYMBIOSIS

An amusing argument has been carried on by the scientists over the question: Is the fetus a true parasite in its relation to the mother, or does it develop in harmonious symbiosis giving some compensatory physiologic benefit to the mother? Both sides and the middle have been ably defended, but the truth seems to be that the fetus can be parasitic or symbiotic, depending on conditions.

For example, it has been shown that there is a reciprocity between the internal secretions of the mother and fetus. In diabetes in the mother, the pancreas of the fetus is able to compensate for her own lack of pancreatin.

The pancreatic glands were removed from a group of dogs and they all promptly died of diabetes except one slut. She was pregnant and manifested no signs of diabetes until the birth of her whelps, whereupon she also promptly died of diabetes. The pancreatic glands of her embryo pups supplied the needed pancreatic hormone to her body so long as they were within the womb. When their connections with the mother were severed, she could no longer draw upon them for this hormone and, so developed diabetes and died. This is a remarkable example of the harmonious symbiosis that exists between mother and fetus.

Dr. Feldman says that "during asphyxia of the mother, the fetus sends oxygen to the maternal blood." The amounts of both nitrogen and phosphorus retained by the pregnant woman is greater than during her non-pregnant state. The same is true of iron and sulphur and perhaps of all elements of the body. It is the rule that a woman's nutrition is improved during pregnancy and it is not uncommon for her ailments to disappear during this period. Investigators claim to have demonstrated the existence of placental antibodies in the mother's blood. Antibodies are supposed to increase the resistance to germs and toxins.

PARASITIC FOETUSES

Within certain limits, pregnancy may prove positively beneficial to a woman. On the other hand there are conditions in which pregnancy will prove to be her undoing. There is a vigorous tendency of the embryo to maintain, at whatever cost to the mother, the calcium content of its own organism. This is the reason that the pregnant woman, inadequately supplied with lime salts, loses part of her teeth. In severe cases of deficiency, she may even develop osteomalacia.

THE SCIENCE AND FINE ART OF FOOD AND NUTRITION

There will be a loss of lime, iron and other elements from the pregnant woman's tissues unless her own diet is rich in these. The fetus behaves somewhat as a parasite if the mother is not well-fed. If the food is insufficient or deficient, or if other unhygienic factors disturb the mother's nutrition, the metabolic balance will become disturbed in favor of the fetus. Depletion of the maternal bone-calcium occurs where the mother's diet does not contain a sufficient amount of assimilable calcium. The feeding of inorganic calcium (lime water and other lime containing drugs) to the pregnant woman does not benefit.

Experiments with rats have shown that the calcium content of fœtal rats remains normal when the mother's are inadequately supplied with lime salts. When the diet of female rats is deficient in calcium it does not affect the calcium content of the young rats unless the deficiency has persisted for a long time prior to pregnancy. If such prolonged deficiencies have existed, the entire development of the young is seriously impaired.

Dibblet, feeding diets very poor in calcium to pregnant dogs, found the skeleton of the new born dogs possessed a normal calcium content, although the mother invariably suffered with osteomalacia, so greatly had the vigorously growing fetuses robbed her blood and bones of lime to supply their own bone-building requirements. As much as 30 per cent of the calcium was withdrawn from the mother's bones.

Whether the fetus is to develop in harmonious symbiosis, or antipathetic symbiosis (parasitically) depends upon the mother's nutrition. It lies within the power of the mother to determine whether her child shall be a parasite or a symbion. She is eating and living both for her child and herself. Surely this is a subject worthy the study of every prospective mother.

CALCIUM

Hinds will often eat the shed antlers of the buck. In Mr. Macpherson's book on Red Deer, he says: "The immense quantities of bone deer will eat is proved by Mr. Williamson's statement to Mr. Harvie-Brown, that in a few months they had completely eaten the bones of a horse in the Hebrides, and Mr. Harvie-Brown remarks that this great appetite displayed may be accounted for by the total absence of bone-producing elements in the geology of the Hebrides."

Hinds, when gravid and while suckling their young, require considerable lime, and where the soil is deficient in this element so that it is lacking in their regular diet, they turn to bones. In certain parts of the British Isles the hinds will eat the horns off the heads of living stags, so lacking in lime is the soil. P. Y. Alexander, M.A., L.L.D., quotes one Whitaker as saying "both bucks and does will pick and chew shed horns. I have seen them also chewing old rib-bones of beef."

A sufficient restriction of calcium in the diet of gravid rats renders delivery so difficult and painful that they die in trying to give birth.

Dr. Melville C. Keith, who was much ahead of his time in his dietary views, has left us this observation, *Seven Studies*, 1900; "Caries, or rotting of the teeth from insufficient material, is more familiarly seen, and more universally experienced, in the woman who bears children and is fed with scanty tooth material while the child is growing within her. The skeleton of the child demands bone and it is not in sufficient quantity in the blood of the mother. And, the mother's body being unable to respond to the demand for the bone material, her own bony system is drawn upon, and hence the disintegration of the teeth to supply the child with the needful bone material. So, also, are her bones absorbed for the same reason.

"The direct cause and effect are to be seen in the shell of an egg. Take a hen and deprive her of all material containing lime, and the egg will be so very soft shelled as to mash up when it is laid. Not having shell material enough, the egg shell is deficient and the hen, if not supplied, will die after laying a few months.

"When the shell is very soft, give the hen powdered oyster shells, or lime, or old bones, in a shape for the hen to swallow, and the eggs will soon have a tough, thick shell.

"So with cattle. I have seen cows on the Prairie of St. Landry, Lousiana, devote a couple of hours to chewing up a bone while they were carrying a calf. The proper thing in these cases is to supply these animals with bone producing material."

This should show us how urgently necessary it is to supply the pregnant mother with adequate calcium in her diet. As phosphorus is as essential as calcium to the bones and the latter is usable in proportion to the amount of the former that is present, it is equally essential that the mother's diet contain ample phosphorus. Women who crave something sour during pregnancy and who insist on satisfying this craving with pickles, vinegar, etc., rob their bodies of calcium instead of supplying this needed element. Those who satisfy their craving for sweets by eating candy, sugar, cakes and such, instead of eating dates, figs, raisins, bananas, etc., are thereby assisting in the calcium depletion of their bodies. White sugar is especially a calcium-thief.

The use of lime water will not help either the mother or the fetus in such cases. Indeed, the use of inorganic lime-salts, with the exception of calcium carbonate and tri-calcium phosphate, produces "acidosis." Large doses of calcium chloride induce severe losses of calcium from the body and may even result in osteoporosis or osteomalacia. Chloride of lime, if given for a long time, results in severe losses of calcium, even in bone deformity. Calcium chloride induces hyperacidity within the body and the alkalies of the bones and other tissues are used in neutralizing the acids. There is only one source from which to secure your calcium − namely, natural foods.

SOURCES OF CALCIUM

It is now the vogue to feed pregnant and nursing mothers milk to supply them with lime for their babies. Year after year, this milk is narrowed down, more and more, to pasteurized milk, which supplies practically no calcium. Dr. Claunch gave it as his view that if a pregnant woman takes a glass of milk a day during her pregnancy, she will have a large baby, one too fat for an easy birth. Besides producing an over-sized baby, milk is by no means the richest source of calcium.

Physicians also prescribe calcium tablets for mothers in order that they may secure sufficient calcium with which to build the bones and teeth of their babies. This calcium is in the form of an inorganic salt and is not only not useful, but is positively injurious.

The need for calcium by the pregnant mother is greatly exaggerated. The amount of calcification, both of the bones and teeth, of the baby before birth is not great. Calcification has hardly begun in the teeth at the time of birth and the bones are still soft at this time.

Most fruits are considerably lower in calcium than is milk. The same is true of nuts. Yet if a mother received no more calcium than she derives from a diet of fruits and nuts she will secure all the calcium she and her baby require. There are several vegetables that contain twice as much calcium as milk. Some of them run nearly three times as much calcium as milk. All of the following vegetables are much richer in calcium than milk: Cabbage, red cabbage, savoy cabbage, celery, dandelion, dill, Jerusalem artichoke, lettuce, romaine lettuce, okra, both large and small radishes, sorrel, sugarbeet leaves, swiss chard, tomatoes, turnips, turnip leaves, water cress. A number of other vegetables contain as much or nearly as much lime as milk. All of them contain sufficient to meet the needs of the mother and baby.

IRON

Not only must the mother supply the calcium or lime salts and phosphates, so essential to the development of the teeth and bones of the child, both before birth and during the nursing period, but she must supply every other element the child requires. She must supply the vitamins. She must supply the child with sunshine. And where she fails to secure these for herself, the child will also be deprived of them.

If the mother's diet does not contain sufficient iron, the fetus will draw upon her blood and tissues for its supply. Many anæmic women improve during pregnancy, but if the mother's diet is lacking in iron there is a tendency to anæmia during the latter months of pregnancy.

SOURCES OF IRON

Milk is low in iron. To feed milk for calcium does not supply the needed iron. It will be best to secure calcium and iron from the same sources — this is to say, from fruits, nuts and vegetables. Taking iron tablets is of no avail. Sorrel, lettuce, black salsify and spinach are the richest sources of iron, but all green vegetables are well supplied with this element. Fruits and nuts are lower in iron than vegetables, but contain sufficient amounts to meet the needs of the mother and baby. Asparagus, artichokes and kale are high in iron content. Raisins, despite the advertising slogan, "have you had your iron today," are not rich in iron.

OTHER MINERALS

Eating a diet of fresh fruits and of fresh vegetables, particularly uncooked vegetables, will not only guarantee an abundance of iron and calcium, but will, at the same time, guarantee an abundance of the other needed minerals and of all the vitamins required. Taking sodium or phosphorus tablets, vitamin pills, etc., will be of no avail. Stick to nature's products for best results.

THE SCIENCE AND FINE ART OF FOOD AND NUTRITION

Professor Sherman of Columbia University, in his *Chemistry of Food and Nutrition* states: "The necessity of a generous supply of vegetables and fruits must be particularly emphasized. They are of the greatest importance for the development of the body and its functions. As far as children are concerned we believe that we could do better by following the dietary of the most rigid vegetarians than by feeding them as though they were carnivora. If we limit the most important sources of iron — vegetables and fruits — we cause a certain sluggishness of blood formation and an entire lack of reserve iron, such as is normally found in the liver, spleen and bone marrow of healthy, well-nourished individuals."

VITAMINS

Due to the rapidity with which the child is growing, whether before or after birth, and to the fact that the mother has already attained full growth (at least she should have done so before becoming a mother), food deficiencies affect the child much quicker than they do the mother.

Pregnant animals fed on a scurvy producing diet, develop the disease much more rapidly than non-pregnant ones, and they often die of scurvy before the time of delivery. The sacrifice of minerals by the mother's body may continue to such a state that grave disease, such, for example, as the change from compact into cancellous bone-tissue (osteoporosis), may develop.

When Ingier fed pregnant pigs on a diet "deficient in C," the fetuses developed typical infantile scurvy in ten to twelve days. He found that if the pigs were properly fed until close to delivery, a sudden change to a scorbutogenic (scurvy-producing) diet does not affect the fetuses. These will be born normal. But the milk proves to be inadequate and the young pigs quickly develop scurvy. The circus lioness, when fed on meat alone, brings forth cubs with cleft palates due to calcium deficiency.

Dr. Percy Howe in a paper (1922) on "Decalcification of Teeth and Bones and Regeneration of Bones through Diet," refers to some of his experiments on guinea pigs and states that the use of a scorbutic diet, one containing an excess of carbohydrates, "resulted, in a number of cases, in the absence of eyes in the young. I have had several animals born with only one eye, or one good eye and other sightless or imperfectly formed. Many are born with spots on the outer coating of the eye, which clear up under proper feeding."

—444—

Howe also says: "In animals on the scorbutic diet, eye trouble follows even to the point of pus welling out over the eye during eating. Feeding orange juice is followed by complete clearing up of the trouble."

The vitamins in milk are not synthesized from the mother's own body, like the main nutrients, but are derived unaltered from her food. It is essential that the pregnant and nursing mother's diet contain sufficient of these to meet the needs of her child without robbing her own tissues of their stored supplies. Fruits and green vegetables are the best sources of these. Many children suffer handicaps, defects, deformities and vital weaknesses, as a result of failure to secure in infancy and before birth a diet adequate to supply their needs. An abundance of fresh greens and fresh fruits is essential for the pregnant and nursing mother and for the nursing child.

PROTEIN

If the mother's diet, though containing a sufficiency of protein, contains these in a form which is not fully adequate for promoting growth in the offspring, the maternal organism supplies the foetus with what is lacking by drawing upon the maternal tissues.

The amount of supplementary protein required to make good the inadequacies of the proteins of such foods as corn, cereals, seed, bananas, carrots, etc., is very small. It is much less than would be required if the supplementary food were the sole source of protein. Mothers whose diet is largely cereal require some supplementary protein, but not large quantities of this.

CUMULATIVE EFFECTS

We may go beyond the immediate results of a deficient diet during pregnancy or during lactation. It is really necessary to begin right eating before birth, even before conception. Repeated experiments with animals and numerous observations on humans have demonstrated that certain long-continued dietary deficiencies result in serious impairment of the generative organs. Animals so fed conceive less often and have smaller litters than well-nourished animals. Exclusive diets of fats and proteins and carbohydrates and lime-poor diets have such effects. Defective nutrition may lead to degeneration of the mammary glands with resulting changes in the composition of the milk or a failure of the milk supply.

Short experiments are of little value in determining the value of a dietary. In animal experimentation it has been found that on a given diet the animals may seem perfectly healthy and apparently well-developed and reproduce their kind, and in the third or fourth generation symptoms, the outcome of deficiencies of organic salts, make their appearance. Control animals under the same conditions, except that they are adequately provided with the element or elements deficient in the experimental diet, remain free from the degenerative symptoms.

Osborn and Mendel, as well as McCollum, have repeatedly stated that the thriving of a single generation on a diet is no guarantee that it is a satisfactory one. It may be only slightly inadequate and its effects may become apparent only after the passing of several generations. After the passing of a few generations on a slightly inadequate diet, the animals suddenly cease to conceive so often, and give birth to weakly and short-lived offspring. Finally complete sterility or failure of lacteal secretion occur.

It is often only after the lapse of several generations that all of the evil effects of an unbalanced diet become apparent. It is only then that lessened fertility shows up and the offspring are weak and short-lived. Ultimate sterility and inability to secrete milk ends the line.

Undoubtedly the increasing inability of civilized mothers to nurse their babies is the result of the denatured diet they have been existing on for the past two or three generations. Defective nutrition may even lead to degeneration of the mammary glands with resulting changes in the composition of the milk.

Berg says: "From a communication made to me verbally by Urbeanu I learn that he saw barn door fowls, provided with what seemed a bare sufficiency of calcium, develop for three generations in a way that appeared perfectly normal, but the birds of the third generation were sterile because their eggs had no yolks. Control birds were still entirely normal in the fifth generation" Who can estimate the amount of "degeneration," deformity "hereditary disease," inability to nurse, to conceive or procreate, inability to give birth, nervous and mental disorder, etc., that is due to the faulty diet of those who have gone before? The fathers have eaten inadequate diets and the children's teeth have holes in them.

The effect of deficient diets reach through more than one generation. Female dogs fed on a diet which produces rickets gave birth to pups which were so strongly predisposed to rickets that the feeding of good food for a considerable period did not remove the tendency to rickets. The dietary deficiencies also increased the susceptibility of the young to respiratory troubles, such as catarrhal conditions (these often extending into and impairing the digestive tract) and pneumonia.

Physicians of experience have all seen instances of thin, poorly developed women, who have been sick all or most of their lives and who have conceived, perhaps, only after six, eight, ten or more years of married life, give birth to babies apparently normal, but weak and not able to eat. They have juggled the diets of such infants in every conceivable manner without success, because these children should never have been born and in many instances will not be able to live. I have seen two such children from one such mother and one such child from another such mother. Strangely enough the desire for motherhood is often stronger in these women, who should not have children, than in normal women.

Children born of well-nourished parents have good digestive powers; whereas children of poorly nourished parents are likely to have poor digestive powers. This fact is also attested by stock raisers with reference to their stock.

Well-nourished mothers (this does not mean over-fed) give birth to well-nourished and, therefore, well-developed and vital children. Not merely are the bones and teeth and respiratory organs involved in the results of adequate or inadequate diets, but every tissue in the body is weakened or strengthened, as the case may be, by the mother's food. Mother's nutrition is the real prenatal influence.

McCollum has pointed out that a slightly deficient diet eaten over a period of generations, lowers vitality, predisposes to premature old age, and shortens life. Grant and Goetsch found a slightly deficient diet, when eaten over a long period of time produces pathological conditions which never result from extreme dietary deficiencies. They found that young animals have rickets only when the diet of the mother is of a type which leads to rickets. They proved that the mother's diet governs absolutely the decreased resistance of the young to the effects of deficiencies in their own food. Rickets they found, will not develop in young animals whose diet is deficient in bone material, providing they are born of well-nourished mothers. The rapidity and severity with which rickets develops in young animals, depends very largely upon the depletion of the mother's nutrition during pregnancy.

THE SCIENCE AND FINE ART OF FOOD AND NUTRITION

"Poorly nourished cows frequently give birth to weak, puny calves which are hard to raise," says the U. S. Dept. of Agriculture. "The feeding of the calf, therefore, begins before it is born."

The facts here stated as true of cows and calves are equally as true of human mothers and their infants. The food elements essential for the development of the infant are taken into the mother's stomach, digested and absorbed into her blood, from which they are transmitted to the fetus, through the umbilical cord. If the mother does not consume food of a character to maintain her in a vigorous condition, and at the same time supply the needs of the infant, both she and the infant will suffer. In endeavoring to rear healthy, vigorous children many mothers handicap themselves at the start by not eating properly.

The facts given in this chapter by no means cover all the troubles that may be produced in the offspring by faulty feeding of pregnant women. They are enough, however, to reveal the urgent necessity for mothers and mothers-to-be to intelligently consider and adequately study the vitally important subject of prenatal feeding.

Let the mother not forget that not alone the teeth, but the bones and all the other tissues of her child, its future growth and development, its susceptibility or "resistance to disease," its chances of survival and much else depend upon the food with which she supplies it during the nine months of ante-natal life. Her own health and the integrity of her own tissues, perhaps, even the integrity of her mind is wrapped up very largely in her diet during this period. The mother's responsibilities are great and she cannot shirk them without paying a heavy penalty; and without, also causing her child to have to pay. It is not just a matter of her teeth or of her child's teeth.

DIET AND INTELLIGENCE

Dr. John. Monroe, of Long Island University, during sixteen years of experiment and investigation, subjected five thousand school children to tests at various periods of their lives, and followed seven hundred of these through college and into business. He sums up the result of his work in these words: "Intelligence is not constant, nor is it entirely hereditary. Much of the present shortage in intelligence may be alleviated when it is recognized that the physical and chemical surroundings of the germ plasm prior to birth may hopelessly condition that plasm into idiocy after birth; that the expectant mother probably does require food and health care for the developing embryo in order to produce children of high intelligence; that the vicious food conditions, the sanitation and hygiene, the brutality of many homes appear to be the conditioners of moronity and border-line dullness; and rapidly developing intelligence must be stimulated on all levels incessantly if it is to come to full development."

In Vol. 5, of this series, this subject will be dealt with at greater length. Mother's nutrition conditions to a greater extent than has ever been suspected, the future intelligence of her child.

DIET DURING PREGNANCY

Women who will eat properly and care for themselves hygienically during pregnancy will not only save their teeth and preserve their health and assure themselves healthy, vigorous children, but they will make childbirth safe, easy and, providing, they are normally developed and live fully right, make childbirth painless.

Some years ago a theory was propounded that as a means of making childbirth easy, even painless, the mother should eat no foods during pregnancy that would harden the forming bones of the fetus. The mother's own bones were also to undergo a softening process in order to decrease the resistance to the passage of the child at birth. It was explained that by a proper course of diet after birth, the bones of both mother and child would quickly recover and the bones of the child would become strong enough to support him.

Fortunately, the practice that grew out of this theory was better than the theory. The diet that was thought best adapted to bring about these desired results, was one of fresh fruits and green vegetables. Apples, grapes, lemons, oranges, figs, raisins and other fruits in season were eaten in abundance. Potatoes, beets and other tubers were excluded for it was thought that foods that grow under ground were less fit for food than the foods growing above ground. An exception was made in the case of onions. All vegetables were used abundantly. Cereals were used exceedingly little. No bread at all was permitted and but little meat. Distilled water was used for drink.

The reader will see that such a diet supplies an abundance of bone-forming material. An excess of bases will be introduced into the body and plenty of vitamins will be present. The mother's bones, teeth and other tissues and her health would not suffer mineral losses due to a commandeering of these by the fetus, as would occur if a diet were fed to secure the effects they set out theoretically to secure.

The theory was wrong in principle. The practice was good but not based on the theory itself.

Along with this diet went sunbathing, gymnastics and good general hygiene. The result was that many women, who followed out the complete program, reported absolutely painless c h i l d b i r t h s. It is unfortunate that the great majority of women possess so little regard for their own and their children's highest welfare, that only one in ten thousand is willing to forego their favorite indulgencies in order to have painless parturition and a healthy vigorous child. Although I am convinced that childbirth should cause no more pain than swallowing or a bowel movement, in a well-developed woman, I have been able to secure this effect in only one case, due to the fact that I have been able to get but one woman to follow instructions to the letter and not only partially. In this case three prior births had been long and unusually painful. The fourth was over in twenty minutes and was painless.

Women who are poorly developed or deformed, due to faulty food, lack of sunshine, insufficient exercise, and the deforming influence of corsets or other tight clothes, during the period of development, cannot expect perfect results; but all of these, by proper eating and proper care during pregnancy, will have safer and easier births and assure better health in both themselves and their offspring.

DIET WHILE NURSING

The child depends on the mother's nutrition for its food supply, after birth, for as long as it continues to nurse. Her own diet is as important to her child during the nursing period as before birth. These two periods — gestation and lactation — may be considered, from the trophologic viewpoint, as one. They are one both as regards the mother and as regards the child.

Observers have recorded cases where infants at the breast became affected with scurvy although their mothers were in apparent health. Sucklings have been known to be affected with beri-beri while their mothers were in apparent health. This is attributed to vitamin deficiency. It does not matter whether it is a lack of vitamins or calcium; the mother's diet is certainly inadequate. Children may become rachitic or may develop xerophthalmia (a dry and thickened condition of the conjunctiva) because the mother's diet is inadequate.

That undernourished mothers cannot nurse their babies is proven by the results of fasting, by the experience of mothers in certain parts of war-ravished Europe, by animal experiment and by examples existing all around us. A fast quickly reduces the quantity of milk and impairs its quality. Experiments have shown that after 14 days of fasting the amount of milk secreted is only about one-seventh of the normal amount. The milk becomes poorer in water, protein, sugar and mineral salts. The fat content remains practically unchanged. Lusk found that in fasting goats, the fat content increased. Others have found the fat content of milk to remain practically the same in cow's milk, although the other elements all decreased.

Within wide limits the composition of milk is independent of the food eaten by the mother. For, so long as the needed tissue-building elements are present in the mother's own body, she will be able to produce milk of a definite composition. The mammary glands manifest great energy in extracting the needed materials — whether fats, proteins, sugars, minerals or vitamins — from the tissues of the mother and the source of milk does not "dry up" so long as the mother's organism can yield up the requisite materials for its production.

The quantity of milk produced is greatly influenced by the mother's diet, but this will not greatly affect its quality, so long as her own tissues may be drawn upon to make up the deficiencies. When the supply of any tissue building element fails, the quantity of milk falls off, but the composition remains practically unchanged. If there is complete failure of only one tissue-building element from both the diet and the maternal organism, the secretion of milk is arrested.

Carl Rose carried on experiments on goats over considerable periods. He states that he could not find that extensive variations in the diet resulted in any changes in the composition of their milk. It is certain, however, that no female animal can provide, indefinitely, food elements in her milk, if these are not supplied by her diet. The persistent robbing of her own tissues, to supply the needs of her young, results in their exhaustion, and in serious disease in the mother. The milk suffers and this produces, as shown by Steenbock and Hart, grave debility in the young. Long continued malnutrition in mothers results in degeneration of the mammary glands, as was seen in Central Europe during World War I.

Kauppe, in Germany, examined the milk of a number of nursing mothers during the war, and found the fat content practically normal. He resorted to a fanciful interpretation of psychic influences as an explanation for the failure of infants to thrive on their milk. In Central Europe the half famished mothers during the war were unable to nurse their children. How ridiculous to call in "psychic influences" to account for what was so evidently due to partial starvation.

PRACTICAL CONSIDERATIONS

The energy displayed by fetal organisms in securing the nutritive materials requisite for life and growth even under the most unfavorable circumstances, and the energy displayed in the same direction by the milk glands, the organs chiefly responsible for the nourishment of the young organism immediately after birth, demonstrate how intent nature is upon providing for the "younger generation." One generation exists simply for the next and is sacrificed, if need arises, for the next.

What these facts lead to, as a practical proposition, is the necessity, on the part of the mother, to eat an adequate diet both during pregnancy and lactation. For, if she does not do this, her own body suffers, and after it has been "bled white," the body of her child also suffers.

The mother can supply to the fetal and nursing organism only what she possesses. If its needs are not supplied by her diet, her own tissues and stored reserves become the diet of her child.

Pregnancy and lactation are not "diseases." They do not call for special diets, or for special care or treatment. The mother should simply be careful to observe all the rules of hygiene and the rules for eating and for combining her foods, as given elsewhere in this book. She should supply herself and her child with an abundance of vitamins and minerals, by eating plenty of fresh fruits and green vegetables – largely or wholly raw.

Too many babies are born puny and feeble and lacking in the vigor and sturdiness that should characterize the beginning of life, because mothers are not properly fed. If too little of the fruits and green vegetables are fed during the prenatal period and during infancy and childhood, there results a lasting weakness which shows itself when the child is exposed to stress or strain.

Berg advises "from five to seven times as much vegetables, potatoes, and salt-rich fruits (apples and pears are poor in this respect), as of meat, eggs or cereal products – for otherwise an adequate excess of bases cannot be guaranteed," to supply the needs of growing children.

This standard will be found to be an ideal one for the pregnant and nursing mother. Undernourished or inadequately nourished mothers cannot hope to produce healthy offspring, or to nurse them properly after they are born.

Berg records that "when, at the sun-bath station of the Viennese University Clinic it became necessary during the winter to restrict for eight weeks the supply of fresh vegetables, scurvy appeared with positively explosive violence." This serves to emphasize the tremendous importance of fresh fruits and green vegetables in the diet of everyone, but especially in the diet of mothers.

Cereals, especially, seem to induce defective teeth, particularly when not counter-balanced with large quantities of green foods and fresh fruits.

McCollum says: "There is good reason to believe that the common practice of confining the diet to too great an extent to bread, meat, sugar, potatoes, beans, peas and cereals (before birth and during the nursing period) is in no small measure responsible for the failure of many mothers to produce milk of satisfactory quantity and quality for the nutrition of their infants. There is no hardship (but great benefit) in the restriction of the intake of meats, etc., and the increase of milk, fruits and green vegetables, and the mother who does so will greatly minimize the danger of a break in the healthy growth of her baby."

Mothers are not likely to undereat on starches, proteins and fats, although, on a one sided diet, they may eat only inadequate proteins. A varied diet will prevent this. The food elements that are most likely to be lacking in the diet of civilized mothers are the minerals and vitamins. Living largely on refined and denatured and cooked foods, as they do, mineral and vitamin depletion is one of the greatest evils connected with the mother's diet.

Let her eat acid fruits if she has a craving for something sour. Pickles are not food and will not nourish her child. Sweet fruits will satisfy her craving for something sweet; use these instead of sugar or candy. Every nutritional demand can be supplied by natural foods and by nothing else. Canned fruits are confectionary and not fruits. Their food value is small. Eat fresh ones.

In leaving this subject, let me again emphasize the necessity of good general hygiene of both the mind and body. Abnormal mental states will impair the mother's nutrition as certainly as defective food and, in this way, cripple her child. A want of fresh air or of sunshine, a lack of rest and sleep, overwork, emotional overirritation, sexual abuse or any other enervating and devitalizing influence, will result in a perverted metabolism, toxemia and trouble for both mother and child.

Building the Teeth
CHAPTER XXXVII

That man's teeth are naturally as sound and durable as those of the lower animals was shown in Vol. I. Geologists and paleontologists often unearth the skulls of peoples long dead, the teeth of which show no signs of decay and the enamel on which is often almost double the thickness and much harder than the enamel on our teeth.

Today most of the civilized portions of the race are a race of dental cripples. We are face to face with the fact that our teeth begin to decay in childhood. Indeed they sometimes have cavities in them when they erupt.

In 1913 Dr. A. Freedman Foot examined 1,694 children in six clinics and found eleven of these with normal teeth. In his report to the Second District Dental Society of New York, Dr. Foot said: "The six year molars of nearly every child was broken down wholly or in part. In many instances the molars were decayed when they came through the gums. So extensive and far advanced were the defects that corrective treatment, even if it were applied would have been of little value."

Dr. Louis Goldstein, New York City, declares: "After examining the teeth of not less than 400 school children in my home neighborhood here in Bronx, I have yet to see a perfect set of six-year molars (first four permanent teeth to appear in childhood). These teeth in nearly every instance were entirely decayed. I have never observed a perfect set of teeth in any American child and have but one adult patient showing extremely good teeth. She is a young woman."

The six year molars are the first of the permanent teeth to erupt. They should last throughout the life of the individual. Why should they decay in childhood? Why should they have cavities in them when they erupt? It is evident that such teeth cannot be saved by brushing the teeth. They must be saved before they ever come through the gums or they will not be saved. Something more fundamental than "uncleanliness" of the surface of the teeth and mouth is concerned with the production of tooth-decay. Until this is recognized by the parents of the world, there is no hope of ever saving the teeth of our children.

Hugh W. McMillan, D.D.S., M.D., of Cincinnati, says: "To a careful observer of dental conditions at the present time in clinic and private practice, it is very evident the ravages of dental caries and diseases of the gums are daily increasing, in spite of the increasing number of dentists, in spite of the multiplicity of patented and personally-designated tooth brushes, in spite of proprietary pyorrhea cures and gum massaging pastes, in spite of acid, alkalin, neutral, mucin-dissolving and film destroying tooth pastes and mouthwashes and in spite of the type of periodontologist who aims to prevent by either applying or removing something from the tooth surface in the same manner that some unintelligent physician might expect to cure by external applications a skin disease of general origin.

"Treated by a combination of all these methods dental decay and gum diseases progressively continue, causing pain, discomfort, nervous disorders, impaired digestion and local infection, until after a losing fight the bewildered patient rests edentulous and free from organs which under the present regime may be considered physiologically superflous."

Dr. H. J. Morris, president of the Yorkshire Branch of the British Medical Association says: "The cry that clean teeth do not decay is really absurd, because under the popular method of feeding, the teeth cannot be kept clean. Surely we have seen enough by this time to have lost our faith in the tooth brush, and it is time the people lost theirs too. The old belief should be modified by a new one."

"As a matter of fact," Dr. McMillan says: "the tooth brush does not get in between the teeth or down in the occlusal fissures or around fillings or under the gingival margins. The actual places where decay primarily occurs are not touched by the brush. As ordinarily used, about all the brush accomplishes is to polish the already self-cleansing surfaces.

"Is it sufficient to tell a patient that a clean tooth never decays, when it is often impossible to clean it with scalers? Is it right to tell a child to brush his teeth so that they will not decay, when often patients are seen who brush their teeth several times each day and still caries are rampant?"

BUILDING THE TEETH

I have seen children whose teeth were all but wholly destroyed despite the regular and frequent use of the tooth brush. The enamel was melted off their teeth down to the gum line, the teeth were "eaten" away until they were not larger than needles; along the gums they were black and often covered with tartar. It is foolish for dentists and the manufacturers of tooth brushes and toothpastes to tell these children and their parents that "a clean tooth never decays."

Parents are advised to have the dentists frequently examine the teeth of their children and repair all defective first teeth, because the jaws do not develop properly if the temporary teeth are lost and the second set of teeth will be impaired by this loss. This is a case of getting the cart before the horse. The loss of teeth does not cause the faulty development of the jaws, nor the injury to the permanent teeth. The permanent teeth suffer, the jaws fail to develop properly and the first teeth are lost due to the same common cause.

NOT CAUSES OF DECAY

Sugar and fruit acids do not injure the enamel of normal teeth. Sound teeth have been immersed in a sugar solution and in fruit acids for months without suffering any erosion. Dr. E. Howard Turison and others have proved this.

Sugar can hurt the teeth only by entering the stomach and blood and perverting metabolism. Free sugar (commercial sugar) possesses a strong affinity for calcium. When eaten in considerable quantities it leaches the tissues, including the teeth, of their calcium. Dr. Howe says, "only when general derangement follows sugar feeding does caries occur." Starches, sugars, including candies and syrups, must be eliminated from the diet in treating pyorrhea.

Lactic acid does not injure the enamel of the teeth. No experiments have been able to show that bacteria of any type, when cultured on the teeth, are responsible for dental caries. Bacteria, even if they enter into the production of dental decay, play a very subordinate part and, in conditions which seem to be most favorable to their activity and growth, they are powerless to produce dental decay so long as the resistance of the body is normal.

Tooth decay is attributed to the action of bacteria and their acids upon the teeth. In recounting his experiments on monkeys in which dental caries was produced by a deficient diet and, incidentally, referring to the lactic acid theory of tooth decay, Dr. Howe says: "Before we examine the effects of vitamin-C deficiencies upon the teeth of monkeys, let me remind you that all of our efforts to affect these teeth by fermentation in the mouth for long periods of time by the feeding and injection of microorganisms associated with caries have been unavailing, so long as the diet was normal."

Experiments by Drs. Howe and Hatch (1917) in America, and by Sir James McIntosh, Warwick James and Lazarus-Barlow, working together in England, in trying to produce dental caries by using acid forming bacteria all resulted negatively. Dr. Howe says that "so long as the diet is normal it has been found impossible to cause caries or pyorrhea by maintaining fermentation in the mouth or by feeding or injecting the bacteria believed to be most actively associated with dental caries."

There is a deeper cause for tooth decay than the germs that get onto the surfaces of our teeth. That cause exerts its baneful influence upon the growth and development of the teeth. That cause reaches back into the prenatal life of the child when the tissues of the teeth are being formed and developed.

If these things are not so, why then are so many teeth plainly defective when they erupt. They are small, distorted, overlapped, notched, have cavities in them and present other evidences of faulty structure and of lack of resistance to the forces of decay. It is so common to see the six-year molars, the first permanent teeth to erupt, come through with cavities in them.

Something more fundamental than a tooth brush and a biannual dental examination is required to prevent such a condition as this. Something more than these things are essential to the preservation of such teeth.

The ocean of dental decay is so large and its causes such that it can never be coped with by cleaning and filling the teeth. No amount of scrubbing and polishing can preserve them if nutrition is inadequate. Only a radical program will avail us here.

Cleaning the teeth of tartar, which is intended to save the gums and not the teeth, avails little unless a change in food and water is made. The calcific (lime salts) and food debris deposits (tartar) collecting about the necks of teeth come from the saliva and excess lime in free use of lime water. It often collects rapidly.

TOOTH DEVELOPMENT

It is well to bear in mind that every tooth a man will ever have (except the false ones) is already formed or being formed in his jaws at birth. The teeth actually begin to be formed before any of their supporting structures in the bony alveolar process.

The anlage or germ appears as the dental ridge developing from the cells of the ectoderm, as early as the seventh week of fetal life. Out of this ridge the tooth-buds of the temporary teeth with the enamel organ's begin to be differentiated about the eighth week. These structures, invade the underlying mesoderm and together they form the "dental papilla" which becomes distinguishable during the ninth or tenth week.

The tooth-buds of all the deciduous teeth are definitely formed and the enamel organs of the permanent teeth have appeared by the fifteenth week. At about the twentieth week calcification sets in in the tip of the incisors to be followed by calcification in the canines and premolars in the twenty-fourth week.

The first permanent molars, in their origin and development, follow very closely the development of the temporary teeth. At about the fifteenth week their enamel organs first appear and this is followed two weeks later by the formation of their dental bulbs. The dental follicles of these teeth are complete and their calcification has begun by the ninth month. All of the other permanent teeth have also been laid down by this time and are calcified during early childhood.

Let us briefly review this: At birth all of the temporary teeth are definitely formed and calcification is in process; the six year molars are formed and calcification of their crowns is under way; all of the other permanent teeth have been laid down and await calcification during early childhood.

It is before birth, when these teeth are forming, that we must begin to save the teeth of child and adult. For, not only is it here that those defects are produced which are visible in so many teeth when they erupt, but here also are many of the defects initiated which are to appear later. A soft pre-tooth structure laid down in the jaws of the embryo, due to nutritional perversion of the mother, predisposes the teeth to cavities and decay. Finally calcification, due to nutritional perversions and deficiencies, injures both the temporary and the permanent teeth.

NUTRITION

A faulty diet and nutritional derangements after birth easily results in faulty tooth structure, both in the temporary and permanent teeth. The prenatal months and the pre-school years are, indeed, as they have been aptly termed, the golden age for the prevention of tooth decay. If no thought is ever given to the requirements of children's teeth until after they erupt, the chances are that, on our modern diet, the child's teeth will be defective and short lived.

Upon the mother falls the duty of feeding the teeth during the prenatal months and during the nursing months after birth. The duty and the responsibility are hers. Her duty is not merely to her child but to herself, as well. For, if she does not supply the embryo and perhaps even the suckling, with the necessary elements in her food, nature will manage to take some of these out of her own tissues. Her own teeth will suffer, and perhaps, also her blood and other tissues, due to nature's habit of safeguarding the child at the mother's expense.

Dr. Howe says that: "The deficiencies which manifest themselves in the dental apparatus of the child are generally, in part at least, results of deficiencies in the diet of the mother before the child is born and wrong feeding of the infant. It is more and more the duty of our profession to take care of the dental condition of the expectant mother. The diet which will protect the teeth against the heavy demands of this period is the very diet to supply materials for the bones and teeth of the fœtus."

Mothers tend to lose their teeth during pregnancy and lactation. This is not true of animals and savages and is so in civilized mothers because their diet does not meet the demand for extra calcium during this period.

It is an old proverb among mothers, "with every child a tooth." To this may be added, "for every child several cavities." A British investigator, Dr. Ballantyne, in the study of a hundred cases in the Edinburgh Royal Maternity Clinic, found that ninety-eight per cent of the pregnant women suffered with "dental caries or infection." Ninety-three per cent of this number had had one or more extractions. More than half (53%) of these patients were under twenty-five years of age. Almost as high percentages of carious teeth have been noted in pregnant women in some of our American clinics.

On a deficient diet (experimental), growing animals show such effects as the following − dental caries, cranial caries, mandible caries, caries of other bones, distortion and malnutrition of bones − such as shortened and small ribs, smallness and deformity of the cranium, chest, pelvis, etc. − rickets, distorted and malposed teeth,

BUILDING THE TEETH

crooked nose, etc. Caries is the term for decay or ulcerous inflammation of bone.

Dr. Howe placed animals on a scurvy producing diet and produced "retarded growth, warping of the body structure, lowered vitality, susceptibility to colds and more serious forms of illness." If the diet is bad enough the animals die in four weeks. If not greatly deficient "death does not come immediately or completely, as with entire deprivation (of vitamin C), but comes creeping on slowly, insiduously and progressively, until it involves all the bony tissues, including the teeth. Even the enamel, which is the hardest and perhaps the most resistant tissue in the body, is affected."

"The particular form of starvation which is scurvy dissolves the soft or organic parts of the bones and teeth. In bones there is an organic matrix or frame-work, and the mineral salts, which give stiffness and hardness, are held in this organic material. Even the enamel has such a framework, and evidence which lies before me as I write indicates that there is more circulation in the enamel than we have supposed. When the body is deprived of enough vitamin C for a long time something happens to the matrix, perhaps in tiny spots here and there through the body, and if the deprivation is sufficient, the matrix will break down." — (Howe)

Howe further says: "We have seen that, under the influence of a vitamin C deficiency which has not been sufficiently prolonged to cause recognizable signs of scurvy, the pulp of the tooth in a guinea-pig will undergo changes that are destructive for it and for the dentin. It will shrink forcibly enough to tear the odontoblastic processes out of the dental tubuli and, in the section (a picture of a set of teeth is here shown), something appearing like broken processes may be seen on the outer margin of the pulp. This tearing out of the processes probably renders it impossible for the odontoblasts to continue the functions which may be essential to the metabolism of the dentin, and soon thereafter the dentin begins to liquify and may be extensively or completely destroyed. If similar changes occur in human teeth, is it not probable that dentin in which the functions of the odontoblasts have not been torn away, would offer less resistance to the agents of decay than the same dentin would when in good health? Our experiments show that a complete vitamin C deficiency will visibly affect the odontoblasts in about five to seven days.

"We have seen that very soon after the feeding of orange juice is begun, the pulp, though incapable of returning to its former size or form, resumes some of its functions and initiates the development of secondary dentin, which might be called *dental scar tissue.*"

Animals fed on a deficient diet until they are ready to die, and have sustained great injury to their teeth, improve upon being given orange juice. Dr. Howe says that within twenty-four hours after the first feeding of orange juice, the pulp of the teeth begins to resume its dentin-building function. I have seen great improvement in the condition of the teeth of adults follow improved diet. Howe tells us that "when the nutritional balance is restored, the destructive process from within can be stopped and, if it has not gone too far, may be repaired. It is quite possible that you may do that with these other teeth if you will prescribe liberal quantities of fresh whole milk, unpasteurized, orange juice and green vegetables. Keep the protein in the diet low. Excess protein in the diet of experimental animals is always a disturbing factor."

Howe and others have shown that animals fed on the conventional American diet of refined cereals, pasteurized milk or cream, white sugar, meat and eggs, bread, coffee and sweets, with a deficiency of minerals and vitamins, develop rickets, scurvy, etc., and decay of the teeth. If the diet is very bad, the animals develop not only dental caries, but caries of the cranium, ribs, spine, and of the bones of the limbs.

Dr. E. A. Crostic, New York City, observes: "No one in New York City is eating the proper food these days. Foreigners who come here with a history of natural foods, behind them possess solid tissues.

"Thirty years ago when the occasion arose people could sit in a dentist's chair and have several teeth extracted without wincing. Today, so lacking in nerves, energy and vitality are our women, that almost any of them after the ordeal of one or two extractions is on the verge of collapse."

Faulty food weakens the nerves as well as the teeth and lowers resistance to pain and shock. I am sure that if people would have their teeth pulled without the use of anæsthetics, there would be far less after-suffering and no deaths from anæsthesia.

Dr. Howe was able to produce bone destruction in various parts of the body by faulty diet. He was also able to demonstrate bone regeneration following an improvement in diet. Some of the de-

BUILDING THE TEETH

structive changes were so like osteomalacia that they could not differentiate between the "two" conditions. The conditions are probably identical. By the same faulty diet he was able to produce dental caries; and by a change of diet he produced a degree of dental regeneration.

Each tooth is a highly specialized piece, of bone, a part of the bony system of the body, and receives its nourishment from the blood, just as do the other bones of the body. The teeth are subject to the same laws and nutritional requirements as the rest of man's bones and are affected for good or ill by whatever affects the nutrition of the body as a whole.

The teeth are leached of their salts from the inside until there is only a shell left. The decay begins on the inside. The teeth may be practically destroyed from within. Cavities form inside, then the enamel breaks through. Scrubbing the surface of the teeth cannot build sound teeth. The healthy human mouth is self-cleansing and bacteria cannot thrive therein.

Howe fed growing animals on deficient and adequate diets alternately and produced stripes of hard structure and soft structure in the teeth representing the periods of feeding. He placed guinea-pigs on a deficient diet and says: "We found that soon the teeth became decalcified, lost their hardness, could be easily penetrated by a sharp instrument, or a pin and that they were so soft they easily bend. Distinct cavities formed in some and the dentin was badly disintegrated.

"We found the alveolar process, or semi-bony structure that holds the teeth firmly in place had been gradually absorbed, so the teeth became loose and could be easily pulled out with thumb and finger whereas ordinarily they are set in very tightly, as are healthy human teeth.

"Inflammatory and degenerative changes occurred resembling pyorrhea. In the experiments where we injected micro-organisms, into the gums of guinea pigs, no such results occurred, showing that pyorrhea is a result rather than a cause.

"Irregularities of the teeth occurred, in one case the teeth crossed each other, making a letter X. Putting this animal back on a normal diet recalcified these teeth, set them hard in their sockets and so fixed them permanently in this abnormal position.

"We examined the jaws of some of these animals after they had died. The jaws showed that while the guinea pigs had been on a vitamin deficient diet, the bony structure of the jaw had been mined of its calcium and when the normal diet was restored, areas of calcium had been replaced, showing very definitely that the body calls on the bones for calcium when it is needed in the blood, and that the blood gives calcium back when there is an abundance of this element."

Zilva and Wells fed guinea pigs on a scorbutic diet and noted the following changes in their teeth — pronounced cellular disorganization, with disappearance of nuclei and of interstitial cement substances. The disintegrating process involved the nerves, cells, bloodvessels and odontoblasts, their places being taken by a new firm, fibrous structure devoid of cells, nuclei, or regular arrangement of constructed parts. Similar pathological changes have been observed to occur in the various organs of the body.

Let us understand, once and for all, that decay of teeth is a result of a disturbance of calcium metabolism, from whatever cause. It may be and often is due to a faulty diet; and may be and often is due to many other factors and influences that pervert metabolism. I have seen the rapid breaking down of the teeth in cases of marked chronic digestive troubles. Hyperacidity of the stomach is a frequent cause of crumbling of the teeth. Animal experimenters point out that those animals that develop caries, also develop acute gastrointestinal disturbances, diarrhea with mucus and blood in their stools. The best diet that can be fed will fail to nourish the body if it is not digested. It follows, logically, that whatever deranges digestion and perverts metabolism may be responsible for tooth decay.

Dr. C. R. Kelley, New York City, observes, "Periods of disease in children marked for general nutritional disturbances in which tooth nourishment is for a time completely shut off, leave their traces like sign-posts on developing teeth."

Defective teeth are always present in rickets. This is true in children, in dogs, in pigs and in other animals. The pig is most susceptible to rickets of all domesticated animals. At the Rowett Institute, in England, it was not found possible to produce any symptoms of rickets in any animal, under any environment, favorable or unfavorable, on a diet which contains a sufficient amount of alkaline salts. Mineral deficiency brings about rickets, and injures the teeth.

Artificial infant feeding tends to produce decay of the teeth. Children in England and Scotland show about 85% decayed teeth. American children who are breast-fed to six months or more show

42.6% decayed teeth; if they are nursed under six months they show 42.9% decayed teeth. Children fed on sweetened condensed milk show nearly 73% decayed teeth. The vital necessity of nursing your child is thus made manifest. But, it is also necessary that you feed yourself properly.

In certain tribes who chip their teeth off and point them in their effort to add to their beauty, so long as their broken teeth are well-nourished, they do not decay. An animal may break a tooth in a fight or otherwise, but it does not decay.

There is only one reason why civilized children cannot have as good teeth as savage children—the refusal of pregnant and nursing mothers to eat proper foods and take adequate care of themselves and their failure to properly feed their children up to the sixth year of their lives.

Flourine starvation may often be responsible for a thinning of the enamel of the teeth. But there is no excuse for flourine starvation. Nature certainly supplies us with abundance of this in *natural* foods.

Mrs. Mellanby (of England) declares, "the more cereals that are eaten, other things being equal, the worse formed are the teeth." I think this applies to all cereals and to all cereal foods, but it particularly applies to all denatured cereals. The present diet of civilized peoples is largely acid-forming, and the excess of the acid radicals in our diet makes a great demand on the alkaline bases of our bodies. White flour has been robbed of most of its alkaline salts and is much more acid-forming than whole-wheat flour. But even whole-wheat is an acid-ash food.

The mineral salts of white bread have a higher acidity than that of other cereals. It is, no doubt, for this reason that in countries that subsist largely on white flour, tooth decay is more prevalent than where other cereals (also denatured) are used.

Investigations have revealed that those races whose diets include no cereals have teeth and mouths practically free of any kind of disease, while those races whose staple diets are cereals and meat with relatively small amounts of fruits and vegetables have jaws and teeth like those so common in America. Wheat is the most damaging of all the cereals, regarded from the point of view of its acidity. Little meat and cereals and an abundance of fruits and vegetables produce teeth like those found in Polish and Irish peasantry and those of the vegetarian races of the Orient.

Chalky decomposition of the enamel of the teeth is the result of calcium and phosphorus deficiency over a period of years. It is not always possible to arrest the decomposition or to improve the teeth. Indeed I recall having seen but one case where marked improvement followed a revolution of the diet. If this condition is to be prevented in children the mother must have ample mineral-bearing food during pregnancy and lactation.

If, in the quotations from Dr. Howe, we substitute the words fresh fruits and green raw vegetables, for the term vitamin C, we have a practical working basis upon which the mother may feed herself and her child. All denatured foods rob the body of minerals. All excess of acid foods rob the body of calcium and other bases. Fruits, green vegetables and nuts are best for the teeth.

EXERCISING THE TEETH

Soft diets, which require no work of the teeth and jaws in chewing, aid in producing dental decay. No tooth can have adequate nutrition unless it is used. Mush-eating does not give the teeth proper exercise. Raw foods are best. A tough, fibrous diet not only gives the teeth and jaws needed exercise, but also cleans the teeth. The conventional, unnatural and highly refined, cooked diet leaves the mouth and teeth dirty.

IRREGULARITIES AND MALPOSITIONS

By the time a child is five or five and a half years old its baby teeth should be well spread apart in front to make room for the permanent teeth, which will soon begin to erupt. If the child's diet and care have been proper, so that his or her development has been normal, this will be so. But how often do we see it otherwise? The vault of the mouth is so often high rather than broad and flat, as it should be. There is not room in the jaws for the permanent teeth. As a result these are crowded or overlapped, malposed and irregular. They must also be defective, for the same developmental failure which resulted in a faulty dental arch, also produces defective teeth.

Dr. Howe says that: "Under favorable conditions, the child develops proper cranial and facial proportions and a broad dental arch, and at the proper age the deciduous arch voluntarily widens to form the anterior portion of the permanent dental arch" ° ° ° ° "under unfavorable conditions, facial development in the child may be retarded so that when it is time for the permanent teeth to erupt the arch may not be wide enough to accomodate them and they will be malposed. Such a physical deficiency may arise from any of many causes acting either singly or together, such as poor heredity, lack of sunlight, illness, a deficient diet, and perhaps others."

Prof. E. Mellanby has shown that the structure and arrangement in the jaws of teeth of animals depend largely upon their nutrition during the period of development, so that it is now possible to produce almost any degree of imperfection of the teeth by supervising the diet of puppies.

BASIS OF SUCCESS

I have watched the failure of the efforts to stay the decay of teeth by the use of various diets and various articles of food. A quart of calcium-rich milk a day does not prevent tooth decay. Feeding phosphorus-rich foods has not prevented tooth decay. Giving vitamins C and B has failed to save the teeth. The giving of vitamin pills, calcium and phosphorus tablets, etc., has failed, equally with the diets. Giving orange juice also failed. Feeding cod liver oil does not save the teeth. The result is that many dentists are convinced that no diet can save the teeth. Yet the fact stands out like a sore thumb that people on certain diets do maintain good teeth while those on other diets have poor teeth. What is the answer? Dietary adequacy and not specific dosage with one or two or three nutritive factors. The *Law of the Minimum must* be satisfied.

Good teeth depend upon good health and not *vice versa* as the tooth-extracting fad proclaims. No cause of impaired health, however insignificant it may seem to be, should be neglected if the teeth are to be preserved. There seems to me to be no way to preserve the teeth by any plan that falls short of a complete system of health building. No one-idea plan can succeed. Soundness of the teeth will be preserved by the same mode of living that preserves soundness in all the tissues and structures of the body. We must learn to think in terms of health-building. We must learn to think in terms of health of the whole organism and cease thinking in terms of local health.

The health conditions found in the mouth are local indices of the condition of the tissues throughout the body. There is no such thing as a local tooth disease. The condition that leads to decay is always systemic. More than 75% of children presenting extensive dental caries, also have other serious troubles. Instead of the decay of the teeth being the cause of the systemic derangement and so-called local troubles elsewhere in the body, the systemic derangement is the cause of the tooth decay and other mis-construed local troubles.

So long as we view the teeth as isolated isonomies and forget their relationships with other parts of the body, we cannot hope to find the cause of tooth decay and will continue to fail in our efforts to preserve the teeth. Disease of the teeth is merely part of the disease of the body. Health of the teeth is part of the health of the body. The unsoundness dentists find in teeth which they indict as cause of disease, is merely part of the general pathology of a diseased body.

Searching for a unitary cause of tooth-decay is folly. The basis of good health is, at the same time, the basis of sound structure and normal function in all parts of the body. Teeth, like the eyes, heart, bones of the spine, etc., depend upon the whole of the elemental factors of life.

Any factor, physical, nutritional, emotional, etc., that perverts or impairs nutrition will cause the teeth to decay. Poor health, impaired nutrition, perverted metabolism, however produced, affect all the structures and functions of the body in varying degrees and any effort to preserve or restore integrity that ignores the cause of general impairment must fail.

Health is the basis of sound teeth. There can be no completely sound teeth in diseased bodies. No decay of the teeth can occur in a perfectly healthy body that is maintained in this condition by first class habits. Anything that is essential to good health is essential to good teeth. As the teeth are integral parts of the body their health depends upon the general integrity.

HEALING OF TEETH

Hygienists and others have long held that teeth will heal. Until recently dentists have denied this. There is no longer room to doubt this.

The teeth are bones. Bones do heal and regenerate under favorable conditions. Even the enamel of the teeth, it seems, is able to repair itself, as I have been able to demonstrate on a broken tooth of my own. Self-restoration of teeth with cavities in them have been reported by dentists within the last few years.

BUILDING THE TEETH

Limits must be recognized to the self-restorative powers of the teeth and regenerative conditions established as early as possible. Success cannot be expected, even then, in all cases.

Repair of the teeth depends, not alone upon a diet of fruits and vegetables, but upon a general improvement in health. Every factor that improves nutrition—sunshine, exercise, rest, etc.—will aid in repair.

The Eliminating Diet
CHAPTER XXXVIII

The eliminating diet is now frequently miscalled a fast—a fruit fast, an orange fast, a grape fast, etc. It is also often called a cleansing diet. It is a diet of juicy fruits, or green vegetables or both.

There is a sense in which the orange diet, for example, is similar to a fast in its effects. During a fast the cells feed on the accumulated reserves stored in the body and do not secure their sustenance from fresh supplies which have just arrived by way of the digestive tract.

An orange diet is a true fast in the sense of abstinence from proscribed foods, but it is not an orange fast. Considered, however, from the point of view that such a diet turns the cells away from freshly arriving food supplies to the stored reserves, to meet their food needs, it has very much (not all) the same effects as a complete fast. Milo Hastings has very nicely illustrated this matter in the following words:

"The essential action might be explained by likening the body to a store. If the manager of a store has been too ambitious a buyer he is very likely to have accumulated certain stocks of goods until his shelves are too crowded, and the general efficiency of the store's activities is impaired. So he decides to put on a sale, mark down his prices and have a general housecleaning—all of which is often a very wise move for the health of the business.

"A complete fast or abstinence from all food would be like a clearance sale during which a store ceased entirely to purchase new stocks. But a partial fast would be like a clearance sale during which the store continued to purchase new stocks, but less new stock than the sale was consuming. Good management in a store would indeed often suggest the wisdom of just such clearance sales during which the major inflow of new goods was shut off, but in which the supply of certain new goods much in demand and which had not been accumulated to excess was still continued from an outside source.

"This last condition nicely pictures the argument for the partial fast. But as in store management, so in nutritional management, the

THE ELIMINATING DIET

wisdom of such a clearance or such a partial fast would depend on whether one used wisdom in choosing what new material should be supplied while the old accumulations were being used up."

The purpose of the eliminating diet is not to see how many glasses of juice one can take in a day in an effort to "alkalinize" the body, or to supply an excess of minerals or vitamins. Indeed, this method of drinking juice largely defeats the purpose of the diet. The nearer the diet approaches a complete fast, the more effective it becomes. Juice salesmen and sellers of juice extractors will deny this, but they are in no position to know what they are talking about.

The food substances that are consumed in greatest excess and which are likely to accumulate in the body are fats, sugars, starches and proteins. Proteins can never accumulate in amounts as great as can the fats and carbohydrates, but the excess of protein may be most harmful. The eliminating diet accomplishes more than merely compelling the utilization of excesses of proteins, carbohydrates and fats.

There are two sides to the story of nutrition. One side deals with the building up of the body and the manufacture of secretions. The other side deals with the elimination of waste-matter from the blood and tissues. This latter part is accomplished by the use of food substances that never really become part of the body but are held in solution in the blood. The protein wastes of the cells are carried to the liver where they are combined with the alkaline, organic mineral elements which convert them into soluble salts. These salts are then easily eliminated by the kidneys and skin. A diet rich in bases and poor in acids is an eliminating or "curative" diet.

It is often difficult to distinguish between normal body waste and a mere excess of food. The normal wastes of the body are commonly assumed to be the usual daily excretions from a conventionally fed man. But average conditions are often far from the ideal. In the case of the element, nitrogen, for example, excreted through the kidneys, it was for a long time assumed that the average daily wastes represented normal and necessary wastes from true physiological processes. Later investigations have shown this to be a mistake. It has been found that by reducing the intake of protein, from which the nitrogen is derived, the nitrogen excreted through the kidneys could be reduced to less than one-fourth of the quantity which was formerly assumed to be necessary and normal. Similar facts are true of common table salt and other mineral elements.

These things are quickly brought to light during a fast. After the first few days, during which time there is usually an increase in elimination, the elimination of waste rapidly drops to levels much lower than the amounts daily eliminated by individuals who are customarily over-fed.

A house cleaning process is inaugurated. The body throws off its surplus elements after which it strikes a new balance of elimination, one which probably represents the actual daily wastes of the processes of life. Much of the former greater amounts of waste eliminated presumably represented the overflow of a surplus of material consumed by the individual, which had reached the danger line of active poisoning from excess.

The striking benefits produced by fasting are attributable largely to the cleaning out of these excess materials which have been accumulated by habitually eating in excess of the actual body requirements.

This surplus material may quite accurately be spoken of as toxins or poisons, for it definitely injures the body if it is not promptly eliminated. It may even result in some degree of injury, other than the waste of energy and secretions in handling it, by passing through the body when performing no useful function.

Of the three main groups of food elements (carbohydrates, hydrocarbons, and proteins), carbohydrates offer the least danger of creation of possible toxic substances and proteins the most danger. Both of these are commonly consumed greatly in excess of requirements, the carbohydrates usually in the greatest excess, and these are capable of producing much trouble if they are permitted to ferment in the digestive tract.

Keep in mind that the most healthful food may be harmful if consumed in excess. Excesses of proteins and carbohydrates are especially likely to produce harm. That life continues in spite of the fact that we are constantly putting into the body a surplus of food and introducing poisonous substances therein, is due to its possession of an elaborate system of getting rid of the surplus and toxins.

It is often assumed that the digestive organs are able to reject any substance that would prove injurious to the body. Unfortunately their capacity to do this is very limited. Otherwise, the thousands of drugs poured into human stomachs, would have no effect beyond irritating the lining surfaces of the digestive organs. That they are absorbed by the blood and do produce their injurious effects throughout the body is evident enough.

Most of such substances that are absorbed into the blood are later excreted through the kidneys. Some are oxidized in the tissues and excreted in part through the lungs. Others, after being absorbed from the intestines, are later cast back into the intestines as excretions and pass out into the stools.

All of this is a very wonderful and complicated process. Most "diseases" and deaths are due to an over-strain and breakdown of the organs and functions of elimination, or, more correctly, when the processes of elimination are impaired and the poisons permitted to accumulate, we sicken and die from the accumulation of a toxic over-load. This is equally true of what we designate normal wastes of the body as it is of poisons which should never have been introduced into the organism.

Oranges and other fruits have very minute quantities of proteins while the juicy fruits are all comparatively low in carbohydrates. Their real cleansing and detoxifying effects are obtained largely by forcing the body to consume its surplus of proteins and "fuel foods." As soon as the supply of these foods is cut off and the body is given nothing but fruit juices or fruit, the accumulated excesses are called upon to supply the cells with protein and sugar.

Fruits and fruit juices are rich in alkaline bases and in vitamins and quickly replenish any deficiency of these that may exist and also overcome the acidosis (hypoalkalinity), usually present in those living on the modern dietary.

This principle need not be limited to oranges, or grapes, nor even to juicy fruits, but may also be extended to include all green, non-starchy vegetables. Mr. Hastings says that "All scientifically planned weight reducing diets are in this general class, but weight reducing is not the only purpose for using such types of diets. As temporary measures they may be beneficial to general vitality, even when the weight lost is to be later replaced."

The eliminating diet is as near protein-starch-fat-sugar free as can be fed, in order to enable the body to use up and throw off its surplus of these elements. It is also rich in organic salts and organic acids thus supplying to the body an abundance of alkalinizing elements, so that "acidosis" is overcome and the accumulated toxins in the body are prepared for elimination and thrown out.

The foods most commonly used in eliminating diets are oranges, lemons, grapefruit, tomatoes, apples, grapes, carrots, spinach, chard, lettuce, cellery, cabbage, beet greens, onions, etc. Melons are sometimes used, as are peachs. The fruit chosen is taken at regular intervals during the day in varying quantities depending on the individual case.

All of these foods are valuable for their pure water, organic acids, minerals, vitamins and cellulose. They are all low in fats, carbohydrates and proteins. Since the food elements abundant in these foods are the ones chiefly lacking in the conventional diet and the food elements in which they are deficient are the ones that predominate in the conventional diet, salts and vitamins are supplied while at the same time utilization of the surplusses of carbohydrates, fats and proteins is compelled.

An eliminating diet may be a mono-diet. (The citrus fruit diet is perhaps the best-known of these); or it may be a diet consisting of a variety of the unconcentrated foods.

These fruits are rich in organic salts, which are liberated during digestion, and supply the body with the elements necessary to the neutralization and chemicalization of the toxins preparatory to their elimination. They are at the same time extremely limited in the amount of proteins and carbohydrates which they possess and are well-adapted to a curative purpose. There is absolutely no foundation for the old medical delusion that acid fruits should not be given in "acid diseases." We often find that to give acid fruits where hyper-acidity of the stomach is present increases the distress in the stomach and for this reason are forced to use a diet of a different kind. Hyper-acidity of the stomach is not, however, "acid-blood," and fruit acids (organic acids) do not enter the blood as acids. The fruit diet proper consists of the exclusive use of any juicy or acid fruit.

Acid fruit diets are often distressing to patients with hyperacidity. They are also often hard on nervous patients, making them irritable and preventing sleep. In rare cases the acids seem to get into the lymph unchanged and cause skin eruptions. In cases of this kind, other diets are preferable.

The Orange Diet: The orange, because of its palatableness, because it is available at all seasons of the year, and, because it may be had in all parts of the country, is the most popular, at least in this country, of eliminating diets. Usually as many oranges as one desires are consumed. Sometimes the number is limited. From three to sixteen oranges a day are permitted. Not only the amount of oranges permitted, but the intervals between feedings must be determined by the condition of the patient.

The patient may be fed several oranges at each of three meals a day; or, he may be given an orange every half hour, or every hour during the day. Some may be given the whole orange, others must be given only the juice.

Due, perhaps, to the sugar in the orange, many people are troubled with gas while on this diet. Unless there is considerable distress, this need not cause the diet to be changed. Unripe oranges are likely to cause considerable distress, making lips, tongue and perhaps the stomach, raw in a few cases. I prefer Texas oranges; next to these in the order named, California and then Florida oranges.

The Grapefruit Diet consists in taking grapefruit exclusively. It is given in the same manner as is the orange diet (without sugar), and almost never causes gas.

Grapefruit are often preferable to oranges and many are able to take grapefruit who cannot take the orange diet. Grapefruit seems to hasten elimination even more than do oranges. I prefer Texas grapefruit; next to these, in the order named, Arizona, Florida and California grapefruit.

The Lemon Diet, consisting of eating lemons only, is usually too much for the average patient. The procedure is to begin with one half of a lemon three times a day and increase this by one and a half lemons each day until nine lemons are taken. The process is then reversed and one and a half lemons are dropped off each day until the starting point is reached. After ten days of feeding, this regimen may be repeated if necessary. This diet is especially recommended in rheumatic conditions and in liver disorders.

The Tomato Diet: This diet consists in the use of ripe tomatoes. These are given as in the orange diet. Tomatoes should be employed only during the tomato season. Hot house tomatoes are not advisable.

The Grape Diet: This consists in living for several weeks at a time on nothing but grapes, swallowing the seeds and skins. This diet has won great renown in European Nature Cure Institutions, particularly those in France and Southern Germany. Many, including the author, in this country have used it with excellent success. It was heralded as a specific for cancer a few years ago. This was unfortunate. It is not a specific for cancer nor for anything else.

On the upper Rhine they have Trauben Curen—sanitaria where people are fed almost exclusively on ripe grapes in order to purify their blood. The grapes generally used for this purpose are of the variety known as Musketeller, with big, honey-sweet berries, of a most enticing flavor. It is the opinion of those who employ this diet that their patients cannot hurt themselves by eating all of the Muskatellers they may desire.

Grapes are rich in iron and have proven very useful in anemia and chlorosis. The grape diet has also been found very serviceable in such conditions as gout, rheumatism, dyspepsia, constipation, catarrh, stones and gravels, malaria, liver and lung troubles including tuberculosis. General Booth employed the grape diet to "cure" inebriates. He was not only successful in breaking the drink habit in this way but his patients gained in weight.

Fresh, vineyard ripened grapes should be used. Hot house grapes, and those shipped long distances — from Africa, Spain or South America — being pulled very green, are not so good. The grape diet should be employed only during the grape season.

Five to eight pounds of grapes are fed daily, beginning with a pound and increasing the amount used each day until the capacity of the patient is reached.

Some patients develop large quantities of gas on this diet. Others develop a diarrhea which persists as long as the diet does. In such cases some other diet should be employed.

The Apple Diet, consists of eating apples exclusively. In cases where this diet does not cause too much gas it is excellent.

Fruit-Vegetable Diet: This consists in feeding fruits and green vegetables at separate meals. Any fruit in season may be used. Fruit may be used at one meal and vegetables at two meals; or fruit at two meals and vegetables at one.

The vegetable meal should consist of a large raw combination salad, without oil or dressing, and two cooked non-starchy (green) vegetables. Or, it may simply be a large salad. In some nervous disorders the raw vegetables may have to be temporarily excluded. In other such cases the raw salads may be eaten if lettuce is omitted. Lettuce causes much gas and discomfort in some cases.

THE ELIMINATING DIET

Vegetable broths are sometimes used instead of fruit and with practically the same results. These are used to distinct advantage in those cases where the digestive tract is so sensitive that the acid fruits cause distress.

Vegetable broths are of two kinds — cooked and uncooked. The cooked broths are made by chopping one or a combination of the succulent vegetables up fine and boiling them. It is usually strained after cooking to remove the cellulose.

The uncooked broths are made by finely chopping one or a combination of the succulent vegetables and pressing out their juices.

There should be no great hurry about breaking away from an eliminating diet. One who is actually desirous of regaining health will continue on such a diet long enough to secure the desired results. After the body has been thoroughly cleansed and the forces of the organism recuperated; when all or nearly all symptoms of trouble are gone, then, a gradual return to a normal diet should begin.

Obviously a diet composed exclusively of oranges or grapefruit or lemons cannot be continued as long as a grape diet or a fruit and vegetable diet; although, it may usually be continued long enough to bring about the desired results. (I had one man on a grapefruit diet for forty-five days). Or, else they may be employed for a period and followed by a less frugal diet, after which they may be resumed.

Feeding in Disease
CHAPTER XXXIX

Dr. Philip Norman says: "Possibly the most confusing chapter in medicine today is the one related to the problem of diet. Textbooks on treatment are woefully barren of tangible information. The authors assume that the medical man is sufficiently schooled in dietaries. Instruction concerning diet are usually dismissed with the admonition, 'Of course, the diet must be carefully planned, etc.' The greatest reflection on medical intelligence is to be found in the diet kitchens of the hospitals. The interns, the nurses, and the patients testify volutarily to the short-comings of hospital fare. It is traditionally accepted by patient and physician as part of the disagreeableness to be expected in the process of hospitalization. Dieticians are too often nothing more than cooks, who feebly attempt to enhance the physical attractiveness of food without thought or knowledge of the patients' nutritional requirements.

"The average meal consumed today is the outgrowth of the efforts of cooks who have catered to taste rather than to reason. The basic plan is to combine proteins, carbohydrates and fats. The conception of the calorie has retarded logical and rational reasoning in regard to diet, more so than any single other factor. The calorie is definitely associated with proteins, carbohydrates and fats. The calorific conception is a fuelistic rather than a nutritional conception. Nourishing such a complex aggregation of cells designated as the body differs widely from the problem of burning fuel to make steam."

Conditions are not much better in the ranks of the various drugless schools. Many of these practitioners give no attention whatever to diet and others almost none. Many of those who give great attention to diet know very little about it and to the everlasting shame of many of these, they are guided by what they have learned from lecturers and written works of a swarm of lecture racketeers, who, while they have many patent foods to sell, have had neither training nor experience in trophology. The lecturers are sadly deficient in knowledge of everything except salesmanship.

"Type feeding," "polarity feeding," feeding according to temperament, and similar attempts to feed "individualized" diets, are based on fallacies and errors of the most misleading kinds. In spite of this, their authors have frequently worked out dietaries that are far superior to the conventional diet.

Another group feeds "specific foods" for "specific diseases." Dr. Harry Finkel says: "It is to be hoped that the future doctors will learn the medicinal value of each particular food and prescribe it in the same manner he does drugs." A formidable dietetic-pharmacopea has been worked out — apricots for nausea, obesity and constipation; beets for the kidneys and bladder; cucumbers to purify the blood; pineapple for "sore throat"; leeks for coughs, colds and insomnia; spinach and beet tops for anemia; olive oil for gall stones; lemons and grapes for cancer; celery and fish for nervous troubles, etc. This is a system of medicine — allopathic medicine.

I agree with Dr. Weger that no food has curative properties *per se*, and that "it is wrong to ascribe to food the power to cure." He correctly says, "the person who recommends or takes a certain kind of food to cure a certain kind of disease is still in the elementary or kindergarten stage of food and health knowledge."

No confidence can be placed in the claims for therapeutic virtues in special foods. The theories and claims of those who maintain foods have certain specific effects upon certain organs and tissues of the body have been thoroughly studied and tested by the author and by others. Time and time again we have prescribed these foods and watched for their alleged effects. These effects have not shown up.

Similar to the effort to feed special foods in "specific diseases" is the effort to feed special organs of the body. We are told that there are certain foods to feed the eyes, certain foods to feed the nerves, certain foods to feed the hair, certain foods to feed the nails, certain foods to feed the brain, certain foods to make one magnetic, certain foods to make one sleep, certain foods to fill one with energy, etc. No such foods exist. The ensemble of diet must meet the ensemble of the nutritive needs of the body before any organ can be adequately nourished.

Nothing that is good for the muscles is bad for the nerves, or any vital organ. What is good for the teeth is good for every organ of the body. Foods that promote and preserve beauty of the skin are also best for the brain. Foods that build strong, efficient stomachs are precisely those foods that build vigorous hearts, efficient livers, good kidneys, etc. The good of one is the good of all. That which perfects one organ perfects all the organs. The body is a unit and goes forward or backward as a unit — it must be nourished as a whole, not by piece-meal.

Foods enter the digestive tract and are broken up into their constituent nutritive elements and enter the blood stream as mineral salts, amino-acids, monosaccharides, glycerol and water. These are the things that circulate in the blood and which reach the organs and tissues. The blood succeeds in maintaining a surprising uniformity of structure and composition regardless of the food eaten. It is blood that feeds the organs.

One of the greatest mistakes in those dietaries worked out on the calorie basis is that the chemical reactions which occur in the incongrous combinations usually fed, so change the character and value of the whole mass that the one who eats such menus never receives the calories represented in his meal. The same thing is true of similar menus now worked out with special reference to vitamins.

Due to the prevailing confusion about nutrition and stimulation, many old errors continue to rule the minds and influence the practices of the layman, the dietician and the physician. Dr. Trall protested that physicians were "in the habit of saying to cold, pale, thin, and debilitated patients, for whom some other doctor had recommended a vegetarian diet, that they require a 'more stimulating diet,' meaning, of course, fresh-meat. And I have heard more than one doctor of the 'old school' call 'flesh, fish and fowl' tonic or high diet, in contradistinction to vegetable, which they termed reducing or low diet."

So-called "strengthening" foods stimulate the nerves and muscles, put on fat, color the face and lend a fictitious appearance of health; but they waste strength, "rust" the tissues, distend the blood vessels with plethora, overwork the heart, bring about anterio-sclorosis, and result in premature old age and death.

In dietary matters, as in other matters, it reveals a lack of vision and understanding to consider only immediate and temporary results and not look into the future at ultimate and permanent results. It can hardly be too often repeated that the more you eat, the more you poison yourself and the faster you wear yourself out.

These fallacies about meat and vegetable foods are far from dead and we hear them repeated quite often today. It is no uncommon thing to hear a patient, who is on a fruit and vegetable diet, told that he or she needs "a more nourishing diet," meaning that the patient should have meat or eggs. Nourishment is still thought of in terms not only of stimulation, but also in terms of proteins, carbohydrates and calories.

The term "high living," as commonly employed, means gluttonous indulgence in unhealthful dishes. When those who thus eat become bloated masses of disease or attenuated wrecks of prematurely worn-out bodies, they are said to be victims of "high living." The term and its use implies that it is decidedly vulgar to eat plain, wholesome foods and stay well.

The miserable dyspeptic who has lived on hot biscuits, fried meats, short cakes, plum puddings and other concentrated foods and "knic-knacs," until he is nearly dead, is said to be suffering from the effects of "too good living" — as though healthful living is actually bad. We are told that greasy dishes, gravies, cakes, etc., that prove to be distressing to the digestive organs, are "too rich" — as though foods that are wholesome and good are and must necessarily be poor.

All *Hygienists,* from the days of Jennings and Trall to the present, have been consulted by "poor, wretched invalids," who have suffered for half a lifetime or more, of misery and infirmity, due largely to improper diet, who upon being told that the adoption of and rigid adherence to a senisible diet of fruits and vegetables would enable them to regain a fair degree of health, comfort and usefulness and materially prolong their lives, reply "with solemn, yet almost ludicrous gravity," as Trall put it, that they "had rather live a little better and not quite so long" — as though healthful living is necessarily not so good.

Obviously no man who is in possession of "definite and correct ideas of the relations of food to health, could ever talk in this nonsensical manner." These expressions not only mislead those who hear them, but they indicate an evident lack of clearness and precision in the minds of those who use them.

"Eat what agrees with you" is the usual advice of the physician to those who seek information about their diet. What agrees with us? This advice, like the advice to eat what appetite calls for, usually amounts merely to the advice to eat according to long established habits. In popular estimation as well as in the view of the physician, the absence of distress in the abdomen immediately following the ingestion of food is evidence that it is causing no harm.

There can be no greater fallacy than this advice and this view. The very worst foods that can be eaten, those that are least valuable or most harmful, seldom produce any abdominal distress. Not only is the digestive system capable of withstanding a great deal of abuse, but the true test of food value is: does the food nourish the tissues?

It does not matter how perfectly the digestive organs may function, nor how easy and comfortable one may be after his meals, the body cannot obtain from food, elements that are not there. If the diet is lacking in some of the essential elements of nutrition, the tissues must suffer because of this lack. And this is the reply to those Chiropractors who assert that "if the Chiropractor restores the digestive organs to normal, the patient may eat what he likes." The body cannot take from its food, elements that are not there any more than a plant can extract elements from the soil if these are lacking.

Finally, imperfect digestion may result in fermentation and putrefaction and the consequent poisoning, with no immediate discomfort after meals. Perhaps a little gas a few hours after eating will be the only abdominal discomfort the individual will experience.

A lack of certain food elements, or an excess of others, or the presence in the food of deleterious elements are all that can cause trouble. We must feed the body, not the organ or the "disease."

My friend of happy memory, Dr. Wm. H. Havard, suggested the following practical classification of diets, according to the prime purposes they are intended to serve:

1. *The Building Diet,* or the diet of physical growth, rich in proteins, carbohydrates, minerals and vitamins, for the growing child, the pregnant mother, the convalescent patient and the person who has had a long fast.

2. *The Mature Diet,* or the *Diet of Maintenance,* rich in minerals, vitamins and carbohydrates, but poor in proteins, for the healthy adult individual.

3. *The Curative Diet,* or *Diet of Elimination,* rich in minerals and vitamins and practically protein-starch-sugar-fat free, for the chronic sufferer. The eliminating diet is fully discussed in the preceding chapter.

A chasm too great to be bridged with any possible compromise exists between a feeding system that feeds according to digestive and assimilative capacity and all other systems that endeavor to force-feed in keeping with apparent or theoretical systemic needs without regard for or consideration of the patient's ability to digest and assimilate. *Hygienists* take into consideration, not alone digestive capacity, but also assimilating capacity. We realize that nothing is to be gained from merely passing food that is not used, through the patient.

" 'Nourishment' is the prevailing cry of 'those that would cure us,' " says Adolph Just in his *Return to Nature;* " 'You need more nourishment!' But how can a body be nourished when it is incapable of absorbing, and especially incapable of expelling, that which has been already stuffed into it? The fact is that in nearly every instance the sufferer to whom more nourishment is recommended is one who is already brought low by excessive nourishment — he is actually pining through overplus!"

These patients are not only incapable of absorbing but, also, of digesting food. How foolish to give more food when it cannot be digested, absorbed and assimilated! Not more food, but more ability to assimilate and excrete, is needed and must be first provided through rest, fasting and hygiene before food is to be thought of. Nothing is of more advantage in most cases of "disease" than a fast, often a long one. A reduction of surfeit is essential to the most vigorous manifestations of vitality and to the restoration of vigor.

Many doctors of all schools will disagree with this. Since, however, almost none of them have ever undertaken a protracted fast, nor have they ever supervised a representative number of protracted fasts for the benefit of others, and since few of them have ever really studied fasting, they have no right to put forth considered views upon a procedure of which they know little or nothing from the practical viewpoint. There is really no problem of feeding in acute "disease," for no food should be given in acute states.

The amount of food given the patients must always be graduated in proportion to his strength. The feebler the system, always the less digestive power possessed. Stuffing the sick on "rich" viands under the supposition that they need so much food each day, or that "plenty of good nourishing food" will build them up is a common, but fallacious, practice.

Patients should not be fed according to any arbitrary standards, such as that they need and must have 3000 calories each day, or that they need and must have so many ounces of protein a day, but according to their abilities to utilize the food consumed.

It is essential that we recognize that the nutritive needs of the sick organism vary from the needs of the healthy organism. Greater caution must be observed in feeding or in eating where one is trying to eradicate illness than if we have only to maintain health. A firm resolve on the part of the sufferer to do all that is essential, is required. He must abandon his old ways and stick to a new and radically different program.

Where lack of salts and vitamins has exhausted the tissues and organs and where surplus acids exist in the body, one or more crises must usually develop before real improvement becomes apparent.

After controverting the opinion that fleshiness and the muscular power of the body are to be considered as criteria of the excellence of any regimen prescribed for the chronic individual, and pointing out that to eat increases the pain, inflammation, discomfort, fever and irritableness of the system, and does so in proportion to the amount of food eaten and in direct ratio to its supposed nutritive qualities, and that to fast or to consume non-irritating non-stimulating foods and drinks in moderation reduces the "violence" of the disease and renders recovery more certain, Graham says, *Lectures*, p. 441:

"Nevertheless, the chronic invalid himself, and generally his friends, and sometimes also his physician, seem to think that fleshiness and muscular strength are the things mainly to be desired and sought for, and that any prescribed regimen is more or less correct and salutary in proportion as it is conducive to these ends. Whereas if they were properly enlightened, they would know that *the more they nourish a body while diseased action is kept up in it, the more they increase the disease. The grand, primary object to be aimed at by the invalid, is to overcome and remove disease action and condition, and restore all parts to health*, and *then*, nourish the body with a view to fleshiness and strength, *as fast as the feeblest parts of the system will bear without breaking down again*. (Italics mine, Author). And the regimen best adapted to remove the diseased action and condition, more frequently than otherwise, causes a diminution of flesh and muscular strength (Please note, it is only muscular strength that is diminished. Author's note), while the disease remains, in regulating the general function of nutrition to the ability of the diseased part. But when the diseased action ceases, and healthy action takes place, the same regimen perhaps will increase the flesh and strength as rapidly as the highest welfare of the constitution will admit." The latter increase in weight and strength on the same regimen would not be possible if the previous loss of flesh and strength on it represented an actual loss of vital power. Yet every experienced *Hygienist* knows that what Graham says here is true. The common practice of stuffing the chronic sufferer like a harvest hand is evil. It is even bad for the harvest hand, but much worse for the invalid. Graham disposed of this practice as follows:

"In regulating the diet of chronic patients, however, it should always be remembered that the extensiveness and suddenness of any change should correspond with the physiological and pathological condition and circumstances of the individual; and most especially should it be remembered that the *diseased organ or part should be made the standard of the ability of the system.* If the boiler of a steam engine is powerful enough in some parts to bear a pressure of fifty pounds to the square inch, while in some other parts it can only bear ten pounds to the square inch, we know that it would not do for the engineer to make the strongest parts of the boiler the standard of its general ability or power, and to attempt to raise a pressure of forty pounds to the square inch, because some parts can bear fifty pounds; for in such an attempt he would surely burst the boiler at its weakest parts. He must therefore make the weakest parts the standard of the general power of the boiler, and only raise such a pressure of steam as those parts can safely bear. *So he who has diseased lungs or liver or any other part, while at the same time he has a vigorous stomach, must not regulate the quality of his food by the ability of his stomach, but by the ability of the diseased part.* This rule is of the utmost importance to the invalid, and one which cannot be disregarded with impunity, and yet it is continually and almost universally violated. Few things are more common than to find individuals who are laboring under severe chronic disease, indulging in every improper quality and quantity of food, and other dietetic errors, and still strongly contending for the propriety of their habits and practices, on the ground that 'their stomachs never trouble them.' Alas! They know not that the stomach is the principle source of all their troubles; yet by adopting a correct regimen, and strictly adhering to it for a short time, they would experience such a mitigation of their sufferings, if not such a restoration to health, as would fully convince them of *the serious impropriety of making a comparatively vigorous stomach the standard of the physiological ability of a system otherwise diseased.* (Italics mine, Author). — *Science of Human Life,* p. 440.

There are dieticians and physicians who work on the principle that if we just put enough of the vitamin, mineral and protein containing foods into the stomach, these somehow will be taken into the blood stream and be utilized.

Vitamin A is supposed to be essential to good eyesight. Peaches and cream contain much more vitamin A than the bread puddings so often eaten as desserts. For this reason, peaches and cream are advised as dessert. Yet these foods eaten on top of a regular meal do not guarantee that the eater will get vitamin A from them. They must be digested, and the dietitian who neglects the digestion of foods, is an ignoramus.

There is more to supplying the body with appropriate nourishment than the mere eating of foods, even the best of foods. A whole list of conditions, particularly diseases of the digestive tract, such as acute gastro-enteritis, peptic ulcers, chronic and acute gastritis, diarrhea, loss of teeth, nausea and vomiting from any cause, as in pregnancy, heart disease, etc., lack of appetite from any cause, such as fevers, severe inflammations, visceral pain or severe pain in any part of the body, operations and anesthetics, and states of mental depression such as worry, apprehension, grief and neurasthenia and psychoneurosis, interfere with the intake of food. Migraine not only interferes with eating but often results in vomiting, as does epilepsy. The absorption of food is interfered with by diarrheal diseases, enteritis, intestinal parasites, tuberculosis of the intestine, sprue, liver and gall bladder diseases and ingestion from any cause. Diabetes mellitus, diseases of the liver, chronic alcoholism, Bright's disease, heart disease, nervous troubles of various kinds, and a general toxic state interfere with the utilization of foods. Overacidity coupled with insufficient rest and sleep, hyperthyroidism, pregnancy and lactation, the wasting that occurs in fevers, etc., increase the food requirements of the body without always increasing the body's ability to digest, absorb and assimilate foods. Indeed, in some instances, there is a marked decrease in the total ability to utilize the food eaten. Many of the "therapeutic" measures of the disease-treaters of the various schools interefere with the proper nourishment of the body. Sippy diets and mush diets used in stomach ulcers, certain types of reducing diets, minerals, acids and alkalies given as "medicines," laxatives, cathartics, and drugs given to increase the excretion of urine, interfere with the digestion, absorption and utilization of foods. Any influence that enervates the body will lower digestive ability and reduce the body's assimilative powers. A lack of sunshine, lack of exercise, insufficient sleep, emotional disturbances — these and many other factors interfere with the nutritive processes of the body. Tobacco inhibits digestion and thus prevents the proper utilization of the food eaten.

FEEDING IN DISEASE

Coffee and tea cause a premature emptying of the stomach, thus interfering with digestion. Bitters have a like effect.

This failure of digestion, absorption, and utilization of food is not confined to any particular food factor. Indigestion means fermentation of carbohydrates and putrefaction of proteins. It means that fats decompose and minerals and vitamins are also lost. Failure of absorption from whatever cause means that fatty acids, amino acids, sugars, minerals and vitamins are lost. In diabetes there is chiefly loss of sugar, in Bright's disease there is chiefly a loss of nitrogen, but both of these losses cause a loss of other and correlated food factors.

It is folly to attempt to remedy nutritive failures resulting from any or all of these conditions by feeding concentrated vitamins and minerals. The body's ability to absorb and utilize these substances is not increased by having them forced upon it in concentrated form or in increased amounts. Nor are these substances usable in the absence of the proteins, carbohydrates and fats. The only rational plan of caring for cases of these kinds is to correct the causes that have produced and are maintaining the troubles and permit health to return. With the return of health normal digestion, absorption and assimilation will also return.

Treating patients with doses of vitamins, or with mineral concentrates, or with both of these combined, and ignoring all of the many causes of their troubles is identical with the older drug practice. It is simply another of the medicine man's long efforts to "cure" disease without the necessity of removing its cause. There is no more sanity in trying to *cure* the effects of alcoholism by dosing the inebriate with vitamins and minerals than there is in trying to accomplish the same thing by dosing him with drugs of the older varieties.

Too many dietitians are that only and give no attention to other and important factors of life. They often complain that a particular patient does not or cannot utilize certain food elements or food factors and resort to drugs or some form of drugless stimulation, to gland extracts or to vitamin injections, or some other futile means of treatment and totally disregard the natural factors upon which good nutrition depends. They ignore the need for sunshine, exercise, rest and sleep, peace of mind and a host of other factors of living that are important to nutrition. Tobacco inhibits digestion, hence it interferes with the proper utilization of food stuffs, yet a biochemist will talk about the inability of certain "healthy" tobacco users to utilize vitamins.

True vitamins are not drugs and it is foolish to say that they are used as drugs when prescribed for certain deficiencies. It would be as correct to say water is a drug when used to revive a man famishing from thirst. They are food accessories, first, last and all the time. Synthetic vitamins are drugs; they are never anything else.

I hear and read much about how vegetables, eggs, fruit and milk "cure" many diseases. I have patients coming to me from all parts of the country who are eating these foods prescribed by physicians of the old school as well as by "irregulars" and they are still sick. One of their troubles is that they are still feeding "plenty of good nourishing food to keep up strength." In other words, they overfeed their patients.

In practice we cannot dissociate the effects of deficient and ill-balanced foods from the effects of toxins. The deficiencies and toxemias are so inextricably bound up that they cannot be separated. They are, in fact, Siamese twins. In some of earlier experiments with deficient diets, the addition of wood shavings, blotting paper and other forms of foodless roughage to the diets of animals was enough to clear up pathological conditions and restore health. Graham attributed these pathologies to poisoning resulting from gastro-intestinal decomposition. This is present in most, if not all, cases of avitaminosis.

Overemphasizing a praticular food factor, such as protein, vitamins or minerals, is a mistake. Ideal nutrition is possible only when adequate quantities and due proportions of all food factors are present in the diet. Please note that I said these must all be present in the diet: this does not mean that they must all be present in each meal, as is the thought of those who serve "balanced meals." What is needed is a *balanced diet*. There is interdependence between the various elements of the diets. Vitamins and all other food factors work best in cooperation.

BALANCED DIETS

After discussing the need of the healthy for a balanced diet (please observe that this is not the so-called *balanced meals* of yesteryear) Victor Lindlahr asks: "Is it not logical to insist that sick people, too, must receive enough (and proper percentages) of proteins, carbohydrates, fats and each of the known minerals and vitamins necessary to life? Of course the sick must receive balanced nourishment before any additions or modifications necessary for their specific disease can be made."

Instead of this statement being true, it is often essential that the sick abstain from food altogether or go on a very restricted diet for a period,, before they can hope to recover health. The balanced diet is more appropriate for upbuilding after recovery is almost completed.

THE MILK DIET

Most of the claims made for the curative virtues of the milk diet are false. Milk contains no excess of vitamins or minerals that will compensate for the use of devitalized foods and is wrongly classed as a "protective food."

Laboratory rats fed on an exclusive milk diet developed anemia. The protracted use of an exclusive milk diet tends finally to render children susceptible to so-called infections in later life, even to develop tuberculosis. Berg, experimenting on humans, found that when only so much milk is given to these as is required to supply them with the bodily protein requirement, the excess of alkalies in the milk did not suffice either for growing youth or adult human beings. Berg, says "natural milk contains acid-rich proteins, and unless these proteins are fully utilized by the body (as they are in the suckling undergoing normal growth) the total surplus of bases is not placed at the disposal of the organism." Lyman and Raymond, experimenting on rabbits, which are very sensitive to acids, found that on a diet of cow's milk, the animals died of *acidosis*; but when sodium citrate was added to the food, the acidosis disappeared and the urine contained less ammonia. "Milk," says Berg, "is well known to be adequate in respect to inorganic constituents (minerals) only for the earliest period of life; but for adults is rendered adequate by the addition of a little iron. In my own experience, however, as far as adults are concerned, the richness of milk in protein makes the excess of alkali in this food inadequate."

The milk diet requires a lot of juggling to make it serve at all. It produces constipation in about 80% of those who employ it, and diarrhea in perhaps 10%. It causes much gas, abdominal distention and discomfort. It causes nausea in many, bowel inpaction in a few, catarrh in many, increased blood pressure in all and places a heavy tax upon the heart, liver, stomach, intestine, kidneys, lungs and glands of the body. Most patients gain weight rapidly on it, but such weight is not a gain in healthy flesh and is almost never permanent. It completely wrecks many patients.

THE FLESH DIET

During the last few years the Salisbury meat diet has enjoyed a short-lived vogue in certain quarters. It is now about fifty years since Dr. Salisbury first announced the use of an exclusive meat diet in the treatment of a number of maladies; including arthritis and tuberculosis. He assumed that most human ailments are due to the development of yeast in the digestive tract. He excluded carbohydrates from the diet to starve out the yeast cells. There was and is no scientific foundation for his notion and, although, he and his followers claimed a remarkable success, his method was short-lived.

Dr. Salisbury correctly described the consequences of the ordinary starch and sugar diet as making a "yeast pot of the digestive tract." The fermentation is real under the usual haphazard eating and the evil consequences of the fermentation are no less real. The remedy, however, is not the substitution therefor of a greater evil —acid formation and putrefaction of meat.

SYMPTOMATIC FEEDING

Foods are frequently used, both by laymen and by doctors of all schools, as palliatives, that is, for the relief of symptoms. Honey is used to relieve coughing and dryness and irritation of the throat. Warm milk is often employed to relieve insomnia. Patients suffering with gastric ulcer are fed frequently during the day and sometimes at night to relieve stomach distress. Nervous patients are fed frequently to relieve their nervous symptoms. A large class of incorrigibles eat to relieve headache. These people are food drunkards and are uncomfortable when deprived of the accustomed food. Some food drunkards suffer from nausea when their stomachs are empty. These eat to relieve the nausea. Patients who suffer with gastric catarrh are advised to drink fruit juices or lemonade to cleanse their stomachs of mucus. Food addiction is as real as morphine addiction and produces almost as intense suffering. When deprived of food these addicts suffer the same symptoms as the morphine addict experiences when deprived of his dope. Feeding wheat bran or a lot of bulk and roughage in some other form in cases of constipation, instead of removing the causes of constipation, is a form of symptomatic feeding that has no justification. Symptomatic feeding is like giving drugs to ease or "relieve" symptoms.

The ulcer diets commonly employed are deficient in vitamins and minerals. These diets are devised to avoid mechanical irritation of the ulcer or to use up the excess acid in the stomach, not to provide adequate nourishment for the sufferer. Someday it will be realized that these diets help to perpetuate the ulcer and to make the condition of the patient worse. Such feeding will then be looked upon as malpractice.

It is easily possible to feed a diet that will relieve a symptom and, at the same time, make the patient worse. No better example of this can be given than diets commonly fed in diabetics, which have no regenerative effects upon the pancreatic tissue, but do increase the toxemic condition of the patient. Many of the diets fed to diabetic patients help to keep the urine sugar-free. They reduce the amount of blood sugar. But they are so deficient they lay the foundation for metabolic troubles that are almost as serious as the diabetes.

LIMITATIONS

There is a limit to the possibilities of any trophologic regimen. Even a biologically correct dietary and a complete bionomic program, resorted to at the eleventh hour, may be insufficient to stay the progress of degeneration and prevent its culmination in death.

IDIOSYNCRACIES

It is no doubt true that the normal individual is able to eat anything that anyone else may eat. Few, however, are normal and we frequently meet with those who cannot eat certain foods without suffering. Not infrequently a perfectly good food appears to be harmful to some individual and this seems to lend credibility to the old notion that what is one man's boon is another man's bane. Learned treatises have been written about these supposed idiosyncracies; yet, in most if not all such cases the trouble is not due to the food at all.

Some people develop skin eruptions after eating strawberries and some other foods. These people should be placed on a diet of strawberries and fed strawberries exclusively until the trouble ends.

Some people are so sensitive to eggs that the consumption of only a small amount of egg will cause nausea, vomiting, purging, headache, urticaria, and other distressing symptoms.

Some people are constipated by cheese. This indicates enervation; correct the cause of enervation.

Oranges cause gas with some. Pears and apples do the same for others. Cooked cabbage and cauliflower produce gas in some. Many will have catarrh and a coated tongue so long as they use milk, even if it is but one glass a day. Some fruits cause diarrhea in some patients. Eggs and meat often bring on asthmatic attacks in certain individuals. This is, however, only after such individuals are already poisoned with an excess of protein. Many patients are made uncomfortable (have a heavy feeling in the stomach) when they eat spinach.

Much of the trouble that a certain food is supposed to give is the result of wrong combinations. Sometimes the trouble grows out of eating the food in excessive quantities, or it is blamed for the trouble caused by a too large meal. In some cases trouble is due to suggestion — the fixed idea that a certin food will cause distress. In many cases the trouble grows out of digestive derangements and ceases as soon as digestion has been restored to normal.

All these things have to be considered in planning a diet for a patient. When normal digestion is re-established these things disappear, but while digestion is still impaired, those foods that cause trouble are best omitted from the patient's diet. Often, however, a patient thinks that a certain article of diet causes him trouble, when it is only the wrong combination that produces the trouble. A patient will complain that acid fruits cause gas. Upon inquiry you find that these have been taken with a breakfast of cereal and sugar, and egg on toast. You put the patient upon an acid fruit diet and no trouble results. Wrong combinations are often the cause of trouble.

FEEDING IN CONVALESCENCE

Feeding in convalescence is usually a very simple matter. Caution is required in order not to overtax the weakened digestive powers. Moderation should be the rule. Combinations should be the simplest and foods should be simple and wholesome.

A "diet of growth" is demanded, yet, due to the weakened condition of the digestive organs, it is necessary to institute this gradually.

During the prodromal stage of acute disease, say of pneumonia, there occurs an impoverishment of the patient's blood of alkalies; then follows an impoverishment of the tissues of alkalies. This occurs more or less generally, but localizes itself more specifically in the lungs, or in the organ most affected. These alkali-elements are used in neutralizing and detoxifying the toxins causing the trouble. Some have, indeed, advocated the employment of fruit juices in acute disease to supply the body with alkaline elements and some have recorded cases of acute disease in which there was a definite and distinct call for lemons or oranges or other acid fruits. Whether the general use of fruit juices in acute disease is or is not to be recommended, it is obvious that the diet of convalescence should be rich in alkaline elements to restore those that have been used up in the work of cure. It should be equally obvious that the alkali-depleted diet usually fed to patients is not designed to help, but must always injure the patient.

The conventional diet is more or less deficient in alkali-elements due to the fact that it is made up largely of the concentrated proteins, carbohydrates and hydrocarbons, and to the further fact that these have usually been deprived of their alkaline elements in the processes of manufacture and cooking. Practically all the "staple" articles of food used in America today show a relative predominance of acid-forming over base-forming elements.

Such a diet cannot maintain health. Still less can it restore health. It is predominantly acid-forming and does not contain a sufficient amount of base-forming elements to maintain normal excretion. To bring about increased elimination in a sick body an entirely different diet is required.

It is essential that plenty of fresh fruits and green vegetables or their juices be fed to replenish the body's exhausted alkali-reserve and restore the normal alkalinesence of the blood.

Orthodox "science" considers foods to be "nutritious" and "non-nutritious, according as they yield much or little nitrogenous, carbohydrate and hydrocarbon substances. In keeping with this idea foods are classed as (1) proteins, (2) carbohydrates and (3) hydrocarbons. Fruits and green vegetables are practically unclassified. "The wonderful vitalizing acids (organic acids) and salts" which they contain, are relegated to the "ash" column, and practically ignored.

Dr. Trall declared, that "all good fresh fruits and vegetables are antiscorbutic" which is equivalent to saying that they are "base-forming" or anti-"acidity." Fruits and green vegetables yield to the blood more activating acids and bases than all the "nutritious" foods taken together, and yield them with almost no tax upon digestion, absorption and assimilation. "These particular acids and bases readily travel to the blood and are quickly utilized to build up and repair tissues, to promote immunity to and recovery from disease."

Graham declares: "The question is, how to remove all irritations from the system, and restore each part to healthy action and condition. But almost all the articles of medicine, not excepting those called tonics, are either directly or indirectly irritating or debilitating in their effects on the living body, and therefore should be avoided as far as possible. Many of the articles of diet ordinarily used in civilized life are also decidedly irritating and pernicious; and many of the modes of preparing food, are sources of irritation to the system. In fact, when the body is seriously diseased, even the necessary functions of alimentation, under the very best regimen, are, to a considerable extent, the sources of irritation; and where it is possible to sustain life without nutrition, entire and protracted fasting would be the very best means in many cases of removing disease and restoring health. I have seen wonderful effects result from experiments of this kind." — *Science of Human Life*.

All stimulating and irritating foods should be excluded from the diet. All foods that undergo fermentation very readily should be withheld. No denatured foods — white flour, polished rice, white sugar, degerminated, demineralized corn meal, canned, pickled, embalmed foods, jams, jellies, preserves, pastries, so-called breakfast foods, etc. — should be consumed. All foods eaten should be wholesome, natural foods; condiments of evry nature should be tabooed. Bread, even whole grain bread, is especially bad.

Such fruits as dried apples, peaches, pears, apricots, fancy dates, figs and raisins are bleached with sulphurous acid. Crystalized fruit peels, citron, walnuts and almonds are also subjected to this same whitening process. These should never be used, well or sick. The sulphurous acid disturbs metabolism, destroys the blood corpuscles and other cells and overworks the kidneys.

Commercial apple jam and other jams are made up of sulphurated skins and cores. "Chops," as these are called are composed of about 10 per cent fruit, 10 per cent juice. The rest of the jam is composed of about 10 per cent sugar and 70 per cent glucose. The whole is held together and given a jelly-like consistency by phosphoric acid. Amrath, a coal tar dye, gives it a bright strawberry color, while it is prevented from decomposing by benzoate of soda. The government permits one-tenth of one per cent of benzoate of soda to be used and requires that it be stated on the label. It is usually indicated in very fine print. Sulphuric acid is present in almost all commercial syrups and molasses. These syrups have little food value and are harmful in many ways.

It can easily be seen that the use of such foods by either the well or sick cannot result in anything else but harm. We have not yet discovered a way to prepare foods, to add to them and subtract from them, that will make them better than they are as Nature gives them to us. Our preparations only impair their nutritional value. Until such a method is found it is the part of wisdom for us to stick to the natural foods.

Such a diet cannot be made adequate by the addition of synthetic vitamins nor by the addition of vitamins extracted from their natural carriers. Neither will the addition of mineral concentrates nor mineral concentrates and vitamins render adequate a diet made up of such foods.

The Three Year Nursing Period
CHAPTER XL

In each species the nursing period bears a definite relationship to the time required for the animal to reach maturity. Animals that grow slowly and are longer in reaching maturity have a longer nursing period; while those that grow rapidly and reach maturity early have a short nursing period. Compare, for example, the nursing period of a few weeks for the puppy with that of nine months for the calf, and an even longer nursing period for the colt. The slowest growing animal of them all, the human, which takes longest to reach maturity and requires two years to develop sufficient teeth with which to chew solid foods, should have the longest nursing period of them all.

In the "Moral Precepts of Ancient Egypt," as recorded by Ptahhotep, a high official in the reign of Assa, a king of the IV Dynasty, about 3360 B. C., are these words: "When after thy months in the womb thou wast born . . . for three years her breasts were in thy mouth." In the Boulek Papyrus (1500 B. C.) the Egyptian sage, Kneusu-Hetep, in counseling his son, says: "Three long years she carried thee upon her shoulder and gave thee her breast to thy mouth, and as thy size increased her heart never once allowed her to say, 'why should I do this.'"

William J. Robinson, M. D., in *Woman: Her Sex and Love Life,* tells us that in Egypt and other Oriental countries "it is no rare sight to see a child of three or four years old interrupting his work or his play and running up to suckle his mother's breast."

Thus we see that during more than five thousand years of recorded Egyptian history, Egyptian mothers have continued to nurse their children for from three to four years or more.

So far as I can learn from my researches, the long nursing period, three to five years, is universal among those people who have not learned to substitute the mother with a cow or a goat. A few examples will suffice.

A patient of mine, a native of Macedonia, informs me that in his country mothers nurse their babies two or three years and even longer. A cousin of his was nursed for six full years. I may add

THE THREE YEAR NURSING PERIOD

that since I started my investigations I have met three American women who nursed their children for more than two years. A Hebrew patient, who was born and reared in Turkey, tells me that Turkish women nurse their children two years and longer. Dr. Kellogg points out that "pictures of young children standing at the breast of savage mothers are common." In France, Italy, Japan, and among the Slavs, the prolonged nursing period is the rule.

Westermark tells us *(History of Human Marriage):* "Very commonly, in a state of savage and barbarous life, the husband must not cohabit with his wife till the child is weaned. And this prohibition is all the more severe, as the suckling-time generally lasts for two, three, four years, or even more."

He mentions a number of such people and attributes the long suckling time, not to the natural needs of the child, which nature has provided for, in the same manner that she has provided for a supply of milk from the maternal breast, for as long as needed in the case of the lower animals, but "chiefly to the want of soft food and animal milk."

Westermark points out, however, that this is not always the case saying: "But when the milk can be obtained, and even when the people have domesticated animals able to supply them with it, this kind of food is often avoided." He gives, as an example, the Chinese who "entirely eschew the use of milk."

The Macedonian, previously referred to, assures me that, although his native people have and use goat's and sheep's milk, they never think of feeding it to an infant, providing the mother could nurse it, or of voluntarily cutting short the nursing period because these milks could be substituted for the mother's milk.

Dr. Robinson attributes the long nursing period among Orientals to the desire to prevent conception. This assumption has neither biological nor historical basis.

Before the coming of the white man to America there were no milk animals. (The deer and buffalo were here, but were not domesticated.) Indian mothers were forced to nurse their children because they had no milk from other sources to aid in weaning. They nursed them for two to three years. Among the Sioux Indians mothers were sometimes known to suckle two children at the same time. This same thing has been observed among the Guiana Indians of South America who as a rule nurse their children three to four years.

Catlin says: "It is a very rare occurrence for an Indian woman to be blessed with more than four or five children during her life; and, generally speaking, they seem to be contented with two or three." Westermark tells us that "this statemnt is confirmed by the evidence of several other authorities; and it holds good not only for the North American Indians, but, upon the whole, for a great many uncivilized peoples."

Catlin also says, in combatting the charge, made by some half-informed people, that there was an enormous infant mortality among the Indians, "Among the North American Indians, at all events, where two or three children are generally the utmost results of a marriage, such a rate of mortality could not exist without soon depopulating the country."

Replying to the charge made by some that the "slight degree of prolificness" observed among the North American Indians, and some other savage tribes, was due to "hard labor, or to unfavorable conditions of life in general," Westermark says: "That it is partly due to the long period of suckling is highly probable, not only because a woman less easily becomes pregnant during the time of lactation, but also on account of the continence in which she often has to live during that period."

Mr. John McIntosh tells us in his *The Origin of the North American Indians* (1844), page 118, that, "when a woman is with a child, she works at her ordinary occupations, convinced that work is advantageous for both herself and her child; her labour is easy, and she may be seen on the day after her delivery with her child at her back, avoiding none of her former employments. They suckle their child until they are at least two years of age."

I hold that the natural nursing period of the human infant ranges from three to five years, depending on whether it is born in the tropics or in the far north; its own mother's milk should constitute all or a large part of its diet until the child has reached a definite stage in its physical development. I believe, also, that the period during which child or animal should take milk bears a definite relation to the length of time required to complete its physical development.

Apes nurse their young from five to seven months. Their first teeth are complete by the third month. Young camels nurse for a year, although they begin to eat with their mothers a few weeks after they are born. A similar fact is seen with cow and horse.

THE THREE YEAR NURSING PERIOD

"Primitive" people and animals nurse their young for some time after the complete eruption of the first set of teeth. Dr. Felix Oswald (*Physical Education*, page 29) declares that "the appearance of the eye-teeth (cuspids) and lesser molars mark the end of the second year as the period when healthy children may be gradually accustomed to semi-fluid vegetable substance. Till then, milk should form their only sustenance. But mothers whose employment does not interfere with their inclination in this respect may safely nurse their children for a much longer period."

In support of this he says: "The wives of the sturdy Argyll peasants rarely wean a bairn before its claim is disputed by the next youngster and the stoutest urchin of five years I ever saw was the son of a Servian widow, who still took him to her breast like a baby."

Dr. Page said: "In the absence of particular circumstances compelling premature weaning, I believe that the mother's milk providing the mother be in fair health and the babe evidently thriving on her milk, is the best food for the infant during the first eighteen months, and even until the end of the second year."

Dr. Kellogg says: "among primitive people nursing continues until the first teeth are complete, or for three years, although considerable other food is eaten."

Prof. Sherman, of Columbia University, says: "In China, nursing is continued for two full years and not rarely for three full years. The child thus has ample time to become adjusted to the consumption of a variety of vegetable foods before its maternal milk supply is entirely cut off."

The practice of nursing babies two years or more was, until quite recently, very common in Canada, as it was in this country forty years ago. Indeed, the long nursing period has everywhere prevailed until the practice of giving animal milk was substituted for that of the mother.

I have no patience with the theory that mother's milk becomes unfit for the child after the first year, and that a longer nursing period is injurious to the mother and child. The healthy well-fed woman can nurse her child for the period nature intended without harm to herself or child; and during this period, her own milk, if normal, is better for her child than that of any cow, goat, mare, camel, sheep, ass, or other milk animal used by man. I hold that it is the duty of every healthy mother to nurse her child during the whole of this period and that for her to lay down on the job is to rob her child of its birth right.

I do not mean that the child should exist exclusively upon milk during this whole period. It, like the sucklings of other animals, should gradually include more of other foods in its diet as the maternal supply diminishes.

It is the duty of every woman to nurse her child as long as she can. Even after the child is eating other foods it should still be receiving its milk supply from its mother's breasts. If her milk is insufficient for the needs of the child and she is forced to supplement this with the milk of animals, it is still her duty to nurse her child so long as her milk supply holds out. Mothers who refuse to do this commit a grave crime against their children.

Milo Hastings declared in an article in *Physical Culture* ("The Extravagance of Meat"), a few years ago, that, "The natural period for nursing the human infant is three to four years. And as the mother rarely conceives during the nursing period she would under such circumstances only bear five or six children in her lifetime. Civilization shortened the nursing period with the aid of the cow and has now in many instances eliminated it altogether. Two results followed this change. First, our utter dependence upon the cow; second, the absolute need of birth control to prevent too frequent child bearing. Someday under a perfectly rational civilization the longer period of nursing the human infant may return, but there is little chance for it in our time and hence the cow is a necessity for the nutrition of our children."

Lactation is not a fully reliable means of preventing conception, but it is as reliable as the harmful artificial means now in almost universal use and has the advantage of being harmless, if not actually beneficial. I am not sure that sexual intercourse during lactation is desirable, however,

Cow's Milk

CHAPTER XLI

The food essential to healthy development and growth of every infant mammal, including human infants, is produced for it in its own mother's breasts. The milk of each species differs widely from that of every other, as we shall show later, and each is especially fitted to meet the needs of the young of that species. The infant continues, for some time after birth to feed upon the substance of its mother.

We are prone to take it for granted that man began to feed cow's milk or the milk of other animals to babies shortly after Adam and Eve were kicked out of the Garden of Delight and that he has continued to do so ever since. We may even imagine that the practice is universal. We could hardly make a worse mistake.

We know, for example, that few Chinese and Hindu mothers have cow's milk or the milk of other animals for their babies. We know that the North and South American Indians had no milk animals and their children received no milk after they were weaned from their mother's breasts. In many other parts of the world the same fact holds good.

It may come as a distinct surprise to most of my readers, that the early American colonists made very little use of milk. The Pilgrims landed in Plymouth in 1620. It was not until 1624 that the first cattle were brought over by Gov. Winslow. These increased rapidly and were added to by fresh shipments from England, so that by "1632 no farmer was satisfied to do without a cow; and there was in New England, not only a domestic, but an export demand for the West Indies, which led to breeding for sale. But the market was soon overstocked, and the price of cattle went down from fifteen and twenty pounds to five pounds; and milk was a penny a quart."

This last statement about milk means very little for Albert S. Bolles, from whose *Industrial History of the United States* (p. 115) the foregoing statement is taken, tells us, on the next page, that cows were seldom milked at this period, being raised principally for their hides, and secondly for meat, only very incidentally for milk.

THE SCIENCE AND FINE ART OF FOOD AND NUTRITION

So far as the record of history can show us, a man by the name of Underwood is the first to have risked the experiment of feeding cow's milk to infants. This was in the year 1793—only 154 years ago. This was before the invention of the rubber nipple and we may well imagine what a fine time he had feeding this calf-food to a human infant.

Prior to that memorable date—1793—if a mother died and left her child to be nursed, this was done by another woman—a wet nurse and not by the cow. Since then, the cow has not only become a foster mother of the American and most of the European portions of the human race, but we have develped the absurd notion that "a baby is never to be weaned." It must have milk, not merely through the period of infancy, as nature designed, but also throughout childhood, adolescence and adult life as well.

Milk is loudly proclaimed the one and only "perfect food" and from every direction we are urged to drink milk. It is the "perfect food" for the infant, the child, the athlete, the office worker, the invalid and for everyone. There is a strong commercial influence back of all this hue and cry about the magic virtues of milk. We need not take too seriously the mouthings of those who are actuated by the profit motive.

Milk (cow's milk) is not the perfect food for either infant or adult. But we have so endowed it with super-potentiality that we even insist on nursing mothers also nursing. A quart a day, and even more, is sometimes prescribed for the nursing mother. This slavish adherence to milk has been brought about as the result of a frame-up between the doctors and the dairymen, of which, the following item taken from the *Ice Cream Field*, (National Journal), of July, 1927, and entitled "Dairy Council Plans Education Work," is only partial evidence:

"Latest developments in the health education and increasing the use of dairy products in the nation's diet were discussed at the sixth annual summer conference of national and regional dairy council at Buffalo, N. Y., June 11 to 13. Speakers at the conference included M. D. Munn, President; Dr. Charles H. Keene, professor of hygiene, University of Buffalo; Miss Mary E. Spencer, health education specialist, Washington, D. C., Dr. W. W. Peter, associate secretary, American Public Health Association; Dr. H. E. Van Norman, president Dry Milk Institute; Clifford Goldsmith, writer and lecturer; Miss

Sally Lucas Joan, health consultant, and officers and trained specialists of the council organization.

"Many new posters, leaflets, exhibits, moving pictures, health stories, plays and other educational means of presenting the Dairy Council story of the importance of the 'protective foods' in the diet were presented and discussed during the conference. An analysis of the type of work being done by the council organization and how it helps the dairy industry was presented by W. P. B. Lockwood, New England Dairy and Food Council, Boston, Mass. Business sessions of the officers and women workers, as well as a special session on publicity methods, completed the conference program.

" 'The Dairy Council is reaching the point now,' stated Dr. C. W. Larson, director, 'where its corps of trained workers must devote most of their time to the presentation of interesting and instructive projects and material which can be supplied to schools and colleges, health and welfare organizations and similar groups to be presented by them in their own localities throughout the United States. Formerly, most of our time was spent in school work. Now, that is only one phase of the enlarged activities of the Dairy Council.' "

This is a cold-blooded business affair which raises the cry of health as a means of increasing the profits of the dairying industries and the doctors that are associated with these industries, and which unblushingly labels their propaganda, *education.*

Milk, is not an "adult food" but is a temporary expediency in the life of the young animal, lasting it until the time that it evolves teeth for independent mastication and is able to secrete digestive juices of a quality and character to enable it to digest the foods it will naturally live on for the remainder of its life .

Cow's milk is not only not a perfect food for the human adult; it is not the best food for the human infant. It is not even the best milk from the lower animals for infants. Instead of talking about the importance of "protective foods" in the diet, they should devote their "educational (sic) campaign" to telling people of the dangers of the denatured foods. That their campaign is merely an effort to sell more milk and not an effort to tell the people the truth about their present denatured diet gives the whole show away.

It is wholly unnatural for cows to give the large quantities of milk, rich, in fat, as our dairy cows do. By selective breeding and forced feeding, they are induced to give large quantities of milk and to produce this far beyond the normal nursing period for calves.

Indeed, many of these cows are never "dry," but continue to produce milk, that is sold in the market, from one calf to the next, year after year. I have seen cows milk for ten or more years, without once being dry, and having a calf a year during this time.

This constitutes a drain on the cows which makes it impossible for one of them to be healthy. They are especially prone to tuberculosis and have their lives greatly shortened. While almost all dairy cattle are tubercular, this disease is extremely rare among the range cattle of the plains.

Added to the evils of excessive milk production, is the evil of overfeeding on a one-sided and high protein diet. This tends to produce disease in the cow and to greatly impair her milk also. An excess of protein in the mother's diet impairs her milk for her baby, then certainly an excess of protein in the diet of the cow, whose milk already contains far more protein than that of a woman, is bad for the child. An excess of fat is also bad for the infant. Our dairy herds have been so bred and they are so fed that their milk contains a great excess of fat.

Dairymen and farmers produce milk to sell and the more milk and butter-fat a cow produces the more profits there is in it for them. Farmers and dairymen are not different to owners of coal mines or cotton mills—they are interested only in increasing their profits. They will produce only that kind of milk and those quantities of milk that brings in the most money for them, regardless of its evil effect upon the users of the milk.

Cows from which certified milk is produced are kept throughout the year in sunless barns, are permitted a very limited amount of exercise and are fed chiefly on dry food, being given little or no fresh green fodder. This sickens the cow and assures the deterioration of her milk. Cows need green grass, exercise, fresh air and sunshine. Dr. Hess, of Columbia University, showed that milk from cows fed on pastures in the sunlight maintains the health and growth of animals, whereas milk from cows maintained out of the sun and fed on dry fodder will not.

The best of cow's milk can be obtained only from healthy, range-fed cows, which get plenty of green foods, an abundance of sunshine and fresh air, and are not tuberculin tested (poisoned) and are not stuffed on protein-rich foods to over-stimulate milk production.

Dairy cows and particularly "certified" herds, are now all tuberculin tested—that is, poisoned and sickened. The tuberculin test is a fraud. It is not a reliable test for tuberculosis, as every doctor well knows. Give it to animals in large doses and they "promptly die with symptoms of an intense intoxication," in "moderate doses," "the animals display the symptoms of a profound intoxication, but gradually recover, with a mild and chronic form of disease."

Tuberculin is the putrescent resultant of decomposing beef broth containing glycerine and is preserved with carbolic acid. It is not merely a poison, it a whole array of poisons.

The very best of cow's milk is poor enough as infant food, without making it still worse by pasteurization. Pasteurizing milk leads to carelessness and assures us dirty milk. This will be more fully discussed in the next chapter.

Milk also undergoes deterioration after it is milked and permitted to stand. Its food value is markedly impaired by being frozen.

Present methods of producing and handling milk make it next to impossible to procure good milk in the markets. These present methods are largely the results of the work of physicians who urge us to use more milk. Do not censure me too strongly, then, when I declare that the medical profession is determined that there shall not be a healthy child in America and that no child shall be permitted to have good food.

The word "protein" is a very indefinite term and it is known that the same amount of protein and calories from different sources may have very different food values. Cow's milk possesses a different and inferior protein to that found in mother's milk and, while well suited to the needs of the calf, is poorly fitted to the nourishment of the infant.

Both the mineral content and the vitamin content of cow's milk, the milk most commonly used in this country, vary greatly, perhaps more than those of any other food product. They vary with food and season. Milk may be almost entirely lacking in vitamins. This is especially so in winter when green foods are lacking. Certified milk, produced by cows kept in sunless barns and fed on dry foods, is very deficient in vitamins. Malnutrition is common among certified herds. Milk also undergoes considerable deterioration by being exposed to the air and from being chilled.

Biological tests have shown that cow's milk is poor, as compared to other foods, in growth-complettin (vitamin) B. The same is true of human milk. Of course, the milk of a normal, well-nourished mother or cow possesses enough of this vitamin to supply the needs of infant or calf, but when cow's milk is diluted, in preparing it for the infant, this food quality is dangerously reduced.

Cow's milk forms a large, hard, tough curd that is difficult for the infant to digest. Human milk forms small, soft flocculent masses which are easy of digestion.

These different physical and chemical characteristics of the milk of the two mothers are designed to meet the different requirements of the young of the two species and the two milks are not, therefore, interchangeable. It follows, logically, that the cow is not the best mother of the human infant and when she adopted our children, she did them an injury.

Many investigators, among them Freise, Mattill and Conklin have reached the conclusion that after a certain age has been attained, milk is unsuitable as the sole source of protein. Some of these investigators think that this is due to the fact that the milk protein is not sufficiently concentrated. Berg says that their experiments do not reveal any inadequacy in the composition of the milk protein, but that the results they obtained are due to the modified requirements of the adult organism in the matter of the mineral requirements. Without determining which of these conclusions is the correct one, it is obvious from the results of their experiments that milk is not a good food for the non-suckling organism. After the normal nursing period has been passed, milk may be profitably dropped from the child's diet.

There is everywhere a tendency to exaggerate the value and importance of milk. All the virtues ascribed to milk, as a food for the infant and growing child, belong properly to the milk of the healthy well-nourished mother and to no other milk. Diseased and inadequately nourished mothers do not produce adequate milks. Breast-fed infants often develop rickets during the latter part of winter, due to insufficient "vitamin C" in the mother's diet. Milk from cows fed on a "vitamin D" deficient diet will neither prevent nor cure nor allay the course of clinical rickets in infants. Both breast-fed and bottle-fed infants on an exclusive milk diet may develop rickets.

It is apparent that milk possesses no exceptional factors of safety against certain deficiency diseases. Infants have developed deficiency disease while being nursed by mothers who were apparently well-nourished. On the other hand, the current manner of feeding dairy cattle and the present methods of treating milk affect the vitamin C of milk. Straining, cooking, pasteurizing and re-pasteurizing milk damage it in many ways. So, also, does the freezing of milk. Oxygenation occurs in milk as it stands—nature provided for milk to flow directly from the producer to the consumer, without all the delay, preserving and tampering. Some types of containers are said to render catalytic action a possibility.

Milk is poor in iodine and in iron. Anemia has resulted in animals restricted to a diet of cow's milk. Infants are born with a rich store of reserve iron, providing the mother's diet and tissues have been able to provide this. Otherwise the infant may not possess a rich surplus of iron and the exclusive milk diet may result in anemia. For these reasons, among others, I have for years advocated supplementing both mother's milk and cow's milk with fruit juices—not a few drops or a few teaspoonfuls a day; but large quantities of juice to supply minerals, carbohydrates and "vitamins." Fresh grape juice for iron and sugar, orange juice for "vitamin C," prune juice for calcium and sugar, etc. All of these juices contain minerals.

Due to the failure of milk in the winter, I advocate having all babies born in the early spring, so that their period of most rapid growth shall have been passed before the milk failure sets in. Here in the Southwest, where we are blessed with an abundance of fresh fruits and green vegetables throughout the whole year, this control of birth is not nearly so important as in the North, where most babies develop rickets. Here in San Antonio and vicinity we have plenty of winter sunshine to supply "vitamin D."

Pasteurization

CHAPTER XLII

In the process of pasteurizing, milk is heated to 145 degrees F., and maintained at this temperature for a half hour, or longer. This produces some very important changes in the milk itself, none of which are beneficial. The process is intended to destroy bacteria which are supposed to cause disease. It does destroy some of the germs in milk, including the lactic acid bacilli, which are the natural protectors of the milk. The destruction of these lactic acid bacteria permits the milk to rot—it will not sour.

Welch's Bacillus and various putrefactive germs are present in pasteurized milk and, due to the absence of the protective lactic-acid germs, these set up putrefaction in the milk, which then becomes poisonous. Diarrhea is perhaps only the least of troubles resulting from such poisoning.

FUTILITY OF PASTEURIZATION

Many bacteria or their spores are not killed, even by boiling. I put no stock in the germ theory, but it was this theory that started this pasteurizing monkey-work, and I want to show its folly, even from this angle.

Pasteurization does not render milk sterile—that is bacteria-free. Not even boiling for a few minutes will do this. We are assured that 99% of the bacteria in milk are destroyed by pasteurization. This is true only under ideal conditions and these often do not prevail in commercial practice. This assurance, however, is very misleading in that it omits to mention the fact that most of the bacteria destroyed are the harmless lactic acid bacteria, while those that remain are largely the very bacteria that are said to be harmful. The statement also hides the fact that those bacteria that survive even ideal pasteurization multiply rapidly thereafter, so that within several hours after pasteurization the number of bacteria in the milk may be considerably larger than before.

In proof of this I shall appeal only to the most orthodox authorities. In their official publication: *A Study of Bacteria Which Survive Pasteurization;* Ayers and Johnson of the U. S. Department of Agriculture, say:

PASTEURIZATION

"Four distinct groups of bacteria, the acid forming, the inert, the alkali forming and the peptonizing, survive pasteurization . . . .

". . . . Streptococci from milk and cream were much more resistant than those from other sources."

The works of three noted medical authorities, Rogers and Frazier and Prucha have revealed that certain types of what the medical profession regards as dangerous streptococci and other groups of bacteria actually flourish at the temperatures of pasteurization.

Dr. Chas. Sanford Porter, who is considered an authority on milk, declares that pasteurization destroys the lactic-acid forming bacteria and that "these bacteria are not dangerous to health, and the methods of restraining or destroying them are without effect on the bacteria of consumption, typhoid, or other fevers that might contaminate milk in certain places."

Dr. Kellogg declares that: "Present methods of controlling the milk supply are by no means entirely satisfactory. This is especially true as regards the bacteriological examination of the milk. At the present time this examination usually extends no further than the determination of the total number of bacteria present except when a special research is undertaken, the number of bacteria present is no criteria whatever of the character of the milk as regards its safety to life and health. In general the greater number of bacteria present are ordinary sour germs which are entirely harmless.'

Dr. Kellogg's words mean that it is not customary to make a differential count. Most of the germs present are lactic acid bacilli and not so-called typhoid germs nor so-called tubercular germs, etc. Pasteurization kills the wrong germs.

PASTEURIZATION HASTENS GERM GROWTH

The lactic acid bacteria are often referred to as protective bacteria. Many medical men of outstanding ability think that by destroying the lactic acid bacilli, which destroy the other forms of bacteria, pasteurization may actually increase the "dangers of milk."

Discussing "Antiseptic in Milk" in *The Drug Trade and Cosmetic Industry* (July 1938) Wizaman and Kneiner point out that raw human and cow's milk do not support the growth of many bacteria, such as the diphtheria bacillus, streptococci and others, or permit but slight growth of these bacteria. The factor in human milk inhibiting bacterial growth has been given the name, *inhibins*. These men showed that this factor is inactivated by heating to temperatures lower than those employed in pasteurization. A higher temperature was found necessary to destroy the *inhibin* in cow's milk in seven minutes.

DESTRUCTIVE EFFECTS OF PASTEURIZATION

Only victims of the bacteriophobia created by medical men and bacteriologists are much interested in what happens to the bacteria of milk when this is pasteurized. What happens to the milk itself and what effect this has upon the user is of vastly more importance. These are the serious effects of pasteurization. If pasteurization only killed a few harmless germs, nobody could offer any serious objection to the process.

I shall rely upon the most orthodox authorities to show that the chemistry and physical structure of the milk are greatly altered, its vitamins destroyed, its calcium and phosphorus rendered useless, its digestibility impaired, its proteins rendered less valuable and its value as a food greatly reduced. The sugars of the milk are broken down and carmelized and to some extent the colloids are agglutinated. The original structure of the milk is broken down and the cream line is slightly reduced.

MILK PROTEIN SPOILED

Parsons and McCollum demonstrated that the protein of milk is partially coagulated by "sterilization" and that the coagulated portion is precipitated with the salts and clings to the walls of the container. They found also, that when milk is boiled, its antineuritic principle is destroyed more rapidly than its growth-factor. In feeding cow's milk to rats, it was found that 50 per cent more of dried milk is required than of raw milk to maintain normal growth.

The partial coagulation of the protein of milk and its precipitation, the precipitation of the salts of the milk, the practical destruction of the milk albumen as food and the disturbance of the mineral balance of the milk renders it very unsatisfactory as a food. Many evils flow from this impairment of the food value of the milk.

CALCIUM SALTS DESTROYED

There is a great and physiologically important reduction of the bone-nourishing salts of the milk. Its calcium-magnesium-carbono-phosphate is broken up into its constituent salts an at least three of these — calcium phosphate, magnesium phosphate and calcium carbonate — are practically insoluble and their usefulness almost destroyed Pasteurization renders the mineral salts of milk insoluble and non-absorbable.

PASTEURIZATION

In the *Journal of Biological Chemistry*, 1928, Martha M. Kramer, E. Latzke and M. M. Shaw in "A Comparison of Raw, Pasteurized, Evaporated and Dried Milks as Sources of Calcium and Phosphorus for the Human Subject," noted not only a striking calcium inadequacy for infants in pasteurized milk, but also a less favorable calcium balance for adults as compared with fresh raw milk. They further observed that milk from cows kept in the barn for five months gave a less favorable calcium balance than did fresh milk from a college dairy herd. This is but another evidence that certified milk from cows kept in sunless barns and fed on dry foods is an inadequate food.

In the *Lancet* (London) for May 8, 1937, it is shown that chilblains are practically eliminated when raw milk rather than pasteurized milk is used in the diet of children. This is attributed to the higher calcium value of raw milk or to the improved calcium assimilation when raw milk is used.

Milk drinking is advocated as a means of assuring good teeth. The drinking of large quantities of milk by infants, children and adults is not preserving the teeth of the people of this country. The evidence for this is all around us. One reason for this is that most of the milk consumed is pasteurized milk. The *Lancet* (London) for May 8, 1937 says that in children the teeth are less likely to decay on a diet supplemented with raw milk than with pasteurized milk. In his *Vitamin Theory and Practice* (Cambridge, University Press, 1935) L. J. Harris says: "Dr. Evelyn Sprawson of the London Hospital has recently stated that in certain institutions children who were brought up on raw milk (as opposed to pasteurized milk) had perfect teeth and no decay. Whether this was due actually to the milk being unheated, or possibly to some other quite different and so far unrecognized cause, we cannot yet say; but we may be sure of one thing, that the result is so striking and unusual that it will undoubtedly be made subject of further inquiry."

PASTEURIZATION DESTROYS VITAMIN A

In the article previously quoted from in this chapter, Krauss, Erb and Washburn say: "According to S. Schmidt-Neilson and Schmidt Neilsen (Kgl. Norske Videnskab, Sels k, Forhandl, 1: 126-128, abstract in Biological Abstracts, 4:96, 1930), when milk is pasteurized at 63 degrees C. (145 degrees F.) was fed to mature rats, early death or diminished vitality resulted in the offspring.

"Pasteurization of milk destroys about 38% of the B complex according to Dutchera and his associates". Again, "Mattick and Golding (Relative Value of Raw and Heated Milk in Nutrition, *Lancet*) reported some preliminary experiments which indicated that pasteurization destroys some of the dietetic value of milk, including partial destruction of vitamin B^1. These same workers found the raw milk to be considerably superior to sterilized milk in nutritive value."

They add "On the 7.5 cc. level two rats on raw milk developed milk polyneuritis toward the end of the trial, whereas three rats on pasteurized milk developed polyneuritis early, which became severe as the trial drew to a close. On the 10.0 cc. level none of the rats on raw milk developed polyneuritis, but three on pasteurized milk were severely afflicted." Again they say "Using standard methods for determining vitamins A, B, G and D, it was found that pasteurization destroys at least 25% of the vitamin in the original raw milk."

PASTEURIZATION DESTROYS VITAMIN C

E. O. Jorda, in the twelfth revised edition of his *Textbook of General Bacteriology* (page 691) says: "Current objection to pasteurization is mainly on the ground of vitamin destruction. Vitamin A (fat soluble) and B (water-soluble), both abundant in milk, are quite resistant to heat, but the antiscorbutic vitamin C is weakened or destroyed by pasteurizing temperatures. Infants fed exclusively on a diet of pasteurized milk will develop scurvy."

PASTEURIZATION DECREASES RESISTANCE

Hess points out, in a statement to be quoted in a later section of this chapter, that children fed on pasteurized milk have less resistance to "infections" than those fed on "raw" milk.

The *Lancet* (London) of May 8, 1937, states that resistance to tuberculosis increased in children fed raw milk instead of pasteurized, to the point that in five years only one case of pulmonary tuberculosis had developed, whereas in the previous five years, when the children had been given pasteurized milk, fourteen cases of pulmonary tuberculosis had developed. It thus becomes apparent that pasteurization does not protect against tuberculosis.

F. M. Pottenger, Jr., says in *Clinical and Experimental Evidence of Growth Factors in Raw Milk, Certified Milk*, Jan. 1937: "It should be determined experimentally, if possible, whether health and resistance are undermined by pasteurization. If so, in our attempt to protect the child from milk-borne infections, we may be denying his heritage of good health by removing from his milk vitamins, hormones, and enzymes that control mineral assimilation and promote body development and general resistance to disease. It is also possible that these same elements are as important to the adult invalid who needs milk as to the infant . . . We cannot afford to pasteurize milk if it is found that pasteurization diminishes the potency of the growth-promoting factors that determine the skeletal development of our children . . . and resistance to respiratory infection, asthma, bronchitis and the common cold when factors preventing them are present in greater amounts in properly produced, clean, raw milk than in pasteurized milk."

These are considerations that should have received attention before the campaign to pasteurize all milk sold in commerce was started. Pasteurization was born of fear and frenzy and pushed by the large dairy interests for profit. Few stopped to ask the important question: What effect will it have upon the health and development of those who drink this milk? Pottenger says that many experiments, such as those made by Cattel, Dutcher, Wilson, and others have shown that animals fed on pasteurized milk show deficiencies. He himself, presents three babies, one of which was breast-fed, a second of which was fed on raw cow's milk, and a third that was fed powdered milk, pasteurized milk, boiled certified milk, and canned milk. The first two babies were healthy and developed normally. The third "was always sickly" is small and at the age of eight months developed asthma. This is not enough evidence upon which to condemn pasteurized milk, but it is additional evidence of the evils of tampering with milk.

PASTEURIZATION AND GROWTH

Pottenger thinks that "the strictest bacteriologic standards for milk should be maintained" and that there should be "closer cooperation between raw-milk producers and public-health officials so that the growth-promoting factors of raw milk can be studied." He says: "We cannot afford to pasteurize milk if it is found that pasteurization diminishes the potency of the growth-promoting factors that determine the skeletal development of our children" and destroys the factors that protect children against "respiratory infection, asthma, bronchitis and the common cold." He says that the factors "preventing them (aforementioned respiratory 'infections') are present in greater amounts in properly produced, clean, raw milk than in pasteurized milk."

THE SCIENCE AND FINE ART OF FOOD AND NUTRITION

W. E. Krauss, J. H. Erb and R. C. Washburn in their *Studies on the Nutritional Value of Milk and the Effects of Pasteurization on Some of the Nutritional Properties of Milk*, Ohio Agricultural Experiment Station Bulletin 518, page 7, Jan. 1933 say that " . . . Fisher and Bartlett point out by a statistical treatment that the response in height to raw milk was significantly greater than that to pasteurized milk. Their interpretation of the data led to the assertion that the pasteurized milk was only 66.0 per cent as effective as raw milk in the case of boys and 91.1 per cent as effective in the case of girls in inducing increases in weight, and 50.0 per cent as effective in boys and 70.0 per cent in girls in bringing about height increases."

Daniels and Laughlin found the same thing to be true in young rats fed on evaporated milk, pasteurized milk and long heat-treated milk, as they report in the *Journal of Biological Chemistry*, 1920. The rats failed to grow normally. Holmes and Pigot include these experiments in their studies of "Factors that Influence the Antirachitic Value of Milk in Infant Feeding" published in *Oil and Soap*, Sept. 1935 and show that the heating of milk precipitates the calcium salts of the milk, rendering the calcium unavailable.

PASTEURIZATION AND ANEMIA

Krauss, Erb and Washburn, in their studies of the "Nutritive Value of Milk and the Effects of Pasteurization on Some of the Nutritive Properties of Milk," (Ohio Agricultural Experiment Station Bulletin, Jan. 1933) tell us that "pasteurization was also found to affect the hematogenic (blood producing) and growth-promoting properties of the special milk." This "special milk" was raw milk from specially fed cows which did not produce nutritional anemia.

PASTEURIZATION AND RICKETS

In 1926 McCollum stated in a lecture in Pittsburgh, that since the city of Baltimore had passed an ordinance requiring the pasteurizing of all milk sold in that city, the cases of rickets among children had increased 100%. This increase in rickets flows naturally and logically from the destruction of the vitamins of the milk and the precipitation of its lime salts. The addition of cod liver oil and synthetic vitamins to the diet of the infant fed on pasteurized milk can not compensate for all the losses from pasteurization.

PASTEURIZATION AND SCURVY

In the *American Journal of Diseases of Children*, Nov. 1917, A. F. Hess of Columbia University, in "A Study of Pathogenesis of Infantile Scurvy," says: "Some have questioned whether pasteurized milk is really involved in the production of scurvy. The fact, however, that when one gives a group of infants this food for a period of about six months, instances of scurvy occur, and that a cure is brought about when raw milk is substituted, taken in conjunction with the fact that if we feed the same number of infants on raw milk, cases of scurvy will not develop — these results seem sufficient to warrant the deduction that pasteurized milk is a causative factor. The experience in Berlin, noted by Neumann (Neumann, H. Deutsch,, Klin., 7: 341, 1904) and others, is most illuminating and convincing in this connection. In 1901 a large dairy in that city established a pasteurizing plant in which all milk was raised to a temperature of about 60 degrees C. After an interval of some months infantile scurvy was reported from various sources throughout the city. Neumann writes about the situation as follows:

"'Whereas Heubner, Sassel and myself had seen only thirty-two cases of scurvy from 1896 to 1900, the number of cases suddenly rose from the year 1901 — so that the same observers, not to mention a great many others, treated eighty-three cases in 1901 and 1902.'

"An investigation was made as to cause, and the pasteurization was discontinued. The result was that the number of cases decreased just as suddenly as they had increased."

The reader will note that the fact that pasteurized milk causes scurvy in infants has been known for forty six years or more. It was no new discovery that Hess proved by his tests, involving damaging experiments of helpless infants. In spite of this knowledge, in 1912 a Medical Commission declared that in feeding infants, heated milk is the full equivalent of raw milk. A Hebrew orphan asylum in New York, sometime thereafter, began the feeding of infants upon cow's milk which had previously been heated to 145 degrees Fahrenheit for thirty minutes. After a few months on this diet there occurred (1914) an "outbreak" of scurvy in these infants. Dr. Hess recommended the addition of orange juice to the diet. The scurvy cleared up rapidly following the addition of the orange juice.

Hess points out that the infants developed scurvy on a diet of pasteurized milk and adds: "This form of scurvy takes many months to develop and may be termed subacute. It must be considered not only the most common form of this disorder, but the one which passes most often unrecognized." He says also, that "one of the most striking clinical phenomenon of infantile scurvy is the marked susceptibility of infection which it entails — the infrequent attacks of 'grippe,' the widespread occurrence of nasal diphtheria, the furunculosis of the skin, the danger of pneumonia in advanced cases," constitute evidences of this susceptibility. A study of the widespread epidemics of the Middle Ages reveals that they followed in the wake of widespread scurvy, a condition that was very prevalent in those days .

Hess thinks that although pasteurized milk "is to be recommended on account of the security which it affords against infection, we should realize that it is an incomplete food." Is it not strange that a man can show that the feeding of a diet of pasteurized milk produces scurvy and greatly increases liability to infection and then, at the same time, state that pasteurized milk affords security against infection? He recommends the feeding of "an antiscorbutic, such as orange juice . . . or potato water" to the pasteurized milk diet and says, "In order to guard against it (scurvy), infants fed exclusively on a diet of pasteurized milk should be given antiscorbutics far earlier than is at present the custom, even as early as the end of the first month of life."

Why wait a full month before beginning to protect the child against the deficiencies and inadequacies of pasteurized milk? Infants can take orange juice and other juices from the third day after birth. It is my practice to start juices this early if there is reason to think the mother's milk is inadequate or if the child is placed on cow's milk, even raw cow's milk.

Berg says of the scorbutogenic diet, "the addition of milk to the diet will prevent the onset of scurvy; but this prophylactic power is more or less completely lost if the milk be boiled, condensed or dried." The antiscorbutic property of milk is ascribed to its vitamin C, which is destroyed even by pasteurization. Discussing the influence of heat on this complettin, Berg says: "this makes it obvious why the pasteurization of milk greatly reduces the C content of the nutriment and why infants and children fed on pasteurized milk are so apt to suffer from scurvy. Of course in the process of condensation, the antiscorbutic qualities of milk are gravely impaired. In young monkeys, and also in guinea-pigs it induces typical scurvy."

The addition of sodium citrate, lime and other alkalies to milk further impairs the milk, besides interfering with its digestion. Berg says: "Since the complettin C is sensitive to alkalies, we can readily understand that it is completely destroyed when milk is sterilized after addition of sodium citrate, which has an alkaline reaction.

PASTEURIZATION

Generally speaking, the sterilization of nutrients impairs their antiscorbutic power, being more injurious in proportion to the height of the temperature. Tinned meat and tinned milk are therefore invariably scorbutogenic." Barnes and Hume showed that the drying of milk reduces its antiscorbutic efficacy to approximately two-fifths the original. Hess and Unger showed that this does not occur if the milk is dried in a few seconds.

Berg refers to a four-year-old child which developed scurvy while fed exclusively upon a diet of soups, coffee and boiled milk. He says "such cases are, in truth, far less exceptional than might be supposed." Many mild cases developed in Germany during the war, while, reports of "epidemics" of scurvy in orphanages exist.

R. M. Overstreet, in *Northwest Medicine*, June, 1938, as abstracted by *Clinical Medicine and Surgery*, "The Increase of Scurvy," says: "Within the past few years an increasing number of patients affected with scurvy have been brought to the Oregon Children's Hospital. As the prophylactic amount of vitamin C (15 mg daily) is contained in 300 cc. of breast milk, scurvy is rarely found in breast-fed babies.

"The vitamin C of cow's milk is largely destroyed by pasteurization or evaporation."

In the *Journal of Nutrition* for Dec. 1939, in an article dealing with "The Destruction of Ascorbic Acid in Commercial Milks," Warren W. Woessner, C. A. Elvehjem and Henry A. Schuette say: "Samples of raw, certified, certified Guernsey and certified vitamin D milks were collected at the different dairies throughout the city of Madison. These milks on the average are only a little below the fresh milks as recorded in table 1, indicating that commercial raw and certified milks as delivered to the consumer lose only a small amount of their antiscorbutic potency. Likewise samples of commercial pasteurized milks were collected and analyzed. On an average they contained only about one-half as much ascorbic acid as fresh raw milks and significantly less ascorbic acid than the commercial unpasteurized milks.

"It was found that commercial raw milk contained an anti-scorbutic potency which was only slightly less than fresh raw milks and that pasteurized milks on the average contained only one-half the latter potency. Mineral modification and homogenization apparently have a destructive effect on ascorbic acid."

PASTEURIZED MILK KILLS

The London *Lancet* reported, a few years ago, some experiments by an English physician who fed a number of kittens and puppies on pasteurized milk. They died. Kittens and puppies fed on raw milk thrived well.

The digestibility of the milk is markedly impaired. It produces constipation and if fed exclusively, scurvy, rickets, scrofulosis and kindred diseases. Dogs fed pasteurized milk develop mange and other disorders. The same litter, fed on raw milk thrived. Pasteurized milk is simply not capable of sustaining life, health and growth for very long.

The infant death-rate in Toronto, Canada is 20 per cent higher than that of London, England, and double that of rural Ontario. Toronto uses pasteurized milk while both London and rural Ontario use natural milk. When pasteurized milk was substituted for raw milk in Toronto, the death rate in three of the city's largest homes and hospitals for children increased.

In many instances there is nothing wrong with babies except that they are being starved by being fed pasteurized milk. Babies do not thrive, and cease to thrive on heated milk. These same babies do well when changed to raw milk.

DIGESTIBILITY OF PASTEURIZED MILK

S. L. Harris, bacteriologist, Janesville, Wis., says that "pasteurization destroys some of the very important constituents and makes them indigestible. The albuminoids are coagulated. The sugars are broken down, and to some extent the colloids are agglutinated."

PASTEURIZED MILK DIRTY

The standards of sanitation demanded of the producers of Grade A raw milk are much higher than those demanded of the producers of pasteurized milk. Dirty milk is almost assured by pasteurization. The false sense of security created by faith in the protective power of the process discourages rigid cleanliness and promotes carelessness in handling on the part of the producer and all concerned. A high standard of cleanliness is not demanded by friends of pasteurization. Milk produced under all kinds of conditions, even though pasteurized afterward, is not as desirable as raw milk produced under sanitary conditions. Pasteurization does not make unclean milk clean.

"By milk I mean safe milk," says Alfred W. McCann, "and the only scientific way of insuring safety is by the process of pasteurizing."

PASTEURIZATION

McCann knows that safe milk depends upon: (1) a healthy cow, (2) proper food, sunshine, fresh air and exercise for the cow, (3) clean handling. He knows that healthy dairy cows are extremely rare; that no dairy cow is properly nourished; that their food is always denatured and unbalanced; and that milk is not always handled in a way to keep it clean. What then does he mean by calling pasteurized milk, "safe?" He means this:

If the cow is sick, pasteurize the milk and use it.

If the milk is deficient, due to a deficient diet or lack of sunshine, pasteurize it and use it.

If the milk is dirty, pasteurize it and use it.

We reject such plans and programs as this. If we are to use milk, let us have clean milk from healthy, well-nourished cows. It is not impossible to get such milk.

McCann says: — "In early infancy, during an exclusive milk diet, a few teaspoonfuls of sweet orange juice strained through a clean linen cloth, will offset any so-called disadvantages that here and there the enemies of pasteurized milk have charged against it."

This is ridiculous, although it is the attitude of Sherman, Mc-Collum, Howe, and most other experimenters who recognize the impairing work of pasteurization—and these "so-called disadvantages" are not merely charged against milk by its enemies; they are admitted by its friends.

A few teaspoonfuls of orange juice, or tomato juice, or lemon juice will not and cannot replace the destroyed and impaired substances in pasteurized milk. Dr. Howe says: "If milk is to come from unknown sources, I prefer to have it pasteurized, because I can compensate for the loss of vitamin C by taking enough orange juice." But there is more loss to milk through pasteurization than the mere loss of vitamin C and orange juice and tomato juice cannot entirely take the place of the qualities lost. The whole theory of denaturing some of our foods and "offsetting" these with foods that have not been denatured is false and ridiculous, whether we are dealing with milk or with white flour.

Assuming that orange juice, lemon juice, or tomato juice will prevent the development of scurvy in infants fed on pasteurized milk; this is not enough. We don't want our infants merely to escape recognizable scurvy. We want the maximum of health and development. A child may present no recognizable signs of deficiency, may appear normal, and still not have the high standard of vigorous positive health that is always desirable.

The false sense of security that the process of pasteurization gives people who use such milk, is only one of the evils of this process. It puts a premium upon carelessness and uncleanliness in the handling of milk.

In those parts of the country where the big dairy interests, with the aid of the Board of Health, have succeeded in getting raw milk outlawed, so that nothing but pasteurized milk is available, there is nothing left for mothers to do except to supplement the milk. This can only be done by feeding orange juice, grape juice, and other juices in much larger quantities than those commonly prescribed.

Mother's Milk

CHAPTER XLIII

Milk, the normal food of the young of all mammals, is prepared by the milk glands of each species to meet the specific and peculiar growth and developmental needs of the young of the particular species. The milk of one species, while it may be used by the young of another, is not adapted to the needs of the young of any other species. The great differences between the chemical compositions of the milk of the various species, differences that are accompanied by physical differences equally as great, may be partially seen by a glance at the following tables:

COMPOSITION OF HUMAN AND ANIMAL MILKS

	Water	Protein	Fat	Carbohydrate	Mineral Matter	Total
Human	87.75	1.60	3.95	6.25	0.45	34.70
Cow's	87.30	3.55	3.70	4.88	0.71	55.50
Dog's	75.60	11.20	9.60	3.10	1.35	55.30
Swine's	82.30	5.90	6.90	3.80	1.10	65.00
Sheep's	80.80	6.50	6.90	4.90	0.90	47.40
Goat's	85.70	4.30	4.50	4.40	0.80	70.00
Mare's	91.50	1.30	1.20	5.70	0.41	48.20
Rabbit's	69.40	15.50	10.50	2.00	2.60	85.00
Buffalo's	82.20	4.40	7.10	4.70	0.85	48.00
Camel's	87.10	3.60	2.70	5.30	0.75	58.15

Composition of mineral matter in 1,000 parts of water free substance of human and animal milks.

	Acid binding elements		Acid forming elements						
	Potassium	Sodium	Calcium	Magnesium	Iron	Phosphorus	Sulphur	Silicon	Chlorine
Human	11.73	3.16	5.80	0.75	0.07	7.84	0.33	0.07	6.38
Cow's	13.70	5.34	12.24	1.69	0.30	15.79	0.17	0.02	8.04
Dog's	5.70	3.25	18.20	0.80	0.08	19.75	0.25	0.15	6.55
Swine's	9.35	6.95	21.35	1.20	0.25	16.20	0.30	0.25	9.15
Sheep's	5.03	4.65	11.70	2.15	0.17	17.70	0.20	0.10	5.70
Goat's	15.60	3.45	13.90	2.30	0.60	21.05	0.30	0.20	13.50
Mare's	12.05	1.60	14.25	1.50	0.20	15.00	0.15	0.05	3.65
Rabbit's	11.40	7.75	33.60	1.75	0.07	22.80	0.40	0.30	7.00
Buffalo's	6.60	2.88	15.95	1.50	0.08	16.15	1.37	---	3.47
Camel's	10.50	2.00	15.48	2.70	0.12	17.20	2.05	---	8.10

Studying the tables it will be noticed that the protein content of the various milks varies from 1.30 to 15.50, being highest in that of the rabbit, the young of which is one of the most rapidly growing mammals. Note, also, that the milk of the rabbit contains the highest percent of fat and mineral matter. The human infant is the slowest growing animal on the earth. Note that the milk of the human mother is lowest in protein and low in mineral matters and fat. The milk of the various species is adapted to meet the particular growth needs of each species.

Human milk resembles cow's milk but differs from it in several important particulars. It is much sweeter than cow's milk, has no odor, and varies in color from a bluish white to a rich, creamy yellow. One, however, cannot judge of the quality of milk from its appearance, for the yellowest milks owe their color to a substance called *carotin* which is found in certain vegetables used for food.

MOTHER'S MILK

The composition of human milk is very much the same throughout the whole of the nursing period. The greatest variation is in its protein content which diminishes as time passes. The composition of the milk varies from day to day and even from one feeding to the next, as well as from the beginning to the end of each nursing.

Human milk, on an average, contains about 7 per cent milk sugar, 3 to 4 per cent fat, 1.50 per cent protein, and 0.20 per cent of salts. The percentage of whey or soluble proteins in human milk is much more easily utilized by the baby than are those of the cow's milk. Its salts are in a form much more easily utilized by the baby than are those of the cow's milk. There is sufficient of these salts for the baby's needs except that of iron. But, since, the child is born with a good supply of iron stored in the liver, it does not suffer, at least for many months, due to this deficiency. This is, indeed, a remarkable instance of the precise adaptation of the milk to the needs of the child.

The most important differences between human milk and the milk of cows or goats are qualitative rather than quantitative. Cow's milk contains too much casein and not sufficient albumen for the human infant. It is also deficient in milk sugar. The amino-acid content of its proteins is different, also. Mother's milk is peculiarly adapted to the needs of the human infant. Cow's milk is not.

While the human infant is normally of very slow growth, the human brain is larger at birth than that of any other animal and its rate of growth is greater. In mother's milk nature has provided for the greater demands made by the rapid growth and important size of the human brain in infancy and she has not made these provisions in the milk of any other animal. In other words, mother's milk is peculiarly fitted to nourish the brain of the infant, while that of the cow and goat are not. Not merely is human milk more digestible, but it is more complex than the substitutes. In it are found lecithin bodies in peculiar properties, which serve for the construction of the large human brain.

The minerals of cow's milk are not readily assimliated by the human infant so that one-third of the mineral elements of cow's milk is lost in the bowel discharges. This may not be as important as it appears at first glance, as cow's milk is richer in most minerals than mother's milk.

In view of the superior fitness of mother's milk to nourish the human brain, it comes as no surprise to learn that mentally, breast-fed children are brighter and indefinitely superior to bottle-fed children. Bottle-fed babies are more neurotic, have more of the "diseases of childhood," and a higher death-rate. It has been repeatedly shown that breast-fed babies are physically and mentally superior to bottle-fed babies. Except for height, bottle-fed babies rank lowest in all physical traits measured.

Human milk is peculiarly and specifically adapted to the needs of the human infant. No other milk is so adapted to the nutritive requirements of the baby. Owing to the peculiar composition of human milk, it is impossible to secure a substitute that is "just as good." It is a terrible thing for a mother to fall down on the duty of nursing her baby. Cow's milk, despite all the virtues attributed to it, is a terrible food for child as well as adult.

Human milk is secreted for the use of the human infant and under normal conditions, in healthy mothers, will be secreted in sufficient quantity, and proper quality and over a sufficiently long period of time to supply the entire milk-needs of the infant.

The secretion of the breasts during the first few days after birth is somewhat different to ordinary milk and is called *colostrum*. It is scanty in amount, thicker than milk and of a deep lemon-yellow color. Its chemical composition differs greatly from that of the later secretion. It is supposed to have a laxative effect upon the child.

Colostrum changes gradually into true milk which is thinner and bluer. The flow of milk is usually well-established by the end of the first week while the complete change is finished by the end of the second or third week.

As the child grows the secretion of milk gradually increases in response to his demands. Much of the milk is actually formed while the baby nurses and is secreted in proportion to the vigor, strength and persistence with which he sucks.

Mother's milk varies with the food eaten and with the season. Her glands secrete about 2¼ to 3 pints of milk a day between the third and sixth months of lactation. This amount gradually increases up to the end of one year. If the mother's diet is rich in phosphates, or in lecithins, the milk will possess large amounts of these constituents. Her milk is also readily affected by tobacco, alcohol, coffee, teas, narcotics, and nearly all drugs. These should be avoided.

Analyses of mother's milk to determine its quality are of no practical value unless the whole of several nursings are used. Samples taken in the evening are likely to be different from those taken in the morning. At the beginning of the nursing the fat in the milk varies from 6 to 10 per cent.

Considerable variation in the composition of the milk of various women is found. But babies thrive well on all of these. A baby that was thriving well on its mother's milk will thrive equally as well on the milk of a wet nurse. It is also true that one baby may thrive well on milk which, for some reason, another baby failed on. A baby may even take the milk of several wet-nurses and thrive well on all of them.

There can be no absolute standard for good milk. Unless some extreme variation exists, chemical analysis of the milk cannot determine its fitness or unfitness for the baby. Most of this laboratory monkey-work is just part of commercial medicine.

There is only one test for the adequacy or inadequacy of milk, and this is the feeding test. If a child is growing normally and thriving on the breast milk it is receiving, it is quite evident that the supply is adequate. But if it is not growing it is possible that the supply of milk is insufficient.

The amount of milk the baby receives may be determined by weighing it before and after nursing. Usually the baby receives one-half its meal during the first five minutes of sucking. During the second five minutes it gets an added quarter of its meal.

FAILURE TO NURSE

The custom of not nursing their babies is growing among women. Many babies are not nursed from the start. Others are nursed but a few weeks, or at most three or four months. There is a common superstition among women, fostered by the medical profession, that it is bad for both the mother and the child for it to be nursed longer than a few months. There are women who refuse to nurse their children for fear it will ruin their figures. Most of them have no figures to ruin. Others refuse to nurse their children for the reason that it hampers their social activities, prevents their participation in bridge, or their attendance at the theatre. Many of the "emancipated" ones, that is, those who have become wage slaves and are being killed in the factories, do not nurse their babies because this would interfere with their wage slavery.

Thousands of women protest that they want to nurse their babies but jump at every slight pretext for not doing so. Their readiness and willingness to discontinue nursing their babies upon the flimsiest excuses reveals that their protests are lies. Failure to breast-feed is, in most cases, deliberate and in many other cases the subconscious desire not to nurse prevents the secretion of adequate milk. Much "inability" to nurse the baby is due to carelessness, neglect or ignorance.

The delactation of mothers is due to a variety of causes, some of them deliberately employed by the mothers, themselves; some employed, either deliberately or unwittingly, by physicians. Their function-depressing treatments and their wholly inadequate dietetic prescriptions prevent the production of an adequate supply of milk.

Physical degeneration and defective functioning account for but an insignificant number of those women who bottle-feed their babies instead of supplying them with superior food from their own breasts. Lactation can be established and maintained in almost every woman. If mothers care for and feed themselves properly and give adequate attention to the essential details, the milk glands of nearly all of them can be brought into the required degree of activity. If women fully realized the value of natural feeding they would soon find the capacity for breast-feeding to be practically universal among them.

Much "inability" to nurse the baby is sheer unwillingness to do so. Many mothers can find the greatest number of flimsy excuses for not nursing their children. These must be made to see the great importance of breast-feeding babies. They must be brought to a full realization of the great advantage of breast-feeding over all other methods of feeding babies.

Except for those "emancipated" women who prefer their club activities, the theatre, or to be exploited in factory office and store, to caring for their children, breast-feeding is much more convenient and much less work than washing and sterilizing bottles and nipples, making up formulas and feeding baby with a bottle. Nature's plan is as simple as it is superior. Women were very foolish to permit the he-women, the physicians, dairymen and manufacturers of prepared baby-foods to induce them to abandon the natural method of infant feeding.

Unfortunately the medical profession does not fail to identify its own best interests with the perpetuation and aggravation of our present disabilities. In accordance with its own financial interests it has neglected (and discouraged in all others) any effort to restore natural conditions in order that functions may be normal, and has employed all of its ingenuity in the task of producing an ever-increasing array of artificial "aids" to function. Under the tutelage of this profession we watch a year after year increase in the number of mothers who have recourse to the bottle instead of the breast in feeding their infants. Babies are thus fed more and more upon inferior foods.

The first thing the physician does is to give the mother instructions for bottle-feeding her baby. She leaves the hospital with a can of powdered milk and a formula by which to feed her baby. No effort is made to induce or enable her to feed her child from the fountains of superior nutrition.

ASSURRING AMPLE MILK

There are only two ways of increasing the supply of milk—namely, an improved diet, and the complete emptying of the breasts at each nursing. Water drinking will not help. There are no drugs to be taken internally or applied locally and no patented foods that will stimulate milk production.

EMPTYING BREASTS

The complete emptying of the breast at each nursing is the most effective means of increasing the production of milk. If the breasts are not emptied each time, the secretion of milk gradually decreases. Farmers and dairymen have known this fact, with relation to cows, for ages. Some women, like cows, give more milk than others, but aside from this, the amount of milk secreted depends very largely upon the demands of the baby — increasing when more is consumed and decreasing when less is taken.

Unfortunately what farmers and dairymen know about their cows, few physicians know about women and few husbands and mothers are aware that the same principle is as true in relation to milk production in women as in cows. A dairyman who knows enough to thoroughly empty the udders of his cows at each milking will sit by and watch his wife neglect this in nursing her baby and wonder why her glands "dry up."

I have tried to emphasize the necessity for the complete emptying of the breast each time the baby nurses. Too many mothers allow their baby to nurse one breast for a few minutes and then give it the other breast. Neither breast is ever fully emptied and they both rapidly dry up. The child should be given one breast at one feeding and the other breast at the next feeding. See that it completely empties each breast before giving it the other breast, if one breast does not supply enough milk for the feeding.

It is highly important that the breast be completely emptied at each nursing. It seems a little strange that every farmer and dairyman knows that failure to completely empty the udder of a milk cow at each milking will cause her milk production to steadily fall off, but we fail to recognize the same fact in woman. Milk secretion is largely in response to demand.

If the breasts are not thoroughly emptied at each nursing, the supply of milk will quickly diminish.

Emptying the breasts at each nursing will increase the quantity of milk more certainly than anything else.

DIET

One of the most important factors in assuring an adequate milk supply is the mother's diet. This is of prime importance in the production of milk of good quality — possessing all the required nutritive factors in adequate quantities. Dairymen who know how to feed their cows to assure quantity and quality milk-production will put their own babies on a bottle and take the word of ignorant physicians that their wives are unable to produce adequate milk for their babies. This is one of the paradoxes of our day.

Eating large quantities of rich foods is useless. These only derange digestion and destroy the mother's appetite. The one class of foods that greatly increases milk production in animals, and there are reasons for believing they will do so in woman, are green foods. An abundance of these should be eaten.

Prof. McCollum says: "There is good reason to believe that the common practice of confining the diet to too great an extent to bread, meat, sugar, potatoes, beans, peas and breakfast cereals (before birth and during the nursing period) is in no small measure responsible for the failure of many mothers to produce milk of satisfactory quantity and quality for the nutrition of their infants. There is no great hardship (but great benefit) in the restriction of the intake of meats, etc., and the increase of milk, fruits and green vegetables, and the mother who does so will greatly minimize the danger of a break in the healthy growth of her baby."

McCarrison says: "When, as is sometimes the case, mother's milk is itself harmful to the child, is it not largely the result of her own disordered metabolism that in many cases results from improper feeding before, during and after pregnancy? For mother's milk may, like the milk of animals, be deficient in certain respects if her food be deficient. The milk of stall-fed cows is not so rich either in vitamin A or in vitamin C as that of cows fed in green pastures."

Speaking of the long period (two to three full years) over which the Chinese mother nurses her child, Prof. H. C. Sherman says: "It is not improbable that the free use of green vegetables with their high calcium and vitamin content in the food of the mother may be a factor in her ability to nurse her children through such a long period.

"This must be true because McCollum has found that the vitamins of milk are not manufactured by the cow, but are taken directly by the cow from her food."

In treating of the causes of rickets, Dr. Eric Pritchard, of England, notes that the diet of the English is deficient in the alkaline minerals and contains an excess of acid radicals. Commenting on the effects of this upon nursing he says: "It is also worthy of note that, concurrent with the deterioration of teeth in this country (England) there is to be observed a decreasing ability on the part of mothers to suckle their infants. The production of milk entails an extraordinary drain on the calcium resources of the body; when these resources are depleted, the inability to produce milk is a natural sequence."

Good milk, upon which the life, health and growth of the baby depends, cannot be produced out of a diet of tea and toast, coffee, vinegar, pickles, pastries, gravies, condiments, canned foods, greasy meats, white flour and sugar, fermented bread, wines and beer.

Fruits and green foods are our richest and best sources of alkaline bases and should do for the human mother, in the matter of milk production, what they do for other mothers. Fruits and fresh raw green vegetables should form the bulk of the diet of the mother during both gestation and lactation. Aside from this the mother's diet should consist of the usual natural foods. Nursing is not a disease and does not require special diets. She should, however, especially avoid habits of eating which derange her digestion.

Dr. Page says: "The woman who lacks a reliable appetite for any sort of plain wholesome food, is not a well woman; if she indulges in that which is unwholesome, she cannot maintain good health; if she is overfed, abnormally fat and plethoric, she is a sick woman; and such mothers cannot supply a perfect food for the nursing child." "Much sloppy food, hot drinks, profuse drinking between meals to force the milk,' are injurious to both the mother and child. Much animal food is not advisable either in winter or summer, and in the latter season especially should be avoided altogether." "Nausea, lack of appetite, fitful appetite, 'gnawing' at the stomach — the latter so generally mistaken for a demand for food — all result from excess or the use of unwholesome food or condiments."

An excess of protein in her diet may result in an excess of protein in her milk and this is likely to cause trouble in the child. That this is true is well attested by observations upon human beings. In animals it has been tested in the laboratory. Hartwell, one scientific investigator, found that an excess of protein in the mother's diet during lactation is detrimental to the well-being of her young. L. T. Anderegg, of the Laboratory of Physiological Chemistry, Iowa State College, says: "Evidence obtained in this laboratory shows that it is a matter of considerable importance that the ratio of fat to protein be within certain limits if optimum results are expected. If the proprotion of fat to protein is too high, growth may be normal in the first generation, but the animals produce few or no young. Evans and Bishop and Mathill and Stone employed diets in which the ratio of fats to protein was too high for best results, and as a consequence few or no young were produced.

"Hartwell showed that the young were not reared when the mothers were given high protein diets at the time of lactation. The young went into spasms and examination of the alimentary tracts showed the cessation of the flow of milk. It has been observed repeatedly in this laboratory also that diets high in protein and comparatively low in fat are detrimental to the rearing of the young."

Nervousness or lack of exercise may also result in too much protein in the milk.

The value of a particular protein depends upon its amino-acid constituency. Since the animal body is unable to synthesize aminoacids, it must receive these ready made from the vegetable kingdom. The green grasses and green herbs, eaten by the cow in the spring, when naturally this is her whole source of food, must contain all of the amino acids essential to the production of the superior protein of milk. Trypotophan, so vitally essential to the human infant, and found also in cow's milk, must be present in the grasses and weeds that she eats.

Green vegetables, nuts and fruits yield these same needed amino acids to man when he eats them, as they do to the ape, squirrel or cow. The much vaunted high-grade protein of the animal, or its milk, are synthesized out of the amino acids it derives from green vegetation, fresh fruits and nuts. We must not forget that man is capable of doing the same thing. The mother's diet should contain an abundance of these foods.

The percentage of sugar in milk cannot be increased or decreased by any means. The amount of fat cannot be increased except in mothers who are much underfed. It may be reduced, however, by cutting down the whole amount of the mother's food. There is probably great variation in the amount of salts in milk produced by diet, while it seems certain that its vitamin content must vary greatly.

SUNSHINE

Physicians and dairymen have recognized for a numer of years now, the importance of sunshine in the production of good milk by cows, but nowhere, outside of *Hygienic* circles, is the value of sunshine in the production of good milk by human mothers stressed. Daily sunning shuold be indulged by all mothers, during both pregnancy and lactation. This will mean better health for the mother and better nourishment for the baby.

EMOTIONS

Anger, fear excitement, rage, etc., may greatly diminish or completely suspend the secretion of milk; or, these may so alter the composition of the milk that the baby will be made ill. I often wonder if some women don't fail to nurse their children due solely to their fear that they cannot and to worry over the thought that they cannot. Nervous and excitable women are liable to have too much protein in their milk, and this will derange the baby's digestion.

It is recorded that angry mothers have killed their children by nursing them. Worry and anger may so derange the milk as to cause convulsions in the baby. Any influence that depresses, or excites, or over-stimulates the mother, will ruin her milk and make her baby sick.

It is imperative that mothers and mothers-to-be cultivate and maintain poise. A cheerful, optimistic disposition will help to maintain normal function of her milk glands.

FATIGUE

Fatigue impairs the function of the milk glands. Women who are over-active in any type of activity, or who are overworked in factory, mill, store, or home will fail to nurse their children. One of the most outstanding evils of the modern industrial system is its destructive effects upon womanhood and motherhood. The exploitation of women in industry robs babies of the care and companionship of their mothers and robs them of their mother's milk so essential to normal development.

Mothers should receive sufficient rest and sleep to maintain a state of wellbeing at all times. Night nursing, that robs them of rest and sleep, also trends to reduce the milk supply. Night life, gay parties, theatre parties, etc., rob mothers of the ability to nurse their babies. Women who do not want to be mothers in the full sense should refrain from incurring the responsibilities of motherhood. They make better mistresses.

ALCOHOL FOR BABY

Mothers are often advised to drink beer, wine, ale, cocoa, chocolate and malted drinks, to increase and improve their milk supply. This advice is pernicious in the extreme. "It is a question," says Dr. Wm. J. Robinson, "if a mother partaking of considerable quantities of alcoholic beverages may not transmit the taste for alcohol to her children." Certain it is, the alcohol finds its way into her milk and is imbibed by the baby along with the milk. Mothers should be careful what they take into their stomachs while they are pregnant and nursing, even if they are unwilling to live sensibly at other times. A woman who becomes a mother assumes certain vital responsibilities to her child, even though, in modern times, this responsibility is taken lightly.

NICOTINE FOR BABY

Repeated tests have shown that nicotine is contained in the milk of smoking mothers. The amount present varies with the amount of smoking done by the woman. Since the tendency to chain smoking is great in women, most women who smoke know few limitations to their indulgence. For the sake of her baby, she should give up the filthy habit completely. Indeed, it should be discontinued as soon as she finds herself pregnant, for there is ample evidence that there is a much higher death rate among babies whose mothers smoke than among those whose mothers exercise more intelligence in their living. Woman's slavery to *Lady Nicotine* (one of the most powerful narcotics known) is nothing to boast of. This kind of slavery is poor "emancipation" for the "free" woman.

MOTHER'S MILK

DRUGGING BABY'S FOOD

Many drugs taken by the mother are excreted in the milk. Alcohol, opium, atropin, iodid of potash, salicylate of soda, the bromids, aspirin, urotripin, and antipyrin are among the drugs which find their way into the mothers milk. Cathartics and laxatives taken by the mother are likely to produce colic and loose movements in the baby. Nicotine finds its way into the milk of mothers who smoke.

Mothers should be careful not to take drugs and poison their babies. We are told by medical men that these drugs never occur in the milk in sufficient quantities to do harm to the baby, but this must be viewed as merely a defense of their drugging practice. Anyway, they never recognize the harm from a drug unless the drug nearly kills.

Should Baby Be Weaned?
CHAPTER XLIV

Elsewhere I have pointed out the advantages of breast-feeding over unnatural feeding. That the natural food of a baby is its own mother's milk is so obvious it hardly needs emphasis. It is, then, certainly the duty of the woman who brings a baby into world to do the best she possibly can in caring for it. Breast milk being the ideal food for the infant, it is certainly her duty to promote a sufficient supply of good milk for her child.

A woman whose maternal instincts have been lost or have failed to develop, and who has not attained a degree of moral and ethical responsibility, which compels her to protect her child, should not become a mother. If she does not feel the responsibility for giving her child the best antenatal and postnatal care she should not bear children. Men who are lacking in a sense of responsibility, in aiding their wives in the proper care of their children, should refrain from becoming fathers. They are better off single.

Mothers who turn their babies over to the tender mercies of a nurse or a day nursery while they go to business, and deny their children the benefits of their breast milk, are not deserving of children. There are cases where the mother is the support of the family and in such cases she cannot avoid this, no matter how much she desires to do so, but there are probably many more of the other kind. Mothers who deny their breast milk to their babies and who dry up their breasts so that they can shine in social functions or be forever "on the go," or because of the mistaken notion that nursing will ruin their figures (as though the figures of their children are not of more importance than their own caricatures of the human form), are fiends. If a woman is unwilling to sacrifice her parties, swimming, club work, drinking, and chocolate and indolence for the sake of the health and normal development of her child, she is morally and biologically unfit for motherhood. She should avoid it.

No woman of sound mind and normal instincts would ever think of refusing to nurse her child if she fully realized how much more likely it is to live and develop normally and how much less likely it is to be sick and die, when it is breast fed than when it is bottle-fed.

SHOULD BABY BE WEANED?

Nursing a child benefits the mother, as well as the child. Mothers who cannot or who will not nurse their children are deprived of these benefits. There is, first, an improvement in the nutrition of her own body. Second, nursing the baby assists in the involution of the uterus. The uterus of a nursing mother returns more quickly and more perfectly to its normal prepregnancy condition, than the uterus of a woman who does not nurse her child. It is claimed that the reciprocal affection between mother and child is greater, if she nurses her child, than between babies and mothers where the mother does not nurse her child. This is not a far-fetched claim and it is quite likely true. I put no credence in the claim that the nursing mother transmits, through her milk, traits to her child which the non-nursing mother does not. Not only is proof of this entirely lacking but I can find no grounds upon which to base such a belief.

Too many women are looking for an excuse to give up nursing their children and there are too many physicains who encourage them in this. They give up nursing their children on insufficient grounds, because they do not want to nurse them. They wean their babies too early because they do not want to go on nursing them to the normal limit of the nursing period. In this they are encouraged by doctors and manufacturers of patented baby foods who tell them that their milk is not good for the baby after a certain period.

They are advised that the baby should be weaned for its own sake as well as for it's mother's sake at about nine months to twelve months. "By this time the child should have become accustomed to artificial feeding from the bottle, gradually introduced as the breast is gradually withheld so as to avoid a too sudden change."

This is pernicious advice and is usually followed by the equally pernicious advice to "try some of the prepared foods," "if the first substitute food does not agree with the child," and lastly, "when certified milk cannot be had, give the baby one of the standard makes of condensed milk or baby foods." The advice to take an infant off the wholesome milk of its mother and put it on such stuff is criminal, and any mother who follows such advice, after learning the truth, deserves to lose her baby.

Women often give up the effort to nurse their babies because there is no milk, when, if they will persist for a few days the milk will be forthcoming. The supply may be small at first and will later increase in amount.

Other women are unwilling to bear the discomforts of cracked nipples for a brief spell. Doctors and others frequently tell them that it will make the child ill if, where the mother does not have enough milk for the childs needs, she feeds it both from the breast and from the bottle. The information is both false and pernicious. The baby will fare all the better for receiving the mother's milk. Babies should have the advantage of the mother's milk in addition to the other foods used, as long as possible.

There are many women who make up their minds that they cannot nurse their baby long anyway, so they give it up at once. Such a thing cannot be too strongly condemned. A mother's milk is of more importance to her child during the first few weeks of its life than subsequently.

It sometimes happens that a woman could not nurse a prior baby and she gives up the duty of nursing the present one, because she thinks she can not do it. Inability to nurse one's first baby, for example, does not mean she cannot nurse subsequent ones.

Some women imagine themselves to be too nervous or too delicate to nurse their children. But many of these "too nervous" women have good milk while many delicate women will find their health improved while nursing. "Delicate" and "nervous" women owe it to their children to at least make an honest effort to nurse them.

Small breasts do not constitute a reason for not nursing one's child. There is no necessary relation between the size of the breast and the ability to nurse one's child. It is a fact that many women with small breasts secrete more and better milk than women with large breasts. The normal breast is not a large pendulous bag, anyway. There are of course, women who have no breasts. The glands never develop and their chests are adorned with nothing more than the nipples. Such women, if it is possible for them to become mothers, should avoid motherhood.

The resumption of menstruation is, due to the persistence of ancient superstitions about this function, often considered a cause for weaning. It is estimated that almost half of all nursing mothers begin to menstruate again as early as the third month after birth. Children should not be weaned because of this. They do not suffer because of the menstruation.

SHOULD BABY BE WEANED?

A slight and brief illness should not cause the mother to wean her child or to withhold her baby from the breast. Only serious illness should cause her to wean her baby.

Pregnancy need not result in the immediate weaning of the child. Although, this is usually advised, on the grounds that it is too much of a drain upon the mother to nourish two lives besides her own, and her breast milk is likely to become too poor and scanty to nourish the baby properly, I am sure this objection to nursing during pregnancy is valid only if the mother is eating the denatured slops advised by those who make the objection. Most of the drains blamed on pregnancy and lactation are due to a denatured diet and lack of hygiene.

There are a few conditions which demand the weaning of the child. Dr. Tilden says: "Convulsions in nursing children, not traceable to objective causes, will usually be found to come from slight septic infections of the mother, due to injuries incident to child birth; hence it is well to carefully investigate all unaccountable sickness occurring in young children soon after birth, with a view of locating the trouble in a blood derangement of the mother and discovering, if possible, whether it comes from septic poisoning."

Again he says: "Many, if not all, children born under conventional circumstances, are more or less encumbered with flesh; instead of weighing 5 or 6 pounds, they weigh from 10 to 12 pounds and because of this overweight mothers have long, tedious, and painful labors, and too frequently are forced into instrumental deliveries. As a sequel these mothers suffer greatly from bruises, contusions and lacerations. It matters not how careful the physician who officiates at such confinement is to be scrupulously clean, these women usually have enough septic infection to cause their milk to be unwholesome, and even if they escape having a slight septic infection the severe labor breaks down so much tissue that the blood is deranged and the secretions, including the milk, are impaired to such an extent that before the doctor and the nurse are suspicious that anything is wrong the baby is very sick. This necessitates taking the child from the mother's breast, which is equivalent to weaning it, for the mothers are usually as much encumbered with flesh as the children, and because of this encumbrance plus the blood impairment described above, they cannot be restored to health until long after they have lost their milk."

Many women who have prolonged and painful and even instrumental deliveries are able to nurse their children well, however.

Women with tuberculosis should not even try to nurse their children. Of course such women have no business having children, in the first place. Any acute or chronic "disease" which deranges the mother's milk should cause her to wean the child. Insanity and epilepsy are listed as reasons for not nursing one's baby, but I think these are even better reasons for not having children. So-called syphilis is not a reason for weaning the child.

Babies with lip deformities and premature babies that are too weak to nurse are best fed their mother's milk after this has been expressed from her breasts. The milk should be forced from the breasts by the use of the hands. The breasts should not be massaged in this operation.

The breast pump is not advisable. It injures the tissues and invariably causes the breasts to dry up prematurely. Dr. Tilden says of this: "I found that when the pump was used the breasts were more or less bruised and that the bruising caused inflammation and suppuration. In time I proved to myself that there were more abscesses following the use of the pump than when it was not used."

No Starch for Infants
CHAPTER XLV

Dr. Prospiro Sonsino, el Pisa, proved years ago, by a number of experiments, that there is a "physiological or normal dyspepsia to starchy food (absolute inability to digest) in the first portion of infant life." Certain it is that, since starch of all foods, requires thorough and complete mastication and insalivation, it should not be fed to infants before they have teeth. This view was supported by Dr. Routh, professors Huxley, Youmans, Dalton and perhaps by all who ever examined the subject.

Dr. Page was particularly bitter against the practice of feeding starches to infants. "Farina, corn-starch, fine flour, and refined sugar," he declared, "are the fashionable materials of the infant dietary; but a worse selection could hardly be made." He cautioned against the injury to the vital organs resulting from "prematurely feeding the infant on even the best selected articles of the general table," and added: "It is not uncommon for infants to be given cakes and candies and even pork, fried fish, cabbage, ham, potatoes, etc., while the teeth are blamed for the ensuing gastro-intestinal disorders."

It will not do to feed mashed potatoes, corn meal mush, farina, and the like to toothless infants, and imagine that because these things can be swallowed without chewing, the problem is solved. They are also swallowed without being insalivated and are eaten by one whose digestive juices are ill adapted to starch digestion.

The fact that Nature makes no provisions for the digestion of starches before full dentition, should be sufficient evidence that she does not intend it to form any part of the infant's diet. Before the teeth are fully developed the saliva of the infant contains a mere trace of ptyalin, the digestive ferment or enzyme that converts starch into sugar. There is just enough of this ptyalin present in the saliva to convert milk sugar into dextrose. It is this almost total absence of starch-splitting enzymes from the digestive juices of the infant that accounts for the great amount of digestive disorders which result from feeding starch foods to infants. When starch digestion is impossible, starch fermentation is inevitable. This poisons the baby.

If we limit the following remarks of Page's to the milk from a healthy, well nourished mother, he is eternally right. He says: "Milk is the food for babies and contains all of the elements necessary to make teeth, and until they are made, it should continue to be the sole food. It is not enough that two or three or a half dozen teeth have come through, that they should be expected to do any part of a grown child's work."

Dr. Densmore, who did not favor starches, even for adults, says of them for infants, *How Nature Cures,* p. 55; a diet of cereal or grain and all starch foods: "is especially unfavorable for children, and more especially for babies. The intestinal ferments which are required for the digestion of starch foods are not secreted until the baby is about a year old; and these ferments are not as vigorous for some time as in adults. All starch foods depend upon these intestinal ferments for digestion, whereas dates, figs, prunes, etc., are equally as nourishing as bread and cereals, and are easily digested — the larger proportion of the nourishment from such fruits being ready for absorption and assimilation as soon as eaten."

Dr. Tilden is equally as strong for what he calls the no-starch-for-babies plan. He says: "It is a mistake to feed starchy food too soon — before the end of the second year; for young children cannot take care of too much starch." "Children under two or three years of age have trouble in converting starch into sugar. They should get their sugar from fruits; fresh fruits in summer, and the dry sweet fruits in the winter — raisins, dates and figs."

In my own practice I make it a point never to prescribe starch food of any kind for babies under two years of age. In my own family I have never fed my children cereals. The cereals are the most difficult of all starches, unless it is beans and peas, to digest. There are strong reasons to think that cereals cause the production of poor bones and teeth.

Babies do not need starch foods and cannot utilize them to any advantage. Many of the troubles from which children suffer are due to the practice of feeding them starch. Cereals with sugar and cream or sugar and milk are especially bad — the cereals and sugars are usually denatured and the milk is pasteurized, to add to the evils.

NO STARCH FOR INFANTS

"Upon no consideration," says Dr. Page, "should any of the farinaceous or starchy articles be added until the mouth bristles with teeth; then it may be justly considered that he can handle something of the adult diet."

Macaroni is a "slippy, glutinous mass of starchy acid which is never chewed, and equally of course is never digested," and should never be eaten by child or adult. Cakes and cookies, breads and pastries, jellies, jams, custards and the like should never be fed to children or eaten by grown ups.

If cereals are fed to children only the whole-grain cereals should be given. It is a crime to feed denatured cereals to children. Doctors who advice them are either ignorant incompetents, or else knaves who have their eyes on the money they derive out of the sickness caused by these.

All starches should be served dry, to insure thorough chewing and insalivation. They should be taken with green vegetables, raw or cooked, but never with acid fruits, proteins or milk. Jellies, jams, etc., should not be fed with them. Cream and sugar should never be served on cereals. Raw starches are easier to digest than cooked starches and require more chewing; this probably accounting for a part of their greater ease of digestion.

Three Feedings a Day
CHAPTER XLVI

The baby that is healthy at birth possesses the power and ability to digest and assimilate, easily and continuously, an amount of food necessary to produce normal growth. This rate of growth cannot be exceeded, although it may be and often is retarded, by feeding the child excessively; for, as many children have growth checked by too much food as by a deficiency.

Most people have a mania for fat babies; they like to be able to say the baby gains a pound a week. This gives rise to excessive feeding. Most of the gastro-intestinal disorders in infants are due solely to too much nursing and can be remedied simply by giving the digestive organs a much needed rest.

When a baby is increasing in weight during the first three months after birth from a half to a pound a week it is merely a rolling on of fat — disease — and is not healthy growth. It is always abnormal and is a snare and a delusion. Fat children do not have great resistance to disease.

From time immemorial it has been thought necessary to keep babies stuffed with something, to keep them growing and fat — they must be fat. From the time they are born until they die, the greatest anxiety has been to keep their little bodies full of something. During the first year of their lives, infants are, as a rule, stuffed early and late. This is the chief cause of the great mortality at this time.

After the first year they are allowed more time between meals and hence a less proportion of them die. About one-third of the deaths are in children under one year and only about one-fifth between the ages of one and five. After the age of five, children are fed on something like a three-meal plan and comparatively few die between the ages of five and twenty. It is true, as a rule, the toughest and therefore the "fittest" do survive.

Dr. Page says:— "The farmer who wants to raise the best possible animal from the calf, lets the creature suckle in the morning at milking-time, and again, at night. He is wise enough to feed his calf only twice and the result is, the calf thrives from birth, and sickness is unknown.

"The same farmer has a baby born, and a contrary course is pursued, with a contrary result. Even before nature supplies the food — before the mother's milk comes — the ignorant nurse undertakes to supply the seeming deficiency, and doses the baby with sweetened water, cow's milk, safron, or the like, instead of giving nothing but what nature supplies, which for the first few days at least is sufficient.

"The dosing referred to results in stomach-ache, and the cries of pain being mistaken for cries of hunger down goes another dose, until finally, when the mother's milk does come, the child's stomach often is in a condition to revolt at anything. If the little victim goes along for a few weeks or months, it is generally fed every hour or oftener, unless it happens to be, as is often the case, in a lethargic state for several hours, sleeping off the surfeit as an adult sleeps off a 'drunk.'

"It is often the case that an infant is eating and vomiting. alternately, from morning till night; indeed, so common is this that it is regarded as altogether natural. It is expected that the child will 'throw up' continually, at least after being fed, and the nurse declares that it is all right — nature takes care of all of that."

"It is not all right; it is all wrong. Nature indeed revolts at this barbarous treatment of the baby's stomach. Early and late. often during the night, as through the day the stomach is kept full and distended, every hiccough is an attempt of the stomach to eject its overload, or evidence of an undigested residue, and the habitual vomiting is simply the result of cramming, until the little, helpless babe has become a confirmed dyspeptic. The mother or nurse habitually flies to the sugar-bowl to relieve the infant's hiccough. But the remedy is worse than the disease; and although the hiccough may disappear, it will, if the habit be continued, be succeeded sooner or later by symptoms of deeper disease in the form of so-called cold. feverishness, etc., the result of the excess of food and excess of saccharine matter."

Happily such gross feeding has disappeared among the better informed classes with a consequent improvement in the health of our babies. But it is still all too true that babies are greatly overfed and are frequently dosed. There are no reasons for doubting that dyspepsia which Page calls "the parent of nearly all our ills," is the result of overfeeding in infancy, confirmed by continued overindulgence through life.

However well intentioned mothers and nurses may be, the almost universal custom of constantly feeding infants is extremely cruel, and we may be sure that were such mothers and nurses compelled to take food as often and in the same excessive quantities that it is forced upon the baby, night and day, the abuse would soon be ended. The cruelty of the practice would soon be apparent.

Children thus punished sooner or later arrive at a condition where their digestive organs are unable to function efficiently. The constant overwork will impair and cripple them. Then it is that we see children literally starving to death on five, six and even more meals a day. As paradoxical as it may seem, many children starve because of being overfed, just as many adults do.

Dr. Tilden well says: "If mothers could be made to see the fearful price they pay for keeping their babies fat they would hasten to learn a better plan of feeding. Children who are overweight are more susceptible to disease influences than smaller and lighter children. The fat, chubby baby, everything else being equal, is always the one to take the croup, tonsilitis, diphtheria, scarlet fever and, when a few years older, pneumonia, rheumatism and other forms of common diseases."

In his *In A Nut Shell*, Dr. Dio. Lewis relates the following experience of his: "When I was a boy my sympathies were awakened by what I thought the cruel starving of calves. They were fed only twice a day, morning and evening. Eating all day myself, I thought it very cruel to tie up these poor helpless things, and give them no food or drink from morning till night.

"Each of my brothers had a calf, my sister had a calf, and I had a calf. The others were satisfied with John's assurance that twice a day was enough. I knew better and made such a fuss about their starving my poor little Sam, that the 'powers that be," ordained that the feeding in the case of young Samuel be as his owner directed. Upon the proclamation of this ukase I determined to show 'em what's what, and to make sure I fed Samuel myself, and gave him all he wanted once in two hours.

"At the end of six weeks how the rest of 'em did crow over me. It was true, as they said, that at the beginning of my sausage-stuffing system, as they called it, Samuel was the biggest calf in the

THREE FEEDINGS A DAY

lot, but at the end of six weeks what a fall was there my countrymen. Even my smallest brother's little Fan could give Samuel odds. To cap the climax, when we untied and turned them all out together, little spotted Fan went at my Sam, upon whom my hopes had centered as the bully of the yard, and walloped him in no time. For a long time they wouldn't stop plaguing me about that good-for-nothing calf. My little sister asked me one morning at the breakfast table, 'how's 'ep 'opher Sam'el this morning.'

"From that day to this I have never advocated the frequent feeding of calves. They do best on two meals a day, and now I have no doubt that some calves I wot of would do vastly better on two meals a day."

At my father's dairy we fed the calves twice a day and they thrived well. I do not recall that we ever had a calf to die and only one or two to ever be sick. I recall an occasion or two when a calf escaped from the pen and got too much milk, whereupon it would develop a severe diarrhea known among farmers and dairymen as the "scours." In our home the babies were fed every two hours during the day and everytime they cried at night. Colic, constipation, diarrhea, hives, feverishness, croup, colds, and more severe types of disease were as frequent among the children as they were rare among the calves.

In those days the medical profession urged two hour feedings and night feedings as well. Many older peoples have not gotten away from this view yet. They still think that children should be gorged until they are surfeited and sickened or else they are not fed enough.

Long prior to this time, however, Dr. Page and others had proven that three meals a day are enough for a baby. Asserting that no infant can thrive unless well fed and assuming that a well fed baby is one that secures the minimum amount of suitable food that will suffice to produce a comfortable, happy, thriving baby, with body and limbs well-rounded with flesh, not fat, and whose growth shall be uniform throughout its whole life, and until the frame is fully developed, he declared: "It is my belief, verified by experience in the case of my own infant, and from other substantial proof, that three meals a day, with sufficient restriction at each, will accomplish this end, and are all that should be permitted from birth, and the intervals should be at least five or six hours between meals."

He assumed, and probably correctly, that the rate of growth of the infant after birth should correspond with its rate of growth before birth. In the case of his own child, he says:— "Our three-meal infant has doubled in weight at nine months, verifying, to that extent, my theory that the normal growth of infants corresponds to the (normal) fœtal growth. She is taller than the average child at this age, and though less heavy than most children, she is more muscular, and, had I permitted it would have become fat, for she has given abundant evidence of the ability to fatten rapidly on three meals."

He tells us that her sleep was perfect, sound and continuous. there was entire exemption from hiccough, throwing up, colic, constipation, diarrhea, stomach trouble, and all other troubles, and she completely escaped the fat disease, with its pasty complexion. Her limbs lengthened by normal growth, were well-covered and rounded with muscle, her complexion was brown and ruddy from being perfectly nourished and being in the open air during winter, as well as in the spring and summer. She was able to hold her head erect from the fourth day onward, and sat erect on the floor without support at four months.

My own experience corroborates all of this: I believe it to be an invariable rule that babies fed as herein directed grow faster and develop better than the overfed children of the average home. They do not weigh as much, for they are never permitted to become fat. More than once I have stopped all food but orange juice in my own children to counteract a tendency to get too fat.

Any normal baby should be able to hold its head erect at four to six days of age. My own children sat erect in my hand without support, I of course balancing them, at one week. They could stand erect in my hand at three months, and stiffen their little backs and hold themselves out on a perfectly horizontal plane, without support, as I held them just above the knees, at four months. At five months the two boys could, while lying on the back, their feet held down, raise themselves up to a sitting position several times in succession. The girl was practically six months old before she could do this. But she acomplished a new "stunt" I tried. She held herself out horizontally, being held by the legs only, with her back down. All three of them could make a *wrestler's bridge* at four months. These are only a few of the things they did that the average child does not do.

THREE FEEDINGS A DAY

If children are fed three meals a day and are not overfed, the following high standard will be attained: "ease and comfort through the day and perfect rest at night; freedom from hiccough, vomiting, constipation, 'colds,' diarrhea, digestive disorders, skin eruptions, etc." "There will be a steady gain from month to month, by reason of healthy growth, without the abnormal accumulation of fat so surely indicative of disease." There will be the greatest possible happiness for both the baby and those who care for him. It will not be forever fretting and crying, due to the discomfort of gluttony. Its chances of growing into hale and hearty manhood and womanhood, with good health, and splendid physique, will be increased manyfold.

There is no reasonable basis for the statement, often made, that, while some infants thrive on three meals a day, some probably most, infants would starve unless fed more often. We know that in the feeding of hogs, cows, horses, etc., the ration that suffices for one individual suffices for all. Among adult men and women we do not find the need to feed some of them but three meals a day and others six or eight meals a day .

Infants are fundamentally the same. Their bodies are all constructed alike and function in accordance with the same general principles. One man is a type of the whole race. Young animals, like the calf, kid, etc., which grow more rapidly than does the human infant and reach maturity before the infant has passed babyhood, do not require to be fed as often as we are in the habit of feeding infants.

Dr. Page weaned a kitten at six weeks of age and put her on two meals a day of milk and whole wheat bread. Her meals were served at 8 A. M. and at 8 P. M. When she was two-thirds grown, he says of her that she "has outstripped the others of the same litter, who have been fed oftener in thrift and growth, and in muscular activity she excels them all. Certainly no one could well imagine a livelier kitten than 'Topsy.' In flesh her condition has remained about the same as when feeding was commenced."

That overfeeding tends to stunt growth is well proven. Why should we go on stuffing our children in an effort to fatten them or to force them to grow more rapidly than normal?

Dr. Tilden says that: "If a child (on the three meal plan) grows thin and really loses weight after the second week it will not be an indication that it is not fed often enough. My experience has

—547—

been that the mother's milk is deficient is some of the important elements, or that she does not give enough."

In discussing the three meal plan he says: "If an infant is properly cared for from birth it will not be awake oftener than two or three times — we will say three times — in twenty-four hours. This, then, I assume is as often as nursing children should be fed, and I have succeeded in influencing a few mothers to feed their babies according to this plan, and the results have been gratifying, indeed.

"The children are smaller (not fat) and very active, and much stronger and brighter than children fed in the ordinary way."

He also says: "Children fed three times a day will not be troubled with constipation and will not have white curds in the discharges from the bowels."

Feeding of Infants
CHAPTER XLVII

If Nature has prepared milk for the young animal, it is quite obvious that milk is its natural diet, during the period in which it is provided. The fact that shows clearly and convincingly the splendid food value of milk is that during the period of most rapid growth, in the lives of mammals, milk is the sole food. So efficient is it as a food that a baby ordinarily will double its weight in 180 days with no other article of food. A calf or colt doubles its weight in sixty days and a pig in ten to fifteen days on milk alone. It is equally apparent that the milk of the species of which any young animal belongs is the one best adapted to it.

Certain it is that nature did not intend the baby to chew food until its teeth are sufficiently developed to perform this function. Since they reach this stage of development at from twenty to twenty-four months after birth, there seems to be no earlier need for "solid" foods. If earlier need of such foods exist why does nature not supply the needed chewing equipment at an earlier period?

The natural indications are for an exclusive milk diet for at least the first two years. We add fruit juices, not because there is any need for them in nature's scheme of things, but because in our unnatural life, we do not supply them with milk of proper quality. Soft fruits may be used before the teeth are fully developed, but only after they are sufficiently developed to enable the child to mash these up well.

No other food except milk and fruit juices should be given the child for the first two years of its life. At about eighteen months of age soft fruits may, however, be added to the diet. These should form all or part of one meal a day. If four feedings have been indulged in up to this time one of these should now be stopped. No starchy foods or cereals should be given under two years. Artificial sweets—candies, cakes, pies, sugar, etc., —should never be fed to children. It goes without saying that all food fed to infants and children should be fresh and pure. But we do well to remember that the most wholesome food soon become poisonous if taken in excess.

THE SCIENCE AND FINE ART OF FOOD AND NUTRITION

Investigations made in Boston a few years ago, showed that a breast-fed baby has six times the chance of living through the first year as a bottle-fed baby. Elsewhere I have shown the great percentage of infant deaths from gastro-intestinal disorders. Less than ten percent of the cases of death from "diarrheal causes" occur in breast-fed babies, while ninety percent of all infantile deaths are in the bottle-fed babies.

Breast-fed babies have a better start in life. This can be given them by no other means. As a class they are more vigorous and healthy and are more resistant to disease than bottle-fed babies. They develop into better and stronger children.

Statistics show that only two breast-fed babies contract the so-called contagious diseases where five bottle-fed babies do so, and that where such diseases are contracted the chances for recovery are greatly increased in the breast-fed baby as compared to the chances of the bottle-fed ones. Adenoids and enlarged tonsils are also more common among bottle-fed than among breast-fed babies.

American and English mothers are fast losing the capacity to nurse their babies. Investigations have shown that only 12 per cent of American babies are entirely breast-fed, while 28 per cent are absolutely bottle-fed and the residue from both breast and bottle, but many of these insufficiently from the breast. These young citizens get a bad start in life and the results show up very plainly when the call for men comes, as in the recent war. Hardly more than fifty per cent of the young men of this nation were found physically fit. In New Zealand, where breast feeding is the rule, the infant death rate is only half of that in America. This is significant and should lead mothers to a more wholesome mode of living to enable them to suckle their own children.

NURSING BABY

Nurse your child as long as you can. So long as it is thriving well on your milk this should form its food. If it does not thrive well on this alone, give it an orange juice and grape juice feeding each day, in addition to your own milk. Indeed I believe that with the poor milk supply of modern women, these juices should be fed even if the child does seem to thrive well. See directions in this chapter.

Supplement your own milk with cow's milk or goat's milk, if you must, but do not do so, unless this becomes necessary. Let your child nurse as long as possible, even though it gets only a small amount of its food from you. Up to five years, if you can supply it milk, do so.

Dr. Tilden says: "I am compelled to compromise with most mothers, and permit four feeds a day, and then the majority will sneak in an extra feed at night, which, of course, the baby has to pay for with occasional sick spells."

THE WET NURSE

The wet nurse, though now almost obsolete, has saved the lives of many children and deserves to be restored to her former position from which the cow has dislodged her. That the best food for an infant is that of its own mother is undoubted by those who are in a position to know. Next to this, is the milk of a healthy properly fed wet nurse. Indeed, where the mother's milk is defective, that of another woman will be best for the child.

Formerly, wet nurses were more plentiful than now, because there was more demand for them. Unnatural feeding had not then supplanted the natural method. Many babies can be saved if supplied with the milk of a wet nurse, who will be almost certain to die without it. Others that will eventually "pull through," in spite of artificial feeding, will be saved much illness and suffering and the parents will be spared much anxiety if a good wet-nurse is employed.

The qualifications for a wet-nurse are health and cleanliness. It makes no difference what her race, color or religion, or social status is. She imparts none of these to the child through her milk. In the South are many adults who were nursed at the breasts of "old negro mammies," and though we often hear the old mammies say "that boy sure must have some negro in him," it is not so. We do not become cows by drinking cow's milk.

The Wasserman test is unreliable clap-trap and syphilis is a frightful night-mare. Don't worry over this in choosing a wet nurse. See that she has good health and is cleanly. See that she is properly fed.

It does not hurt a child to be given milk from several women any more than it does to be given milk from several goats or cows. Breast milk, put on ice, will keep as well or better than cow's milk. It is also cleaner and more wholesome. Where a wet-nurse cannot be had, milk taken from more than one woman may be fed the child.

Hospitals, maternity homes, physicians and nurses can usually supply one with a wet nurse. In some of our larger cities, Boston for example, there is a directory for wet-nurses. One can usually be found if we seek diligently enough. An ad in the paper will often produce results.

BEGINNING FEEDING

Real hunger seldom appears for two or three days after birth as is evidenced by the fact that the baby will be satisfied by a water diet. During this period nature does not provide real milk, but a secretion called *colostrum*, which probably serves several needs of the child and does not behave merely as a laxative, as it is usually supposed to do.

We hear of a so-called "inanition fever" that is supposed to develop in rare cases during this period, when it becomes necessary to feed the baby artificially. This is a medical fallacy and need not be considered here.

Some ignorant and ill-advised nurses and mothers, thinking it necessary to feed the baby during this period, when nature has not supplied food, give it cow's milk or sugar in water, or other "food." This is a needless and pernicious practice. The baby need not be put to the breast during the first twenty-four hours after birth.

NIGHT FEEDING

Feeding the baby at night prevents both mother and child from sleeping and teaches the child irregularity in sleep. Night feeding saps the mother in supplying the abnormal quantity of milk and in depriving her of sleep. When the mother's sleep is distrubed in this way, she is weakened and normal secretions are interfered with, resulting in an impairment of her milk. The impairment of the milk reacts unfavorably upon the child. Feeding at night is not only not necessary, it overfeeds and sickens the child.

Dr. Dewey says: "The last thing you should do before entering your beds at night is to nurse your child, and that should be the last nursing until the next morning." With the advice not to nurse the child during the night we fully agre, but the advice to nurse the child the last thing before retiring must be qualified. Women retire at different times of the night. Dr. Dewey adds: "As for night nursing it is entirely a matter of habit and a very bad one. There is absolutely no physiological need for food and a night of rest is no less important for the tender life than for the mother. If the habit has been formed it should always be broken and it will require only a short time in most cases."

HUNGER VS. REGULARITY

Regularity in feeding quickly establishes the stuffing habit. It teaches the infant to eat at certain times as a mere matter of habit, and not because there is a real demand for food. It prevents the development and regulation of natural desire which, alone is a reliable guide to frequency in feeding.

If the child does not relish or desire food it is folly to force or persuade it to eat anyway. Never compel a child to eat. If the child is uncomfortable wait until comfort returns before feeding. Children fed in this way will grow up strong and healthy and miss the so-called children's diseases. Overfeeding and wrong food combinations are responsible for most of the diseases peculiar to children. A little intelligent attention to proper feeding will avoid all of these.

FREQUENCY OF FEEDING

Three to four feedings in twenty-four hours are enough for any baby. Babies fed in this way develop faster than those stuffed in the old way. Over nutrition actually inhibits function and retards growth and development. No feeding should ever be done between meals. Every time a child cries it is not hunrgy. Dr. Dewey insisted that three feedings a day are preferable to more and added: "No infant can starve or fail to fully develop on three full daily meals."

An infant is nourished in proportion to its power to digest and assimilate the food supplied to it, and not in proportion to the quantity of nutriment it may be induced to swallow. Not the larger quantity swallowed, but the right quantity perfectly digested and perfectly assimilated can secure best results with infants as well as in children and adults.

In spite of the obviousness of this principle, it is almost an article of faith with many parents, nurses and doctors, a dogma so firmly fixed in their minds that they cannot be persuaded to the contrary, that the infant that is fed most thrives best. If the infant is losing weight it always suggests the need for a larger supply of food, while every cry means hunger and must be silenced with more food.

The cat, dog, cow, hog and all other animals, do not permit their young to suck as often nor as long as they desire. The cat often absents herself from her kittens for as long as six hours, while I have seen dogs deliberately get up from their resting places when their puppies attempted to nurse, and run away from them. On the plane of instinct there is no such folly as the stuff-them-to-kill-them practice, and the animals are more successful than we.

All around us are healthy-born children who are *"starving to death* under the eyes of parents who would pay a dollar a drop for food to restore them." Many of these children are surrounded with every requirement for a healthful life except one—namely, "the knowledge on the part of the attendants of the fact that the Creator did not design that a baby's stomach should be treated like a toy balloon!" They are famishing from too much feasting.

The chief cause of digestive disorders and of all those other complaints that grow out of these is everfeeding. The habit of feeding babies every two hours during the day and every time it wakes up and cries at night is a ruinous one. Such feeding overworks the baby's digestive organs and introduces an excess of food into the alimentary tract to ferment and poison the child. It weakens and sickens the child producing diarrhea, colic, skin eruptions and more serious disorders.

Dr. Oswald considers "involuntary cramming" among the chief causes of gluttony. "Fond mothers," he says, "often surfeit their babies till they sputter and spew, and it is not less wrong to force a child to eat any particular kind of food against his grain—in disregard of a natural antipathy. Such aversions are allied to the feeling of repletion by which Nature warns the eater to desist, and if this warning is persistently disregarded, the monitory instinct finally suspends its function; overeating becomes a morbid habit our system has adapted itself to the abnormal condition, and every deviation from the new routine produces the same feeling of distress which shackles the rum-drinker to his unnatural practice. Avoid pungent spices, do not cram your children against their will, and never fear that natural aliments will tempt them to excess. But I should add here that of absoultely innocuous food—ripe fruit and simple farinaceous preparations—a larger quantity than is commonly imagined can be habitually taken with perfect freedom from injurious consequences." —*Physical Education*, p. 58-59.

ANIMAL MILKS

Over the earth many animal milks are used—mare's milk, camel's milk, reindeer's milk, ass's milk, goat's milk, cow's milk, etc., serve as human food although, in most parts of the world, the feeding of animal milks to children and infants is not a general practice. In this country cow's milk and goat's milk are about the only kinds used. Despite the many claims made for the superiorty of goat's milk over cow's milk, none of the claims have been substantiated. In my own experience cow's milk has served better in some cases and goat's milk in others. For growth and development animal milks serve better than soy milk and other artificial milks.

Cow's milk, when fed to babies, should be diluted. Equal parts of pure, whole, raw milk, and pure, preferably distilled water, should be given to the young child. Absolutely nothing but water is to be added to the milk. If goat's milk, mare's milk, or ass's milk is used, these same rules and regulations should apply.

Milk for babies should be half-and-half—half water and half milk—up to three months, after which time it may be increased to two-thirds milk and one-third water.

Until the child is six months old, milk feeding should be four to six ounce feedings.

At six months these may be increased to six ounce feedings.

At nine months they may be increased to eight ounce feedings.

Babies should never be given over eight ounces.

One is likely to get a more uniform standard of milk where the milk comes from a herd of cows, than if it is taken from only one cow. It does not injure a baby to have its milk come from several cows in this way.

Milk should be prepared as it is used and not prepared a day's supply at a time. Bottles and nipples should be thoroughly cleansed each time but the usual fuss over this thing is ridiculous and born of the fear engendered by the germ theory. All of this boiling and sterilizing of bottles, nipples and vessels belongs to the germ fetich. It is a lot of bothersome foolishness that is possessed of neither rhyme nor reason. Mothers patiently carry out such processes day after day and, then, when their over-fed, over-heated, over-excited, over-treated babies develop diarrhea or cholera infantum, they accept the doctor's verdict that the child is suffering because of some want of cleanliness on the part of the mother. She failed to boil the nipple long enough, or something. If these mothers could watch young pigs and see how they scoff at this thing called sterilization they would demand of the doctor's intelligent reasons for their babies illnesses.

FEEDING THE MILK

"All milk-eating creatures are and should be sucklings," says Dr. Page. Quite right! Milk should never be drunk like water. Nature teaches us how milk should be taken. So long as your child is to have milk, up to five or six years, give it to him or her from a bottle and nipple. This will insure thorough insalivation and prevent the child from gulping it down.

CERTIFIED MILK

The present method of keeping cows for producing certified milk, in sunless barns, feeding them dry food and tuberculin testing them at frequent intervals and force feeding them, assures us a milk of poor quality.

BOILED MILK

Attention has previously been called to the fact that when milk is boiled or subjected to prolonged heating its complex carbo-phosphates of calcium and magnesium, salts indispensible to the up-building of bone, are precipitated in the form of the quite insoluble salts, calcium-phosphate, magnesium-phosphate and calcium-carbonate. This greatly impairs the physiological usefulness of the salts of the milk.

DEFECTS OF MILK

Barnes, Hume, Hart, Steenbock, Hess, Ellis, Dutcher and their collaborators have shown that the amount of vitamin C in cow's milk rises and falls with the season, being highest from May to July when plants are in their most vigorous stages of development, and lowest in winter, the decrease beginning when the hay is ripened. A single pasteurization of milk suffices to rob it of the little C it contains. Berg has pointed out that "it is owing to this scanty supply of C in the milk that bottle-fed infants sometimes become affected with scurvy. Of course the customary practice of diluting cow's milk for the hand-feeding of infants lowers the percentage of C in the food to a dangerous extent, seeing that the C content of cow's milk is already low in many cases."

It should be apparent that if raw cow's milk is fed to infants in diluted form, the vitamins and salts, in which the milk is deficient, must be supplied from some other source. This need is much greater in the case of pasteurized, boiled, condensed and dried or powdered milk; for, these milks are usually diluted, in addition to being heated. The mere addition of demineralized and devitaminized sugar or syrup, and insoluble lime to the milk will not compensate for these deficiences. It only adds to the deficiencies.

It will be objected that most doctors now give orange juice, or tomato juice, or both. While this is true of many of them, it is alas! also true, that they give these for their vitamins only and, as only small quantities of vitamins are supposed to be needed, these juices are given in quantities too small to make up for the mineral deficiencies. Nor is any effort made to render the protein adequate.

Will it be replied that they feed potatoes and grains as early as possible? I answer: these should not be fed before the end of the second year, because of the a b s e n c e of the starch-splitting enzymes in the child's digestive juices up to this time. There is barely enough ptyalin in the saliva of an infant to convert the sugar of milk into primary dextrose. Feeding these foods to infants and young children is a most prolific cause of gastro-intestinal disturbances. Not only are the starch-splitting enzymes absent, but even were they present, such foods would not excite the flow of saliva and its ptyalin, for they are habitually fed in the form of mush or gruel—boiled and soaked.

ADDITIONS TO MILK

Lime water has been added to the milk of infants for several generations, because the doctors ordered it. The lime is not only of no value to the child, due to its crude form, but it is also an irritant as well as a nutritive evil. An excess of lime, even of the organic lime salts, interferes with the mineral balance in the body. This is of particular importance to young babies. Besides these considerations, cow's milk contains three times as much lime as human milk. The giving of lime salts to children produces acidosis.

Bicarbonate of soda added to the milk of an infant is an unjustifiable stab at the baby's digestion. It increases the alkalinity of the milk and calls for greater effort in digestion. It overworks and impairs the gastric glands. It also destroys some of the vitamins of the milk.

Milk with corn starch, or arrow root, or crackers, or rice, or barley water, or cereal water of any kind, or farina, or oatmeal is an abomination. Babies so fed suffer and die from wasting gastro-intestinal disorders. These foods set up fermentation, diarrhea, etc.

Sugar should never be added to milk. It tends to produce fermentation and all of the resulting evils. A child may be given all the sugar it needs in fruit juices.

When medical men learned that cow's milk contains about twice as much protein as human milk, they began to dilute cow's milk with water when feeding it to infants. But diluting the proteins also dilutes the carbohydrates of milk, so they add sugar, karo syrup and other sweets to the milk. Diluting the milk fifty per cent, reduces its calcium by this same percentage. Lime water is added to make up the deficiency.

Due in part to its greater abundance in the indispensable amino-acid, tryptophan the protein of mother's milk is superior to cow's milk. The growing child needs fairly large amounts of tryptophan and when the protein supply contains only small quantities of this amino-acid, the growth of the organism runs, to an extent, parallel to the ryptophan content. Although the protein content of human milk is little more than half the protein content of cow's milk, the absolute tryptophan content is considerably more in human than in cow's milk. This partly explains why babies grow more rapidly on their mother's milk than on the milk of the cow. Diluting cow's milk reduces the tryptophan content.

As pointed out in a previous chapter, the amino-acids (lecin, lysin, cystin, tyrosin, tryptophan, etc.) are utilized by the body only in proportion to the amounts of other constituents in the diet, which enable the body to synthesize them into proteins peculiar to man. Every dilution of the salts of the milk, which is not made good from some source, renders the milk less adequate as food.

Cow's milk contains nearly four times as much lime as human milk and only about one-half as much iron. Yet, it is the practice, when diluting cow's milk for infants, to add lime and ignore the iron. Children need more iron than adults just as pregnant and lactating women require proportionately more iron than men. When milk is diluted all of its salts are diluted and not merely its lime.

FRUIT JUICES

Dr. Tilden says: "If we ever get on to a rational plan of eating, children up to two years of age will be fed on an exclusive milk diet, with orange or other fruit or vegetable juices."

Fruit juices supply minerals, vitamins and sugar. Grape juice, for example, rich in grape sugar, also supplies, in addition to other minerals iron that is so deficient in diluted milk.

Fruit sugar, or levulose, is predigested and ready for instant absorption and use in the body. It is this predigested sugar that instantly refreshes and revives the greatly fatigued man or woman. The best source of sugar for the infant is found in grapes. Take the required amount of fresh, ripe grapes and crush them in a vessel. Squeeze the juice out of these and strain it. Put it into a bottle and give it to the child just like it takes its milk. Do not dilute the grape juice. Small babies may have four ounces of this at a feeding; older babies, that is after six months, eight ounces. Never give bottled grape-juice. Never cook the grape juice.

When grapes are out of season, unsulphured figs, dates or prunes may be used instead. These should be soaked over night in the usual way, then crushed and the juice strained off. This juice should be fed in a bottle and may be given in the same amounts that the grape juice is given. These sweet fruit juices should not be given with the milk but should be given three or four hours after the milk feeding.

Orange Juice is one of the most delicious and attractive foods that can be fed to babies. It contains pre-digested food that is ready for absorption and utilization when taken. This, perhaps, explains why a glass of orange juice is so refreshing to the tired person or to the man who has been on a fast. The sweeter the orange, the more refreshing it is. Oranges are rich in lime and other alkaline salts and prevent or overcome acidosis. Ignorant doctors who decry oranges because they "make the blood acid" should be prohibited from practice.

The regular eating of orange juice results in the retention of calcium and phosphorus in the body, and in the assimilation of nitrogen (protein), out of all proportion to the amounts of these elements contained in the juice. The juice actually enables the body to utilize the elements better than it could otherwise do. Nothing can be more helpful to children, and particularly undernourished children than orange juice — not two or three spoonfuls a day, but from a glassful to three glasses full. Don't be stingy with the orange juice; stop kidding yourself and the child with teaspoonfuls of the juice.

Orange juice, grape juice, etc., may be given to infants from birth. The two week's old infant should be given the juice of one-half an orange, about two ounces, undiluted. By the time the child is three months old it should be taking four ounces at a feeding, of undiluted orange juice. At six months it should be taking eight ounces. Never add sugar or other substances to the orange juice.

Lemon juice, lime juice, tomato juice, grape fruit juice, melon juice or the juices of other fruits may also be used, but are not always to be had, as is orange juice. Most children will relish grapefruit juice, although many of them refuse tomato juice.

Never give canned or cooked fruit juices to infants and children. Never add sugar, oil or other substance to them.

If four milk feedings are given these juices should be given, not less than thirty minutes before the second milk feeding of the morning and afternoon, or three to four hours after the milk feeding.

FEEDING SCHEDULE

Baby's feeding schedule should be about as follows:

6 A. M. Milk.

10 A. M. grape juice or other sweet fruit juice. (In the south fresh fig juice may be used in season.)

12 Noon, Milk.

3 P. M. to 4 P. M., orange juice or tomato juice or grapefruit juice, or other juice.

6 P. M. Milk.

ARTIFICIAL INFANT FEEDING

So artificial are we in our habits of thinking and acting and so afraid are we of food products as Nature prepares them, that it is becoming more and more the practice to feed infants on artificial food substances. Indeed it is now the practice of physicians to give mothers formulas for preparing artificial foods at once and not wait to see if they can nurse their babies. Booklets by the manufacturers of prepared baby foods or evaporated milks are supplied every mother when she leaves the hospital. The practice actually discourages breast feeding and causes women to distrust raw, fresh milk. Indeed, there are physicians who tell mothers that the evaporated milks are the only safe milks.

I once sat and listened to a physician explain to a young mother the procedures for preparing milk for the hand-feeding of her two-weeks old boy. He talked of Klim, Eskay's Food and other proprietary foods — dried, and condensed milk. When he was asked about raw whole milk, he thought this might be permissible if one was not near a drug store and could not get the dried and condensed varieties.

FEEDING OF INFANTS

Doctors are the victims of the commercial exploiters of baby foods, and patent medicines (proprietary remedies), as often as the public. Only ignorance of nutritive science permits them to "fall" for the claims of the manufacturers of "proprietary foods" for infants. I frequently run across babies that are being fed on pasteurized and even boiled milk, upon the advice of the doctor.

Artificial infant foods are undesirable. Dr. Robert McCarrison of England, says that the "seeds" of *diseases* that inevitably kill their victims in middle life are often introduced into the body with the first bottle of cow's milk or artificial baby food — and he is not referring to germs, either. Dr. Page condemned the various artificial foods, advertised as "substitutes for mother's milk" and, although, "many infants manage to subsist on them, and in many cases thrive on them," he did not consider that such foods are good.

Some years ago Dr. Fischer, in his *Infant Feeding,* gave analyses of some of the powdered milks and infant foods then on the market. "Nestle's Food," "Horlick's Malted Milk," and "Milkine," were shown to be far inferior to mother's milk as food for infants.

Dr. Tilden says: "There are many brands of artificial foods on the market, and there are tons of these foods used in this country every year, but so far as being of real benefit is concerned, it is doubtful if they are beneficial when it comes to supplying a need that can't be supplied by something of greater food value.

"I do not say this from lack of experience, for I have had years of experience. I once believed that most of the better brands were really of great use, but I discovered after a thoughtful retrospection that I have gradually and unwittingly abandoned the use of all of these foods, and it has come about not because I love them less, but because I love natural foods more, and, of course, secure better results with them."

McCarrison says: "I would ask you to consider °°° the increasing tendency in modern times to rear infants artificially — on boiled, and dried milks, on proprietary foods which are all of them vastly inferior to healthy mother's milk in substances essential to the well being of the child — inferior not only in vitamins, but also in enzymes, thyroid derivatives and other essentials."

Mendel says:: "In the preparation of some of the present-day proprietary infant's foods — products so numerous and presented with such conflicting claims that the physician and mother alike are bewildered as to choice — there is considerable 'juggling' with facts in novel ways. Novelty should not be a bar to recognition; but are we on safe ground in the ready acceptance of the newest commercial tendencies?"

In U. S. Dept. of Labor Bulletin No. 8, *Care of Children* series, are these words about artificial baby foods: "The general concensus of opinion among authorities seems to be that one or another of these baby foods may be temporarily used if fresh cow's milk is not available, as in traveling or in the tropics, but their continued and exclusive use is to be condemned. All are expensive and many of them do not give the baby the required food elements, nor the proper proportion of these elements, while the use of some of them is known to be followed by various forms of illness."

Scurvy, rickets, anæmia and malnutrition are often the results of the use of artificial foods. Many children seem to thrive on them for a while, may actually appear to do better than those fed on their mother's milk, and then disaster overtakes them. Be not deceived by the advertisements of those who have infant foods to sell. These concerns exist for profit and not for baby's welfare.

Condensed milk, evaporated milk, dried milk and other artificial foods are unfit for the baby and no intelligent mother will ever feed these to her child.

SUMMER FEEDING

Hot weather is accused of having much to do with the fearful slaughter of the human animal — a distinctly tropical animal and certainly well adapted to a hot climate.

Blaming hot weather for certain "diseases peculiar to children" and for the deaths in these conditions, is a very misleading way of saying, as Page puts it, that, "the excess of food that can be tolerated under the tonic and antiseptic influence of cold weather, *engenders disease during the heated term.*"

Hot weather favors decomposition, cold weather retards it. But, on the whole, we are hurt almost, if not quite as much by food excess in the winter as in summer. We are more likely to have bowel diseases in summer, respiratory diseases in winter—this is the chief difference.

Adults usually instinctively eat less in hot weather than in cool or cold weather. They often miss a meal or two altogether. How often do we hear one say "it is too hot to eat!" We find the adult also, without any scientific knowledge of Trophology, living largely on green vegetables, fresh fruits, melons, etc. They consume bread, potatoes, meats, cereals, etc., in less liberal quantities. They frequently omit the noon-day meal.

How many parents exercise as much common sense in feeding their infants and children during the summer? How often do we see the suffering infant crammed with as much milk as during the winter? Then when the baby is made sick—there is diarrhea or fever—we see it dosed and drugged to drive the demon of disease out of its little body.

FEEDING DIFFICULTIES

The feeding method in vogue is a hit and miss system. It is a case of "try this" and "try that" and then try something else. The mother, the nurse and the physician chase "from pillar to post" and tax themselves to the uttermost to find a suitable food. If they find a diet that fits they do not know why is fits. If the diet fails to fit, they are equally in the dark. So long as the child appears to do well on a given diet they are satisfied; but if it develops a diarrhea or an "upset stomach," a change is made and another food tried. This continues until all known foods have been tried out. The little victims of the guessing and abuse who are fortunate enough to survive in spite of such handicaps, finally arrive at the period when they are taken off the baby foods and then the death rate is lowered. Credit for the child's salvation is attributed to the baby food that chanced to be used last.

Much of the troubles in hand-fed infants, which apparently call for modification of the milk, are due to extra-feeding factors. They may be due to overfeeding, in which case the digestive tract requires a rest. They are frequently due to physical and psychological factors that demand attention. Too much noise, too much excitement, over heating, undue chilling, overclothing, lack of rest and sleep, "infection," congenital weakness, lack of fresh air, harsh care, too much bathing, etc., are factors that tend to upset the digestive systems of infants, as of adults.

The healthy, hungry infant can digest almost any sensibly modified milk mixture. The unhealthy infant often needs changes in its care and environment more than in its food. Regularity in feeding often leads to over-feeding and trouble. Mothers and physicians have developed the insane notion that babies should be fed regularly, whether or not there is any actual need for food. They do not allow for the normal from day to day variations in physiologic demands.

Mothers are cautioned to awaken the baby promptly at feeding time (as determined by the clock) and most of them are foolish enough to do so. This teaches the child to eat as a matter of habit and not to supply any existing need and also disturbs its sleep.

The present popular method of feeding is what really makes the problem of infant feeding a difficult one. There is no way to adapt even the most wholesome and easily digested food to an infant when it is fed in such quantities. With proper feeding it is but little trouble to find a food that will " agree" with the baby.

What is the great secret of success in feeding babies? Dr. Tilden well expresses it thus: "Fit children to the food and never attempt to fit the food to the children." How? Easy! Watch these few simple rules:

1. Feed the child natural, that is, uncooked, unprocessed, unsterilized, unadulterated, undrugged, foods.

2. Do not stuff the child. Feed it three moderate meals a day.

3. Feed simple meals. Do not feed foods that are mixed in such a way as to cause fermentation.

4. Do not feed between meals, nor at night.

5. If the child is upset, or feels bad, or is excited or tired, or over heated, or chilled, or in pain or distress, or is sick, don't feed it. If there is fever, give no food.

Feeding Children from Two to Six Years
CHAPTER XLVIII

At the zoo here in San Antonio there are signs warning visitors not to feed the animals. The signs read as follows: "All birds and animals are scientifically fed the correct foods — in proper quantities to insure best physical condition." "The feeding of tid-bits and wrong kinds of food by the public is very harmful — and represents a cruel practice — which the Zoological Board cannot allow."

In this same city, as in all other cities, there are thousands of children who are fed haphazardly, unscientifically and inadequately. The children are sickly, undeveloped, undernourished and deprived of many of the joys of life.

Everywhere one goes he sees children eating cookies, candies, crackers, ice cream and other worthless things. "With hands full of cookies and pockets full of peanuts" they gorge and stuff, filling their little bodies with these acid-forming foods and robbing their tissues of their precious alkaline elements. Children are frequently made into a veritable dumping ground for all the various patented foods, emulsions, and even drugs that clever advertisers offer to the public and to physicians.

Parents often feel sorry for their children when they see them deprived of certain foods, but they are wasting their sympathies. Such sympathies are tantamount to wishing for them a continuance of disease. "When parents are intelligent enough to know their duty to their children," says Dr. Tilden, "they will not feel sorry for them because they are not eating in a way to make them sick." Too many parents are ruled by their emotions and sentiments and not by knowledge and reason. Give children those foods that are good for them and do not cultivate in them an appetite for harmful foods.

If you desire to bring up your child without the need of a doctor, with perfect digestion, freedom from disease, good teeth, a splendid body and alert mind, follow the advice given herein and keep away from sugars, refined starches and all processed foods. If you are fond of adding to the incomes of physicians and also of seeing your children suffer and die, follow the "good old fashioned way" that is the vogue all around you.

FRUITS AND VEGETABLES

Beginning with the second year fruits and vegetables may be added to the child's diet. Any fruit in season, if well ripened, may be fed. There is no reason to fear fruit of any kind; peaches, plums, apricots, cherries, figs, apples, pears, grapes, berries, bananas, and so on through the whole list. Give the child the pulp and all —not merely the juice. Water melons, cantalopes, honey dew melons and melons of all kinds may be given. All kinds, of nuts, except peanuts, which are not nuts, may be given.

Any or all fresh vegetables may be given either raw or cooked, preferably raw. Spinach, chard, kale, cabbage, beet tops, turnip tops, asparagus, celery, lettuce, tomatoes, onions, squash, fresh green beans, brussels sprouts, cauliflower, etc., may all be given the child. Carrots, peas, fresh corn, (not canned corn or peas), beets, parsnips, salsify, etc., may also be fed. Ther is no reason to fear to feed your child vegetables, provided they are fresh and properly prepared.

Berg advises "from five to seven times as much vegetables, potatoes and salt-rich fruits (apples and pears are poor in this respect), as of meat, eggs or cereal products—for otherwise an adequate excess of bases cannot be guaranteed," to supply the needs of growing children. With this I concur. The pregnant and nursing mother should make up her diet in the same way, if she wishes to supply her child with adequate bases.

PROTEIN REQUIREMENTS

The growing organism requires a little more protein than the adult organism, but it has been clearly and definitely shown by numerous tests that the difference between the minimum amount required to maintain weight and the optimal requirement for growth is not great. Any excess of protein above the optimal requirement for growth does not increase the rate of growth. Nothing is to be gained from overfeeding on proteins. "Nitrogen, the chief ingredient of protein, is universally a good servant, but a bad master," says the British biologist, H. Reinheimer. It is therefore, best to avoid overfeeding of protein.

MASTICATION

The child should be taught early to thoroughly masticate all food. This is best done by giving it foods that require chewing when the child first begans to eat solid food. Many mothers feed their children mushes, gruels, and foods that have been put through a sieve (perhaps because the child specialist has ordered it), which may be swallowed without chewing. The result is they never learn to chew. Never give a child mashed food or mush. If the child can't chew its food it is not ready for that kind of food.

NUMBER OF MEALS

Give the child three meals a day, including his three nursings which are simply supplemented with these foods.

COMBINATIONS

It is necessary to observe the same rules for combining foods, when feeding these to the child as when feeding them to the adult.

VARIETY

This varied or general diet idea has been and is being greatly overworked, both as regards children and adults. At no previous period in history did man have the great variety of foods he now has. But he does not need to eat every food that grows just because they are now available.

Children quite naturally eat monotrophic meals. They like to make a meal on one thing. Parents usually do not permit them to do this, being under the variety "spell" and being convinced that we must have our variety all at one meal. If children were given natural foods they could safely be left to follow out their instinctive monotrophic practices. But to permit a child to make a meal on jam and bread, or on cake, or on cheese, or macaroni, would be no good.

ADAPTATION

My observations have led me to believe that children adjust themselves to the diet the mother has taken during pregnancy and lactation, more readily than to other diets. Certain experiments with insects have shown this to be positively so among these. Further study will show whether or not my observations of infants are accurate. If they are accurate they open the way for parents to adjust their children to the best diets.

INSTINCTIVE EATING

It would be safe to turn children loose and let them eat what and when they will, just as animals do, provided they are supplied with natural foods, are not urged to overeat and their sense of taste has not previously been perverted and the stuffing habit has not been cultivated in them. Don't season and sweeten their foods to stimulate a false appetite and induce them to over eat.

Supply them with plain, wholesome natural foods and no other kind and leave it to their natural instincts to teach them to eat foods that are good for them. Set them a good example—they will follow a good example as readily as they will a bad one.

FORCED EATING

One of the most common crimes against children is that of compelling them to eat when there is no desire nor demand for food. Many mothers complain that their children will not eat. They have to coax or force children to eat. If there is no desire for food, none should be given. Children may be depended upon, always, to take food, if and when they are hungry. If the child is not hungry let him go without food. His own sense of hunger is a better guide as to when he should eat than all the science of all the ex-spurts in the world, who know all about the thing, and know it all wrong.

Morse-Wyman-Hill say children "must be made to eat what is given them, *** whether they like it or not, because it is most important for older children and adults to eat a general diet. *** A baby should be made to eat its foods as they are given to it, even if its nose has to be held in order to make it swallow."

This is criminal advice and if followed, is a sure way of creating in the child an antipathy towards its food or some food and a spirit of antagonism. The spirit of children is not so easily broken and subdued as these authors assert. They resist coercion long after an adult has submitted himself to the yoke and become a slave.

Children who refuse to eat at meal times are those, usually, who are permitted to munch crackers, cakes, candies, and other such dietetic abominations between meals. They are not hungry when meal time arrives. But there is a more profound reason why this type of diet "spoils the appetite." It loads the body with an excess of denatured carbohydrate and, in self-defense, nature cuts off the demand for food.

There is no indispensible food. If a child does not like spinach and many of them do not, there are other foods just as good, or better, that he will like. I have seen a baby's nose held to force it to swallow a poisonous drug prescribed by a doctor, and I don't believe in this method of forcing a distasteful food down a child's throat any more than I believe in its use to compel the child to swallow the doctor's dope.

LACK OF APPETITE

McCarrison regards loss of appetite as an evidence of food deficiency. We noted in a previous chapter that animals fed on a mineral-free diet soon refused their food and had to be force fed. Experimenters who have, themselves, gone on a deficient diet, a white-bread diet for example, note the same thing. McCarrison says "It seems to me that 'loss of appetite' is one of the most fundamental signs of vitamin deprivation. It is a protective sign; the first signal of impending disaster. It should at once excite suspicion as to the quality of the food in any patient who may exhibit it."

The head of a boarding school for children here informs me that children come to the school, thin, pale and without appetite and that on the abundance of fruits and green vegetables, they receive at the school, they gain weight, become normal in color and develop good appetites. I have seen the same thing occur many times in my own practice when mothers have brought their puny children to me with the wail that the children will not eat— "I have to make him (or her) eat." If a child is obviously undernourished and refuses food, it must be because its protective instincts have rebelled against more of the deficient food. Only a well nourished child can have a truly normal (or natural) food-demand. A finicky appetite should cause parents to become suspicious of the child's eating.

McClendon noted among American soldiers in the trenches, that when theier rations were restricted to eggs, sugar, chocolate and dried milk made into a sort of biscuit, a craving for fresh foods became overpowering within two or three days and caused them to refuse their rations. He considers that in a state of nature this craving has tremendous survival value for man and animal.

Children do not have to be forced to eat that which is wholesome and good, if they have been fed properly from the start and have not had their appetite and sense of taste spoiled by sugar, salt, pepper, spices, etc. Too many children have their appetites for plain food spoiled by the vulgar habit of seasoning their foods and cultivating in them the same perversions of the sense of taste and the same abnormal cravings that are seen in adults. Jam or jelly is put on their bread or crackers, sugar is put into their milk, sweet cookies are fed to them often, they are given candy or ice cream or little knick-nacks between meals, or they are given sugar out of the sugar bowl. Mayonnaise or other such slop is smeared over their food. Their appetites become so cloyed and their sense of taste so perverted that they no longer enjoy simple foods. When they grow older their perverted taste and jaded appetites and overstimulated bodies will demand tobacco, alcohol, and petting; also sex-slush in their movies and novels.

Children are victims of the fallacy that they require lots of fats and sugars and starches, which has evolved the present onesided and deficient diet. This diet is virtually robbed of mineral salts and vitamins and then doctors and parents add a few teaspoonfuls of tomato juice, or orange juice and nauseous cod-liver oil to this diet, to make up for its deficiencies. Cod-liver oil and other fatty emulsions added to a diet already over-burdened with fat only helps to make the child sick.

FOOD FEARS

A few words may be said about the foods that people have unfounded fears concerning.

Fruits are especially valuable for the mineral salts, sugar, organic acids, vitamins and distilled water which they contain.

I once saw a little child pick up a luscious ripe cherry in a fruit store and start to eat it. Her mother immediately said: "Don't put that in your mouth; it is not good for you. I will give you a cake when we get outside, but don't eat that."

Such lamentable ignorance! Most people deserve to lose their children. My sympathies are for the children. Any parent can have the truth about the proper care of children who will seek to acquire it. Most of them are too brain-lazy and indifferent. It is so much easier to follow traditions and customs.

If this mother desired to teach her child not to take fruit from the store, she certainly went at it the wrong way. The idea that she conveyed to the child was not that it should not take the fruit, because it should never take that which belongs to another; but that she should not eat the fruit, because it was not good for her—would make her sick.

Bananas have long been condemned by the medical profession as indigestible. This was declared false by the Hygienists who highly recommended them. "Orthodox" experimenters now declare that the banana, when fully ripe, is easily digested. But the average physician has not found this out. Bananas are very wholesome food and rank high in vitamins. They should only be eaten when thoroughly ripe, and should never be cooked.

Apples are among the choicest of foods. They are rich in phosphoric acid and are especially valuable for nervous and rickety children. They contain much iron in its most assimilable form.

Strawberries are delicious and contain a sweet acid that makes them popular as food. They are rich in food-iron and food lime, excelling all other fruits, except the raspberry and fresh figs, in richness in iron. They are also richer in iron than most vegetables, being excelled as a source of iron only by green peas and fresh lima beans. They are also rich in vitamins.

Dewberries, blackberries, raspberries, huckleberries, and all other berres are fine for children. They should always be fed raw, never cooked, and never with sugar.

Preserved Fruits are confections. Do not consume these abominations with any thought that they represent fruit.

Sugar and honey should never be eaten with fruit of any kind. Fermentation is almost sure to result.

Nuts are also very bad and very indigestible, if we listen to the antiquated pill-peddlers and serum squirters, who claim to have been commissioned by the Almighty to look after our health. Nuts are not indigestible. They are the best of foods, and if thoroughly masticated, and not eaten at the end of a hearty meal, are easily enough digested.

Raw Starch is not indigestaible as is generally taught and believed. It is well known that cattle digest raw starch more easily and completely than cooked starch.

PERNICIOUS FOODS

Do not give the child any processed starches, refined sugars, so-called "breakfast foods." Corn flakes, puffed rice, puffed wheat, bran foods, cream of wheat, cream of barley, wheatena, etc., are not good foods for child or adult. All the great claims made for them are false. For heaven's sake never feed these things to your child. Oatmeal is perhaps the worst of all cereals for child or adult. Cereals are among the most difficult of foods to digest. These certainly do not belong in the diet of infants and young children when the ability to digest starch is so low.

The cracker-habit usually follows the sucking habit. Baby discards its nipple and takes up the cracker. If he is taken to church, to the theatre, to the park, to a friend's house or goes to see grandma, he must have his cracker. Mother carries a whole box of crackers—nice white ones, well salted, or "graham" crackers, well sweetened—along with her, for baby must have a cracker every few minutes. If he does not get a cracker he is pulling at mother's dress and crying and fretting. The cracker is given him to solace him and keep him quiet. Poor mother! Poor child! They are both undisciplined and ignorant. Mother is the slave of her badly spoiled child and is as badly spoiled as the child.

The whole program of living of such children is wrong and in need of correction from the ground up. Can such mothers be induced to make the needed change? Have they the moral courage to let the baby "cry it out" and adjust himself to a better life? I fear not. Their emotions would get the best of them.

Children are given tea, coffee, cocoa and chocolate to drink and eat, doctors often advising these poisonous substances. These things are properly called drugs and produce definite "physiological" effects when taken into the body. It is certainly not desirable to start children off with poison-habits of this kind. No good can come from the over-stimulation, loss of sleep and overwork of the kidneys these produce.

Sugar: Dr. Wm. H. Hay says: "Without a doubt the greatest curse of the early years of child life is the general impression that sugars are good for active children, furnishing many calories of energy, either this or the use of pastries and the two evils are one, for the same objection that holds against the sugars holds equally against the pastries."

One's heart must grow faint when he sees the children of this country stuffing bon-bons, cakes, crackers, bread and jam, candy, ice cream, soda-fountain slops, and similar stuff down their throats at all hours of the day. What do parents mean by giving these things to their children?

Children soon cultivate a "sweet-tooth" and are not long in learning that they can get what they cry for, if they only cry loud enough and long enough. How many mothers and fathers have the moral courage to listen to a baby's cry? Not many. They are ruled by sentiment and emotion, rather than by knowledge and reason. It is so hard for them to listen to the cry of the baby; they feel so sorry for the poor child. They don't want their baby to cry. It is so hard on their nerves to listen to baby cry. They are just moral cowards and sentimental jelly-fish, who injure their children physically, mentally, emotionally, socially and morally, because they have not disciplined themselves to do what is right. They take the easiest course for the present, little reckoning that they have to pay for it later.

Baby soon learns that if it will only cry for a few minutes it does not have to eat spinach, but can have cake instead. Mother will give it ice-cream or candy if it only cries for it. What a terrible moral lesson to teach a child!

Morse-Wyman-Hill say: "There is no food which causes more disturbances of digestion in childhood than sugar. As money is said to be the root of all evil, so sugar may be said to be the root of all disturbances of digestion in childhood. Further than this, sugar is a very common cause of loss of appetite, and destroys their appreciation of proper food. It also, more than any other one thing, is responsible for the decay of children's teeth. Candy, therefore, should never be given to children. It can do them no good and may do them much harm. It is idle, of course, to claim that two or three pieces of candy a day will disturb the average child's digestion or prevent its normal development. Children that have two or three pieces, however, usually want more, and are quite likely to get more. It is true that some kinds of candy are richer and more indigestible than others, but they are all made of sugar, and plain sugar is bad for children. Children should be brought up not to eat sugar on anything. There is no objection to putting a little sugar in the food during its preparation, but no sugar should be put on it when it is served. (This is a case of splitting hairs—sugar is just as harmful when put in the food as when put on it. H. M. S.)

"It is often said that sugar is a necessary article of diet for children. This belief is fostered by the manufacturers of sugar and candy. It is, however, not true. Carbohydrates are advisable for children as a source of energy. They are not absolutely necessary, however, as is shown by the fact that Eskimo children grow up without them." (Eskimo children do not grow up without carbohydrates. H. M. S.)

Sugar, candy, syrup, etc., inhibit gastric secretion and impair digestion. This is true of cakes, pies, etc. It is just as true of brown sugar, maple sugar and cakes and cookies made of wholewheat flour and brown sugar or honey, as of white sugar and white flour products.

Two or three pieces of candy a day may not perceptibly injure children; but when it is added to the cookies, cakes, pies, jams, jellies, white bread, denatured cereals, saturated with white, or even brown sugar, mashed potatoes, pasteurized milk and other denatured products, it only adds to an already preponderantly acid forming diet and further leeches the child's body of its precious alkaline elements.

Many candies contain poisonous dry-stuffs, adulterants, flavors, etc., as well as nuts, milk and other things that form, with the sugar, bad combinations.

Ice-cream is an abominable mixture of canned milk, powdered milk, pasteurized milk, gelatin, sugar or syrup, coloring matter, flavoring extracts and often canned fruits. It is no good for child or adult.

The following is quoted from *The Ice Cream Field*, the National Journal of the ice-cream manufacturers, for July, 1928; and is headed, "Baby Specialist Favors Ice Cream:"

"Ice cream has been prescribed for infant food for several years by Dr. Luther R. Howel, of Columbus, Ohio, one of America's leading baby specialists. Dr. Howel states that ice cream has proven an ideal food for undernourished babies and in several instances was a means of saving their lives. He says that the homogenization of milk and cream, as carried out in the manufcturing process of ice cream, makes the food particularly digestible, an important factor in infant feeding."

This is just plain ordinary bunk and known to be false even by the man who made the statement. In *McCall's Magazine*, July, 1926, Dr. E. V. McCollum wrote: "These is no more attractive way of serving milk to your family than in good ice cream. We have constantly emphasized the importance of drinking more milk, for the average amount consumed per person is still far too low. The more frequent serving of ice cream at the family table is one of the easiest ways of getting milk into the diet, especially for children who do not like milk and for persons who demand food with marked flavors."

Men who have been stung by the milk-bug don't care how they get milk into you, so long as they get you to take it. Why do children cease to like it? If milk is so necessary, why does nature cut off both the supply and the demand? In opposition to this rank nonsense about ice-cream, I offer the following words of Morse-Wyman-Hill, who say:

"Ice-cream, ice-cream soda and other sweet drinks **** are always inadvisable for and usually harmful to children. They are harmful chiefly because of the sugar which they contain, partly because they are too cold, partly because they are too rich, and partly because they are usually taken bewteen meals. Children would be better off without any of them. Ice-cream is probably less harmful than the others. Vanilla ice-cream is not as rich as the other kinds. The majority of people are so willing to take the chance of injuring their children's health in order to give them temporary pleasure that we have found it useless to attempt to cut ice-cream entirely out of the diet of children. We therefore compromise and allow the children to have plain vanilla ice-cream without any sauce on it once a week."

It was asserted at a dental meeting a few years ago that slaughter-house offal and scraps are now bought up and the fat rendered out of these and used in ice-cream instead of the cream of milk—cooked animal tallow, suet and lard are now sold to your children in ice cream!, while subsidized ex-spurts lure you on to "eat a plate of ice-cream every day," and tell you that ice-cream is a "health food."

Give no sugar, salt or soda with anything. The practice of neutralizing the acid of lemons, by adding soda to the lemon juice, is both useless and injurious.

Meat should never be fed to a child under six years of age, and better never at all. Meat broths have practically no value. They act as excitants rather than as nutriments and should not be fed to children. Eggs are not good foods for children any more than for adults. Pickles are indigestible and unfit for food.

FISH OILS

Cod Liver Oil is not to be regarded as a food. Its use as a *medicine* covers several centuries but its magic virtues are recent discoveries. For a few years it was a specific for rickets, both preventing and curing the disease. Now it must have the aid of better food and sunlight, or at least lamp light. There is not really much attention given to sunlight.

Mr. Harter's statement that the giving of "from six to ten drops of cod-liver oil every other day, increasing the proportion as the child becomes older, until at the age of twelve the child is taking" a half tea-spoonful three times a week "sounds a little like witchcraft," is good. He adds, "It seems only a step from oil from fish livers to the extract of frogs' tongues and newts' gizzards."

THE SCIENCE AND FINE ART OF FOOD AND NUTRITION

I have never used cod-liver oil, but it has fallen to my lot to care for children to whom it had been given for longer or shorter periods without benefit. I have seen troubles that I am convinced resulted from its use. I advise all parents not to give it to their children.

When the Hawaiian Islands were first discovered, these people, among the finest in the world, had no milk, no cod liver oil and no grains. Their diet had lacked these things for centuries, perhaps since about 1 A. D., when the first people are supposed to have arrived on the Islands. Their splendid bodies and great vigor proved these "indispensibles" not to be indispensible.

Man Shall Not Diet with Food Alone
CHAPTER XLIX

Radiant health depends on a number of factors. It is not a matter merely of adequate vitamins, or correct diet. Fresh air, sunshine, exercise, sufficient rest and sleep, emotional poise, freedom from devitalizing habits—these are all essential to recovery of health as well as to maintenance of health.

Every physico-chemical process of the body is correlated with others and any failure in one spells a corresponding failure in the correlated process. It is a symbotic principle that a failure in any of the functions of life, due to a failure of the conditions upon which function depends, results in a crippling of the symbiotic support which the (failing) function normally gives to all of the other functions of the body.

The normal activity of all the functions of the body is based upon the supply of all of the natural conditions upon which function depends and a failure in only one of these conditions reduces the effectiveness of all of the other cooperating and interacting conditions. Due to the interrelations and interdependencies of the organism any interference with the functions of an organ, either as a result of unnatural "stimulation," or as a result of a lack of natural "stimulation," is interference with all of them.

In a previous chapter we learned of the "synergistic actions" of the various food factors. It is necessary for nutritionists to learn the synergistic relationships that exist between other factors of living and food. Man does not live by food alone. He breathes, drinks, works, plays, sleeps, rests, thinks, emotes, reproduces, misbehaves, etc. He lives in the sun or in the shadows. He is not what he eats; he is the sum total of the effects of all the factors of life. Exercise improves his assimilative power. If he is fatigued or enervated, rest has the same effect. Sunshine helps him to assimilate his foods. It helps him to convert certain pro-vitamins into vitamins. A state of toxemia prevents due utilization of his foods. A fast is often the surest and only means of restoring normal nutrition.

Our dietitians have not yet learned to prescribe for their patients a *balanced life,* hence their patients miss the benefits that flow from the synergism of all the factors of living. Bear always in mind that in a simple, well-balanced and well-ordered life all the synergisms of all the factors of living are at work.

No doubt, too, all wrong factors of life have "synergistic actions," so that in a disordered life, all the synergisms of wrong living habits and wrong influences work together in tearing down and weakening the body.

Life is not purely a matter of food, as was shown in Vol. 1, and all efforts to treat man by diet alone must fail. It is significant that practically all the remarkable successes obtained with "diet cures" have been in experimental animals and children. It is equally significant that "diet cures" are far more successful in animals than in children.

There is a reason for this: A reason that is seldom suspected by the gum-willies of the "food research" laboratories and the cure-mongers of the ancient order of Aesculapius. With their specific and entitative diseases, produced by specific causes and requiring specific cures, they flounder hopelessly in a sea of confusion of their own making.

The life of a human being, child or adult, is much more complex than that of any experimental animal in the laboratory. His environment is more varied, his contacts greater in number, the influences to which he is subjected more numerous and the resources of that environment much greater.

Even the animal is not a mere test-tube. *Statistical regularity* is all that can be secured in experiments with these. "Because you get a result in animals with fair uniformity," says Dr. Howe, "it does not necessarily follow that you will inevitably and uniformly get identical results in humans from the same procedure. Every little while something occurs to show me anew that the animal is not a mere test-tube. He is apt to take a part in the process going on in his body, and he may sometimes take the part by means of a mechanism or a product about which we know little or nothing."

Faulty diet is the chief, though, by no means the sole cause of lowered resistance and disease in children; in adults it is one of a whole series of crippling influences of which it is often difficult to determine which is producing most harm, but all of which must be corrected before good health can be restored. Efforts to cure the effects of dissipation without correcting the dissipation, by administering a diet cure, is so ridiculously childish that it ought to appear so even to medical cure mongers, dietitians and other like cooties.

In the laboratory, the self-styled "research worker" takes a group of healthy, vigorous young animals, places them under the most hygienic conditions and, then, feeds them deficient diets. He proves that by a deficient diet he can produce certain types of disease, and by correcting the diet he can cure these so-called "diseases." Indeed, McCarrison found that by deficient diet he could produce, and by correct diet, remedy practically every "disease" from which man suffers.

The fact is that, while there is a fundamental unity in all animal life, from amoeba to man, there are specific differences, even between closely related species, that make animal experiments often misleading. There is only one experiment that can be relied upon in man and this must be performed on man, not on guinea pigs or rats.

The last experiment must always be upon man, testified Professor Starling before the British Royal Commission Investigating Vivisection. Why? Because what works on animals does not always work an man.

Pharmacologists follow, literally, the old advice to "try it on the dog" and try out their drugs on various kinds of animals. They long ago discovered that the same drug induced or provoked different reactions in different kinds of animals. The only way they can determine what action it will occasion in man is by trying it out on man.

A pigeon can take enough morphine to kill several men and fly away as though nothing happened. Hogs can take without apparent harm enough prussic acid to kill many men. Rabbits grow fat on belladonna, but if we included it in the salads fed our children, we would soon be without children.

What is known as the "biological test" in feeding, that is, trying it out on the dog, turns out as much fallacy as trying out drugs on the dogs. I have often wondered what the "biologists" would feed us if they used sewer rats as experimental animals. If they were to use buzzards in their experiments they would discover that rotting meat from a hog that had died of cholera is good food. Dogs eat bones and digest them with ease. It is doubtful that man could get away with a bone diet so easily. Tobacco worms live on tobacco—you try it, worm.

Anything we desire to prove can be proved on the lower animals if we only use a sufficient number of kinds of animals. Rat-pen (or guinea pig) dietetics has simply led the dietitians astray in more ways than one. They have worked out their solutions to human problems in their test tubes, guinea pigs and rats, and not in the human body. As a consequence, they do not even know dietetics.

Dr. Pearl T. Swanson, of Iowa State College reported that "Experiments with rats indicate that 'complete reproductive failure' results when mother animals lack meat." She adds that the "deficiency" is "not made up by pork." Beef should be eaten. Her experiments "showed" that the diet must be made up of 30% protein. To such a result, we answer: Rats! Tell it to the old gray mare and hear a real horselaugh. Tell her that her colt will be born dead, or that she will be unable to suckle her colt, or that her grandchildren will be sterile, unless she eats beef. Tell it to the wild ass and listen to his bray. Tell it to the old cow whose calf is busy extracting the lactic juice from her over-distended udder. Try to convince the dairyman whose prize cow gives seven gallons of milk each day that unless he feeds her on beef, she will not be able to supply sufficient milk for her calf. Tell the story to the ewe that without beef her lambs will be born dead. Tell the mountain goat that if she does not eat beef her kids will starve for lack of milk. Remind the doe that her fawns will be sterile in the third generation if she does not eat enough beef. Tell the story to the musk-ox, the elephant, the rhinoscerous, the giraffe, camel, bison, buffalo, rabbit, the great apes, parrot, etc. Publish the story far and wide. Let all the earth know that a woman out in Iowa has "discovered" by "research" and "experiment," that she has proved by the "scientific method," that if female animals do not have an abundance of beef in their diet, their young are born dead, they are unable to supply sufficient milk for their young and in the third generation their offspring become sterile.

Go into crowded India and China and tell the vegetarian millions of these lands that in another three generations their countries will be depopulated unless the mothers of these lands eat beef. Tell the news to the many vegetarians of America, some of them fourth generation vegetarians, that they are headed for rapid extinction along with the horse and cow, if they do not eat beef. A rat-pen dietitian has proved it, and let no one doubt the findings of the infallible "scientific method."

It would be folly to say their animal experimentation has not provided some knowledge or that it has not supplied leads that have been useful, but the tendency is to rely too much on the results of the animal experiments in feeding men, women and children.

The laboratory man's problems are simple. He makes them himself and solves them quite readily. He deals with controlled experiments and knows all the elements of his experiment. Compared to this, the life of even the youngest child is a complex mosaic of interlacing influences that are not dreamed of in the laboratory man's philosophy. The experimenter has proved that a deficient diet will produce disease, but he has been too prone to overlook the significant fact that a perversion of nutrition, due to any other cause, will produce disease; so-called defiency diseases, as well as other types, despite a theoretically perfect dietary.

Anything that increases the body's food needs, such as growth, hard work, extreme cold, wasting disease, and anything which tends to hinder absorption, such as gastro-intestinal disorders from whatever causes, predisposes to scurvy, beri beri, malnutritional edema, rickets, pellagra, tuberculosis, anemia, atrophy, polyneuritis and other nutritional diseases.

Decadence of functional power follows upon any artificial or vicarious interference which seeks to supplant the natural functions of the body. The best diet possible can be aborted in its health-building potentialities by the presence of excitants and artificial "aids" to the functions of life.

We are safe in saying that every case of leanness is due to under-nourishment; but we would be far wrong if we asserted that the under-nourishment is due, in every case, to insufficient food. The majority of such cases are due to nervous depletion brought on by a hundred and one different causes. Grief, worry and excessive mental activity almost always leads to loss of weight. Sexual excesses and abuses lead to nervous depletion, digestive impairment and loss of weight. Indigestion, due to long continued over-eating, is a frequent cause of faulty nutrition. So, also, is a lack of sunshine. There are so many causes which are not considered in these laboratory experiments.

Trophology should consist of more than merely a consideration of foods, for a failure in any of the important nutritive factors will abort the health-building potentialities of the best of foods.

In the sick room, in the sanitarium, in all the departments of life, in every phase of health-disease, we do not deal in controlled experiments. Our subjects are not "controls." Our problems are not self-made. We have hundreds of factors and influences to consider that the laboratory man knows nothing of. The problems we are required to solve are as complex as his are simple. The problems increase in complexity as the age of our patient advances and his sphere of activity widens. We know, even if the curemongers and peddlers of diet-specifics do not, that the correction of the diet of a patient, however helpful this may prove, is almost never sufficient to restore sound, vigorous health.

Man is not what he eats any more than he is what the thinks. He is a complex product of heredity and environment and into his make-up there enter many different kinds and qualities of building stones. He is largely what he lives and what he fails to live. The man who said tell me what you eat and I'll tell you what you are did not know what he was talking about. He was as far wrong as was the man who declared that "as a man thinketh in his heart so is he." It is time we abandoned our one-sided views of our many sided lives. Life is too complex to be reduced to such simple formulae.

The search for diet-cures is part of man's age-long quest for a savior—something or some one to save him in his "sins" and not require him to give them up. Money grabbers who have piled up fortunes at the expense of those whom they have pillaged and impoverished, when their dissipations have wrecked their lives, imagine that money can buy health for them. Like the pair in the New Testament who tried to buy the "gift of the spirit," the truth is never pleasing to these men and women of the Croesus-complex, who think their money can command for them all that their hearts desire.

They exchange their loot for a "showy commercialized professionalism" which some graduate of a "class A" medical college palms off on them as knowledge and skill. From one dissapointment to another they turn until their sufferings are so great they can no longer bear them. Every savior having failed them, for every treatment they have received has made them worse; the yeast and diet cures have failed, the manipulations and elctrocutions have been all in vain, the serums and drugs have added to their miseries and the operations have increased their torments; they come, these scraps and derelicts, these wrecks and incurables, to the Hygienist and want to know "how long will it take you to cure me?" Imagine their surprise when they are informed that there are no cures, no saviors, and that they must forget their old faith in vicarious atonements and cease their "sinning."

MAN SHALL NOT DIET ON FOOD ALONE

"Doctor, if you can cure me you can name your own price." Yes indeed! But this calamity will never befall our race. The time will never come when cures will be produced; the discovery will never be made that will restore potency to the sensualist while permitting him to practice sensuality; that will sober up the inebriate while he continues to drink; that will save the gourmand while he continues to hog it. A body vitiated by indulgencies cannot possibly be restored to sound health so long as the indulgencies are continued.

A reasoned conception of law and order would save mankind from the pitfalls of false religion—theological or medical. There is too much of the *Shaman* in "modern religion;" too much of the *medicine man* in "modern medicine."

Beauty and ecstasy of life come from a clear mind and a healthy body. Plain, orderly, abstemious living and high thinking make life more beautiful and good and add to the joys of living. To abandon these for the flesh-pots of sensualism and then demand to be cured of the results while still in your "sins," while pleasing to the thoroughly commercialized professional healers, is a display of asinity rather than of wisdom and sound judgement.

Our Denatured Soil
CHAPTER L

Man is made of the "dust of the ground." What he is must depend very largely upon the kind of soil of which he is made. We get our soil after it has been prepared for us by the plant kingdom. The plant is limited in its preparation, to the soil at hand.

The composition of the soil not only determines to a large extent the character of plant development, but it equally determines the character of the development of man. Soil culture will finally come to be recognized to be equally as important as soul culture. Someday the ethnologist and the preacher will come to the trophologist and agriculturist and ask to be taught of these. Sylvester Graham, who was among the first to point out the evils of our present fertilizer follies, declared plants are deteriorated on such soil and that the meat, milk and butter of animals fed on these plants are deteriorated and adds: "Surely the immediate effects of such deteriorated vegetable aliment on the human system must be very considerable." He also declared that it is "most certain, that until the agriculture of our country is conducted in strict accordance with physiological truth, it is not possible for us to realize those physical and intellectual and moral and social and civil blessings for which the human constitution and our soil and climate are naturally capacitated."

When vegetables are grown in soil and their produce removed each year, the soil is sapped of its minerals. The soil is denatured. Efforts to restore a denatured soil by the use of an even more denatured fertilizer is as absurd as would be the effort to restore a body, suffering from mineral deficiencies, to normal by feeding it white flour, polished rice, canned goods and pasteurized milk. Sylvester Graham, Baron von Liebig, Dr. Julius Hensel, Dr. Lahmann, Otto Carque, Prof. Frank M. Keith, Sampson Morgan and others, have warned of the evils of our present agricultural madness.

Plants derive their carbon and nitrogen largely from the air, their minerals from the soil. A crop of wheat yielding 20 bushels of wheat and 2 tons of straw per acre removes 259.2 pounds of minerals from an acre of land. A crop of oats yielding 40 bushels of oats and 2 tons of straw per acre removes from an acre of soil 283.6

pounds of minerals. Some crops cause a greater drain upon the soil than do wheat and oats. The growing and harvesting of crops represents a steady drain on the minerals of the soil and a steadily diminishing fertility until, finally, it becomes incapable of producing wholesome foods.

Much of our soil is denatured. Our crops are being fed a "white flour" diet. They are suffering from "scurvy." An orthodox food scientist says: "Vegetables may be lacking in those necessary proximate principles if grown upon soil unsuited for their proper nutrition, or if deprived of sunlight. Milk may be lacking in these principles if the cow is fed upon provender grown upon impoverished soil. The same is true of the meat of animals fed upon faulty provender." The health and development of man and animal is determined by the soil upon which they feed.

The fertilizing of the ground of Warnham Park (England) with bone dirt every alternate year, "added 70 per cent to the nutrimental qualities of the grass, accounting for the immense improvement since Mr. F. M. Luca's plan was tried, a four-year-old Warnham stag being better than and adult animal in most other English parks."

Texas cattle are, on an average, much larger than Florida cattle, but there are differences almost as great between the cattle in one county and those of another, and perhaps adjoining county in Texas. In a county where the soil is poor, cattle are smaller than those in a county possessing fertile soil.

These facts teach us that the proper fertilization of land is of most importance to those of us who eat the produce of the soil. If the soil is poor, our foods will be poor and our health and development will be correspondingly poor.

The food value of vegetables depends largely upon the soil in which they are grown. Continued cultivation depletes and impoverishes the soil. So does the washing away of the soil by water which is unimpeded by timber. Prevailing methods of fertilization actually unbalance the soil and introduce into it three or four elements only. Most of the valuable minerals needed by plant life are not returned to the soil by commercial and barn yard fertilizers.

Our farmers and agricultural experts insist on making us out of manure and animal waste from the packing houses. Manure-fed plants mean manure-fed minds and bodies. For many years agricultural ex-spurts have taught that nitrogen, potash and phosphoric acid are the three elements necessary to add to the soil in order to assure

THE SCIENCE AND FINE ART OF FOOD AND NUTRITION

maximum crop yields. During the same period farmers have had to deal with ever lessening crop yields despite the unlimited use of manures and fertilizers. They are also confronted with a progressive lessening of the resistance of their crops in insect pests and plant diseases.

Nitrogen-potash-phosphoric acid fertilizers act largely as stimulants. They produce rapid, rank growth, but the plant is lacking in strength, stability and resistance to insect pests. The plants do not acquire stiffness and strength and their organs lack "a certain solidity and power of resistance against those external causes which endanger their existence." Plants really need but little phophoric acid and an excess does them harm. The first world war cut of our potash supply and we learned that we could grow crops without this.

Animal fertilizers introduce an excess of nitrogen into the soil. This lays the plants liable to insect pests and deteriorates their qualities in every important particular. Luther Burbank says: "What happens when we overfeed a plant, especially an unbalanced ration? Its root system, its leaf system, its trunk, its whole body is impaired. It becomes engorged. Following this, comes devitalization. It is open to attacks of disease. It will be easily assailed by fungus diseases and insect pests. It rapidly and abnormally grows onward to its death."

An excess of nitrogen retards the formation of roots, tubers and grains and produces sickly plants. In cereals it "leads to a bright green color, to a copious growth of soft sappy tissues, liable in insect and fungoid pests (apparently because of the thinning of the walls and some change in the composition of the sap), and to retarded ripening." Too much straw is produced and the grain is of poor quality. A similar thing is seen in clover.

Potato plants produce more leaves as the nitrogen supply is increased, but no more roots and no more tubers. Under like conditions tomato plants produce an abundance of leaves, but very little fruit. Excess nitrogen unfits cabbage, spinach, lettuce, etc., to withstand the rough handling of the market.

Plants are cross-feeders and thrive best on mineral food. Soil is disintegrated rock (mineral) and v e g e t a b l e amalgamations (humus). It is clean, as Mr. Morgan points out. This kind of soil does not produce the weak, watery, unhealthy plants of the food market. Mineralized humus will produce clean soil. Nothing else will.

OUR DENATURED SOIL

Soil is not an inert mass. It is teeming with life and pulsating with change. Purification of the soil, as of sewage, is a biological rather than a physical and chemical process. Plants thrive in active symbiosis with soil bacteria.

Mineral fertilizers—rock, volcanic lava, wood and coal ashes, saw filings, etc.,—if added to the soil, in connection with leaves and other plant substances, give a better yield of food stuffs—foods that are richer in minerals and which possess greater resistance to parasites than do those raised on manure-fed lands.

The application of mineral fertilizers to the soil raises the "ash" content of plants. Stone dust fertilizers have been repeatedly shown to cause worms to cease infecting fruits. The use of stable manure as fertilizer deteriorates their quality and causes them to become infested with bugs and worms.

"The New Soil Culture," "clean culture," as Sampson Morgan, of England, often called it, produces from six to eight times as much per acre as does the old filth fertilizer—"animal, bird and human excrement, reinforced with nitrates and phosphates."

Without sufficient calcium no sugar or starch can be formed; without iron and lime no albumen can be formed; without silica no fibre, or plant skeleton, can be formed; and so on to end of the list of plant minerals—sodium, magnesia, manganese, iodine, etc.

Our denatured soils are lacking in iron, sulphur, silicon, magnesia, lime, manganese, sodium, chlorine, iodine. If these are not present in the soil in sufficient quantities they will not be present in our foods.

Berg, Ritter, Truninger and Liechti have shown that cultivated plants, when "too exclusively manured with nitrogenous fertilizers," or when treated with liquid manure (poor in alkalies), or with ammonium sulphate, are greatly deficient in bases and become positively acid.

An acid grass is produced in a soil rich in nitrogen, but poor in minerals. Grasses ordinarily rich in alkaline salts acquire an acid reaction if grown in deficient soils. Animals fed upon pastures, the soil of which is deficient in lime and potassium, become seriously ill.

Foods grown on such soils are not proper foods upon which to feed our bodies and those of our children. In accordance with the Law of the Minimum, the development of our bodies must correspond to the character of the soil upon which we feed.

THE SCIENCE AND FINE ART OF FOOD AND NUTRITION

A complete growth depends upon a complete diet. Perfect fruits, nuts, vegetables, cereals and other eatables, depend, not upon an oversupply of one or two of the minerals as our potash-phosphorus fertilizers seem to indicate, but upon a proper proportion of all of them.

Pfeifer prepared various solutions of the minerals that are contained in plants and placed seeds in these to grow. He proved that the absence of only one of these elements, from the solution, injured the plant.

Chlorophyl, the green coloring matter of plants, corresponds with the hemoglobin, or red coloring matter of the blood. Without chlorophyl plants cannot live. Like hemoglobin, it depends upon the presence of iron. Pfeifer found that plants grown in solutions devoid of iron suffer from faulty nutrition. Potassium leads to the development of stems, flowers and fruits; its absence stimulates the growth of leaves. In the absence of potassium the crop remains backward and the fruit does not develop. The absence of any element from the soil means that it will also be absent from the plant and, therefore, absent from our food.

Dr. Lahmann was right when he wrote: "What is wanting in the plants? Mineral substances. These have in many places been entirely drawn out of the soil, which has been exhausted through generations, *** and yet these mineral substances are absolutely indispensible for the formation of healthy cells and tissues." "To remedy the present degenerative condition of agriculture we should plough and dig deeper and use mineral manure, that is supply the soil in natura, those mineral substances which are wanting in it."

Soils in various parts of our country vary in fertility, largely as a result of erosion and of faulty agricultural methods. In many parts of the country, due to the wasteful destruction of our forests, the rains have washed the soluble elements of the soil into the sea. Some parts of the earth have been so completely demineralized by ages of washing away of their minerals by water, that they have little left for plant life.

So great has been the mineral-loss in the soil of certain of our Middle-Western states, due to washing of the soil by rains, this washing unimpeded by forests, that one of the State Agricultural Experiment stations of one of these states, found it necessary to secure and analyze specimens of foods from many parts of the country in their efforts to determine a fair average content of such foods. These averages are very low and will not sustain life and growth in an ideal manner, while the present methods of fertilizing the land only assist in further denaturing the soil. Our North Central states are also badly depleted.

Prof. Geo. W. Cavanaugh, head of the Agricultural Dept., of Chemistry, Cornell University, says: "I have experimented with vegetables grown in different parts of the country and have found carrots, for instance, as unlike each other as they would be were they unrelated. It is the same with beans, squash, rhubarb—with every vegetable. They can only be as rich in minerals as is the soil in which they are grown. A man may starve to death while eating them."

Early American colonists settled along the Atlantic coast, farmed it for a few generations and then moved back as far as the Appalachian Mountains where they exhausted the fertility of that vast region. From there they swarmed into the fertile Ohio and Mississippi valleys and after skimming the cream off the rich soils here they totally abandoned many farms here just as had previously been done in New England. Some of these New England farms remain abandoned to this day.

From here our soil-wasting farmers swarmed to the virgin lands east of the Rocky Mountains, where they soon greatly reduced some of these seemingly inexhaustible soils and practically ruined others. They swarmed over the Rockies into the fertile valleys of the Pacific Coast. Reducing these valleys they then started northward into the fertile plains of Canada.

They surged westward until they could go no farther and turned north. When they could not go farther north then, like a receding wave, they rolled back East and sought out and soon exhausted portions of the various states that had been previously overlooked in their westward march of destruction.

They entered the mountains, cut down the trees of the rich forests, scratched the sloping earth with a plough and planted beans and corn. Rains came in the form of tearing, pouring, thunderstorms and let loose from one hundred to four hundred tons of rushing water per acre in a single hour and the loose earth, deprived of its protection from trees was washed away and fertile hills that, with proper cultivation, might easily have nourished a thousand or ten thousand crops, became so poor in a few seasons that the laborous work of the poor mountaineer now gets only a meagre crop.

Nature put trees there, but the farmer wanted a level-land agriculture. Tree agriculture alone is fitted for the hills. The hillside was certainly never meant for the plough.

Modern agriculture is all in the direction of exploitation, rather than of concern for the well-being of the soil, the animal or the plant, or man and we frequently run in opposition to natural forces and cosmic influences in our desire to exploit Nature. There is a limit to the stimulus that may be applied to soils for the forcing of crops. Animals instinctively avoid eating grasses and vegetables growing on dung-heaps and heavily manured places, such as an old cow-lot.

What has happened to the soil of America? It has gone the way of her forests and the bison—wasted by the most extravagant people of all human history. In the short time that has elapsed since Europeans first began colonizing the North American continent, we have lost an average of over three feet of the top soil of the whole United States. Erosion by wind and water is blamed for this loss, but back of the wind and water has been the destruction of the forests and ploughing of the land. What Faulkner properly calls the *Ploughman's Folly* prepared the soil for water and wind erosion. Carelessness has caused many forest fires that has destroyed many thousands of acres of productive land. Much of the rich Everglades of Florida were destroyed by fire. Every year our irrational methods of sewage disposal sends millions of tons of the best top soil of the country out to sea. Year by year our land grows less and less fertile.

To offset this, we resort to commercial fertilizers that poison the plants, undecayed animal offals that sour the soul, and have neglected the true sources of soil. Soil is disintegrated rock. From the the rock and from humus or properly decomposed compost comes the finest fertilizer for our soils. We prefer to enrich the manufacturers of chemical fertilizers.

Coupled with this diabolical agriculture, are the devastation of forests, destruction of wild life and the reckless waste of earth's mineral resources. If this folly continues for another five hundred years the earth will have become uninhabitable.

Dr. Rudolph Steiner, of Germany, late founder of the Anthropophysical Society, and his students, have presented evidence to show that there is benefit to be derived from planting fruits and vgetables in juxtaposition instead of, as at present, growing only one thing in a field or patch. For example, they plant nasturtiums among the apple trees and horse radish by the potatoes and claim that the flavor of both fruit and vegetable is improved thereby. There may be some symbotic counter-service rendered by plants to each other that has heretofore been over-looked.

More valuable to the health-seeker than climate is soil. He should go where he is sure that the fruits and vegetables of the region are rich in the health-giving, body-building minerals, rather than to a popular resort where climate is the only appeal. The Southwest offers the health-seeker both soil and climate. Sunshine and an abundance of excellent fresh fruits and vegetables are available the year round.

Bulletins No. 94-95 of the Defensive Diet League of America say: "We know definitely that lettuce, spinach and other products grown on the comparatively exhaustless soil of Texas and the far West are so much more valuable as food that is seems almost unbelievable, as, for instance, such a comparison of vitality as one to ten thousand. Of course, loss in shipping long distances must be taken into account."

The Rio Grande Valley is fertilized from the mineral laden waters of the Rio Grande River, as these bring the minerals from the mountains which they drain. This soil, the richest in the world, produces oranges, grapefruit and other fruits, as well as vegetables, that cannot be surpassed in flavor and food value. The Winter Garden district, lying south of San Antonio, produces fruits and vegetables that supply the health seeker with the precious minerals of life in great profusion. The year around abundance of sunshine assures, not merely mineral assimilation by these fruits and vegetables, but, richness in vitamins and deliciousness of flavor. As rainfall is not excessive, vegetables and fruits are not rank watery, tasteless, foodless foods.

This is not a book on agriculture, else would this chapter be greatly extended. I include this brief chapter merely to aid in arousing our readers to an awareness of the need for agricultural reform as a part of dietary reform.

About the Author

No one was ever better qualified to write a book about food and nutrition from the Natural Hygiene perspective. Herbert M. Shelton ranks among the foremost authorities on this subject. For over fifty years, he managed his own institution where people from all parts of the world, in varying states of health and impairment, came to learn how to build and preserve their health.

Born in 1895, Herbert M. Shelton was a persistent and uncompromising student and teacher of Natural Hygiene. Early in life, he discovered the errors and inconsistencies of all the various therapeutic systems and began to explore, on his own, the ramifications of the fact that health is maintainable only by healthful living.

A prolific writer, he authored innumerable articles and more than 40 books. He was both editor and publisher of the *Hygienic Review* from 1939-1980. For more than 50 years he was the director of Dr. Shelton's Health School. Here he pursued his foremost goal of eliminating people's fear and ignorance of disease and teaching them how they could help themselves to the health which is their birthright.

About the American Natural Hygiene Society

The mission of the American Natural Hygiene Society is to teach its members and the general public how to live the happiest, healthiest lives possible. Founded in 1948, it is the oldest natural health organization in the United States promoting a vegetarian diet.

With nearly 10,000 members around the world, the Society is the foremost international center for information about Natural Hygiene, which means literally "the science of health." Natural Hygiene is the only total-lifestyle health system centered on the following fundamental principles: *health results from healthful living,* and *healing is a biological process.*

The Society publishes the award-winning *Health Science* magazine; conducts International Natural Living Conferences and Seminars; publishes and distributes Natural Hygiene books and tapes; and operates the Herbert Shelton Library (an historical library tracing the history of Natural Hygiene to its origin in the 1830s).

To become a member of the Society, or to get your free copy of the Society's book and tape catalog, contact:

American Natural Hygiene Society
P.O. Box 30630
Tampa, FL 33630